TOUR:SMART

★★★ AND BREAK THE BAND ★★★

TOUR:SMART

 **AND BREAK THE BAND**

MARTIN ATKINS

FIRST EDITION

:SMART BOOKS

:Smart Books is a division of Soluble, LLC.
PO Box 16840
Chicago, IL 60616

Art Direction: Martin Atkins
Layout and Design: Karen Barth, Mike Johnson
Additional Graphics: Mike Johnson, Mitch O'Connell, Adam Watkins
Cover Design: Don Weigand
Editor: Margot Olavarria
Production Assistants: Andrea Cochran, Katie Conlin, Kate Wilhelm
Peer Editors: Jon Allegretto, Martin Bowes, Brit Bursh, Katie Conlin, Ben Coughlin, Jade Dellinger, Susan Ferris, Thomas Fricilone, Joel Gausten, Rachel Hammon, Dan Johnson, Mike Johnson, Pei-Lun Liao, Michelle Mangulabnan, Simon Mattock, Steve McClellan, Alexandar Mihajlov, David Nicholas, Ben Prendergast, Chris Ramos, Geoff Smyth, Virginia Thomas, Chris Tisone, Pat Van Hulle, Tara Watkins, Kate Wilhelm, Stephanie Wilkins, Sarah Williams
Research Staff: Rebecca Farber, Kristina Gallapo, Jason Scovel, Frank Snover, Jamie Weissinger

I always say never underestimate the difference you as an individual can make to any situation that you choose. For everyone who has helped in any way, thank you. You know who you are.

ISBN 978-0-979-73130-3

Visit the Tour:Smart websites for online updates, forums, and discussions!
www.tstouring.com
www.myspace.com/toursmart

DEDICATED TO:

Katrina, Ian, Harrison, and Sidney for saving and inspiring me every day.

Mum and Dad, after all of these years, anywhere from 100 to 6,000 miles away, interesting to find out that wherever I am there's a large piece of both of you inside of me. Thank you for starting me on this path.

THANK YOU:

To Mike Bertucci, for suggesting this.

To Janet Leder, for helping me keep my head on straight.

To Katie Conlin, for being the hub of the office with all of this on top of everything else – understanding, deciphering, energizing, helping, and not freaking out every single time I added another new chapter.

To Mike Johnson, for going the extra mile and staying engaged.

To Kate Wilhelm and Karen Barth and everyone at the office who has worked so hard to make this a reality.

To Don Weigand, for so much creativity on the cover.

To Margot Olavarria for your expertise and kindness always.

To Charlotte Scherer at Art Forms for pulling me out of the shit.

To the interns who come in and make a real difference with whatever is going on.

To this year's class that, I think, suffered in direct proportion to the book's progress.

To everyone who contributed pieces of themselves to this, big and small. The fact that you did is inspiring and I know will be helpful to the lunatics that follow! I'm so proud and lucky to have your words and experience in here.

And finally, to Phyllis Johnson at Columbia College Chicago, for pulling me into the world of education that sparks me and continues to set my head on fire.

Peace, love, and respect

Martin Atkins
May 2007
Chicago, IL USA

TABLE OF CONTENTS:

INTRODUCTION

You should fail because your band is shit or because you don't have the balls. You shouldn't fail because of a lack of some basic advice and a bit of planning. Your music, your band, might be important to some people, very important to a few, mildly important to a few others, but it will never be more important to anyone than it is to you. Apply that principle to everything. It is ugly. It is difficult because there are so many things that need to be watched and nurtured. But at the end of the day, even if you are totally justified in blaming a bad agent who booked you in the wrong club or a slacker manager on a tour where the only thing blown was your cash, it is YOU, your band, and your music that is going to suffer the worst consequences.

So take responsibility for all of this NOW!

That's a common thread that runs through this book. What better person than you to navigate the dangerous waters ahead, as you steer your unique vision through the shallow streams of compromise and the deep oceans of sell-out? This book will help you to avoid the wrecks of ambition, as you steer towards the constantly moving "X" on the tissue paper treasure map. This book will help you know when a random collision of events is creating opportunity or danger, whether to go for it or blow your nose on it, crash on the rocks or grind them up and snort them. With the advent of MySpace you don't have to do anything, but with over two million other bands on there, if you don't start doing something, you will be invisible in that crowd, unheard, overlooked and, soon ..... over.

The problem now is how to get attention in a sea of attention seekers. You have to reinforce whatever attention that you are getting. How do you get face time at the group therapy session? You've just got to set your hair on fire. That way, if the flames and screams don't get people's attention, the smell sure as fuck will. Indeed, it is touring, physically putting yourself in front of people and each tiny incremental move forward that will get you where you need to go. You are not trying to sell 10,000 CDs or 100,000 downloads—you are trying to individually sell one CD or one downloaded track, to thousands of different people, thousands of important times, one at a time. The method and the path aren't complicated, but they are time and energy intensive. Do you want to build a cathedral that will stand for time everlasting, or an Acme Quick Church-in-a-Box?

This book contains a stained glass reflection of what it takes to tour successfully and make it—whatever that means. It is part basic knowledge, part math, part poetry, part alchemy, and part understanding of each and every one of the limitations placed upon you by terrain, physical distance, your bank account, head, heart, yourself, and your willingness to choose to ignore the things that stand in your way. In pulling all of this apart over the last 30 years, I reached a delightful conclusion: it's still only the people who are prepared to risk that will be rewarded.

The enormity and quantity of the tasks at hand, the level to which some people will sink and lie and cheat and steal and apologize and do it all over again, will overwhelm you. YOU WILL CRY. But I guarantee you; it is better to be working at 4 am on the process of taking charge of your band's future, than it is to be bouncing off the walls, wondering. Boxing Champion Jim

Braddock said it very well, "At least in the ring, I can see who I am fighting." The things you pick up along the way, the understanding and insights you gain, will give you the life skills to create a better situation, as you continue to grow as an artist and as a person within any piece of this business, or this world, that you choose.

Sure, things are always in a state of flux: concert attendances are down, Miss America is arrested for underage drinking, astronauts diaper-drive across the country on a failed killing spree and the increasingly A.D.D. world is halfway between being entertained and hypnotized half of the time in a half-ass Frito-Lay-way. Clubs are closing. NASCAR is the next wrestling. Generation X(presso) is glued to its screens and everyone is a DJ or a film-maker. Fifteen minutes of fame has been replaced by a moment on MySpace and a killer night is now a kilobyte. Bloggers are influencing elections—the new top twenty! And the candidates are still out there shaking hands, kissing babies, and sexually harassing their staff.

Record stores are selling books, coffee, and product placement. Record labels, what's that? The stakes are high, the same as they always were. Those obsessed with the spreadsheet forgot the columns for grooviness, reputation, and vibe—or did they decide it wasn't important? Those obsessed with the art frequently forget the business or despise its reality. Neither is the path. Each can help the other. Opportunity is fluid and fleeting, the hardest part of the entrepreneurial eye test is seeing that flash in your peripheral vision. By the time you question its existence, someone else has taken out an ad for the product it inspired them to make ten seconds ago.

Having realized the depth of these changes and learned many road lessons the hard way, I share them with you in these pages. This book is the distillation of a million thoughts, tried and tested ideas, mistakes, and catastrophes that you DON'T have to make along with some that, inevitably (difficult bastard), you do. I found that my learning curve needs more than one cattle prod to get me to the point of real understanding and that most people need to register something a few times for it to become clear. If by repeating something twice it sinks in and saves a band, a relationship, or a gig, then that seems like a small editorial price to pay, especially when repeated from different sources. I tried very hard to forget the fact that this is a textbook. I had to talk about things not traditionally spoken about in a learning environment. But Jesus Christ! Every student astronaut has to ask, "Where on earth do we take a shit?" It's got to be in a NASA textbook somewhere! So I apologize if any of the imagery or language in this book offends you, but if it does… then maybe a life on the road isn't for you!

ORGANIZATION OF THE BOOK

You can't write an incomplete, lame-ass, bullshit book about seatbelts or airline safety—it's against the law. The same isn't true for any book about the business of touring which is unfortunate for you and fortunate for any lame-ass who has spent three weeks in a van. There are no airbags in the touring industry. When it goes wrong, your head is going through the windshield.

If knowledge springs from mistakes and shared catastrophes (more than shared triumphs and self-congratulation), then it's easy to see why the music business is filled with people making the same mistakes over and over (and over) again. Someone on my SuicideGirls' column said it best: "You don't hear skinheads talking about an interesting thing that happened the last time they were severely beaten up…" And it's rare to see anyone in the music business sharing anything (except really bad drugs). I haven't been afraid to admit those mistakes. Somewhere in here is the story of a tour during which I lost $60,000, and accounts of three instances where having a pre-tour band agreement would have saved my ass. Somewhere in my column I casually mentioned not signing Disturbed (they went on to sell 4.5 million albums). There is more to be gained by sharing these lessons than by holding on to a picture of me shaking hands with Dick Clark.

Maybe it's so tough at the beginning that it's really difficult to give another band advice that could help them get the gig, the slot, or the audience that you want. I understand that. And the people who benefit from keeping artists frightened and in isolation can cynically fuel the competitive nature of the business for their own benefit. But really, the way forward is to make your own Stairway To Heaven (or Downward Spiral), not by using the crushed hopes and broken bones of the failures of your fellow artists as a platform.

One man's ceiling becomes another man's floor; one man's wall is another man's door.

There are two things that make this book quite different from many others that I have seen. One: my being completely unplugged from any need to reinforce any existing knowledge or conform to any institutional guidelines for what a textbook should contain. For example, there's not much on legal issues in here; contracts don't protect you without leverage, so there is a load about gaining leverage. Two: I don't shy away from the fact that I don't know it all (pretty unusual for a label owner, huh?) and that I'm excited to have over 100 people from all over the world and all levels of business share their insights. That's humbling as all hell for me and cool as fuck for you.

There are bits and pieces all throughout the book that I have never thought of or didn't know, other pieces that are great to have confirmed, and some that inspire me to reach higher, and learn more! Promoters tell you what they want to hear, journalists give you advice, soundmen tell you how to get a better sound, managers tell you how it is, and others give you thousands more tips from over 100 industry professionals. Take the time to read their comments and, in however many days it takes you to read the book, you could be six hundred years wiser.

Sprinkled throughout the nuts and bolts of advice, there is insight into state of mind and state of body. That's the cool part: the in-between-the-cracks stuff. It becomes so real you can almost taste it! There is no such thing as an insignificant detail. Small things can become big things. If you don't believe me, follow me to the rear lounge of the bus!

However the learning process works, I know that I could say to you, "I regret punching the metal elevator door and crushing two knuckles on my right hand" and it doesn't mean that you won't. Everybody has their own process and their own throbbing painful reminders. Maybe it will just be good to know you're not alone in this. I can't be standing next to you when all of the shit goes down but, through this book, I and a hundred other contributors who care can watch your back and be your psychic network. Can you hear me now?

The website will have updates, news, and developments as things inevitably keep changing.

That's a good place to stay up to date with my appearances, and other information. The business is moving so quickly that during the final editing process we added the "Stop Press" section at the back of the book. This is going to keep on unfolding and that's exciting. We also decided to have the purchase of this book include free downloads of the next two updates. Go to *www.tstouring.com* to register.

In some cases, the extra shit you didn't plan for will eventually weigh you and the band down and you will, sadly, be done. In some cases, the crazy insane shit that no one in their right mind would try and pull off ends up saving you! Ah, isn't that beautiful? The yin and the yang, the revolving/revolting equation, the dualistic do-do. That shit's going to drive you crazy... take my word for it.

It's the wildest drug you will ever do.

 For some, it is the only place to be, a very special rarefied place that, on a good day, fuels the soul, and in one glorious night makes up for five years of horrible shit. It makes your head tingle like you just accidentally did everyone's speed.

So, get real, roll up your sleeves, pull on that long plastic glove, squeeze out a generous helping of KY, and stick your arm up the cow's ass that is the music business!

Be careful, watch yourself, and don't be an asshole.

Get on the road, and send me a story!

Peace, love, and respect,

Martin Atkins

"...the hardest way to make an easy living."
 -The Streets

WHAT THE HELL DO I KNOW?

Any time I'm guest lecturing I tell students to always consider the source of information that is being presented to them. That's good advice.

Rupert Neve the creator of Neve audio engineering products coined the phrase QBE— "qualified by experience"—because that's what he is. So if I were you, my next question would be "what experience…?" I don't usually twitter on about the things that I've done, I'm usually busy working on the next things that I'm doing. You can (and you should) read my bio and a list of everything on the web site. But here's a quick overview so you can determine the validity of any of this:

I started playing drums at the age of nine, playing in bands and cover bands in the North East of England gigging many nights a week and backing strippers while (hello Snake Lady) doing my homework in the dressing room. I moved to London and joined Public Image Ltd. in 1979 just in time to co-write and perform one song on *The Metal Box* ("Bad Baby"). My first live show with PiL was recorded and released as *Paris au Printemps* and within the first six months we performed live on BBC TV's *Old Grey Whistle Test* and ABC's *American Bandstand*. I co-wrote and performed tracks on the *Flowers of Romance* album, the *Commercial Zone*, co-produced *This is What You Want, This is What You Get* and appeared on and co-produced the first 32 track digital live recording *Live in Tokyo*. I toured the world with PiL until leaving in 1985. At some point in the early eighties I packed two suitcases, jumped on a plane and moved to The States.

I had my own alter-ego, Brian Brain from 1978 to the late '80s. We toured the U.S. and Europe and had nine releases.

I started Invisible Records in September 1988. Just as things seemed to be settling down for me in the U.S., I received a phone call from Killing Joke asking me to join the band. I flew to the UK (risking the ability to return as my resident alien paperwork was in process) and eventually became the band's manager as we collaborated on the *Extremities, Dirt, and Various Repressed Emotions* album and several tours. I began to design t-shirts and scenery for the band.

nine inch nails broken

A Chicago Killing Joke show led to an invitation to work with Ministry on 1990's legendary *Cage Tour* documented in the *In Case You Didn't Feel Like Showing Up* video.

Now things started to get crazy. The day the Ministry tour ended, Bill Reiflin and I took most of the participants from that tour into the studio with Steve Albini producing with the addition of Trent Reznor of NiN, and David Yow of Jesus Lizard.

During the next six months, I appeared in Nine Inch Nails' "Head like a Hole" video, performed on the Grammy award winning "Wish," and toured the world again with Pigface.

I taught myself to engineer and started to record, mix, and produce Invisible bands as well as my own projects. Pigface grew. The tours got crazier. The lineup kept changing: Danny Carey from Tool joined for 10 days in 1994, Trent Reznor showed up for a couple of early dates, Flea jammed on a studio track in Hollywood, Shonen Knife contributed vocals from Japan. In 1995, I started to create and promote multi-band package tours complete with sound reinforcement, video projections, and an outbreak of spinal meningitis.

In 2003, the work load from package tours prompted me to visit Columbia College in Chicago to present our touring activities and ask for interns to help in return for credit and experience. Phyllis Johnson asked me to begin teaching "The Business of Touring." That's when I finally began to learn. Not just about teaching and how much that fueled me, but by paying attention to the lessons I'd already learned at great cost.

I'm still out there doing it, either taking my SuicideGirls column on the road (I'll be sitting on a disgusting smelly couch near you soon!), drumming, guest lecturing, presenting my gallery show, working on a new sound library, reading the "Fuck List," DJing, or sitting in my studio dubbing a new track inside out, messing around with beats, and fucking things up. That feels like a pretty big difference too… I'm still smiling.

University of Colorado Denver, CO

Belmont University Nashville, TN

HOW TO USE THIS BOOK

All of the concepts expressed in this book are the fruits of many years of ideas, execution, examination, lessons, and application of the new information to start the cycle again. It's great that you don't have to go through all of that – but, it's not possible for you to dive into this, digest it all, and take all of these strategies on at the same time. It took me a while to build up a tolerance for alcohol and reach a point where I could drink very large amounts of beer, vodka, or anything really, and I was 12 or 13... so, be careful. The consequences to you of trying to do all of this at once could be the same – dizziness, vomiting, clutching the toilet, sweats, and an aversion to peach schnapps. The ideas for promotional CDs evolved over a period of five years and had a staff to execute the tasks involved. So, yeah, be ambitious... you have to be – but carefully ambitious!

Look up the "Grains of Wheat on the Chess Board Story." In short, a king offered a farmer a large amount of gold to do something. Before getting paid the farmer gave the king an opportunity to pay him in wheat instead by placing one grain of wheat on the first square of a chess board, two on the next, four on the next, eight on the next, and so on, doubling the grains on each square. Easy right? Actually, no. By the time you get to the last square, you will need more wheat than there is in the world and a six story, 25 square-mile building to put it in.

OK. So, here is an analogy for you: Fame and fortune – Christina Aguilera, Bruce Springsteen, Green Day, Elvis Presley (I know I keep mentioning him), and U2. For your purposes those are all unattainable, 25 square-mile wheat warehouses. Forget it. Stick with me on this stuff and I guarantee you that you will advance further along the chessboard. Has anyone ever said that? I'm guessing not. They'll dangle something impossible to hook you in and sell you something. That's not right, not cool, and not going to happen. You can't conceive how to go about going from where you are now to U2 status. Well, neither can I. But, you can get two extra pieces of wheat on the next square, can't you? OK let's start there.

So, here's a couple of suggestions:

1. As you go through this some areas will speak to you and you'll say, "Oh, yeah, I can do that." Others won't. They will be time consuming and freak you out – skip those for now. Mark them down as an area you need to go back to. I'd suggest implementing some of the merchandise booth strategies first along with some of the strategies for a more successful show. This way, you'll be getting better results and there will be a little bit more money. That's always a bit of stress relief. The next time -- the next show – you can add two more strategies to your list and ditch one that just didn't work for your band. Build.

2. It's tough when one person is driving a band's process. It may be the case with song writing in the studio or practice space, but it doesn't have to be all the time with everything. Read this book as a band. Divide up some of the areas that people have skills in. Four of five people working together can accomplish more than five times the workload of one person when each is fueling and supporting the other. This is where band stuff crosses over into "Three Musketeers" territory – not that you are covered in chocolate – but that you are "all

for one and one for all" dangerous motherfuckers. Still, take it step by step and grow the business of your band.

3. Hit the drummer on the head with it.

4. Execute some of the strategies in a :smart way – gradually. Instead of trying to add ten shirts to your merch booth for an important show, design ten (or come up with basic ideas at a band meeting) and execute four or five. If you really believe that you need and want ten – that's great. The last thing you need is to have printed all of the backs of ten new shirt designs, but, exhausted, you don't have time to print the fronts. Lots of the work, none of the benefit. So, design ten, execute four or five. If this is your first time screen printing, start with one simple design, work it through, then do another. Finish one thing first.

5. Never stop. Get into the groove of this. Crazy things now that take all night and all of your energies will become routine next time. Take the 'typing the guest list' example. The first few times you do it you'll be cursing me and your printer because you have the extra cartridge but can't find the cable. But, pretty soon you'll be typing the guest list for NYC while doing an interview with some huge magazine, anxious to know exactly how many special ways this book helped you.

Lastly - however, whatever, wherever, all of it, bits of it, just USE IT!

ⒸⒽⒶⓅⓉⒺⓇ········❶

WHY IT IS ESSENTIAL TO TOUR

There's one great plastic, fantastic reason for you to get out there, make a noise, jump up and down, meet people, shag people, smile at people, listen, interact, make friends, expose yourself, push, push, push, and make your music as important to other people as you can…

IF YOU DON'T DO IT WITH YOURS…
SOMEBODY
ELSE
IS DOING IT WITH THEIRS.

You don't need to look far for an example of how important it is to get out there, tour, and do the work. Do you think for one second that, if it wasn't essential, that any politician in the country would ever leave home? Can you imagine the torture they endure? The lengths they go to protect themselves from air-borne and hand-borne germs? Most of those guys can't even bring themselves to think about other people, let alone touch them—unless it's on the ass. So the only reason they are out there is: 1. More ass or 2. Every one of their advisors has told them that they have to, shown them the evidence, and pushed them out the door.

"But," you ask, "How does this affect me? I'm not into politics; I'm just making music!" Shut up, get real, and get in the van. Every single element affecting your career and your ability to continue is helped by touring:

- The record store is more likely to stock your music and put up a poster.

- The local paper is more likely to review your CD or mention your show.

- Anyone anywhere is more likely to check out your MySpace page if they see you are coming to town.

- Any promoter in any other city is more likely to give you a gig if they see you are performing in other parts of the country.

- People on the web write about things that happened at shows they went to, not shows that didn't happen, that they couldn't go to….

- You'll have direct and immediate feedback from a real, live audience, either smiling and jumping up and down because the songs you thought were great really are, or screaming and throwing things because you are delusional and your songs are shit. Either way, this is way more valuable than a bunch of people on your MySpace page plugging their own albums.

- People are more likely to buy your CD or listen to it somewhere, anywhere! So they can sing along with their favorite songs at the show and look like they've known about you for years.

- If they buy the CD before the show, they're more likely to buy a t-shirt at the show and a copy of the live album.

- Your manager, if you have one, will prioritize you over another band because you are working harder (unless the other band is Radiohead).

- You can be the eyes and ears for your label, if you have one... or for other bands. You can tell them where responses are good, let them know where no one has your music, and at the same time give them a real reason to tell retailers why they should stock your music, like: "We just played to 450 people on a Tuesday night! People went crazy! We sold three times the CDs we usually sell from the booth because no one can find it around here."

- Your agent, if you have one, will pay more attention if you show him you are going to do seven shows a week. That means if he can get you to a point where you are earning $1,000 a night, then you have the potential to earn him $1,000 a week.

- You are creating more of your own content... you can't release a Live in Paris album if you don't go and play there!

- The more you play, the better you get!

"The first time through, you're generating smoke. If you don't do something with that smoke, it dissipates."

MARTIN ATKINS IN A ROCK STAR JOURNALISM INTERVIEW:

RSJ: You've said that it only makes sense to do one tour if you're going to do three more. Explain the reasoning behind that philosophy.

MA: The first time through, you're generating smoke. If you don't do something with that smoke, it dissipates. People's memories are short. You've got to be better the second time to seem as good as you were the first time to the people who already saw you. Then you need to go back the third time to have those people bring their other friends and the guy from the paper who couldn't come the first time. Then you've gotta tour the fourth time because if you don't, that good review is wasted because you haven't turned it into some t-shirt sales.

"As an independent artist, it is ALWAYS best to focus your energies on a handful of areas in which you can build your audiences and develop relationships with the right club bookers, store owners, and radio staff. New technologies now allow you to have your music heard around the world via the internet, but nothing beats human interaction to get the word out about your labor of love."

    - CIMS (Coalition of Independent Music Stores)

"Nothing beats human interaction to get the word out about your labor of love."

STEVE BLUSH, AUTHOR OF AMERICAN HARDCORE

"YOU'VE GOT TO GO TO THESE PLACES AND SHOW THEM."

You gotta go on the road. You've gotta work. You've gotta get out of town and play a lot. You can be a big fish in a small pond, and it doesn't matter. I mean it's nice to be big in New York, but it doesn't mean anything. I say you've got to go to Austin, TX, and Portland, OR, five times before anyone gives a shit.

Let me tell ya, I was out on the road doing my Hardcore show, and I was doing very well because people want to know about Hardcore, but I hooked up with good shows. For the book tour, I do a slide show to which I tell the story of Hardcore. I would show up at the clubs; I would show up at bookstores; I would show up at record stores. I did some pretty big rooms and just about every city in the country. You've got to be a Road Warrior. You wanna go to other cities because coming from New York is a big deal, but you don't wanna stay at home because it doesn't mean anything. People read a little about New York, but basically you've got to go to these places and show them.

"...you've got to go to Austin, TX, and Portland, OR, five times before anyone gives a shit."

"The DIY legacy left by the punk scene is one of the best blueprints. It starts with the live show - you build an audience that way. Bands shouldn't be in too much of a hurry to move to Los Angeles or NYC, where the competition for gigs and attention is fierce. Build a story in your own community. Tour regionally. Save a little money and record a CD. Come to the labels with good songs and an audience."
  - Larry White, Pil, Davy Jones Manager

"Let me know if the band is actually out playing gigs. Honestly, if your band isn't playing live shows, you are a long way away from any commercial air play."
  - Chris Payne, Q101 Chicago

Martin Atkins: "How do you see the role of touring?"
Jeff McClusky: "Critical"

"One of the easiest ways to protect your investment in an indie co-op deal is to let the record stores know that you'll be on tour and stopping by within a month."
  - Martin Atkins

C·H·A·P·T·E·R······2

BUILDING BLOCKS: BASIC CONCEPTS AND IDEAS

1. THE RUBBER EQUATION

Here's a central issue: and maybe a reason why there hasn't been a book like this before. Anytime I feel like we come to a concrete conclusion about anything, I immediately feel that there's an exception to that rule. Like, "Don't go west, head east!" Except if you are getting radio play in Phoenix or San Diego, then head west! It's crazy to drive from Nashville to Denver for a Wednesday night! But, maybe Wednesday night in Denver is the big, monthly event for your genre of music and there's a radio station involved, and… and… and… So, tear up the map and the budget and for fuck's sake, get there!

Rather than randomly deciding to do something, there needs to be a reason.

2. TAKE RESPONSIBILITY

Take responsibility for everything. There's no such thing as traditional efficiencies when dealing with the world of art and music. You need to begin by taking responsibility for everything. As things grow, you will learn not only the things that can be delegated and the way to communicate those tasks, but you will also begin to learn who can be trusted with them. If you hear yourself saying "that's not my job," staple your hand to a tree, call me, I'll come down there… You can scream "please help me, my hand is stapled to a tree," and I can say, "that's not my job… sap!"

3. AVOID CONFORMITY

The challenge is to understand some of the rules before you can start to make them flexible. You need to think about breaking the mold rather than neatly slotting into pre-allocated holes. SonicBids is convenient, but you have a finite number of choices of how to present your band (The same choices that other bands are making right now). It is the really cool, unusual packages that will stop the traffic in my office and be a talking point for a few minutes. Understand where to avoid conformity, that's the trick. Pay attention to the red light. But don't listen to anyone telling you to stop.

4. AIM LOW, GET HIGH

(Another great t-shirt and an important thing to remember).

The best way to get high up the ladder is to start at the bottom and slowly work your way up to the top. Tortoise vibe. There is no way to bypass the first 36 rungs unless you have James Bond's rocket-powered jet pack or the best drugs on the planet. Every instance of someone I know getting somewhere in this business (or staying in it) has begun in a very small, humbling way. Carrying ice up stairs; answering a telephone; doing something you don't want to do

> "Pay attention to the red light. But don't listen to anyone telling you to stop."

TOUR:SMART TIP
for more information go to:
www.tstouring.com

diligently, without complaint. I'm not saying don't have respect for yourself or your ambition. I'm just saying that the chances that are going to be offered to you might be surprising in their mundane and trivial nature. But don't forget—this is the music business. The trick is to get inside the building, not to be outside claiming you are on the guest list. It's only a matter of time before everyone in the building freaks out on drugs, runs off with a band, or decides to settle down. So, Aim Low, Get High. Wear the shirt!

5. TOUR TIME IS DIFFERENT FROM OFFICE TIME

This idea is explained very well with a chart in the merchandising section, but it applies to everyone on a tour. Simply being aware of this is helpful. When anybody needs to communicate with the tour, you don't call at 9 a.m. or 10 a.m. The tour might not have gone to sleep until 5 a.m. Use e-mails and text so that your message is waiting when someone wakes up. If it is important, call ahead to the venue or hotel.

On the road, days melt and blur. It's easy to forget which business is closed for the weekend and when the weekend actually is. After all, you're trying to make every night be a Saturday night. You cannot alter this fact, it just is, so creatively deal with it wherever you can. Just help.

6. MOVE TO BOISE

A horrifying catchphrase to most of you, hell-bent on an office on Sunset Boulevard or 5th Avenue, and I guess this is the geographic equivalent of Aim Low, Get High. I absolutely don't mean to imply that Boise doesn't have the quality, the amount, or the impressive array of entertainment that you'll find in LA or NYC, it absolutely doesn't. It's a fact. And no, I don't have any property in Boise nor am I a member of the Boise Chamber of Commerce. But, when compared to someone's alleged plan of achieving success by moving to either LA or NYC, moving to Boise is a fucking stroke of genius (as you will see from the figures here and in the *Appendix*).

City	Number of Bands performing each week
LA	1764 to 2940
NYC	741 to 1235
Boise	39 to 65

***Data taken from www.villagevoice.com, LA Weekly, and Boiseweekly.com (See Appendix for expanded charts).

How thrilling to meet DJ Doc Martin in Denver. Did he remember me for my drumming with PiL, for my production with Killing Joke or Pigface or for my appearance on the Grammy Award winning "Wish" with NiN? Nope, he started calling me Mr. Idaho!

7. THINK OF YOUR PARENTS BEFORE GETTING SHAGGED

This one is way more fun than any of the other ones. It's good practice, before spending any chunks of cash, to think of what your parents might say. If you're dropping $10,000 on a radio campaign, a producer, a publicist, or some kind of opportunity, think of that as if it was a car. What would your parents do? They'd look at the odometer to see if the amount of miles for the year indicates excessive driving. They'd look at the maintenance records to see if the oil had been changed regularly. In the absence of any records, they would conclude that maybe the oil had never been changed. They'd kick the tires and, in general, be cautious. Then, chime in with some anecdotal information like, "Oh my God, that's that car that keeps exploding," and then someone might actually suggest running the VIN number. This all seems perfectly reasonable and wouldn't take more than half an hour or so.

In the music business, none of these things are going to take place. You are more likely to end up prematurely celebrating the success that you believe is just around the corner than doing any research to give you real information that might dissuade you from parting with the money… shut up, you know it's true.

So, hear that voice of reason inside your head, be smart, and investigate. Think of your parents before you get shagged!

This strategy has the added benefit (like a pop song that uses an odd time signature to confuse your brain and embed the hook of a chorus) to completely fuck up your sex life. In the case of an erection lasting more than six hours, please call a doctor.

8. SELFISH PHILANTHROPY

Once you move away from a blaming mentality (and that's no easy thing for many bands to do) and you start to take responsibility for everything, you start to employ selfish philanthropy whenever you can. It's described in the chapter on riders. It's basically the act of helping someone (whose time and energy is important to you) to accomplish their tasks in a more efficient way so that their time and energy becomes available to you should you need it. Worst case scenario, that person gets an extra hour to chill. Reduce your carbon copy footprint.

9. ALWAYS ASK EVERYONE (AND YOURSELF) WHY?

We end up back at the great big golden rule which is: always ask why.

WHY – are you heading west?

WHY – did you choose this agent?

WHY – didn't you book this yourself?

WHY – did the ticket price get that high? Are you worth it? Would you pay that much to see you?

WHY – is it time to make another album, how many has the last one sold?

WHY – don't you buy three copies of this book?? Just in case you lose two…

Why, why, why, why, why?

> "…always ask why."

10. ADOPT A WAR-ROOM MENTALITY

That is what a tour is. You are at war with:

• Other bands looking for attention, an audience, and t-shirt sales.

• Other agents looking to book their bands.

• Your own situation.

• Service providers.

And once the tour starts, you are at war with:

- The elements.
- People (in and out of your band).
- Illness.
- Human frailty.
- The world.

11. FRONT END LOADING

Look at the incremental build up of costs (financial and human) with an understanding of the total investment needed for a two year commitment for your band. Then, apply some of the budget you'll need to slog through year two onto the front of year one. If done intelligently, you will be in a much different place by year two. You can use this strategy on a smaller scale with a single show or tour…more money spent earlier will help more.

12. ALLOCATION OF RESOURCES

You need to know what shows are selling poorly early enough so that you can do something about it. You also need to know what shows are selling well. If a show is selling well, you can ease off on the number and frequency of promotional packages, phone calls, etc. When a promoter informs you that tickets are not selling, you can respond with a truthful, "That's weird; the other three shows in California are going great." This will give you the beginning of a problem-solving, fact-based conversation with the promoter. You might discover that the three shows that are selling have ticket prices of $5, while the show that is not selling has tickets at $12.50. Why? Perhaps it is because the agent over-sold the show to the promoter. Maybe your rider and sound reinforcement requirements are so overblown that it has weighed the cost of the show down and shot the ticket prices up. Maybe no one is paying attention. If you understand the markets you are in and have accurate information you can brainstorm with the promoter on how to increase ticket sales. Believe me, any promoter still in business will appreciate and embrace any realistic attempt to fill his venue.

13. RISK ASSESMENT

One of the first things we do is put up a huge board in the office and start to track the shows. We look at the day of the week, the capacity of the venue, advance ticket sales, past performances, any special web-packs that have sold, proximity to other secondary markets, and the number of street teamers we have in a city to help.

The definition of a low risk show is another one of those Rubber Equations. The following things can help to make a show date less of a risk:

- Thursday, Friday, and Saturday (less of a risk than Sunday, Monday, Tuesday).
- More than two or three street teamers in a city.
- One or two secondary markets close by—each with one or two street teamers.

- A low-capacity venue (in terms of the shows you have and expected levels of attendance).

- A low ticket price.

- A well-established, well-attended regular night.

- A traditionally good market for your band with good e-mail address coverage.

The guarantee or the "deal" for the show is a Rubber Equation within itself. A high guarantee doesn't mean that much unless you've received a substantial deposit on the show. Then, you are reasonably assured that the promoter will bust his nuts to make sure that the night goes well so he can get his money back. Too high of a guarantee might precipitate a reduction. On the other hand, a door deal with no guarantee might relax the promoter in terms of his risk to the point where he doesn't do the expected level of promotion for your show. Instead, he concentrates on two or three other shows for that week for which he's paid too much money. Or, you might have a situation at the door where too many people are being let in for free.

A high risk show isn't just a show on a Tuesday night (although it might be). A high risk show is a show on a Tuesday night where the capacity is much larger than you are comfortable with, you only have one street teamer, and there aren't any secondary markets close by. In terms of risk, this beats a show the following Tuesday at a smaller capacity venue.

Risk, is two-fold. The first part is financial: in terms of a guarantee and merchandise sales that are in jeopardy. But there's also the second part: risk in terms of your reputation in a particular market. And, just like the melting icecaps, things can accelerate and spiral downwards rapidly.

Look through the whole tour and assess risk. Be prepared to constantly re-evaluate the risk level as you get closer to show date and more information becomes available. This is as close as it gets to an episode of *The West Wing*. You have finite resources you can deploy to protect the good shows and reinforce and help the shows that need it. Be careful to remember that you have (hopefully) more than two weeks worth of shows! I need to invent a name for the phenomenon which we shall call, "Everybody Concentrating on the First Ten Days of a Tour" Syndrome. Ten weeks before a six week tour starts, you have ten weeks before the first show, but 16 weeks before the last. Use this to your advantage. It might not feel like you need to worry about the last week of shows…you have plenty of time, but be careful. You're going to get pulled into a swirling world of shit and before you know it will be too late to effectively promote these shows.

14. THE POWER OF THE CAR PARK

Awareness of other events in the area (either geographically or within a genre) is the first step to anything. You don't want to be performing across the street from the largest show that ever happened! But, once you realize that something else in the world is happening other than your show, you can use this information. You can car-park it. You can create an "After Huge Show Party," which makes everyone think that everyone from the big show will be at your show, (instead of sleeping on the bus halfway to the next gig). Or, you can use both of these events to publicize your show, which you have now decided to be one week (or better yet one pay period) away from the really large event. You are the little fish swimming alongside the shark. You can either have all of your street teamers driving over a 50-mile radius to promote your event, or you can use a smarter approach and target like-minded, sympathetic, niche audiences. Cover the cars, have some people there talking it up, handing out information.

15. GET A USEFUL INTERNSHIP

Sometimes it might not seem like there is a direct path from where you are to where you want to go. Try not to get discouraged. Take an internship in a seemingly unrelated field. You might be surprised how useful this could be. See the appendix for a list of suggestions, and send me more examples!

> "You are the little fish swimming alongside the shark."

C·H·A·P·T·E·R 3

PLANNING AND ROUTING: SAVED BY GEOGRAPHY

"Do not go into battle unless you are certain of the outcome."
  - Sun Tzu

AMERICA IS BIG...

...really, really big. In a business where there are so many things that will derail you, it seems silly spending years mastering sampling , drumming, singing, or improvised guitar techniques, but not spending a little bit of time understanding elements that will affect your life on the road every day—Geography and Demographics. Look at a map. Keep looking at it. Think about how long it is going to take to drive from Minneapolis to Seattle. Imagine yourself playing the board game of "Touring USA!" What would your strategies be? Because, for some reason, when someone shows up in a van or buys a guitar, all common sense flies out the window!

Before you do anything, assemble information that will help you communicate with an agent (if you have one) or directly with a venue. If you see a gap between two groups of places that you want to perform in, reach out to a local band to bridge that gap. Understand that any show will be poorly attended unless you use some of the strategies outlined in this book, or make up some of your own. Developing new markets is costly and time consuming, but you must allocate resources accordingly. Suggest a free show for these dates, get involved in an established evening, play every day, twice a day if you can, or better yet, get involved with an established evening with a cheap ticket and a popular local band.

FACTORS TO BE AWARE OF BEFORE YOU PLAN A TOUR

- Size of city and proximity to other cities and secondary markets.

- Mileages.

- Best locations for your specific niche.

- Established events that can help you.

- Other tours within the same time period to use and avoid.

- Weather patterns.

- Your goals as a band.

- Your past history.

- Touring patterns.

GEOGRAPHY

It is only 300 miles to the next show, but is it all up hill in 110 degree temperatures? Is one route clearer than another? Is there snow through that mountain pass? How many cities' rush hours are you going to hit? Is there a time difference?

We thought it was pretty much the same mileage from San Francisco to LA either by the coastal route or the I-5. It ended up being an entire day's difference: I-5 is a mindless toolbox-on-the-accelerator drive; whereas, route 101 is comparable to a drive in the Italian Alps or for those of you unfamiliar with them, the part of *Grand Theft Auto* where your car always ends up in the lake.

All of these things need to be taken into consideration in advance and get logged into the itinerary while you are still able to think. Once you get out on the road, you will have enough information and awareness to say, "We can't do an after show party tonight. We have a difficult drive through a treacherous mountain pass, two rush hours, and an early load in... please put your panties back on."

> "We have a difficult drive through a treacherous mountain pass, two rush hours, and an early load in... please put your panties back on."

CLIMATE

You need to factor climate into your planning. Drives are different across Texas and Arizona in the summer. It's dangerous to go across Colorado, Utah, and Washington from December onwards, not just dangerous in terms of not being able to make it to a show, but... dangerous... Once you understand all of this, you might make a decision to tour in the face of the possibility of bad weather because there will be less competition from other bands who stayed home. …or you might decide to stay home… either way you are making decisions based on information.

EMERGING MARKETS

Population and geographical changes in many markets are fluid. There are many businesses moving in order to find other, cheaper places to operate. This isn't to make more money, this is to survive! Slowly (but noticeably), secondary markets have started to have a scene and some major markets are declining or the emphasis is moving to the suburbs. Boise has grown 2% in the last year, Atlanta 3.3%, Phoenix 4%, just about every city in Florida is growing… New Orleans, tragically, has shrunk by 22%, Detroit and Buffalo are shrinking too. Go and play emerging markets! You're certainly going to get a enthusiastic response (See *Appendix*).

PLACES TO AVOID

It seems that most bands want to head to New York City or Los Angeles to prove that if they can make it there, they can make it anywhere. Well, maybe. But the cards are stacked against you in both cities. People there are less likely to show up to see an unknown band and you might find yourself playing with five other bands. They are cities where people display their support not just by showing up and applauding, but also by leaving after the band they came to see has performed. Put these cities on the back burner. You don't want the catchphrase associated with your band to be, "We can't make it there; we can't make it anywhere," because it's just not true.

Places to Avoid (for now):

New York City – "Nobody cares, dude!!!"

Los Angeles – "Dude, what was the question?"

Austin, TX – Two weeks before and two weeks after SXSW (South by Southwest).

SECONDARY MARKETS

There are two definitions used here for Secondary Markets:

1. Smaller cities.

2. Cities that are close by or competitors with a primary city. (A primary city might not be the largest, it's the one you have a show in. So if you have a show in Athens, GA, then Atlanta becomes the secondary market).

I am still learning about the geography and the flexible equations of time and distance in different parts of the country. It is not simply defined by city vs. suburbs, or by miles vs. hours. These considerations are overlaid by what can be a regionally unique mindset. In Manhattan, 25 blocks can be way too far for someone to travel. In Utah, people will drive eight hours to see a band they love. Rochester to Buffalo is 78 miles. This seems like a trek, but there is one club in Buffalo that is just off the highway, making it a straight-shot one hour drive. This creates a cross-promotional opportunity, a secondary market, and, depending on what you do, either a problem or a solution.

> "We can't make it there; we can't make it anywhere."

Using your geographic knowledge, along with information on secondary markets, will help you to ensure that:

1. The tour has a greater chance of success.

2. The tour has less of a chance of failure because of stress, miles, or money.

3. Less wear and tear on machinery and people.

4. There is less chance of someone dying during a 12-hour overnight drive.

Some venues will have a non-competing clause in their agreement that will state that you can't play within 60 miles and 60 days or 80 miles and 80 days of another show. You need to understand why that clause is in your agreement. A club in Manhattan will argue that a show the week before or the week after in Long Island or Brooklyn will dilute the audience base for their show. They might be right.

Further upstate: if you play Rochester on a Friday and Buffalo on a Saturday, unless you are careful, the Buffalo promoter will advertise in the Rochester paper, and cheapen the ticket price. If it is a hotly-anticipated show, the Rochester promoter will advertise the show in Buffalo and try to get people who cannot wait one more day to see the band to jump on the highway and see his show. If you are not careful, you can decimate earning potential and upset a promoter.

If you are smart (and if you're reading this then you are already smarter than the guy reading *Tour:Stupid*), you can plan your touring activity to take advantage of secondary markets. Plan to hit Rochester first (or whichever is the smaller club where you have the best connections in the surrounding markets). Promote that show in Buffalo. Do not announce a Buffalo show until you are on stage in Rochester. Sign everyone up to your e-mail list and hand out postcards. If you are playing to a few hundred people a night, then perhaps 50 people from Buffalo will be at the Rochester show. They want to support the band and, after all, you have not announced the Buffalo date yet. So, you have a happy promoter in Rochester, the people from Buffalo get to see you early, and the Rochester show was so well attended that 60 of those people come down to see your Buffalo show.

Throw in some incentives like a live or remix CD that is only available at the merchandise booth or a special shirt that can't be bought on the web and you are really creating your own destiny... unless you are crap and your shirts suck. Then you are walking through jello... creating your own density.

DATE	CITY	ATTENDANCE
Regular way...		
Dec 11	Rochester	200
Dec 12	Buffalo	200
	TOTAL	**400**
The TOUR:SMART way...		
Dec 11	Rochester	250
Jan 15	Buffalo	325
	TOTAL	**575**
	DIFFERENCE	**175!**

ATTENDANCE

At the Rochester show, there are now 200 people, plus the 50 people from Buffalo because you advertised there, told your street team, and had a special advance CD.

At the Buffalo show, there are 250 people from Buffalo, more than usual, because their friends had told them about the Rochester show, plus 60 kids from Rochester make the trip and 15 kids from another town who heard how crazy it was, for a total of 575 people! Just by adding in a few weeks and planning (See the *Ultimate Routing* later in this chapter)!

TOOLS - DON'T BE ONE, USE ONE
THE RAND MCNALLY DIST-O-MAP

For fewer than ten dollars you can get a *Rand McNally Dist-O-Map*. It is not some new, gimmicky tech tool, its way cooler, very much like the cover of Led Zeppelin's *Album III*. It has the advantage over map-questing in that you can sit on the phone, run a budget, and dial up distances at the same time. It will also show you options that you might not have thought of previously. If you are lucky enough to be traveling by bus, you will be able to

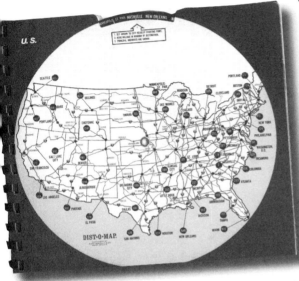

easily see which cities lie within the magical 450-mile overdrive mark. I cannot think of one single agent I have ever met who doesn't need this tool (or frighteningly, one that already has one when I meet them!) Think about that for a minute (especially after you realize that this costs $7.95). It has been the catalyst for the rerouting of several tours, which not only reduced the overall mileage, but put us in the right venues on the right nights. The other reason you need one is to dial up the total distance covered on a tour, divide that by the gas mileage of your chosen vehicle, multiply that by the average cost of gas, and begin a budget. Can't wait, can ya? Go to the chapter on *Budgets* to work through some examples.

> **Note to self:** when trying to communicate effectively, try to avoid analogies and examples from 1970.

Dist-O-Map® is a registered trademark of Rand McNally & Company.

> *Dial up the mileage and you will be able to see potential problems ahead of time. I can guarantee that your longest drive will be the night of the show with the latest curfew and the night before the all ages show with the earliest doors ever. That's just the way it is and always will be (See Murphy's Law).*

DEMOGRAPHICS
REGIONAL DIFFERENCES

Regions have unique differences. For instance, some towns have strict curfews that will shred your audience halfway through your show. Some cities have transportation restrictions that compound curfews. Some cities' bars are open late, some bars in Chicago stay open until 4 a.m. L.A.'s only until 2 a.m. The curfew laws in Boston just changed. Venues cannot have an over 21 show on the same night as an all ages event. An all ages event cannot end later than 11 p.m. There are changing socioeconomic elements, too. The first time you go to El Paso, you will understand that, even though every other show on the tour is a $15 ticket, El Paso is too expensive at $5. The military is gone, all the jobs have gone a couple miles across the border. The state of Michigan isn't far behind with thousands of jobs disappearing from the automotive industry. You need to be aware of when the market will only bear a $5 ticket or more than a $15 ticket, because the extra $5 you pick up in New York helps with the extra $10 you don't pick up in El Paso. And Youngstown, Ohio doesn't even exist. If you want a building in Youngstown, Ohio, the city council will *give you one!* But, before you reach for the phone, realize this: you don't want a building in Youngstown, Ohio.

It is not an answer to not play the smaller markets. You have to play every night within a reasonable traveling distance of the last and next show. A day off is the easiest way to shred a budget, and creative people get bored. Boredom gets expensive. Expensive is bad... bad is not good...

You might find that an enthusiastic small crowd in a city without a record store or a Hot Topic is exactly the place you need to be to build your audience, sell loads of merch, and keep the business of your band running!

ROUTING

Your plan (and for fuck's sake please have one!) needs to layer the unique elements of your band's strengths and weaknesses, the location of your fans, the availability of good clubs, and other bands to play with the inner needs of the band itself.

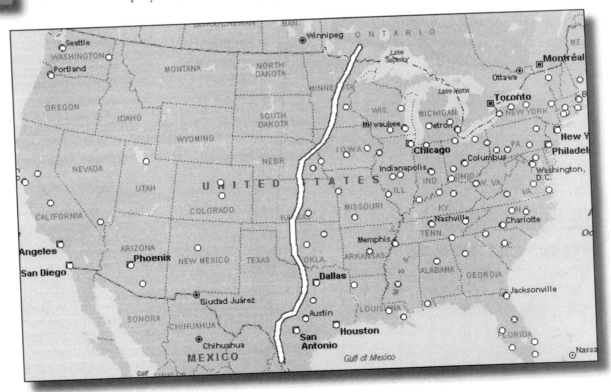

TOURING PATTERNS

The map on the facing page shows the one hundred largest markets in the U.S. as white dots (See the *Appendix* for the list of U.S. cities by population). If you draw a line from Minneapolis to Texas, only 15 of those cities lie west of that line. All of the miles, the exploding transmissions, the melting brains, the people left behind at the side of the road, the dangerous mountain passes closed by three feet of unexpected snow, are to the west of that line. Not to mention eight of the ten most expensive states to buy gasoline are west of that line and eight of the ten cheapest places to buy gas fall east of that line. If you think this is splitting hairs, right now there's a $0.68/gallon difference between the most expensive western state and eastern state. A huge decision you can make is to stay east of the line (Read the section on *Project .44*, a Chicago-based band, in the *Case Studies* chapter).

We can all draw nice patterns on a map, but it gets shredded when you start to book events, a certain club only has Thursday nights for your type of music so you have to double back. An important radio show can only happen on a certain day. You just have to fit the tour to the opportunities at a certain level rather than trying to fit the opportunities to your pre-conceived plan. Does this mean that you shouldn't make a plan? No, you need to be aware of all of these decisions.

TOUR:SMART TIP
for more information go to:
www.tstouring.com

You can tour:

• REGIONALLY

Usually involves a band staying close to their home base and slowly traveling further away in concentric circles.

• WEEKEND-PLUS PETAL PATTERN

Weekend Hit and Runs

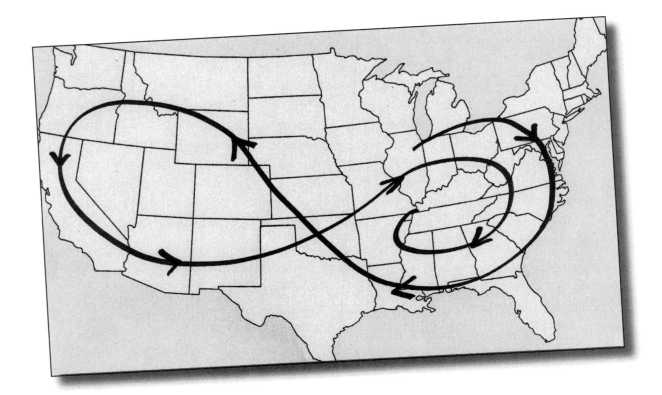

• THE ULTIMATE ROUTING

This expresses the idea, not the specific routing. It's easier to get the idea with this schematic before you tackle the routing.

The next maps illustrate the routing for an eight to 12 week long tour. In this example, we acknowledge and use the markets that are close together. There are about 13 primary/secondary markets like Rochester/Buffalo. For example: Boston/Providence; Baltimore/DC; Toledo/Detroit; San Antonio/Austin; Milwaukee/Chicago; etc.

The first set of dates fuels the second set of dates four to seven weeks later. If you're on top of this strategy, you can be your own advance team in San Antonio with the singer announcing from the stage, "See you in Austin in four weeks motherfuckers!" Your merch crew could be giving out flyers and hanging posters for the next date in the bathrooms. Your most important street team members from Austin could be invited to the show as a thank-you kick-in-the-pants, as well as an opportunity for them to pick up cool merch and more flyers if they need them. You'll be able to see at a glance who's enthusiastic and working and who isn't.

If you extrapolate the difference in the Rochester/Buffalo market (a difference of 175 people) over 15 similar markets in the U.S., this routing could generate over 2,500 more people coming out to see you on your next tour. The second loop on the figure eight adds about four or five thousand miles to the total distance traveled over a ten week period when compared to a regular "shortest distance between two points" or Hamiltonian Routing.

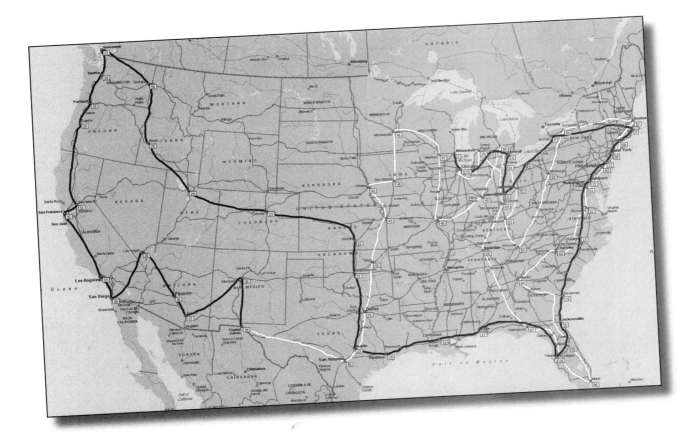

Florida

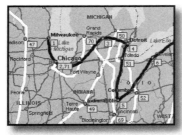

Midwest

Northeast

Texas

"The first set of dates fuels the second set of dates four to seven weeks later."

HOW CAN WE MAKE AN EXTRA $220 A DAY?

Just to show the impact that Excel can have on your tour, your art, your music, your ability to do this again, the probability that your band won't implode, the chances that your girlfriend won't leave you, and to convince you to come to grips with it, have a look at the following question:

#days	day of week	Date	City	State	G'tee
1	Wednesday	11/05/03	Dundee	IL	$1,000
2	Thursday	11/06/03	Cincinnati	OH	$3,000
3	Friday	11/07/03	Columbia	MO	
4	Saturday	11/08/03	Cleveland	OH	$6,500
5	Sunday	11/09/03	LaCrosse	WI	$2,500
6	Monday	11/10/03	Toledo	OH	$2,000
7	Tuesday	11/11/03	Detroit	MI	$5,000
8	Wednesday	11/12/03	Boston	MA	
9	Thursday	11/13/03	Washington DC		$5,500
10	Friday	11/14/03	Rochester	NY	$5,000
11	Saturday	11/15/03		NJ	$5,000
12	Sunday	11/16/03	Philadelphia	PA	$4,500
13	Monday	11/17/03	New York	NY	$5,000
14	Tuesday	11/18/03	Pittsburgh	PA	$4,000
15	Wednesday	11/19/03	TBA		
16	Thursday	11/20/03	Atlanta	GA	%
17	Friday	11/21/03	Tampa	FL	$7,500
18	Saturday	11/22/03	Ft. Lauderdale	FL	$5,500
19	Sunday	11/23/03	Jacksonville	FL	$5,000
20	Monday	11/24/03	New Orleans	LA	$1,750
21	Tuesday	11/25/03	Houston	TX	$3,500
22	Wednesday	11/26/03	Dallas	TX	$5,500
23	Thursday	11/27/03	Austin	TX	%
24	Friday	11/28/03	Tulsa	OK	$5,500
25	Saturday	11/29/03	San Antonio	TX	$4,500
26	Sunday	11/30/03	El Paso	TX	$5,000
27	Monday	12/01/03	Albuquerque	NW	$2,500
28	Tuesday	12/02/03	Tempe	AZ	$4,000
29	Wednesday	12/03/03	Hollywood	CA	$8,000
30	Thursday	12/04/03	San Diego	CA	$1,500
31	Friday	12/05/03	Fresno	CA	$3,500
32	Saturday	12/06/03	San Fran	CA	$5,000
33	Sunday	12/07/03	Portland	OR	$1,500
34	Monday	12/08/03	Seattle	WA	$8,000
35	Tuesday	12/09/03	Salt Lake City	UT	$4,000
36	Wednesday	12/10/03	Denver	CO	$7,000
37	Thursday	12/11/03	Springfield	MO	$5,300
38	Friday	12/12/03	Minneapolis	MN	$3,300
39	Saturday	12/13/03	Chicago	IL	$16,000
40	Sunday	12/14/03	Milwaukee	WI	$4,000
					$166,350
			Number of Shows		40
			average per show		$4,158.75

"How can we make an extra $220 a day?" In class, all of the answers concerned insisting on more cash from promoters, telling the agent to get you more money, paying the opening bands less... Every idea came with a backlash or a consequence that could end up costing you more. If you confront anyone, it needs to be as a last resort, not because you didn't look at your Excel sheet. So, look at your Excel sheet and think of a few solutions before you look at the next page...

By canceling the Columbia and Boston shows that didn't seem to have guarantees, moving the Dundee show from the 5th to the 7th, and moving the Cincinnati show from the 6th to the 12th we were up $220 a day. Aside from illustrating the value of Excel or just simply paying attention, another essential part of this lesson might be that the agent didn't suggest this. He doesn't lose money on a day off; he isn't rewarded for reworking shows for better routing and more efficient use of your time; that's your job. It's your job if you're in a van and it's your job when you're going out and grossing $200,000 over a six week period.

#days	day of week	Date	City	State	G'tee
1	Friday	11/07/03	Dundee	IL	$1,000
2	Saturday	11/08/03	Cleveland	OH	$6,500
3	Sunday	11/09/03	LaCrosse	WI	$2,500
4	Monday	11/10/03	Toledo	OH	$2,000
5	Tuesday	11/11/03	Detroit	MI	$5,000
6	Wednesday	11/12/03	Cincinnati	OH	$3,000
7	Thursday	11/13/03	Washington DC		$5,500
8	Friday	11/14/03	Rochester	NY	$5,000
9	Saturday	11/15/03		NJ	$5,000
10	Sunday	11/16/03	Philadelphia	PA	$4,500
11	Monday	11/17/03	New York	NY	$5,000
12	Tuesday	11/18/03	Pittsburgh	PA	$4,000
13	Wednesday	11/19/03	TBA		
14	Thursday	11/20/03	Atlanta	GA	%
15	Friday	11/21/03	Tampa	FL	$7,500
16	Saturday	11/22/03	Ft. Lauderdale	FL	$5,500
17	Sunday	11/23/03	Jacksonville	FL	$5,000
18	Monday	11/24/03	New Orleans	LA	$1,750
19	Tuesday	11/25/03	Houston	TX	$3,500
20	Wednesday	11/26/03	Dallas	TX	$5,500
21	Thursday	11/27/03	Austin	TX	%
22	Friday	11/28/03	Tulsa	OK	$5,500
23	Saturday	11/29/03	San Antonio	TX	$4,500
24	Sunday	11/30/03	El Paso	TX	$5,000
25	Monday	12/01/03	Albuquerque	NW	$2,500
26	Tuesday	12/02/03	Tempe	AZ	$4,000
27	Wednesday	12/03/03	Hollywood	CA	$8,000
28	Thursday	12/04/03	San Diego	CA	$1,500
29	Friday	12/05/03	Fresno	CA	$3,500
30	Saturday	12/06/03	San Fran	CA	$5,000
31	Sunday	12/07/03	Portland	OR	$1,500
32	Monday	12/08/03	Seattle	WA	$8,000
33	Tuesday	12/09/03	Salt Lake City	UT	$4,000
34	Wednesday	12/10/03	Denver	CO	$7,000
35	Thursday	12/11/03	Springfield	MO	$5,300
36	Friday	12/12/03	Minneapolis	MN	$3,300
37	Saturday	12/13/03	Chicago	IL	$16,000
38	Sunday	12/14/03	Milwaukee	WI	$4,000
					$166,350
			Number of Shows		38
			average per show		$4,377.63

MISTAKES TO AVOID

TAMAR, THE COUNTDOWN NYC

TOURING EXPERIENCE

We got hooked up with some friends from NY through MySpace. We wanted to play a show together so I contacted a promoter in NY (again through MySpace) that booked this club called RARE in the meat packing district. A very cool area from everything I had heard. In fact, RARE used to be the infamous NY club, The Cooler. So I was excited. Our friends found some other great bands and it looked like it was going to be a great night.

When we got to the club, I asked how we were going to get paid. The guy at the door said that in order to get paid, we needed to have 15 paid friends that would come to the door and say they were there to see us. There were five bands on the bill and each band had a half-hour time slot with some change over time in between. So essentially, anyone that came to the show had to go up to the door guy, tell them which band they were there to see, pay ten bucks, and he would mark a little line next to that band's name to show that one person paid for that band. It made for a terrible night. All of our friends were on our guest list, and we weren't going to make them pay! And to make matters worse, most of the people who did come out came to see a specific band left immediately afterwards, so much for building any camaraderie among bands or fans. I noticed at the end of the night only one band got paid out of five bands.

:SMART TIPS

1. **Play every day,** twice a day if you can! It is not an answer to not play the smaller, poorer markets. Play every night within a reasonable traveling distance of the last and next show.

2. **A day off is the easiest way to shred a budget.** Creative people get bored. Boredom gets expensive.

3. **Always ask why!**

4. **Buy a Rand McNally Dist-O-Map!**

5. **Be careful about the number of people in your band.** Two to five people is easier than ten to twelve. Except if you are Gwar or Pigface.

6. **If you draw a line from Minneapolis to Texas,** there are only 15 of the largest cities west of that line. Stay east of the line.

7. **Play secondary and smaller markets. It is not an answer to not play these places.** You have to play every night within a reasonable traveling distance of the last and next show.

8. **The first set of dates fuels the second set of dates four to seven weeks later, be your own advance team!**

CHAPTER 4

TRANSPORTATION: BROKEN DOWN

Martin Atkins
Private Collection.

TOUR BUS

"Sometimes pirate ship, sometimes cattle truck, sometimes love bug."

Let's start with the tour bus. If you are in a car or a van, you don't want to read about it. If you haven't toured yet, you can still fantasize that you will be touring in a bus.

Be careful that you are not traveling in a bus too early in the massive exponential curve of your meteoric career. Why? Well, number one, nothing makes sleeping on a bus over a long overnight journey sweeter than having spent a few years driving in a crappy vehicle, eating dust and unidentifiable truck stop food.

Reason number two is more intangible. It has to do with social structure and part of the essence of the flimsy rubber band that holds this together. When you are in a bus, it becomes a traveling cocoon. People like to be safe and comfortable in all understandable things everything is there: cell phone, fridge, toilet, and band members begin to magnetize to it. When you are in a van, you need people to stay with. You'll find those people by staying in the club longer, interacting harder, being more alert, smelling better, and not drooling. Yes, free accommodations also come with obligations, but it's these social obligations that interlock and weave their way through the fragile endeavor of "Breaking America."

I don't mean this to sound careerist or mercenary because that's not what I mean at all. I don't remember many of the people I bumped into drunk or shagged in my last 25 years. But it is the people who I stayed with that I still have interaction with today. And that's a special legacy from that time in my life. There is an unwritten underground contract that strangers in a city honor when they trust and open their hearts, homes, showers, beds, washing machines, and high-speed DSL lines to a beat-down band on the road. To deny that contract, to deny that 5 a.m. conversation, to deny their ability to make a massive difference with a bed, a blanket, a bagel, and a bath is to deny the bond that will reverberate for years afterwards. Maybe part of touring in a band has nothing to do with the music. Maybe it has more to do with meeting people, seeing differences across the country, and discovering their changing attitudes. All you see inside the bus is the changing landscape, the mold growing inside the refrigerator, and the bass player's growing porn collection.

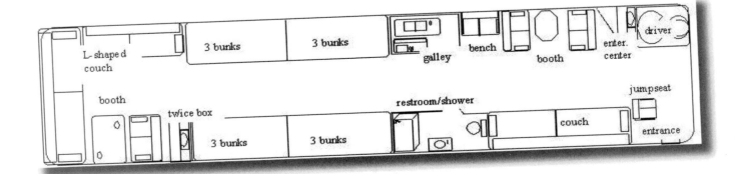

Before you even call a bus company, make sure you have a proposed routing. You should be able to tell the bus company the approximate total mileage before you pick up the phone. If you cannot, then you already look like someone who doesn't have a clue, because literally— you don't. It's only by dialing up the distances and looking at the touring spreadsheet that you can get any idea of what will make or break your budget. Be aware that in addition to the driver's daily bus rate and any overdrives, you will be paying for generator services (one or two a week), the driver's hotel (which he must have every day), a taxi for the driver to the hotel after load in, and a taxi from the hotel after you have loaded out. You will also be responsible for washing the linens once a week. This is not a place to save money, as you will discover.

Some companies have a tiny per mile maintenance fee, which can add up. You will also be

> "We spent two weeks on a Pigface bus crazy mad on chocolate almonds and the strongest strawberry daiquiris ever, then we realized we were paying for all of it. Including pizzas bought by the driver as an apology for getting us so lost we missed dinner."

required to pay any damages, which can be $200 per cigarette burn when you were in the back of the speeding bus while looking at gas prices, or the etched polar bear bathroom mirror that was smashed by your guitarist when he broke up with his girlfriend, the rearview mirror that was crushed while reversing into a telephone pole, the vomit stains on the front carpet, etc. Drivers will require at least enough float for a full fill-up and more. Most buses hold 140+ gallons of diesel at $2.60/gallon ($364), so you need to be giving them at least $500 at a time. You're going to get about 1,000 miles per fill-up.

Also beware: There is also something called "deadhead," an allowance of time for the bus to arrive from wherever it was to wherever you need it to be. This is usually two days on the front and two days on the back. I agreed to that several times rather than ask, "What the fuck is that?" You will be paying for two plus two extra days of bus, and two plus two extra days of driver. A bus averages $475 a day. That's $1,900 for four days of bus, and $740 for four days of driver, which makes $2,640 coming out of your pocket, or your stupid amplifier fund, all because you didn't ask. But wait, your driver will arrive with a bag full of receipts from the two days of deadhead and expect to leave the tour with bus float for hotels and gas on the way home.

Beware of cheap bargain vehicles, buses, vans, anything... If you are at a level where you should be traveling in a bus instead of just pretending you are... get a decent, safe, and reliable one.

> **"Anytime the driver disappears into K-mart, Wal-Mart, or any kind of Mart (except me), the receipt will go into your envelope (that means you bought the chocolate raisins fatty!)."**

"It was my birthday. I was exhausted. I vowed to never again skimp on the tour bus. You will pay for it many times over in the end. If the deal seems too good to be true, it fucking well is." - Dave Baker

You should be concentrating on your career and your war with your body and mind, not dealing with maintenance issues. Whoever negotiated the bus deal with the Killing Joke '88 tour, thanks! I am sure you thought you did a fantastic job. But your foot didn't fall through the floor of the toilet while pissing at 60 miles an hour. You were not aware that a loose pipe was dripping gallons of piss onto my drum kit. You weren't on stage when the drum kit was hit by the light system (and pure candle power that only a New Jersey night club on a Tuesday night can provide), creating clouds of steaming piss! Breathe deep! Oh yeah!

At least if you are dealing with a large reputable company when things go wrong (not if, not if, not if), they will have the machinery and financial cushion to deal with you. Keep your cool; write everything down. List everything as it happens so that you can communicate the details effectively. You might not remember all of it when you are swimming in the middle of the problem. Same with a van rental company, when your van explodes, at least you can get a larger company to deal constructively with the problem.

> *You need to look at the potential savings when working with small companies in terms of what will happen when you have a breakdown on a Friday afternoon the night before your biggest show with no prospect of help from a company 2,000 miles away from their one and only office, where everyone leaves at four o'clock and won't be back until Monday. Gottit?*

NEGOTIATING

Don't be afraid to negotiate. Get a few different quotes from people, but make sure you lock in and nail down the actual bus you are going to get. The less you pay, the more tempted the company will be to send you out in 'Old Daisy'... no joke... ever seen mushrooms growing in a coffee pot?

"I usually keep asking for reductions until someone tells me to fuck off, then I dial it back a click."
  —Martin Atkins

**"If the deal seems too good to be true, it fucking well is."
– Dave Baker**

In this example, I've listed all of the problems day by day for the bus company and for myself. It's easy to list the cost of a hotel or a replacement RV, but I go on to make several points more difficult to quantify that are real costs to your career: there was no networking in New York City, we had to switch buses (one of the most stressful things you can do on the road, somebody always loses something), one promoter refused to ever work with us again, and during another show, we went on stage after an 18-year-old-age-limit curfew. If you can point this out without being hysterical, you make your point more effectively.

Bus Problems Free for All Tour

Location	Days	Cost	Condition/Credit For
	20	$ 500.00	est gas running generator all night at 1 gallon/hr
Albuquerque			no a/c, no generator day 1
San Antonio			no a/c, no generator day 2
			tire loss
		$ 760.00	rv + driver rental
		$ 50.00	rv driver bonus
		$ 75.00	rv gas
Dallas			no a/c no generator day 3
			no notification from driver who knew at 6pm
			bus left with no power
		$ 25.00	running engine all night
			no emergency contact from ▮▮▮▮ from 3a.m. & 7am calls
			couldn't empty trash
Tulsa			baND ARRIVES AT 8PM - 7 O CLOCK DOOR!
			club very upset – ▮▮▮▮ service nearly costs us the show - band go on past 18 under curfew
			chuck at Cains said "he will never work with us again"
			no generator day 4
		$ 445.04	hotel tulsa
Springfield			bus switch
	4	$ 1,440.00	4 days bus credit
			**please note only one nights hotel - NOT 3
		$ 180.00	additional fee taken from rv deposit for driver
New York City			no power to lights or TOILET
			forces us to leave 3 hours early = no networking in NYC!!!!
TOTAL		$ 3,475.04	

"...very quickly, it was go time!"

Sitting here now, I remember how frustrating it was to be trapped on a bus with no A/C and have the garbage literally overflowing back into the bus (the driver had parked the bus with the garbage door blocked by a light pole). No one could sleep. It was horrible. It was like something out of one of those submarine movies (Run Silent, Run Deep). A stick-your-head-in-an oven kind of experience. The next morning I really lost it with the driver. I threw pizza boxes into the front well of the bus. The driver reacted as if I had thrown a hot, bubbling pizza in his face! He pulled over and, very quickly, it was go time! Cars were honking. We realized we were standing on the grassy knoll in Dallas! It was the only thing that stopped a big fight.

OVERDRIVES

Bus drivers are only allowed to travel 450 miles per day then they charge you double their day rate. This is called an "overdrive." Anything over 600-650 miles in one blast is called a "double overdrive." That's when you pay the driver three times the daily rate. So before you allow your agent to explain how amazing the Denver show on a Tuesday night is going to be, make sure the potential upside isn't swallowed by double or triple bus fees and 100 extra gallons of gas!

I WANT MY MPG

Most buses get (around) nine miles to the gallon. This is true of well-maintained buses, which will cost you more per day because they probably look nicer, but someone claiming on the phone that their 1972 deathtrap is going to get nine miles to the gallon, only needs to be two miles to the gallon off to cost you, nobody else but you, thousands of dollars that you could otherwise spend on drugs and the latest fancy equipment.

mpg	9.00	7.00	7.00
cost per gallon	$2.60	$3.00	$3.50
total miles	15,000.00	15,000.00	15,000.00
total cost	$4,333.34	$6,428.58	$7,500.00

The average U.S. tour at 15,000 miles at nine miles to the gallon is 1,666 gallons of fuel. At $2.60 a gallon that's $4,333. If ("Please God, no, how could it be!"), the owner of the bus exaggerated the efficiency of his vehicle which only gets seven miles to the gallon and maybe gas prices just increased 40 cents... well that's not very much of a difference is it? Yes it is, you are going to need $6,428—a difference of $2,095! What will happen as you make these calculations half way through the tour because you are bored or up all night speeding? CNN will tell you that gas prices are going up to $3.50 a gallon. Now that's $7,500 of gas, a difference of over $3,000. (You can have so much fun doing things like this with your new Excel prowess!) With gas prices set to rise to $4.00 per gallon this year, the total cost rises to over $8,500... but that won't happen... an agent told me so.

I WANT MY MPG MILES PER GALLON

BUS ETIQUETTE

A bus is tiny; the usable common areas are very small. The corridor in the bunk space has a door at each end and is going to be dark with boots, some kind of horrifying underwear hanging from a peg, arms, and God knows what else, all potentially very dangerous. Any kind of roommate laws having to do with space and mutual respect should be underlined twice and highlighted in yellow. One of the great benefits of a bus to a budgetary-challenged, hard-working band is a full size refrigerator. It enables you (when a promoter does provide you with the rider) to take perishables with you for the next day when the next promoter doesn't. It also means you can eat cheaper, better, and stock up with essentials. It also opens up some of the catering rider strategies (discussed in the *Riders* Chapter) but someone, if not everyone, needs to pay attention to the refrigerator and the trash!

HERE'S THE DEAL.....

WHEN THE TRASH STOPS MAGICALLY DISAPPEARING – THEN IT IS TIME TO EMPTY THE FUCKING TRASH!

THE GARBAGE CAN IS IN A CUPBOARD IN THE SECOND BAY, THE TRASH BAGS ARE RIGHT NEXT TO IT. BY THE TIME THE TRASH IS VISIBLE IN THE BUS – THAT MEANS THERE ARE PROBABLY 20 BOTTLES READY TO RAIN DOWN ON WHOEVER IS DOWN THERE TRYING TO DEAL WITH IT.

> **An overlooked benefit when one venue feeds you well, you can take the lasagna away for the next day!**

From Mark O'Shea NIN Tour Manager

- **Do discuss the smoking rules of the bus before you get out on the tour.** Where and what is to be smoked where and how. This is a group meeting discussion.

- **Don't let strangers on your bus** or you will eventually be sorry. You should develop a set of rules as a group for how and why visitors are allowed on the bus (your home away from home).

OTHER BUS RULES

Guests on a bus: limit guests to the front lounge only. This keeps the rear lounge as a safe haven for valuables and anybody who needs to chill. It also prevents guests from trudging through the aforementioned dark corridor in the bunk area. Do not ever transport anyone from one city to another, excluding the occasional partner.

Bus Keys: for some reason, even though there will be 12 people on the bus, the driver only arrives with one or two keys. Everybody on the bus should have a key. If you don't ask the driver to arrive with 12 keys, he won't. And it might be three or four days into the tour before

> **"Everybody on the bus should have a key."**

TOUR:SMART TIP
for more information go to:
www.tstouring.com

you actually have time and an open locksmith to get you the keys you need. The last thing you need to deal with in the first few days on a tour is people who are like, "Well, I didn't lock the door because I didn't have a key."

TIPS FOR A SAFE RIDE

- When traveling in a van, always wear your seat belt.

- When traveling by bus, always make sure your feet are facing the driver; otherwise, if he brakes quickly you could snap your neck.

Actual Daily Cost of a Tour Bus

Variables		
Days of Tour		70
Weeks of Tour		10
Total Overdrives (451 - 599)		6
Total Overdrives (600+)		2
Deadhead days		4

Charge	Rate	Total
Daily Costs	$ 475.00	$ 33,250.00
Bus lease/day	$ 36.00	$ 2,520.00
Insurance	$ 185.00	$ 12,950.00
Drivers Wages/day	$ 185.00	$ 1,110.00
Overdrives (between 451 miles and 599 miles)	$ 185.00	$ 370.00
Overdrives (600 miles+)	$ 25.00	$ 1,750.00
Trailer charge/day to driver	$ 45.00	$ 3,150.00
Trailer rental/day	$ 10.00	$ 700.00
Tracking Satellite Service/day	$ 25.00	$ 1,750.00
Bus driver taxi to and from hotel	$ 85.00	$ 5,950.00
Bus driver hotel		
Weekly Costs	$ 45.00	$ 450.00
Bus wash/week	$ 45.00	$ 225.00
generator service/100 hours	$ 45.00	$ 450.00
interior cleaning/week		
Deadhead Charges	$ 475.00	$ 1,900.00
Bus lease/day	$ 36.00	$ 144.00
Insurance	$ 185.00	$ 740.00
Drivers Wages/day	$ 25.00	$ 100.00
Trailer charge/day to driver	$ 45.00	$ 180.00
Trailer rental/day	$ 10.00	$ 40.00
Tracking Satellite Service/day	$ 85.00	$ 340.00
Bus driver hotel		
Misc Costs	$ 500.00	$ 500.00
Floats	$ 60.00	$ 200.00
Carpet cleaning/every three weeks	$ 750.00	$ 750.00
End of tour cleaning costs		
Crap (paper towels, bowls, toilet paper, spoons, cleaning supplies, etc)	$ 500.00	$ 500.00
Actual daily cost of bus/trailer is:		$ 1,000.27
TOTAL		$ 70,019.00

MONEY SAVING TIP

Save money on a day room or shower room by using the bus driver's room as a shower room. You are paying for the room, and as long as you are courteous and inform the driver that at 3 a.m. after load-out you will be using the shower, he can return the courtesy by not trashing his room. Inform the hotel that you will need extra towels in the driver's room/day room. Even if there is a shower at the venue, there will always be someone in the touring party who forgets to shower, or is too busy to shower, or is so sweaty that they could use another one. One band came to this method a few months too late. They cut short a planned tour for their new album just as they were starting to get radio play because of a $10,000 budget shortfall. In the preceding three months of touring, they had one or two day rooms each day, easily costing them the $10,000 they needed. The tour stopped and the band broke up.

EXAMPLE:

One and a half rooms per day (that's one room one day and 2 rooms the next) on an average of $65 per night, is $97.50 per day. That's $8,775 over 90 days.

I am going to keep saying this stuff again and again and again. It is not the big stuff that will make or break you. It is the stuff between the cracks. Neil Young said it best, "Rust never sleeps."

TOUR:SMART TIP
for more information go to:
www.tstouring.com

CAR

The ideal, man oh man, not many people, no nine m.p.g. of a giant bus to deal with, no parking problems... what could possibly go wrong?

I just dialed up car rentals for 28 days (it said that was the maximum rental and just on an economy car within the Chicago area). The rate per week varies from $179.99 per week down to $147.99 per week within the same company! So, if you are embarking on a cross country trek you might want to do more than pick up a car from the handy place around the corner!

Over the course of 10 weeks, that's a saving of $320 dollars.

Shop around for the best m.p.g. See the appendix for some examples.

VAN

The first step up is essential if there are four or more of you (plus sound, lights, merchandise, etc.). The cost of the days on the road starts to rise, but you have some flexibility in carrying some special elements of the show and some extra people. (Van rentals will vary from $500 per week and up.)

Be careful to consider that it will be a member of the band that is going to be driving, as well as having worked and performed that day. You want to leave town as soon after the show as you reasonably can, but that increases the dangers from fatigue. Probably one of the band and crew will become the night guys, someone else will be the morning person.

The driver controls the music—always!

If it's a long drive have someone not get blasted that night and take a nap in the afternoon so that you can have a driving buddy. It's much safer that way.

As you start to gig and travel more, look into purchasing a van, customizing it for your needs, and hiring a driver/merch person/soundman.

A FEW WORDS ABOUT VAN AESTHETICS

You may think that it's punk-as-fuck to stencil your band name in huge letters on the side of your '88 Ford cargo van, and to spray paint a huge anarchy symbol across the rear loading doors. Don't do it! I guarantee you that your fans will not appreciate your sense of vehicle aesthetics nearly as much as they will appreciate you actually making it to your show on time. If you've spent any time on freeways in this country, you know full well that everybody speeds, and only a few people are actually stopped and ticketed. Nothing in the world says 'pull me over and give me a ticket' like a punked out touring van. You do not want to encounter the police as you make your hurried drive from Minneapolis to Chicago (especially if your driver has a green mohawk and a 'Fuck The Police' patch on the shoulder of his stone-washed denim vest!). Make your artistic, political, personal, and aesthetic statements on stage, not with your vehicle. Camouflage the fact that you are a touring band! If you have any leftist political bumper stickers on your van, remove them! Even though nobody gives you a second look in NYC, that "No Blood For Oil" bumper sticker might just get you hauled into jail by the red neck sheriff as you drive through the middle of nowhere Georgia on your way to a great show. Feel free to add a yellow ribbon magnet, some 'Bob Dole '96' bumper stickers, or a Jesus fish. This not only greatly reduces your chances of a run-in with law enforcement, expensive traffic tickets or worse, it also protects your gear and merch from theft. You will often have to park your vehicle overnight with your gear inside. If you make the mistake of letting your van look like a band vehicle, you are advertising the fact that there is probably stuff inside that is worth stealing! Make your van blend in, and for extra security when you have to park your van at night, try to back it up against a building so that it is impossible for anyone to break open the rear door.

- Mike Johnson, Invisible Records

The next step up is a van with a trailer, but now you start to accumulate potential problems. Make sure you get a double axle trailer. The cost vs. risk of going with a single axle just isn't worth it. When one tire explodes, you shall have 3. Now you have the van keys, the padlock for the trailer key ("I thought you had the key for the trailer padlock!"), the wear and tear on the trailer tires, the rear trailer lights, reversing into that tight spot in Chinatown, down that alley. The rear of it will be wrecked within four weeks so don't plan on selling it for a profit after the first tour. I've been looking at some interesting custom trailers (how fucking sad is that), with a small production office in the end nearest the hitch... and there's always a hitch.

Trailers are cheap to rent but also pretty cheap to buy. This is an investment that could pay for itself at the end of one tour. You can pick up a decent trailer for a couple of thousand dollars or less. You're probably going to worry about padlocking the rear doors of the trailer, and of course you should. But, there have been be many instances of thieves unhitching a trailer using bolt cutters to cut a security chain and taking the whole thing in minutes. Here's something I came across trawling through the internet that might be useful.

Super Tough Trailer Hitch Lock with Viro Locking System
Will resist cutting torch, drilling, deep-freezing, sledge-hammers, as well as bolt-cutters.
$192.50 plus $55.00 s/h… Get one!
http://tirelock.com/dev/productdetails.php?pid=36

If you are cramming too much equipment into your trailer write down the pack and leave the chart in the trailer. Stick some tape on cases and call the numbers from the stage to load. That way, if you're sick, the remaining crew can follow your laminated pack chart and get out of town quickly. If not, they will be all ready to go, high five-ing each other that they managed the pack without you (who could have thought it was so simple)?... then the remaining three cases roll out of the venue and you're there for another two hours trying to mephisto the fuckers into the trailer.

Get a trailer with a fold down ramp door, and put wheels on anything you can!

OTHER METHODS

RV

"Whatever you decide to do about a vehicle, for fucks sake don't buy a Winnebago (shortly before the artist bought a Winnebago)."
— Mark O'Shea

One of the big challenges to touring is setting up transportation. Touring in a van can be uncomfortable, especially if there are a lot of people with you, and you have to do a ten-hour drive. And tour buses are expensive. So we tried compromising between both, and getting an RV. I was told that RVs have a lot of mechanical problems, and they cost a lot of money to maintain, but I decided to give it a try anyway, only later to find out how true this was. After the RV had barely made it to several shows, we had to sit on the side of the road so the damn RV would stop overheating, After one show, while in the parking lot, and turned off mind you, the RV caught on fire—with our driver asleep inside and wearing ear plugs! Fortunately, she got out safely, and the fire department came quickly and extinguished the blaze. But the entire outside of the driver's side of the RV was completely melted by the fire. After the incident, I realized it would have been more cost effective to let the damn thing burn to the ground and collect the insurance money!

— Lacey Connor, Nocturne

"If your RV catches on fire, don't call the fire department! Instead, let it burn to the ground and collect the insurance money."

"RV's? We did it with Killing Joke and Brian Brain. In those days The Chili Peppers did it too... RV's are notoriously unreliable for the longer hauls. Tempting, but be careful unless one of you is a mechanic...you do get the benefit of a toilet, refrigerator and stove..."

– Martin Atkins

FERRY

The most common place you will encounter a ferry will be from Dover to Calais, France or from Liverpool to The Hague (DenHaag) during a European tour. These crossings are subject to weather and so are the people on the ferry. It can be eight to nine hours on a good day. You can book an overnight crossing and sleep on the ferry if you can; it might be cheaper than a hotel room and a missed show.

Carlton P. Sandercock:

In a message dated 12/11/06 9:54:57:

hi marteeeen

last night, I was looking after the surviving members of the MC5 who were to play London's underworld last night. they were at Antwerp the night before and drove down to Calais for the hour and a half channel crossing due to be in Camden about 3 in the afternoon. with the storms we had yesterday the poor bastards were on the ferry for about 6 hours until a naval frigate had to attempt to bring the ferry in sideways another 3 hours in traffic from Dover to London and they arrived just as the support band were finishing.

fuckin storming show though and no whining either troopers !

TRAIN

The Bullet Train in Japan goes REALLY FAST!

I took the train from Portland to Seattle and it was like a two day holiday! It was nice to be on my own, there was great scenery, and I got to stay in the day room from the day before, sleep in, and chill a bit—a gift for sure. As a tour manager, you can always look for ways to alleviate the people pressure of a crowded bus in some cost-effective ways (not just for the person who is off the bus). When two or three people are off the cramped bus, it's a holiday for everybody else left on the bus too. But, be careful. When you split up the touring party, you double the chances of random shit happening.

Martin Atkins Private Collection.

TOUR:SMART TIP
for more information go to:
www.tstouring.com

PLANES

Using commercial flights is always an option. With equipment being trucked over land, the main advantage to flying is that the band will be able to avoid the 2,000 mile drive from Minneapolis to Seattle, and you might gain a larger degree of flexibility in the booking. You will still be dependent on the drive time of the truck and the flights add a second tour to manage: the ground transportation with the truck and a separate schedule of flights, arrivals, taxis, check-in times, and all of those elements. or you can rent equipment and ditch scenery, or FedEx everything.

On a bus tour, you can creatively use a cheap flight to relieve pressure. If you have two days off, look at flying home the person with the relationship problems. It will a be great relief for everyone... if they come back.

Flightstats.com a great tool to avoid delays. It might tell you that a particular flight is late 75% of the time.

PLANES

KATRINA ATKINS

If you're flying, my number one suggestion is to get flights on an airline like Southwest. You will not be charged to change your flight, just the difference in fare and the ticket is good for one year on whoever's credit card it was booked. ATA lets you fly the same day if you miss your flight, for no extra charge at all. Always try to get tickets you can change and flights at sensible hours. When your tour ends, don't book flights out for everyone at 8:00 a.m. the next morning. Chances are good they'll miss their flights and you'll lose your money!

> **"Don't always get the cheapest flight. It can end up being the most expensive if it is not changeable."**

PUBLIC TRANSPORTATION MEGABUS (WWW.MEGABUS.COM)

NATHAN KOCH, EMULSION

If you book three months in advance, it's $1.50 each way! But more realistically for shows (by the time they're confirmed), it's $20-$35 each way. It started in the U.K. and has been really successful there. Now they are testing it in the Midwest, express buses to and from Chicago to eight cities around the Midwest, and it's potentially cheaper than driving if you're a one or two man group. I've been working on getting shows all over the Midwest and using Megabus to get there. Even if it is a $50-100 guarantee, I'm sill doing fine.

Be careful: it's a great, cheap service, but you have to watch the scheduling and there are no refunds if you miss a bus. There are also limits with the number of bags.

These are the stops Megabus makes in the US:

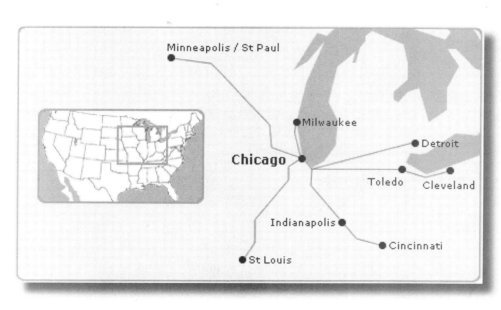

NATHAN KOCH

ONE TIME INVISIBLE WEB/ OFFICE ASSISTANT, AND THE GUY BEHIND 2003's NEW NATIONAL ANTHEM TOUR

ADDITIONAL CONSIDERATIONS

GPS

These pictures tell the story. This is me licking my GPS. I deleted the later ones where I stick it down my pants.

A band can lose time, a sound check, and an opportunity for a great show, simply because they're late. With GPS all you need is gas and that's it. Swerve to the left, swerve to the right, fall asleep at the wheel, poop your pants while you're driving; none of this is a problem for GPS. I wish this had been around in the early 80's when I was groovin' in LA. The smallest cell phone back then was the size of a shoe box. I spent much of my time there driving around lost! Not anymore baby! Except when the GPS lady's voice is muffled by my boxers.

Jack Carson uses GPS on his laptop to track the bus route, especially useful on those questionable overdrives created by a 20 mile detour for the driver to get another bus wash! This is a smart tip to easily avoid unnecessary crap.

TOUR:SMART TIP

OTHER OPTIONS: GREASEL AND CONVERSION VEHICLES

The diesel engine was originally supposed to run on vegetable oil. In fact Rudolph Diesel said in 1911, "The diesel engine can be fed with vegetable oils and would help considerably in the development of agriculture of the countries which use it." What the fuck did he know?

Fuel efficiency doesn't just have an impact on your budget and your ability to get to the next city anymore. It's impacting the planet and whether or not the next city on your tour still exists.

There are companies out there manufacturing conversion kits for diesel engines to straight vegetable oil (SVO) engines. Just like a hybrid car switching from gas power to built-up electrical power, the new models allow you to use gas and/or vegetable oil. New developments every day in this field are making this option more feasible for a band or anyone traveling around the country with deadlines and a time table.

You can check out *goldenfuelsystems.com* and the wonderfully named *frybrid.com* for more details.

GAS CARDS

You might find yourself at a gas station in the middle of nowhere in the middle of the night that doesn't open until 6 in the morning and the only way you're going to get gas is by using your card because that is the only payment the pump will accept.

AAA

A primary membership only costs $54.00 and can be a life saver. From 24-hour roadside assistance, to nationwide arrest bond protection where most jurisdictions and (depending on the charges) will accept your membership card in place of cash for up to $1,000.

MARTIN ATKINS ASKS:

JOLLY ROGER

JOLLY ROGER

TOUR MANAGER

BUS DRIVERS

MA: How do you deal with a bus driver?

JR: Bus drivers are different… different breed of folks… gotta treat 'em like people, ya know? The bottom line is a lot of people treat 'em like they're just some kind of slave or something. You gotta keep the buses clean. And as one of our friends found out that one day, you don't eat crawfish on a bus! (Laughs) Bus driver went to get his gun… the crawfish was gone! (Laughs) The Crawfish Incident.

MA: What about Ministry in Denver in 1990?

JR: The guy's wife drove the crew bus, he drove the band bus. He stayed up with a member of the band doing a bunch of wacky drugs and then he got really drunk once we got to the place. And then he got in an argument with his wife because we pulled in late and she said, "Can't you stop drinking?" So, at one point, he pulled his bus over to the stairway right in front of the main door at the Embassy Suites, and cut all the break lines. So, it took them like ten hours to pull it out from in front of the place. They had only let us stay there, because they wouldn't let rock bands stay there, and I said it was a "Ministry," (Laughs) They weren't too happy about that! Then he came up and he was slapping his wife around and he threw the wedding ring at her, and it raised a big welt on her head right then. And I said, "You know, you gotta calm down." So, he punched me in the mouth. I said, "Man, you're not makin' it any better, you gotta calm down." He punched me in the gut. I said, "Listen, you gotta calm down!" He punched me again! And I just straightened out my arm and hit him and I saw him go in slow motion towards the door. Outside the door was about four feet of walkway and then it was the atrium maybe six, seven floors down. And at that point, I saw myself in prison for the rest of my life for killin' this fucker. And just as he got to the doorway, two security guys came walking in. "What's goin on in…" BAM! They knocked him over.

> **"Bus drivers are different… different breed of folks… gotta treat 'em like people, ya know? The bottom line is a lot of people treat 'em like they're just some kind of slave or something."**

LEASE A SOLUTION, NOT A PROBLEM

JOHN AIKIN

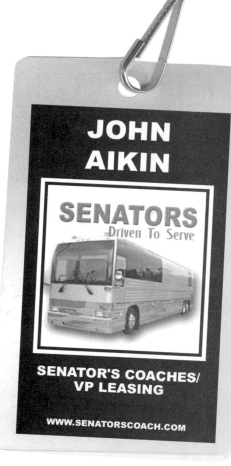

JOHN AIKIN

SENATORS
Driven To Serve

**SENATOR'S COACHES/
VP LEASING**

WWW.SENATORSCOACH.COM

- **Stick with the larger** and more established companies.
- **Realize that you get what you pay for,** and that low cost usually means low quality.
- **A disgruntled driver can disrupt your whole tour;** either make him happy or get rid of him fast.
- **If your passengers are new,** clue them in ahead of time about the basics.
- **Space is a valuable commodity** so travel very light. You cannot leave your stuff out, because it will get in someone's way.
- **Bus plumbing systems do not handle solid waste well.** If you need to take a dump, ask the driver to stop at the next rest area or truck stop. Your fellow passengers will appreciate it. Also, smells tend to linger in the bus, so let the driver know how immediate your situation is. In drastic emergencies, a garbage bag dump may be necessary. Tie it up securely and throw it away later.
- **If your aim is bad, clean it up.** There is nothing worse than bare feet on piss in the middle of the night.
- **Be extraordinarily considerate at all times.** Tempers can be short when confined to a small space for a long ride.
- **A great driver can make a not so great bus drivable,** but it does not work the other way around. A good experienced driver is a must, but attitude is more important than experience.
- **All passengers need to know to not exit the bus in the middle of the night without making sure the driver knows they exited.** Everyone has a story about someone being left in a truck stop in Montana in the middle of the night. Most coaches have a system, like leaving something in the driver's seat, etc.

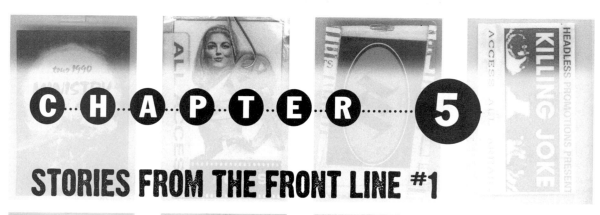

C·H·A·P·T·E·R ····· 5

STORIES FROM THE FRONT LINE #1

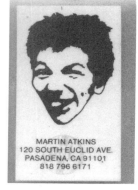

MARTIN ATKINS
120 SOUTH EUCLID AVE.
PASADENA, CA 91101
818 796 6171

P.I.L

JAPAN TOUR

#2

Van Production
TOKYO
☎ 03-470-0681

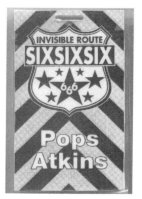

THE FLAMING TV STORY

JACK CARSON, TOUR MANAGER

The band I was working for had a small run of dates in Texas. As you know some of the distances are massive there. So there are a few choices regarding transportation. I should note here that this particular artist had a fairly sizeable budget and prefers comfort over economy. When I am selecting the mode of transport for a short run or any run for that matter, I take a few things into account. In no particular order these are:

- Artist comfort
- Crew practicality
- Gear requirements
- Cost
- Stress factor for me

So my choices for Texas were:

- Charter Airplane (In this case too expensive for the # of dates).
- Commercial Flights (Pain in the ass for me).
- RV (Too small for number for band and crew).
- Couple of Vans (Not any fun).
- Tour Bus (Just right).

I looked around and called all my usual contacts for bus quotes that would not include an arm and a leg in deadheads. All the good ones based nearby were out. I have a mate who owns an older XL Prevost who lives in Texas. I called him and his bus was available. Let me first tell you about the bus. It is old, I think one of the first XLS, it has the 8v90 motor *vs.* the Detroit 60. Those facts alone would usually be enough for a "thanks but no thanks." But, I know the bus, it has an OK interior and looked the part on the outside. This bus had been on a tour I was on as the support band's transport. So I called my mate and basically bullied him into a deal. The call went something like this :

ME: Your bus available for these dates ?

MATE: Yes.

ME: I'll pay $250 a day for the bus, I'll give you $150 a day to drive. You have to drive and I'll buy all the fuel as we go as well as fuel for your trip out and home and you have to throw in Satellite service. I don't even want to hear about end of tour service or bus washes.

MATE: ....

ME: WE have a deal?

MATE: I guess so...

I know this deal sounds harsh but I knew the bus had been sitting for a while and in the end was mutually beneficial. Truth be told this guy liked to go out on the road occasionally and I knew he was a fan of this band.

Next order of business was to call the band and tell them about the crappy bus I had hired for the week. I have always found that if the artist is prepped for something not to be great then they are less miserable when that something is, indeed, not great.

First show went well and we were all en route after an early bus call.

Around 4:00, I was awoken by an acrid stench like burning rubber and static electricity. My first thought was we blew a tire and the driver had not noticed. I jumped up and grabbed my flashlight. The bunk hallway was filled with thick smoke. I looked down to find the source of this smoke and to my shock, it was bellowing from the singer's bunk!

I ripped back his curtain and yanked him out of bed, You should have seen the look in his eyes!

At the foot of the bunk, the tv set was smoldering! I reached in and tore it from the wall and ran to the front of the bus tossing it from hand to hand like a big square hot potato. With the bus still cruising down the highway at 50 mph, I opened the door and threw the tv out. We were in the lane nearest the curb.

The driver remained stone-faced. As far as he knew, the tour manager had just flipped out and thrown his tv off the bus. Perhaps he did not like what was on tv? After we pulled over, things became clearer to the driver. His bus nearly caught fire.

Moral of this story: With tour buses, you get what you pay for. You can always negotiate cheap deals but don't start out with a cheap bus!

> **"Moral of this story: With tour busses, you get what you pay for. You can always negotiate cheap deals but don't start out with a cheap bus!"**

"If you are the last to leave the bus (or no one is in the front lounge when you leave), lock the door. There have been plenty of times random people have 'broken into' a bus because of unlocked doors, and things get stolen. The same rule applies if you get on your bus, but won't be hanging out in the front to watch over things, and there's no one else there. Lock the door behind you. It takes two seconds."
   - Sarah Dope

NEVER SKIMP ON A TOUR BUS: 1998 BIRTHDAY REMEMBERED

DAVE BAKER

Pigface embarked on a tour in late '98 covering most of the United States in three hectic weeks before the holidays. This one came on the heels of the *Lowest of the Low* label tour that spring. It also defied the prevailing wisdom that our bands, bands just about everywhere for that matter, should not tour in December. We bloody well knew that the probability of incurring all kinds of otherwise avoidable problems was heightened with the bad weather we would almost certainly encounter in many markets. Although I don't recall exactly, I can say with some confidence that there were no days off. However, for those of you familiar with Pigface and Invisible Records tours over the past couple of decades, this should be familiar territory.

The tour included many of the usual suspects and some new ones among the band, crew, and label staff and followed the October release of a Pigface live album. Jolly Roger, Martin Atkins, and several members of the crew traveled by plane to each city ahead of the scheduled arrival of the rest of the tour to ensure that each day's load-in and set up proceeded without incident. The tour also leased an extended cargo van for the transport of tour merchandise and some personnel. On one particularly long stretch of highway between Detroit and New York City, "some personnel" meant me.

In addition to the financial constraints faced by independent labels and recording artists every day, this tour was made more challenging by the routing and the travel it dictated. As I mentioned before, there were no days off on this tour. We needed to have a gig booked everyday for the tour to just break even. With daily tour expenses somewhere north of $5,000, a day off quickly translated into considerable losses for the tour and, in turn, Invisible Records. The tour began in the Midwest, and then made its way to the West Coast. Following the Los Angeles concert, we caught an early morning flight to Tulsa, OK, to arrive just in time for an early afternoon load in and sound check.

Following the Tulsa show, the bands loaded out into a new bus (the lease on the first one ended in LA as planned) and departed for Chicago. It was December 21st.

The concert at The House of Blues was sold out. Pigface was well received and at the end of the evening, after a number of days away on the road, I went home to spend the night in my apartment. I turned off my cell phone.

> "This tour was made more challenging by the routing and the travel it dictated."

DAVE BAKER

LABEL MANAGER
INVISIBLE RECORDS
1994-2000

When I awoke just a couple of hours later, I was greeted with a number of anxious cell phone messages. Instead of leaving Chicago for the overnight trip to the next gig in Detroit as scheduled, the bus was still at The House of Blues. Apparently, the bus driver failed to consider the frigid temperatures in Chicago during the month of December. Instead of leaving the generators running during our stay in Chicago, the bus was turned off. As a result, the fuel lines had frozen, rendering the bus immobile for some time to come.

Upon receiving the news, I contacted the bus company. The Detroit performance was just 12 hours away. The bus company arranged to provide a new bus. It was a few hours from Chicago.

Mercifully, the second bus arrived shortly thereafter and the transfer of personnel and equipment from one bus to the other was completed quickly. It was mid-afternoon by the time the tour bus, bound for Detroit, left the venue. They were late, but with the effort of the crew and the staff already on-hand in Detroit, the show was not in jeopardy. Not yet.

Having previously planned to spend the day in Chicago to attend to other tour and label business, I was working out of the Invisible Records' Chicago office. Then, I left for Midway Airport to catch my scheduled flight to rejoin the tour in Detroit. En route to Chicago's Midway airport, I received another call. The new bus had broken down just miles from The House of Blues. Now, the Detroit show was in jeopardy. And with 1,000 tickets sold, we were not going to cancel it.

We improvised in typical fashion. After some discussion with Martin and Jolly to determine what was still possible to salvage the evening, I asked the members of Pigface to grab whatever equipment they could and jump in cabs to meet me at Midway. The band arrived within the hour. Once the tickets were purchased and the bags were checked-in, we made our way to the gate; though not before Jared and I convinced airport security that we had identification for all ten musicians. Apparently, Levi failed to bring his along for the journey. Nonetheless, we made it through this little episode unscathed.

Just after we got through security, Bob Dog Catlin, the Evil Mothers' guitarist who contributed to numerous Pigface tours, told me that he had neglected to loosen the guitar strings on his guitar prior to checking his guitar case. At altitude, this would likely result in the neck of the guitar cracking. However, he had realized this problem too late and the ticketing agent advised him that there was nothing that could be done until the bags were unloaded in Detroit.

This being another in a growing series of misadventures over the past 24 hours, I returned to the counter to speak with the agent and her supervisor. After explaining our predicament and the financial ramifications (with which I took great liberty) of this situation if not resolved, the supervisor relented and asked that I instruct the guitarist to meet an airline crew member at the boarding gate. From there, the guitarist was able to board the cargo area of the plane to make the necessary adjustments to his guitar. I doubt that an airline would be quite so accommodating today. Bob Dog was elated. I was relieved.

In Detroit, the venue had arranged for two stretch limousines to meet us at the airport. After all of the crap that day, it made everyone feel like "rock stars" for a few minutes on the short

"...the fuel lines had frozen..."

trip to the venue. The band hit the door, Martin quickly finished his spoken word performance (which he had been doing in an effort to buy the rest of us some time to arrive), and 15 minutes later, Pigface was on stage for what proved to be the best show of the tour. Triumph in the face of adversity! Again.

At the end of the Detroit show, I got into the cargo van and drove a long stretch of highway to New York City for the last show of the tour. It was my birthday. I was exhausted. I vowed to never again skimp on the tour bus. You will pay for it many times over in the end. If the deal seems too good to be true, it fucking well is.

Also see Dirk Flanigan's piece in *Tour Dairies*.

A ROAD TO HELL WELL TRAVELED
REV. JOHN WHEELER

This is neither a cautionary tale, nor a sob story from yet another artist boo-hooing about how difficult it is to make it in the world of music today. If you hear the call, there is no cautioning against going out into the wild world to display your talent and craft, and it is well-known that if you choose this path in life, there are far greater occasions that call for tears. No, this is a story of true grit and determination, and even a reaffirmation of why we were out there to begin with.

The other members of Screaming Mechanical Brain and myself, had just released a brand new album on a brand new independent label and were about to embark on a brand new independent tour. All of this was very exciting because we had never put out a record with any sort of distribution; and after some good opening slots on larger tours, we were packing some smaller venues around the country. We were to head from Minneapolis, MN down to Chicago, Indianapolis, Lexington, KY, Atlanta, and end the first week by doing Tampa, Orlando, and Fort Lauderdale, FL before heading back out west.

Naturally, things did not go exactly as planned. After waking up and leaving Chicago in our trusty (or not so much) 15 passenger van, we had not made it two hours on the road before we heard a loud bang. I thought we had run over a muffler that had fallen off of another vehicle. However, this was not the case. After we pulled over to the side of the freeway, we found the van would no longer get into gear. This smelled like a transmission problem, but we all convinced ourselves that since we had put in a new transmission not five months ago, that it must be something else, something that could be fixed today and off we'll go to continue our journey.

Three hours later the tow-truck arrived and informed us that there was a mechanic shop ahead in Zionsville, IN. Of course it was closed by now, and of course he could only bring two of us with in the truck. So he hooked up the van and we pulled away watching as the other two band members and our merch guy prepared to walk along the freeway for five miles. While in the truck we talked to the driver and discovered that he was friends with people we knew in Indianapolis, though they all lived too far away for us to stay with. I also remembered that it was time to start canceling shows. Indy was surely a goner, and Lexington's days were numbered. I hate canceling shows, I truly do. Possibly because I am effectively our booking agent and it's so much work to get them in the first place, that it feels like I am cutting off one of my own fingers when I have to cancel. Before I knew it us and our broken down touring van were being dropped off at a closed repair shop to wait through the night.

"...we were now driving around with people illegally stashed in the back of a U-Haul for all to see, and every time we went over a bump, the rope stretched and the door opened and slammed shut. All the while semis and other cars were flashing their brights and honking, as if we were unaware of what we were doing. We knew damn well though, and I thought for sure we were going to get pulled over and arrested."

CHECK OUT THE REST OF THE STORY ON THE WEB AT WWW.TSTOURING.COM!

CHAPTER 6

GOOD
Advice
...FROM BAAAD PEOPLE

TIPS FROM

HENRY ROLLINS

IN NO ORDER:

- **Prepare for a tour.** Don't do a warm-up show in front of an audience who paid to see you deliver the cut stone, not the diamond in the rough. Do that show in front of a garage door at band practice.

- **If you don't want to tour, don't.** No one wants to sit through a band who is dialing it in. An audience can always tell.

- **Don't mix drugs and touring.** If you do, then don't expect to be very good for very long. You can try and have my band open for you and we'll blow your fuckin' doors off every night.

- **Touring is compression.** There's not a great deal of personal space so don't bring anything you're not willing to carry on your back besides gear.

- **Keep some kind of journal.** Memories are made of times like these.

- **Don't insult the people who sparsely fill the venue.** Your tour is bombing, but some people showed up. Rock them hard.

- **Don't worry, be happy.** Touring is very hard and not many people can hack it. Chances are you cannot hack it. Cheer up, if you're any good perhaps you'll get to do it again some time.

- **Keep your eyes on the prize.** There's no money in touring. Just the opportunity for adventure and sacrifice.

- **There's a reason some people are successful for so many years on the road.** They love it and they show it to the audience. People like Ozzy are still around for a reason.

- **Just do it or don't. Either you have it or you don't.** You'll never know until you try and you'll know soon enough.

HENRY ROLLINS

ROLLINS BAND / BLACK FLAG
RADIO DJ / AUTHOR / ACTOR /
SPOKEN WORD ARTIST

www.henryrollins.com

CONTACT WITH LAW ENFORCEMENT WHILE TOURING

CHRIS LEE OF CHRISTOPHER LEE AND THE ODDITIES – LAW ENFORCEMENT OFFICER FOR THE PAST FIVE YEARS

When touring cross-country by ground transportation, whether it be commercial bus or personal vehicle, the sheer amount of miles traveled means that at one point or another you will probably be subject to being contacted by Law Enforcement. Should this occur, remember a few things:

1. **Approach determines response:** if the first impression a police officer gets from a rider in your vehicle is negative, his attitude towards this encounter is going to be the same. It may sound like common sense, but be polite and respectful towards the officer. Anytime an officer directs you to do something, he more than likely has the legal authority to do so. If you believe your rights have been violated either ask to speak to the officer's supervisor, or get the officer's name and contact a lawyer later.

2. **Turn on your interior lights or roll some windows down** if you are stopped while traveling after dark or if you have dark tinted windows, A traffic stop is one of the most dangerous parts of a Police Officer's job, and if they can see that there is nothing in your vehicle that poses a threat to them they will be more at ease, which will hopefully make your stop shorter and less intrusive.

3. **Make sure that there is someone onboard who can act as a spokesman if your vehicle is stopped** either during a traffic stop, or at a checkpoint. If you are traveling in a large vehicle with multiple occupants, remember how you look to the outside world. Touring is a professional venture, so be sure that you have the ability to articulate your purpose when asked. This person should have all the information such as destination of the tour, origination of the tour, who your point of contact is, and insurance and registration for the vehicle.

4. **Know the laws of the area you will be in.** Most (if not all) states have laws against possessing open containers of alcohol in a motor vehicle, laws regulating speed, or some type of safety belt enforcement. This will help keep your performers from getting stopped, getting citations, or going to jail. If you have a professional driver in a commercial bus, this puts the responsibility on him/her and not on the performers. Depending on the area of the country you are in, a divided vehicle like a bus or limo allows for the passengers to the rear

CHRIS LEE

FORMERLY OF CHRISTOPHER LEE AND THE ODDITIES HAS BEEN A LAW ENFORCEMENT OFFICER FOR THE PAST FIVE YEARS

of the driver to consume alcohol while the vehicle is in motion. Also, in other areas of the country, there are set speed limits (Texas), reasonable and prudent speed limits (Arizona), and little or no speed limits (Montana).

5. **The most important piece of advice is to never drink and drive, take drugs and drive, or drive tired.** Once again this is a good justification for the added expense of a professional driver. Much of touring is done late at night and in the early morning, leaving one town after a show and getting to the next town just in time to shower and then go do a sound check. These are prime hours for Police Officers to be doing DUI enforcement. Aside from the legal aspects of dealing with police, there are accidents to worry about. The National Highway Transit Safety Administration reported that there were just under 17,000 fatal accidents in the US in 2005 where alcohol played a role. One needs only look into the history of bands like Metallica and Def Leopard to see how vehicle accidents have drastically affected their existence.

MYTHS ABOUT TOURING

MARK SPYBEY

"Spinal Tap is best watched on a tour bus."
 - Mark Spybey

TWO BUS TWO, 1997: ON THE ROAD WITH PIGFACE - THE LOWEST OF THE LOW TOUR.

MYTH ONE: ROCK MUSIC TOURS ARE GLAMOROUS.

On the Pigface tour of 1997, I was one of several support acts. I lived in Vancouver and the tour started in Tulsa, Oklahoma, so my wife and I flew down. I had sent my gear down by airfreight to Chicago a few days before. I was assured that I did not need any special customs clearance. I checked and double-checked. Touring musicians often have to purchase a 'carnet'. This costs a lot and keeps the Customs officials happy. So, when the guys from Invisible Records went to the airport to collect my gear, Customs refused to release it, claiming I needed a carnet or that we'd have to pay several hundred dollars in import duty for it to be released.

When I arrived in Tulsa, I had absolutely no idea if my gear had been allowed to leave O'Hare and if it had made it to the tour bus in time.

It had got stuck in a freak snowstorm and was delayed.

I wasn't the only band to have problems. FM Einheit, or Mufti to friends, lost half his band due to the vagaries of work permits. They turned up several days later.

Despite my saying that rock music tours are not glamorous, we started by playing in the legendary Cain's ballroom, bedecked with the most gorgeous dance floor you've seen and pictures of various country stars on the walls. It was here that Sid Vicious beat a guy with his bass on the ill-fated Pistols tour of the USA. I proceeded to make a huge accidental scratch on the dance floor with a flight case.

MYTH TWO: TOUR BUSES ARE GLAMOROUS.

My wife and I were dispatched into Tour Bus Two. Was that deliberate? I'm a Therapist by trade; my wife a Nurse and I wondered if our skills would be required during the trip.

MARK SPYBEY

"I AM NOT ANTONIN ARTAUD" I AM MARK SPYBEY

They were.

We are squeezed into a bunk. It's hot and claustrophobic. Everyone, apart from us, seems to smoke all the time. I know several of our fellow travelers quite well; others I know by reputation.

Of course, it is ridiculously exciting to travel in a tour bus. You play a show, shower (If you are very lucky), drink, and make food out of the leftovers from the rider. I excelled in making creative compositions using rye bread, salsa, and peanut butter. When you're tired, you just crawl into your pit and sleep. Theoretically.

The party animals just want to party. You can do this for a while before you exhaust yourself and you get sick.

More of that later.

I just wanted to go to sleep.

As soon as someone walks down the bus, you wake up. When someone goes to bed and makes a racket, you wake up. When the bus travels down a pot-holed stretch of road, you wake up. When someone sings or hollers, you wake up. If you're lucky. Generally, you don't get the opportunity to go to sleep.

Everyone is new to this and no one wants to talk about showing respect to others or making a few house rules. You just grin, curse under your breath, and say to yourself that tomorrow is another day. Maybe they'll get tired or something.

You wake up tired. It's early. Very early. The bus has stopped. You get up and piss (no shitting on the bus, absolute rule, the toilets can't flush it away and the bus driver has to get rid of it manually and an angry bus driver is your worst enemy... believe me). It's cold. There are clothes everywhere. Stale smell of tobacco and beer. All you want to do is get out and breathe some fresh air.

The bus is parked outside another venue and it's not as early as you think. It's lunchtime and you're hungry. So you go for a walk and scope out the neighborhood. You eat.

By the time you get back to the bus the rabble has roused and they are sitting around in exactly the same seats they were last night and they are still smoking.

Everyone wants to play their own music and it all sounds so painful.

As soon as you're allowed into the venue you burst into life and get excited. This is why you're here, to play music. I scope out every nook and cranny and soak up the atmosphere. This is glamorous. It's dirty, it's smelly, but it's so intoxicating.

MYTH THREE: EVERYONE GETS ALONG.

Tours manufacture extreme behavior. Those who you think are likely to explode do so with remarkable consistency and those who seem less likely do so in their own way. One member of the crew was the most mild-mannered guy you could hope to meet: a sweet, caring, and contemplative sort. At a sound check, I saw him attempt to rip the head off the tour manager (verbally, you must understand: our tour manager was 6 foot plus of living legend). The red mist descends and, while it has you in its grip, you do foolish things that you later regret. It's part and parcel of the Tour Bus Syndrome.

Touring musicians merely condescend to cohabit. You deal with the boredom and the tension in your own way: some seek answers in copious amounts of alcohol; some go giggling in gangs to the back of the bus and engage in nocturnal activities that I do not want to know about.

At times, tensions arise between bands or factions within bands. You find yourself spending more time with like-minded people and then you're accused of forming cliques.

You have a good show and everything feels good. You can even cope with the post-concert tour bus party. You have a bad show and you're calling up airlines and checking out flight availability. When you learn it's going to cost you 500 bucks to get a red-eye home, you quickly sober up.

MYTH FOUR: SUPPORT BANDS NEED SOUND CHECKS.

When you're supporting a band like Pigface, sound checks are often non-existent. It's not because of malice, but because of the logistics of sound checking a band with as many members as your average football team. I accepted the situation and made sure that all I had to do was plug in a couple of DI boxes and perform. It's not exactly rocket science. Some folks will go to their graves feeling hard done by, but as a support band, you have to learn to go with the flow.

MYTH FIVE: YOU ONLY WORK FOR AS LONG AS YOU'RE ON STAGE.

Touring is work. Sure, you get ferried all over the place and generally taken care of. If you want to, you can sneak in a bit of sightseeing and hanging out with friends but at all times you're working. That's what infuriates me about some of the guys who would not contribute to what I call the maintenance of touring. Supporting each other. Taking time to make sure everyone is OK. Pulling together to pull off a great show. Respecting the audience.

I'd also suggest that taking care of yourself is an important part of your working day.

We were scheduled to stay in Vancouver after the show and rejoin the tour about ten days later in Washington, D.C. One of the support bands didn't show up, so we agreed to travel down to Los Angeles and flew back to Vancouver from there.

By the time we arrived in D.C., most of the touring party was deathly ill with the dreaded tour flu bug that always (and I mean always) seems to kick in after a few weeks of hedonistic excess. Mufti had ruptured his Achilles tendon on stage and was wearing a moon boot adaptation so that he could walk.

The guys decided to give my wife and me the large room at the rear of the bus to sleep in. Bliss!

The bus was a mess, the crew was a mess, but at least we had a clean and relatively quiet place to sleep.

MYTH SIX: MUSICIANS WHO SMASH HOTEL ROOMS ARE ALWAYS MORONS.

One of my friends, Dave, was suffering with the dreaded tour bus flu bug and he checked into a hotel room to recuperate in Rochester, NY. It transpired that he had viral meningitis and, in delirium, proceeded to pull his hotel room apart. My wife was called and, when she arrived at the hotel, was greeted by a team of paramedics who were convinced that they had another musician suffering from a drug overdose. She convinced them otherwise, good job, as their intended form of treatment would have probably killed him. He was diagnosed with viral meningitis and was in a coma for five long days. We had to leave. His band mate stayed with him. Anyone showing the same signs of the illness had to have a spinal tap. We were all visited by the Public Health Doctor in our next port of call, Montreal, and given some really evil antibiotics that stained our piss and tears a violent orange color. The toilet seat in the bus was pock marked with little orange drips. The least of our worries.

We rallied. Every show became a tribute to Dave. The crowds joined in with "Get Well Dave" chants. This became the defining moment of the tour. Every tour has a defining moment. A particularly bitter or dramatic squabble. A run in with the law. A bus driver driven to distraction, one insult away from throwing everyone off the bus.

The defining moment wasn't Dave getting so seriously sick but Dave waking up from his coma. He wasn't in great shape but he was alive.

Before Dave's illness, there wasn't a great deal of harmony on Tour Bus Two but after, my memory is that we became a slick machine.

MYTH SEVEN: WANTING ORDER MEANS THAT YOU ARE A FASCIST.

I know this because I toured with another band as support a couple of years later. They had a strict no smoking rule on the bus, well, in the Winnebago. Folks turned up on time. If we had problems, we were able to discuss them.

Things could have been different in Tour Bus Two. For a start, every time I suggested we needed a few "Ground Rules," I was accused of being a control freak.

When musicians tour, they work hard and they play hard. Most of the stereotypical images that you might conjure up in your head exist. The overwhelming feelings are of intense excitement and overwhelming tedium. Sitting around in tawdry venues, trying to amuse yourself. Making up games. Trying to scope out decent food. Just existing. Nursing your wounds, physical and psychological.

MISCELLANY

- **Musicians have the worst,** and I mean the very worst, smelling feet.

- **Pouring vodka on smelly things** does not make the smell go away.

- **When you have the opportunity to shower, shower.** You may not see another shower for 2 weeks.

- **The bus driver is your best friend,** and I mean your very best friend. Treat him with respect.

- **The tour manager is also your best friend,** and I mean your very best friend. Treat him with respect.

- **The members of the road crew are your best friends,** and I mean your very best friends. Treat them with respect.

- **No fans on the bus.** Never. Ever. They always shit in the toilet.

- **No shitting on the bus.**

- **Spinal Tap is best watched on a tour bus.**

If all of this sounds a tad negative, you need to remember that touring is a privilege. You earn the right to do it and despite the illnesses, the smells, the fights, and the tedium, it is an experience that is absolutely priceless. I cannot begin to say how marvelous it was to stand in a desert or to play at the Fillmore in San Francisco or to sit in any of the nameless diners in small town America and watch the world go by. I left the tour with a warm, rosy glow. Richer for the experience.

C·H·A·P·T·E·R····7

PROMOTERS AND VENUES IN THEIR OWN WORDS

In the same way there are certain people in radio, record stores, and labels who can give you good advice... club owners and promoters have seen two to five bands a night five to seven nights a week... any opinions and advice should be sought out and looked on as a blessing. Try to separate the two halves of your brain, put your ego on the shelf, staple your mouth shut, and listen.

PROMOTERS

I called on nationally-known promoter Joe Shanahan here in Chicago to get some insight and a deep dish slice of his experience for you:

JOE SHANAHAN, METRO CHICAGO

"There are still human beings in the business, people who care about the show, but you have to be careful. There are sharks here, just as there are in corporate America. Most people in bands will be around two, three, four times. Hopefully, you'll make a friend, a connection as an artist. You see the same people on the way down that you see on the way up. My advice? Try and be professional. Have a good heart and a good soul. Look at it as a business of synergy; you need to know you'll be dealing with these people time and time again."

Like Joe Shanahan said, it's a small business, a core group of people with long memories. Some people believe they only have 15 minutes to take everything they can. This is exactly the wrong attitude to have. You need to form relationships and slowly build a base.

> **"Put your ego on the shelf, staple your mouth shut, and listen."**

"It's a great place to be on a good night watching something new and inspiring. The business is full of people who have to watch the bottom line, but are still NOT BLIND to originality and VIBE."
 – Joe Shanahan, Metro Chicago

"It's a business of building bridges."

My first encounter with Joe was in the early '80s while touring from the U.K. with my 3-piece outfit, Brian Brain. Lots of fun: all the drums were on quarter-inch tape so all we had to do was drink a lot and collide into one another. It was a late afternoon show on a Saturday. We had a four song, 12" vinyl record available on import only, so there was no label involved. The Cubs were playing. So, while the neighborhood was jam-packed, the venue wasn't. I stumbled into the office to ask Joe for our "guarantee" of $750. Joe said to me, "Here's $250, Martin. There's nobody here. Be happy you're getting this." I don't remember what I felt at the time, but talk about learning a valuable lesson early on. Thanks Joe.

MARTIN ATKINS ASKS:

MICHAEL YERKE – #1 TALENT BUYER IN THE COUNTRY AT HOUSE OF BLUES CHICAGO.

MA: What would be your first piece of advice to a new band?

MY: Have a good CD. Put your best song first. This might sound ridiculous but it happens on most bands' first CD.

TOUR:SMART TIP

MA: It would be useful if bands could stop thinking of their CDs as some glorious work of art, but begin to think of them as an enhanced business card. Michael Yerke is going to listen to track one and make a decision. That information has to be in your brain.

MY: We want local bands that have built up a following. Be as marketing savvy as possible. You have one chance.

MA: So, understand the venue that you are approaching. The HOB has a 1,100 person capacity. If you approach them for a show and are lucky enough to get a response, be careful. If you are headlining, you will be expected to come close to filling the venue. If you're not capable of that, lower your sights to a smaller capacity venue that you can fill and start to build your audience. Don't contact HOB or a larger venue until you are confident you can do that.

MY: Some people become overly persistent. It's a fine line. The tough thing at HOB is that many of the shows are already packaged with a 3-band lineup, so we're not able to put a local band on the bill.

I asked Michael if there were some really bad things that would be very difficult for a band or artist to recover from, aside from the obvious no fan base. He said that breaking any laws is obviously crossing the line. They're running a business; they can't have bands sneaking minors in because of liquor laws. He advised for artists to be respectful of the law and any in-house rules.

> **"Be as marketing savvy as possible. You have one chance."**

WHAT A PROMOTER WANTS TO HEAR TO BOOK YOU

DAN STEINBERG - SQUARE PEG CONCERTS, SEATTLE, WA

- **Our label will do** a ticket buy.
- **We are worth 150+ tickets** in your town (and really mean it).
- **We will play for free.**
- **We have the guy** from "The OC" in our band.
- **We are getting air play** in your town.
- **We will buy** our own pizza.
- **We will be buying ads** to support the date.
- **We will hand out flyers** everywhere in town.
- **We want to show you** we can draw a crowd, give us a shot on an off night.
- **Our record is selling** in your city.

THE BASICS ARE MISSING
KEVIN LYMAN, VANS WARPED TOUR

- **Right now there are so many young bands on the road** and I was just talking about how basics are missing.

- **Check your oil in the van** whenever you put gas in it, or you will blow up your engine. Happened to a young band on tour with us yesterday.

- **Buy a club or other steering wheel locking device.** This is not a guaranteed deterrent to getting you van stolen but will discourage people.

- **Back your trailer up to a wall** this will help keep people out of it.

- **If you are a crew guy finish your gig.** Don't jump from tour to tour for a few extra bucks.

- **Tour support is the worst loan you can ever get.** You pay about 900% interest back to your labels.

- **If you do some demos** don't hand them to someone and say, "we're way better then these but thought you might like to hear them." Represent yourself in the best possible way you can.

KEVIN LYMAN

FOUNDER OF VANS WARPED TOUR KEEPS BRINGING SHOWS TO A PARKING LOT NEAR YOU

> "Represent yourself in the best possible way you can.."

THE POWER OF SOUP:

JOHN J. CHMIEL - WATER STREET MUSIC HALL ROCHESTER, NY

JOHN CHMIEL

WATER STREET MUSIC HALL
ROCHESTER, NY
www.waterstreetmusic.com

After you put in all the time and effort promoting a show and you cannot do anything else, a club owner must create the proper atmosphere for a band to give a truly great show. This is done by the attitude of the entire staff whether you are winning or losing. You must always be upbeat! Your attitude towards the bands sets in motion a chain of events from the moment they walk in and can either make the show or cause for a poor performance. The show must go on. If you make money *or lose,* it should not reflect on the treatment of the band. You must learn to relax and enjoy the show, then worry about it later. If you are trying to build a band, a good performance means everything. If you don't care, remember that the band members may end up playing in other bands that might make you money another time. When band members talk about your venue to other people, it has to be positive. Ultimately, it is your reputation on the line. Believe me, the agents talk and it ends up being a very small world.

One of the easiest things you can do to make a great impression is to have a pot of soup on when the band shows up. I can't tell you how many times I have seen a smile come from a band or crew member's face when they have just woken up on the bus or van and here is this hot pot of soup waiting for them. Several bands now request it when they get booked at my place. I also prepare good homemade food. I love it when they say that they look forward to coming to Water Street Music Hall because they know the food will be good.

We had a pet cat for about six months. It amazes me how a person's attitude can change when a cat is present. Must be the unconditional love that does it, but I've seen more tired, worn-out people just do a 180 when the cat was just hanging out. OHHHH, Kiddy!

Attitude and catering – it's not that hard. But from the horror stories I hear, it can be. Treat bands and crew the same way you would want to be treated. It will come back to you ten-fold, not to mention boost your karma.

MORE EVIDENCE OF THE POWER OF SOUP:

Brian Brain performed several times at a venue in Providence, RI, called The Living Room. Randy was the promoter there. Each time we played, Randy's mother would make a home cooked meal: chicken, potatoes, salad, pasta, something healthy and real! Not many venues did this at the time. It could have been viewed as an unnecessary expense, but when it was time for PiL to perform somewhere in Rhode Island, he got the show. We didn't even look at offers from many other promoters looking to do the date. Margot Olavaria referenced the same venue... 15 years after we were there.

ALL LOCAL BANDS/ARTISTS

URSULA RODRIGUEZ AND RAMONA DOWNEY, BOTTOM OF THE HILL, SAN FRANCISCO

Once you've booked a show at the Bottom of the Hill, make sure you come down to the club before your show. You may think of special requirements or get some great ideas about your presentation. The Bottom of the Hill is pretty well equipped to make your show here a special event.

Pick up the calendar and check for your listing on TicketWeb. *(www.TicketWeb.com)* Make sure your band name is spelled correctly. As we all know, band names can be quite oblique and that's all well and good, but you shouldn't expect the whole world (specifically our bookers) to know instinctively how to spell your band name. For example, if your band is called "The Isle of Ewes," it's not really cricket to call up the week of the show all upset because you saw an ad where it appeared as "The I Love Yous." We're not mind readers, and as a general assumption... No, we haven't heard of you. So please spell out your band name to us, even if it seems obvious to you. After years and years of drug abuse, we have diminished mental capacities.

Here are some, hopefully, useful guidelines which apply to almost every show that's booked at the Bottom of the Hill. There are exceptions to these rules so please make sure you've checked with the bookers about your specific show.

Most of the time we have three bands on the bill for any given night. Sunday through Thursday shows usually start at 9 PM. On Fridays and Saturdays, shows usually start at 10 PM. Sometimes we may have an early show in the afternoon, starting at 3 or 4 PM.

For most shows, the Headliner loads-in and sound-checks first. The support band follows suit a half hour later and the opener a half hour after that. The following chart works as a guideline for most shows we do at the Bottom of the Hill. Again, there are many exceptions to this, so please always check with the bookers about the specifics of your show.

You should pick one person in the band (or a road manager, agent, etc.) to be the point person for the band. There will be forms to fill out, drink tickets to get, guests to accommodate, etc. It's easier if there is a designated person for each band. When you get to the club, the first thing your point person should do is find our sound engineer. That person is the stage manager for the evening. Introduce yourself to him or her. At that point, you will be asked to load

URSULA RODRIGUEZ & RAMONA DOWNEY

BOTTOM OF THE HILL

BOOKING FOR BOTTOM OF THE HILL IN SAN FRANCISCO
www.bottomofthehill.com

your gear to the area directly in front of the stage. Drummers should start setting up their hardware.

Band	Load-In	Sound-Check	Set Time	Set Length
Headliner:	6:30 PM	7:00 PM	M/Tu: 11:00 PM W/Th: 11:30 PM F/Sa: Midnight	Up to 1 hour
Support:	7:00 PM	7:30 PM	M/Tu: 10:00 PM W/Th: 10:30 PM F/Sa: 11:00 PM	40 minutes
Opener:	7:30 PM	8:00 PM	M/Tu: 9:00 PM W/Th: 9:30 PM F/Sa: 10:00 PM	40 minutes

Please be as flexible as you can. Realize that unexpected things come up all the time so you may need to sound check at a different time than you expected. Or you may need to switch your set time. When problems arise with the logistics of the show, it's best to be patient and as flexible as possible. We want to try to preserve a good vibe for the night. Work with the sound person to come to a suitable compromise if these situations arise. Realize we all want a good show for you. No one is working against you.

TOUR:SMART TIP
for more information go to:
www.tstouring.com

HOSPITALITY

Your point person needs to know what to expect with regards to hospitality. All the details of your hospitality will have been worked out at the time the show was booked. Here are some important points to remember:

- If you have a contract, you should know your hospitality rider. If not, there will have been a verbal agreement with the booker.

- The dressing room is our office by day. If you need to use it, then you need to make that arrangement in advance with the booker. On some nights, we simply do not have enough staff to open the dressing room.

- We assign our hospitality based on the number of people in the band. (That means people who perform on stage.) Please don't show up the day of the show and ask for drink tickets for sound people, light people, video people, merch people, backstage sex-slaves, indigent dwarfs, Red Cross volunteers, etc. If you need hospitality to include these people, then you need to make that arrangement with the bookers in advance of the show.

- Before we can pay the band, we need a representative of the band to fill out a couple of forms.

- The first of these is the Guest List. On the top of this form is a section where you fill in the names of each of the people in the band. Each of these people is allowed two guests. Again, band members include performing members of the band only. Road crew members belong on your Guest List. We have been known to make allowances in this regard, always ask in advance.

> **"Be patient and as flexible as possible"**

There is more from Bottom of the Hill in *Booking*. Look at the input from Canadian promoter Gary Topp in *Touring Internationally,* and good stuff to read in *Creating Your Own Event,* and *When You are the Opening Band* that touches on relationships with venues and promoters.

LESSONS LEARNED
STEVE McCLELLAN

In terms of tour management, after 32 years of being at the receiving end of thousands of tours at First Avenue and in the 7th St. Entry, I learned some valuable overviews from artists and tour managers.

First of all, look for solutions, not who to blame when things don't go as planned. Things are in a constant state of flux. Anything from equipment to the weather will be cause for adaptation on the road and both the venues and artists should be aware of the need for flexibility.

Secondly, the old win/win axiom always worked for me, as it was "magic" when a venue's staff and a touring artist staff clicked and the basic feel after a show was "Let's do it again!" This is in terms of both financial satisfaction and just the ease of working with people you enjoy working with again and again.

Thirdly, pay attention to the details, as both a touring artist and a busy venue need to minimize the wear and tear that constant touring and continual concert presentations cause to staff, equipment, and other resources. When things are coordinated, advanced, and prepared to focus on the goal of a successful concert, all parties feel good after the show that no matter what, effort occurred on both sides.

Finally, I've always found that making it about the people more than the dollar resulted in my enjoying my work a lot longer than many I've watched burn out in a business that is notorious for burning out people.

I guess that would have to be my four main lessons learned...

STEVE
McCLELLAN

MCNALLY SMITH COLLEGE OF MUSIC, MUSIC BUSINESS DEPT. FORMER GENERAL MANAGER AND TALENT BUYER AT FIRST AVENUE NIGHTCLUB, MINNEAPOLIS, MN

:SMART TIPS

- **Have a good CD and put your best song first.** This might sound ridiculous but it happens on most bands' first CD.

- **Pay attention to details!**

- **Learn from your mistakes (or mine).** Have common sense and be able to think on your feet!

- **Know what promoters want to hear** in order to get your band booked!

- **Represent yourself in the best possible way.** Don't hand your demos to someone and say, "We're way better then this, but thought you might like to hear them."

- **Don't be in a big hurry to play to no one.** That's what happens when you play before you are ready.

- **Start a mailing list!**

- **If no one will book you, book yourself.**

- **The first and most obvious way of making a show special is by not playing too much!**

- **Don't send a demo too early.** It will just end up in a pile of hundreds of others. It won't do you any good, save you any time, or make anyone's life any easier.

CHAPTER····8

CONTRACTS

What is a guarantee? I like to ask the class and watch all of the hands go up... 'It is the amount of money that you are absolutely guaranteed to receive from a venue.' The answer tilts the axis of the students' world...

"There is no such thing as a guarantee."
- Martin Atkins

The main purpose of the contract is to set out the ideal conditions under which you can perform —the stage size, the ticket price, the things you need, the equipment, the considerations for safety and security, etc. The catering requirements, the technical requirements, stage plot, and the line input list are separate riders attached to the main contract.

There are many ways to defend yourself and ensure that you get what you need from a venue or a relationship. In none of these situations is a contract any form of protection. Use it as a simple letter to confirm the key elements of the show and compensation. Make sure it's fair and expressed clearly, at least then you have a chance that everyone will agree. A contract without leverage is useless. It will not defend you if ticket sales are bad. Good ticket sales are your best (and maybe only) defense if things go wrong. Sorry, did I say if things go wrong? I meant when!

> "Good ticket sales are your best defense."

KEEP IT SIMPLE.

Don't think that the larger or more complicated the contract the more you are protected. The reality is, unless you are at a $5,000 guarantee level and above per performance—and sometimes even then—this is all based on relationships and leverage. If a promoter rips you off for $2,000, you have to consider if you are going to hire an attorney in that city, and be prepared to have it cost you more than you might get, to get back that money...

> "...did I say if things go wrong? I meant when!"

Put these items in your contract:

- Performance length. Minimum and maximum.
- Day, date, time, and location of the performance.
- Venue name and address.
- Promoter's name and address (it might be different).

- Ticket price and compensation (percentage of door or combination and ability to check the validity of these numbers).
- Amount of deposit, if any, and when and how it should be paid.
- Cap (or limit) on house guest list in the event of a door deal.
- Deny or allow recording, photos, etc.
- Right to sell merchandise in a location of your choosing and house percentage if any.
- Number of guests that you are allocated.
- PA (sound) requirements and who pays for it.

> *You don't want to specify every element of the PA—we sometimes just put that we want it to sound loud (115db) at the back of the room and be able to handle the low end of electronics… If you need extra equipment – you are going to have to pay for it one way or another so be careful…*

- Parking, permits to be provided and paid for by the venue if necessary.
- All permits and licenses, etc. to be covered by the venue/buyer.
- Acts Of God, War, Weather, Illness, etc.: a clause that protects both parties if any of these events should occur.
- Control of other acts on the bill. Maybe you want to make sure the evening works, this won't be allowed until you actually have an audience.
- Dressing room security.
- Insurance—confirm that the venue has liability insurance, etc.

SOME EXTRA THINGS WE PUT IN THE CONTRACT:

"In the event that a special, limited edition, 'hand-screened' poster is created for the event, then the venue will provide the band's representative with one hundred not folded flats, of the poster, the day of the show."

This exists because I am still seeing limited posters by Kozic, etc., that were created to promote shows, being sold on eBay. I'm also wondering if, in some cases, we might have paid for these posters as part of the expenses of the show! I am fine with venues creating galleries of these posters and making money, they need revenue streams, too, but, the band or label should get some as well!

Photo by Daniel Dorough.

DRESSING ROOM HEATING AND COOLING

You can just ask for climate control. This isn't pop star bullshit; the bigger the tour, the greater the risk. You don't need to jeopardize the tour over a dressing room that's too cold. Hot, sweaty people coming off stage do not need to get sick… or even hotter!

LOCAL INFORMATION AND MEDIA LIST

Within five days of signing the contract… venue agrees to fax or e-mail a local contact/media list to artist so that we can allocate our resources to most successfully promote the event. This list will include record stores where tickets are being sold (they are more likely to put up a poster), print advertisers, local papers, local radio with contact information, hotel with any special venue rate and contact info, tattoo/clothes/piercing outlets, and any other useful contacts and web sites to help promote the event.

This is also a great litmus test. A good promoter will fax or e-mail you something the same day, wouldn't you if someone was asking for information to help make your show succeed? If you don't receive anything after a few days and a reminder calls, make sure that you send a fax or e-mail. Then, I'd print it out and bind it into my itinerary or copy it to my tour folder so that if there is a problem at settlement (because the promoter says we didn't do anything and he did everything he could) you can show him the e-mail. Right about that time is when you glance up to the shelving unit behind his head and see the FedEx box of posters and promotional materials that cost you $24 to overnight to him so he would have the flyers for the genre-related show six weekends ago... of course, you don't even have to look. The box is still sealed.

CLEARING THE HOUSE/MERCHANDISE SALES

We put this in after a particularly horrible house clearing in Milwaukee, WI, at the RAVE: "In no event will the venue be cleared prior to 30 minutes after the end of the main band's set." What? Well, you can't write down the exact time that the main band finishes the show, but you can ask for 30 minutes of sell time after the show. This, after all, is when you are going to make some money.

SECURITY MEETING

The best time to address any security issues is in a meeting with the security team before the doors open. You can find the head security guy and ask him when you can address his guys. You should make them all aware of your policy towards photographers, people jumping on stage (it's fine with Pigface even if they want to pick up some drum sticks, etc.—but for other bands its absolutely not acceptable). So, it's your job, or your tour manager's job, to make sure everyone knows what's up. Communicate!

If in doubt, I will repeat myself or do an extra sign or something: the only problem you will ever get from double checking is maybe pissing someone off that is actually really good at their job. But, if they are, they'll understand why you are repeating yourself and you can easily apologize.

BARRIERS, ETC.

I have had more band members injured by barriers than any fans have been saved by its presence. But this is a case-by-case basis with the venue. Sometimes it is an insurance requirement.

TICKETS ON SALE

Make sure that you confirm that tickets will be up on sale within five days of signing the contract. Let the venue know that this is an important issue for you. Do not breathe a sigh of relief when the contract is issued. You have to get tickets on sale. A signed contract is no guarantee that this is happening. You have to check by looking at the web site and communicating with the club.

> "The bigger the tour, the greater the risk."

> "You have to get tickets on sale."

PAYMENT TO BE MADE IN FULL IMMEDIATELY PRIOR TO PERFORMANCE

If there is a problem, the only leverage you have is the potential mayhem that a rioting, pissed off audience might create if you don't play... sometimes it works, sometimes it doesn't.

ALL OF THE ELEMENTS OF THE AGREEMENT ARE FLEXIBLE...

...even at a high level. If a promoter asks for a reduction, that means he wants to change the "guarantee" to $5,000 instead of $10,000. If you don't agree, he might not agree to open the doors to the venue. So, you'd be agreeing to a 100% reduction. You have to deal with this situation professionally, entrepreneurially, and on a case-by-case basis. I have renegotiated dates the evening of the show with promoters (once at gun point!) and, understanding the overall situation, have sometimes managed to make the situation better for me. Sometimes you are lucky to get out of there with a pizza and your merch sales. Sometimes you need to be prepared to lose the battle, win the war, and live to fight (and I do mean fight) another day.

See the Chapter on *Settlements* for more!

MULTIBAND PERFORMANCE AGREEMENTS

You need one voice for the tour. It has to be a benevolent dictatorship. This means you have to have the right and the ability to do the things that you need to do without consultation but you will do so in a kind, humane, and generous manner.

The first time I heard that phrase was from my first attorney, Michael Toorock. I honestly thought he'd gone mad. Dictatorship is one of those words with anyone in a band. I didn't even hear the word benevolent for a couple of years. When you understand both words together, honestly, it's the only path you can take. Once you realize that all of the responsibility, the financial repercussions, the moral, intellectual, and whatever-the-fuck baggage from these endeavors is going to sit across your shoulders (and maybe your family's), then it's absolutely right to have the full ability to make decisions that directly affect the tour.

It's very important that you have an agreement from all of the bands and elements that make up a package tour; otherwise you're leaving yourself wide open for problems. This has happened to me three or four times, so pay attention. On a longer tour, one band can increase in popularity as another decreases, leading to inequality in scheduling of the bands, disrupting the flow of the evening, and generally fucking with your world.

You must have a non-competing clause in your agreements, meaning the artist is prevented from playing within a certain distance of a contracted show for a certain period of time before your contracted date, for instance, 60 days and 60 miles or 80 days and 80 miles. You might think, "That would be crazy! Why would do they do that? No one would do that!" Well, when you put a package tour together, you're responsible for paying people whether people show up or not. It's all on your head. Some people can respond by joining in the fight with you to make it a successful tour, while some people treat it as a holiday. You also need the agreement to apply to the time after your tour.

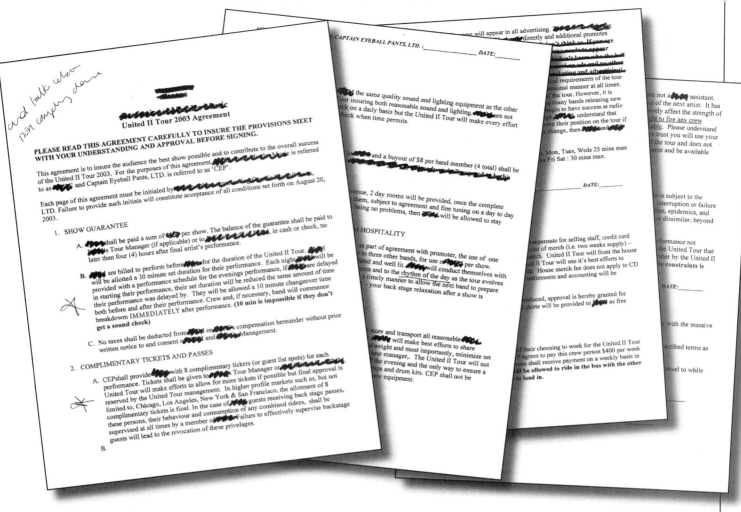

KEY CLAUSES IN THE AGREEMENT

B. ████ are billed to perform before ████ for the duration of the United II Tour. ████ will be allotted a 30 minute set duration for their performance. Each night ████ will be provided with a performance schedule for the evenings performance, if ████ are delayed in starting their performance, their set duration will be reduced the same amount of time their performance was delayed by. They will be allowed a 10 minute changeover time both before and after their performance. Crew and, if necessary, band will commence breakdowm IMMEDIATELY after performance. **(10 min is impossible if they don't get a sound check)**

COMPLIMENTARY TICKETS AND PASSES

A. CEPshall provide ████ with 8 complimentary tickets (or guest list spots) for each performance. Tickets shall be given to ████ Tour Manager or ████. United Tour will make efforts to allow for more tickets if possible but final approval is reserved by the United Tour management. In higher profile markets such as, but not limited to, Chicago, Los Angeles, New York & San Francisco, the allotment of 8 complimentary tickets is final. In the case of ████ guests receiving back stage passes, these persons, their behaviour and consumption of any combined riders, shall be supervised at all times by a member of ████ Failure to effectively supervise backstage guests will lead to the revocation of these privelages.

B.

1B – DURATION OF SET

Specify the set length. Also, by using this language, we're providing incentive to a band to be on time, not creating another job and another responsibility for ourselves. The key words are "If the band is ten minutes late in starting their performance, their set duration will be reduced by the same amount of time."

2A – GUEST LISTS

Define the number of complimentary tickets each band will receive. Also, make backstage access contingent upon the band not creating any problems.

5. HOTEL ROOMS

    A. If there are no showers in the venue, 2 day rooms will be provided, once the complete touring party has finished with them, subject to agreement and fine tuning on a day to day basis & conditioned upon there being no problems, then ~~████~~ will be allowed to stay overnight in 2 of these rooms.

    A. CEP shall furnish where possible , as part of agreement with promoter, the use of one dressing room, to be shared with up to three other bands, for use of ~~████~~ per show. These rooms should be clean, ventilated and well lit. ~~████~~ will conduct themselves with respect to the other bands and vice versa and to the rhythm of the day as the tour evolves and vacate a shared dressing room in a timely manner to allow the next band to prepare and focus for the show. REMEMBER – your back stage relaxation after a show is someone elses vital preparation time.

    B. As far as scheduling and the aesthetics of the tour and technical requirements of the tour allow,and subject to ~~████~~ conducting themselves in a professional manner at all times: ~~████~~ will perform directly prior to ~~████~~ for the duration of the tour. However, it is understood that, in some cases, during a longer tour, with so many bands releasing new music to co-incide with the tour, that one other band may begin to have success at radio or press that will cause the equilibrium of the tour to change. ~~████~~ understand that they are able to create this success for themselves to preserve their position on the tour if they wish. In the event that market forces dictate an order change, then ~~████~~ and ~~████~~ will conduct all discussions in a professional manner.

    B. In the event that a tour shirt/'event' shirt is produced, approval is hereby granted for ~~████~~'s name to be included on the shirt. 12 shirts will be provided to ~~████~~ as free goods in full compensation.

5A – HOTEL ROOMS

Here we're allowing a band who is traveling separately from the buses to use the day rooms after the touring party has left. This is a $250 bonus to the band, but benefits are, and always should be, considered only on the condition that there are no problems.

6A – DRESSING ROOMS

Once again, the language outlines what you hope to accomplish, allows you latitude if it is not possible, and introduces the idea of respect and rhythm to the day.

8B – SCHEDULING AND AESTHETICS OF THE TOUR

While you want to present the tour and everybody in it, a promoter might decide the best use of his column inches is to make the headlining band's logo as large as possible. You have to let them make that call.

9B – MERCHANDISING

You have to control the merchandise booth. It's not about grabbing a percentage of somebody's t-shirt sales. The merchandise booth controls the information flow outward from the tour, enables you to fulfill (in a professional manner) any sponsorship obligations you have made, and also, as producer of the tour, allows you to easily give merchandise to anybody who deserves it, making it easier for the next time.

IF YOU ARE THE OPENING BAND

If you are an opening band, you might not be able to confirm your exact time slot in terms of the 24 hour clock, but you should make sure to clarify which bands are performing directly before and after you. Then, even if the show is delayed for two hours or John Lennon comes back from the dead to do an acoustic set, you are still performing before band X or after band Y.

> "...benefits are, and always should be, considered only on the condition that there are no problems."

CONTRACTS/SETTLEMENTS
JOLLY ROGER

MA: Have you ever relied on a contract for protection?

JR: No, I mean if somebody gives me their word, that's it. If you lie to me, you got a problem. You know? I don't go anywhere unless people say what I want them to say. You know, the stuff I want to have happen.

MA: What about the worst case of being ripped off by a venue? Once a month, once a year, never?

JR: You gotta be on top of all that stuff. As you get bigger, you have to have somebody count the door. You gotta look at all your receipts, all your catering. You gotta know about where it is in each city and just because you can do a whole backstage for $700 in Oklahoma City doesn't mean it's gonna cost that much in Chicago.

I talked with Jolly about the prickly subject of getting paid before you play. If you're nervous about getting paid after your show, then you are in a delicate situation where just expressing this feeling could push the club owner over the edge and into a self-righteous rant. Because you are basically saying, "Everything that happens at this point makes me nervous about the possibility of not getting paid and I'm not sure I trust you..."

JR: Yeah, you're basically calling someone a thief before they have a chance to rob you. You have to be very careful about insulting people on their honesty. So then, what I do is, I made up that saying and I've used it with every band ever since. And I've said it with your name in front and Rick Nielson's (from Cheap Trick). "He knows he's not gonna see any of the money; he just wants to smell it before he goes on stage." And it's just a quirky, "Give me the guarantee and we'll go." And you know, they never argue about that! Now, if you go in and you go, "Oh, I heard there was a problem two weeks ago..." you've got a problem.

INTER-BAND AGREEMENTS
GRETA BRINKMAN

"Oh, that'll never happen to us... we're friends!"

My band blew up in tears and hatred when the other members refused to sign even a one-page partnership agreement, which meant that Joe Serling (Moby's lawyer in NYC) couldn't represent us even though he thought it had potential. Then the other members went completely off the deep end, stole the master tapes from the studio, and broke into my house to steal the safety tapes! Then they tried to record over my parts on the original tapes, but got in a fight with that studio for not paying and lost custody of the tapes instead.

I randomly met one of the owners of that studio in the hardware department at Lowe's and he remembered me and gave me the master tapes back for free. I am so lucky... sometimes in a weird, backwards way. Needless to say, I am never speaking to or working with those clowns ever again and I've been just giving away my 400 copies of the CD to anybody who seems like they might like it. I can laugh about it now, but I was so hurt and upset I could barely even talk about it for over two years! I'm better now and the other members are still playing the local bar once a month in a Johnny Cash cover band, so, ha!

A band needs to have a partnership agreement in place before any money comes in or plans get made? It's a pretty important point and one that not a lot of bands get ("Oh, that'll never happen to US... we're friends!")

GRETA BRINKMAN

BASS PLAYER
MOBY / L7 / DEBBIE HARRY / PIGFACE
INTER-BAND AGREEMENTS
www.bassgodessgreta.com

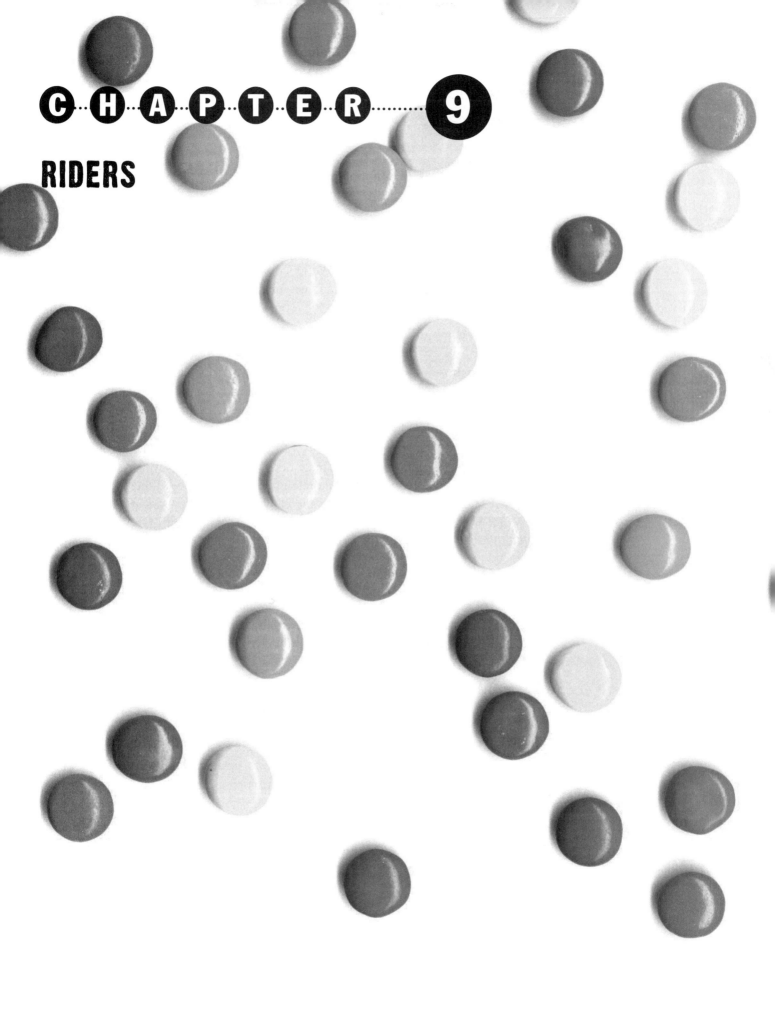

C·H·A·P·T·E·R 9

RIDERS

"Where's the vodka?"
  - Lee Fraser

PART 1: CATERING RIDERS

Something happens at the mention of the word rider that sends even the smallest band on some fantasy island bullshit voyage. It's like a scene from *Dog Day Afternoon* (or is it *Benny Hill*) where the bank robbers demand cash, a helicopter, hot chocolate, a hamburger, gummy bears, and a video of England winning the World Cup in 1966. Every item on the rider has a cost to you! And someone needs to go out and get it, rent it, buy it, unwrap it, and put it on a stage or on a table or in a basket in the dressing room.

Bands' riders are exciting to look at for fans, providing a voyeuristic look into the private backstage world that so few have access to. It was the chapter on riders from another book that pushed me over the edge and made me decide to put this book together. The author cited a band requesting M&Ms—but no brown M&Ms—as an example of excess and silliness on a rider!! Well, c'mon, first off, if that's as bad as it gets, deal with it! Sort out the brown M&Ms! However, he completely missed the purpose of this particular request. It is genius! A litmus test for a busy tour manager who has 200 things to check on each hour. Any one of them can derail a performance, a mood, or a legitimate need. So, rather than waiting for the day to unfold, the tour manager could walk into the dressing room and glance at the bowl of M&M's. If he saw brown M&Ms, he would know that the clown organizing the show hadn't read the rider... time for a meeting before something lands on someone's head or, "I thought it said 200 watt power amp... you really need 20,000 watts?" Watch *Spinal Tap* (again). That Stonehenge shit is real!

Each touring entity has unique requirements. While assembling multi-band package tour riders, I have seen requests for baby wipes, cucumbers, and blue Gatorade. I thought each was a silly indulgence; until I saw Godhead use the baby wipes to remove white makeup, and The Enigma pour the blue liquid down his nose through a tube and slice the cucumber in two off of someone's back with a machete.

As a band member or tour manager, you need to make sure these essentials are not obscured by other elements (two cases of micro brew beer or three different kinds of cheese). As your band grows, you will start to get a good idea of what is really helpful on the rider, what you don't need, what you could use more of, and what is so essential that you don't need to worry about a promoter getting it. As your audience base grows, you could and should ask for more of the things that make your life easier, safer, more productive, and groovier, but this will be at an ultimate cost to you.

> "If you feel like some interesting cheese and your guarantees are high enough to get it, that's great. But it's going to end up with someone's cigarette stubbed out in the middle of it."

If you feel like some interesting cheese and your guarantees are high enough to get it, that's great. But it's going to end up with someone's cigarette stubbed out in the middle of it. I would suggest stocking the bus with these things, then you only have to worry about the band and crew scarfing them! Realize you are paying for all of this anyway and the largest difference will come to you, not in a $400 savings of cereal, but in a greater understanding of the nuts and bolts of the business. Maybe you can take better care of the crew and yourself, maybe you can reduce ticket prices which could lead to a larger attendance, a better show, a bigger buzz, and maybe you will get to do another tour. Oh ok, suddenly a bit more interesting is it? How do you spell Cristal?

C. J. from Drowning Pool just told me they have a goat on their rider!!!
BAAAAAAA!!

JADE DELLINGER, ART CURATOR

As a collector of concert memorabilia and tour-used artifacts, I've always found contract riders particularly entertaining. As I researched my book on Devo, these riders gave interesting insight into the personal whims, perceived necessities and backstage antics of a working band. With commercial success, these demands frequently become more elaborate and often border on the absurd. Of course, the rider gives specifications for the sound system, lighting and stage, but it's the artist's "wish list" for accommodations and meals that's most revealing. It's hard to imagine, but I own original documents from the Pistols 1978 U.S. tour hand signed by Mr. Rotten and John Beverley which state: "Artist would greatly appreciate cold beer, a platter of meat, cheese and fruit and various juices prior to the show and towels for the stage. Your kind cooperation is kindly appreciated by us." Of course, Christina Aguilera asks for chewable "Flintstones" vitamins; Jane's Addiction requests clean boxer shorts; Kansas requires prune juice; and Janet Jackson insists on an arrangement of tulips, roses, gardenias, and lilies.

JADE DELLINGER

ART CURATOR & CO-AUTHOR "WE ARE DEVO!"

SMOKINGGUN.COM
ANDREW GOLDBERG AND WILLIAM BASTONE

You've probably seen *SmokingGun.com,* They've posted 200+ examples and funny bits about contract riders at:

http://www.thesmokinggun.com/backstagetour/index.html

From Smoking Gun: "While possibly a typo, might freaky Trent Reznor & Co. actually enjoy some bowels pre-show? Also, who knew that industrial/Goth rockers like NIN were part of that pernicious juicing cult? And as for those boxes of corn starch, well, we're not sure why they are so 'Very Important!' [On Marilyn Manson's Contract Rider They Say]: Frankly, we expected a lot more from Marilyn Manson, the self-proclaimed Antichrist Superstar. With the exception of two bottles of absinthe, what kind of Satanist stocks his dressing room with Haribo gummy bears, mini chocolates, Doritos, and 2% milk? And it's odd that air conditioning is 'Really important!!' to a guy who has pledged fealty to Lucifer himself. Oh, and don't even get us started on the post-concert 'Manson Bus' food. Manwich mix?! Soy milk and microwave popcorn? Sweet Jesus, where are the chopped-up kittens and pints of pigeon blood?" Check it out.

> **"...what kind of Satanist stocks his dressing room with Haribo gummy bears, mini chocolates, Doritos, and 2% milk?"**

For a new or small band… just try asking for nothing… everything you get at the beginning is a favour… everything after that you pay for.

An oversized rider could be a large contributing factor to a ticket price that's three dollars more than it needs to be on a Tuesday night. If you do not sell tickets in advance, the catering rider will be one of the first things to be cut (that means you won't get anything except maybe water). You might have to cut the rider simply to keep the show alive. However, it is not possible to cut a ticket price once it's been announced. You should also be prepared to make on-the-spot adjustments to the rider if the venue has an in-house restaurant but, you should already know about this because you advanced the show didn't you?

Here are several sections to the larger catering rider:

1. 'Upon Arrival' – What you want to be ready at the venue at the pre-arranged load-in time.

2. 'The Evening Meal' – The meal portion of the day usually after soundcheck and before the doors open.

3. 'In the Dressing Room' – Anything specific to the band close to show time.

4. 'Available Throughout the Day' – Everything from coffee with cream to garbage cans.'

MULTIPLE BAND RIDERS

You are going to need to pull out your spreadsheet. If you are in a van and there are four or five of you, you might not need much.

> "Be prepared to make a compromise in everything except the things that affect the show and the attendance."

But you should put it down and at least take time to start practicing budgets, contract building, and communication.

We have spent days coordinating multiple band riders. You need to make sure which elements are essential to each band. Look at the budget and determine some reasonable dollar amount. Trim things down where you can. You can always finagle an extra pizza for the crew, more scotch, and more wine when a show has gone well. When things are bad, no one feels like celebrating, so all of the crap that's on the rider to fuel the backstage party becomes redundant and ultimately pisses off the promoter who has paid for it—before he bills it all back to you.

Quantity	Item	Cost	Total	Total Cost$ X # of shows (38)
UPON ARRIVAL - UNITED II				
7	Large loaves of bread (3 white, 2 wheat, 1 raisin, 1 lo-carb)	$1.40	$9.80	$372.40
4	Packages of bagels	$2.32	$9.28	$352.64
6	Large boxes of cereal (specifically include Raisin Bran, and a choice Meusli, Smart Start, Chex, Cheerios)	$3.00	$18.00	$684.00
2	Boxes of individual packages of microwavable oatmeal			
3	Gallons of milk	$3.29	$6.58	$250.04
1	Case of yogurt	$2.75	$8.25	$313.50
4	Boxes of toaster waffles	$9.99	$9.99	$379.62
2	Pounds of bananas	$2.99	$11.96	$454.48
1	Large bowl of fresh fruit	$0.69	$1.38	$52.44
1	Small jar of crunchy peanut butter	$10.00	$10.00	
1	One jar of jam (Strawberry – M/W/F, Grape - T/TH/Sa/Su)	$2.49	$2.49	$130.58
1	4 pack of butter	$1.99	$1.99	$75.62
1	Large tub of margarine (low fat)	$1.99	$1.99	$75.62
	Sliced sandwich meats (ham, turkey, beef - Ind. packaged)	$1.99	$1.99	$75.62
	Sliced sandwich cheeses (amer., swiss, etc. - Ind. packaged)	$8.99	$8.99	$341.62
2	Tubs of cream cheese	$8.99	$8.99	$341.62
2	Cans of tuna	$1.79	$3.58	$136.04
1	Jar of mayonnaise	$1.99	$3.98	$151.24
	Fresh coffee, tea (hot & iced), milk, non dairy creamer & regular creamer, sugar & sweet & low available ALL DAY LONG until the end of sound check	$1.99	$1.99	$75.62
48	Cans of assorted pops (including diet sodas) ALL DAY LONG	$0.25	$40.00	$1,520.00
5	Cases of bottled water	$12.00	$12.00	$456.00
1	Case of Iced Tea	$7.00	$35.00	$1,330.00
2	Gallons of Orange juice	$12.00	$12.00	$456.00
	Paper towels - 6 pack, Paper plates - 100 pack, Paper bowls - 40 pack, Spoons, forks, and knives - multi pack/100 ea, Can opener, Napkins - 250 pack	$2.99	$5.98	$227.24
2	Toasters			
	Microwave			
2	Garbage cans			
Totals			$226.21	$8,631.94
SPECIFICALLY IN PIGFACE'S DRESSING ROOM				
3	Cases of domestic beer	$12.00	$36.00	$1,368.00
1	Case of imported beer	$20.00	$20.00	$760.00
1	Six pack of non-alcoholic beer	$6.99	$6.99	$265.62
1	Bottle of Absolut	$18.99	$18.99	$721.62
1	Bottle of Jim Beam	$11.99	$11.99	$455.62
2	Bottles of good red wine (Shiraz, Cabernet, Montepulcciano, etc…)	$7.99	$15.98	$607.24
1	Bags of tortilla chips (no Doritos) & 1 jars of salsa	$5.00	$5.00	$190.00
6	Cases of bottled water	$7.00	$42.00	$1,596.00
6	Large bottles of Gatorade	$1.50	$9.00	$342.00
24	Cans of pop	$0.25	$6.00	$228.00
1	Carton of baby wipes	$2.99	$2.99	$113.62
	Clean ice, LOTS of cups			
25	Large, clean towels (bar towels not acceptable)			
	Mirror with good lighting			
Totals			$174.94	$6,647.72
SPECIFICALLY IN DOPE'S DRESSING ROOM				
2	Cases of Budweiser	$12.00	$24.00	$912.00
1	Pabst Blue Ribbon (or Budweiser)	$11.00	$11.00	$418.00
1	Gallon of Orange juice	$2.99	$2.99	$113.62
1	Gallon of Cranberry juice	$2.99	$2.99	$113.62
24	Cans of Coke	$0.25	$6.00	$228.00
1	Large bag of plain potato chips	$1.99	$1.99	$75.62
1	Large jar of ranch flavored dip	$1.99	$1.99	$75.62
1	Mixed nuts, dried fruits, power bars, any kind of healthy munchies!	$2.99	$2.99	$113.62
1	Case of (24) bottled water, non carbonated (ROOM TEMPERATURE)	$7.00		
6	Full length fluffy towels (dark color)		$7.00	$266.00
Totals			$60.95	$2,316.10
SPECIFICALLY IN PMM'S DRESSING ROOM				
1	Case of bottled water	$7.00	$7.00	$266.00
6	Large bottles of Gatorade	$1.50	$18.00	$684.00
1	Bottle of Vodka	$10.99	$10.99	$417.62
1	Bottle of red wine	$7.99	$7.99	$303.62
1	Bottle of cranberry juice	$2.99	$2.99	$113.62
6	Clean towels (bar towels not acceptable)			
Totals			$46.97	$1,784.86
SPECIFICALLY IN RACHEL STAMP'S DRESSING ROOM				
1	Case of bottled water	$7.00	$7.00	$266.00
1	Case of premium domestic or imported beers	$12.00	$12.00	$456.00
6	Cans of brand soda	$0.25	$1.50	$57.00
6	Cans of diet soda	$0.25	$1.50	$57.00
1	Assortment of chocolate candies (Reeses, M&M's, Kit Kats, Twix, Snickers)	$2.99	$2.99	$113.62
6	Well drinks from bar			
8	Clean bath towels (bar towels not acceptable)			
Totals			$24.99	$949.62
UNITED II TOUR EVENING DINNER				
	2 course dinner (main course with salad & bread, etc.) to be provided between 4pm and 7pm after consultation and confirmation with tour manager. It should be a sensible selection of nourishing food for 36 adults without a day off. There are approximately 10 vegetarian/vegans in the touring party. Dinnerware, napkins and a clean, comfortable place to sit and eat will be provided. This portion of the dinner may also be bought out for $12.50 per person.			
Totals			$450.00	$17,100.00
UPON ARRIVAL TOTAL			$226.21	
DRESSING ROOM TOTAL			$307.85	
DINNER BUYOUT			$450.00	

UNITED II SHOPPING LIST

BREADS/BREAKFAST FOODS
7	Large loaves of bread (4 white, 2 wheat, 1 raisin)
4	Packages of bagels
6	Boxes of cereal (specifically 1 box of Raisin Bran & a choice of other generic cereals including Cheerios, Smart Start, Muesli, etc...)
2	Boxes of individual packages of microwavable oatmeal

FROZEN SECTION
4	Boxes of toaster waffles

PRODUCE
2	Pounds of bananas
1	Large bowl of fresh fruit

DELI
	Sliced sandwich meats (ham, turkey, beef – Ind. Packaged) FOR 36 PEOPLE
	Sliced sandwich cheeses (amer., swiss, etc. – Ind. packaged) FOR 36 PEOPLE

DAIRY
3	Gallons of Orange juice
3	Gallons of milk
1	Case of yogurt
1	4-pack of butter
2	Tubs of cream cheese
1	Large tub of margarine (low fat)

CANNED GOODS/SNACK FOODS/CONDIMENTS
1	Large jar of ranch flavored dip
2	Cans of tuna
1	Mixed nuts, dried fruits, power bars, any kind of healthy munchies!
1	Bag of tortilla chips (no Doritos)
1	Large bag of plain potato chips
1	Jar of salsa
1	One jar of jam (Strawberry - M/W/F, Grape - T/TH/Sa/Su)
1	Small jar of crunchy peanut butter
1	Jar of mayonnaise

BEVERAGES (JUICES, SODAS, WATER)
2	Large bottles of Cranberry Juice
12	Large bottles of Gatorade
1	Case of Iced Tea
5	24 Packs of assorted sodas (including Coke, Diet Coke - or other Diet name brands, Sprite, etc...)
14	Cases of bottled water - 24 pack

BEER
2	Cases of Budweiser
1	Pabst Blue Ribbon (or Budweiser)
3	Cases of domestic beer
1	Case of premium domestic
1	Case of imported beer
1	Six pack of non-alcoholic beer
3	Bottles of good red wine (Shiraz, Cabernet, Montepulcciano, etc...)

MISCELLANEOUS ITEMS
	Napkins - 250 pack
	Spoons, forks, and knives - multi pack/100 ea
	Paper bowls - 40 pack
	Paper plates - 100 pack
	Paper towels - 6 pack
	Can opener
1	Carton of baby wipes
	Clean ice
	LOTS of cups!

LIQUOR
1	Bottle of Vodka (well)
1	Bottle of Absolut
1	Bottle of single malt whiskey (Mon, Wed, Fri)
1	Bottle of Jim Beam

RIDER STRATEGIES

TWO GREAT THINGS TO DO WITH A CATERING RIDER!

1. When you are putting a large tour together, four pages of dressing room requirements might seem excessive. Any good promoter faced with the prospect of a 28-person touring party won't make an offer until they see the rider requirements. When a promoter starts screaming, "Oh my God, this is a $1,000 catering rider!" You can follow up with, "No, we have totaled this all up based on a Chicago supermarket. It will cost $450 in all." If you do have a $450 catering rider, have some contingency plans ready to use in a negotiation. It is great to have fresh juice, cereal, bananas, five kinds of bread to toast, yogurt, etc., for the "upon arrival" portion of the rider. But when it comes down to it, three gallons of coffee and a couple of boxes of donuts one day and a couple of bags of bagels the next still works. This saves time on runners and set up, too.

2. After itemizing each band's requirements, we sort everything into a shopping list for each section of the supermarket. A human being is going to end up with the list getting you (or not getting you) your rider. For a 60 date tour, taking the time to sort a four band rider makes sense. For example: cereal, fresh fruit, produce, beer, wine, meat, deli, it communicates to the promoter your awareness of the massive accumulation of tiny minutia that go into any day, maybe the runner will spend one less hour at the supermarket (or not need to go back because the lactose milk was on another page), and then be able to take the keyboard player to the hospital or help the drummer do laundry... I call this selfish philanthropy.

During the first two package tours we put together, there was a fight between people who wanted smooth peanut butter and people who wanted crunchy. We'll use peanut butter as an example and then we can extrapolate. Let's say we are doing 60 shows.

LEVEL ONE– This would be to have a jar of crunchy and smooth peanut butter on the rider. Every day. Everybody is happy, right? The manager has covered his ass!

Super Chunk $2.55 ($153) and Whipped $2.40 ($144) = Total: $297

LEVEL TWO– I return home from the tour with 14 jars of peanut butter. For a few minutes there I feel like a great provider for my growing family. But every single jar had one spoonful out of the top. Which led to a new strategy for peanut butter: throw away the 14 jars and...

LEVEL THREE– Buy two jars of peanut butter at the beginning of the tour, put them on the bus, and when they are close to being empty, buy more.

"But every, every single jar had one spoonful out of the top. Which led to a new strategy for peanut butter..."

I think I might have bought six jars of peanut butter on the whole tour. Instead of $297 I paid $15.30.

A total savings of $281.70!

This might not seem like much, but apply the same philosophy to coffee. You don't need an industrial size jar of crappy coffee everyday, anyway. And cereal, a big touring party only needs six or eight boxes of cereal every few days not every day, etc. The difference is huge, not just in money, but in a promoter being able to accommodate the show and pressure removed from the ticket price.

> Promoters assume that you'll eat anything put in front of you. Make them pay attention. Be specific but be realistic: you need cases of bottled water but it doesn't have to be Evian. Once again, call early, call often and never assume. Locate a nearby back-up source for meals and have petty cash for your runner should you need to scramble. And, as always, sometimes you simply have to laugh and muddle through.
> – *Kathleen "Burt" Bramlett, Production Manager for Penn and Teller*

TOUR:SMART TIP
for more information go to:
www.tstouring.com

CATERING Once you start to see a budget for a multi-band package tour you realize, it's not out of the question to look at bringing catering out with you. The only reason we haven't done this so far is because of limitations of space and facilities. Even on the three bus tours, most of the buses will be pulling a trailer. But the economics of catering makes sense and, if you factor in the health, comfort, and vibe benefits, it's a no-brainer.

"CUISINE TO MANGLE YOUR MIND"

METAL CHEF – ADRIAN H. MERRILL

ADRIAN H. MERRILL

CUISINE TO MANGLE YOUR MIND

www.MetalChef.com

This photo was taken on July 5, 2005 at the POUND SF (San Francisco). I was catering for the VIPS/BANDS at the 2005 Thrash Against Cancer Benefit (Hirax, Vicious Rumors, etc.)

Here is a brief overview of my services. First of all, the band has to have kitchen facilities on their bus/RV. For three meals a day, I charge $500/wk (cash) plus food (most often paid for with buy-out money so the only cost incurred by the band is my wages). I have done a lot of high-protein/low-carb cooking for bands, as there tends to be a lot of beer consumed (which obviously accounts for the majority of carb intake). In addition, I have done a few personal diets for certain band-members some people don't like "this" or "that," and I like to accommodate as best as I can.

As for health tips: If you're not used to eating raw garlic, don't do it when you're drunk... ha ha ha ha! I was out with a band with a guitarist who was fairly health-conscious and was on this raw-garlic kick (eating a tablespoon of raw, crushed garlic everyday), but their singer wasn't. He tried this endeavor before a night of reckless abandon and puked Goldschlager and garlic all over the outside of the RV.

A "Rough Weekly Budget" for 30 people:

Food Cost: ($1,000/wk food cost is a per-meal cost of $2.38) will range between: $800-1,000

The cost of my services for one week: (30 people/wk x two meals/day x seven days): $1,050 (cash)

Total Estimated Weekly Budget: $1,850-$2,050: (not bad for 420 meals, eh?)

At your service, Adrian "Metal Chef" Merrill

See other catering options online at *www.tstouring.com*

MORE SOUP

When putting together the rider, be careful. When I put together the rider for the PiL European Tour, I was living in New York City and missed the comfort of Heinz Tomato Soup which, for some reason, you can't buy in the States. Day three of a forty-plus city tour and I sank lower and lower into my seat at the large dining table as members of the crew began to grumble, "What the fuck?! Tomato soup again?!" I knew we were in for another 30 days of it. "Yea, fucking tour managers."

PART 2: TECHNICAL RIDERS

WRITING A TECH RIDER PEOPLE WILL READ...

KATHLEEN "BURT" BRAMLETT, PRODUCTION MANAGER FOR PENN & TELLER

KATHLEEN BOYETTE BRAMLETT "BURT"

PRODUCTION MANAGER

...You can't. Think of a technical rider as the fine print on the back of a credit card agreement: it's important, it explains a host of obligations and responsibilities —and no one ever reads it.

You can increase the chances that someone at the venue will pay attention to your rider by keeping it short, concise, correctly punctuated and spelled, and well-organized. But never assume. Call early, call often. Talk to the technical director, the lighting and sound departments, the house manager and wardrobe. Above all, be friendly, be flexible and have fun. You might be playing an ill-equipped venue with Mrs. Moore's ninth grade class as your crew, but it's a gig and this is what you do and there's no better life on this planet.

Organize your rider thusly:

GENERAL STAGE REQUIREMENTS

Specify that the stage should be cleared of excess stored scenery and equipment. Few promoters will pay attention but occasionally you'll be pleasantly surprised.

Briefly state your requirements. Be specific, do your homework but be prepared to move "The Cherry Orchard" out of your way before you unload the trucks. Never assume. And ask those seemingly obvious questions.

> On a dark and stormy morning in Northern California, I arrived at the venue du jour to discover no safe, reliable access from the stage into the house and an abyss, commonly called an orchestra pit, disconnecting the two. It hadn't been noted in the venue's tech rider (which I had read), nor had it been mentioned in any of the numerous conversations I'd had with various departments at the venue. Silly me. I never asked, "Is there an orchestra pit we have to bridge with a truck ramp, plywood and two by four stilts because the house to stage step units you tout as useable are actually built into hidden coves just downstage of the proscenium that haven't been opened in a decade?"

DRESSING ROOMS, GREEN ROOMS, WARDROBE

Understand that unless you can convince the promoter to hire movie set trailers or RVs, you're going to have to make do with whatever you get. Having said that, do state your dressing room

> "You can increase the chances that someone at the venue will pay attention to your rider by keeping it short, concise, correctly punctuated and spelled, and well-organized. But never assume."

needs and ask questions. If the dressing rooms are inadequate, how about Mrs. Moore's ninth grade biology lab next door? It's got high tables, high stools, electrical outlets, plenty of light. Send someone to K-Mart for cheap full-length mirrors, balance them lengthwise on the tables using trays of dissected frogs and voila, a dressing room. Be creative. It's part of the joy of touring.

Ask about a washer and dryer but be prepared for howls of laughter. Laugh along, ask the location of the nearest coin laundry and start your tour with a sock of quarters.

LIGHTING AND SOUND REQUIREMENTS

Unless you're lucky enough to carry all your own equipment, demand a current inventory of lighting, sound and communication gear in each venue. Determine what you need to add and call, daily if necessary, to insure said equipment is ordered, delivered and that the promoter has scheduled time to install what you require before you get there.

Other departments, props, wardrobe, and merchandising, travel with everything they need for a performance, which limits the problems they face to those of space, time and personnel. Lighting and sound have to get past hurdles with the promoter, the budget, the performance schedule in the venue and the rental vendor before they get to worry about those little issues of space, time and personnel. Follow up, call the rental vendor, suggest options to the promoter.

Think. Offer solutions. Don't simply point out problems.

CREW REQUIREMENTS

State what you need, understand you'll be surprised and know you'll have to manage. Though it seems obvious (and nothing is) state that the backstage running crew must wear black clothes and shoes.

Confirm crew and schedule with the promoter and the technical director. Determine whether your preferred schedule fits within local union regulations, make any changes necessary and keep your sense of humor.

HOUSE MANAGEMENT, BOX OFFICE AND MERCHANDISING

These folks make your patrons either happy or resentful. Talk to the house manager, the box office manager, the head usher and security. Explain whether your performers wander through the audience during intermission, sign autographs post show, allow photography or encourage cell phone calls during the performance. Do you sell souvenirs? Do you carry a bank or expect the venue to provide small bills for change? Explain and arrange. You don't want to be surprised by the venue, so keep the surprises you have for them to a minimum.

Ask the obvious questions.

There are few jobs in which you reinvent the wheel every day or so. This is one of them. That challenge will stretch you beyond your self-imposed limitations. Aside from learning to fall asleep in seconds and under any conditions, is there anything more rewarding?

Think. Offer solutions; don't simply point out problems.

TOUR:SMART TIP
for more information go to:
www.tstouring.com

TOUR:SMART TIP
for more information go to:
www.tstouring.com

THINGS A HOUSE PRODUCTION MANAGER MUST DO TO MAKE A SHOW RUN WELL

JIM DARDEN, HOUSE OF BLUES CHICAGO

JIM DARDEN

PRODUCTION MANAGER

HOUSE OF BLUES CHICAGO

- **Know your venue** – sounds simple, but the more you know about your venue the more you can make the day run smoothly, not just the stage and dressing rooms, the whole place, it's history, how to get around the place, who are the house managers, maintenance, on and on and on. If the touring personnel see that you know your place, they will feel their day will be easier, and be confident in your actions.

- **Advance, advance, advance** – be thorough, precise, do not forget the little things discussed, keep all notes and e-mails and records of phone conversations. Do not be caught with your pants down, with a good advance you avoid most deviation from what is expected for the smooth execution the show.

- **Expect changes** – Musicians and/or actors or any combination of these, are of a different breed. They are guided by "muse" rather than the real world we live in. The touring production staff will expect some adaptability to meet their artists' needs.

- **Know your budget/have close communication with the promoter** – Do not go spending your promoter's money foolishly, or you won't be working for him very long.

- **Know your staff** – Match the right personalities of your staff to the type of show you have. If your staff likes the band, or genre of the performer, they are more inclined to want the day to go well. This doesn't mean bring on "groupies," just people who might be excited about working with that show. This would also include making sure you have a good mix of veteran staff on and some younger guys. Teach the young ones, they are your staff of the future.

- **Know your neighborhood/city** – Everyone wants to know what to do and where to go, this includes, but not limited to, theaters, bars, nightclubs, laundry mats, grocery stores, hospitals. You should also know where to get tour supplies, instruments, and "nerd gear" of all kinds. Have good vendor lists and build relationships with these folks.

- **As my mother taught me: It's nice to be important, but it's more important to be nice** – Many people come off the road tired, dirty, demanding, abrasive, needy, and think that they are the most important people on the planet. Help them the best you can, be as nice as possible and hopefully these grumpy peoples demeanor will change when they see you are the one trying to make their day better. On the other hand, some people are just assholes. If this is the case, just remember, they will be gone at the end of the show and with luck tomorrow's show you get to deal with a better class of people.

It is nice to be important but more important to be nice.

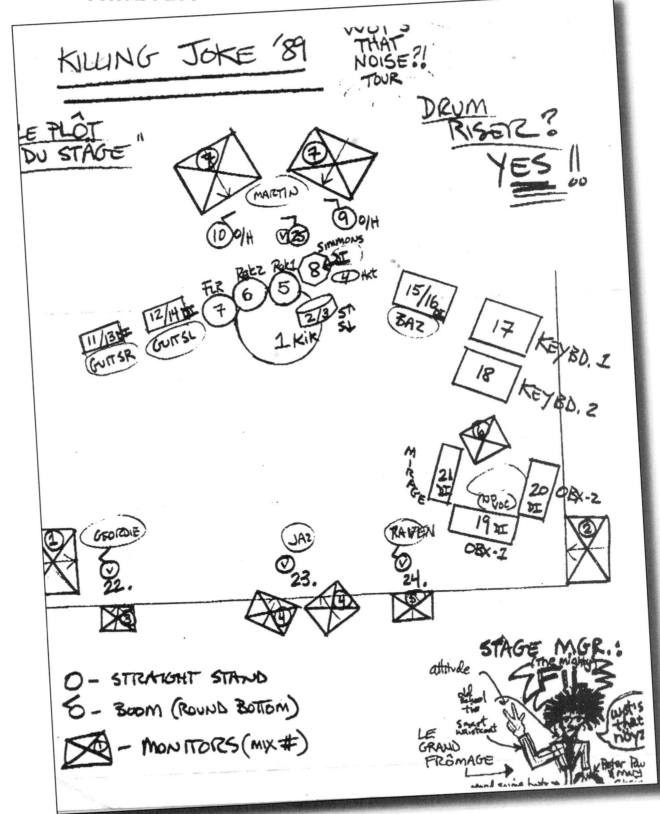

THE LOWEST OF THE LOW INPUT LIST

	F.O.H. INPUTS	NOTES		MONITOR INPUTS
1	KICK	B52A, M-88, D112	1	KICK 1
2	KICK (TRIGGER)	COUNTRYMAN DI	2	KICK (TRIGGER)
3	SNARE	SM 57	3	SNARE
4	HI-HAT	SM 81	4	HI-HAT
5	RACK TOM 1	SM57, EV-408, MD-504	5	RACK TOM 1
6	RACK TOM 2	SM57, EV-408, MD-504	6	RACK TOM 2
7	FLOOR TOM	SM57, EV-408, MD-504	7	FLOOR TOM
8	OVERHEAD	SM 81	8	KICK (2ND KIT)
9	KICK	B52 A, M-88, D112	9	SNARE (2ND KIT)
10	SNARE	SM 57	10	HIT-HAT (2ND KIT)
11	HI-HAT	SM 81	11	BASS-LEVI
12	RACK TOM 1	SM57, EV-408, MD-504	12	GTR-BOBDOG
13	RACK TOM 2	SM57, EV-408, MD-504	13	SITAR-BOBDOG
14	FLOOR TOM	SM57, EV-408, MD-504	14	GTR #2
15	OVERHEAD	SM 81	15	CELLO-GUS
16	LEVI BASS	COUNTRYMAN DI	16	SAMPLES-L
17	BOBDOG - GUITAR	421, 409	17	SAMPLES-R
18	BOBDOG - SITAR	COUNTRYMAN DI	18	LOOPS
19	GUITAR #2	421, 409, SM57	19	FM EINHEIT-L
20	GUS - CELLO	COUNTRYMAN DI	20	FM EINHEIT-R
21	SAMPLES - L	DI	21	MARTIN VOX
22	SAMPLES - R	DI	22	VOX 1 - MEG
23	LOOPS - L	DI	23	VOX 2- JARED
24	LOOPS - R	DI	24	VOX 3 -?
25	FM EINHEIT - L	DI	25	VOX 4 - ?
26	FM EINHEIT - R	DI	26	NOT BREATHING - L
27	?		27	NOT BREATHING - R
28	?		28	BAGMAN - L
29	?		29	BAGMAN - R
30	MARTIN VOX	SM 58, OM-5	30	SCORN - L
31	MEG - VOX 1	SM 58, OM-5	31	SCORN - R
32	JARED - VOX 2	SM 58, OM-5	32	F.O.H. TALKBACK
33	? - VOX 3	SM 58, OM-5		
34	? - VOX 4	SM 58, OM-5		
35	NOT BREATHING - L	DI		
36	NOT BREATHING - R	DI		
37	BAGMAN - L	DI		
38	BAGMAN - R	DI		
39	SCORN - L	DI		
40	SCORN - R	DI		

- **Think. Offer solutions. Don't simply point out the problems.**

- **Realize you are paying for all of this.** Ask for as little as you can if you are starting out.

- **After itemizing each band's requirements,** sort everything into a shopping list as a service to the venue and as insurance for you that something is less likely to be forgotten.

- **Don't treat the rider as some kind of yardstick/comparison between other bands.** Or as an emotional crutch for your artistic insecurities.

- **Get what you need. If it's really crucial, bring it yourself!**

- **It is always good negotiation to make a compromise** in everything except the things that affect the show and the attendance.

- **Take time to start practicing contract building and communication.**

- **Question anything in a deal that might inflate the cost of the show** and ultimately the cost of a ticket! It will reduce attendance.

- **If you feel like some interesting cheese** and your guarantees are high enough to get it, that's great. But it's going to end up with someone's cigarette stubbed out in the middle of it. I'd suggest stocking the bus with these things. Then you only have to worry about the band and crew scarfing them!

- **Don't insist on yelling all your needs to the house guy** - listen for a second. You might need six loaders at most venues. But at House Of Blues Chicago you're dealing with a small elevator load-in. They'll let you know that more than four loaders is a waste of your money, if you'll let them.

- **Advance! Advance! Advance!**

- **You don't want to be surprised by the venue –** so keep the surprises you have for them to a minimum.

C·H·A·P·T·E·R ···· 10

BOOKING: DIY VS. AGENTS

"I never found anybody who could manage my career any better than I could."
 - Steve Miller (Steve Miller Band)

Thanks Steve, but we're talking about booking here...

A small band trying to get somewhere can do much better using their own resources, friends, and other bands because a smaller band cannot be a priority with an agent. Booking yourself is the best way to protect your band, and your future.

Good agents are increasingly rare these days, they are all overworked. Right now, there are a bazillion bands and tomorrow there will be a bazillion and ten. If you want to develop a larger audience and an increasingly better show, you're going to spend whatever time it takes to carefully make sure that your first shows are in the right places with the best chance of success. That is not necessarily the goal of an agent.

What do you get from an agent? You get a human being... a human being that can't really protect you and probably has less knowledge of the geography of the U.S., and certainly your band than you do. In terms of your career, it might ultimately be worth spending three months slowly working on getting a show at a prominent nationally-known venue. For an agent, it's worth the commission.

"I know the tour doesn't work - I know. But I need to make a boat payment."
  - Agent

The quote above says it all. This agent doesn't care about the damage he is doing to a band's career and is very far away from providing a nurturing, managerial relationship for the band. How successful was the tour? Well, the agent has got to make his boat payment.

Whether you are looking for an agent or booking yourself (or both):

Keep a detailed history of your shows and activity—the attendance, the ticket price, the day of the week, the weather, the guarantee, notes about the venue, how many shirts you sold, what size, and how many CDs you sold, is essential information for you to be able to pitch: "In the Midwest, we play to 300 people a night, have this many street teamers, and 3,000 kids on our

> "What do you get from an agent. You get a human being... a human being that can't really protect you and probably has less knowledge of the geography of the U.S., and certainly your band than you do."

mailing list. We could make sure that the dates for X band from Europe go really well." This is a really important building block in understanding the business of your band : the strong points and, just as importantly, the weak points.

Are these sales enough to justify or subsidize a buy-on with another band and larger audience?

Hype and bullshit doesn't count. Honesty does.

There is no benefit to having the agent or promoter expecting 200 people on a Tuesday night if only 120 people show up, it's a failure. If you honestly think you're good for 20 people and 47 people show up, it's a success. Professionals are used to seeing a band develop, they will be more excited by the possibilities of twice the attendance you expected than they will be by half of what you hoped for.

So get busy.

You're not going to find an agent unless you get out there and start to do the work. A good agent is going to want to know the details and the peculiarities of your business so he knows some of the areas in which he can negotiate; does he have to concentrate on a better sound system? More lights? Vegetarian food on the rider? The only way you (and then your agent) can talk knowledgably about these matters is for you to have been out there and to have done it.

BOOKING YOURSELF

If you book yourself, you can use your connections to help yourself and an out of town band that is useful to you. You can make decisions based on the long term good of the band, not the commission. It's a quick learning curve, just like cocaine, the more you do, the more you'll know.

START EARLY

Start the process a minimum of three months before the first show. Work through planning, ideas and information before that. In the pre-planning stage, before you pick up the phone you should identify the markets you think you can do well in and why. That's the first step to being able to convince somebody else. Let the information you have speak to you and follow its advice. If your initial tour plan targets Dallas and all of your fans are in Denton, play Denton. It might not look so cool on the back of a shirt, but it's going to feel an awful lot better when people show up. Plan carefully. You only have one chance to make a first impression, and you can't afford changes to your plan once some shows have been confirmed. By the time you realize the Thursday night would've been better than the Tuesday, the club might be booked up for the next two months.

Be organized about the way you communicate, software, charts, different colored pens, use anything and anyone that helps. Contact more than one venue in each market. You might think you know the right venue, but when you're just starting out, the right venue is the one that will give you a show.

PACKAGES

Research venues on the web and submit materials in the way that is the most convenient for them. If you can afford it, track packages. If you wait two weeks to call to make sure a package has been received, that's when you find out the booker is only there on a Wednesday and Thursday. You called on a Friday, so you call back the following Wednesday and that's when you find out that the package hasn't been received, you just blew three weeks. FedEx is expensive, but you can FedEx Ground something for $7 or $8 or add delivery confirmation from USPS for $0.60; you can allocate your resources. FedEx packages to the ten or twenty most important venues and use a cheaper method for the additional packages.

Make sure you follow up within a reasonable time after your submission.

TOUR:SMART TIP
for more information go to:
www.tstouring.com

> **"...concentrate on the hard facts— not the opinions. Opinions are like DJ's — everybody is one.**

PREPARE FOR THE CALL

Read the *"Promoters and Venues"* chapter. Those guys are telling you what they want! It's priceless! Always remember that what you're asking for is a favor. Know your information—concentrate on the hard facts—not the opinions. Opinions are like DJ's—everybody is one.

TOUR:SMART TIP
for more information go to:
www.tstouring.com

AGENTS

> "The agent told me it was a beautiful old theatre and it was - just completely wrong for our purposes."
> - Martin Atkins, Pigface Tour 1995

You might actually want to ask yourself, "Do we need an agent or do we just think we need an agent?" Either way, a detailed record of your history—is essential . A good agent will point you in the right direction, suggest other bands for you to play with, and have good, almost managerial input for you.

> "Gas prices will go down."
> - Agent

You might be thinking that an agent will protect you if you don't get paid. This might be true to a certain extent, but there are only so many venues, your agent needs to be calling that same venue the next day about another show, so be realistic and be humble. An agent is not going to jeopardize relationships with a venue that he has had for five years (and hopes to for another five) for you!

> **"An agent is not going to jeopardize his relationship with a venue that he has been dealing with for five years (and hopes to for another five) for you!"**

Earlier in the book, I suggested you buy a *Rand McNally Dist-O-Map*. I have never met a single agent that knew of their existence (What does that tell you?). Remember, they're not liable for the cost of horrific, lazy routing, you are. So look at the routing you're presented and pay attention before you're sitting in a van going backwards and forwards on the same highway. . Look at the PIG case study and apply those simple ideas to any tour you are presented with.

If and when you get an agent it is not time to relax, it is time to stay involved! And really pay attention.

WHEN YOUR AGENT SUGGESTS AN OPENING BAND

Be careful. This is an easy way for your agent to get 30 shows for another one of his bands, get them off his back, and get more commission. Check for yourself to find out some information about the band:

- Do they have a label?

- Is that label going to help in any way at all?

- Have they sold any CDs?

- Do they have a following? How many people are on their MySpace page (divide by two)?

- Have they played in these markets before?

- Do they have a street team?

- Do they have posters? Or will they contribute to printing posters (saving you each half)?

- Do they have mountains of equipment, throw vegetable oil all over the stage, or have a reputation for causing problems?

Do your homework! You might be better off with a strong local opener in each city, at least you'll have a chance at a place to stay!

> "El Paso will be great."
>   - Agent

"It just depends on the agent, really. There's a couple that have been really good, but for the most part, they are people who give away whatever they can to make the deal. They'll take away from your advertising budget or your catering budget and they'll add it to the overall fee. The only reason they're doing that is to get their percentage. And that is way too widespread."

    — Jolly Roger, on the role of agents

MICHAEL YERKE – House of Blues, Chicago

MA: What makes a good agent?

MY: A good agent will try to get the best for their artist and will also have an understanding of where that artist is in the marketplace. A good agent is fair. If a show is obviously going to do poorly (because of poor advanced ticket sales), a good agent will get on the phone before the catastrophe occurs and perhaps talk about a reduction in the fee and a way to reduce the hit to the venue. There are some agents who won't consider a reduction under any circumstances. They will allow a venue to take the hit and offer up some false promises like, "We'll catch you next time around."

BUILT INS

This is a night with a built in crowd. A promoter has identified a market and nurtured it with events, drinks specials, and rewards to the devoted, even if it means he has had to subsidize the evening himself, building loyalty. The good side is that there will be a good crowd of people there the night that you play. The bad side is that these kids will pretty much be there whether you play or not. So, the ticket price can only be a couple of dollars more than it usually is; otherwise, the attendance will decrease. The promoter knows he has something valuable: an asset that has taken him time, money, and effort to build. He might offer you much less than another club to play there. You will be wise to take the show. Make sure that your merchandise is reasonably priced you have good quantities to take advantage of the situation, and have plenty of promos to give away.

Some of our bands want to get straight into one of these tastemaker venues. I suggest that they go to three to five cities located close by to start with, smaller venues with limited risk and limited downside, using my five-pointed star inward crush strategy (see next page).

EXAMPLE

Let's look at this for a club in Cincinnati For a show there, I'd want to play a show in Dayton, OH (49 miles away), a show in Richmond, IN (63 miles away), a show in Lexington, KY (88 miles away), and maybe a show in Louisville, KY (106 miles away) or any other closer, small market in a 60-mile radius.

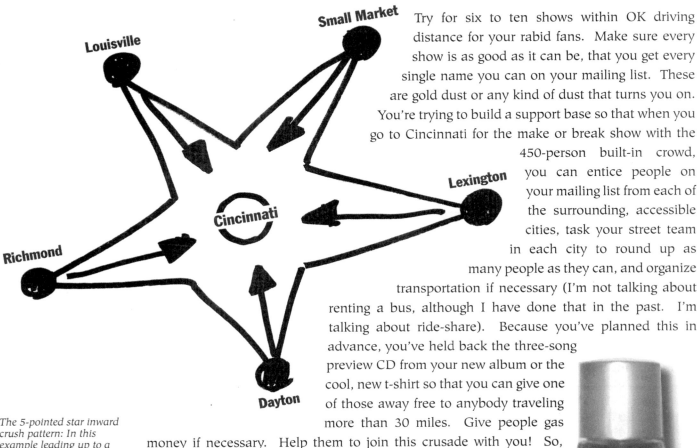

Try for six to ten shows within OK driving distance for your rabid fans. Make sure every show is as good as it can be, that you get every single name you can on your mailing list. These are gold dust or any kind of dust that turns you on. You're trying to build a support base so that when you go to Cincinnati for the make or break show with the 450-person built-in crowd, you can entice people on your mailing list from each of the surrounding, accessible cities, task your street team in each city to round up as many people as they can, and organize transportation if necessary (I'm not talking about renting a bus, although I have done that in the past. I'm talking about ride-share). Because you've planned this in advance, you've held back the three-song preview CD from your new album or the cool, new t-shirt so that you can give one of those away free to anybody traveling more than 30 miles. Give people gas money if necessary. Help them to join this crusade with you! So, when you hit the stage you have 200 extra people at the venue. The promoter will notice the increased attendance. The bar staff will notice the increased revenue. The 450 kids who usually go will notice the larger crowd and get pulled in. End result: you've done something other than talk and hype and the next time the promoter is looking for a solid band that works hard with a good following to help a national show that might be struggling, he's going to call you. That's it, simple. As Sun Tzu would say, "Never take your country to war unless you're sure of the outcome."

The 5-pointed star inward crush pattern: In this example leading up to a show in Cincinnati, the points of the star represent the shows in Dayton, Richmond, Louisville, Lexington, and another nearby market.

> "Never take your country to war unless you're sure of the outcome."

Or, you can go into the same venue unprepared, with no strategy other than a new aftershave called *Strategy for HIM*, and create such a horrible first impression that you will never be considered for anything there ever again.

Although it makes perfect sense to you to play two more shows per week (because that's $500 more in gross income a week, four more pizzas, more beer, and more t-shirt and CD sales), it doesn't make sense for the agent. Faced with a choice of booking that sixth show for you or using that same amount of effort to book the five easy shows for a different band that week for the same $187.50 commission. It's really simple—you are fucked!

Show #	Hours Worked	Commission	Total Hours Worked	Total Commission	Agent's Hourly Wage
1	1	$ 60.00	1	$ 60.00	$ 60.00
2	0.5	$ 37.00	1.5	$ 97.00	$ 64.67
3	1	$ 37.50	2.5	$ 134.50	$ 53.80
4	2	$ 37.50	4.5	$ 172.00	$ 38.22
5	3	$ 15.00	7.5	$ 187.00	$ 24.93
6	4	$ 0	11.5	$ 187.00	$ 16.26
7		$ 0	11.5	$ 187.00	$ 16.26

FIVE VS. SEVEN SHOWS PER WEEK

If I told you I could get you in front of 6,000 extra kids next year, you'd think I had scored you the opening slot with Tool in Chicago. The reality is just as great, but not as sexy.

You need to play every day. The difference between playing five shows a week and seven shows a week could be the difference that breaks your band, as long as you don't overplay your local market.

Consider what happens when you look at 5 vs. 7 shows per week:

5 Shows/Week

# Shows	Gtee	Door %	Com. 15%	Shirts (#)	CDs (#)	Hotels	Food	Profit
1	$400	n/a	$60	13	12	stay with fans		
2	$250	n/a	$38	16	11	stay with fans		
3	$250	n/a	$38	11	14	$150		
4	$250	n/a	$38	13	15	stay with fans		
5	$100	n/a	$15	8	7	stay with fans		
6	$0		$0	0	0	$150	$60	
7	$0		$0	0	0	$150	$60	
Totals	$1,250	$ -	$188	61	59	$450	$120	$ 1,997.50

Now add events on days six and seven

7 Shows/Week

# Shows	Gtee	Door %	Com. 15%	Shirts (#)	CDs (#)	Hotels	Food	Profit
1	$400	n/a	$60	13	12	stay with fans		
2	$250	n/a	$38	16	11	stay with fans		
3	$250	n/a	$38	11	14	$150		
4	$250	n/a	$38	13	15	stay with fans		
5	$100	n/a	$15	8	7	stay with fans		
6		$475	$0	16	21	stay with opener		
7		$250	$0	8	11	stay with headliner		
Totals	$1,250	$725	$188	85	91	$150	$0	$ 4,112.50

This is what we get after adding in the band side of things (shirt sales, CD sales, and occasional hotel if there aren't any fans to stay with, and food expense if there isn't a venue to provide at least pizza and beer).

So by the band getting involved and booking (or creating) two door deal shows, the revenue for the band has gone up over $2,000 for the week. They sold 32 more CDs and 24 more t-shirts. It's not about the money. You will sell more CDs! At $10/CD and $15/t-shirt, that's $680 more from merchandise, $725 more from ticket sales and expenses have gone down. More pizzas, more beer. You don't need to spend $300 on hotels, and you save $120 on food. You saw the chart where the more shows per week an agent booked, the more time it took to make less commission. You are unplugged from these considerations. You are investing in your career and creating relationships, possibly for decades. Now let's look at that difference spread across 40 weeks.

Now extrapolate that across 40 weeks

5 Shows/Week

# Shows	Gtee	Door %	Com. 15%	Shirts (#)	CDs (#)	Hotels	Food	Profit
1	$16,000	n/a	$2,400	520	480	stay with fans		
2	$10,000	n/a	$1,500	640	440	stay with fans		
3	$10,000	n/a	$1,500	440	560	$6,000		
4	$10,000	n/a	$1,500	520	600	stay with fans		
5	$4,000	n/a	$600	320	280	stay with fans		
6						$6,000	$2,400	
7						$6,000	$2,400	
Totals	$50,000	$ -	$7,500	2440	2360	$18,000	$4,800	$ 79,900.00

7 Shows/Week

# Shows	Gtee	Door %	Com. 15%	Shirts (#)	CDs (#)	Hotels	Food	Profit
1	$16,000	n/a	$2,400	520	480	stay with fans		
2	$10,000	n/a	$1,500	640	440	stay with fans		
3	$10,000	n/a	$1,500	440	560	$150		
4	$10,000	n/a	$1,500	520	600	stay with fans		
5	$4,000	n/a	$600	320	280	stay with fans		
6		$19,000	$0	640	840	stay with opener		
7		$10,000	$0	320	440	stay with headliner		
Totals	$50,000	$29,000	$7,500	3400	3640	$150	$0	$ 143,510.00

For a hardworking band on the road for 40 weeks, the difference is $63,610. If you wanted to completely book yourself you'd save another $7,500 in commissions. You'd sell 1,280 more CDs, and 960 more shirts. The value to this in trying to break a band is huge. You simply can not sit around and complain about your agent. You must take the responsibility.

You might be sitting down wondering how you could possibly pull off seven shows per week. You want to know what I'm thinking? What would happen if you could do eight or nine shows?

BUY-ONS - PAY THE PRICE!

"Even if you have to pay money to get on a bill, just do it. If you think you're too good to pay anyone money to play a big major event, then you'll just never play any major events."
— Jeffrey A. Swanson, Creator of GothicFest

The buy-on is an opportunity that has more and more value as the business grows clogged with bands screaming for attention. It's really simple: if a headlining band is performing to 1,000 people per night, there is a chance for an up and coming band to play to that larger audience. In the harsh real world of touring economics, these opportunities are sold.

It is not always directly about money. A few hundred or a few thousand dollars helps with the bottom line, but it does not mean a thing if the venues are empty. You are going to need a combination of cash and assets that you can bring to the table to secure a buy-on slot, so carefully assemble your building blocks. If you have a group of reliable street teams, a well-maintained mailing list, an active MySpace page, the ability to draw an audience, and a supportive record label, these are all valuable to the larger promoters and tours who need to off-set risk. Your hard-earned assets can be the deciding factor between your band getting the slot over another band with more money but less real resources.

To be able to examine the value of a buy-on to you and your band, you need to know several things:

- How many people do you usually play to?
- What happens if you play to 100 people?
- How many shirts and CDs do you sell?

If you are a good band with cool shirts and a well put together CD, then your biggest problem is the growth curve of building an audience. A smart buy-on can dramatically shorten this curve.

Let's look at why a buy-on can be attractive.

EXAMPLE ONE: NO BUY-ON
Go to Cleveland and play to 11 people on a Tuesday night. Impress the club owner and hopefully meet someone from the radio station, newspaper, or anyone who likes your band. Find some people who are interested in being on your street team. Do not get into a fight with the band you are opening for. Build a relationship with them, and perhaps stay at their house.

Eight weeks later: Go back to Cleveland after having e-mailed your new street team with flyers. Play the right venue this time with the band that you met. Play to 60 people and sign up 35 people to your mailing list.

> "It is not always directly about money. If a band is looking for a buy-on, a few hundred or a few thousand dollars helps, but it does not mean a thing if the venues are empty."

Ten weeks later: (One member of the band has to fly to Amsterdam, go to a wedding, take a final, or broke his wrist punching a wall). Go back to Cleveland and play the same club where you now have a relationship with the promoter who likes you. He puts on you a bill with two other bands and feeds you. There are 250 people there and they love you. Things are really looking up. Your agent just booked some shows in Florida during which the van explodes.

Five months later: Go back to Cleveland. You are tired, beaten-up, and you have forgotten all of the lessons that you learned from this book and play the wrong club. Go back to two steps. The owner of the club that you should have played shows up to say hi and buys you a pizza anyway.

Three months later: Play at his club, get back on track, and play to 300 people. That's over a year and you haven't been to the West Coast yet!

That is one way to do it. If you are trying to conquer America, it might be two years before you can play Cleveland five times.

EXAMPLE TWO: USING A BUY-ON TO GROW YOUR AUDIENCE

> "The Lessen Lesson"

Buy on to five regional shows of a national tour with a larger band within your genre that plays to 1,200 people per night. Call smaller venues in those markets and book shows for 10 weeks after the larger show. Print flyers and announce the shows from the stage. Go back to those cities and perform to 220 people. Go back six weeks after that and play to 350. You just saved nine months, and used money to accelerate your growth curve. Momentum keeps morale up and lessens the chances of your awesome bass player leaving.

If you are confident that the only thing holding your band back is exposure, then a buy-on to play with a larger band within your genre can be a good investment.

BE CAREFUL!!

> Means send an e-mail, not have a wake!!

Memorialize the agreement before you do anything (time slot, number of guests, length of set, etc.). You might assume there is only one band opening (you!), when there might be three with your band on first. Send an e-mail with all of your questions.

You could be pushed on stage a couple of minutes after the doors open, at which time there are more people standing in line outside than there are in the venue. You could perform to these people for free, outside!

Be open to new ideas! Think outside of the box... and the venue!
Interestingly enough, when I ran out of time and space on stage on the Lowest Of The Low Tour, I suggested to one of our two-piece bands that they should think about performing before doors opened to the people standing in line. It would be great exposure! The duo was outraged that I would suggest such a thing! I guess they would have rather played to no one but be inside the building. Talk about literally not thinking outside of the box!

Define some of the elements that are essential to showcase your band in a positive light. What about the lighting? Can you use it all? Probably not. No one wants every band to use strobes all the time. It will make the main band's strobes seem tired. Ditto smoke, etc. Will the volume be at a realistic level for the room or will the main band's sound guy pull the faders all the way down? You would be surprised and horrified at how often that happens. It is reasonable for an event to increase in tempo and volume as the night unfolds, but there are respectful limits to that curve.

> *I did an open-air show with Killing Joke, opening for the Mission UK, at some huge park in London. We had a double-decker tour bus and Henry Rollins was opening. We did our show and then I went back to the bus to try and have a bit of a nap. All of the sudden, I heard this amazingly loud, thunderous sound. I asked one of the crew guys what it was. "Oh," he laughed, "they just turned the rest of the PA on!"*

I have listened astounded to the opening band's set as the soundman checked out his brand new effect while the unsuspecting opening band's bass drum is flanged, phased, delayed, or doubled. Pay attention. Do your homework. Do not convince yourself that a band that is asking you to buy-on is doing well. Try to look at Pollstar or Soundscan information to make sure they are selling records in the markets in which you are considering a buy-on. Those might be their weakest markets. Just because you know they do well in New York, Omaha, Baltimore, and Los Angeles does not mean that they are going to do well in Atlanta, Charlotte, or any other cities you have been asked to buy-on to.

Get some anecdotal information from the internet, a friend, or a record store owner. You can learn a lot from a band's message board. How does the band do when they are in town? The band could be cool, but their label might totally suck. You are probably not going to get a sound check, plan for it! And definitely read the chapter on *When you are the Opening Band.*

The problem with purchasing an opportunity is that it is difficult to quantify exactly what the opportunity is, especially in the music business. If it doesn't turn out OK, bear in mind things probably aren't turning out OK for the main band either. This could be an opportunity for you to have a real scream and try and get some money back (which is unlikely if things are bad). Or you can think this through and realize that the most you can probably get out of this is some points for being unbelievably cool about it. No one wants their problems rubbed in their face or compounded with more problems.

MERCHANDISING AND MATCHING PRICES

You are also going to want to look at merchandising and how many shirt designs or items you can have. Be careful if you are asked to "match price." That means you need to sell shirts at the same price they do. If you are touring with a band that has expensive shirts, you might be asking your fans to pay more to see you in terms of the ticket price and shirts. A shirt that has been $12 could be $20-$25 because you agreed to match price. Think about a two to three song sample CD, you could give away to this larger audience as an effective price reducer... "CD is $7.50... or free with any t-shirt!"

> **"You are probably not going to get a sound check, plan for it! "**

Advice from Tub Ring:

We were treated extremely nice and fair and even got to do another tour without buying on (later). It was a bit of a costly investment, so we were worried. However, we made about five times our buy-on amount in merch sales by the end of the tour, which made the whole thing extremely lucrative for us in the end. Not to mention, all the new fans we made which would be at future shows and increase future sales. There have been bad buy-ons. What people have to really be careful of is finding the right band to buy-on with. You need to buy-on to a tour that's going to have a crowd that will (in general) like you. I've seen other bands buy-on a tour, not connect with that tour's audience, and walk away from the whole thing without any financial progress or positive exposure.

OTHER KINDS OF BUY-ONS—PAY TO PLAY

There are more and more venues across the country who are using the pay to play technique. You purchase a set amount of tickets from the venue and sell them. Some venues are creating second stages where five or six local openers compete for a slot to be on the main stage opening for the main event. One club does it very simply: the band that sells the most tickets gets the slot! This is the real world; it ain't like Little League where everyone gets a trophy. The other five bands play in the side room. I know of several venues across the country, from east coast to west coast, that are doing this right now. Be careful: not all of them seem to be totally up-front about the fact that you might not be on the same stage as the main band. You might not even be in the same room. However, if you have your shit together, you will at least be inside the same building, legitimately, so you and your helpers can get more names for your list and offer to help in any way you can.

"As far as I know right now, this is common practice in LA, Connecticut, Milwaukee, Phoenix, and, I'm sure, many other parts of the country."
    -Martin Atkins

"Going on tour with your mates because they love the band, really means "let's take these mugs out so we can get someone to pay "tour support." So, in effect it's no longer taking your mates out because you like their band; it's a profit centre!"
    - Steve Beatty, Plastic Head Distribution

While trawling around the internet, I came across the website for the Bottom of the Hill in San Francisco. The advice that they had for bands was so good, I asked them for permission to reprint the information from their website: *www.bottomofthehill.com*

HOW DO I GO ABOUT GETTING A SHOW AT THE BOTTOM OF THE HILL FOR THE FIRST TIME?
RAMONA DOWNEY AND URSULA RODRIGUEZ

THE GROUND RULES:

Do not send a demo unless it has been requested. The Bottom of the Hill has no "foot traffic." We mean zero, a null set. No one comes to the club except to see the bands. You should feel very confident that 40 to 50 people would come to see your band on a Monday night. If you don't feel that's the case, you should wait a bit before playing this particular club. You shouldn't be in a big hurry to play to nobody, and that's what happens if you play before you're ready. Until then, be patient.

When you play B.O.T.H. for the first time, you are making a statement about your band. These are some things we would be looking at:

1. What does your music sound like live?
2. What size crowd do you draw?
3. What kinds of people come to your shows?
4. What other bands are you friends with or do you go well with?
5. How easy are you to work with?
6. How loud do you play?

When we put together a show for your first time, we're trying to get a good vibe going. You should establish a rapport with other bands and musicians.

BUILD YOURSELF A NAME FIRST

How do you do that? Start small. Play the smaller clubs: the Sushi Sundays, the rent parties, the (Lord, help us) frat parties, and start a mailing list. Target your audience. Figure out who is likely to like your stuff and concentrate on those types of events. When you start getting shows, play the room. You won't do anyone any favors by blowing their eardrums while keeping your integrity intact.

Make sure you go see other bands. If you like their work, introduce yourself. Give them a tape of your music. Often times your first fans will be other musicians.

If no one will book you, book yourself. Throw a warehouse party! We can only accommodate roughly 90 acts per month. So keep in mind that there are alternatives to playing in established "rock" venues. Bob Dylan built his reputation at cafes, Crash Worship at warehouse parties and raves, and Ani DiFranco playing every little corner of this fair land out of a beat-up VW bug.

SHOULD I TAKE ANY SHOW THAT'S OFFERED TO ME?

No. Be smart about the shows you take. In the beginning, it's not wise to be too choosy, but before long, you should start turning down shows that don't make sense. Realize that more is going on than just a show being played. You are being associated in the minds of the audience with the other bands on the bill and with the venue.

WHO GETS CREDIT IF A NIGHT DOES WELL?

The most important thing for any band is to be associated with is a good night. At the Bottom of the Hill, we typically have three bands on the bill per night. If each band's crowd only comes for their set, then we only ever have 40 people in the club at any given time and the club looks like we're holding a wake. Encourage your crowd to come early to see the opener or stay after your set to watch the next band.

ONCE WE'VE PLAYED THERE AND DONE WELL, WHAT'S THE NEXT STEP?

The next step is to do it again under slightly different circumstances, a bit later in the week, with a different band or two perhaps. Keep in mind that no one plays the Bottom of the Hill every month, so it's important to use some strategy when you plan a show. Our job is to maximize the impact of each show. The first and most obvious way of making a show special is by not playing too much.

IF YOU AGREE TO PLAY A SHOW AT THE BOTTOM OF THE HILL, YOU SHOULD NOT HAVE ANY OTHER LOCAL SHOWS AT LEAST TWO WEEKS PRIOR TO THE SHOW AND ONE WEEK AFTER.

Specifically, this means two weekends before and one weekend after. Many times, we have seen bands announce to an empty room: "Um... this is our last song... come see us at the Boomerang this Friday." First off, why announce such a thing when the only people there are employees of the Bottom of the Hill? Secondly and most importantly, could the fact of having another gig in just a few days have something to do with the fact that no one came to your show?

Another way to make a show special is to make it a party. Is it a CD release? Is it someone's birthday? Is it someone's last show with the band? Did you get some press? People will come out on a Monday if there is a compelling reason.

HOW DO WE LET YOUR VENUE KNOW ABOUT US IF YOU'RE NOT ACCEPTING DEMOS?

At the earliest stages, it's more important just to let us know you're playing, getting press, and building a following. After you've played a few shows and sent a communiqué or two, then you should call the booking line. If you send a demo too early, it ends up in a pile with hundreds of others.

"... you shouldn't be in a big hurry to play to no one."

TOUR:SMART TIP
for more information go to:
www.tstouring.com

WHAT TO DO WHEN IT'S IMPOSSIBLE TO GET THROUGH ON THE BOOKING LINE DURING THE BOOKING HOURS:

- Leave a message during off-hours. If you need to get through to us, we will eventually make that call back. It may take a few tries, but we will.
- The most important thing when you leave a message is to leave your name and telephone number. Everything else is secondary! When you leave your telephone number, enunciate. (Hence, "five" can sound like "nine.")
- The volume of calls on the booking line is enormous. Sometimes we get as many as 60 messages a day. If you've already left a message, don't leave another. You will hear from us if we have a show for you. We cannot call everyone just to say we don't have any openings right now. We realize this system is imperfect but we are working at the practical limits of what we are capable.

WHEN CAN I CONSIDER A SHOW CONFIRMED?

Many times when you call for a show, the bookers will give you a tentative date saying something like: "Why don't we shoot for the third? You ask the other people involved and I'll make sure the date is clear and we'll talk again to confirm it." That is not a confirmed show. A million different things can happen on both sides of that conversation. The drummer is out of town, you forgot you have a show too close to that date, etc. We don't consider a show confirmed until we have discussed the full bill (opener, support, and headliner), load-in/sound-check/set times, what each band can expect to be paid, and what the ticket price will be. It's often happened that bands have sent mailings or done posters for shows that weren't confirmed. Please make sure you have talked in person with one of our bookers to confirm your show. Phone messages aren't reliable.

When you confirm a show with us make sure you know the following things:

- Date of your show
- Ticket price
- Load-in time
- Sound check time
- What your payment is
- What the bar telephone number is in case of emergency
- How to get to the Bottom of the Hill

When we confirm a show with you, you also need to tell us how many people are in your band, roughly what the stage plot is (typically "guitar, bass, drums with two vocal mikes up front"), and any special arrangements you will need for your set (i.e. "We're sharing a drum kit with the opening band" or "We need a direct box for our Electric Latrinophone").

OUT OF TOWN BANDS

The important thing when you're on tour is to play to new people. That is an objective that is not achieved if you play to an empty venue. We do our best to put together bills that make sense and it's very difficult to put a band that no one's heard of, with no draw, on a bill that would be better served with a local band. It is wasteful to send packages without contacting

> "Did you get some press? People will come out on a Monday if there is a compelling reason."

> "Sometimes we get as many as 60 messages a day. If you've already left a message, don't leave another."

the bookers first and it is almost always a waste of money to send packages overnight. The volume of mail that we receive means that it takes us a few days to get to packages in the best of circumstances. We are usually booked eight weeks in advance. It doesn't hurt to check for openings on short notice, but they only happen rarely.

IS IT IMPOSSIBLE FOR A BABY BAND FROM OUT-OF-TOWN TO PLAY AT THE BOTTOM OF THE HILL?

The best way to do it is to make friends with local bands that have some draw. We encourage you to identify yourself with a scene, whether it's Brit Pop or Heavy Metal. It's a good way for people who've never heard of you to know something of what you sound like. As you make connections in the area, you can start getting your records played on local radio stations, place your music in local music stores, and eventually the momentum will start moving towards you. Consider that just as knowing a local band can help you get shows in this part of the world, knowing you will help them get shows in your part of the world.

COULDN'T MY BAND OPEN FOR ONE OF THE BIG NATIONALS COMING THROUGH YOUR CLUB?

Basically, no. For purely business reasons, we need bands that draw on those big bills as openers to bring the crowd out early. We have seen many shows where the 10 p.m. band plays to just about nobody and then 400 people show up at 11 p.m.

Copyright (c) 1999, Bottom of the Hill, all rights reserved.
(Bottom of the Hill's ultimate capacity is 325 people.)

1. **Have information that outlines your strengths.**

2. **The main function you want to achieve through booking** is developing a larger audience and an increasingly better show.

3. **You shouldn't be in a big hurry to play to no one.**

4. **Be smart about the shows you take.**

5. **People will come out** on a Monday if there is a compelling reason.

6. **Fully research a buy-on opportunity.** You need to use every tool that you have to evaluate the value of the buy-on. Examine the larger band's reputation online.

7. **Do not be afraid to ask questions.** There is no such thing as a stupid question.

8. **Confirm everything ahead of time.** Advertising, your place on the bill, your guest list, etc. Do not leave any surprises for the night of the show!

9. **Ask yourselves, "Do we need an agent or do we just think we need an agent?"** Don't bullshit yourselves or anyone else!

10. **Look at the roster the agent has.** Does he have bands in a similar genre?

11. **When you get an agent, it is not time to relax –** it is time to stay involved! And really pay attention.

12. **Double check everything.** Your agent doesn't have time.

13. **Remember, agents are not liable for the cost of horrific, lazy routing, you are.**

C·H·A·P·T·E·R ···· 11

MARKETING I - REVENUE STREAMS

"Making money is art, and working is art, and good business is the best art" - Andy Warhol

There are opportunities everywhere if you are touring! And looking! Not only can you sell your CDs and merch, you can sell space on posters and postcards. You can agree to hang someone's posters in the bathrooms of clubs all across the country and help other businesses too.

Opportunity is the big word here (even though it's only in ten point type). You might not think that the fact that you are going out on the road for eight weeks is a big thing but, there are many bands that are not making the effort. Get on it! You are going to be somewhere that somebody else isn't... use that!

There are three kinds of revenue streams:

- The basic selling of a physical item for an amount of money (Traditional).

- The increasingly valuable stream of selling opportunities (Non-Traditional).

- Reducing expenses, affects the bottom line in the same way.

TRADITIONAL

CONCERT/TICKET SALES

Maybe, hopefully, possibly, you might get paid for a performance! The capacity of the venue multiplied by the ticket price gives you the GP or gross potential. In a smaller bar type venue you might just receive a percentage of the door (say 80% of the door cash) if the ticket is $10 and 100 people are in the venue, then that's $1,000 x 80% that's $800 right? Yeah!... Thirty of those people are the regulars that the doorman let in for free, eight of them are your guests and ten are the other bands, that's a gross of $520 x 80% = $416 less your bar tab. Ooops. But the bar sure makes a killing! Use a clicker to accurately count the number of people in the venue. Or take the first ticket that is on the roll at the door, then look at the last one at the end of the night. The difference in the numbers is the total number of people that the doorman randomly decided to charge admission.

As the venues get larger, they will start to charge you for the sound system, insurance, promoter profit etc etc. Your rider will be paid for by, errrrrrr, you!

Another kind of payment is a straight guarantee, it kind of means that, however many people show up, 10 or 300, you'll still get paid as if the 500 people your manager and agent convinced the club would show up, did. Great in theory. In practice, the promoter will cancel the show, or just offer you what amounts to a percentage deal anyway: "Look, there are 50 people here, 30 of them paid $10 to get in, I'll give you $200 less your bar tab... which right now is $320." There is no such thing as a guarantee; the name is misleading and counterproductive. From now on, let's call guarantees Helicopters. There isn't going to be one of those at your show either.

MERCHANDISE: T-SHIRTS, WORKSHIRTS, HOODIES, JACKETS

The soft goods, or, anything that isn't a CD or DVD, you count in at the beginning of the night, you count out at the end. The difference is the number of shirts that you sold, less any that you gave away. Some venues will just allow you to tally your sales as you go and then settle with the house percentage (anywhere from 0% to 35%) at the end.

You also have to factor in that all of your "profit" might be contained within the 180 XXL shirts you still have (and will always have) left in your basement. Or in the 100 girly shirts that always seemed to be two cities behind you.........?

CDS

Create interesting packaging that makes your CDs more desirable. Selling CDs at shows is going to become a main point of purchase of physical product. Your display at shows will fuel activity on your web site. Your label might 'front' CDs to you and expect payment 30 to 60 days later. Pay attention to details like this, you don't want your supply of CDs to be cut off half way through the tour. You might be paying wholesale price for the CDs, which could be $7.90 and up. If you are running your own business and manufacturing your own CDs, then your cost will only be around $1 per CD. A good stock of CDs is also an opportunity to give a few away if an important DJ or journalist shows up. You should always try and have a good stock of special items not easily available and a few live recordings, which you can burn on an as needed basis, so you don't have money tied up in extra stock. Of course, you want new fans to buy the new disc but you want stuff for the old fans, too. Always create new items for your fans.

DVDS

Live shows are a great place to sell live DVDs. Make sure you have a selection. People in Cleveland might be really excited to buy a DVD of the last Cleveland show—they might be in it!

POSTERS

Here's a good idea: make a great poster and you can sell it! We create limited edition screen-printed posters (you can also do these very quickly while you are waiting for your professionally-printed posters). Have the band autograph them and sell them from the merch booth. Keep them and archive them, you'll be pleased you did if your band stays around for a few years. Sell them individually or bundled with a concert CD/DVD.

The first time we did this was for the first *Sheep on Drugs* tour. You can see a brief description of that process and some examples in the chapter on *How to Screen Print*. Here comes the first lesson in momentum, grooviness, and systems checking. We got an unexpected benefit—phone calls from the venues after the first weekend, saying that they had received their posters, put them up, and had them stolen immediately. This wave of activity certainly got everyone's attention. It also dawned on us that three or four venues had not called. So we took the initiative and called them to check. Sure enough, one venue had not put the posters up yet. We were able to inform them that the other venues were calling and reporting that the posters were being stolen immediately. So we warned them to be careful; but most importantly, it enabled us to identify two venues whose packages had been sent to the wrong address.

It is only once you understand the value of each extra day's worth of promotion, that you can appreciate just how important that information was. Sometimes one day lost can cost you a weekend's worth of promotion—so stay on it! After a while, we memorialized some of the posters in a mass-produced version.

Fast forwarding to the *Preaching to the Perverted* tour: I had purchased a bunch of four-color calendar blanks. The graphic gave me the perfect punk rock juxtaposition: a semi-naked slut over iconic religious images. This time, rather than just banging these out and apologizing for the small amount of posters available, I signed and numbered the limited edition silk-screen prints. We sent out roughly a dozen posters to every venue, making a fantastic display with the repetition of the overprint images on top of different backgrounds. This encouraged venues to create a larger display, rather than simply putting up two posters. With the lessons learned from the *Sheep on Drugs* tour, we followed up as quickly as possible with the printed commercial version.

> **"Sometimes one day lost can cost you a weekend's worth of promotion..."**

PROGRAMS

Programs can be pretty cool souvenirs of a concert event. They seem to be more popular in Europe and only confined to sporting events in the U.S. However, for a band that's been around for a while, programs serve both as memorabilia and as a take-home source of information about available albums and merchandise (potentially leading to follow-up sales).

You can promote your web site, sell advertising space in them, get one of the other bands to split the printing costs with you and feature the companies who are sponsoring you..

STICKERS, BUTTONS...

These are just cool things to have around to give to fans. Merch guys like them because they can give them to people instead of change. Most revenue from them doesn't come from their use individually but comes from their use as an add-on "Free Sticker with T-shirt," so overprice them; $2.50 might be too much for a 2" x 5" sticker, but when you give one away free with a t-shirt, it feels like you're getting $2.50 off the price. Don't forget, you can print on the backs of stickers, too, for example: "New album coming soon!"

Always be on the lookout for cool things that could be printed to expand the brand of your band. Jackets? Cool! Just don't print too many. Find a supplier that will turn them around quickly for you. Coffee mugs? Great! But be careful, they break! Don't forget belt buckles, DJ bags, trucker hats, knitted hats, 7" singles, Zippo lighters, pens, combs, whatever.

WEB SITE

The web is the internet equivalent of your merch booth. Treat it as such. Have it be the place where people go for information, updates, free downloads of music. It will not only be a revenue stream in and of itself. It will fuel other revenue streams. See *Using the Web* for more.

NON TRADITIONAL
POSTCARDS

On our first package tour, we had 20,000 cards. We sent them out to street teams and venues all over the country. Trying to get the best price on printing was all we had to do. Check out the web... we use *www.M13graphics.com* You can get five thousand postcards for $199 and ten thousand postcards for $398. You can share a flyer with them if you want, with their ad on the back you get a substantial discount.

On the next tour, I called four or five other businesses to see if they wanted to take the back of the card (or "the other front"). We called *Pleasurable Piercings, SpookyGirls.com,* another band touring at the same time, Emulsion, and a couple other bands on the label. They each agreed to split the cost of five to ten thousand cards. So, in terms of promoting the tour, we'd gone from 20,000 cards to 60,000 cards without increasing the cost. This felt like a triumph, until I was sitting in a restaurant in Detroit and I saw the five postcard fronts meticulously and prominently displayed on the free postcard rack by the door of the restaurant. I realized that I wasn't selling half of a postcard. The value was the placement and peer-to-peer physical distribution of the card. Then, I felt like an idiot.

On the next tour, I presented the opportunity differently, 10,000 to 20,000 postcards distributed across the country to a target market, the price includes printing. By this time, we were breaking even on the printing and distribution of the postcards. We teamed up with Jägermeister, who would supply us with 10,000 to 20,000 postcards. We were printing six different postcards for the tour, and presented different ads on the other side so that people who had seen card one or two would then pick up card three or four and absorb the information again.

We stickered every postcard with the correct information for the show - we didn't want to trust this task to the venues.

Now, we had another problem. First, you have to sticker 10,000 to 40,000 postcards. Second, now you don't just have a great big mountain of postcards anymore, and you have to keep the postcards sorted by city. You also need to make sure that you don't sticker all of the cards. You might need 400 postcards in Chicago and two thousand in Los Angeles. Or, you might have ten amazing reps in New York, but three reps without transportation in Atlanta. This is about allocation of resources.

PROMOTIONAL CDS

The first time we did CDs, it was just to distribute electronic press kits (EPKs). Then, we evolved to mass producing CDs. The first was the *United Tour* and, while we still did postcards, we mass-produced CD sleeves which began to take their place. One tour we did ten thousand, the next tour fifteen thousand.

We put on two tracks from each touring band, along with some promotional materials, and I realized that we had created an opportunity of massive value to another band or label within the genre. Figure it out: To have fifteen thousand copies of one of your songs distributed across the country! Man! If you wanted to do that on your own, it would cost ten times that! For any band, $1,500 is a fantastic deal so, we called a couple of labels and bands and more than subsidized the undertaking.

For the *Free for All* tour, Jägermeister printed the CD jackets for us.

POSTER PLACEMENT

In the same way that you can place other bands' or other labels' music on a promotional CD or postcard, you can place "Mini's" across the bottom of a poster. You could combine a postcard/cd /poster opportunity.

EBAY

eBay is also a strategy and tool deserving of more examination. See the chapter on *Using the Web* for more information!

VEHICLE WRAPPING

A common idea, usually three weeks before a tour starts, when it's too late to do anything, is: "Let's wrap the vehicle!" This is a way that you can subsidize a touring opportunity, but most of the larger companies will want to have some control over the routing. No one wants to have an expensively-wrapped bus that is the centerpiece of an advertising campaign parked behind a stadium in an inaccessible, "Crew/Bands Only" parking lot, invisible to the thousands of fans streaming into the venue. There are more and more companies looking to wrap vehicles and participate in non-traditional ways of advertising. Log on to *www.clockworkbanana.com*. Input your schedule and routing and see if it meshes with any of the opportunities up there.

SPONSORSHIP

Sponsorship is more of a chance to save money than generate money. It is a chance to form constructive relationships that will help with the larger picture. Sponsors may pay some expenses as an incentive for bands to perform in their priority markets. More and more companies are seeking opportunities to market through music so stay aware of opportunities (Also, see the chapter on *Sponsorships*).

TOUR SUPPORT

This is another source of revenue for a touring band. Be careful—this could cost you a lot. Many labels—including mine—do not give cash as tour support (we give merchandise for the bands to sell). Make sure that your budget is accurate. Explain why you need help, petition for it, and make it happen. Understand that all of this needs to be paid back. It might also be the reason that your band is eventually dropped. If you agree to pay for merchandise on a 30 or 45 day billing, do it!

If you ask your label for $10,000, you're going to have to pay all of it back. Why did Kevin Lyman say it's the most expensive loan you'll ever get? Well, first off it seems like free money so you're not going to spend it as carefully as you would if it was money you had earned from shifts down at the gas station or Kinko's. Secondly, if you ask your manager to get you tour support, then he's going to commission 20% of it. If he has to go to New York to talk the label into giving it to you, then he's going to commission it, bill you for a flight, hotel, cabs, dinner, breakfast, coffee, drinks with your publicist, and maybe a second night's hotel. So you might only actually get $6,000 or $7,000 to benefit the tour. But you're going to owe $10,000, comprende?

> "Tour support is the worst loan you can ever get.
> You pay about 900% interest back to your labels."
> – Kevin Lyman

BUY-ONS

If your band starts to gain some notoriety and success, you'll be able to sell opportunities to other bands to help subsidize your touring activities. (See the section on "Buy-Ons" in the *Booking* Chapter).

SELLING OTHER BANDS' MERCH

You can agree to sell other bands' merchandise for a percentage of the gross. The other band gets use of the credit card machine and avoids the cost of bringing an additional merch person. Be careful with accepting credit cards, it is convenient as all hell, but if a charge is challenged by the cardholder, then you only have 21 days to provide the bank with proof that the charge is legitimate. If you don't, then the charge will be refunded to the customer. You need to factor in this cost, along with the lease of the credit card machine, your merchant account, the rolls of paper, etc. into all of this.

LOGISTICS/SERVICES

If you are routing and investigating all of the ways to book the best, closest hotels and travel, you can provide this service to the other bands or labels for a small fee and help them avoid the problems that you have already worked through.

BEGGING

Well, not really begging. Sheep on Drugs obtained a bright blue donations bucket and labeled it, honestly, "Alcohol Fund – Please Give Generously." They received between five and fifteen dollars per night from their amused fans. I'm not recommending this to solve your budgetary problems. But I am holding it up as an idea for a revenue stream and I'm willing to bet you wouldn't have thought of in ten years of banging your head against the wall.

REDUCE YOUR EXPENSES (LESS OUT = MORE IN)

The simple, yet often overlooked concept here is that spending less money is just as good as bringing in more money! If you want to make an extra $50 a day, you can accomplish that by selling 5 more CDs every night, or by reducing expenses by $50 per day. Here are some ways to reduce expenses on the road:

SELL OFF OR RENT OUT ADDITIONAL BUNK SPACE

If you are trying to make a budget work and you have 9 people on the bus, you can either use the three extra bunks to put all of your crap on (these are called JUNK BUNKS) or you can hire a two piece band as an opener and provide transportation to them for a cost that is 2 x 12ths of the cost of the bus. (See *Transportation* Chapter for estimated bus expenses.)

> *The first time we did this we had five members of another band use some of the spare bunk space in one of three busses. I just divided up the cost of the bus and the driver by 12 and then multiplied by the number of bunks we were selling. As I started to pay out for fuel, trailer, driver's hotel, bus wash, trailer rental, etc., I realized that I had given the other label way too good of a deal!*

Run your budgets. Do your homework. Be fair—but be fair to yourself, too. It is a great situation for an opening band not have to eat the dust of a tour bus and drive all night to the next show. It's safer and way cooler to be on the bus. Also, if you are tour managing a package tour, you can make sure that the other band is there!

SHARING EXPENSES

By sharing crew members, you can save money or get better, more professional help. Two bands can share a soundman, but you have to be professional about it and not play any silly high school games. You can share a vehicle, a crew member, or a merchandise person.

You can share advertising expenses with another band or label. Instead of two bands each printing and mailing their own posters, why not reach out and split the costs of printing and mailing? That's massive! But, you have to understand some of the forces that you are dealing with. When I did the posters for the *UNITED* tour, the Pigface logo and the My Life With The Thrill Kill Kult logo were exactly the same size (I measured them, so did the graphic artist). But, I knew that this was the first promotional item anyone from either camp was going to see, so we kept making the MLWTTKK logo larger and larger until it absolutely looked as big and, if anything, larger. I didn't need the headache of someone in the band thinking they were being disrespected. Avoiding small problems like is priceless.

C·H·A·P·T·E·R ···· 12

MERCHANDISING: THE ENGINE

"This isn't about being able to jump up and down on a bed of money and light cigars with $100 bills-this is about having the ability to replace the exploding transmission, to bail somebody out of jail, to replace the stolen instruments, or to pay for the producer of your dreams. If it is all purely about your art, then get a clue and make some money so you can communicate your art the way you want without explanation or apology. 'It would have sounded much better if we could have afforded mastering...' fuck off!"

— Martin Atkins

Merchandising is an essential part of the touring process and promotional campaign. It is the backbone of information for a new band with no track record. It is no longer about trying to sell 10,000 CDs to 10,000 people. It is about selling 10 different CDs to 1,000 people, selling more things to fewer, more-invested people, in a shorter amount of time, before attention is distracted. Frightened? You should be. Everyone has ADD! Everyone is jacked up on (if you're lucky) coffee.

Make sure that you have cool new stuff for people to buy and that your booth is manned. When I see a band that I like, especially if I know they are in a van and struggling, I want to buy the CD and a shirt to show my support. If that stuff isn't there, or the person they have selling it is at the bar or someplace else, then I feel kind of cheated. This has to do with the circle of support. Your job is to make sure that you are creating and selling merchandise to complete the circle. It's not just about the music or the money, it's about memorializing the experience in a tangible way.

A well-stocked merchandise booth with unique, cool, and hard-to-find items will be another powerful reason for people to come to the show...and you need every reason.

It is surprising how many bands have no clue about the unique elements associated with their merchandise. Many bands will present their loyal fans with only one

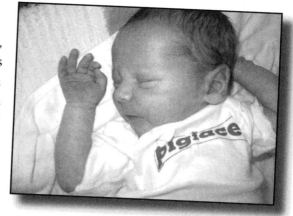

or two items, or return home from their largest, best-attended tour and reward their local fans with whatever is left: their poorest selling shirts in a wide array of sizes, and their best selling shirt in XXXL. It's impossible to predict every aspect of merch sales, but I do know that:

- If you offer five items, from shirts to baby onesies, rather than only offering one or two items, you will sell more.
- If you are attentive to size range, you will sell more.
- If you give people a choice of payment methods: credit cards, etc., you will sell more.
- If you have items in the $5 to $70 range, you will sell more.
- If you give away some items for free, you will sell more.
- If you have good information from your last one or two tours, you will make less of the sizes that don't sell and you will sell more.
- If you have a knowledgeable, polite merch person who is happy to give information, you will sell more.
- If you pay attention to the location and visibility of your booth, you will sell more.

THE BOOTH

Once you realize the importance the merchandise booth has to the momentum of the band, the loyalty of your fan base, and the bottom line, you will begin to pay more attention to its location. I have had more fights with promoters in the last year over this issue than anything else. If the merchandise booth has to be in an out of the way place, make the club owner explain to you why before you agree to that location. He will not be at the gas station when there is no money for food or another oil change, you will. Use that knowledge to drive your discussions.

YOU NEED YOUR MERCH BOOTH TO BE:

- In a traffic stream
- Close to the entrance
- Well lit, but not too bright if it's a very small venue and you're close to the stage

I have seen enthusiastic merch people set up in a place where they get the best view of the band. This cannot enter into determining the best location.

- If your merch is in a corner somewhere, make sure that you or the band stop the show halfway through and let people know all of the cool items you have for sale and where that booth is.
- Make fliers listing the cool, unique, hard-to-find merch you have at the booth and leave them at the bar, at the door, and on the tables. That's something I learned in Japan.

A cute girl in a rubber dress might help drive the traffic to a merch booth, but if she isn't watching the inventory and you end up running out of stock for your big weekend. Then don't

> ## "...this is a filter, an information distribution point and a smart people-person helps."

bother! Have someone knowledgeable about your band work the booth. Just like your favorite record store, this is a filter, an information distribution point and a smart, people-person helps, not just to sell stuff; they are there to help customers choose wisely. I always try to guide people through the labyrinth of Pigface releases so that only the rabid, completist fans are exposed to the more esoteric releases.

Your merch person will be the first person to set up and the last person to tear down. If you are a tour manager or a band leader, make a few stops at the booth throughout the evening. Make sure they have eaten or have water if they need it. They might just need a bathroom break so, relieve them (if you know what I mean). If you are in an opening band, offer to help; this could be the difference of you working with the band again or not. Tour managers: try and keep a loader later to help the merch person.

Do not be embarrassed to sell your merchandise. If you are, please stop reading now and give up. In one way or another, all you will be doing, literally or figuratively, is selling yourself and your music from the moment you put this book down. If that is not for you, fine, then enjoy making music in your bedroom and at smaller venues around your town, or go do something else. You have to have the common sense to drive the bottom line.

PROBLEMS

Things are going great. You are well stocked with a range of merch, then, you experience the synchronized "security sweep." At a show in Milwaukee, five minutes after the show, eight side doors opened and five security guards walked from the right to the left hand side of the room and cleared it in less than five minutes. I did not realize what was going on until two things happened: first, I saw two security guys high-five each other saying, "Three minutes, twenty seconds! It's a record!" And second, Curse Mackey, an entrepreneur and father, came into the room screaming because there was simply no one left to buy anything. It cost him $150 that night and the tour $3,000. A concerned security guard ran out into the parking lot to try and get people back into the building. What a sad waste of time and energy. Frightened people ran into their cars and sped off as fast as they could. After that night, I came up with the following clause in my contract that you are welcome to use:

> "In no event will the venue be cleared prior to thirty (30) minutes after the end of the main band's set finishing completely."

What?! Well, You can't write down the exact time that the main band finishes the show, but you can ask for 30 minutes of sell time after that. This is when you are going to make some money. Make sure you communicate your needs to the staff before doors open, as the owner of the club or security chief might not have done so. You will suffer if he has not.

DISORIENTATION ON THE ROAD: ROAD LAG

I want to call attention to the disorientation people feel when they're on the road. For example, t-shirt supply: after noticing the need for a restock of t-shirts, the band may contact a supplier on a Friday afternoon. This oversight will cause them to be out of stock for a week because the shipment will not go out until Monday and will not arrive until Wednesday. This is not just a problem of having the merch guy pay more attention. Things that seem obvious or routine while sitting in an office can seem difficult, if not impossible, when you're on the road.

At 2 p.m. every Wednesday—not 10 p.m., 2 p.m., because *tour time is different from office time*—we talk to the merch guy and look at how much we've been selling vs. how many shows we've played. If we've been selling ten CDs a night and we only have 80 left, we're going to order a restock after show number four. Instead of looking to point out where someone is failing in their job, we try to work on the positive and see what we can do to make things easier on a weekly, or daily, basis. Remember, sitting in your office, you are maybe 20 feet from a toilet; on the road, you could be 20 miles away from one! Priorities change!

You can prevent the cost of your tour skyrocketing! Out of stock problems can cause crisis after crisis. A huge cost of touring is not taking into account the importance of paying attention to these details.

> The window of opportunity for the tour to communicate with the label office in New York City and the tour in California.

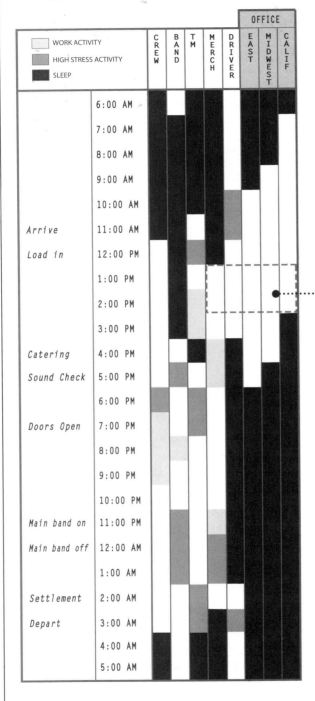

"Tour Time is Different from Office Time"

		CREW	BAND	TM	MERCH	DRIVER	OFFICE EAST	OFFICE MIDWEST	OFFICE CALIF
	6:00 AM								
	7:00 AM								
	8:00 AM								
	9:00 AM								
	10:00 AM								
Arrive	11:00 AM								
Load in	12:00 PM								
	1:00 PM								
	2:00 PM								
	3:00 PM								
Catering	4:00 PM								
Sound Check	5:00 PM								
	6:00 PM								
Doors Open	7:00 PM								
	8:00 PM								
	9:00 PM								
	10:00 PM								
Main band on	11:00 PM								
Main band off	12:00 AM								
	1:00 AM								
Settlement	2:00 AM								
Depart	3:00 AM								
	4:00 AM								
	5:00 AM								

Legend: WORK ACTIVITY / HIGH STRESS ACTIVITY / SLEEP

"You tend to lose complete track of time, which I think is very hard for people back home to understand when they're like, "You haven't called in a month!" And you're like, "Really? didn't notice! Sorry!"
—Nixon Suicide

MERCH % TO VENUES

Many venues will be looking to take 10% to 30% off the top of your shirt or soft goods sales. Sometimes this can be creatively negotiated. If you cannot negotiate around it and a venue takes 30%, make sure that you know your gross merch sales for the night (or at least the amount that you are going to report) and keep that figure in mind during settlement... If the promoter is complaining about the door takings or something you can add in "yes, but everyone here drank like a fish, one of your bartenders told me you had to bring in an extra person, and, you're making $600 off my merch too don't forget"... they haven't, and now they know you haven't either.

"Limit the number of designs that each band can have at the booth..."

PACKAGE TOUR

If you put together a package tour, then you should take responsibility for creating a merchandise store and displays. You want to control the information flow and presentation.

1. CREATE A PACKAGE TOUR NAME

And a range of event merchandise. Have the terms written into your agreement with the other bands. A larger band on the tour might get 10% of the net. A smaller band should be happy to get their name on the shirt and a dozen freebies.

2. SPACE/DESIGN LIMITATIONS

Limit the number of designs that each band can have at the booth. The first band should have just one or two shirts and two CDs.

3. STOCK LEVELS

Have each artist be responsible for re-ordering and coordinating deliveries. For example, a package could arrive at a venue or hotel when no one knows to expect it. A helpful person may put it into the office for other people to deal with on Monday morning. One thing leads to another and it could take five to seven days to reroute a package to a "safe" location. So you will need to have the merchandise company send *another* package of new shirts so that they can have them for the weekend... and then someone will be paying FedEx next day shipping rates... guess who?

4. PAYMENTS/ACCOUNTING

Account merchandise at the end of the first ten days, and every seven days after. Getting a larger tour up and running will kill you financially, and you do not need to be accounting to three other bands in the first five to seven days of the tour. It's going to be tough for all of the other bands, you don't need their stress compounding yours. There are too many other considerations to deal with: tweaking the merch display, finalizing the band line-up, dealing with the promoters, fine-tuning the set times, firing the crazy drunken crew guy and finding a replacement, keeping pressure on the agent to fill in those last two days off in six weeks time... errrr, etc. Therefore, having that extra cushion of three days is invaluable.

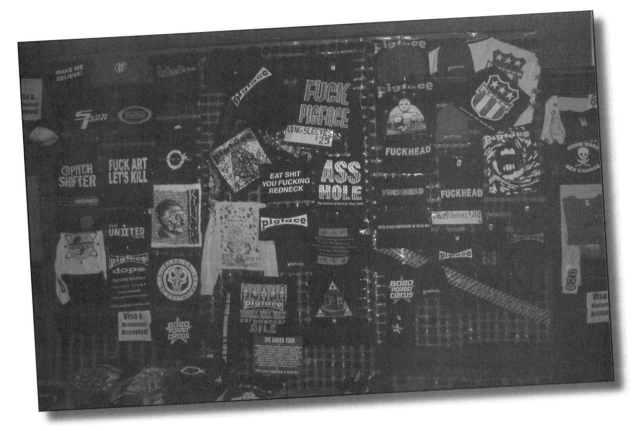

REAL-LIFE MERCHANDISE STRATEGIES
MAKE IT SPECIAL

Create unique items for sale on tour only or have advance EPs of two or three songs from the up-coming album. With *The Damage Manual.* We were very successful selling EPs and albums before the tour started. This concerned me. I wanted to have great sales from the shows too, not only for financial reasons, but also to report to Soundscan and use the numbers as a stick to poke our distributors. I created an etched Zippo lighter which would only be available at the shows. The only way to get it was to buy the EP and the album for $15. This was a great deal even if you already had both releases. People ended up buying the two CDs in order to get the lighter and gave one or both of the CDs to friends. This is exactly what you want to happen with physical product: peer to peer file sharing. The Soundscan numbers were great.

THE *ONLY* WAY TO GET A SUPERFUCKINGCOOL DAMAGE MANUAL ZIPPO LIGHTER IS BY BUYING A DM FULL LENGTH AND EP FOR A MEASLY $15 !!!

On the *Preaching to the Perverted* tour, we had people check a box on the mailing list to let us know if they were interested in buying a panel of the scenery at the end of the tour. For $75 a panel, it was a really nice piece of art and memorabilia. The scenery ended up paying for itself.

BOTTLENECK!

Place a member of the band in front of the merch booth to sign autographs. This has the great result of slowing down the traffic in front of the merch booth, encouraging sales (people want to buy something for the band to sign), and will also temper the security guards' moods (they are less aggressive when the band members are around). This may get you an extra 15 minutes of selling time—that could equal an additional $200/night, $1,400/week, $5,600/month!

SUBLIMATE THE BAND NAME

Once you have a range of merchandise, create more merch that's linked to the band but not obviously (…obviously to a fan, but not obviously to somebody else). Then you have two elements, one, a chance to sell more t-shirts and two, the motivation that drives me: the performance art aspect of having someone who has never heard of or actually dislikes the band wandering around in a t-shirt. Some good examples of this are:

- I ♥ Damage.
- Damaged.
- America Runs on Damage.
- Eat Shit You Fucking Redneck.
- Asshole.
- Got Dub?
- Fuck Art, Let's Kill (Chemlab).
- Suck! (from the Pigface/Trent Reznor song "Suck").
- Drink, Fight, Fuck (The Countdown).
- Pervert.

If you're writing lyrics, there should be six t-shirts on every album. It's a pretty good yardstick in a pop hook-y world. If your songs are full of complicated layers that don't belong on t-shirts, then in a commercial environment, maybe they don't belong on an album. I don't mean to tread on your art; I'm just trying to make sure your art doesn't tread on your business.

> **"I don't mean to tread on your art…"**

> **"…there should be six t-shirts on every album."**

EXPERIMENTS AND EVOLUTION

Be open to experimentation. After a few nights of everyone screaming, "Eat shit, you fucking redneck!" on tour with Pigface we turned it into a song. Then, Curse said to me, "That should be a shirt, dude!" I called the t-shirt printer and a week later, it was. We didn't get into any discussions about font size or art. It was just a simple message on the front of a shirt. It sold

**EAT SHIT
YOU FUCKING
REDNECK**

pretty well every night of the tour. On the *Preaching Tour*, someone had suggested making some Pigface work shirts. We had 50 made to experiment with at the merch booth. Then, at the last minute, I pulled all the shirts from the booth and gave them to the other bands and crews on the tour. It's pretty amazing how unifying a small gesture can be. A couple of years later, we began to produce used work shirts. The shirts did well. Around the office, I saw people reserving shirts either from cool, fucked-up sounding companies or with cool name patches. I pulled aside a shirt in the print shop marked "Betty" for Betty X. I have a bunch that say Martin, but sometimes I like to be Pete or Steve. It seemed like the big part of the attraction of these shirts was people choosing a company or a name patch that resonated with them. So, I suggested that we put up two racks of the shirts instead of just one pinned-up on the display board. This way people could flip through the many different options. This was, of course, a complete pain in the ass for the merch guys, who smartly tried to deflect the additional workload by cautioning me about the possibility of theft. I wasn't having any of it. The shirts did well. People seemed happy with their individual choices. The racks, just like the "5 CDs for $20" bin, magnetized people to the booth, creating a comfort zone where people could browse and listen to the conversations and information without being pressured to buy... like the "just looking" sticker at a car showroom.

ACCIDENTAL DISCOVERIES

You might have more time in the morning as you leave town than in the previous days late afternoon, lost, trying to find the venue. The day of a show in Portland, we stopped in at a record store (where the DJ and the promoter also worked) to do a spoken word appearance and drop off some CDs. It was a great show and I decided to stop by that record store to say hi, bye, and grab some coffee the next morning. It so happened that there were a couple of titles that the DJ/buyer saw at our well lit, well stocked, and well laid out merch booth the night before that were not in his record store. Right then, he placed a $70 order before we headed to our next stop on the tour...plus they had great coffee!

INTANGIBLES

Really it is all intangible (actually that was a great big lie as none of this is intangible. It is as hard as a concrete block to the head). If you work at these ideas and conquer all of the problems associated with a larger booth, you will not only generate much needed revenue, you will have a wider, cooler selection to give to a DJ, a hot girl or guy, friends of the promoter, or someone at the venue who has been marvelously helpful to you all day. Groovyness all around... another circle completed.

CELEBRITY MERCH BOOTH

Jared from Chemlab came out to sell merchandise on the *Damage Manual* UK tour. He had just released the *Covergirl* album, so he made sure it was the first CD on after the doors opened. We allowed him to have it and some other stuff at the booth, and we had the bonus of him sending out e-mails to everyone that he was going to be there.

Check out "Merch" in the "Cyanotic" section of *Case Studies* chapter.

> "The racks, just like the "5 CDs for 20" bin, magnetize people to the booth, creating a comfort zone where people can flip through, browse, and listen to the conversations and information without being pressured to buy."

THE ULTIMATE STRATEGY

The evolution of every strategy was embodied in the *Free For All* Tour, now the subject of an independent documentary. There was a general atmosphere around the office that concerts like Skinny Puppy, Nine Inch Nails, Ministry, etc., were too expensive to afford. I wanted to do something that made sense for us and rewarded our fans. In addition to keeping ticket prices low, we gave two coupons to everyone who bought a ticket. One coupon was for $5 off any CD from the merch booth. The second coupon was for the balance of the ticket price off a t-shirt. If the ticket price was $15, then everyone was given a $10 coupon off any t-shirt and $5 off a CD. For a $20 ticket, fans received a $15 coupon off of a t-shirt and $5 off a CD. This was a great reward for our biggest fans—the ones who always plan on buying a shirt and a CD. Either it meant that they could put some money in their pocket, buy more beer, actually afford parking, or buy another CD and another shirt. For the fans on the fringes, it was an incentive to try something at less of a financial risk. Either way, it was a great deal. I spent days, nights, and weeks checking figures and looking at scenarios to avoid recreating the infamous Hoover Promotion in the U.K. (it bankrupted the European firm).

I liked the *Free For All* brand... it was clever. In retrospect, we would have gained more by simply calling it FREE... I don't think anyone really thought the shows were going to be free and the more complicated name confused some.

MERCH TIPS
LUKE STOKES AND CHRIS RAMOS

MA: *I called up Luke Stokes and Chris Ramos to ask them to put some of their years of experience down for me. They're both featured in the Free For All Documentary. Luke has been on the road with Dope, Pigface and countless others as merchandiser and tour manager. Chris Ramos has worked at the Invisible offices and has been out on many tours.*

HAVE MORE THAN ONE SHIRT

You should have at least two t-shirt designs, plus hoodies, girl shirts, bags, etc. Make sure you have a range of sizes (at least M-2XL). Remember, America is big!

DON'T STOP BRINGING OUT A SHIRT THAT SELLS

Just because people have seen the shirt doesn't mean it won't sell. If it has been a decent seller, bring it out. People get bigger, smaller; they lose things, ruin things. You might have the same guy buy the same shirt three times. You can stop bringing the mesh half shirt that has yet to sell.

Keep track of what you sell and what sizes. We have used Excel and QuickBooks for this in the past. Get the attendance figure from the tour manager so you can estimate what to print on future tours.

MAKE THE BOOTH A REASON TO GO TO THE SHOW

Cool shirts, free samplers, and stickers are all extra incentives. Make sure people know you're going to have a cool booth to add one more reason why they should not miss your show.

HIRE A MERCH PERSON

Paying 10% of your merch sales to keep from losing 20% to 30% in missed sales and theft is a good idea.

> **Jolly Roger**
>
> **MA: What about being ripped off by a venue? Once a month, once a year, never?**
>
> **JR:** You gotta be on top of all that stuff. As you get bigger, you have to have somebody count the door. As you get bigger, you have to have somebody you really trust on merchandise because a merch guy can not only rip the venue; they can rip you every night. Guys can put away three, four hundred bucks a night and you won't even know.

DON'T PUT AN ASSHOLE IN YOUR MERCH BOOTH

The merch booth is the information booth. The merch person is always the easiest to find so they need to be able to handle themselves in a professional manner when talking to club owners, street teams, promoters, or for that matter anyone. They should keep the booth open from doors until there are no fans left.

BE CREDIT CARD ENABLED

The guy buying Jäger Bombs for everyone in the band with his MasterCard will buy shirts and CDs if you let him. The best way to do that is to give him the option of plastic. It may cost close to $1,000 to set this up, but most bands make the money back in credit card sales shortly after if they are touring.

THINGS TO HAVE AT THE MERCH BOOTH:

1. **Mailing List** – Name, city, state, zip, e-mail.

2. **Lots of Pens** – People have a tendency to take your pens.

3. **Sharpies.**

4. **Packing Tape** – Tape it down or it will get stolen

5. **Staple Gun always helps** (don't forget extra staples).

6. **Envelopes** (9 1/2 x 11) to keep track of mailing lists, etc.

7. **Scissors.**

8. **Paper.**

9. **Receipt Paper** – if you have a credit card machine.

10. **Table** – Folding tables take up less room in the van or trailer. Go to Home Depot.

11. **Painter's Clip Light** – Bring a backup and some extra bulbs. I like to use 75 to 100 watt light bulbs to light up the merch board. Most clubs hate when you use bright lights to sell merch, but they are not paying for gas with merch money; you are.

12. **Extension Cords** – One or two 20-foot cords and a power strip or two. The club's power situation may be shoddy at best.

SIGNS WILL HELP

Put prices, sizes, and other pertinent information on your merch board. Make sure it is big enough and legible enough to read from 25 feet. If you have a credit card machine, make sure to have extra signs that say you take credit cards. Avoid overkill on the description of the merch. Price, size, front, and back are helpful and will enable fans to complete a transaction quickly.

More Transactions = More Cash.

COMP THE CLUB

Don't be afraid to give shirts and CDs to the club you're playing. A cool shirt goes a long way when you're trying to negotiate your guarantee, your rider, or (God forbid) another show there.

NEVER STOP SELLING

OK, you finished the tour and you have merch left. Just because your tour is over doesn't mean you can't still sell. Sell merch through your web site or outsource it to another company. They may take a percentage, but let's face it: most venues are going to take a percent of your merch as well. I highly recommend using your web store to sell old merch as well as the new designs. It's a good way to test new designs and move "vintage" ones. Imagine if your favorite bands had a place where you could purchase their old tour shirts from over the years. You know you want that Black Sabbath tour t-shirt from '78.

MERCHANDISING: CREDIT CARD TIPS

In this day and age, a credit card machine is a no-brainer. You'll increase your merchandise revenues by 15-25%. If I knew anything about video games, this would be one of those moves that gives you the extra boost that enables you to do more ninja kicks into the old lady's face so you can steal her drugs. That's how good a credit card machine is. You can lease the machine, but be careful. There are some scams out there, I think I might have paid $8,000 for a credit card machine we leased in 1996 and forgot about.

You can still get the ancient ones with the paper and the carbon copies, but I just have visions of the air ripping through a touring vehicle and everyone's credit card information blowing away in the wind for anyone to grab a hold of. The satellite version gets you instant approval unless the club is two flights of stairs down in a basement and then your merch guy will have to run outside and stand in the middle of the street once in awhile.

Here's a mistake to avoid: anyone can dispute a charge on their credit card statement. If they do so, you will be sent a notification and you will have 21 days to dispute their dispute. We created a touring company that my kids named "Captain Eyeball Pants, Ltd." So, large amounts of people had no idea that they bought anything from Captain Eyeball Pants, Ltd.

How could they? We didn't tell them! I came home to 50 or 60 of these disputed charge notifications just in time to do nothing about it."

It's pretty simple to set up an account with your bank allowing you to accept credit cards. Funds will be deposited each day. Companies charge you a small percentage of the sale, usually between 2% and 3%. They'll also charge you a monthly minimum of around $30. If they have $20 in their commissions, they'll just be taking another $10 off of you. But bear in mind, when you are off the road, you'll have your lease payment on your machine and your monthly minimum commission. There can also be a transaction fee of $0.30 per transaction.

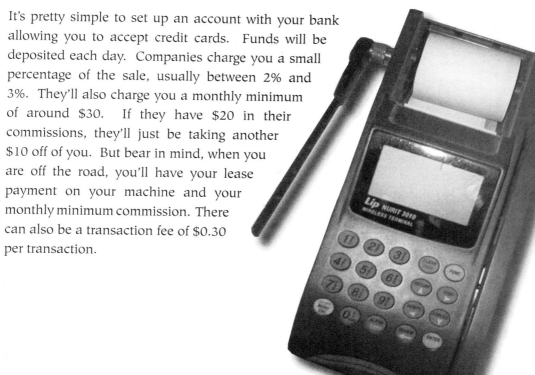

"You've gotta be business savvy really, or else you get the piss taken out of you."
  - Melanie B, Spice Girls

THE HOT TOPIC PHENOMENA
MICHELLE YOON

MA: So Michelle, you mentioned something in class that we pinned a label on: "The Hot Topic Phenomena." What is that?

MY: Even though the shows that occur in markets without Hot Topics stores are smaller in comparison to major and secondary markets, there is the potential for higher merchandise sales. People are willing to travel for hours to catch a glimpse of their favorite artist and will always leave with a souvenir from the show as a reminder of the night. However, in major markets such as Los Angeles, you come across the jaded music consumer who is inundated by numerous choices. On a daily basis, they have a multitude of events occurring within their city. Fans in smaller markets do not have the same luxury. The gross sales per head in these smaller markets are astonishingly similar to major markets.

They understand that the artist may not be back for a few years.

MA: What percentage of merchandise do you think is sold after the main band finishes? I know it's a rush, but any idea on a figure?

MY: From what I have experienced, most kids will buy their merch right after the band they are there to see plays. For instance, on a tour where the band I'm working for is opening or playing the slot before the headliners, most of the merch I sell will happen right after the band performs, with very little happening after the main band performs. .

When I have worked for headlining acts, I have noticed that it's continuous throughout the show. However, about 60% to 75% (a rough estimation) of sales will happen at the end of the evening, beginning a few songs before the end of the set.

The image on the left is a lanyard ID badge reading:

MICHELLE YOON

TOURING MERCHANDISE MANAGER

MERCHANDISING

AME

I was merchgirl for the band Aqualung. I came onto the tour with just three weeks to go. When I met the band manager who was heading back to London the next morning, he explained all the different merchandise they had and how he wanted me to keep everything stocked and all those type details. As we were talking, someone brought him a box. He was so very excited to show me what was in this box, telling me that he just knew we were going to sell cases and cases of them. They had just gotten this idea a few weeks ago and decided to go with it and he was so fucking positive this was going to make some serious money. Well, he opened the box and what he had ordered was pretty cool: this lovely little English pop band had made mugs, yes, ceramic mugs. Unfortunately, out of that first case (he had ordered three cases with 36 mugs in each case), I think there were about 16 mugs that were not broken. That was pretty much how every case was so, of course, his logic was to up the price of the mugs to make up for the broken ones. No one is going to pay ten fucking bucks for a mug at a concert... well, a few people did. But I would say in the three weeks I was there, we sold about 20 of the mugs at $10 and the rest were either broken or just given away. So while I have no idea how much they spent on these mugs, I can almost promise that it was more than the $200 we got from sales. The idea was good. People liked it. The most common response I got was, "Can I just go home and buy it online?" People did not want to carry a mug with them at a show!

T-SHIRTS!

Same band, same time... different merch issue...

This time it was the T-shirts...

When I arrived the first night with just three weeks left to go, we had a pretty even amount of girly T's and a good variety of sizes. I had a great first night at the merch booth. By the third night, I was running out of girly T's. Now let me just explain this band a little bit. They are an English pop band with the front man being very cute, very adorable, and therefore making most of the audience teenage girls. And yes, we sold out of girly shirts right away. When I let their manager know that we needed to get more girly shirts, he said, "OK, no problem. They will be at the next venue." So I was pretty happy with that, being a merch girl, and told that the more I sold, the bigger my bonus at the end of the tour would be. I told him at least 36 more girly T's!!!

The next day, there was no box, no shirts, no nothing. The manager called and told me that they would be at the next venue. We had a day off in between and the next venue was a Christian college, with about 1,000 seats, sold out (because they had sold tickets at $7 a piece and, again, it was teenage girls). When I got to the venue, the box was there and in it were 36 of the same boy shirts that I already had an overabundance of and they were L, XL and yes, even XXL! So here I am at a college show filled with about 800 girls and no girly shirts! The opening bands had plenty of girly shirts. (I was doing merch for all three bands). So, yes I sold more of the opening band shirts than the main band. Then, when I tried to explain why sales were so low, the manager just did not see why little girls would not want a L, XL, or XXL shirt. I asked him to send me some girly shirts. He said, "No, you need to move what we have..."

We had a little over two weeks of the tour left and at least 40 shirts of all the big sizes and zero girly T's! I tried to sell those shirts. The tour manager and I decided to discount them a little, offer promotions: "Buy a CD, get a shirt for ten bucks!"...whatever we could do to move these shirts. But the main problem was that they were not really right for their audience. They were more of a boyish design, large sizes, and girls were just not interested. On a side note, I also ran out of CDs numerous times on this tour—to the point that we had to go buy some from record stores just so we had some to sell. Luckily, they gave them to us wholesale, but still quite a pain to spend the day trying to track down CDs that we should have had plenty of.

At the end of the tour, I was talking to the main guy of the band and explaining all of the merch issues. I suggested a new idea for a t-shirt, told him to make it girly and put some shiny writing on it with a good phrase from one of his most popular songs. On the next tour, he used my idea and told me that they were selling out of them almost nightly... but they were still stuck with a ton of the large-sized and (to be honest) ugly t-shirts that they had while I was with them. So the point of the story is: if you are a band, managing a band, or whatever, be sure that your shirts match your market. They do not need to be fancy or way cool or expensive. Just think of your audience and what they would like and always be sure you have plenty of stock! Track your sales so you know what sells, and know your market and the area you are in. Do a little research and it will pay off!

A valuable lesson learned for all involved... except maybe the band manager that just could not see why no one bought the ugly large shirts... which on another note, I think were his idea... ha!

BODIES! FROM COVENTRY TO CAIN'S
SIMON MATTOCK

I got asked "What it's was it like working merchandise on a Pigface tour?" I answer:

Intense, chaotic, exciting, exhausting, exhilarating, and challenging all at once. I saw everything from where Sid Vicious punched his way through a wall at Cain's Ballroom in Tulsa, invitations to go to a party by a punter at 3 a.m. (using her bare breasts to sweeten the invite), surviving on only three hours of sleep per night, dealing with Detroit at -20 degrees Celsius, offered a chemistry set of illegal substances, seeing rocks stars peeing in the headlights of the tour bus, punters trying to drive to an all-night club after copious amounts of liquor then crashing into a wall on the side of someone's house (only making a total distance of about 15 meters from the venue we had just left), hearing about various sexual swapping activities and mind-bending fantasies, being bombarded with faxes, phone calls and memos. On top of this I saw a 9mm Magnum and piercings where piercings shouldn't

> **"I saw a 9mm Magnum and piercings where piercings shouldn't be."**

be. I saw crazed kids, mad dogs, and the backs of heads, fists and feet. I saw money being shoved, pushed, and slipped into jackets, bags, and hands. And finally and best of all I saw one of the goddamn best live shows on the planet: Pigface.

Not bad for a nine-day trip! And I lived (after 14 hours sleep the day after the tour). These things can change your life forever!

HEEBEEGEEBEEZ INPUT:

I think the shortsightedness in knowing/forecasting their target audience can be the main problem with a group's inability to fully benefit from their merch potential. There are other factors as well that can't always be completely expected but should be planned for. Many avenues could and should be pursued to make a tour not only more profitable, but more successful.

JONATHAN PUST

HEEBEEGEEBEEZ
OWNER

CURIOSA FESTIVAL
VENDOR COORDINATOR

C·H·A·P·T·E·R 13

BUDGETS: DO IT ON PAPER

"There is a dance between art and business.
You need to learn to cha-cha."
   - Martin Atkins

Traditionally, artists shun businessmen. But, the cool, artsy guy needs some of the skill sets that the businessman has, and the businessman could certainly learn fluidity, creative thinking, and computer marketing skills from the artist. The smart ones seek each other out. In the early days of punk rock, we were all throwing stones at the buildings that housed the major labels. It was fun, but not really dangerous in a meaningful way. Pretty soon I was inside those buildings learning, absorbing, and using their phone lines. Ultimately, that's way more subversive and constructive to your goals.

Sometimes an artist will say to me, "I'm not interested in the business. It's my art and my music that is important." But, if someone isn't watching out for the business, there won't be any art or music. Yes, you can express yourself and jot down ideas and sketches visually or musically. But the more ambitious and original the idea, the more important it is delivered clearly and not confused by technical issues, poor presentation, and flat-out mistakes. If you can't afford another four hour session in the studio, or that extra piece of equipment, you might have to go with a flawed performance that compromises your artistic vision. The same applies to touring and the presentation of a show.

The budget for the tour is not supposed to prove that anything is a great idea. It is designed to

> "The more ambitious and original the idea, the more important it is delivered clearly and not confused by technical issues, poor presentation, and flat-out mistakes."

let you know where the problem areas will be. There are many variables on a tour. It's important to get some of the concrete items in your budget as early as possible. Look at your method of transportation (see the Transportation Chapter to get an accurate estimate of cost). Determine how long the tour is going to be and multiply out the figures. To do this, I use Excel. I set up columns for Item (Column B), Total Cost (Column C), Daily Cost (Column D), and Weekly Cost (Column E). If you haven't used Excel before, you may want to jump ahead and read the chapter on Excel basics before proceeding... I'll wait for ya.

Don't start fantasizing about hotel rooms or paying yourself.

The first thing I want you to do is chart your tour with a row for each day – not a row for each show. This will train you to see your days off (your worst enemy). See the PIG Tour in the "Case Studies" chapter.

MILEAGE (SHEET 1)

The purpose of this part of the budget is for you to figure out how far you are going to go and how much it's going to cost you. Work out the mileages from city to city using your *Rand McNally Dist-O-Map*. If you are hoping to travel by bus, mark the number of overdrives you expect so that they can be added into the budget. Now you can see your routing with mileage, including days off. To quickly total up the miles in Column E (Mileage), you enter a formula into Cell E42. Put your cursor there and then type "=" (this tells Excel that you are about to enter a formula). Then, type SUM(E2:E41). Farther than you thought, huh?

BUDGET – EXPENSES (SHEET 2)

Budgets can be tricky, but I have found that this is an effective way to organize them. Some of the items on a budget have a Daily Cost, others have a Weekly Cost.

> "Don't start fantasizing about hotel rooms or paying yourself."

	A Date	B Day	C City	D State	E Mileage	F overdrive
2	14-Apr-09	Wed	Palatine	IL		
3	15-Apr-09	Thur	Palatine	IL	0	
4	16-Apr-09	Fri	Cleveland	OH	344	
5	17-Apr-09	Sat	Detroit	MI	175	
6	18-Apr-09	Sun	Pittsburgh	PA	288	
7	19-Apr-09	Mon	Rochester	NY	287	
8	20-Apr-09	Tues	Hartford	CT	356	
9	21-Apr-09	Wed	Richmond	VA	443	
10	22-Apr-09	Thur	Washington	DC	105	
11	23-Apr-09	Fri	Atlanta	GA	657	1
12	24-Apr-09	Sat	Tampa	FL	480	
13	25-Apr-09	Sun	Gainesville	FL	260	
14	26-Apr-09	Mon	Talahassee	FL	490	1
15	27-Apr-09	Tues	New Orleans	LA	405	
16	28-Apr-09	Wed	Houston	TX	365	
17	29-Apr-09	Thur	Austin	TX	162	
18	30-Apr-09	Fri	Oklahoma City	OK	394	
19	1-May-09	Sat	Denver	CO	619	1
20	2-May-09	Sun	Salt Lake City	UT	512	1
21	3-May-09	Mon	DRIVE DAY			
22	4-May-09	Tues	Seattle	WA	883	1
23	5-May-09	Wed	Portland	OR	178	
24	6-May-09	Thurs	San Francisco	CA	639	1
25	7-May-09	Fri	San Jose	CA	90	
26	8-May-09	Sat	San Diego	CA	524	1
27	9-May-09	Sun	W. Hollywood	CA	121	
28	10-May-09	Mon	Phoenix	AZ	398	
29	11-May-09	Tues	Albuquerque	NM	457	
30	12-May-09	Wed	San Antonio	TX	727	
31	13-May-09	Thur	Dallas	TX	272	
32	14-May-09	Fri	Tulsa	OK	258	
33	15-May-09	Sat	Springfield	MO	182	
34	16-May-09	Sun	Covington	KY	566	1
35	17-May-09	Mon	Winston-Salem	NC	493	1
36	18-May-09	Tues	New York	NY	567	1
37	19-May-09	Wed	Boston	MA	213	
38	20-May-09	Thurs	Ithaca	NY	331	
39	21-May-09	Fri	Buffalo	NY	457	1
40	22-May-09	Sat	Columbus	OH	338	
41	23-May-09	Sun	Chicago	IL	313	
42	Totals				14,049	11

For example, a soundman at $100 per day vs. a van rental at $750 per week. Other items, like posters, are presented with a Total Cost. However, if you have any one of these three items, you can drive the other two using the form we will set up with the budget.

Every single band or touring entity is different in terms of its physical needs, equipment, artistic needs, support crew, lighting, scenery, mental space issues, or any kind of general quirkiness. However, if there are four people in your band touring in a rented van with a soundman, your budget categories could look something like this:

	A	B	C	D	E
1	Example Budget - Band in Van				
2		gas per gallon			
3		vehicle mpg			
4		# gigs			
5		# days			
6		total miles from routing sheet			
7		Total Mileage plus 15%			
8					
9					
10			total	per day	per week
11		EXPENSES			
12		Transportation			
13		Van Rental			
14		Gas			
15		Oil			
16		Trailer			
17		taxis			
18		Other Travel (Flights, etc)			
19		Misc Travel			
20		Hotel			
21		Wages			
22		Per Diems			
23		Crew - Soudman			
24		Crew - Roadie			
25		Crew - TM			
26		band wages			
27		Promotions			
28		Phone			
29		Posters			
30		Postage			
31		Internet			
32		Musical Supply			
33		Rehearsal space			
34		equipt rental			
35		Musical Supply (strings, heads etc)			
36		Misc			
37		Add'l Food/Supplies			
38		Agency Commission			
39		Management?			
40		Contingency			
41		TOTAL EXPENSES			
42					
43		REVENUE			
44		Gtees			
45		Shirts			
46		cds			

Now, you can start to fill in your budget for gas cost. This is easy in Excel. You can link the Total Mileage Cell which we just created (Cell E42) on your Mileage Sheet to the Gas Cost in your Budget Sheet. Put your cursor in Cell C6 of your Budget Sheet and type "=." Then, switch to the Mileage Sheet and click on Cell E42. The number in that cell will automatically appear in your Budget Sheet. Now, if the mileage changes, the total on your Budget Sheet will change, too. In Cell C7 on your Budget Sheet, type "=C6*1.15." This adds 15% to your mileage because you are going to drive back and forth from the hotel, to a store, get lost, etc.

Now, we need to enter the cost of gas (Cell C2) and the mpg the vehicle gets (Cell C3).

	A	B	C
1	Example Budget - Band in Van		$2.90
2		gas per gallon	19
3		vehicle mpg	
4		# gigs	40
5		# days	14,349.00
6		total miles from routing sheet	16,501.35
7		Total Mileage plus 15%	

Now, you can enter a formula in the Gas Cell C14 under Expenses. Put the cursor in that cell and type "=C7/C3*C2". The result is the total mileage divided by the mpg your vehicle gets and multiplied by the cost of gas per gallon.

	A	B	C
1	Example Budget - Band in Van		$2.90
2		gas per gallon	19
3		vehicle mpg	
4		# gigs	40
5		# days	14,349.00
6		total miles from routing sheet	16,501.35
7		Total Mileage plus 15%	
8			
9			
10			total
11		EXPENSES	
12		Transportation	
13		Van Rental	
14		Gas	2,518.63

As mileages and gas prices change, you just have to type in the new numbers. All of the cells relate to each other. You can look at what happens if you change to a vehicle that gets nine mpg, like a tour bus. All you have to do is type "9" in Cell C2. The formulas do the rest.

Start to add in some of the other elements of the budget. Maybe you are paying your soundman $100 a show, the van is $750 a week, etc. Add in the van rental to Cell E13. Then, enter a formula in D13 "=E13/7". This gives you the Daily Cost of your van. Now, add in the total number of days on the road in Cell C5 (not the number of gigs, the number of days).

Enter this formula into cell C13: "=D13*C5". This result will give you the Daily Cost of the vehicle multiplied by the number of days you're going to have it. Sometimes I'll add in a couple of days if there's a bunch of driving around before and after the tour just to be safe, but I haven't done that on this example.

	A	B	C
1	Example Budget - Band in Van		$2.90
2		gas per gallon	9
3		vehicle mpg	
4		# gigs	40
5		# days	14,349.00
6		total miles from routing sheet	16,501.35
7		Total Mileage plus 15%	
8			
9			
10			total
11		EXPENSES	
12		Transportation	$ 4,285.71
13		Van Rental	$ 5,317.10
14		Gas	

	A	B	C	D	E
1	Example Budget - Band in Van		$2.90		
2		gas per gallon	19		
3		vehicle mpg			
4		# gigs	40		
5		# days	14,349.00		
6		total miles from routing sheet	16,501.35		
7		Total Mileage plus 15%			
8					
9					
10			total	per day	per week
11		EXPENSES			
12		Transportation	$ 4,285.71	$107.14	$ 750.00
13		Van Rental	$ 2,518.63	$62.97	$ 440.76
14		Gas			

Start to fill in some of the other blanks. With the trailer at $35 a day, enter "=D16*7" to get the Weekly Rate. Enter a formula into Cell C16, multiplying your Daily Cost by the number of days on the road (=D16*C5). This gives you the Total Cost of the trailer for the tour. Add in the soundman. You've agreed to give him $100/day. Add in taxis at $20/day and per diems for the band (four band members plus four crew members at $15/day each). You know the posters cost $350. Let's budget in $60 for an oil and filter change every 3,000 miles. I wouldn't normally do this on a budget. However, since we're

◇	A	B	C	D	E
1		Example Budget - Band in Van			
2		gas per gallon	$2.90		
3		vehicle mpg	19		
4		# gigs	40		
5		# days			
6		total miles from routing sheet	14,349.00		
7		Total Mileage plus 15%	16,501.35		
8					
9					
10					
11		EXPENSES	total	per day	per week
12		Transportation			
13		Van Rental	$ 4,285.71	$107.14	$ 750.00
14		Gas	$ 2,518.63	$62.97	$ 440.76
15		Oil	$ 330.03	$8.25	$ 57.75
16		Trailer	$ 1,400.00	$35.00	$ 245.00
17		taxis	$ 800.00	$20.00	$ 140.00
18		Other Travel (Flights, etc)			
19		Misc Travel			
20		Hotel			
21		Wages			
22		Per Diems	$ 4,800.00	$120.00	$ 840.00
23		Crew - Soudman	$ 4,000.00	$100.00	$ 700.00
24		Crew - Roadie			
25		Crew - Merch			
26		Crew - TM			
27		band wages			
28		Promotions			
29		Phone			
30		Posters	$ 350.00	$8.75	$ 61.25

practicing, let's enter a formula of the Total Miles plus 15%, divided by 3,000, and multiplied by the cost of the oil/filter change "=C7/3,000*60" in Cell C15.

Now, you can figure all of the corresponding formulas for Total Cost by day and week. Multiply a Daily Cost by seven to get a Weekly Cost. Multiply a Daily Cost by the number of days on the road to get the Total. Divide the Total Cost (like posters) by the total number of days to see how it affects the tour.

FORMATTING YOUR BUDGET

When you enter a formula to get your Average Daily Cost of gas, you're going to get a number with nine figures after the decimal point. You need to format the column. Click on the letter "E" at the top of Column E. Choose "Format" from the Main Menu. Your options will be Cells, Rows, Columns, Sheet, Autoformat, Conditional Formatting, and Style. You want "Cells." A window will open called "Format Cells." Click on the tab that says "Number." Under Category, choose Currency. Hit OK. You can do the same thing for Column D. However, be careful with Column C—only format from Cell C11 down. You have mpg figures that are not dollar-related. On some versions of the program, you can highlight the cells and click on a dollar sign on the toolbar.

Now you're starting to see some real world shit like $4,800 in per diems, $800 in taxis, and close to $1,500 for a trailer rental. Keep adding in the rest of your numbers.

Add in $450 to Other Travel (Flights, etc.) because your soundman is flying from somewhere or the guitarist can only do the tour if you can fly him to San Francisco at the end of the tour, or whatever. Put hotels in at three rooms per night at $85/room. Your roadie and merch person each get $50/day. The tour manager gets $125/day. The band wages—forget it. Add $300 for

TOUR:SMART TIP
for more information go to:
www.tstouring.com

phone. Add $1,200 for postage to venues, street teams, record stores, etc. Add $60/month for internet ($2/day). Add one week of rehearsal space at $100. Add equipment rental: you rent a guitar rig for $150/week because you don't want to shell out $800 to buy one and it seems like a good compromise to get the tour out. Musical supplies can vary widely from tour to tour. I try and change my drum heads once or twice per tour. A crazy, physical guitarist might need to change the strings on all five of his guitars twice per show. But for now, let's just put that in at $50/show as an average cost of replacing things as they break.

Because we're trying to make the budget work by playing everyday, you can use the number of days as a multiplier for that daily figure. If you're in a band that only performs five times per week, you can either multiply by the number of shows or still use the number of days as an added cushion or contingency.

Additional food and supplies is zero because we're playing everyday and we expect to get fed and watered like any good work-horse. Plus, we've allowed a $15 a day per diem.

	A	B	C	D	E
1	**Example Budget - Band in Van**		$2.90		
2	gas per gallon		19		
3	vehicle mpg				
4	# gigs		40		
5	# days				
6	total miles from routing sheet		14,349.00		
7	Total Mileage plus 15%		16,501.35		
8					
9					
10			total	per day	per week
11	**EXPENSES**				
12	**Transportation**		$ 4,285.71	$107.14	$ 750.00
13	Van Rental		$ 2,518.63	$62.97	$ 440.76
14	Gas		$ 330.03	$8.25	$ 57.75
15	Oil		$ 1,400.00	$35.00	$ 245.00
16	Trailer		$ 800.00	$20.00	$ 140.00
17	taxis		$ 450.00	$11.25	$ 78.75
18	Other Travel (Flights, etc)				
19	Misc Travel		10,200.00	$ 255.00	$ 1,785.00
20	Hotel				
21	**Wages**		$ 4,800.00	$120.00	$ 840.00
22	Per Diems		$ 4,000.00	$100.00	$ 700.00
23	Crew - Soudman		$ 2,000.00	$50.00	$ 350.00
24	Crew - Roadie		$ 2,000.00	$50.00	$ 350.00
25	Crew - Merch		$ 5,000.00	$125.00	$ 875.00
26	Crew - TM				
27	band wages				
28	**Promotions**		$ 300.00	$7.50	$ 52.50
29	Phone		$ 350.00	$8.75	$ 61.25
30	Posters		$ 1,200.00	$30.00	$ 210.00
31	Postage		$ 80.00	$2.00	$ 14.00
32	Internet				
33	**Musical Supply**		$ 100.00	$2.50	$ 17.50
34	Rehearsal space		$ 857.14	$21.43	$ 150.00
35	equipt rental		$ 2,000.00	$50.00	$ 350.00
36	Musical Supply (strings, heads etc)				
37	**Misc**		$ -		
38	Add'l Food/Supplies				

Now, let's assume that the agent is receiving 15% commission and you're averaging $750/night as a guarantee. By that, I mean a $1,200 Saturday night, a $200 Monday, etc. You can add in the fees onto your mileage sheet as they come in. We're just going to add in an average total at the bottom of the mileage sheet.

Now, you can enter a formula in the cell for Total Agency Commission. Put your cursor in Cell C38 of your Budget Sheet and type in "=". Then,

42	Totals			14,049	11		
43	Avg Gtee					$	750.00
44	Total Gtees					$	29,250.00

go to your Mileage Sheet and click on the cell that has the Total Gross from the tour (G44) and type in "*.15".

You can see your agent is getting over $4,000. Now, let's add in totals for Day, Week, and Total. In Cell C42, type "=SUM(C41:C11)". BAM! The spreadsheet is swearing at you. You get ########. This means there isn't enough room to display the number. You simply have to go to the top of the sheet, click on the line furthest to the right of the letter in the column until you get a double arrow cursor, and can expand the column width. You need to know how to do this anyway for really long names on your Guest List.

39	Agency Commission	$ 4,387.50	$109.69	$ 767.81
40	Management?			
41	Contingency			
42	TOTAL EXPENSES	$ 47,059.01	$1,176.48	$ 8,235.33

For now, we're leaving Management blank, but if you have management and they take a percentage of your gross guarantees, you use the same method. Contingency is just another safe guard. You can add in an extra 10% of expenses or just leave with a zero balance credit card.

Here comes the fun part. Add in your Revenue from the Mileage Sheet. Put your cursor in Cell C45 and type "=". Now go to your Mileage Sheet, click on Cell G44, and hit enter. In Cell C49 (Total Revenue),

42	TOTAL EXPENSES	$ 47,059.01	$1,176.48	$ 8,235.33
43				
44	REVENUE			
45	Gtees	$ 29,250.00		
46	Shirts			
47	cds			
48	misc			
49	TOTAL REVENUES	$ 29,250.00		
50				
51	TOTAL	$ (17,809.01)		

type "=SUM(C45:C48)" to get your Total Revenue. In Cell C51 (TOTAL), type "=C49-C42" to get the profit or loss for the tour. So right now, you're $17,000 in the hole.

Before you start fantasizing that your merch will cover it, let's solve some problems first.

Drop your per diems to $10/day. Cut your hotel budget to a total of $4,000. Ask the soundman and the tour manager to take $10/day less. Ask the agent to take a 10% commission.

	A	B	C	D	E
10			total	per day	per week
11		**EXPENSES**			
12		**Transportation**	$ 4,285.71	$107.14	$ 750.00
13		Van Rental	$ 2,518.63	$62.97	$ 440.76
14		Gas	$ 330.03	$8.25	$ 57.75
15		Oil	$ 1,400.00	$35.00	$ 245.00
16		Trailer	$ 800.00	$20.00	$ 140.00
17		taxis	$ 450.00	$11.25	$ 78.75
18		Other Travel (Flights, etc)			
19		Misc Travel	3,400.00	$ 85.00	$ 595.00
20		Hotel			
21		**Wages**	$ 3,200.00	$80.00	$ 560.00
22		Per Diems	$ 3,600.00	$90.00	$ 630.00
23		Crew - Soudman	$ 2,000.00	$50.00	$ 350.00
24		Crew - Roadie	$ 2,000.00	$50.00	$ 350.00
25		Crew - Merch	$ 4,600.00	$115.00	$ 805.00
26		Crew - TM			
27		band wages			
28		**Promotions**	$ 300.00	$7.50	$ 52.50
29		Phone	$ 350.00	$8.75	$ 61.25
30		Posters	$ 1,200.00	$30.00	$ 210.00
31		Postage	$ 80.00	$2.00	$ 14.00
32		Internet			
33		**Musical Supply**	$ 100.00	$2.50	$ 17.50
34		Rehearsal space	$ 857.14	$21.43	$ 150.00
35		equipt rental	$ 2,000.00	$50.00	$ 350.00
36		Musical Supply (strings, heads etc)			
37		**Misc**	$ -		
38		Add'l Food/Supplies	$ 2,925.00	$73.13	$ 511.88
39		**Agency Commission**			
40		**Management?**			
41		**Contingency**			
42		TOTAL EXPENSES	$ 36,396.51	$909.91	$ 6,369.39
43					
44		**REVENUE**	$ 29,250.00		
45		Gtees	$ 8,000.00		
46		Shirts	$ 6,400.00		
47		cds			
48		misc	$ 43,650.00		
49		TOTAL REVENUES			
50			$ 7,253.49		
51		TOTAL			

Now, the figures look a little bit better. You're losing $8,600. But you have to be careful. There is a human cost, too. If your soundman isn't an invested fifth member, you just took $400 off of him and removed a substantial level of comfort by slashing the hotel budget. Let's add in merchandise and see how we're looking. I'm going to base merchandise on the assumption that your average guarantees are $750/night and you are playing to 150-250 people per night. Let's say you sell 15-25 shirts per night and the same with CDs. You can sell the shirts for $15 and the CDs for $10. The shirts cost you $5 each and the CDs cost you $2 each. In Cell C45, type "=C5*20*10" which is the Total Number of Days multiplied by the Average Shirt Sales multiplied by the Profit per Shirt ($15 minus $5). Do the same for CDs. You should be aiming to sell more merchandise to your fans. See the *Merchandising* chapter for some tips.

You are now making a small profit. Give the soundman and the tour manager back their $10/day and take some positive steps to make sure a small profit doesn't mutate into a large loss. You might not make twice as much money, but you will be twice as sure to make the amount you're projecting and that's a good thing.

> **"You might not make twice as much money, but you will be twice as sure to make the amount you're projecting and that's a good thing"**

See if there are any door deals or guarantees vs. percentage with a good enough break point for you to increase revenue with some applied thought and effort. If you can think about the future, maybe you can buy a trailer for $1,000. That's a savings of $400 this time, but next time it costs zero. Maybe you can find a deal on that guitar head you're renting. You could pick one up for $450 instead of $500 from a sympathetic store owner or find one online. Same deal: save a few hundred and build for the future. I know it's tough to get a tour out the door, but bite the bullet. Throw a "Please Help Us Go on the Road" benefit for your band, and sell something! It's going to help you in the long run. You could cross off another couple of grand in hotels. But you get the picture. Do it on paper beforehand.

Once you run the example, you can start to play around with ideas like: "Wow, if we tour for longer than a year, it would really make sense for us to buy a van." You may even begin to look at the various parts of the country you want to tour. Once you get used to inputting and saving information, you realize (just like names and addresses on your mailing list) that this is a valuable resource. I am always asking bands if they sell t-shirts or CDs at their shows. The answer is most often yes. But when I ask how many and of what design, that's when it all gets a little vague. A record needs to be kept of how many people are at each show, how many CDs and shirts you sold, and in what sizes. That information can be used for leverage later to analyze future opportunities and more accurately predict the size range of shirts and quantities of CDs you will need. There are ways to make more money and there are ways to avoid wasting it. Both put more in your pocket and increase the chances of you surviving through problems.

If the budget shows you that by performing 45 shows, you only break even, then you need to carefully track expenses as the tour progresses. If the budget makes sense and you have two hotel rooms a night, but if a couple of shows get cancelled and gas prices go through the roof; you will know that if you do not do something immediately, things are going to get worse and you are going to come home owing a lot of money. Knowledge of the budget allows you to make adjustments in a timely manner. If you are on top of your figures and realize that driving from Minneapolis to Seattle to have two days off, a show in Seattle, a day off, a show in Portland, and drive back to Denver is actually going to lose more money than doing nothing, then you can make the agent aware of these facts and reschedule later. The crucial time to make changes and act is before the tour, not after.

> "Touring on a budget means sleeping in crap holes or in the van, playing in front of ten people, all of whom look like they don't want to be there, get paid nothing, sound is crap, food nonexistent, and a long drive back after you got paid a tenth of what you were promised...was all great back then!" - Steve Beatty - Plastichead Distribution, bassist with October File

"There are ways to make more money and there are ways to avoid wasting it. Both put more in your pocket and increase the chances of you surviving through problems."

"Knowledge of the budget allows you to make adjustments in a timely manner."

"The crucial time to make changes and act is before the tour, not after."

HOTELS

Look at the hotels. Do you need hotels every night? Are there people you can stay with? If necessary, do a separate sheet for that. Allocate your resources! You know that hotels are way more expensive in NYC than El Paso, factor that into your budget. Make sure that you know if a venue has a shower and if there is hot water. Then, make sure that the hot water doesn't get turned off before the end of the night when all the crew wants to shower! If there are showers, you don't need hotel rooms that day. If your budget is very tight and you are traveling on a bus, you can save money by asking the driver if you can use his room as a shower room after the show. You cannot disturb the driver during the day (he is sleeping and downloading porn). But after the show when he is rested, his room becomes available because he is behind the wheel waiting for the merch guy to finish up! This tip might have kept a few bands from calling it quits. And could save you over $2,000 per month!

Do not plan a day off! A day off will just happen when a show falls through, you don't need both!

TOUR:SMART TIP

for more information go to:

www.tstouring.com

OTHER CONSIDERATIONS

On larger tours, type in a separate line for every member of the crew. Some of them might be earning different rates. The soundman is making more than the on stage crew guy. The lighting guy may be somewhere in between depending on what he's doing. The tour manager is probably the highest paid person on the tour. By giving everybody a separate line, you can itemize what everyone is being paid and adjust where necessary. You might want to employ the soundman a week early to be involved in rehearsals and to make sure he's advancing the dates; same with the tour manager. You might need to make adjustments here before the tour gets started. Do you need three on stage crew guys? Do you have to have a monitor guy? What about lights? For bands using computer-controlled backing, midi light packs are a great option to have a synchronized light show exactly locked to your music. So you don't need a light guy, but someone has to set up the lights. It's a good, cost-effective way to put on a more professional show at a smaller level. Be careful though, it might not look as impressive on a larger stage.

On tours involving international travel, you're going to want to put exchange rates somewhere on the sheet. The critical variables will change with band, situation, and country. The exchange rate of the U.K. pound to the U.S. dollar has fluctuated wildly over the last 20 years, going from $2.40 to the pound to $1.18 to the pound.

Here's a quick vehicle comparison you can mess around with:

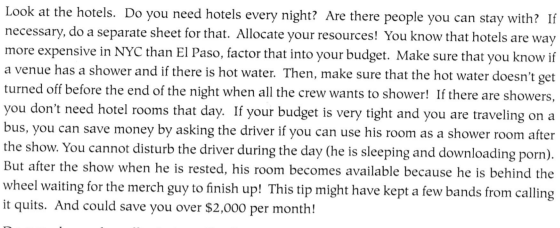

This is where it gets very cool. If you entered 7 mpg (because that's what some rinky-dink bus company told you the 1980 Eagle Bus that Van Halen slept in gets), see what happens when you enter 9 mpg:

gas price		1.89		
vehicle	bus		prius hybrid	
mpg		7	47.00	
total miles	14000		14000	
price per gall	1.89		1.89	
total gallons	2000		297.87	
total cost	$3,780.00		$562.98	

See? Fun, isn't it?! This is good for looking at gas prices and mpg. You can run this little piece of the chart to look at some "What ifs" between vehicles, a Prius, a van, etc.

By entering some pretty easy formulas, you can take some of the strain out of all of this. This is where you decide to fire the band and put everything on an iPod. Make sure you're performing seven nights a week.

BUDGET - STOP THE BLEEDING
CURSE MACKEY

Once you're on the road, the band basically bleeds cash until you find ways to stop the bleeding. That means developing your guarantees and door percentages through better attendance, with continued periodic performances in whatever markets you are working, while building your merchandise sales at the same time. The bigger the crowd, the more you make from the club and from merchandise. As this happens, you'll start spending more: hotels, better vehicle, additional crew, lighting, new gear… it never stops. The bigger the show, the more it costs. In order to not lose your ass, it is ideal to know how to manage your cash. This is where the Excel spreadsheet comes in.

Mastering Excel is not a glamorous task, but it must be done. Make a list of everything you spend money on while on tour. It will add up to 50+ items. Then, make a list of the ways you make money—that list will be way smaller. Excel allows you to add up the cost of expenses vs. income. It is also the best way to forecast how much money you need to do that trip to SXSW that you are so hyped on. You can see how big of an effect a $0.30 increase in a gallon of gas will cost you, or having hotels three times a week vs. finding free places to sleep and things like that. It will really paint a picture of the harsh financial reality of touring.

CURSE MACKEY

TOUR MANAGER
WOODSTOCK TATTOO &
BODY ARTS FESTIVAL
EVIL MOTHERS / PIGFACE
www.actionartsagency.com

SAVE MORE MONEY ON HOTELS
KATRINA ATKINS

KATRINA ATKINS

HOTELS & TRAVEL

First, when I hear that there is going to be a tour, I instinctively go into a panic. I have seen more money go out the door simply because people do not care (especially if it is not coming out of their pockets). Find someone who truly cares about the bottom line! I don't care if it is your mother. I used to stand by and watch people get paid to do a seriously bad job booking hotels and flights. Not only were most hotels booked by an agent expensive, they almost always seemed to be way too far from the venue which is a problem for so many reasons. If you are traveling by tour bus or van, it doesn't matter; someone is going to not get a shower, get left behind, or be late for sound check. Cabs are expensive (if they show up). One badly booked hotel can cause a whole world of shit. People like to have a shower once in awhile. If you're booking hotels, walking distance is the way to go. I can't tell you how many times I've been out to visit a tour and noticed a hotel across the street from a venue and some dumb-ass has booked the band five miles away! They might have saved $20 initially, but it has been blown out by cab fares or the room just being left because you were late, stuck in traffic, or the drive was longer than you thought. A few more instances like this and the hygiene problem kicks into high gear.

Go on *Expedia.com* and click on hotels. If you put in the exact address, you can see the distance of the hotel from the venue. I did this on the last tour and it worked out pretty well in most cities. If there is nothing or something is too expensive, you can always call the venue and see if they have a rate. Promoters sometimes do, but the venues seem to be more helpful if you can reach them at a decent hour. One thing about Expedia is that you have to prepay to get the rate they are selling. Go into hotel information and get the number and book it yourself. Sometimes you can get the Expedia rate but still have the option of cancelling the rooms. Otherwise, if you don't make the gig, you're still paying for the rooms. Make sure whoever is in charge of checking in gets the correct information and always get cancellation numbers. A few times, we have been charged when we have cancelled rooms and it all makes a difference.

Another thing: make sure whoever is in charge is smart and responsible (if you can). One asshole can screw up your whole hotel budget in one night. Once, a tour manager either didn't

> "If you are traveling by tour bus or van, it doesn't matter, someone is going to not get a shower, get left behind, or be late for sound check. Cabs are expensive (if they show up)."

get the hotel information in time or lost it and there was a convention in this particular city. Our three bus drivers ended up staying in suites at the Omni downtown for $1,000 when I had prepaid rooms already booked at a closer hotel for $50 each. So, there you go, three weeks of non-stop work saving money only to be blown by a tour manager who was out of his mind.

DAVE CALLENS' QUICK BUDGETS!
DAVE CALLENS

After years of wondering why label executives and reps always came back with questions that I thought were thoroughly answered in my pre-tour budget, I decided I would send a Fred Flintstone budget and see what happened. Well, I never lost a tour after implementing this. It was me: I totally missed the point of simple and easy numbers. No flashy spreadsheet for me after that. While I'm on the road, I would just use an expandable Excel spreadsheet with self-calculating formulas and finalizations. There was one drawback to this, though. I had way too much extra time on my hands. Tour accounting became boring.

Check out Quick Budgets on the *www.tstouring.com!*

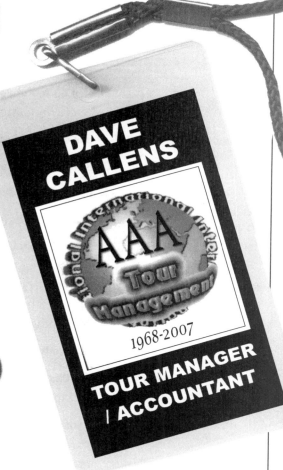

:SMART TIPS

1. **Do a budget!**

2. **The budget for the tour is not supposed to prove that it is a great idea.** It is designed to let you know where the problem areas will be.

3. **It's better to do it on paper than with people.**

4. **Include a line in the budget for every day, not every show!**

5. **Include a column for days of the week.**

6. **Be realistic. This isn't time for putting in figures of what you hope for.** There is no such thing as a guarantee. Didn't you know that?

7. **Enter a formula where the total number of guarantees** is divided by the total number of days on the road, not the number of shows.

8. **Stay on top of your budget as things change.** The crucial time to make changes and act is before and during the tour, not after!

9. **One of the easiest ways to make a budget work better is to do seven shows a week!**

10. **Using the driver's hotel room (for showers!)** can save $75/day!

11. **Use the information you have to keep the agent on track. Know your shit!**

12. **Add 15% to the total mileage for the tour to allow for running around, getting lost, etc.**

13. **You will probably estimate travel times based on 70-80-90 mph.** The reality is that every time you stop for gas and get more caffeine, two members of the touring party who are awake will buy something, go to the bathroom, etc., and just as you are about to leave, wake up the others who didn't know they had a store here, or have to go the bathroom, or something, which will drop your miles per hour average to an AARP approved 55 mph.

14. **Choose the highest average for gas prices, not the lowest!**

15. **Don't include merchandise revenues in the incomes** until you have done 50 shows and you can extrapolate or guesstimate them. Even then, use a figure of 50% of what you are hoping.

16. **If you are very nervous and not sure of your abilities to deal** with problems once you are on the road, remove the highest and lowest paying shows from the income list. Make sure you are sitting on the toilet when you do this as you watch your budget shred.

17. **Do not schedule arbitrary days off.** One will happen on its own when you can not find a show or a show is cancelled.

C·H·A·P·T·E·R — 14

PRESS AND PUBLICISTS:
AN INSIDE PERSPECTIVE

"Writing about music is like dancing to architecture."

— Guru Melvin Ranchero

When dealing with anyone—especially anyone in the press, be nice! I met Jason Pettigrew when he was a young journalist for a small raggedy paper run out of someone's downstairs apartment in Cleveland called *Alternative Press*. He was sent out to cover Killing Joke, but there were some strange things going on that night that caused the interview with the rest of the band to be postponed and then cancelled. I apologized a few times and eventually did an interview at 4 a.m.—by which time there were free morning donuts at the hotel. So we scarfed a few and after all these years, we are still friends. And here he is contributing some valuable advice for the book later in this chapter. That's karma... and donuts!

> *"... anyone reading your press kit that can really help you, has between 5 and 15 seconds... so make it count."*

PRESS KITS

- Remove all mention of when the band started – unless it was in jail or somehow involved Charles Bukowsi or Angelina Jolie.

- Sonicbids is an online music community that allows musicians and promoters access to each other's materials. You have to use Sonicbids, but remember: it is the interesting packages that get opened in my office and the interestingly packaged CDs that get into the player.

- Include some brief information about how the band is doing in a particular market. It implies that, given a chance, you could be successful in another market too.

- Nebulous hyperbolae and smoke screens are easily identified as just that... crap.

- Remember that anyone reading your press kit who can really help you has between five and 15 seconds, so make it count.

Instead of FedExing press kits all over the place, we have an "Image Bank" up on the website where anyone can look through images of the bands, preview, and then download high resolution versions. We put this information on the CDs we send out to promoters when we are preparing for a package tour.

ELECTRONIC PRESS KITS

An electronic press kit *(or EPK)* is a press or media kit equivalent in electronic form. Press kits include materials that will make it easier for someone to understand your project quickly

"Take a step back, consider why, and fix it."

and elements that will enable and encourage them to write a longer and larger piece about you and your band. You can make your band's EPK stand out by using graphic elements, photos, etc. Chop together a five minute informational video... communicate in the way that makes the most sense for your band. If you find yourself apologizing all over your press kit, take a step back, consider why, and fix it. You only have one chance to make a first impression.

> "Do not blow off any interviews or photo ops. The press, even though it may at times not seem so, is very advantageous to your touring career. This is part of your job anyway."
> - Mark O'Shea, NIN Tour Manager

PUBLICISTS

"If you fuck it up and play pop star sometimes neither the interview nor your career can be rescheduled."

Many of the overall guidelines before finding an agent apply to finding a publicist – especially in the beginning. A good publicist, because of relationships at different magazines, etc., might be able to get you more press than you can on your own. But if you're a young band starting off, your main requirements for a publicist should be making sure that the venues have your shows listed correctly, that your CD goes to the right person doing the review at the local paper before your show, and that someone from the paper is invited to do a review for a show in the first place. Now, that's a lot of work if we're talking about two or three local papers. Then, multiply that by 25 shows on your first tour, and add in all of the web sites, newsgroups, etc. That need feeding. This task is probably best handled by you, the band, or someone that wants to help the band. It only takes a few shows in front of an audience of three people to motivate *somebody* to do *something*. It's actually quite gratifying to send those packages out eight weeks early, make a follow up call to make sure they've been received, sit on the computer typing until your hands freeze, and know that there is one more thing out of 50 that's going to help your show, rather than e-mailing your publicist two weeks before the show to see if it has been done or not.

Once you do have a publicist, you need to remember that once again, you're dealing with a human being. If they get you a 4 a.m. interview with a magazine in Germany, do it and smile. Doing any interview is good practice and you're letting your publicist know that once an interview is set up for you, you'll do it without making him or her look like an asshole. If you fuck it up and play pop star, sometimes neither the interview nor your career can be rescheduled.

Look at your guest lists. You want to see how well your publicist is performing, not how many packages they've sent out. You want to know the results. If you set up your guest list correctly, your publicist should be sending you a list of people from relevant magazines. Give creative, positive feedback. Steer! Ask for advice about the interviews you are doing. Do they have any feedback or input for you? A bad publicist can just start putting anyone on the guest list. They can put Elvis fucking Presley on the guest list; he may or may not show up.

TEN POINTS TO CONSIDER WHEN DEALING WITH THE PRESS:

JASON PETTIGREW

JASON PETTIGREW

EDITOR IN CHIEF

ALTERNATIVE PRESS MAGAZINE

1. **Check your website/phone service/e-mail** for any last minute guest list additions or interview requests, at least once in the morning, and then again 90 minutes before you go on stage.

2. **If a writer is coming to the show to review it,** see that they get a copy of your set list. Most reviewers from daily papers will bug the soundman for it. This isn't to undermine your set, but to check the correct song titles for the review itself.

3. **Do not make a writer wait longer than ten minutes for ANYTHING.** Show up or call on time for your interviews. That writer probably has someplace he or she would rather be as well, Baby Cobain.

4. **Never cop an attitude with a writer** unless you are 100% positive that the person you are talking to will be the future lawn and garden manager at your local Home Depot. (Why do you think people hate that guy from Third Eye Blind so much? Besides the obvious reason...)

5. **If you believe the good stuff written about your band,** you automatically have to believe the bad stuff. Read and learn.

6. **Never publicly dis a magazine or writer on stage.** Even addressing them negatively still acknowledges their alleged power. Don't find out the hard way that a lot of periodicals have a larger life span than a typical rock band.

7. **Rock critics are not your friends.** If one of your word-processing "buddies" slags your new music, it's because it's his or her job. Repeat #5.

8. **At starting level, press kits that are larger than a bio, an 8 x 10 photo, and one page of cuttings (photocopies of stories written on your band) are wasteful.**

9. **If you are actively seeking press, don't mail your disc blindly to a random selection of outlets.** You don't shop for golf clubs in a jewelry store; why are you sending your techno project CD to a punk-rock fanzine? Be aware of specific magazines and writers who are sympathetic to the kind of music you make. Address your packages accordingly.

10. **Never, ever use advertising in a magazine as a promise for coverage.** "Well, we bought an ad." Guess what? I tipped a rude server at a restaurant last week, but that doesn't mean I was entitled to a 30-minute grab-ass session in the cloakroom with her.

> **"If you are actively seeking press, don't mail your disc blindly to a random selection of outlets. You don't shop for golf clubs in a jewelry store... "**

WHAT MAKES AN ARTIST/PUBLICIST RELATIONSHIP WORK

MARIA FERRERO, PUBLICIST ADRENALINE PR

I cut my teeth in the '80s with Metallica, Testament, and Anthrax; the '90s with Ministry and KMFDM; and the 2000's with Lamb OF God. Tenacious perpetuate of success.

Adrenaline PR is a full service public relations firm turning artists into household names since 1983.

What makes a relationship work, I will speak for myself, is honesty: honesty with the clients and honesty with my contacts. Integrity plays a huge part and interacts with honesty. My clients get the real deal from me and my contacts respect that. When I take on a client, I believe in them. I'm not just "working a client/project" for the cash, ever! I'm very picky about who I take on as a client and therein lies the integrity part. If my name goes on something or if I am pushing something, I have to believe in it. I have a track record and a reputation that I will not compromise.

Then, the honesty ties back in and I cannot push something I do not believe in.

The type of client who should seek publicity is any artist who wants to become known. This is a no-brainer. You need to create a buzz, people talking about you. The publicist is the facilitator of that.

Services that I provide are getting the word out by any means, carrier pigeon, skywriter, television ticker, e-mail, letter, fax, phone call, follow-ups (repeated if necessary), with the willingness to walk away before I piss someone off with my tenacity.

The silliest mistake any artist should avoid is not knowing, not being authentic in who you are, and having any fear—fear kills. Kill the voice in your head—follow your heart!

MARIA FERRERO

ADRENALINE PR - OWNER
TIPS ON DEALING WITH A PUBLICIST
www.adrenalinepr.com

> "... fear kills –
> Kill the voice in
> your head – follow
> your heart!"

PET PEEVES - AND HOW TO AVOID THEM:
GAIL WORLEY

PET PEEVE #1: LACK OF PUNCTUALITY

As a journalist and someone who has also had a hand in the publicity end of the business, I think it's important to be on time for your interviews with the press, whether the interview is in person or on the phone. It's the biggest drag in the world to be kept waiting in some record company office or hotel bar and even worse to be forced to loiter by the phone in anticipation of a call that doesn't come in at the scheduled time because Mr. Big Rock Star is recovering from a hangover. Sometimes there's a legitimate excuse or scheduling conflict— say, a sound check that's delayed or a television interview taping that runs over—but if that's the case, it's important that a representative of the band notify the journalist that the call will be coming in late and to make alternate arrangements if possible. If you were stupid enough to get plastered to the gills the night before and can't lift your head out of the toilet and crawl to the phone with something clever to say, you don't deserve the media exposure. My time is just as valuable as yours and if you're too busy or clueless to keep an interview appointment with me, well, there are certainly a hundred other deserving bands I could write about. Your band probably isn't that good anyway. Don't waste my time.

GAIL WORLEY

ROCK CRITIC AT LARGE

www.worleygig.com

If you want me to name names, I can cite a situation when I had a scheduled interview with Chris Summers, drummer from the Norwegian garage rock band, Turbo Negro. When Chris was unavailable (i.e. not answering his phone) at the time our interview was scheduled (I was asked to call him), I got hold of the tour manager on his cell. The TM said he'd look around for Chris and then called me back within half an hour to say that Chris had been partying hard the night before and was "asleep." After two more unsuccessful attempts to reach Chris on the TM's cell and then in his hotel room, the interview finally went ahead four hours late. I missed a show I was supposed to see that night and the interview was so bad, I didn't even bother to transcribe the tape. Instead, I found a drummer from another band who was both punctual *and* coherent and wrote my column about him. The '80s are over. Partying until you're obliterated doesn't impress anyone. Go fuck yourself.

> **"The '80s are over. Partying until you're obliterated doesn't impress anyone. Go fuck yourself."**

PET PEEVE #2: RETARDATION

Another pet peeve of mine is the interview subject who either doesn't know how to talk or has nothing to say. This happens more often than you can imagine. Though I've come to understand that drummers are often the most interesting and technically knowledgeable members of a band and make the best interview subjects, there have been a few times when I've been prepared to conduct an in-depth interview for *Modern Drummer* magazine (a publication any drummer would cut off an arm to get coverage in) and the guy has nothing to say. He can't talk about his drums, how a certain pattern was played, his influences, or what's going on with his band. Yawn City. Advice: if you know you're going to be talking to a writer for a magazine that could literally make or break your career, take a minute to think about what you do and the impression you'd like to make with your fans and peers. Most of the time, unless I'm asking you to solve a math problem in your head, "I don't know" is neither a desired nor acceptable answer.

PET PEEVE #3: CELL PHONES

I hate cell phones but I understand and accept that, these days, the world revolves around the little fuckers. I've gotten used to doing interviews with interviewees on cell phones and losing the signal when the tour van goes around a mountain or missing every third word the guy says but, seriously, if a land line is available for an interview, do yourself and the interviewer a big favor and use that. The enlightening revelations that spill forth from your lips mean shit if they're unintelligible on my tape.

Gail Worley

HERE ARE A FEW EXAMPLES OF PROMOTIONAL HYPE!

Last Temptation of Christ: Worldwide uproar! The Catholic Church organized a relentless, hysterical campaign against the movie, which they later admitted created more publicity for the movie than any of the producers could have dreamed of... or paid for!

Sinead O'Connor: Tore up a picture of the pope on Saturday Night Live. Whilst receiving worldwide criticism, it didn't translate into sales. This might be the first recorded instance of bad publicity not translating into sales, or maybe it's the bad publicity in combination with a really bad haircut.

Nine Inch Nails: If this was engineered, it was genius. During filming of the video for "Down In It," Chicago film crew H. Gun Video were faking a helicopter shot by using a camera tied to a weather balloon. The shot was a pull away of singer Trent Reznor lying in an alley looking like he was dead. The wind caught the weather balloon and took it to Iowa where a farmer took the camera to police. The FBI thought it was a snuff flick and next thing you know, it's all over *Hard Copy* (a fore-runner to *Access Hollywood* airing each day at 4:30 p.m.). Before this video, I think Nine Inch Nails sales were 8,000-9,000 units; after, they went through the roof.

OK GO!: When their label refused to release a video for a single, the band filmed a video themselves and put it up on YouTube. Their follow-up, featuring a performance piece on treadmills, inspired a Saturday Night Live knock off. The treadmill video has been viewed over 12 million times and won MTV's award for "Best Short for Music Video" in 2007.

Bow Wow Wow: During the recording industry's hysteria over blank cassette tapes and piracy, Sex Pistols manager, Malcolm McClaren, poured gasoline on the issue by having his band, Bow Wow Wow (already stirring controversy with a 14-year-old Vietnamese girl, Annabella Lwin, on vocals), release a song called "C-30 C-60 C-90 Go," which encouraged kids to record their favorite music and not buy it. The song was instantly banned. Sound familiar?

Janet Jackson/ Justin Timberlake: Justin accidentally exposed Janet's breast during a move they practiced for five days straight.

Master tapes of the new albums have been stolen: Left in a taxi in London/New York City (Fill in name of city here)... or left in an airport by the singer. U2 did this in 2004. During a photo shoot in France, U2 lost a CD. Police hysteria etc...etc... (Thanks Jamie Wysinger)– Update: Trent Reznor just left flash drives with songs on them in bathrooms!

Brandon Block: Storms the stage of the Brit Awards in 2000—pretending he had mistakenly heard his name.

Dixie Chicks: Got worldwide publicity after stating they were ashamed that President George W. Bush is from Texas. This strategy hasn't harmed them at all. In fact, it's done quite the opposite. After the 2007 Grammy awards, their album moved from #72 to #8. It also spawned a documentary, *Shut Up & Sing,* which in turn spawned another round of media frenzy when NBC refused to air ads for the documentary. Kerrrching!

Madonna/Britney Spears: Madonna and Britney Spears kiss during the opening act of the 2002 MTV Video Music Awards. No stranger to controversy, Madonna had gained worldwide publicity when she released *The Sex Book,* an overtly sexual video, etc. etc. etc.

William Castle: American film director was famous for promoting his low budget movies with tricks and gimmicks. To promote *Macabre* in 1958 there were ambulances parked outside the theatre in anticipation of audience members collapsing or dying of fright during the film. For *The Tingler* in 1959 he equipped the seats in theatres with joy buzzer devices. And in 1961 for *Homicidal* he inserted a 45 second break in the movie with a voiceover informing the audience how much time was left for them to leave and receive a refund for being too frightened.

Adult Swim: Company in Boston placed electronic light boards giving people the middle finger around the city to promote the television series Aqua Teen Hunger Force. This caused the closure of bridges and a section of the Charles River, and cost the city hundreds of thousands of dollars responding to bomb scares. Whether it was intentional remains a question, but the show received massive prime-time publicity.

Prince Charles: Was on a tour of the United Arab Emirates. There wasn't much excitement about his trip until he suggested banning McDonald's during a conference for the launch of a public health campaign, prompting worldwide publicity and comments from the McDonald's Corporation.

Sex Pistols: The band signed their contract with A&M in a ceremony held outside of Buckingham Palace. Under pressure from its own employees, artists, and distributors, A&M broke the contract with the Sex Pistols three days later. Then during a concert on a boat on the Thames River, the boat was raided by police and the band and many others were taken into custody. Oh, and lead singer Johnny Rotten said "Fuck Off" on prime time national TV.

Bruce Springsteen: When his label refused to release the single, "Born To Run," his manager leaked a copy to some radio stations. Public demand and pressure on the label forced them to release the single.

The Beatles: Performed in the center of London on the roof of Apple Records office, prompting complaints and a visit from the police, all captured in their movie "Let It Be."

So, I'm now announcing the launch of my new book: *Fuck McDonalds, Fuck George Bush, And Fuck You! (A Guide To Touring).* It's an all naked experience, the totally pink book constantly vibrates, ticks like a bomb, and will be super-glued to Madonna's naked ass.

MARTIN ATKINS' HOW TO GIVE GOOD INTERVIEW

You have practiced your instrument, worked out, put piercings and ink in the most (and the least) prominent places, and checked through the stills of the photo shoots to find the position of your head and butt that best displays them. You've practiced hard with the band. You can throw your microphone stand in the air and nonchalantly catch it as if you hadn't practiced it 7,000 times in front of a mirror. But have you given any thought to giving a better longer interview?

First, understand that this is your job. You need to practice and prepare just like a good comedian riffs on certain ideas, bounces them around a bit, then tries them out on a small audience before deciding if it should be included in a regular set. You need to treat your interviews the same way.

Research

Look at all of the magazines and websites within your genre. Get to know the main journalists/ contributors and reviewers. Who are the up-and-comers? Start to read what they have to say. You'll be better prepared for their style of interview and it will help you find a way in or, during the interview, a way out. It will also help you better target the press kit packages you are sending out.

Imagine some of the questions you might be asked and think about your answers.

When you read interviews with artists you don't particularly like would you think: "I still don't like this guy, but he made some interesting comments" or "Wow, this guy really is a dick!?" Be prepared to deal creatively and graciously with anyone's questions even if they demonstrate a basic lack of knowledge of your band. They're still there (either in front of you, at the other end of a phone line, or being transmitted through a computer terminal) and interested enough to ask.

Interviewers

You might have a very nervous interviewer. You don't want a freak-out and a two-question, three minute interview. Think about helping the interviewer through the process so you can get what you need; 20 questions and two pages in the college paper.

With a more experienced interviewer, it's a poker game. You need to be thinking about where they're taking the interview, anticipating, realizing if their questions are designed to reinforce a pre-conceived idea of what you are all about so that they can have an arty, clever piece in their paper. You have to block and then steer carefully without showing your 'tell.'

You need to be comfortable with the basics so your mind can bounce around, see what's around the corner, and come up with the creative insights for which you will surely become known. You need to be doing all of this whilst looking at the clock (because you've got four other interviews scheduled and you still haven't sound checked) but not appearing as if you're in a hurry. Keep mental track of the cool phrases and ideas you are floating. You don't want to keep repeating the same themes to every interviewer in each city—spread it around.

> "You can throw your microphone stand in the air and nonchalantly catch it as if you hadn't practiced it 7,000 times in front of a mirror. But have you given any thought to giving a better, longer interview?"

Practice

Another reason to practice is the same reason that you practice stage moves in the rehearsal room before you're on stage, you don't want to look like a complete ass when you land on your hole, physically, mentally, verbally, and musically. You want to realize that you sound like a complete prick at two o'clock in the morning listening back to the micro-cassette recording of your fake interview; not when you are reading your half-page interview in the latest copy of your favorite magazine. The former is fixable; the latter is not.

Have a Purpose

You need to decide what your message and purpose is and be sure to hit those points during the interview no matter what the questions are. For example:

Interviewer: You guys drive a vehicle that runs on vegetable oil?

Band: Yeah, it's really amazing and saved us a lot of money, thank God—because the studio we used on the new album was soooo expensive.

Interviewer: So, you guys have been to Japan?

Band: Yes, it was crazy. We lost the lyrics for the new album and had to have them faxed over to us so they could be translated for one of the four different covers that we are giving away...

Interviewer: We have to stop the interview, my head is on fire.

Band: That's exactly how I felt when the drummer joined the band—it was so right my head was tingling.

Interviewer (from Knitting Magazine): Err...

Band: That's why I feel an affinity with your readers. They do amazing things with wool. We're weaving a sweater made of musical notes and words. Both things give you a warm feeling in the tummy.

Interviewer (Train Enthusiast Monthly): Err...

Band: The band is a train, fueled by the coal of ideas and excitement, every city is a station on our track to success. Yeah sure, sometimes there's a tree on the tracks or a problem with the signals, but we just have to deal with it.

Tricks For Knitting On The Road!!

Knitting

August 2007 | www.knittingforwankers.com

Knit Your Own Stage Scenery

Interview With Martin Atkins

Interviewer: I'm from FOX news.

Band: Hundreds or twenties?

It's your job to get what you need from the interview. Not to complain because the interviewer was lame—that's lame. What—I'm lame, you're lame, you lame, lame-o

Lame-o-llama! Lame-o-pallooza? Last Temptation of Lame-O… (See? Keep practicing and you'll be a master wordsmith, too).

Lame-o.

After all of that advice really, the only thing that communicates and cuts through the crap is being honest. Intensity and passion are the building blocks of communication and it's impossible to get that fire in your eyes over something your manager told you to say. Anyway, after awhile, you'll be too tired to remember all of the lies about you and Burt Bacharach… But in order to be honest and project the answers you want to give, you have to be comfortable— not just in your chair, in your skin. Have a look around inside that bag of stuff between your spiky hair and your horribly smelly feet. You'll be glad you did… eventually…

…lame-o.

- **When dealing with anyone in the press, be nice.**

- **If you fuck up and play pop star,** sometimes neither the interview, nor your career, can be rescheduled.

- **Do not make a writer wait more than ten minutes for anything.**

- **Never publicly dis a magazine or writer on stage.**

- **Offer online electronic press kits (EPKs)!**

- **Create a buzz**—you want people to be talking about you!

- **Rock critics are not your friends.**

- **Have something to say.**

"Never turn down an interview with anybody. Even a shoddy interview with an ill-prepared interviewer from a tiny fanzine in the middle of nowhere is practice for you and more column inches than none."

– Martin Atkins

C·H·A·P·T·E·R····15

STREET TEAMS

"You can never have perspective on everything...
so listen! shut up and listen!"

We started our first street team as early as 1993, which was way, way ahead of the curve. We called them "field representatives," or field reps. A great field rep, just like a great intern, can evolve into a crew person, a merchandise person, a band manager, or just a good friend—so pay attention!

> **Field Rep=Street Team; two titles, same people!**

We have acquired field reps in person, through our mailing list, by asking people to check a box or send an e-mail if they are willing to help. Sometimes people just wander into the office or a venue at the right time.

Treat your street team with respect. They are helping you because your music has spoken to them. There is a magical feeling of camaraderie that exists when people who are not involved in the music business are able to substantially help people whose music they love. Do not trample on this magic. Try and think about them when you *do not* need any help. Send them a remix, an advance track, a t-shirt, some news, or a Christmas card!

In the same way that there are people who need to be pirates on the high seas of touring and risk everything, there are people who want to help from a safe distance. If someone lets you use their home, shower, internet, or bed, be thankful. Dye your hair purple at the Motel 6. Do not puke or piss in their bed because you are drunk. Do not abuse the cat, dog, or internet connection. Do not hit on your field rep or your field rep's girlfriend or boyfriend! Keep track of these people and make sure to put them on the guest list the next time you are in the area. If you are unwilling to take on the responsibility that accepting this help demands, then do not accept it.

> **"In the same way that there are people who need to be pirates on the high seas of touring and risk everything, there are people who want to help from a safe distance."**

When you ask for help, try to be specific. Some people have no idea of what is involved in helping and might be intimidated. "Oh my God, I don't know how to fix a sampler!" or "I have no idea where the best Thai food is!" when we e-mailed our street team and explained. One time, we felt like our lives had been saved by a box of donuts. When we explained to our mailing list the huge difference it made, I think the penny really dropped. People who had no idea of how to help a band on the road suddenly got it. A box of donuts for $6 became do-able. The circle was completed.

> **"In some of this, you get what you gouge. In other bits - you get what you give."**

"To have any promotions stopped over two slices of bread or a gallon of gas seemed crazy."

During the buildup to a tour, I received some e-mails from reps that said they had driven over 50 miles to distribute flyers, but had to go home because they were hungry and didn't have money for food, gas, or more copies, etc. I decided to offer Subway coupons, $10 gas cards, and Kinko's cards or reimbursements (with receipts) to anyone who needed it. My office manager expected this would cause an avalanche of free sandwiches, gas, and Xerox art experimentation parties at our expense. I didn't really care. Our package tours are a huge undertaking. To have promotions stopped over two slices of bread or a gallon of gas seemed crazy. The response was honestly more fueling to my soul and more uplifting than any great review. Instead of a flood of revved up, gassed up, all-you-can-eat sandwich xerox parties, what we got was a bunch of people ecstatic that we cared enough about them to cover their expenses. It felt pretty good. We ended up sending out a few gas cards, Kinko's cards, and Subway coupons. A couple of people came up to me at shows with Kinko's receipts for reimbursements. There was one person in Detroit who had a $90 Kinko's receipt. We had 980 people show up at that show, and he was one of the reasons why. Instead of giving the guy $90, I gave him $125 worth of merchandise. It worked out great for everyone.

A good street team will also act as early warning signs for problems. I try not to delegate this communication.

"If you can create an environment that allows you to solve problems eight weeks out – that is priceless. Whoever that was: THANK YOU!!"

> *Before one tour, I ended up typing till 4:00 a.m. My hands were frozen like claws. A field rep had e-mailed me that a show in Houston was double-booked with another band. I replied saying that it was a probably a mistake (because that is what I thought our agent would say), but thanked them for the heads up. The rep e-mailed me back again saying that the show was listed on this other band's web site, too. It seemed like too much to be just a coincidence. I was able to take this information and by 10:00 am the next morning, our agent was able to fix the mistake that he had made. If you can create an environment that allows you to solve problems eight weeks out on the road, that is priceless. Whoever that was: **THANK YOU!!***

One of our reps, Greg Zarret pointed out that putting pictures of semi-naked girls and using the word "fuck" in 3.5 inch high letters on the back of a postcard is very funny, but some record stores will not let anyone put those cards in their stores… oops. So, think about that for a moment. I just had something really obvious pointed out to me by a field rep. This is a really important thing for you to think about, especially you assholes who dismiss everyone. "You can never have perspective on everything… so listen!" Shut up and listen!

I WISH I COULD DO IT AGAIN TOMORROW
MICHAEL GALLINA

Being a field rep has been a remarkable experience. I've met a great number of people, been to cities I've never been before, made some great friends, and have had the right to lay claim to more odd experiences than an anti-social geeky white boy should be entitled.

The value of a good street team is huge. It allows you to create a physical presence where you aren't. While the Internet and other telecommunications have made distance easier to bridge, it has also created solid mediums for transfer of flyers and songs. However, the importance of having someone who can put up flyers, get tracks to college radio for airplay, and talk to record store and coffee shop owners and employees is still paramount in ensuring a real presence for an artist or label.

I'm coming up on ten years of doing this work for a variety of bands, running a time frame that predates my ability to buy cigarettes and continues through my ability to rent cars. I have awesome memories ranging from following Pigface in 1998 with a great friend and driving band members around, "borrowing" from the beer stash and sharing other indulgences, to showing up on stage and singing some of my favorite songs. All I had to do was distribute flyers at record stores and coffee shops, speak favorably and passionately about the artists I care about, give out free CDs here and there (and who doesn't love free CDs!), and show up at concerts with free reign to help out all those to do their thing. By doing this, I am representing an artist or label who I know and love. How can this not be awesome?

Many times I've felt completely fucking exhausted after a show, but I've never collapsed without thinking I wish I could do it again tomorrow. It also blows my mind to consider that I have, in some manner, contributed to the success of something I believe in. It continues to be a privilege to be involved with something that matters so much to me.

MICHAEL GALLINA

PATH OF INDETERMINISM
GENERAL TECHNOLOGY
ANARCHIST
www.indeterminism.org

"...have the right to lay claim to more odd experiences than an anti-social geeky white boy should be entitled."

YOU CAN BE A PARTICIPANT
DAVID NICHOLAS

I got involved as a field rep probably in the most pure, organic way possible, without ever really declaring myself one. It just happened because of the music and my love of it. When the *Damage Manual* EP was released, I knew there was something very special happening and I wanted everyone to know about it. The best part of being a field rep is that you can be more than just a fan and consumer; you can be a participant. It also breaks down the walls between artist and audience. Just the chance to be able to express exactly how much the Damage Manual impacted me face to face with Chris, Martin, and Geordie was value enough in itself and I cherish that more than I can ever say. But to also be given a chance to spread the word as a field rep made it even better. There were so many people, places, and networks that I knew would love this music if they got a chance to be exposed to it—and they did. As a field rep, you get to make that exposure happen instead of just wondering, "What if...?," doing that is an honor and privilege.

> "The best part of being a field rep is that you can be more than just a fan and consumer; you can be a participant."

DAVID NICHOLAS

WASHINGTON DC ANTI-SCENE AGITATOR, DUB ADDICT

You also get to see all sides of the music and touring business. Not everyone shares the same level of enthusiasm. Jaded clubs and record stores go out of their way to make field reps feel unwelcome when they are putting up flyers around town. The interesting discovery I made is: don't let them waste your energy. Move right along to a slightly different path, like clothing or book stores of all kinds. I found people there to be more appreciative of field rep work and I know for a fact that it brought out people to shows who otherwise would not have even known about them. The lesson is that it pays to go places that are not so obvious. You can meet some really great people that way.

A FEW WORDS FROM STREET TEAMS

Dean W. Battaglia - Baltimore, MD

Being a musician myself, I can appreciate the hard work and dedication it takes to pull off a mediocre show, let alone what I have seen Pigface pull off over the years. There is nothing quite like being a part of that one show that people say was "magical" or "mind blowing."

Helping a band like Pigface load in equipment, run to the store, or design a flyer or handbill is very rewarding.

Brian Haugh

The definite high is being a part of the scene and making a difference as opposed to just watching the scene from afar. It's even better when you see a great turnout after posting fliers all over a city, when somebody uses a prop on stage that you picked up, or even just picking up food for someone. I've had the opportunity to interact with musicians the way you never can after a show. The perks of being a rep greatly outweigh any difficulties on our part.

Brandon Pruett

After posting flyers and talking to people for more than two weeks, I got a rep pass even though I already had a ticket. The day of the show, I unloaded the trucks and then helped the venue. I was exhausted by the time I got to the show, but as soon as the first band started, I felt a surge of energy and knew it was all worth it!

Ryan Newcomb

Highs: Being part of something bigger than you; helping excellent musicians reach people; and usually being able to belly up to the bar and meet the band is a pretty cool deal, as well.

Lows: Busting your ass in every way you thought possible and having nobody show up and then feeling like a tool when you're one of only a dozen people in the crowd.

Tim Brummet

I had the pleasure of booking a show for Evil Mothers at the Brass Mug, a local dive where many bands broke their teeth, some figuratively and some literally. I've been a field rep for years. I've loaded and unloaded gear, set up t-shirt stands, sold shirts, worked as security, and worked the crowd for signatures. It has been educational, emotional, and extremely entertaining.

Greg Zarret – Wildomar, CA

Positive:

1. Flyering (the postcards are the best). Passing out flyers and postcards at other shows at the venue

2. Getting local radio and college stations to drop names of shows in the area.

> "The definite high is being a part of the scene and making a difference as opposed to just watching the scene from afar."

> "It has been educational, emotional, and extremely entertaining."

Negative:
1. Don't ignore your rep.
2. Get the flyers, postcards, etc. to the rep in plenty of time. Sending them out in waves (instead of a few hours) would be up in the positive.
3. If you print 'FUCK' in 3 1/2 inch letters or print 99% nude girls on your flyer and/ or postcard, Tower Records and similar record stores probably won't put them up.

Andrew Grover

The best thing about being a rep is seeing that a band gets what they need. Offer your house if they need showers or their laundry done. Remember that they are going out of the way to see you, too.

Promote the show online and through tattoo parlors and record stores. I have gotten personal phone calls from bands months later just to say thank you.

James (Jay) DeVoy

* *Ability to meet and interact with people who are considered deific by the field rep.*
* *Unparalleled access and networking opportunity.*
* *Unfettered view into the realities of touring.*
* *Ability to sequentially see all phases of a tour, from booking to promotions to day-off logistics.*
* *Ownership of peer-to-peer promotion of show, responsible in part for success or failure of tour date.*

> **"... it is love and connection that drives a street team..."**

I was excited at the beginning of the *Preaching to the Perverted* tour to interact with other labels and learn and to see how the other labels did things. They said, "We didn't hire a street team for this tour." How totally silly. It is love and connection that drives a street team, not cash! This is a great way for a band to go into the massive hole of unrecoupment—there are plenty of others. It's also a great way for CDs and postcards to be crunching under your feet like snow on a winter's day. Communicate with your reps!

> **"...never underestimate the difference that you as an individual can make to any situation!"**

:SMART TIPS

- **Treat your street teams with respect.** Don't trample on their trust and respect.

- **Send out communications when you don't need help.**

- **Communicate clearly what help you need on the road.**

- **Don't hit on field reps or their partners!**

- **Don't be an asshole.**

- **Make sure that reps get into the shows** and that the venue knows about the rep passes. Check outside to make sure your loyal rep isn't left hanging by an oversight, or that an out-of-town rep has traveled to see the show and can't get in.

- **Try and spend some time with them in the afternoon,** unless you know you are going to feel up to it after the show.

- **Nothing is better than face-to-face contact.**

- **Listen to the reps. Make some time for them.** Their input is priceless, priceless, priceless!

- **Instead of telling your team what you need, ask them what they can hook you up with.** On one tour a street teamer couldn't come to the show, but stopped by for sound check with two massive trays of lasagne. In some of this, you get what you gouge. In other bits, you get what you give.

- **Have a street team!**

C·H·A·P·T·E·R·····16

MAILING LIST: EVERY PERSON COUNTS

"A strong, healthy mailing list will give you more options."

Your mailing list is priceless! It will not only give you the tools to promote shows yourself, but it will also provide you with a network of people who care and more options when it comes to putting a street team together, which in turn will give you invaluable information about a great new club that has just opened, or let you know about a shaky promoter who is about to go out of business. You have to communicate with your mailing list while you are on the road. There is usually a lot of activity before a tour starts, but it is important to keep the kettle boiling throughout the tour with news about how the first shows have been doing, and more communication with the cities to come. A tour is not the time to pack away the computer and go crazy. It is not a holiday; this is the time when the work really begins. It is war!

> "...this is the time when the work really begins. It is war!"

The day of the show is not just the time you finally get to wind up the volume on your brand new guitar rig, wind up the tour manager, or whatever it is that you do. It is also a very small window of time, a gift to you, when you are actually in a city that you are going to want to go back to. Instead of screwing around and pretending to be a rock star, you can do a number of things:

GRAB A LOCAL PAPER: One of the free ones like *The Reader* in Chicago, *The Voice* in NYC, etc. There has to be one at the venue. Look for the name of the club you should have played, or if you played the right venue, the names of places you can send promotional materials to: record stores, tattoo parlors, hairdressers, book stores, coffee shops, or wherever. The great thing about these papers is that you can see and decide immediately if these are places that might be receptive to what you are doing. I like trying to find places that are not used to getting free tickets, free CDs, posters, etc. This way they will be happy to get promotional materials from you. One of these places might want to get involved in some cross-promotions by using the back of a postcard.

> "You already know something very important about these people – they actually go to shows."

MEET PEOPLE: Get out of the dressing room and network. Use the opportunity to do every single thing you, and the people you are with, can do to collect as many names as possible for the mailing list. This is your best chance to do it. You already know something very important about these people—they actually go to shows. You need to aim for collecting 50%+ of the names of the people at the show.

CREATING AND EXPANDING YOUR MAILING LIST:

- **Shoot the (pretend, inflatable) dolphin.** See *Using The Web* chapter.

- **Make sure you have a mailing list.** I have come across this so many times, I am not going to apologize for stressing this point: have a mailing list, you idiot.

- **Creatively entice people to sign up for it,** by having a competition or give-aways.

- **Have a few street teamers trawling the line outside the venue.** People are bored. Give them an incentive to sign up, like a free CD.

- **Have postcards at the booth for people to take away with them.** They might not want to hang around and sign up but might do so later.

Luke Stokes of Dope had tickets printed to win the Marshall amplifier that Edsel Dope used to record guitar on their first album. He sold tickets for $2 a piece and it was a great success. An e-mail is required to notify the winner. Not only do you have people paying $2 a ticket to win a Marshall amp, but you have many more people than usual signing up for the mailing list and taking care to print their information neatly.

Aspire to this level of ingenuity and entrepreneurial business, or steal Luke's idea.

Mailing List Sign-Up – Please Write Clearly!
Members of our mailing list get discount offers from our online store, opportunities for free tickets or passes to Invisible / Underground related events, exclusive downloads, and more!

Name	E-Mail	Address

- **Make sure you get e-mails, city/state and zip codes!** You don't want to bombard people in Portland with news of all of your cool shows in Florida! It's worth taking the time and you need the geographic data.

- **Make sure people have an unsubscribe option.**

- **Clean your list occasionally.**

CHAPTER 17

MARKETING II - USING THE WEB

The web is the ultimate cool tool enabling instant and direct communication between artist and audience without the filters of label, radio station, or record store. But... the easier the communication, the shorter the shelf life. It's easy to be the flavor of the day or the minute, but much harder to be the flavor of the year. For that, you need to use the web as one of many tools at your disposal. In addition to staying on top of and enhancing traffic to your own web site using key words, cost-per-click advertising, banner exchanges, MySpace, YouTube, Facebook, blogs, and message boards, etc., there are many other things that you can do to maximize your presence on the web in an innovative way to solidify your transient base. Make no mistake, the web alone is very powerful, but it is in conjunction with physical world strategies that it is the most potent.

The web is having an increasing force in the world of politics. Bloggers had a large and direct impact on the Joe Lieberman-Ned Lamont Campaign. They are credited with changing the course of that race working in tandem with news media and a blur of personal appearances by both candidates.

FROM CBSNEWS.COM:

"Let me tell you what that meant to me," Lamont said. "At 52, I didn't know too much about the blogs" early on in the race. Lamont said that when he was invited to speak at Naples Pizza in New Haven, he expected 15 or 20 people to show up. But thanks to blogs, there were "120 people hanging from the rafters. And it was thanks to a lot of grassroots energizers like Chris… that all of a sudden across the state we have all sorts of people turning out."

It's all about content, content, content. Type, blog, video yourself blogging, blog yourself filming, write about the experience of filming yourself while you blog, make a sculpture celebrating the event, and then film it's destruction on the first anniversary of its creation and write about how that makes you feel. You have to move between the web world and the real world. Gracefully, effortlessly, you have to shoot the (pretend, inflatable) dolphin!

With the ocean as the web, the air representing the physical world, and the dolphin as the delivery method, the object of the game is to shoot as many information darts into the dolphin

> **"You have to move between the web world and the real world. Gracefully, effortlessly, you have to shoot the (pretend, inflatable) dolphin!"**

before he disappears below the surface. The more darts, the more people with high-powered rifles you can add to your team. So the next time he surfaces, you can pepper his shiny body with hundreds more message darts, until the dolphin is an unrecognizable message porcupine and the ocean runs red with your marketing genius... OK?

MySpace is a really easy way to look like you have a lot of fans, but it is only one of a great number of communication tools. Don't mistake hits or friends for people who are going to get in a car, drive, park, pay for a ticket, and then hang around in a venue for hours until you play... then buy a shirt or a CD... that's way more effort than clicking a mouse. There are over 100 million members of MySpace and not all of them are coming to your show.

> "Have you uploaded any music videos to YouTube yet? MySpace is so yesterday." - Randall Scott

EBAY

TICKET/CD/MERCHANDISE COMBINATION

As soon as a show is confirmed, we put up a super gig pack, two tickets to the show, an album from each of the bands, a t-shirt, and a poster for a great price. The idea is not to make money; the idea is to get people to commit to going to the show.

If you set the auction up to immediately re-list (using a software solution like Marketworks) you will get the best initial response. The closer you are to the date of the show, the less time you have, and the cooler you need to make your gig pack! Add the most value to the pack without adding the most cost. Bundle the tickets with a live disc that you mastered and burned yourself in a screen-printed sleeve, charge $20 and it's a cool unique deal.

You will also benefit from having cash from advance sales before the show happens, Carefully track the winners and remember you'll need to do a ticket buy the night of the show to reimburse the promoter for your tickets, but the positive cash flow at a critical part of the tour preparation is invaluable. Remember that anything you do on the web is most effective in the middle of the month (farthest removed from rent being due).

Another important benefit of this is early ticket sales and an external barometer for each show.

Example:

Denver is looking great: you have sold ten gig packs and tickets are doing well. You are still four weeks out, same in LA. you have sold 11 gig packs in Albuquerque, but the promoter hasn't sold any tickets. This is a great sign that something is wrong in that market. call the promoter and ask, what's the problem? He might tell you that he had a problem with his ticket printer or the ad just went in the paper. But in any event, you are telling him that you are watching the date and it is not going to be acceptable for him to end up the night of the show shrugging his shoulders, unable to pay you, and saying that he guesses that people in Albuquerque just don't like your band...

Hell, it'll be the first time you actually know of a problem date before show time, right?

KICKING IT UP A NOTCH

Once you regularly practice these basic techniques, it will be easier for you to kick it up a notch in the case of a problem date. Everyone who bought a gig pack from the web site for an important show was entered into a drawing for a $200 iPod loaded with our songs.

Make sure that you let the promoter know what you are doing and that the only unacceptable thing to you is a dead room. Don't get pulled into a situation where you end up buying a ton of tickets to give away—that's for the major labels to do! You are helping the promoter to fill his room with people who drink!! You will be surprised at the leeway this will get you. A full club means food and drinks for the band, merch sales, and an idea that you and the promoter are in on this together. Wonderful.

OTHER STRATEGIES

On Eric Idle's (*Monty Python*) *Greedy Bastard* tour, they eBayed opportunities for audience members to sing the Lumberjack song on stage with him. They raised a substantial amount of money for charity, while promoting the tour and increasing the excitement level around it. Different things work for different bands/acts/audiences. Make sure it's a good fit and it will help!

WEDDINGS

The band Local H had the idea of auctioning off a show somewhere along the route of their tour (see their story later in this chapter). I thought that even if the band didn't end up performing at some fans picnic in their back garden, the idea that they might, or they would, created enough publicity to do the job of publicizing the tour.

So, what could we do that would be different? We started to auction weddings. "Want to get married on stage with Pigface?" It started when a couple, Scott and Kimberly Massie, from Pittsburgh asked if they could

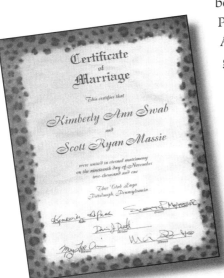

be. I think they met and shagged to Pigface, so it seemed natural to them. An interesting thing happened, we got completely sucked in. I mean, how can you not? The nerves spread; we set them up with tour laminates, champagne, wine coolers, some balloons and 25 tickets to the show. Thank God it was in Pittsburgh; NYC ticket prices would have killed us!

Anyway, we all really liked it; it felt like a real Pigface thing to do. So we kept on doing it!

Four members of the band, past and present, are ordained ministers and the show is so flexible that it lends itself to a wedding at the beginning, halfway through, or at the end. And, honestly, after you've dealt with 45 shows in 45 days, a rotating lineup of 300 members, six trees, and an eight-foot-tall light-up cross, throwing a wedding and making sure that the party (sometimes as many as 30 family and friends backstage) is having a good time is a piece of cake. And yes, we provided that, too.

Overall, we probably lost money every single time we did it, but, holy shit! Do we have some stories… (See *www.tstouring.com*)

> "Overall, we probably lost money every single time we did it, but, holy shit! Do we have some stories…"

THE MAINSTREAM STRANGLE-HOLD ON ALTERNATIVE CULTURE HAS BECOME CHILLINGLY OMNIPRESENT.

JEAN ENCOULE, TRAKMARX

Excerpt from "The State We're In" Address Dec 2006

MySpace, initially the spawning ground for raw, unfettered, underground talent and the virtual exercise yard for zealous self-promotion, has become a brothel of enterprise haunted by cyber A&R men who no longer even have to leave the confines of their plush offices to earn their not-inconsiderable crusts. Like chat-room pedophiles stalking their prey, these masters of virtual reality can turn a challenging idea into a piss-poor marketing concept on the turn of a record. On top of all this, Rupert Murdoch now has an exhaustive collection of sensitive files and information to trade with the security services of the free world, and he hasn't even had to look the word "subversive" up in the dictionary. Not bad for a dude that pays about 1% in taxes!

EBAY
CHRIS RAMOS

CHRIS RAMOS

DOPE GEAR INC.
TOUR MERCH
WEB SALES

Provides a Great Supplement to Online Sales

Pre-selling tickets can be done using eBay. If you use an online tool like Marketworks, you can re-list items automatically. So you could put up a pack that includes a CD and admission to an upcoming show with a "Buy it Now" price that makes sense to you. Every time this item is purchased, a new one will go up and you will be notified by e-mail. This helps you sell tickets while you are working on the other numerous problems of the day.

You can sell gear, clothes used on stage, or other interesting items . You can also package items together in limited quantity in order to make them more attractive to your customers. A pack that includes a shirt, a CD, and a sticker is a great deal for a fan and is an excellent way to move merchandise.

One strategy that has been employed by eBay sellers is to list similar bands in parentheses in the title of the auction. For example, if your band is similar to a commonly searched band such as the White Stripes, you may list it as such Band Name CD w/ t-shirt (The White Stripes). This is not approved by eBay and they may ask you to take this down. When listing Rx CDs, I listed them with (Skinny Puppy, Pigface). This would seem all right to anyone familiar with the band, as it is Ogre of Skinny Puppy and Martin Atkins of Pigface that comprise the band. eBay took issue with this and, after tons of back and forth, the auction listing had to be changed. The way around this is to list your influences in the body of your auction. It is not as effective, but eBay does not have a problem with that.

Marketworks, an online eBay tool, can be very useful.

Adobe Photoshop and a program such as DreamWeaver can also be useful in creating auctions, as the appearance of your auction is quite important. In case you had not noticed, millions of people use eBay, so there is competition.

As I said, eBay is a great supplement. I would not advise you to make it your web store. And do not forget, there needs to be a demand for your items for eBay to be a source of revenue. Therefore, you may want to get out, play some shows, and create a fan base to whom you can sell everything you own on eBay.

EBAY AND LOCAL H
BRIAN ST. CLAIR - LOCAL H

I was a Star Wars freak when I was a kid. I had to have every toy that came out that had the Star Wars logo on it. I didn't just stop there. I wanted to have doubles and sometimes triples of each toy. I would open one to play with and the rest I would display (unopened) on my dresser. The toys were cool. But if you recall, the boxes and packaging of the toys were equally as exciting.

BRIAN ST. CLAIR

TRIPLE FAST ACTION

LOCAL H

tourtimeproductions.com

As I got older, I moved on to record collecting. As a punk rock kid in the 'burbs of Chicago, I was one of few in the early '80s to call himself a punk. I would go to Wax Trax Records in Chicago and Rave On Records in Wheaton any chance I got to buy the newest punk 45s and LPs that I read about in *MRR* (*Maximum Rock & Roll*). While there, I would always pay attention to the record sleeves and, if something stood out and I had enough money, I'd pick that up, too. I got some really cool stuff that way.

When I moved to NYC in 1998, I had all this stuff. Anyone who has been to NYC and has been to or lived in a typical dwelling there: you know what I had to do next. I could have put everything in storage which would have set me back about $200-300 a month, or sell it. After selling most of my records, I learned about eBay. I wish I would have heard of it sooner. I could have made a ton of money on those records. Luckily, most of the records I sold are available on CD now, but that's another story.

I looked to eBay as a way to sell my Star Wars Collection. I spoke to my friends and went online to ask questions to everyone that had an opinion on eBay. I watched auction after auction to see how people bid. When I felt comfortable enough, I started slow. I would put up a record, an old lamp, a punk rock button, an old concert t-shirt, etc. In five months, I had about 30 positive marks to my name on eBay. I knew if I were to get the best price for each Star Wars toy, I'd have to look good to the eBay-ers out there. When I got to this point, I was ready. It took me about six months to sell it all. I wanted to spread it out so that someone could bid week after week with each paycheck they got. I knew no one would have been able to get it all, so I gave lots of opportunity to everyone to bid. I even opened the auctions up to the world, not just the U.S. This way, someone with money in Japan or London could have a bidding war with that kid on the East Coast.

In the end, I was able to pay for my entire wedding at the Ritz Carlton in Cancun, Mexico. We had 26 guests and I still had some money left over.

Local H was in need of a publicity push and some extra cash. We were trying to figure out what we could do. We had just toured and we couldn't go out right away.

I started to think, why couldn't we sell a show on eBay? I mapped it all out. It would cost $500 to get us anywhere we needed to go in the lower 48 states. If the show ended up on the West Coast, we could make a run out of it. If it landed on the East Coast, it could be one show in and one out. Or if in the Mid-West, it's a one-off. We wrote up an auction description with the help of our old manager, Eddie Applebaum. He ran with it. He told our label what we were going to do and that we wanted any and all press to know about this. He e-mailed and called all of our fans at papers and magazines to let them know to watch eBay on the opening date. You can link to stories about this on *pollstar.com, mtv.com,* and *goliath.ecnext.com.* The auction raised eyebrows and got us an amazing amount of press, not only online and in print, but MTV did a few TV news spots on the auction. It ended up just shy of $10,000.

We have toyed with the idea of an eBay Tour, but it hasn't happened yet.

- **Learn to build a buzz without spending money!** Pull in other details when you send out press releases. Besides "your band," combine your shows with "events" such as fund raisers, etc.

- **Generate free press!** Cut through the mundane bullshit of all the other regular stories. Think big!

- **Automatically re-list eBay ticket auctions.**

- **Use every avenue open to you.**

- **Be creative**—that's the main energy you need to market virally.

- **Don't relax**—get your information and your auctions up as soon as you can.

- **Good ideas are priceless.**

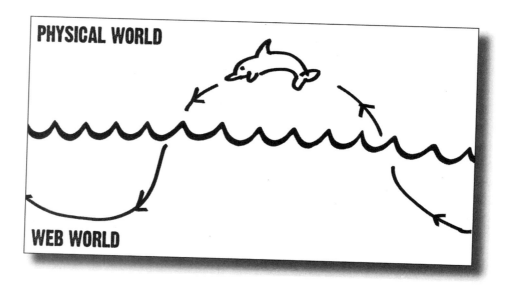

* No real or pretend inflatable dolphins were harmed during the writing of this chapter!

C·H·A·P·T·E·R····18

RADIO: GET HEARD

"If you are looking for a job as a Radio DJ, forget it."

Radio has changed a lot over the last few years. With the consolidation of major markets, an emphasis on playing what people want to hear, and pleasing the advertisers, it's become bigger, big business. It's not some 2 a.m., fuck-off, college DJ connecting distant dots across a wide musical spectrum, driven—not by conformity and the need to fit snugly within a massaged demographic—but by pure delight in music.

There aren't any jobs. I see commercials on TV showing some guy with headphones and "cool chicks" doing what I guess people think DJs do on the radio. They might as well run a clip from the old sitcom *WKRP in Cincinnati*. The whole idea is as real as Loni Anderson's tits.

There are more opportunities with internet radio, but there's a fractured, staggered element to the timing in which people discover new things. Satellite radio has shredded the hit power of the commercial stations… More opportunities are there, but with less impact and fewer listeners. There's no such thing as "number one with a bullet" anymore. It's just low-powered buckshot tickling the barn door, not blasting a hole in it. Is this long-tail theory? I like to think of it as the long-tale theory: too long, unedited, unfiltered, and really boring at the end.

MARKETING SERVICES

We've used many different services to market and promote music to radio. You can selectively target these services to hit college radio, specialty radio (which might be the ambient, overnight show), satellite services, commercial specialty, and full-on commercial radio in the same way you would target a club night that is geared toward your genre. To say that this is a grey area would be an understatement. There are good budget services that will get your music out to college radio. We have used Space 380 and others for this. These services are a delegation of workload rather than a cure-all.

As you aim higher, the target gets much harder to hit. You might have some trouble defining what the compensation should be. Larger companies intelligently use artists' hopes, ambitions, and preconceived ideas of the definition of success to extract a high, morally-suspect toll. All of this simply to gain entrance to the freeway that may or may not lead to superstardom. Look at the wording used in their ads. Read everything cynically. One of my favorite glitter-sprinkled come-ons was this: "It takes a lot of work to win a Grammy for Best Rock Song, and here at … we pride ourselves on blah, blah, blah…" I was halfway through the first paragraph

> "The whole idea is as real as Loni Anderson's tits."

> "There's no such thing as "number one with a bullet" anymore. It's just low-powered buckshot tickling the barn door, not blasting a hole in it.."

on the red carpet; my imaginary Grammy was slipping in my sweaty hands. The flashes in my face were making me a little bit dizzy as I smiled at Cindy Crawford and the guy from *24*... before I realized it was total meaningless shit. I read their ad three more times and realized exactly what they were saying: Nothing. Absolutely nothing. In a really big way.

Apply a simple standard to this and everything: It might not be sexy, cool, or fashionable, but think of what your dad would say if you told him you were spending 10,000 on a used car. He'd probably say something about maintenance records, kicking the tires, and would call you back within an hour with some information from a consumer reports website and ask you for the VIN number. I don't want to tell you to always think of your parents before you get shagged, but this would be one of the good times to do that.

There aren't many places to go anymore that will get you any radio attention. But the role of the ones that remain, as a filter and nurturer of the scene, is increasingly important. You will be very lucky to receive time and input from someone like Chris Payne at Q101. Think about it. The guy has listened to everything. In amongst the homogenizing, the consolidating and the other avenues, we lose sight of the fact that instant exposure through MySpace or a band web site comes without advice or guidance. This is not always a good thing. He has some great advice...

RADIO TIPS

CHRIS PAYNE LOCAL Q101

The most important thing that bands must realize is that we (radio people) receive an incredible amount of CDs from bands wanting to get their shit played on the radio. I get about 20-30 and sometimes 40 CDs in the mail every week. No kidding! The first thing I do is open all the mail and put it in a big stack. One on top of the other. I'm rarely able to listen to it all in one sitting; so many CDs will stay in the ever growing stack as each week goes by. Then eventually, I'll get an e-mail or phone call asking if I received the disc. So I'll turn to my "stack" to locate the disc in question. The only CDs I can read are those in regular, large, CD jewel cases. All of the CDs that are forwarded in the paper or thin CD jewel cases are lost from my quick view. Sometimes lost forever. The point here is: if the disc case is too thin to identify the band name on the spine or edge of the jewel case, it will get passed over. It's a pain to go through my "stack" and look at each CD when I could have looked at the edge of the stack of CDs to discover the next Pigface. If you are giving your disc away at a show or to friends on your MySpace, then send them a CD inside a thin jewel case. If you're sending it to radio, put it in a thick jewel case with a spine identifying the name of the band. It will get your stuff heard quicker.

Please don't send a high school style folder with bio and CD info. All I need is the disc, phone number, e-mail, list of clubs played, and track listing. I don't need a list of each musician, his/her bio, and instruments played. Personally, I don't care who is in the band unless they have played in another locally or nationally reputable band. Finally, let me know if the band is actually out playing gigs. Honestly, if your band isn't playing live shows, you are a long way away from any commercial air play.

If a band can somehow get some face time with me, I am more likely to seek out their disc to review for on-air play. The long and short of it, it's harder to ignore a face-to-face meeting than it is to put off listening to a mailing. Also, if I'm out at an appearance and a band gives me their disc, I'll listen to it on the way home after my gig at the local *Pizza Hut* or whatever event I am promoting.

> **"Honestly, if your band isn't playing live shows, you are a long way away from any commercial air play."**

> **"Always put your best couple of tracks first."**

Always put your best couple of tracks first. If your best track is number 4 or later, I may not even get to hear it.

Believe it or not, but gimmicks work with me. I figure if a band takes the time to do something creative to get their CD heard, then I owe it to them to listen to it and sometimes, even if I don't like the disc, I may even be inclined to play it and let the audience decide.

If a band sends a package via express delivery, I typically open it first. I assume it is time sensitive so I'll open it up right away and check it out.

If you can get a band that I already play to vouch for your band and have them give me your disc, it may carry a lot of weight when it comes to my evaluation. I'm going to give a band the benefit of the doubt if a band I already respect and play on the show has vouched for your band.

Please, please, please advise me as to the songs on your CD that have profanity. It does us both no good if I get fired because in the last 15 seconds of a track, which I never listened to before putting on the air, your singer is belting out lyrics with a myriad of profanity. Better yet, if you think the song is "on-air" worthy then make an edit. Even Tool submits an edited version of tracks they anticipate could be spun on the radio. And I'm sure your band isn't as angsty as Tool.

RADIO PROMOTION (FROM SPACE380):

www.space380.com

WHAT IS IT?

The act of researching radio stations, verifying their contact information, sending CDs to the stations, and following up on the status of the CD at each station. Keeping the Music Director at each station informed of the artist's current successes is crucial.

NON-COMMERCIAL RADIO

College, High School, Public, & Community Radio Stations, we actively work with about 500 non-commercial stations.

COMMERCIAL RADIO

Radio stations that run commercials on air to pay the bills. Most stations playing mainstream music found on BET, MTV, VH1, or CMT are commercial stations. We actively work with about 300 commercial stations.

INTERNET RADIO

Radio stations that exclusively broadcast music streams via the internet. We also include other commercial and non-commercial stations that broadcast via the internet, as well as terrestrial means.

SATELLITE RADIO

Stations broadcasting via satellites offering crystal clear, no commercial audio to thousands of subscribers.

Keith Levene, John Lydon, Jah Wobble, Martin Atkins 1980, Boston.

Photo by Phil in Phlash

> ***BE NICE!*** *In 1981, PiL arrived in the U.S. On the second night we were in the country, we had an interview scheduled at WBCN radio in Boston. The late night (or overnight) DJ was Oedipus, his assistant was Carter Alan. Within a few years, both of them had grown into the most influential DJs in the Boston area.*

THE PROCESS OF DEVELOPING MEDIA EXPOSURE

JEFF MCCLUSKY

Our company became the primary dominating company in radio promotion through the 80s, 90s, and the last few years. There are many companies that did the same thing, but we became known as the main company in the industry. It was, throughout that time period, the most important method or vehicle to help support an act to sell recordings. Or course, during that time, an act that was developing a marketing plan had to make sure that their media plan, web plan, and touring plan were all in the proper stages and at the proper time.

The time element is one of the most important factors in radio. Let's say that today radio still had the largest audience concentration and you could monitor radio airplay, impression, audience, and quality with sales. That's still the case. What's shifted in radio, depending on format, is that it has taken a position of conservatism. However, the impact is still there. Someone has to be careful enough to know when to attempt that portion of the exposure campaign. It's important for a band to be surrounded by good advice.

Up until five or six years ago, you had enough formats—especially in new music exposure, rhythm and blues, hip-hop, alternative—that you could get a CD played on specialty and college radio, mixed to create impact. The biggest shift has been that today, the business doesn't work because not a lot of songs are hits. In today's business, it's an audience of one to 100 million. This means developing your song which ultimately means developing your band. Don't underestimate the marketing of just one song. In the business of artist development, the development of the plan and the process of the timing of the *MySpace* page, *YouTube*, the live performance, and attention from *Pitchfork* and *The Reader,* is critical. Because of this, radio is still an important part, but much later in the process and, in fact, more often than not in today's independent music sector, not applicable. Radio is not even trying to be the Discovery Channel; it's just trying to play the hits.

I get calls all the time to help get songs on the radio. I am doing more work with advertising agencies, placements, film, and other parts of that audience of one to 100 million. The conversion of my company and the relevance shift means that I had to be able to maneuver in all those areas. I could still just be a radio promotion company if I wanted to, but I like to be in the artist development business. We have those other facets in the growth stages.

I've worked on some song licensing deals over the last year and a half and we placed some songs in film, but, again, that means we turned down more people than we accepted. If we could help you get on the radio, we would view that in terms of what we perceive to be a proper amount of audience tracking in other areas of media. If you're a band on Invisible and

> "It's an audience of one to 100 million."

you come in and say, "Can you get indie radio play?" My answer would be no. Even if we could with you not having an underlying growth factor or audience acceptance factor, we'd probably fail at radio. We don't want to fail because we didn't have the right foundation.

MA: Everything's tougher now. Are you mindful of your reputation and position in the marketplace?

JM: I like to think that's correct and I think it's important. A fairly significant artist came to me from an indie label and I turned down the work because I believed his release would fail and then I'd have to argue for my retainer fee.

MA: And then the artist is saying "I paid Jeff McClusky $5,000 and I only got five spins."

JM: I'd rather turn the business down. I still find that when you tell people: "Come in for a meeting and let's talk about media, MySpace, etc." I still have people say to me, "Well OK, but can you help me get on the radio?" Those artists who are excited about this new business we're in today have to see themselves as entrepreneurs in the Wild West, where the winners are undetermined. The job description for success in today's business says that you have to work.

In the height of the '90s, the manager could learn his craft by default from the record company people. That doesn't work today. The manager today really has to be the president of the independent artist's business.

I could very well end up moving in publishing. It's the only area of the recorded music business that has seen increases in the past few years. The value of the copyright seems to be growing, hence the incredible interest in BMG and any catalog that's available.

MA: How do you see the role of touring fit in with all the other activities?
JM: Critical.

MA: What's the definition of success in the music business today in terms of developing artists?
JM: There's the artist business and there's the song business and they're not the same thing. That doesn't mean that if I want to be in the artist business developing bands, that merchandising isn't critical to me. I want to go to Beat Kitchen, Schubas, Metro, House of Blues, and then the Riv in Chicago and I want to be able to make the right t-shirt deal or make my own shirts. The biggest revenue generators (not the biggest record sellers) last year were Rolling Stones, U2, and Madonna because of tickets and merchandising.

MA: What do you see for the future?
JM: Years back, the record company was the bank and the bank had a lock on distribution, radio promotion, and superior relationships with retail, A&R, and marketing. Now, the bank is whoever has the check.

The playing fields are more level now. Too many people ask me about things that they don't know that they don't need anyway. If Wal-Mart calls, you'll figure it out. If and when the time is right, you'll know. The major record labels are all bleeding. WB may have 50 people and are licensing music. Artist development campaigns will be through small labels who know how to develop bands at small costs. In the last three years, RCA and Capitol Records closed. What does that say about our industry?

MA: What is your view on opportunities in the business?
JM: It's the best time the business has seen in 30 years. It's an entrepreneurial business where the growth area is artist-owned and based in independent record labels. You have to be able

> "The manager today really has to be the president of the independent artist's business."

to learn and roll up your sleeves. Learn to be the artist, the manager, the associates, the virtual teams. There are virtual teams that can be outsourced for anything, which is exciting.

But the definition of what the business will look like entirely is best described as Chris Anderson's "Long Tail Theory." In the last two years, we saw the top-selling albums go from eight million to four million units sold, so we can see the digital situation. If they don't fix that, there will be no business. Until people can download once and transfer easily, they'll never solve the problem. Whether or not music will be free and sponsored by Coca-Cola depends on the ease of transference. It's a 12:1 ratio. Fifteen billion songs were traded last year. You're not going anywhere with that figure. Giving away downloads is what indies can do. Columbia Records can't say that.

MA: Peter Katsis (The Firm) is doing partnership deals with bands. Maybe that's an answer.

JM: Jury's out on that one. It seems to make sense that a company would partner in all revenue streams. I get the argument that when the record company invests the money to build up the brand and then ends up limited to only one revenue stream. But that's up to the artist. You're not going to get The Rolling Stones or Bruce Springsteen to give up those numbers, but for a new artist it could be attractive. I think that people will fight if there's too much in one pot. I think artists like to have everything in individual pots. More often than not, people like to separate those.

MA: We started acquiring merch rights. It's all gone madly entrepreneurial. I haven't seen that level of thought from artists or bands. Have you?

JM: I'd have to think about it, but I think the answer is yes, such as Arcade Fire, the first million-copy-selling alternative band. JMA will be involved with a small part of radio promotion campaign and radio is appropriate because of four sold-out nights at the Chicago Theater. They shipped 400,000 records and they have a series of press reviews that reminds me of U2 in 1983. The pieces are all in place and radio is kicking through the field goal or giving them the last piece. When I talked about it with program directors who aren't familiar with the band at alternative radio, I say that's irresponsible. You should know this. That's showing some kind of sense of the marketplace.

MA: Do you find that the 400,000 unit ship-out becomes a very important tool in getting someone to listen to you?

JM: So do sold-out nights and front-page articles in *The Chicago Tribune* by Greg Kott.

MA: I suspect there was a time a when you used to tell people how good their music sounds.

JM: Today, I played Arcade Fire to a group of students and told them that it reminded me of U2 in 1983. If your observation is talking about something in terms of, "I want you to hear this music," that's what my business is. It's about finding something we get over the top about. When people ask me what I do, I say, "I tell people about artists and music that I like." Part two is giving them statistics. Should someone listen to Arcade Fire because it shipped 400,000 units or because all I can say is "Wow?" That's the same statement I made in '76 when I was at Columbia: "You gotta hear this: Bruce Springsteen, Journey!"

:SMART TIPS

1. **Call the radio stations** that are playing your music and thank them!

2. **Tour! Get out on the road,** it could be the reason that your CD gets played instead someone else's.

3. **If you're sending your CD to a radio station, put it in a thick jewel case** with a spine identifying the name of the band. It will get your stuff heard quicker.

4. **Always put your best couple of tracks first.** If your best track is number four or later, the DJ will not get to hear it.

5. **If you can get a band that a DJ or radio station already plays to vouch for your band** and have them give the station your disc, it may carry a lot of weight when it comes to the DJ's or station's evaluation. You could also form an alliance with this band by gigging!

6. **Post radio station request line phone numbers,** e-mail addresses, and web site info on your web site to enable your fans to contact them easily.

7. **Roll up your sleeves and work.**

CHAPTER 19

RECORD STORES

The climate at record stores, both independent and chain, is changing everyday. Paul McCartney just signed to Starbucks' new record label (I was hoping he would have held out for McDonalds or at least Subway—so they could introduce the Yellow Submarine). Tower Records filed for bankruptcy in 2006. There are 179 Virgin Records around the world. There are 13,168 Starbucks (7,521 self-operated and 5,647 licensed) world wide and 3,331 Wal-Marts in the U.S. alone. There are web based alternatives, MySpace music/Snocap, CD Baby, and new technologies every day. It's getting tighter everywhere and more expensive to purchase programs to get your CDs in record store bins or on their shelves, and harder to get any kind of attention from anywhere. With other (let's say "less conventional") outlets making CDs available (Hot Topic, the Post Office, for fuck's sake), everyone's feeling the pinch. You need to stay creative and stay on the road where you have your own mini-store set up each night.

> "You need to stay creative and stay on the road where you have your own mini-store set up each night."

INDEPENDENT RECORD STORES

Independent record stores have always been a beacon in the wilderness. Although their role has changed with the advent of the Internet, their role as a filter is still important.

The ones that are still around have diversified and grown into coffee houses and live venues that sell comics, magazines, t-shirts, books, skateboards, DVDs, etc. They still remain an informational hub with a corresponding web presence. However, they are swamped by everyone thinking inside the box. Over the last two years assembling the book, I received calls back from just about anybody I placed a call to. But it was the six or seven indie stores I called that were by far the most difficult people to get any kind of a response from. They are all nice people and fans of great music, they're just really, really, busy trying to keep it going. You have to look at other options to get your music and your message out there

> Jaded clubs and record stores go out of their way to make field reps feel unwelcome when they are putting up flyers around town. The interesting discovery I made is: don't let them waste your energy. Move right along to a slightly different path, like clothing or book stores of all kinds. I found people there to be more appreciative of field rep work and I know for a fact that it brought out people to shows who otherwise would not have even known about them. The lesson is that it pays to go places that are not so obvious. You can meet some really great people that way.
> – *David Nicholas (Field Rep, Washington DC)*

CONSIGNMENT

A common way for small bands to get their CDs into stores is consignment. If the store thinks they can sell some, they'll agree to take some from you on consignment. If they sell, you get paid. It's important to remember that CDs won't sell just because they are in a store, there needs to be a reason. The piece of string is pulled not pushed (thanks Mike J.). Some stores won't do consignment anymore. They're too busy.

INCENTIVES

I had a look at my weekly e-mail from Eric at Criminal Records in Atlanta, a store that has continued to grow and diversify. Have a long, hard look at the free stuff being given away with releases... this is what you are competing with!

FREE. BONUS. STUFF. YAY!

--**FREE numbered limited edition lithography** with purchase of the new Walkmen CD "Pussy Cats"

--**FREE autographed Ben Folds CD sleeve** with purchase of "SuperSunnySpeedGraphic"

--**FREE poster** with purchase of the new Dredge CD "Live at the Fillmore"

--**FREE Deftones lanyard** with the purchase of "Saturday Night Wrist"

--**FREE Mutemath fold out poster** with the purchase of their new self-titled album

--**FREE 7"** with purchase of the new Rise Against album "The Sufferer and the Witness"

--**FREE live 2 song DVD** with the purchase of Robert Randolph's new CD "Color Blind"

--**FREE mini acoustic concert DVD** with purchase of My Morning Jacket album "Okonokos"

--**FREE poster** with purchase of the new Willie Nelson album "Songbird"

--**FREE lithograph poster** with the purchase of the new Sparta record "Threes"

--**FREE non-album tracks bonus disc** with purchase of the new Chrome Children compilation

--**FREE bonus EP** with purchase of the new Mason Jennings CD "Boneclouds"

--**FREE poster** with the purchase of Sean Lennon's "Friendly Fire"

--**FREE remix CD single** "O Menina" with the purchase of Beck's "The Information"

--**FREE lithograph** with purchase of the new Sparklehorse CD

--**FREE bonus EP** with purchase of Citizen Cope

--**FREE Mars Volta poster** with the purchase of their new CD "Amputechture"

--**FREE bonus EP** with 3 unreleased live tracks with purchase of the new Los Lobos album

--**FREE bandana** with purchase of The Bronx self-titled release that is also on sale right now!

--**FREE download of a non-album track & a cool bike plate** with purchase of Cursive's "Happy Hollow"

--**FREE bonus track downloads with the purchase of these artists new releases:**

--The Black Keys "Magic Potion," Jet "Shine On," The Killers "Sam's Town," and Yusuf (Cat Stevens) "An Other Cup," The Decemberists " The Crane Wife"

LARGER INDIE CHAINS AND COALITIONS

There are notable success stories in the indie store world. Amoeba on the West Coast wields almost radio station-like power in the world of grooviness and tastemakers. On the East Coast, Newbury Comics has grown from one or two stores (Boston and Providence) in the mid to late '80s to 27 stores and still prides itself on representing cool, indie music. There are coalitions of indie stores that function as a collective with one voice making it easy to create larger regional coverage while maintaining an indie store relationship. These are CIMS, with 70 stores in 24 states, and AIMS, with 29 stores in 21 cities.

THE COALITION OF INDEPENDENT MUSIC STORES

http://www.cimsmusic.com/

The Coalition of Independent Music Stores (CIMS) is a group of some of the best independent music stores in America. CIMS was founded in 1995; its current membership is made up of 31 accounts that handle 70 stores in 24 states. Many of the accounts have been recognized by the music industry and their local communities for their outstanding dedication to customer service and developing artist support.

One thing many of us have learned from our experiences: we always recommend building a local story before trying to go nationwide. There is little need to have your product sitting on a shelf if you are not able to actively promote it in a particular market, whether it is through touring or radio airplay. As an independent artist, it is always best to focus your energies on a handful of areas in which you can build your audiences and develop relationships with the right club bookers, store owners, and radio staff. New technologies now allow you to have your music heard around the world via the internet, but nothing beats human interaction to get the word out about your labor of love.

ALLIANCE OF INDEPENDENT MEDIA STORES

http://www.thealliancerocks.com

We're the Alliance of Independent Media Stores (or AIMS for short), a group made up of forward-thinking music stores across the country dedicated to bringing you the best music shopping experience possible. AIMS stores are all locally owned and are widely different in "look and feel," but are united in their dedication to putting artistic integrity ahead of mass-market commercial hype. In other words, it's about the music.

AIMS stores are located coast to coast and our membership currently stands at 29 stores in 21 cities. We are not a chain, but rather an association of independent stores working together to benefit our customers and record label partners. Visit any of us and you'll find a wide selection of music that goes far deeper than most mass-market retailers (including formats such as vinyl and DVDs at most of our stores). Through our combined efforts we're also able to work with record labels to bring you special issue CDs that you simply cannot find at any chain store, period. You'll also meet staffers who are passionate and knowledgeable about music, and ready to provide a level of service that you won't find elsewhere. Remember when record stores were cool? We're still living it.

If you're with a record label, AIMS is ready to work with you to help bring your artists to our customers. We offer both audio and video listening station programs, online marketing support, and can tailor a promotional program to your specific ideas. Inclusion in programs is determined by a vote of all AIMS members, ensuring the integrity of our marketing efforts. All of our stores are Soundscan reporters, and most also report sales to CMJ and StreetPulse. Our sales chart appears weekly in *CMJ New Music Report,* as well as being an element of the *Billboard Tastemakers* chart.

CHAIN STORES

Here's the reality at chain stores. Music isn't in the chain stores to sell music; it's in the chain stores to sell toasters, microwaves, and flat screen TVs. It has always cost a lot of money to participate in a program at the chain store level. Now, the chain stores are demanding Soundscan sales performance of at least 750-1,000 units in the first week. They're looking to bring in a quantity of 5,000 units; below that and they're just not interested. Whereas we used to have CDs sit at stores for six or nine months, Best Buy is interested in your initial first week and a two or three week supply after that. If you have a CD that doesn't sell, that's it. It doesn't matter if you put Elvis fucking Presley on your next CD. It's going to take an awful lot of convincing and more money for you to get any chain store to stock it. The phrase "You only get one chance to make a good first impression" has never been more true. Bands that petition me for a deal based on nothing but the idea that if I get their CD into a well-known chain they will sell more just don't get it. If I could convince a well-known chain to take 5,000 units, it might cost me $5,000 plus the cost of the 5,000 CDs plus whatever print, radio, and other activities I would have to finance to try and make sure those CDs left the store very quickly. That's a $15,000 roll of the dice I'm not prepared to make.

INSTORES

AS A BUILDING TOOL

Forget it. I spoke to an owner of one of the "Top 20 Indie Stores in the U.S." He said that there was not much you could do as an unsigned band even if you advertise in a local paper. The real underground shuns advertising. Those bands sell stuff at shows and maybe just put some flyers in the stores. And as far as instores go, they cost money and they are business killers for the store, sometimes with only three or four people showing up. He remembered one band

with several albums out on a major independent label that had eight people show up—two of whom were parents of the band members. He said that people are too busy to check out something they haven't heard of. The indie stores don't buy product from touring bands anymore because "you just get stuck with the fucking product."

The store owner asked not to be named.

FOR MORE ESTABLISHED BANDS

More prominent artists are doing short acoustic instore appearances before their band's larger venue appearance later that night. This only works if your band already has a draw and acts as a cool, supportive thing you can do for the indie store while they are being cool and supportive of your band. But, pay attention. Look at what just happened to your workload. Now, after sound-check at the venue, you need to jump into your transportation to the store. Do you have the acoustic guitar? Who's got the picks? Where's the tuner? Is it easy to get a cab back over to the venue? Does the singer get to eat? (See the piece from my SG column in *Personality, Ego, and Charisma*).

AUTOGRAPH SEEKERS—Public Image obliges fans with autographs and some merry chit-chat at the New England Music City in Boston. The British group was in town as part of its first American tour.

CO-OP ADVERTISING
YOU PAY FOR PLACEMENT (NEAR THE FRONT OF A RACK, LISTENING STATIONS, EVERYTHING!)

Co-op advertising is the name given to advertising in stores to guarantee (yeah) better placement within the store, a listening station, or inclusion in a multi-cut ad.

> **"But, pay attention. Look at what just happened to your workload..."**

A simple co-op here in Chicago could be with *The Onion* paper and the Chicago-based Reckless Records store where they would feature your CD for sale at their two stores, take out an ad, and mention the show at a local venue. At least the chances of monetizing that are better either from increased ticket sales at the venue, increased shirt sales at the venue, CD sales, etc. You might just have a better chance at booking a show if the venue knows you and/or your label is advertising on your behalf. The cost for something like this can be $200 to $400 depending on the city and the paper. A label would usually coordinate this.

Other typical indie co-op deals would be:

- One cut in a multi-cut full page ad in the local paper with one month CD sale pricing between $180-$200.

- Listening station—around $100/month/store.

- Other stores will come up with a package deal—an ad in their instore paper maybe with a decent review. Four weeks of sale pricing and positioning, a piece of a multi-cut ad, and placement on the website would typically cost around $1,000 for a two to three store chain.

> **"Its important to remember that CDs won't sell just because they are in a store—there needs to be a reason."**

YOU HAVE TO POLICE YOUR PROGRAMS

All of these programs need to be policed. Once again you're dealing with human beings and if you're not following up on a listening station then the response might have been great but the store could forget to re-order. One of the staff might have replaced your CD with theirs. One of the easiest ways to protect your investment in an indie co-op deal is to let the record stores know that you'll be on tour and stopping by within a month.

> *During the campaign for Sheep On Drugs, we spent $3,000 to participate in a chain-wide video campaign where we would furnish 3 x 30 second clips from three different songs which would be featured three times each on a one hour video loop that would be played chain wide, tagging that the CD was available in stores. We asked our street teams to go out to as many of the stores as they could and send us a report. It was horrifying:*
>
> *"My manager says the system isn't working right now."*
>
> *"They didn't receive the tape this month—they are still playing last month's."*
>
> *"We lost the tape." Etc.*
>
> *It was so bad that, after typing up all of the information sent to us by our street teams and submitting it to Caroline Distribution, the company concerned gave us an extra month. Quite how they made that happen I didn't want to find out. The last thing I wanted to do at that point was send the reps out again to see what the results were...*

WHAT MAKES A GOOD INSTORE AND MORE
MIKE JOHNSON, RECKLESS RECORDS, CHICAGO

MA: What makes a good instore?

MJ: The most important thing to keep in mind when trying to set up an instore appearance is that record stores are places of business, and an instore is always disruptive to that business. What makes an instore worth doing from the store's perspective is if the artist brings fans or customers into the store who otherwise would not have been there. It's also obviously not very worthwhile for the artist to do an instore appearance if the only people there are the staff and five customers who are just trying to shop.

If you feel that you have enough fans in the town you are visiting to try for an instore, there is a clear benefit to advertising the event, not just by having flyers distributed, but actually taking out an ad in whatever local paper people read for show listings. Not only will it help people to find out about the event, but a record store will be much more likely to entertain the idea of doing an instore if you (or your label) are willing to put some money towards advertising the event and the store.

MA: When should a band do instores?

MJ: As I mentioned before, if you do not have enough of a following in the town you're going to in order to bring people out to the store for the event, then you shouldn't bother trying to do it. Focus your energy on promoting the tour in other ways, try to get onto a college radio show, make sampler CDs advertising your tour date and send those to someone at the record store to give away, ask the record store to hang posters for your show, etc. These are things that may help your band which may encourage the record store to stock your CD. (Important to keep in mind: if you do an instore and nobody comes to see you play for free, how likely is the record store going to be to stock your CD?)

MA: What makes a bad instore?

MJ: An instore with no fans. An instore with a band that plays way too loud (acoustics are much different in a small record store than in a night club). An instore with a band that plays way too long. Bands that continually encourage people to "Come up to the front!" This is annoying enough when it happens at night clubs (usually if you're playing to 150 people at a club, but there is a 20-foot space in front of the stage with no people, there's a reason for that... best not to call attention to it over the mic), but it's even worse when the people you're bugging to pay attention to you are only there to shop anyway!

MA: Have bands been rude (or worse?) at instores? How does that affect your future dealings with them?

MJ: Every occasion I can remember, the bands that I've dealt with from instores have been really nice, and I've never had any negative experiences. Obviously if a band did come to our store and acted like jerks, we wouldn't have them back and we would remember that when making purchasing decisions, etc. But, like I said earlier, record stores are businesses first, and even though it's not particularly fair, there's obviously got to be an exception if it's some huge buzz band that's going to get a ton of kids into the store spending money... So I guess we get back to the age-old rule of rock 'n' roll which is, unfortunately, if a ton of people like your band, you get to do pretty much whatever you want.

MA: If a band has a poor-selling CD, does that affect the quantity of the next cd you bring in?

MJ: Absolutely.

MA: Do you like to be invited to shows?

MJ: It's always nice to get invited... even if we don't go to the show. Another great thing to do is, if you have the ability to add more people onto your guest list, ask the store if they can give away a few free passes to the show for you, either by sending something out to their e-mail list or by putting a small box on the counter where people can fill in their name for a drawing. This is not only great promotion for your show and gives the store a chance to give something away to some of their customers, but if the store gets many responses from people interested in getting the free passes, it may very well impress upon the staff that you have some fans who might buy your CD if it is stocked!

MA: How do you feel if you are invited but someone has forgotten to put you on the list?

MJ: That's completely annoying, unprofessional, and happens more often than you would think. If you aren't going to follow through on an invitation for a guest list spot, don't even think about making the offer in the first place.

MA: Do you hang posters for every band coming to town?

MJ: We would like to, but with how many shows there are in Chicago, we only have space for about a third of the posters we get... make your posters look rad and they're way more likely to get some window space.

MA: How many packages a week do you get from bands that want you to listen, order, and put up a poster?

MJ: A ton. It's never a bad idea to call the store ahead of time and ask if you can send a package (they'll almost always say go ahead), because then you can find out someone's name to send the package "attn:" to. It's also a good idea to write on the outside of the envelope something like "Dated materials for show on August 15th."

MA: How has the internet affected your store?

MJ: In so many ways, it's probably a more involved question than I can really go into here in all aspects... Like many record stores, we do mail order online, we have a MySpace page, and we constantly use the Internet to gauge pricing for rare records that come into the store. It doesn't seem like online retailers have that much of an impact on retail record sales. People still shop at record stores and I don't see that changing anytime soon.

CHAPTER····20

GUEST LIST

The guest list is where you place record store owners, radio DJs, press, retail, fan club, street teams, friends, and anyone else you want to come to the show and see the band. It allows you to invite people who might not want to pay to see your band, but may come to your show if it is free. It is important to make sure that you can meet these people face to face. Any problem with the guest list is a big one and it will probably unfold in front of a crowd. You will probably embarrass the person you most want to impress in front of, at best, a line of people; and, at worst, their friends and a line of people. Therefore, you must pay attention. This is your responsibility. Why? Because you will pay the price.

> When I'm invited to a show but they forget to put my name on the list, it's completely annoying, unprofessional, and happens more often than you would think. If you aren't going to follow through on an invitation for a guest list spot, don't even think about making the offer in the first place. **–Mike Johnson of Reckless Records**

When I'm out with a package tour, I walk ten miles a day, or at least it feels like it. I try to make three or four trips to look at the guest list at the door of the venue, especially in the first 30 minutes after doors open. (Take two or three trips in the first hour if you can). This is helpful in case there is a problem. Hopefully, your guests will wait around for a little while to try and get the problem resolved. You are also communicating to the door staff that this stuff is important to you so that it will become a little more important to them. The earlier you do this, the better.

Set up an Excel spreadsheet with the first name and last name in separate columns so you can alphabetically sort the list for the door man. Put additional guests for each person in a separate column. I also like to keep track of where the person is from in a category column and who put that person on the list. For instance, you may have people from local record stores, tattoo parlors, and radio stations, not to mention journalists or band guests. This allows you to look back and see what was what. You will also need it sorted by category for settlement if it's a large list. On a package tour, you want to have the other bands and labels involved all harassing you for larger and larger guest list requests. This means that they are doing their job and people want to go. The guest list Excel sheet is also where you should allocate backstage passes, after show, all access, photo passes, etc.

In the case of an extensive guest list on a Friday night in New York City, you are going to want to be able to alphabetize the list at the last possible minute, bump up the type size to 16-point font, and hand it directly to the doorman. The repercussions of an important person being missed on the guest list are so easy to avoid, it is crazy not to take the extra step. The doorman

> "The repercussions of an important person being missed on the guest list are so easy to avoid, it is stupid not to take the extra step."

will know you are trying to help him when you hand him a 160-name, five-page list that is neatly typed *and* alphabetized. Also, it makes all of the other so-called professionals with their handwritten, torn, coffee ring-stained, multicolored pen guest lists look like wankers. At the end of the night settlement, get the marked-up list back to see if the record store guy showed up or if your street team showed up, etc.

> *I remember a manager who was determined to use a North American tour as a signing platform for her European artist. However, on the entire tour, she only asked us for four guest list slots. That's all you need to know that she was simply not doing her job. The band didn't get signed.*

As a package tour producer, or just a guy in a band, you are going to want to sit down with the promoter, go over your guest list during the settlement, and argue that local press and record store staff, etc., should be on the house list. This negotiation can only happen if you have the information and keep track of it.

First	Last	Guests	Reason	Company
Heather	Ash		Whatever Tattoo 1	
Shelley	Ashton	1	ryko	
Dawn	Avagliano		ryko	
Mark	Babec	1		
Les	Barany	1	HR Geigers Manager	curse
Bruce	Bart	3		curse
Damien	Bart	1		curse
James	Beck	1	online	
Mike	Bellamy	1	Triple X Tattoo	curse
Christopher	Blosser		email	
Steve	Blush	1		curse
R.H.	Boeckel		Bile	krztoff
Steve	Bonge		Tatooist	
Greta	Brinkman	1	moby	
Bill	Burcalow		email	
Michael	Caccavale		email	
Michael	Carasquillo			esch
Arrow	Chrome		Scenester	enigma
Nicole	Civitano		field rep	
Joe	Coleman		Artist	
Julie	Cox		email	
Susan	Curcio		email	
Jim	Curcio		email	
Tony	Denier			krztoff
Randy	Derebegian		ryko	

WHY COMPILING A MULTI-BAND GUEST LIST IS A PAIN IN THE ASS

KAMELA LISE KOEHLER

KAMELA LISE KOEHLER

VOCALIST, TOUR MANAGER ASSISTANT

When I was on tour with Pigface, we had two to three tour buses, each sleeping 12 to 14 people. Plus, at any given time, there was one or two groups traveling in satellite vehicles. So that's anywhere from 30 to 40 people who all know people who wanted to get into the show for free. Even if everyone—band members, managers, roadies, merch people, etc.—had just two guests, we were looking at 60 to 80 people such as Then there's all the outside people that need to be accommodated—local press and retail, club contacts, street teams for the label, scenesters, it goes on and on. It's easy to see how prioritizing can be a problem. It was more complex than I ever thought possible when I agreed to do the job.

For example; say the club gives us limited spots without penalty, but after that the tour will be charged. Does the performer's girlfriend or the magazine reporter his publicist has sent get higher priority? What if said reporter only really wants to come if he can bring HIS girlfriend and her best friend? There was an element of personal vs. professional, and often times in the music business that is (to say the least) a blurred line.

Or, try explaining to an intimidating, six-foot-plus bass player who has been a veteran of the road for 15 years that he can't put the sexy young thing he met down the street on the list, Never mind that he is already drunk and really wants to get laid. I can say no, but he will probably go around me and hand in his own guest list… which will result in the tour getting charged because when that extra guest list surfaces at 3 a.m. during settlement, the club will not overlook it.

It was particularly difficult for me to do this job at times because I had to deal with people who I had idolized before I was in the band. I was glad to help manage the tour because I wanted to learn and I needed the money. I was no stranger to the highway, but I had never done anything on this scale. I did not bargain for how hard it would be to say no to some of those who's records I had danced to in my living room when I was 14 years old.

Plus, it was weird for me to be simultaneously in the band and on the crew. I enjoyed the versatility for the most part, but sometimes it seemed like people didn't know how to treat me. Also, there were times when I would be in the middle of getting dressed or doing my makeup and someone would need to add somebody to the list or there was a dispute about a missing name. More than once, I had to walk into the open venue with one eye of makeup done or something. It was hard to have enough time do all of my roles.

With the exception of a few greenhorns, nearly everyone on the tour was an experienced road rat. This meant that nearly all of them had multiple acquaintances in most of the cities we went to. Also, each of their own bands would often be headlining their own tours. So, they

> **"Martin always said that touring was war and it sometimes felt like a battle trying to balance it all out in the cramped, makeshift office in the back lounge of the bus. All the while, someone is digging under the table for their boots and someone else is leaning over me to do their makeup in the mirror behind my head."**

were all used to more freedom with the guest list than the Pigface tour could offer. Of course, people always wanted extra spots in their hometowns.

Each band was allowed a certain number of guests per night and they were expected to figure it out amongst themselves and then give it to me once it was settled. It rarely went that smoothly. Mostly, people made a point of pushing their limits. If they did that too much, the tour would have to charge the band per guest.

Sometimes, in the smaller or more obscure towns, we had relatively few people on the list. But in big cities like New York, LA, and Chicago of course, the list was several pages and took on a more weighty importance. Martin always said that touring was "war" and it sometimes felt like a battle trying to balance it all out in the cramped, makeshift "office" in the back lounge of the bus. All the while, someone is digging under the table for their boots and someone else is leaning over me to do their makeup in the mirror behind my head.

> Clubs could be very uptight about when the list was turned in and making sure it was enforced. I remember getting yelled at by the club lady in San Francisco for turning the list in just a few minutes late. I was late because I had tried to catch a cab back from the Haight for over an hour only to eventually be picked up by a cabbie who refused to bring Fi (from Dragster) and I back to the club. He said that he could not in good conscience bring us to that part of town because the place was down on the docks, and would be dangerous for girls like us. Meanwhile, Martin was growing livid with me because the club wanted the list. When I finally got back, I had to turn in a crumpled, handwritten mess, and nobody was happy. That was a bad night.

Depending on our deal with whatever club we were at, the list could be a high security affair, with me even having to watch the door some nights. Sometimes it was we, the tour, who had to be uptight because the club was letting people in for free who weren't on our list and that could cost us money. Other times, it was much more lax.

Door Clicker

What was really interesting about the whole thing was that, even though compiling the guest list is a big job, it is a relatively tiny part of the management of the tour. I said I was amazed at the complexity of it all, in part because the intricate business of the guest list barely scratches the surface of what it takes to operate a project on the scale of the Pigface tour. There was a sense that the pressure never lets up which is kind of exciting. Before I participated in the tours, I had no idea how much the art of the music and the passion of the stage show can seem all but overshadowed by the business of the music business.

"...the list could be a high security affair, with me even having to watch the door some nights. Sometimes it was we, the tour, who had to be uptight because the club was letting people in for free who weren't on our list..."

:SMART TIPS

- **Start assembling the guest list in Excel** even if there are only a few guests, get into the practice.

- **Be ready to bump up the font size.**

- **Take a few trips over to the list to check up on it.**

- **Separate first and last names.**

- **Save the guest list in your tour folder.**

- See *61 Strategies for a More Successful Show* chapter for more information on guest lists.

C·H·A·P·T·E·R 21

MARKETING III - CREATING YOUR OWN EVENT

GETTING TRACTION FOR YOUR BAND

If you can't get any traction for your band, try pushing in a different direction. Look at the abilities and assets that you have. Maybe you are incredibly wealthy (not for long); maybe your Dad owns two tour busses; maybe you have a great PA and light system or a rehearsal space, a free copier, a house with a Jacuzzi or something that you can leverage or barter. Maybe you just have some great ideas and local contacts... use all of it!

GIVE IT A NAME

Killing Joke had a fantastic show at the Ritz, a venue in NYC with a capacity of 1,400. Six months later we were looking to come back at short notice for another great show. All of the larger venues had been booked for awhile, but many of the smaller venues were available and delighted to move things around to accommodate us. It looked like it would be two or three nights at the Cat Club (600-700 capacity) and a throw down at CBGB's. The idea took on form when Jaz Coleman, the singer, dubbed it *"Seven Days of Sweat and Madness."* We added a Spoken Word/acoustic event/press conference at the Thirteenth Street Playhouse with a beer and wine reception, and a crazy show at the tiny Maxwell's in Hoboken. Then it really was sweat and madness. The christening of the scattered, smaller events created a larger cohesive event and, made a much more impressive poster.

WE DON'T HATE THE GARDEN STATE!

Brian Brain had a similar situation when we played a few dates dotted around New Jersey. My alter ego used the same idea to give what would have otherwise been a lackluster series of events a purpose. It should have been a t-shirt, too, but this was before I was screen printing. And, in hindsight, I'm not sure how much any kind of name—printed up, sprinkled with glue, and dusted with sequins and glitter—could have disguised the fact that, after all, these were a series of shows in New Jersey. But, we tried.

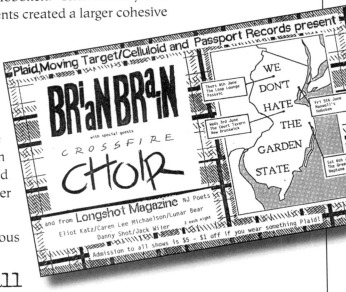

Let's start with a single event. We'll proceed onto more ambitious package tours in the next chapter.

> *"The only art is the art of doing all of it. The artist who isn't aware of the 25,000 other things going on is an escape artist on a fantasy vacation...this is three dimensional multi-tasking on acid." - Martin Atkins*

CURSE MACKEY, ONE OFF EVENTS

CURSE MACKEY

TOUR MANAGER
WOODSTOCK TATTOO &
BODY ARTS FESTIVAL
EVIL MOTHERS / PIGFACE
www.actionartsagency.com

The thought of launching a band from its most infantile stages to its first show is a daunting task. And that is just to get to the stage. How do you get an audience there other than telling them that your band rocks and they should like you?

Creating a themed event based around your performance is a definite method to increase attendance. Give the event a creative title based around your musical vibe or perhaps a holiday that it may be taking place around. Book additional bands as well as something else: a DJ, a VJ, some dancers, a comedian, or a local guest celebrity. Offer prizes; get some giveaways from local sponsors like gift cards from a music store, clothing store, or tattoo shop. Put the logo of the shops who donate gifts on the flyer. Do some ticket giveaways to your event on the local college radio station. Create a guest list of the 25 coolest people you know three to four weeks in advance of your event. Then these influential types will become part of your promotional team. The more frequently you can pull this off and get a system that works together, then you can take the exact same theme to the next market that you are planning to tackle. It's more work than just showing up to play, but it is worth the effort and can help launch your project to a higher profile. But again, if you suck, book lame talent, have a lame looking flyer and have a crappy band, this may not help at all. Regardless, you'll learn something for next time… or you'll learn that this isn't the right path for you before you are in over your head.

With the move towards becoming a real promoter or executive producer of full-scale events comes greater risk. The grander your vision, the greater your risk. With Woodstock Music Festivals, Vans Warped Tour, Ozzfest, Lollapalooza, and arena rock concerts happening every night in every major city, these events come with huge financial risks and public safety liability that ultimately falls on the person guiding the financial vision. The person who stands to gain the most also stands to lose the most, in most cases.

I experienced this firsthand when I produced the Woodstock Tattoo & Body Arts Festival in legendary Woodstock, NY.

To read more on this event see Curses' bit in *Stories From the Front Lines*.

> "…you'll learn something for next time… or you'll learn that this isn't the right path for you before you are in over your head."

MARTIN ATKINS ASKS:
JEFFREY A. SWANSON,
GOTHICFEST CREATOR

MA: What made you create GothicFest?

JS: I worked for a magazine called *New Metal Magazine* and covered the Milwaukee Metalfest years ago. Cradle of Filth and Kittie performed and the place was just mobbed with a bunch of cool freaks. The line was around the building to get an autograph from Cradle of Filth and their following appeared to be more goth than metal. This event may have sparked my idea. OK. Put together a gothic festival and expo in an arena setting here in the US.

What to call it? Why, Gothicfest, of course.

MA: Was it successful?

JS: A major success! We made history and did something that many industry people thought could never happen. There were over 1,000 attendees. After the five page article came out in *Spin* magazine we knew we had done something big.

MA: How much work was it?

JS: Huh! A lot! A year in the making, I thought it was going to kill me. My partners Bill Gingrich and Blair Lehman were burned out as well. We hired a PR firm, did magazine ads, radio spots, internet promotion, street teams, and interviews. And as for the production end of it: lights, sound, stage, banners, video production and audio recording. Then there was all the biz with the sponsors, exhibitors, bands, etc... A lot of late nights!

MA: Would you do it again?

JS: Yes!!!

MA: What would you change?

JS: Keep the lighting darker, be able to leave the venue and come back in at any time, make it a two day festival.

MA: How were the bands to deal with?

JS: Great, and we really had a great time with the event.

MA: Where did the biggest problems come from?

JS: Getting someone to insure the event was a big problem. We almost had to cancel. It was less than a week before we locked in a seven-figure policy.

MA: Are you in a band and how did that help your situation?

JS: Yes, I'm the singer and guitarist for Slave Driver and we had a great time slot, imagine that. We seemed to go over pretty well! We even got a big picture of our band in *Spin* magazine, as

---

well as many other publications and web zines. I also head up Dark Star Records so this was a great thing for our artists.

MA: Anything you would suggest for a band trying to get around the country—or at least, get out of their town??

JS: Look into some festivals online. There are some cool events out there. Even if you have to pay money to get on a bill, just do it. If you think you're too good to pay anyone money to play a big major event, then you'll just never play any major events. I would suggest you first make a full length CD and then get on the road anyway you can.

CLIFF SIELOFF (THE MAN WHO FILMED IT) ON GOTHICFEST:

CLIFF SIELOFF

FILMMAKER
FREE FOR ALL
GOTHICFEST
TERROR VISION

Gothicfest took place at the Odeum Expo, which holds over 5,000 people. Many big-name national acts have performed there including KISS, Sugar Ray, and Rammstein. Gothicfest had no business being held there. Its headlining acts Hanzel Und Gretyl and Slick Idiot are unable to sell out 800-900 max capacity clubs. The rest of the bill featured garage bands that paid the organizers of Gothicfest to perform 40-minute sets. These start-up bands had zero drawing capabilities. The 15 bands performing, the dozens of vendors at the event, and the stage/sound/film crew accounted for at least one third of the attendance. All of the stadium/bleacher seats were vastly empty!!!

But was it a success? I'd have to say "yes." Being such an odd, pseudo-one of a kind event, it received a fair degree of international press/media attention. Gothicfest became the subject of a multi-page article in *SPIN* magazine! It solidified a national DVD deal!

MA: *So, that's pretty interesting isn't it? Two very different views of an event. But five pages in SPIN Magazine created a great foundation for next year's event. With a bunch of lessons learned and the resources to do it again and take it to the next level, it's just like working on a song in the studio: you might not want to have everyone listen to the first version.*

U-35
V. MERCY, APOCALYPSE THEATRE

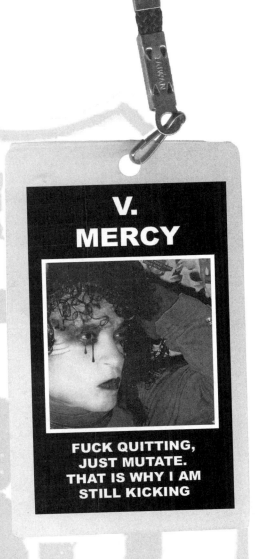

V. MERCY

FUCK QUITTING, JUST MUTATE. THAT IS WHY I AM STILL KICKING

WHAT IS U-35?

We are staking claim to the highway I-35 now re-named U-35—Underground 35. It is the Highway that connects The Northlands, The Ghostlands, The Wastelands, and The Heartlands. Our alliance is rich with many types of artists, business-minded misfits, dreamers, and alternative lifestyle pioneers.

WHO IS RESPONSIBLE FOR THIS CONCEPT?

"V. Mercy" and Hope Hillman developed a strategy that focused on the center of the nation. This area was more known for endless cornfields, oil fields, twisters, ghost towns, and bible thumpers. Mercy discovered that there were unique pockets and clusters of those who appreciated alternative, underground lifestyles and were bursting with undiscovered talent and opportunities. With a willingness to take risk, to share the cost, and to keep a hungry eye out for others. Many bands, DJs, and promoters are joining the call of the wild, helping to promote deeper into the heartland.

The path is being cleared and the future is looking much more lucrative. The Lone Star Caravan (Texas) is forming and a St. Louis, MO, chapter is building up its tribe. Further east of U-35, a new path is being forged down highways 90 and 94, now dubbed "U-90." These are exciting times and, with the inclusion of the Wild, Wild South West Corridor (West Texas, New Mexico, Arizona, and Nevada), it is only a matter of time before enough capital and interest from outside investment is raised to bring it to the next level.

This is only the beginning.

~Mercy

More information can be found @ *http://www.undergound35.com*

"Remember that, although you are solving one problem by creating your own event with a couple of larger bands, you might be creating 65 new problems for yourself. Be Careful! Your head and your bank account might not be able to take it!"
    —Martin Atkins

Check out *www.tstouring.com* for more examples of bands making their own situation work.

Martin Atkins' "Religion Of Marketing" Gallery, Chicago, IL Spring 2007

CHAPTER 22

Advice
...FROM BAAAD PEOPLE

THE PROBLEM WITH MUSIC
STEVE ALBINI

This is a well known, well thought-out piece from Steve... thanks for allowing me to re-print it.

Whenever I talk to a band who are about to sign with a major label, I always end up thinking of them in a particular context. I imagine a trench, about four feet wide and five feet deep, maybe sixty yards long, filled with runny, decaying shit. I imagine these people, some of them good friends, some of them barely acquaintances, at one end of this trench. I also imagine a faceless industry lackey at the other end holding a fountain pen and a contract waiting to be signed. Nobody can see what's printed on the contract. It's too far away, and besides, the shit stench is making everybody's eyes water. The lackey shouts to everybody that the first one to swim the trench gets to sign the contract. Everybody dives in the trench and they struggle furiously to get to the other end. Two people arrive simultaneously and begin wrestling furiously, clawing each other and dunking each other under the shit. Eventually, one of them capitulates, and there's only one contestant left. He reaches for the pen, but the Lackey says "Actually, I think you need a little more development. Swim again, please. Backstroke." And he does of course.

Every major label involved in the hunt for new bands now has on staff a high-profile point man, an "A & R" rep who can present a comfortable face to any prospective band. The initials stand for "Artist and Repertoire." Because historically, the A & R staff would select artists to record music that they had also selected, out of an available pool of each. This is still the case, though not openly. These guys are universally young [about the same age as the bands being wooed], and nowadays they always have some obvious underground rock credibility flag they can wave.

Lyle Preslar, former guitarist for Minor Threat, is one of them. Terry Tolkin, former NY independent booking agent and assistant manager at Touch and Go is one of them. Al Smith, former soundman at CBGB is one of them. Mike Gitter, former editor of XXX fanzine and contributor to Rip, Kerrang and other lowbrow rags is one of them. Many of the annoying turds who used to staff college radio stations are in their ranks as well. There are several reasons A & R scouts are always young. The explanation usually copped-to is that the scout will be "hip to the current musical "scene." A more important reason is that the bands will intuitively trust someone they think is a peer, and who speaks fondly of the same formative rock and roll experiences. The A & R person is the first person to make contact with the band, and as such is the first person to promise them the moon. Who better to promise them the moon than an idealistic young turk who expects to be calling the shots in a few years, and who has had no previous experience with a big record company. Hell, he's as naive as the band he's duping. When he tells them no one will interfere in their creative process, he probably even believes it. When he sits down with the band for the first time, over a plate of angel hair pasta, he can tell them with all sincerity that when they sign with company X, they're really signing with him and he's on their side. Remember that great gig I saw you at in '85? Didn't we have a blast. By now all rock bands are wise enough to be suspicious of music industry scum. There is a pervasive caricature in popular culture of a portly, middle aged ex-hipster talking a mile-a-minute, using outdated jargon and calling everybody "baby." After meeting "their" A & R guy, the band will say to themselves and everyone else, "He's not like a record company guy at all! He's like one of us." And they will be right. That's one of the reasons he was hired.

These A & R guys are not allowed to write contracts. What they do is present the band with a letter of intent, or "deal memo," which loosely states some terms, and affirms that the band will sign with the label once a contract has been agreed on. The spookiest thing about this harmless sounding little memo, is that it is, for all legal purposes, a binding document. That is, once the band signs it, they are under obligation to conclude a deal with the label. If the label presents them with a contract that the band don't want to sign, all the label has to do is wait. There are a hundred other bands willing to sign the exact same contract, so the label is in a position of strength. These letters never have any terms of expiration, so the band remain bound by the deal memo until a contract is signed, no matter how long that takes. The band cannot sign to another laborer or even put out its own material unless they are released from their agreement, which never happens. Make no mistake about it: once a band has signed a letter of intent, they will either eventually sign a contract that suits the label or they will be destroyed.

One of my favorite bands was held hostage for the better part of two years by a slick young "He's not like a label guy at all," A & R rep, on the basis of such a deal memo. He had failed to come through on any of his promises [something he did with similar effect to another well-known band], and so the band wanted out. Another label expressed interest, but when the A & R man was asked to release the band, he said he would need money or points, or possibly both, before he would consider it. The new label was afraid the price would be too dear, and they said no thanks. On the cusp of making their signature album, an excellent band, humiliated, broke up from the stress and the many months of inactivity. There's this band. They're pretty ordinary, but they're also pretty good, so they've attracted some attention. They're signed to a moderate-sized "independent" label owned by a distribution company, and they have another two albums owed to the label. They're a little ambitious. They'd like to get signed by a major label so they can have some security you know, get some good equipment, tour in a proper tour bus—nothing fancy, just a little reward for all the hard work. To that end, they got a manager. He knows some of the label guys, and he can shop their next project to all the right people. He takes his cut, sure, but it's only 15%, and if he can get them signed then it's money well spent. Anyway, it doesn't cost them anything if it doesn't work. 15% of nothing isn't much! One day an A & R scout calls them, says he's 'been following them for a while now, and when their manager mentioned them to him, it just "clicked." Would they like to meet with him about the possibility of working out a deal with his label? Wow. Big Break time. They meet the guy, and y'know what—he's not what they expected from a label guy. He's young and dresses pretty much like the band does. He knows all their favorite bands. He's like one of them. He tells them he wants to go to bat for them, to try to get them everything they want. He says anything is possible with the right attitude.

They conclude the evening by taking home a copy of a deal memo they wrote out and signed on the spot. The A & R guy was full of great ideas, even talked about using a name producer. Butch Vig is out of the question-he wants 100 g's and three points, but they can get Don Fleming for $30,000 plus three points. Even that's a little steep, so maybe they'll go with that guy who used to be in David Letterman's band. He only wants three points. Or they can have just anybody record it (like Warton Tiers, maybe—cost you 5 or 7 grand) and have Andy Wallace remix it for 4 grand a track plus 2 points. It was a lot to think about. Well, they like this guy and they trust him. Besides, they already signed the deal memo. He must have been serious about wanting them to sign. They break the news to their current label, and the label manager says he wants them to succeed, so they have his blessing. He will need to be compensated, of course, for the remaining albums left on their contract, but he'll work it out with the label himself.

Sub Pop made millions from selling off Nirvana, and Twin Tone hasn't done bad either: 50 grand for the Babes and 60 grand for the Poster Children-- without having to sell a single additional record. It'll be something modest. The new label doesn't mind, so long as it's recoupable out of royalties. Well, they get the final contract, and it's not quite what they expected. They figure it's better to be safe than sorry and they turn it over to a lawyer—one who says he's experienced in entertainment law and he hammers out a few bugs. They're still not sure about it, but the lawyer says he's seen a lot of contracts, and theirs is pretty good. They'll be great royalty: 13% [less a 10% packaging deduction]. Wasn't it Buffalo Tom that were only getting 12% less 10? Whatever. The old label only wants 50 grand, an no points. Hell, Sub Pop got 3 points when they let Nirvana go. They're signed for four years, with options on each year, for a total of over a million dollars! That's a lot of money in any man's English. The first year's advance alone is $250,000. Just think about it, a quarter million, just for being in a rock band! Their manager thinks it's a great deal, especially the large advance. Besides, he knows a publishing company that will take the band on if they get signed, and even give them an advance of 20 grand, so they'll be making that money too. The manager says publishing is pretty mysterious, and nobody really knows where all the money comes from, but the lawyer can look that contract over too. Hell, it's free money. Their booking agent is excited about the band signing to a major. He says they can maybe average $1,000 or $2,000 a night from now on. That's enough to justify a five week tour, and with tour support, they can use a proper crew, buy some good equipment and even get a tour bus! Buses are pretty expensive, but if you figure in the price of a hotel room for everybody In the band and crew, they're actually about the same cost. Some bands like Therapy? and Sloan and Stereolab use buses on their tours even when they're getting paid only a couple hundred bucks a night, and this tour should earn at least a grand or two every night. It'll be worth it. The band will be more comfortable and will play better.

The agent says a band on a major label can get a merchandising company to pay them an advance on t-shirt sales! Ridiculous! There's a gold mine here! The lawyer should look over the merchandising contract, just to be safe. They get drunk at the signing party. Polaroids are taken and everybody looks thrilled. The label picked them up in a limo. They decided to go with the producer who used to be in Letterman's band. He had these technicians come in and tune the drums for them and tweak their amps and guitars. He had a guy bring in a slew of expensive old "vintage" microphones. Boy, were they "warm." He even had a guy come in and check the phase of all the equipment in the control room! Boy, was he professional. He used a bunch of equipment on them and by the end of it, they all agreed that it sounded very "punchy," yet "warm." All that hard work paid off. With the help of a video, the album went like hotcakes! They sold a quarter million copies! Here is the math that will explain just how fucked they are: These figures are representative of amounts that appear in record contracts daily. There's no need to skew the figures to make the scenario look bad, since real-life examples more than abound. income is bold and underlined, expenses are not.

The band is now 1/4 of the way through its contract, has made the music industry more than 3 million dollars richer, but is in the hole $14,000 on royalties. The band members have each earned about 1/3 as much as they would working at a 7-11, but they got to ride in a tour bus for a month. The next album will be about the same, except that the record company will insist they spend more time and money on it. Since the previous one never "recouped," the band will have no leverage, and will oblige. The next tour will be about the same, except the merchandising advance will have already been paid, and the band, strangely enough, won't have earned any royalties from their t-shirts yet. Maybe the t-shirt guys have figured out how to count money like record company guys. Some of your friends are probably already this fucked.

Advance:	**$250,000**
Manager's cut:	$37,500
Legal fees:	$10,000
Recording Budget:	$150,000
Producer's advance:	$50,000
Studio fee:	$52,500
Drum Amp, Mic and Phase "Doctors":	$3,000
Recording tape:	$8,000
Equipment rental:	$5,000
Cartage and Transportation:	$5,000
Lodgings while in studio:	$10,000
Catering:	$3,000
Mastering:	$10,000
Tape copies, reference CDs, shipping tapes, misc. expenses:	$2,000
Video budget:	$30,000
Cameras:	$8,000
Crew:	$5,000
Processing and transfers:	$3,000
Off-line:	$2,000
On-line editing:	$3,000
Catering:	$1,000
Stage and construction:	$3,000
Copies, couriers, transportation:	$2,000
Director's fee:	$3,000
Album Artwork:	$5,000
Promotional photo shoot and duplication:	$2,000
Band fund:	$15,000
New fancy professional drum kit:	$5,000
New fancy professional guitars [2]:	$3,000
New fancy professional guitar amp rigs [2]:	$4,000
New fancy potato-shaped bass guitar:	$1,000
New fancy rack of lights bass amp:	$1,000
Rehearsal space rental:	$500
Big blowout party for their friends:	$500
Tour expense [5 weeks]:	$50,875
Bus:	$25,000
Crew [3]:	$7,500
Food and per diems:	$7,875
Fuel:	$3,000
Consumable supplies:	$3,500
Wardrobe:	$1,000
Promotion:	$3,000
Tour gross income:	**$50,000**
Agent's cut:	$7,500
Manager's cut:	$7,500
Merchandising advance:	**$20,000**
Manager's cut:	$3,000
Lawyer's fee:	$1,000
Publishing advance:	**$20,000**
Manager's cut:	$3,000
Lawyer's fee:	$1,000
Record sales:	250,000 @ $12 = $3,000,000
Gross retail revenue Royalty:	[13% of 90% of retail]: $351,000
Less advance:	$250,000
Producer's points:	[3% less $50,000 advance]: $40,000
Promotional budget:	$25,000
Recoupable buyout from previous label:	$50,000
Net royalty:	**-$14,000**

Record Company Income:	
Record wholesale price:	$6.50 x 250,000 = $1,625,000 gross income
Artist Royalties:	$351,000
Deficit from royalties:	$14,000
Manufacturing, packaging and distribution:	@ $2.20 per record: $ 550,000
Gross profit:	$ 710,000

The Balance Sheet: this is how much each player got paid at the end of the game.

Record company:	$710,000
Producer:	$90,000
Manager:	$51,000
Studio:	$52,500
Previous label:	$50,000
Agent:	$7,500
Lawyer:	$12,000
Band member net income each:	$4,031

"THE KNOWLEDGE" INVENT, BUILD, SOLVE PROBLEMS, PREPARE!

KEN LOPEZ

CREW

KEN LOPEZ

ENTREPRENEUR, EXPLORER, INVENTOR, MUSICIAN, PROFESSOR AT USC THORTON SCHOOL OF MUSIC

Touring in the '70s was exciting and largely based on problem solving. We had to invent and build everything. The most common items of today were major challenges back then. I once had the occasion to share stories over dinner with many of the founders of the industry including Clair Brothers, Showco, Audio Analysts, and others. We all shared our story of the microphone snake and, of course, they were all the same. That is because we were solving the same problem and independently arrived at the best solution. We compared time-lines and found that we had all "invented" the snake with-in a year of each other. We all then went on to invent monitors, amps, mixers, rigging, lighting, loudspeaker systems, and, in so doing, an industry. That spirit is still alive to-day and is one of the reasons touring is less harrowing than it might be. The moral is to pay attention to what others are doing. The best solutions rise to the top.

Another mic snake story: Early on, it was general practice to run the output of the console back down the snake to drive the amps. That works with 100-foot snakes—not with 300-foot snakes where the extra length creates a form of electromagnetic feedback. Arriving at an outdoor festival with a brand new 300 foot snake, we confronted this new problem. The solution was to recruit the audience to carry the entire mixing platform forward toward the stage and use the old snake. Problem solved. It's amazing what 100 people will do to make sure the show goes on.

In one of my prior careers, I was a VP at JBL. I cooked up a promotional tour with an all-star band, sound, lights, and crew to tour North America playing private gigs for dealers. We literally had veteran musicians—members of Toto, Pink Floyd, Tower of Power, and other bands—largely doing this for fun. When I asked why, they all said in unison, "No lead singer!"

On the same tour, I realized that those of us who had done this before knew what to expect. But the folks back at the factory had no idea. So, I brought them out for a week at a time in rotation. The credit manager, account administrators, service manager, and office people, all traveled on the bus, slept in the bunks, worked on the shows, packed and unpacked gear, met a great many people, and generally left exhausted but enlightened. To this day, they understand what is really going on out there and are much more helpful as a result.

The Allman Brothers played a show in Paris in which, during the encore, the JBL guitar speakers caught fire during a solo moment before the end of the song. The guitar tech called and explained, "It was so cool. The audience loved it. How can we do that every night?"

At one club gig, a guitarist/singer who had been carrying on relationships with three women was confronted with the sight of all three arriving at the club and then getting acquainted with each other. As they all realized that they were there to see the same guy, they turned to the stage and stared daggers at him. He started forgetting words and generally became flustered, sure that he would be skinned alive. At the end of the set, an enterprising roadie smuggled him out of the venue inside the Hammond organ case, along with a bottle of Jack Daniels. Crisis averted. The wait in the truck wasn't so bad either.

BUS

On one tour, a female guest joined us and brought along an enormous green suitcase. As she rolled it onto the bus, pulling it by a strap, the driver said in his Texas accent, "That sure is an ugly dawg you got there, lady." Then he promptly and very diplomatically offered her a smaller suitcase and sent the "extra" stuff back home via UPS. Bus drivers have to be a combination diplomat, confidant, Scout Master, and Zen Master.

At the beginning of one tour, a brand new crew member exclaimed his joy at being able to "see the country" not knowing that we would be traveling mostly at night.

A veteran bus owner/driver, Blair Camp, had driven for many major tours. He loved to tell "campfire stories" about bus crashes to scare the daylights out of newbies. He always used to say, "If you see me running to the back of the bus, you better follow."

One night, at the beginning of a long drive, another crewmember had gone up to ride shotgun and closed the curtain. Then they changed places. The Driver burst through the curtain yelling, "Run for your lives, we're gonna crash!" The new crewmember, a look of horror on his face, nearly ran the driver down in his dive for the rear of the bus. We all had a good laugh at his expense. Sometimes touring is just like camping out, scary stories and all.

BOOKING: PAY TO PLAY

Many young bands and performers think that "Pay to Play" is just a greedy way for club owners to take advantage of them. They think that once the tickets are paid for it doesn't matter how many people show up. That is a dangerous and false assumption based on an incomplete knowledge of how clubs operate.

Clubs have many expenses included in overhead: insurance, payroll, supplies, rent, and more. Generally, clubs and other performance venues operate on very small profit margins – even large and famous ones. "Pay to Play" is just a method used to try and ensure a crowd. Once the crowd is in the venue, it is expected that they will buy food and drinks. This is known as the Per Capita Expenditure of the patrons. Drinks are what pay the bills. No crowd, no drinks sold.

Clubs will calculate their monthly operating expenses, then divide by the number of show days in the month and arrive at a figure called the nightly House Nut. That is the minimum figure that pays the bills for the night. The entertainment is expected to bring in patrons who will each spend enough to cover the House Nut, and some for profit. No patrons, no profit. If your band doesn't bring in at least 80-100 people for your set, then you won't be asked back. It is a life and death issue for the club and ultimately for the band as well. Like it or not, you are in a partnership with the club.

STRATEGIES FOR SUCCESS

The best preparation I got for touring, and for life, was the Boy Scouts. We had life and death situations occur in the wilderness. Being prepared meant survival. Preparation included gear, maps, and supplies. But it also included readiness in the form of knowledge.

"Being prepared meant survival."

On a long back packing trip, a boy was bitten by a rattlesnake. The 25-year-old leader immediately took charge. He knew that we were 50 miles from medical help but only 18 miles from a radio. He knew that I had run long distance in school and immediately recruited me to run the trails to the location of that radio. While I was gone, he gathered a pre-selected group of scouts to help him save the boy's life, and console the others. He had researched our backgrounds and knew in advance who would be useful in an emergency and who would not. He had done his homework and was prepared. He would make a great tour manager. By the way, the boy survived, the snake did not.

In touring, like back packing or camping, gear is important. Knowledge is important, both technical and organizational. Knowledge about artists and crew is often the most important. Choosing people who are cool and effective in adverse circumstances is great insurance. I think about that Boy Scout leader every time I have to choose an employee or work mate. The right people make the difference in every situation.

One of my favorite quotes:

My long time friend Charlie Morgan of Morgan Sound in the Seattle area recently called me. He was going camping for the weekend and asked "Hey Ken, how much PA should I take?"

During a series of shows with the legendary fusion band Mahavishnu Orchestra in the '70s, I asked the drummer Billy Cobham how he managed to count the complex rhythms. "Count? You can't count this stuff. You've got to feel the music. If you count, you're lost…" This is true in life as well as music.

TOP TIPS FOR TOURING
GEOFF SMYTH, BRIAN BRAIN

GEOFF SMYTH
GUITARIST BRIAN BRAIN

…belated advice for those poor/lucky bastards who decide to go on tour:

- Love what you do.
- Whenever possible, do it with people you love.
- Make friends.
- Do not suffer fools gladly.
- Visit thrift stores often.

THE ART OF MUSIC BUSINESS
CURSE MACKEY

The following text is geared toward musicians and tour managers, but much of this pertains to anyone operating a small business based around their interest in the arts. As a new band, you are basically starting a new business. Some basic business and financial skills are crucial to having a shot at not losing your ass in the first thousand miles of performance.

Here are some general suggestions that I have found helpful to me:

1. **Get a checking account.**

2. **Learn to balance your checking account.** Don't over withdraw – ever.

3. **Use and manage credit cards properly.** You'll need at least one for vehicle, gear rentals and hotels.

4. **Build good credit with your credit card** by making at least the minimum payment on time every month.

5. **Learn to use Microsoft Excel** to create basic budget spreadsheets.

6. **Learn how to make your own show flyer and business card** in Adobe Photoshop.

7. **Get your business cards printed now!**

8. **Learn some basic HTML.**

9. **Use spell checker.**

10. **Build a team of people that share a common vision and goal,** no matter how distorted it may be.

11. **Align yourself with people more successful than you** and let them know you are available to them if the need for help arises.

12. **Read books about the industry** you want to develop a career in.

13. **Read books about success stories** and people you admire.

14. **Read trade magazines.**

15. **Network your ass off with out being an annoyance.**

16. **Get to know the people in your city** that are working in your field.

17. **Become the big fish in the little pond first.** Get your shit together in your own city before moving to LA, NYC, or going on tour.

18. Don't quit your night job. (Be a bartender, waiter, telemarketer, flyer guy for a club, etc.) Having a flexible job that you can make fast cash in between tours is highly recommended for all band members.

19. Attend trade shows like NAMM, SXSW, CMJ, and local events related to your field.

20. Figure out why anyone would care about your project, talent, or skills and be able to say it and write it in 50 words or less.

Somewhere, within the allure and day-dreamy haze of rock 'n' roll success, there is a vital architecture that one must explore if any degree of success is to be achieved. I am not talking exclusively about making millions of dollars and selling millions of records. Chances are – you won't… in fact, I am betting against you right now. Regardless of how you define success, there are things that you need to have an understanding about and the above list can help develop focus towards having your act together at both a performance and business level.

I've never been about conformity and I have worn many self-made hats in my career. I have defined my success by the body of work I have created, the people I have met, the places I have traveled to, the money I have made, and the freedom I have afforded myself by being relentlessly motivated to continue to evolve as an artist and to educate myself about running an artist-based business.

By this I mean: I have been a vocalist, keyboardist, re-mixer, DJ, soundtrack composer, barback, bartender, tour manager, record producer, festival and event producer, concert promoter, art exhibit curator, sponsorship seller, published writer, book and art publisher, and magazine editor. I've had to gather as much information along the way to self-educate myself on how best to perform in each of these roles. There is no better teacher than experience, but having as much information ahead of time is highly advised. For example, if you are going to tour manage a band for the first time, spend as much time reaching out and meeting other tour managers before you go. Experience itself can be very costly.

This business is all about who you know. So get out there, make friends in the biz, go to shows, meet the crew, the DJ, and the radio programmers, go to trade shows, meet the instrument manufacturers, the people who work at instrument stores, the owner of your local indie record store, your college radio people, local club owners and employees, and all of the bands that are in your area—in your genre or out of it.

If you can deliver the goods on what it is you are telling people that you do and can make a positive impression on the people making it happen in your city, you can also become one of the big fish in your small pond. However, if your band's music sucks or you have no skills as a soundman or you are unreliable, then you're fucked no matter how nice you are and maybe you are best served picking a different industry, taking the time to really find out what it is that you want to do, or taking some more time or classes to develop your skills.

TOP TEN THINGS THAT I HAVE LEARNED FROM BEING ON TOUR:

LACEY CONNER

- **Don't date someone who is in your own band!**

Being in a relationship is difficult enough. But if you are in a relationship with someone who is also your bandmate—add on top of that the stresses of being out on the road, and that can make for some tricky times! The biggest challenge is dealing with fans who want to hit on your man or on your woman. One night after a show, these two hot young chicks who were practically Barbie twins came up to me and said "Where's your guitar player? We want to take him home with us!!" What I really wanted to say to them was, "Back off bitches! That man is mine!"

However, they had just had me autograph a CD that they had purchased from me moments earlier, and they were fans of the band, so I just had to bite my tongue (literally), force a smile, and in my most sincere "fake nice" voice that I could pull off, I said to them, "Oh, yes, he's over in the back stage area... I'm sure he'd love to meet you both!"

- **If your RV catches on fire, don't call the fire department! Instead, let it burn to the ground and collect the insurance money.**

One of the big challenges to touring is setting up transportation. Touring in a van can be uncomfortable, especially if there are a lot of people with you, and you have to do a 10 hour drive. And tour buses are expensive. So we tried compromising between both, and getting an RV. I was told that RVs have a lot of mechanical problems, and they cost a lot of money to maintain. But I decided to give it a try anyway, only later to find out how true this was. After the RV had barely made it to several shows—one time in particular we had to sit on the side of the road every half hour so the damn RV would stop overheating, while trying to make a 350 mile drive—and eventually the RV had finally had enough. After one show, while in the parking lot, and turned off mind you, the RV caught on fire—with our driver asleep inside and wearing ear plugs! Fortunately, she got out safely, and the fire department came quickly and extinguished the blaze, but the entire outside of the driver's side of the RV was completely melted by the fire. After the incident, I realized it would have been more cost effective to let the damn thing burn to the ground and collect the insurance money!

> **"Don't date someone who is in your own band!"**

- **Don't drink beer, and then wine, and then vodka, and then Jägermeister, and then more beer,** then lie down on the back of the tour bus while the bus has just started moving and turning corners, and expect to not vomit.

- **If this happens, and your friends clean up your mess, this tells you who your true friends really are.**

- **Be careful what you video tape while on tour.** I really screwed up after one of our tours was over and asked one of my Dad's friends if he could transfer what was on the videotape onto a DVD for me. When I got the DVD back and started to watch it on my TV, from scene 1, I was like "Whoops! Don't want Dad to see that!" then scene 2, "Oh dear God, I really don't want Dad to see that!" and so on and so on.

- **The two people that you never want to piss off in life are: A soundman at a club you are about to perform at, and the person taking your order at the fast food window.**

- **No going "number two" in the toilet of the tour bus.** And if someone on your tour bus asks you if you know what "shit-bagging it" means, say "no" and quickly walk away.

- **No matter how hard you try, you can't cram more than seven people into one bunk of a tour bus.** I know, I've tried. Don't ask why—it seemed like a fun challenge at the time.

For more stories about Tour Buses, check out the *"Transportation"* Chapter.

- **At the end of a tour, you'll never want to eat pizza, tacos, or Denny's ever again for the rest of your life.**

- **Some of the most incredible, talented, inspiring, and unforgettable people can be met while out on tour** – from fans, to promoters, to tour managers, to the band members of the other bands you are on tour with, and so on. I personally have met some amazing and brilliant people while on tour, who I know will be my friends for life, and I wouldn't trade those experiences for all the money in the world.

WHAT TO PACK: ACCESSORIES AND ATTITUDE

The one or two things that stop your head from exploding are different for everyone. There are some no-brainers that are common to every touring experience. For instance:

How about something to stop your ass exploding? At some point, on every tour, somebody eats something or does something that has gastrointestinal consequences. The pills to combat this emergency are tiny and I'm at the point now that any bag that I pick up has four or five somewhere in it—Imodium AD. I have the newest kind… Imodium ADD!

On the other end of your body, bring something for your brain: a book, a favorite DVD, some photographs, an effective communication tool. Decades ago, it was a roll of quarters. More recently, it was a cable to plug my laptop into my cell phone or a map of the nearest Starbucks with Wi-Fi. Now it's a card in your computer. It's always great to communicate and talk to someone outside of the tour (just make sure it isn't a journalist).

Throughout the book, several industry professionals have listed important, yet oft-forgotten items that can save a tour. Here is a summary of some good ones:

• A zero balance credit card—Curse Mackey.

• Emergen-C and Vitamin D—Greta Brinkman.

• An iSight camera for your laptop—Jason Novak.

• Any Medications and a Copy of your Prescriptions—Chris Tisone.

• Birth Control—Debby Herbenick.

• Cell Phone Charger and, if possible, a Chargepod.

• Dist-o-Map.

• AAA card.

• Trail mix–it'll either keep you going or you can throw it down in front of the wheels in the snow! (Thanks Ken Waagner)

You gotta have string, you gotta have rope, you gotta have straps. (Laughs) You gotta have whiskey... oh, did I say that? You gotta have two kinds! (Laughs) You gotta have vodka, you gotta have candy, you gotta have mouthwash. You gotta have earplugs, you gotta have...
    - Jolly Roger

STEVE TRAXLER:

BEFORE LEAVING HOME FOR A TOUR, THESE ARE THE TOP ITEMS TO CONSIDER PACKING AWAY IN YOUR CASE:

1. Open Mind

2. Sense of Humor

3. Flexibility

4. Sincerity

5. Common Sense

6. People Skills

7. Quick Thinking

8. Patience

9. Confidence

10. **Egos** (It's best to consider leaving this one at home since you will find many people carry one with them already and will gladly let you share theirs).

And don't forget creature comforts which should come in handy:

11. A set of Bose noise-canceling headphones

12. An iPod loaded with your favorite music

13. **A computer with a wireless modem and DVD player**, and especially make sure it has an Excel program, probably the most common and utilized computer program on a tour (more uses than a Swiss army knife).

14. A selection of classic DVD's you never have time for at home

15. A great toothbrush

Before you go on tour, change your cell phone plan to nationwide so you don't incur massive roaming charges!

AND DON'T FORGET THE ULTIMATE TOOL TO SOLVE EVERY PROBLEM:

Photo by Jono Podmore

THE ULTIMATE TOUR MANAGER'S TOOL KIT

CHAPTER 24

HOW TO GET A BETTER LIVE SOUND

A GOOD SOUND STARTS WITH GOOD GEAR

LEE POPA, FRONT OF HOUSE SOUND

LEE POPA

HOW TO GET A BETTER LIVE SOUND
FRONT OF HOUSE SOUND FOR MINISTRY
@ LOLLAPALOOZA '92, KMFDM, KILLING
JOKE, ZILCH, LIVING COLOUR

Ministry, Killing Joke, KMFDM, Living Colour, Macy Gray, Pigface, Bad Brains, RHCP, 24-7SPYZ, Beyonce, Outkast

Get your sound before the show:

- Balance all of your sounds at your practice place.
- If your drummer is playing and you can't hear him or her, your amp is too loud!
- Is the bass too boomy?
- If all you hear is drums, you're not loud enough!
- Is your solo volume too loud? Does your clean sound match your dirty sound? Think and listen!

The vocal mic is the most important mic on the stage: Treat it as such. Sorry, no matter how good your amps and drums sound, if you drown out the singer you have ruined the show.

Stage feedback means it's too loud: If the stage monitors feedback: you are too loud for the system. The clearer you hear the vocal, the better the sound of everything.

Play a sound check like it's the show: When the drummer lays back at sound check then pounds at the show, you would be better off not sound checking. Don't lay back. Jump around and go for it so the settings you save at sound check mean something!

TOUR:SMART TIP

Amps and drums that fit the room: If you are playing clubs and overpowering the room, it makes people hate you no matter how good you are! The Rolling Stones have small amps and small drums when they play the clubs on tour. Having a set of small gear makes you have a good time playing and club owners happy.

In tune in time: Tune up often and together. Pick places in the set to tune up. In the set, everybody needs to tune up at the same time. Two guitars slightly out of tune aren't as bad to the ear as one in tune and one out of tune.

TOUR:SMART TIP
for more information go to:
www.tstouring.com

Practice at home with a click (metronome) and you won't rush during the live set. Your drummer will play better.

Softer will make you sound louder: If the soundperson can't hear you, they will put more of you in the P.A. The smaller the sound on stage, the louder the band is because the sound system is doing the work.

Mark your setting down: Get some tape and mark your settings. Don't fool around with your knobs during the show. If you do, chances are you will be turned down because your sound becomes erratic.

Good help is hard to find: Respect the people that are helping you out. Learn the names of the people and thank them after the show even if you think they did a bad job. They did the best they could. Never yell at someone you don't pay!

Start at the source with a good sound and it will be easy to get a good sound in the P.A.

SHIT IN = SHIT OUT

Always use a name brand. Nine times out of ten, this is what you hear at any big concert or on many live albums!

For Loud and Heavy Guitar Sound: A Gibson Les Paul with a Marshall 100 Watt Tube Amp and Marshall 4x12 Speaker cabinet sounds giant. Mic it with Shure SM 57 just off the center of the speaker and it is a sound you have heard on many hit records and have heard on tour (Led Zeppelin, Guns and Roses, and ZZ Top, to name a few).

For Bass: A Fender Bass with an Ampeg SVT, and Ampeg 8x10 gives you the most heard sound in rock. A DI blended with a Beta 52 mic is a killer sound.

For a Good Drum Sound: Start with a good brand (Ludwig, D.W. Drum Workshop, Tama, Pearl, or Rodgers). Mics that always work and give a good sound are Shure, Beta 52 mic inside the bass drum. A Shure SM 57 on the top and bottom of the snare drum and a Shure SM 98 mics on the toms. They are small and clip onto the toms so they stay out of the way. I recommend SM 81 condensers on the hi-hat and over the cymbals.

For Keyboards and Computers: A keyboard controller with Reason, Ableton Live with a digi 002 or your laptop and Motu Box (these are a staple for electronic music). Roland, Korg, Nord Keyboards always sound great. Take the output of your keys or computer into a Mackie 1602 Mixer, put a compressor on the left and right of the mixer (e.g. DBX, Behringer) with a little compression to 2 direct boxes and you have a sound everybody uses.

EARLY IS ON TIME - ON TIME IS LATE.

DOING SOUND FOR STARTERS
MIGUEL TORRES, MATTRESS FACTORY STUDIO

So you're helping a friend setup a small sound system for a party, or you're doing sound for a small festival in your neighborhood. Either way, you're in charge of how the night sounds. If you're just starting out, it's great to get involved with situations like these. They build you up for different situations and help you think on your feet. Many times, during all the craziness of setting up and sound checking, people forget little things. The guitarist's distortion pedal ran out of juice and you have an extra 9-volt, guess what… you just saved the day (for that moment anyway). The band was in a hurry to get to the venue and they forgot picks, always carry extra picks. The DJ forgot to bring his phono-to-1/4-inch adapters but you have extras. It's difficult to say just what is going to happen at any given time but it helps to be prepared. Unfortunately, the only way to be prepared is by going out there and experiencing it for yourself. Here are a few key things to keep in mind:

- Always keep a set of tools with you: screwdrivers, pliers, a blade, a drum key (this is a big help), etc.

> **"A flashlight is your best friend."**

- A flashlight is your best friend. It doesn't matter what time of day it is, you will most likely have to deal with dark places.

- Take a few extra cables if you have any and always bring plenty of adapters: i.e. RCA to 1/4 inch, 1/8 inch to 1/4 inch (and vice versa), etc.

- Writing materials, a small pad for notes, and a Sharpie!

> **"… be prepared."**

- Batteries, batteries, batteries!

- Some extra picks and some DI's if you have any.

- Earplugs. They're your ears, protect them! Here's a web site that makes custom molded earplugs, *www.etymotic.com*.

All in all, there is no replacement for experience.

TIPS FOR TOURING
DON BYCZYNSKI

Why would anybody in their right mind want to tour? To sit upright for five hours, drive 200 miles, eat at fast food joints or (if you're lucky) a "quality" truck stop, all in a nine-passenger van with a trailer, packing in twelve people and smells that have not even been discovered yet to show up at a club that holds no more than 200 people, yet to find out that the production manager is the brother of the owner and knows shit about running production.

Load-in is 4 p.m., sound check is at 5 p.m., doors open at 9 p.m., and again that asshole "production" manager shows up at 7 p.m. He then has the nerve to tell the band that there is an opening band that was added last night and is a buddy of the booking agent for the club so they get a sound check but we need to hurry up and load in. Never having a chance to eat the bullshit deli tray in the dressing room, it's now time to get the gear on stage and get a line check. A line check is a nice churched-up word for "hope all the mics work by the time the band hits the stage."

DON BYCZYNSKI

ONCE DEATH METAL / HARDCORE GUITARIST TURNED SWING PRODUCER!

SEE HOW AT web.mac.com/producedb

I have had the pleasure of touring and mixing with some mid-level acts from 1998 to 2001. I want to dig deeper into the above statement because this was my life for three years and there are a few pros and very many (x 3) cons of touring on a budget. Don't get me wrong—I would never bitch about it. Hell, I saw the states three times over, met some really great people, and got paid for it… well, sort of.

Most of the acts I toured with wanted the tour bus. Why? I have no idea. I guess, when the bus pulls up, it gives a feeling like, "Yeah, we made it!" However, being on tour with acts that had just gotten a record deal or didn't have a major label backing their tour bus was just stupid. How about a reality check: we are on a club tour to about 200-300 capacity gigs at maybe $500-$700 a show. Five shows a week equals $2,500-$3,500 bucks a week. Great! You can afford a bus, right? Wrong. How are you going to get to the shows? Does anyone in the band have a license to drive a bus?

Now, how about the bus driver? Is he going to sit at the club after driving all night and wait for the show to end? Nope. It was my job to get a taxi and get him to a hotel so he could sleep to haul our ass to the next show. Oh, and remember this all has to get done in time before the line check happens or the band needs to go on stage. OK, now with this cash that is left over, the band needs to pay me because I was a taxi hailer, tour manager, sound engineer, production manager, baby-sitter, and the person who made sure that—while the band was getting chicks and drunk after the show—we got paid by the club.

Let's not forget that most 200-300 seat clubs have the worst sound gear that is sold at Guitar-Center. I have mixed an 8-piece band on a 12-channel Mackie mixer. How, do you ask? Well, you better know your gear and you better know how to strip down the input list on the fly. Remember that when you start off, there is no money in the budget to bring your own gear. I suggest that before a tour, rent a rehearsal showcase room and work with your production crew just in case this happens and yes, it will. I was out with The Damage Manual on tour. At a certain club, one hour before doors, the sound gear was still getting unloaded by the sound company the club rented from because the club didn't have their own sound equipment. Again, no sound check that day! I think we all just threw the gear on stage, set up the stage props, and away we went. The show was great, but it is never a good start to the night to have to rush around and really, all the club owner had to do was have the sound company set up the night before. I can safely say, "When booking a return show in that town, you think we'll use that shit dump?"

If you think that starting off touring, even with a major label behind you, will get you Easy Street, then you're truly missing the point of touring. The whole idea behind touring is that you have to work hard and promote yourself. Read books. Talk to someone that knows the ins and outs of being on the road. Talk to bands that are in town from another city. And never think you're going to get rich on tour! Touring on a budget can be a shit ton of work, but it can be a good time as well. I got into a band to have fun. I got into studio and live engineering because of the challenge of making the show a success and having fun making good music. So yes, it is worth all of those sick-smelling van rides. Be smart about it and life on the road is not that bad.

CHAPTER····25

CREW AND PRODUCTION

"How do you know when you need roadies? Well?
How tired are you?"
- Jolly Roger

The inexperienced road person hopes that there will not be a problem. The experienced road person wonders what will be the combination of problems that will need to be solved this particular day—with the knowledge that the tool belt is in place, the batteries are recharged, you've had a 45-minute power nap and there is a spare ink cartridge for the printer…

Each problem solved along the way charges the invisible force field around a good road person, creating an aura, a calmness, that can ripple through a tour, prevent hysteria and the kinds of accidents that hysterical, freaked-out worriers create around themselves.*

The makeup of a crew is as important as the chemistry within the band. Always be on the lookout for people who are on the road but maybe in the wrong position. Some people just have to get on the road but might be better suited to an easier, less stressful—or more stressful—position. People can grow in experience quickly—one crazy tour will put you there. Crew guys can quickly spot people who aren't pulling their weight. If you're tour managing, it will be your job to quickly assess if someone is on a learning curve and decide if you want to invest the time or if someone is stuck in a tape loop, you'll need to quickly cut them loose. Make sure that band weaknesses are cancelled out by strengths with the crew—not compounded.

*Calmly written with one hand jammed in the toaster.

> **"Make sure that band weaknesses are cancelled out by strengths with the crew—not compounded."**

SOUNDMEN:

A good soundman also understands that they cannot know every quirk of a room or the out-of-date sound system that is in it. He will make friends with the in-house staff, and be grateful for any advice and pointers they give to him. And find out where the secret limiters are hidden so you can turn it up! It is important for your soundman to advance the shows. I cannot count how many times I have heard the phrases, "Well if you had only told us two weeks ago," or "We had that very thing up until two hours ago when the rental company took it back." So make sure your soundman calls the club a few weeks before the show, speaks to the production manager and sound guy, and makes the venue aware of any special requirements that the band may have. He should also understand the costs that are involved. Have that talk with him before he orders a bunch of equipment.

If there is something very special, very important, or very difficult to find for your show it might be a worthwhile investment to purchase it for the band so you have it each time you perform. Singers might want to carry their own microphones instead of spinning the roulette wheel of dented, rusty, stinky, or just-been-up-GG-Allin's-ass microphones. As a tour producer and promoter, you do not need to deal with an out-of-commission singer with a throat infection. Good tour managers and responsible soundmen (Thanks Pat!) will carry a bottle of Listerine to swab microphones before show time. Soundmen! Use the most pungent kind of Listerine, you want everyone to know you care! A lot!

> "Sometimes the best deal on a PA is not the cheapest."
>   - Curse Mackey

As you grow, you might want to carry pre-programmed effects or delays. As a soundman, make sure you do not get pulled into the "who's got the biggest box" war. Look at pre-programmed lighting "specials" to make your show stand out.

TOUR:SMART TIP
for more information go to:
www.tstouring.com

- If you're using back-up electronic reinforcement, get an un interruptible power supply!

- When sound-checking, turn on all the lights! That way you can see if the power of everything will cause a short circuit. You don't want to wait until 11:45 to find out that the system can't take it, captain!

FRIENDS, DON'T LET FRIENDS DO MONITORS

Lee Popa used to hand monitor guys a crash helmet. "I don't need that!" said every single one, confused. "You will if Martin has a problem with his monitors; the only way he can communicate is by throwing drums sticks at you!" We got a little bit more attention after that. Sometimes you need some theatre and a little drama to communicate.

But, after many traumatic years trying to get in-house monitor engineers to pay attention and give me more loops in my monitor, I just went out and bought some. Just by raising an eyebrow, I get more or less loop in my own loop monitor, and the in-house monitor engineer can be paying attention to something else in the building or walking his dog during your set. I saw that happen at some club in Texas, the monitor guy took his dog for a walk while Lacey Conner (who was on stage with Nocturne) tried her very best to work with horrifying feedback and no loops for their drummer. Of course (See *Murphy's Law*) this was the night her family was there!

> *Here's another example, on tour in Poland with Killing Joke, Geordie had had enough of trying to communicate with the monitor guy, he was so frustrated he disappeared into the dressing rooms and came out with a very hot iron from the wardrobe room, then placed it on the top of the monitor console and smiled as it slid and melted its way across the console. Don't try this at home, or without a few hit records to pay for it!*

MARTIN ATKINS ASKS:
JOLLY ROGER

MA: If you could give a crew guy advice, what would it be?

JR: You gotta be reliable! It's like my friend Willie G.! He just kept going and going and going. Now he's doing (Mustaine's) guitars and he's doing Scott Knott's guitars and stuff like that. You just have to be true and you have to stick to it. You have to know when you're being ripped off and when you're not and that's something you just learn by being ripped off a bunch of times, I guess. I did one of those symposiums and this guy goes, "How do you know when you need roadies?" And I said, "Well? How tired are you?" (Laughs) It's that simple! You gotta work everyday!

MA: What was the first tour that you did?

JR: Uh… probably when I got back from 'Nam, I worked with a band. We would get a gig somewhere, drive there, meet people, stay at their apartments, and then find a gig at another city and then go there.

MA: What's the biggest band you've toured with?

JR: Styx was the first band. I was with them when they had three albums in a row, so, five million. No one had ever done that before. Kansas and Styx. We had 20, 25 trucks. First bands never to do that. You know, well, what's the biggest band? Pigface! We had 45 people on stage once! That's the biggest one! (Laughs) The only one to ever give me a platinum album was Poison. Even though I worked with all kinds of bands that had platinum albums you know from Hart and Styx and Kansas… I was with Foreigner for awhile. I was with Ozzy when Randy Rhodes died.

MA: So how did you get pulled into Ministry? Was it living in Chicago?

JR: Yeah, I was living in Chicago, working at all the places. You gotta think on your feet. I guess that's the only thing I can say. 'Cuz we've been through everything from our poor friend William slashing his wrist to spinal meningitis… we've been through the whole nine yards.

> " You just have to be true and you have to stick to it."

> "I remember when we had that lighting designer that had made the big fire-spitting dragon. When I said, 'How long does it take you to tear it down?' He goes, 'On a good day, I can do it in 8 or 10 hours.' Excuse me?! "I don't think the fire-spitting dragon is going anywhere, sir."
>
> – Jolly Roger

CREW
Curse Mackey

One cannot do it alone. Once the band is ready to add a crew, you need to find cool, reliable people. Guys or gals who can stay up late, get up early, lift gear, know how to work the gear, and follow instructions. In the early days of a band, this can be friends that might want to just come along for the ride to help load-in, load-out, sell merchandise, and grow with the success of the band. In the early days of Evil Mothers, just having someone along to drive and help carry metal oil drums was something to be grateful for.

Regardless of their role, you've got to take care of your crew. Feed them. Make sure they have coffee and water, donuts help too. Get them t-shirts from the club. Make sure they get a shower once in a while. It's a tough job, and being able to develop loyal, experienced crew guys that love your project is one of the best things a band on the way to success can do. To know that there are guys on the side of the stage there to help you be as good as you can be is a great feeling. And good help is hard to come by so do your best to take care of them. One of the best ways to develop crew is by meeting the guys who work in the clubs you play in. Get to know them. I have used crew guys from clubs all over the U.S. and had much success and seen them go onto have great careers by being the right place at the right time. Same thing if you want to get on the road as a TM or crew member: work the road shows, introduce yourself, and have your business card ready.

"Sometimes you just have to pee in the sink."
  -Charles Bukowski

REGARDING ROADIES:
MARGOT OLAVARRIA, BASS PLAYER

Knowing how to plug-in amps and set up drums are only one requirement of a good roadie. An ideal roadie should be an automotive expert, a driver with extraordinary stamina, a person who is not alien to good hygiene and someone who respects women and women musicians. Way back when I played in a bitch band I shall not name, we solved this problem by hiring girl roadies. While in Brian Brain, sometimes it was hard to find good help. Once we cast our fate to the wind and set out without any roadies. Martin, Geoff, and I developed chiseled biceps from unloading and loading all our equipment from New York to Cincinnati, where we found someone willing to join the tour. I remember having to throw away dirty roadie underwear at gas stops after warning them that that's what would happen if they would not keep it in their bag. Another pair of red-neck roadies would not let us play soul tapes in the van. Let them know who's boss.

Then there was Chaz, who was a load of fun except for one thing: his looks attracted unwanted police attention. Chaz had a shaved head except for a small round patch of hair at the top of his head, to which he would super-glue very long braids. This, and his piercings and tattoos, gave him a Mongolian-punk look that no policeman could resist. For example, we got stopped on the freeway in the middle of the night driving out of San Francisco. It seems Chaz was driving 25 m.p.h. in a 65 m.p.h. highway. Having dropped two hits of acid an hour before, he was being extra cautious with his driving. Then there was the time when cops stopped us in L.A. on Santa Monica Boulevard in front of Okie Dog, one of my infamous hangouts when I lived in L.A. This made things even more embarrassing as Martin, Geoff, Chaz, and I were ordered to "assume the position" with our hands on Doris the van and our legs spread while the cops searched every drum case, every guitar case, every bag, every nook and cranny of poor old Doris, probing for drugs. All they found was our stinky Chinese Red Flower Oil for our road-weary backs (since Chaz had probably swallowed any evidence).

So be choosy of whom you hire because on the road it's so important to love the one you're with. Good people make all the difference as you blaze across the country and meet all the unpredictable challenges the road will undoubtedly throw your way. But the main thing to remember no matter how bad things get: for fuck's sake have fun! It's a great way to see the country and make friends.

> "Good people make all the difference as you blaze across the country and meet all the unpredictable challenges the road will undoubtedly throw your way."

MAKE IT WORK "GUITAR TECH"
CHRIS SCHLEYER

CHRIS SCHLEYER

FORMER PRICK / ZEROMANCER
GUITARIST / A PERFECT CIRCLE /
NIN GUITAR TECH / FOUNDING
MEMBER OF AFFECTED
www.affectedband.com

The most important thing to remember is that: You are there to make it work.

Another important thing is to know thy place.

In short, if it ain't broke don't fix it! Routine is the key to a successful tech/artist working relationship.

Here are some more specific tips to remember from someone who's been on both sides of the workbox:

- **Never out play the talent.** Showing up the talent may get you fired!

- **Know the flow.** Know the signal path like the back of your hand. When the artists signal dies you'll need to track down the source of the problem quick. No time for bumbling or you could quite possibly get handed a bus ticket home.

- **Keep the kool.** As an addendum to #2 you will also need to assure the artist that everything is under control when everything seems to be out of control!

- **When things are running smoothly** it can be easy to get distracted and zone out. Make sure to keep your eyes and mind on the game and off the girls in the front row, they are not there for you!

- **Take a bartending class.**

- **Make contact with the artist's endorsement reps** so that when your band needs strings you can get them for artist cost, too.

- **Never take your work home.** The rest of the guys on the crew bus (if you're lucky enough to be on a tour that can afford a separate bus for the crew) do not want to be reminded of "The Show" on their day off. Leave the smashed midi controller on the truck for the next show day to sort out. There's plenty of hurry up and wait time for fixing broken crap.

- **Don't talk to the talent's girlfriend.**

- **Always have a few after-show passes on hand** in case of emergency for when the talent's girlfriend is not around.

- **Last but not least,** if the guitarist is used to having three guitar picks on the left corner of their cabinet and two waters on the right then make sure it's that way every day. If the show ran smooth the night before then that's your model for how the show should run every night.

> "Make sure to keep your eyes and mind on the game and off the girls in the front row... they are not there for you!"

EXCERPTS FROM:
"I WAS AN OZZFEST ROADIE"
PATRICK ALBERTSON, REVOLVER MAGAZINE

"Back in 2006, I recall the last words of advice I received before leaving the Revolver Offices: "You have to beat up the biggest roadie the first day, or become someone's bitch." Immediately, I think of what being someone's bitch entails. Surely, I have made a terrible mistake.

Staying ten minutes ahead is invaluable when orchestrating an all-day metal festival, but what it really comes down to it this: if the show goes over curfew, it's a thousand dollars a minute, which is always bad for the bottom line.

Down on my hands and knees, as I unscrew clamps and pull out pins, I recall that earlier I had witnessed many a gob of spit and mucus fly to the stage. My mind wanders to the dirt, sweat, saliva, and various other fluids and sediments that may be expelled onto this surface during the course of an Ozzfest. I realize that I am fucking filthy. I also now understand why all the stagehands wear black, pushing, carrying, rolling, dragging, and hoisting gear all day makes it a necessity. A strong immune system probably helps, too.

The bus I'm on is at capacity with 12 people, all Second Stage guys and sponsors. I've been assigned the junk bunk, a literal term. It's little more than a sleeping hole about seven feet long and two-and-a-half feet high, and it's crammed with bags, suitcases, cardboard boxes, swag, and all other varieties of crap. I jam my bag onto the crowded, sheet less mattress. It's an eight-hour drive to Alpine Valley in Wisconsin. We fill it with several (perhaps too many) beers.

As I mic up Unearth's kit, I hear some commotion between the audio tech and Dustin. He comes over with a grave expression and explains that I fucked up. It seems I have accidentally swapped the mics for toms 2 and 3. I apologize and tell him that he can tell Steve to blame it on me. Dustin explains that regardless, it is his responsibility; to pass any amount of blame would be pointless and irresponsible. Because I fucked up, he fucked up and that's just how it works.

> " If the show goes over curfew, it's a thousand dollars a minute..."

Theirs is the kind of knowledge that cannot be taught; rather, you must be a student of the road and learn what each venue is like, what the local management is like, and what the logistics of loading in and out are.

There's another reason for doing this kind of work: You can reside anywhere you want, making it easy to live a good life from your earnings. It isn't conventional, by any means: the hours are

Ozzfest 2006

> "The hours are long and the work is demanding, but being on the road seems to bring with it a camaraderie and loyalty that only those who love it can know. "

long and the work is demanding, but being on the road seems to bring with it a camaraderie and loyalty that only those who love it can know. Generally, Chris and the other crew members I talked to share a resentment of the nine-to-five world—something most of them know little about, other than that they are not cut out for it.

As the tour gears up for another day, I cannot help but think of the trucks, the crew, the bands, and all of the logistics involved in Ozzfest that will continue on after I leave tonight. Charlie had told me, "The greatest people in the world ride these buses, the hardest-working people." Later, in the comfort of my hotel room, on the eve of my return to the Manhattan desk I know so well, I thought back on the last three days and I knew he was right.

OZZFEST By The Numbers:

Miles Traveled: 10,747

Venues: 27

States Visited: 20

Personnel (Aprox.): 350

Oxygen Tanks For Ozzy: 2

Golf Carts: 15

Tractor Trailers: 14

Buses: 35

Bath Towels Per Date: 600

Pounds of Ice Per Date: 975

Minimum Number of Crew and Band Beers Required Daily: 464

On a good day, Jim is the embodiment of an ideal person to have on the road – wiring up a new version of the "shit" lights, fixing a disco mirror ball so I could punch it, dealing with guitars, figuring out drums, scenery, and projectors, fixing personal computers… plate spinning. Fucking priceless and awesome…

MARTIN INTERVIEWS JIM SOCHACKI

MA: Jim, give us an overview of the bands you've worked with and what you did with each band.

JS: Pigface: just about everything, except play, guitars, scenery, projections, drums (several kits, often three). Godhead: guitar tech, drum tech, and tapes. Evil Mothers: I was doing everything for them, guitars, drums, and some prop stuff. Gravity Kills: just guitar tech and keyboard. Sheep on Drugs: took abuse from the tour manager. Somewhere, somehow, I found a way to put that projector up. It was basically just roll in the tape machines, set up Lee's guitar rig, set up the video, and set up the projector.

MA: And then hide?

JS: Yea! I did Test Department and, more recently, Dry Cell, which was just a festival tour put on by radio stations, setting up a lot of guitars for them and a lot of drums. That was interesting because they *bought their own bus* and it was supposedly all checked out and everything. We got in the bus in Nashville, drove for ten miles, and it overheated! Ten more miles—again it overheats! We were trying to make it to Milwaukee for Summer Fest! We could only go ten miles in a jump. I'm with a band I've never met before and I'm suddenly going through their stuff and trying to find what's essential for this show. We find a small plane and we're playing musical chairs, what's in what bay, so we can balance the plane perfectly so it would go.

We finally get to Milwaukee and now we're in a van. There are huge gates at the show location that are shut for the day and (of course) the security isn't there. The band had a half an hour set and a 45-minute slot to pull it off. We're in the van outside the chained-up gates and its 5:00. They need to be on at 5:15 at the latest. Still no guards, I'm freaking out.

MA: Was there a Tour Manager? What the fuck was he doing?

JS: He was on the phone trying to stay calm. I was already freaking out. That was a lot of fun.

MA: Did they do the show?

JS: Yea. And the bus finally got fixed three days later. A couple more flights. Our gear went with Sevendust. The drummer knew the guy from Filter so we borrowed their third drum kit – lucky.

JIM SOCHACKI

DRUM AND GUITAR TECH FOR GRAVITY KILLS, DRY CELL, GODHEAD, AND PIGFACE

MISTAKE TO AVOID

Don't buy your own bus!

Drum Tech-ing vs. Guitar Tech-ing

MA: What about setting up drums? You set up drums for me, Godhead, who else?

JS: Gravity Kills.

MA: How does that differ from guitar tech-ing?

JS: If there's a problem with the guitar, it's a lot easier and quicker to fix than drums. With drums, there's so much more involved. If there's a lug out of place, the whole thing could go out of tune; the wing nuts could fly off…

MA: You can have twelve spare guitars all in tune ready.

JS: It's a lot easier than having a drum kit on backup. You can change out a guitar in no time. Changing an entire drum set could take 12 minutes.

MA: I break a lot of things onstage. Always be prepared; have a spare. But just because you are prepared doesn't mean there won't be a problem.

JS: Everything needs to be right there so no one's standing around looking like a fool waiting for you to show up. Yea, you've broken stands before on stage, you know how long it takes to change one. Even though once onstage with Godhead, I changed a snare drum out with no one knowing! I always have extra snares, cymbals, etc., on stage and ready to go – not in cases.   I swapped the snare out and no one knew.

MA: Did anyone say "you're fuckin' awesome?"

JS: Naw, it was just me and the drummer. It was a quiet part of the song and literally no one knew except us.

MA: But you want people to know that you saved that song!

JS: The drummer knew and he was the one paying me!

Tour Manager/Agents

MA: Anything with a Tour Manager? Something you've seen that's been like, "Thank God that guy's here." And something that's like, "What the fuck is this guy thinking?"

JS: One guy might have been both of those. At times, he gave me a lot of moral support and helped me keep my sanity. At other times, he took away moral support and helped me lose my sanity. He would say things… We were an hour late driving into a show and I'm still in my bunk sleeping. He goes, "Hey man, it's 5! Where you been? We loaded in already! Martin's really mad!" Just trying to fuck with me like that and making me freak out and jump out of my bunk. As I started to wake up, I realized the bus was still moving, I'm like, "Fuck you, we're still moving!"

MA: Any agent experiences—good or bad?

JS: Agents? Not directly, no, but whatever the tour manager's dealing with, if it's affecting the tour, it's gonna affect me. Anything from more shows, cancelled shows, less budget…

> "I always have extra snares, cymbals, etc., on stage and ready to go – not in cases."

Days Off

MA: What's something that really affects everyone in the crew—the catering being late?

JS: Rest. We would work 18 hours a day for months and then we really took a day off! We'd usually need a day off after the day off!

Advice?

MA: You've worked with drum kits, guitars, keyboards, and staging. Do you have any advice for anybody that would want to do that?

JS: Don't do it. Stay in school. Get a degree. Become a doctor or a lawyer or a computer engineer or an electronic engineer—something that pays.

MA: When it pays, it pays OK. Is the trick to keep work lined up?

JS: Yea, I've run into people that tech for big bands like Pearl Jam and Def Leppard and Van Halen.

MA: So how do you get to work for a big band?

JS: Have social skills - which I have none of.

MA: Or a card!

JS: Yea, a working phone helps, too... lack of mental illness. I guess having a mental illness might help you relate...

> "Don't do it. Stay in school. Get a degree."

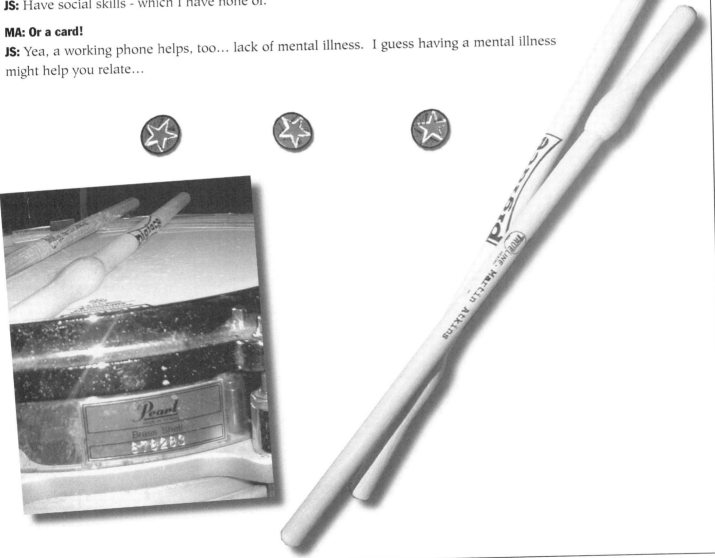

CHAPTER 26

SCENERY AND STAGE DECORATION

"You have to brand your environment. If you don't, you'll be standing in someone else's."
— Martin Atkins

"Good ideas can be cheap and effective. They can help brand your band, make your show cool, and provide a revenue stream."

Maybe it's because I know how to screen print, but it seems like this area is always overlooked by bands. Good ideas can be cheap and effective. They can help brand your band, make your show cooler, and provide a revenue stream.

In the early days of Killing Joke, I saw what could be done by an ingenious lighting designer. When he saw his budget shredded from several thousand dollars to eight hundred dollars, he created a set with nine ten-foot sticks of 3/4 inch conduit (metal pipe), three catering-sized woks with the handles cut off, some long extension cables, and cans of Sterno provided by the venue. He made a tripod by drilling three pieces of conduit together with small chains to prevent them from opening all the way out. With a wok on top, he placed four cans of Sterno in the wok. Three quarters of the way through the show, when things were getting sweaty and the audience was starting to move as one, he would run around the back and plug in the extension cable to an electrical outlet which began sparking inside the wok, creating a crude electrical ignition device for the Sterno fuel. The result was fantastic on small and large stages alike. Of course, I'm not recommending you do this now (this was 1987) pre-Great White. I'm trying to illustrate that what you need to make a great show and effective scenery is really nothing, except a great big bag of ingenuity.

"What you need to make a great show and effective scenery is really nothing, except a great big bag of ingenuity."

The multi-panel backdrops we do now cost less than $500 to create five 4' x 30' panels. They look good in smaller venues and amazing in a theatre setting where you can allow the full drop.

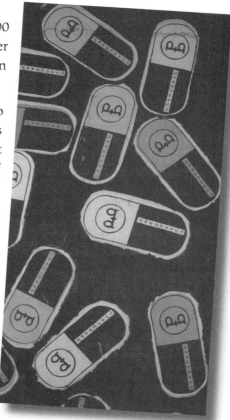

With creative use of inks, you can add other elements to a show. On the Phenobarb Bam-ba-lam Tour with Chris Connelly, WaxTrax Records struggled to get the tour out the door. I liked the idea of dancing pills. Conscious of the fact that we had no light guy or money, I used UV/Florescent inks to print the pills and then filled in the background in black. We took out three UV strip lights (black lights) with the effect that, whenever the house lights came down, the pills would glow.

In 1983 David Jackson created a huge bathroom set for *Public Image Limited*. He stretched white plastic on large frames and then created a tile "grid" using electrical tape. We added a bright projection of the *PiL* logo to the angled ceiling of the stage. When we arrived in London, we added a couple of urinals at the front, which a couple of the audience members used.

Scenery from Chris Connelly tour by Martin Atkins

SHEEP ON DRUGS

With the *Sheep on Drugs* tour, they were using video projections and had their well-known Sheep on Drugs neon sign. I wanted to create an environment for them where the projections would be more effective and we wouldn't be showing all the elements of their show the moment they walked on stage. I designed a show for them which used a box out of metal conduit that had white curtains across the front and was screen printed with Japanese lettering in a special glow-in-the-dark ink. Charged by light it radiates once the lights are turned off—just like the glow-in-the-dark stars you stick on kids' ceilings. The projections for the first few songs hit the white curtains in front. The glow-in-the-dark Japanese lettering provided more interest. It echoed a kind of Bladerunner theme. When the neon was turned on in song number four, it could be seen to be flickering inside the box and diffused through the thin curtains… anticipation.

Two songs before the end, Lee and Duncan, would pull the curtains back so you could see the neon. We built two dancer cages which each had mannequins inside. The strobes inside the white fabric box seemed ten times more powerful. During the last song, Duncan and Lee drew the curtains back and left the stage while the word "Applause" flashed (the audience members are all supposed to be sheep anyway, right?). When the band came on for the two song encore, they drew the curtains back again, we had replaced the two mannequins with two dancers. They stayed frozen for a couple of minutes then started dancing. A nice little mindfuck when they started to move. Total Cost: $600. (Note: they already had the neon and the projector.)

TEST DEPARTMENT

In 1997, when Test Department arrived in the U.S. for their first tour in ten years (and their last), we spent a lot of time with their advance men, Martin King and Gus Ferguson, driving around local scrap yards trying to find materials to make percussive instruments. It wasn't until two days before the tour left that I realized, although they had some projections, there wasn't any other scenery. The band's album, Totality, had phrases all over it. I made 8' X 4' frames out of 1' X 2' wood and stretched mesh across. Then, I retyped all the phrases from the album in Courier Bold Outline font and xeroxed all of the letters experimenting with enlargements to get the right size. Amy Gorman, the publicist at the label, helped me. We used Elmer's Glue and hoped the panels would survive the first week. Total Cost: $150.

When the panels were pulled forward to act as side banners, the shadows of the words danced across the performers. You can see from the photographs how cool it was. I'd love to say it was intentional, but it was one of those glorious happy accidents.

Did the glue hold up? Well, one panel is sitting in my office right now, ten plus years later. The message on this piece of scenery, "The only constant thing is change," another wonderful, happy accident.

PIGFACE SHIT LIGHTS

For the "Feels Like Heaven, Sounds Like Shit" tour, I fantasized about having KISS-style lights flashing behind the band. But, of course, flashing the word "shit." I made it happen using the same "stretch-a-frame" idea as the Test Department scenery, but with chicken wire instead of mesh. Five interns working for several days with Christmas tree lights and garden twist ties saw the project to fruition. We flew the light frames a couple of feet in front of the backdrops and, with the chicken wire and frames painted black, they remained "theatrically invisible" until we lit them. Total Cost: $200 plus pizza and beer for interns (If you buy your Christmas lights on December 27th).

Happy Accident Number Whatever: It was tough not to look around knowing that the word SHIT was illuminated behind me six feet high. As I looked at the crowd, I saw strange looks on people's faces, puzzled, weird… and then, after a few minutes, laughter and yells and fantastic applause. I found out later that the letter "S" wasn't plugged in correctly. So, for the first few minutes, our fans thought we were conceited assholes, flashing the word "HIT" as we played one of the more popular songs. Jolly, who did lights in addition to managing the tour, described it to me at the end of the night. Jim had scrambled around on stage until the "S" flickered and then lit. It took us two more tours and some home engineering from Jim before our light guy would have the ability to sequence and flash each panel, enabling:

- Flashing SHIT
- Chasing SHIT
- HIT

KILLING JOKE

The stage looked bare. I had two banners made (left and right) and then, for the shooting of the video, "Money is not our God," I had a screen shot of a dollar bill (12" X 30") and created the first of the multi-panel multi-image scenery.

We went out and bought white parachute suits (the singer, Jaz, was wearing a khaki suit at the beginning of the tour) and we screen-printed the dollar bills all over the suit. It made for some great pictures and a couple of magazine covers. With the re-release of the Extremities album, these pieces of fabric took on more meaning as memorabilia and will be featured in my upcoming gallery shows.

Geordie Walker, Martin Atkins, Jaz Coleman and Paul Raven.

Martin Atkins Private Collection

PIL

In 1981, PiL performed a show at the Ritz in New York City. I was in London and started to receive phone calls at my flat. "See you tomorrow. Can't wait!" It turned out that John and Keith who were in New York to do some interviews—had been offered to do two shows at the Ritz when Bow Wow Wow cancelled. I guess Keith thought that any drummer could do what I did, or maybe he wanted to save money on a transatlantic flight. In any case, they hired a jazz skiffle drummer from a music store uptown. It was a hot ticket. The Who, amongst many others, were there. We'd been able to pull off the show in Paris with me only having an hour rehearsal with the band but, I knew all the songs inside out and so did Wobble—not so much luck with the Skiffle guy.

Fifteen hundred people watched as the band performed behind the projector screen. It was very cool, anti-rock star, and hip as fuck. It sounded great, too, because (unbeknownst to the audience) the band was miming along with the vinyl-album version of *The Flowers of Romance*. It was a great idea, until the record skipped. People started throwing anything within reach at the $12,000 screen. Very smartly, Keith

Photo by Lisa Haun, New York, NY.

tried the line, "Destroy the screen and you destroy yourselves!" But it was too late for that. Six months later, when I arrived in New York City and rejoined the band, the phone at our loft was still ringing from the people at the Ritz, demanding that we replace the screen.

Ever since seeing photographs of the show that I wasn't at, I've been fascinated with the idea of people not seeing everything immediately, the idea of shadows and anticipation. In one form or another, Pigface has used 8' x 4' stretched white panels across the front of the stage ever since allowing us to:

- Mess around on stage comfortably before the show without being seen.

- Have 25 people on stage with different color flashlights to create an amazing Disney-like backdrop for performances occurring in front of the screen.

- Perform the first one or two numbers with the band in shadow and one or two vocalists up front—while we adjust monitors and levels.

On the Damage Manual tour in 2000, the first time Wobble and I were on stage together since PiL in 1980, we took the screen/curtain idea one step further we used the style screens. When the screens were lowered two songs in, they revealed panels of snow-fencing in front of each performer, once again echoing the shadow-play effect of the Test Department scenery. It wasn't until five songs in that Chris Connelly reached up and snatched the snow-fencing down from in front of the drums… layers… Onions have layers.

Once again, having the right tools, you can create your own environment on stage, from exorcising your Newcastle Brown Ale fetish to shadow-play and dancing glow-in-the-dark pills.

Pigface with guest Danny Carey

CHAPTER 27

SO YOU WANT TO BE A TOUR MANAGER (YOU CRAZY F*#K!)

"Good tour managers enable magic; bad ones necessitate it."

– Martin Atkins

Tour managing puts you somewhere between travel agent, psychiatrist, trouble shooter, imaginative thinker, diplomat, plate-spinner, and accountant; watching the bottom line but then understanding when it doesn't matter. That's a difficult balance. Mixed together with some understanding and hopefully an inner calm that once disturbed becomes a Howling Tiger… like some kind of martial arts deal—walk softly and carry a big schtick!

Really great tour management is unseen. It is the invisible difference of multiplied minutia that either build a higher platform for the artist to jump off of or slowly mount on their backs as a weight to carry, suffocate, and sap. It is a compassionate understanding of the stress of being on the road—not an objective argument for sanity. It is respect first and foremost for the craft and the tradition, the honor, if you like. That means that I can happily insist that someone gets the certain something that makes them happy (for whatever reason) not because I necessarily agree with their needs, but because I understand that this is about something else. Comfort food isn't about how much we like mashed potatoes, it's about a reflected memory flash…

It's being able to view these needs as important—not trivial. When my youngest son Sidney wants to go to sleep, he needs his favorite stuffed animal with the tag and his pacifier—that's it. I don't spend any time trying to convince him that he needs something else or that my perceptions of what he might need are important, he just gets what he needs, end of story. The trick is just to understand this without treating the artist like a two year old; to not disrespect anyone's pre-show set-up psychology because maybe somewhere along the tour you'll learn about why those things are needed.

> "Really great tour management is unseen. It is the invisible difference of multiplied minutia that either build a higher platform for the artist to jump off of or slowly mount on their backs as a weight to carry, suffocate and sap."

"I now approach touring from an almost AA point of view: Accept the things I can't change, change the things I can, and most importantly, have the wisdom to know the difference."

– Chris Tisone

TOUR MANAGEMENT
CURSE MACKEY

Someone in every group of enthusiastic fuck-ups that are out to get drunk, pick-up chicks, and get famous a.k.a. "The Band," needs to be the agreed upon as Leader, a.k.a. the Tour Manager. As nice as it is to have someone else do it for you, in the early going, it often falls on the band to handle matters themselves. It is a good thing to learn how to manage your own tours first. For one, you learn to do it and if you make it to the level of hiring someone, you'll know more about what it is they do and whether they are doing a good job at it. Also, it is helpful for you to have a face-to-face relationship with the talent buyers and club owners. If you are a charming soul, it is going to help you with future gigs and getting these busy people on the phone. There are people that I booked shows with in the mid 90's that I still have active friendships with and it is because I was the guy taking care of the business end of the performance.

CURSE MACKEY

TOUR MANAGER
WOODSTOCK TATTOO &
BODY ARTS FESTIVAL
EVIL MOTHERS / PIGFACE
www.actionartsagency.com

Regardless of who is the tour manager, here are some things you must deal with to have a successful tour. Basically, your job is to make sure the show happens and that the band is properly looked after.

- **Someone needs a credit card** to rent a van, book hotels and deal with emergency situations.

- **Don't let the band trash the club** until you/they can afford to pay for damages.

- **Advance your shows.** Contact with the club lets them know that you are on top of things and are a pro. Call the club a couple of times one to three weeks out to confirm times, promotion, and to build enthusiasm for the show.

- **Have an e-mail sign up sheet** at the merch booth.

- **Bring a briefcase that has a lock** (Don't lose the key, asshole).

- **You must have a cell phone** and always pay your bill on time.

- **Maintain a database of all your contacts, club owners, bands, radio people, and cool stores** in each city and keep adding to it. It's hard to do, but totally essential. After five years, you will have an incredibly valuable resource. Like I said, it's all in who you know and even better if you know how to contact them.

> "It is a good thing to learn to manage your own tours first."

The tour manager is, in essence, the baby sitter, coach, camp counselor, driver, crew chief, all-essential voice of reason and responsibility, and the glue that holds it all together. You need to be able to drive, budget, collect the pay, make sure the merchandise is up and running and ordered, and make sure that the booking agent, publicist, crew, local staff, and band members are all doing their jobs as effectively as possible. Tour managing is one of the most difficult jobs in the business. It comes with a lot of responsibility and very long hours. You need to have serious problem solving skills and be a fast thinker.

EXAMPLE: Doing whatever it takes to make the gig happen, as long as everyone is safe, is the most important part of a tour manager's job.

I was managing and playing keyboards for My Life with the Thrill Kill Kult and we were headed to NYC for a sold out show at Irving Plaza. As we headed out in the a.m. from New Haven, CT, the bus broke down. Once we knew the bus was totally fucked, we realized we could be, too. This was a very important gig and to not show up would cost the band more than five figures in guarantee plus merch sales. I ended up calling four cabs. I sent the band on towards the venue in two cabs so they could get there, relax, and have time to eat and get ready while we dealt with the shit.

The soundman and I cabbed it back to New Haven to get a U-Haul truck. We drove back to where the bus and crew were waiting. We unloaded all of the gear from the trailer into the U-Haul. At the same time, the tow truck for the bus had arrived. Once we were finished and had grabbed the gear, the bus was towed to a fortunately-placed service center. So now I get to drive the 26' U-Haul truck to NYC with the rest of the crew in cabs following us. Of course, this process has put us several hours behind and now we are crashing straight into Manhattan's Friday rush hour. We show up 30 minutes after doors were to open. I maintained contact with the band and the club production manager to let them know to hold doors and also dealt with keeping the local loaders on board and getting the band the hospitality rider. Fortunately, this was a sell-out show so we had the leverage; otherwise, we would have probably had to load in ourselves, as promoters start cutting costs on money-losing shows. We had to cancel the opening band in order to do a brief line check and to insure that the band could do its full set, as the club also had a curfew for the all ages show. Once it was all up and running, we opened doors, the band went on and put on an amazing show, the audience went home happy, and we were paid in full. It was a close call, but fortunately we were able to think fast and did whatever it took to make the gig. Doing whatever it takes to make the gig happen, as long as everyone is safe, is the most important part of a tour manager's job.

"The tour manager is in essence, the baby sitter, the coach, camp counselor, the driver, the crew chief, the all essential voice of reason and responsibility, the glue that holds it all together."

TOUR MANAGER

MARK O'SHEA

THE DO'S

MARK O'SHEA
NIN
TOUR MANAGER

- **Learn the power of three magical words: "Please" and "Thank You."** You will be amazed at how far they can get you, what doors get opened, and how they can smooth out difficult situations.

- **Make a tour budget before heading out on the road.** You need to have a place to start your expectations and know how to monitor them. Learn fiscal responsibility.

- **Talk to your manager, your publicist, and your agent** at least once a day until they tell you not to call so much. These are the life blood connections to the artist and being on the road. Keep them all informed as to "How things are going out there..."

- **Know what all the people at the label do for a living –** that is, what their jobs are, not just the title. For learning and earning is, after all, multi-tasking, isn't it?

- **Kill all you meet with kindness.** This applies a bit back to point number one. But it applies more to the aspect of: you never know where your next job could come from, and ever so closely to: what goes up must come down; those you meet on the way up, you may meet on the way down.

- **Learn how to read your performance contract.** On the one side, it is your job, and on the other, you pay for an attorney already, why not get a bit of free advice one day backstage at a show over some beers and some reading?

- **Learn how to advance your shows properly.** Do call ahead and set up your time schedules, discuss technical concerns, ask directions, and develop a routine way of gathering this information. Respect time and time will respect you.

- **Discuss the smoking rules of the bus before you get out on the tour.** Where and what is to be smoked where and how. This is a group meeting discussion.

- **Remember the code of the road:** What happens on the road, stays on the road.

> "Remember the code of the road:
>
> What happens on the road, stays on the road."

THE DON'TS

- **Don't put any solids in the toilet on tour buses.** All solids are a big no-no. No brown goes down; all paper goes in the garbage. Do your other business elsewhere, usually in the girl's restroom before doors open.

- **Don't condone or conduct underage drinking** or the like in any fashion, especially on the bus. Doing so only leads to many, many headaches (no pun intended), more so nowadays than any time in the past.

- **Don't let strangers on your bus or you will eventually be sorry.** You should develop a set of rules as a group for how and why visitors are allowed on the bus (your home away from home).

- **Don't treat others with any disrespect.** Treat folks the way that you would like to be treated. Easy to remember: what goes around comes around. Keep it professional at all times. If someone or several dudes are being difficult, karma will come to them. You should rise above their level and not bring yourself down. Burning bridges leaves a trail that can allow you to be tracked down and this draws a lot of attention.

- **Don't leave home without cash reserves in your bank account.** You never know when the next emergency could arise. This is advice that should be given to all artists, crew, and touring entities. Most of the time, surprises are unwelcome on the road; routines are what you strive for.

- **Don't screw around at border crossings.** Have your paperwork in order (that goes for immigration and customs). Never be under the influence at the border. Never be disrespectful to either of the officer types (immigration or customs). Never have drugs you're sneaking in or out; too many hassles can ensue, especially nowadays.

- **Don't blow off any interviews or photo ops.** The press, even though it may at times not seem so, is very advantageous to your touring career. This is part of your job anyway.

- **Don't get too worn out before your important shows.** Everything in moderation as you approach larger markets and industry shows along the tour. Bad shows lead to bad things all around. Bad for the relations with label, press, and mostly, the damn fans who keep you out there in the first place.

- **Don't forget about good hygiene and eating habits.** You get sick as a lack of interest in either of these, then the whole tours suffers. Shows get cancelled, fans get bummed, tours get cancelled, and bands get dropped. You get the picture. Simple things that get out of hand snowball into larger things that get insurmountable.

- **Don't break the code of the road.**

Check out the note from Martin on "The Code of the Road" in *Personalities, Ego, and Charisma* chapter.

> **"Shows get cancelled, fans get bummed, tours get cancelled, and bands get dropped."**

SMALL STUFF

Tour managers take note: take care of the small stuff, and you might not need to deal with the big stuff. In fact, on tour, risking life being away from family and loved ones, cat, and a comfortable chair, I don't believe there is such a thing as small stuff.

Tour manager tip: Keep the driver's licenses for the loaders. They are the first to arrive and could be the first to leave if you don't! And most likely to not reappear at the end of the night.

> "Take care of the small stuff, and you might not need to deal with the big stuff."

"There are few jobs in which you reinvent the wheel every day or so - this is one of them. That challenge will stretch you beyond your self-imposed limitations. Aside from learning to fall asleep in seconds and under any conditions, is there anything more rewarding?"

- Burt Bramlett

MARTIN ATKINS ASKS:

JOLLY ROGER

SO YOU WANT TO BE A TOUR MANAGER...

MA: I think that my favorite thing to ask anybody is: if you could go back twenty-five years, what would you say to yourself? What advice would you give yourself?

JR: As far as dealing with people and rock 'n' roll, I like to think that, maybe I'm mellower, maybe I don't yell as much, maybe I yell at the right time, maybe I listen to other people more... That all comes with age—there's nothing you can do about that.

MA: You told me once that you wanted to cook breakfast for everybody. Why?

JR: I like cooking and it would be a real easy job to get up and, as everybody came off the bus, I would cook breakfast and people would tell you what went wrong the day before, blah, blah, blah... you know, and then, after that, move off and take care of whatever we have to take care of.

MA: With that information.

JR: Yea. And that's the whole thing... I don't know why it is, but people just come up and tell me things. Out of the blue, and this would let that kind of stuff happen. Whatever comes with it comes with it. I've never done anything just because it was easy. Some of the projects we've been involved with are some of the hardest projects ever made. You're doing 49 out of 50 days, flying all the baggage to Europe, playing New York one night and London the next... I mean, like in everything we've done, although I couldn't control things, I could adjust behavior, adjust...

MA: You could steer.

JR: Yea, and put some money away... I'll never tell you how much money I got! (Laughs) And you know that. But I'm never gonna. There are no top ten things. You gotta have everything. You gotta think of everything! You gotta have the red wine or white! In case they got a girlfriend. You gotta have a bottle of whiskey in case somebody just says, "It's time to go." You gotta have wrenches, you gotta have pliers, you gotta have testers, you gotta have cables, you gotta put a lot of crap in a little box. You know, it's really hard to just say you know anything you know. I always carry stamps. I always carry hand stamps so you can stamp passes for when some jerk on the crew steals 30 passes—you can get him by putting a sticker on everybody. You gotta have string, you gotta have rope, you gotta have straps. (Laughs) You gotta have whiskey... oh, did I say that? You gotta have two kinds! (Laughs) You gotta have vodka, you gotta have candy, you gotta have mouthwash. You gotta have earplugs, you gotta have...

MA: If someone was thinking of becoming a tour manager, would you say that self defense would be an essential part of that?

JR: Yea, it always is. OK, it's 2007, but when you read about Medieval Europe, I mean, guys used to just travel around and they used to try to take everything you had and there's guys out there right now that don't give a good goddamn and they'll take everything you have. I mean, it's amazing that there hasn't been more problems of that nature. Everything from always knowing where there's a piece of wood or something to smack a fucker with to... I used to carry that big wrench for a long time—a six hundred millimeter crescent wrench, which got stolen last weekend. I can't find it, so I can only assume somebody stole it. Sort of made me upset because it has a long connection… I've had it for a long time.

MA: Have you ever carried a gun on the road?

JR: No. There's too many laws that cross over. You clock a fucker with a piece of iron or something—OK, you're gonna get in trouble for a deadly weapon.

Touring is Warfare

MA: I put in one of the tour books the St. Crispen's Day speech from Shakespeare. And it seemed like this wild connection between touring and warfare. But it's not even a wild connection, it's…

JR: …the same. A lot of friends of mine when I got back from 'Nam, you know, had problems. I never really had those problems because I never really stopped. I was at war again. I mean, once I came in with Cheap Trick, that was '73, '74, or something like that, and we were doing 300 dates a year! We did that for three years in a row before their first album came out. That just makes it a life; it's not a gig or whatever, it's a lifestyle.

TOURING 101
ERIC PERINA

At the age of four years old, my first live audio experience was KISS Alive 2 on 8-Track. My older brother Mark would come home from school and scream at me for figuring out how to work his record player as I was scratching his Ozzy, Rush 2112, and Alice Cooper albums from dropping the needle on them. He gave me four bucks and took me to the local record store—Kroozin Music—and told me to pick out what ever I wanted. I searched around for hours and, after seeing the cover of KISS' Alive 2 up there on stage jamming, I was sold.

Since I was a kid, I've always dreamed about life on the road. I can do this forever. My experience with touring has been close to 20 years. I started working for a local PA company carrying gear for $35 a day and worked my way up to front of house sound engineer. I also do tour management. My first big tour was with the opening act for Cheap Trick. I was a drum tech for that tour and since then have toured with Survivor, Run-DMC, Twista, From Zero, Local H, Kanye West, and many other local and national acts. I mix for major label executives on both coasts and in-between. I have also done runs as a Drummer for many acts, including Killjoy, Voodoo Rain, 32 Leaves, and, currently, Dirtbag.

ERIC PERINA

CHICAGO, IL
CHICAGO MUSIC SERVICE

Traveling is a lot of fun and creates a better assessment of the world other then what you see everyday back at home. A continuous change of scenery is awesome as well as rewarding. It can also be a very tiring and enduring experience if you are not well prepared before you leave or if the party that you are traveling with is unorganized or not self-sufficient enough for your travels.

It is a team effort and the most important part is "you." It takes a self-sufficient person, along with other self-sufficient people, to become a touring team. If one person does not have it together, it hinders the whole tour. I've seen people left behind or sent home because they stayed at the after parties too late and missed a bus call by five minutes. It is a tough decision to make as a tour manager, but it is the right one in order to keep a schedule of 30 plus cities and a touring crew of 10, 20, or more on time.

"You can not organize enough." The one thing on the road everyone has to share is time.

It is a routine: practice it and it will show when you are in Iowa and you have less then 15 minutes to get on stage with possibly no sound check. It takes the pressure off.

Here are some check tips I follow in order to have safe, efficient travels and, most importantly, a great time.

1. **Pre-organize your tours as much as possible** including gear! Downsize as light as possible!

2. **Advance all shows and destinations**. Advances determine details for all scheduled stops—load in time, set times, sound check, etc.

3. **Do not bring extra stuff that could go unused.** It just adds more time to your travels and valuable space.

4. **Pre-organize all of your merchandise including pricing** (organizing out on the road becomes distracting to sales and you will lose money along the way).

5. **Create day-to-day itineraries for all parties attending** (everyone needs to be in the know). Details!

6. **Always use new strings, drum skins, and clean instruments** in order to develop a clean sound every night out on the road.

7. **Pre-check maintenance on all traveling vehicles** (carry a motor club card or tow card for emergency repairs or towing as well as emergency safety kits).

8. **Create contact list for all parties attending** including a contact list for a home base (label, reps, office, etc.).

9. **A front of house pre-snake box with your own microphone set-up** to send to house saves time during change over. Include copies of a stage plot for house production.

10. **If you can, try to pre-rehearse your tour at a soundstage facility** with road crew, set-ups, tear down, and loading and pre-organizing trucks or vehicles.

11. **Always travel smarter not harder.** Drink lots of water.

The Art vs. Business Struggle Continues...

...except that there is NO struggle

ART always wins!
Then, the business of it fails
and the ART loses.
ALWAYS.
Business is not EVIL.
Art is not a badge to wear.
it's a fucking affliction
that does not need to be compounded
by bad business
or worse...
the denial that business exists.
    -Martin Atkins

tour 1990
MINISTRY
all access all areas

THE 4TH RHINO LABEL FEST
JULY 26 & 27, 1996
Martin Atkins
Invisible Records
Chicago IL

PiL
PUBLIC IMAGE, LTD.
JOHN LYDON KEITH LEVENE WOBBLE
NO. 3

TEST DEPT
AFTER SHOW
invisible
x-tacy under duress 1996

KILLING JOKE
BACKSTAGE
EXCESS
ALL AREAS

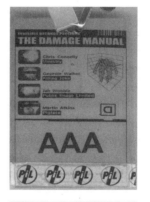

SEE The DAMAGE MANUAL
eWETLANDS N.Y.C. 10/21 11pm
Call The Syndicate
1-888-666-2061

DAMAGE ADDICT
THE DAMAGE MANUAL
D
GUEST

P.I.L
JAPAN TOUR
#2
Van Production
TOKYO
☎ 03-470-0681

DAMAGE ADDICT
THE DAMAGE MANUAL
D
ALL ACCESS

PIGFACE
SCORN
FM EINHEIT
BAGMAN
NOT
BREATHING
PHYLR
DEAD VOICES
ON AIR

THE DAMAGE MANUAL
Chris Connelly Ministry
Geordie Walker Killing Joke
Jah Wobble Public Image Limited
Martin Atkins Pigface
AAA

MCP CONCER
STAFF PASS
ACCESS ALL AREAS
Venue
Authorised by

MURDER INC.
MURDER INC.

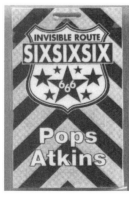

INVISIBLE ROUTE
SIXSIXSIX
666
Pops
Atkins

SHEEP on DRUGS
AFTER SHOW
invisible
x-tacy under duress 1996

pigface
Sounds The Same
AFTER show

ALL ACCESS

KILLING JOKE
10th Anniversary North America Tour
ALL ACCESS

WORKING TOGETHER TO TEAR THINGS APART
underground, inc.
UNITED II TOUR 2003
U
DIFFICULT
FUCKHEAD

Pigface
Team '94
invisible
INDEPENDENCE AND STRENGTH THROUGH DIVERSIFICATION
ALL ACCESS

IN BLUES WE TRUST
PIGFACE
HOUSE OF BLUES
CHICAGO

pigface
dope
PROFESSIONAL MURDER MUSIC
RACHEL STAMP
DIABLO SYNDROME
TEAM '03
THE UNITED TOUR
PRESS

CHILDREN'S TOURING GROUP
CHRIS TISONE

My first true experience with touring came hard and fast. I was the stage manager for a touring children's show based in Chicago. We usually performed for schools and libraries within a one to two hundred mile radius—usually day trips, sometimes an overnight or two, but that was about it. The touring group consisted of me and six actors, three men, three women, and sometimes the director and the writer would come along as well. Really nothing major until one day, the company announced we were going to Florida on an 8-day tour, hitting multiple large capacity venues, in three different cities across the state. At the time, I think we all might have felt like this was going to be a big paid vacation.

The director and the actors were flown down, and I left two days earlier with a 16-foot rental truck and the writer. Our first load-in, in West Palm Beach, was uneventful and we had a good time getting to know the staff at the venue as we put up the set and plotted the lighting. Everyone else arrived safe and sound and we had a great tech rehearsal. Everything was going as planned. We were a bit farther from home, but we had our set up and rehearsal period down to a science; even the Union guys were impressed with how efficiently everyone managed everything. Everyone, for the most part, helped out, even the actors. Some places we physically couldn't do certain things because we were forbidden by Union rules, but more often than not, the cast would help me load the truck up before going to the next venue.

As I mentioned, everything was going fine. The show was ready to go, and since our show was for school children, we had nothing to do but check into the hotel and relax for the evening before the morning show. Later, we met up with some of the venue staff for dinner. Afterward, they wanted to show us around a bit. No one was ready to go back to the hotel yet, so we went to local bar. Now it may or may not surprise you that theatre folk have a tendency to party, and that's the ironic part of what was about to happen to us. We were good that night. We were really good. Everyone knew that we had to get up early to get to the venue in time for warm ups, fight call, and the inevitable arrival of six hundred screaming children for a 9:00 a.m. show. (A side note: After you've done theatre like this for a while, you learn that a hangover and even a couple of screaming children don't mix—imagine hundreds of them!)

I'm always a bit of a "mother hen" when it comes to my cast, even though I like to imbibe as well. If I'm stage managing a show, in town, or on tour, I try to keep at least one sober eye out for any potentially damaging situations, and I can honestly say that everyone was just having a good time and maybe a little slap-happy from all the traveling and hard work. Nobody was drunk or out of control. We even decided as a group to leave relatively early that night.

On our way to the van, we were delayed at the tracks by a speeding freight train. Everyone was shouting and yelling—basically goofing off—while we waited for the train to pass. A couple of the guys, including the lead in the show, broke into an Irish jig. I think Riverdance was popular at the time. It happened so quickly. I think we all thought it was a joke at first. The lead actor kind of stumbled and then a look of excruciating pain came across his face and he crumpled. He'd landed wrong on his left ankle and had what looked to be a major sprain. I got his pants leg up and—I've heard stories of things swelling to the size of various fruits —within moments of the accident, his ankle literarily swelled up like an overripe cantaloupe.

Immediately, as if on cue, all manner of hell broke loose. I decided, upon seeing the injury, that a trip to the ER was our only option. Not only was this injury worse than anything I'd ever encountered before, the visual severity of the injury led me to believe that the ankle could be broken and my even worse fear was that without medical attention, the poor guy could potentially be faced with permanent damage. At this point, everyone decided to chime in. "He doesn't have insurance, you can't take him to the ER." "What about the show tomorrow?" "How are we going to get back to the hotel?" "Let's just put some ice on it and an ace bandage; he'll be fine." "We can't spend the whole night at the hospital." "Will we have to cancel the show?"

I felt like a quick executive decision was in order. Unfortunately, there was no one making that decision. Everyone just panicked, worrying about things other than the current problem at hand. This guy's injury looked to be getting worse by the minute, so I decided to step up and take control of the situation. After getting everyone's attention, I think I had to yell to do that—I hate having to yell—we carried him back to the van. Luckily, we had the light board operator from the venue with us who offered to take us to the hospital so everyone else did not have to. I instructed everyone to go back to the hotel, get some sleep, and plan for a much earlier call in the morning, once we determined what we were going to do.

After a long night in the emergency room, we learned that, indeed, he had a major sprain and, in addition to a temporary leg cast and crutches, he would have to stay off the leg as much as possible. I remember the doctor actually chuckling when we mentioned that we had a show in about five hours. At this point, it was about 4:00 in the morning and our leading man was incapacitated. There were no understudies on the tour and no one who could take over the part. It was too late to cancel the shows that day because the school busses were leaving early that morning. We had to come up with a game plan. After talking to the director, we decided we would wake everyone up at 5:30 a.m. and re-stage the show so that the actor could do it on crutches.

I'm not sure how, but believe it or not, we pulled it off. Had the circumstances been even slightly different, I don't know if it would have been possible. The actor was in so much pain and could not take anything stronger than Tylenol for fear that it would affect his performance —as if excruciating pain wouldn't. If it had not been for his determination to go on with the show, it never would have happened. Hell, I'm pretty sure I would not have been able to do what he did. His character was on stage almost the entire show. We had to quickly change all of the blocking and stage business. Our show was a cautionary tale about bullying and there is a scene where he got beat up by three schoolgirl bullies. The fight culminated with one of the girls smashing him in the face with a lunch box. It was always a high point in the show for kids; they'd just go crazy during that scene. But this time, the children just sat in stunned disbelief that these three girls were beating up this guy on crutches. I will never forget the horrified looks on their faces! Later, in Q & A (it was in our contracts that there was a short question and answer session with the kids after the performance), all the kids wanted to ask about was his injury and why that was part of show (the play was based on a popular young reader book, in which the character is obviously not on crutches)! He always fielded this question and we answered with "Well, the show must go on."

> **"...a trip to the ER was our only option."**

Now you have to remember that all of this happened the first day of our tour. We had six more days to get through and suddenly the whole game had changed. We had to make sure that the actor's leg was up and iced when he wasn't on stage. He couldn't bathe because of the temporary cast, so we had to wrap his leg with garbage bags and duct tape so that he could wash up. During travel, everyone had to cram together with the luggage so that he could keep his leg up in the van. Everything took longer, call times had to be adjusted, and we constantly had to make sure that he wasn't making the injury worse. That was my biggest fear as a manager: that we'd get back to Chicago and the poor kid wouldn't ever be able to walk right again. The doctor, after all, had said that he really shouldn't be on it at all.

Even now, I'm not totally sure how we did it, but we managed. After everyone's initial panic, we all pulled together and made it work. It's just what you do in this business. I think it also demonstrates the randomness of this business. You can plan contingencies for whatever you think is going to go wrong on the trip, but take my word for it: it's never what you think it's going to be. I'd like to say that a tour manager should be prepared for anything and everything, but there is just no way to realistically do that. I now approach touring from an almost AA point of view: Accept the things I can't change, change the things I can, and most importantly, have the wisdom to know the difference.

> **"I now approach touring from an almost AA point of view: Accept the things I can't change, change the things I can, and most importantly, have the wisdom to know the difference."**

EMILY WHITE
TOUR MANAGER FOR THE DRESDEN DOLLS

I don't even know where to start. It's been such a whirlwind three years. I was a music industry major and interned all around Boston like crazy. I met Amanda one night when the Dolls played at my university (Northeastern). I asked if she needed help with anything and she was like, "Please come over tomorrow!" As she had no label, no manager, and had managed to sell 10,000 CDs for the band on her own.

A few months later, they were going on their first "National Tour" which included a stop at *SXSW*, but it was a humble beginning as they were only making $100-$200 a night. I asked if I could tour manage, admitting that I didn't officially have any experience but I could at least sell their merch. Amanda needed to check with Brian and, after a week had gone by, I inquired again (as I didn't know her that well at the time). She said, "I totally forgot!" And yelled across the apartment, "Hey Brian, can Emily be our tour manager?" He said, "Yeah, that's cool" and so it began. That tour was a blast and a great way to get my feet wet. From there, I just grew with the band.

I remember their first big NYC showcase was a big deal as was when we flew out to LA for a west coast showcase. That following summer, we were supposed to go on the Lollapalooza tour, but it was canceled and so we did a regular national club tour. I then took a break for a few months to do an internship at MTV U.K. in London. I came back just in time for some New Year's shows and continued to somehow tour manage them while I was in college. I missed one 6-week tour in my last semester of college, but would still do all their one-offs and weekend shows. The day I graduated from college, the band was playing Coachella and, as I said, we kicked off the NIN support tour, which was six weeks, and also hit Mexico and Europe.

I was 22 and it was obviously very intimidating, but by far one of the most rewarding experiences of my life. I'll never forget standing out in the rain with our sound guy before the first NIN load in when the NIN production manager asked where our banner was. I told him it was in Colorado getting licensed and fireproofed (thinking this was the right answer) and he stormed off saying, "Trent's not going to be happy about this" as I guess they wanted to use our banner to cover their gear. Within the hour, The String Cheese Incident tour manager (who I knew through the management company) happened to live in San Francisco, where we were, and took me all around to the production folks at The Warfield and introduced me. I made a few emergency calls to him on that tour (i.e. "Fuck! How am I supposed to get a bus driver hotel room on the Vegas strip for $100?") and am forever grateful. The NIN production manager and crew came around quickly and I really appreciate everything they taught me.

EMILY WHITE

TOUR MANAGER: THE DRESDEN DOLLS, IMOGEN HEAP. MADISON HOUSE MANAGEMENT CO. NY
www.dresdendolls.com
www.madisonhouseinc.com

From there, we crisscrossed North America, Europe, Australia, and Japan multiple times over the next few years. I love being on my feet at all times and having to deal with whatever is thrown at me. I have friends and business contacts all over the globe as I've traveled so frequently with the Dolls. They didn't even want to go on their international promo trips without me—which was a blast for me!

But my work went beyond tour management, as I did a lot of day-to-day maintenance for the band as well. When I graduated from college, the band struck a deal with the management company that I would work in their office whenever I wasn't on the road so I would always be working on Dolls stuff. I love working at the management company but am not really a TM for hire. I did a tour with Imogen Heap once when their TM had a family emergency, but that's pretty much it. I'm constantly sorting out touring issues for our artists as it's obviously vital to their careers. My experience on the road has proven to be invaluable in life but also in my career at the management company.

SUICIDEGIRLS ON THE ROAD
VICTORIA SANTINO

My first experience of the SuicideGirls Live tour came from sitting next to the original girl who was organizing the tour. I'll call her "Peggy" so as to protect her later when I explain how she fucked up the tour. I think it's fair to protect her name because it wasn't entirely her fault; she simply had absolutely no idea what she was doing. But then…neither did I.

So, Peggy was constantly moaning about how much she hated this tour, the grueling piles of work it entailed, the difficult dancers she had to deal with and the venues that just wouldn't dish out enough money. Auditions were the first step. Thankfully, the owner of an LA club, The Dragonfly, has been a great supporter of us and allowed us to audition (and later rehearse) there, which saved the deficit this tour created quite a lot of money. Seven girls were chosen, two current SuicideGirls who were on tour last year, one dancer who was on tour last year, and four other dancers. The next step was to hope the dancers would be interested in becoming SuicideGirls, since this was the SuicideGirls Live tour after all.

After a bit of convincing and a lot of explaining by Peggy that they "don't have to show their vagina," the girls all agreed to become SuicideGirls. Therein lied the first of many fiascos: The girls didn't want anything to be shown. They covered up their nipples whenever possible and everything else most of the time. Any shots where you can see some butt cheek or cleavage, they wanted taken off the site…SuicideGirls.com…a site of pin-up photos. We learned quickly from this experience who our problem dancers would be. There were three big ones: One ended up quitting, one we let go, and one went on tour and became the bane of everyone's existence. So much so that when we got the offer to tour with Guns N' Roses later, all six of the other girls said "I'll go, as long as she doesn't."

After a mad rush to replace two dancers, the girls were rehearsed and ready to go out on tour. The next problem was that the girl who we had planned on sending as our merch girl couldn't even split a bill at a restaurant. We quickly (though very late in the game) realized she'd fail miserably out on the road. The decision was made to send Peggy instead. The tour had filled her entire work days up to now, so it made sense she go on tour and see her baby through to fruition. The idea wasn't so appealing to her. I remember her crying for several days, she really didn't want to go on tour. Maybe that should have been our first sign that something was not quite right with her, but we missed it and out on tour she went.

I spent several hours creating a beautiful excel document so that she can easily keep track of merch sales. All she had to do was enter the starting numbers of what she brought into each

> "We're not horrible people, just seem to have bad luck with merch girls."

venue and the ending numbers. The formulas did the rest and would tell her not only what she sold but how much cash she should have in her hands. Sounds easy enough, right? Well Peggy decided to tally sales on a beat up notebook, which meant that in the nine shows she handled merch for, she didn't account for over $4,500 worth of merchandise. Good thing we got her off that tour as quick as possible.

Sadly, it wasn't just because she couldn't keep track of sales that she was sent home. She was constantly holding up the van: was the last one out of the hotel in the morning and the last one out of the venue. She seemed to have a hard time counting: merch, money, pretty much anything. She was often high and rarely slept. One of her tasks while on tour was to put the playlist of songs for the show onto the $500 iPod SG had bought for her... for this exact purpose, to play the songs which the girls dance to... kind of the point of the whole tour. Well, she first wouldn't let the dancers use her iPod, then couldn't figure out how to put the playlist on the incredibly simple piece of Mac equipment. The last straw was dropped when she didn't FedEx the merch cash as she was instructed. After several warnings and Peggy still not able to get her shit together, we sent her home.

I had the fun job of picking her up at the airport and bringing her to the office to talk to Missy. She was in the car about five whole minutes before she asked "Am I getting fired?" I played dumb, knowing damn well that she was going to be taking a "sabbatical" one she'd likely never return from. I believe her sabbatical officially ended just a few days later, when we realized that she had scheduled one day of rest to make a 23-hour drive. That was a fun moment, when I

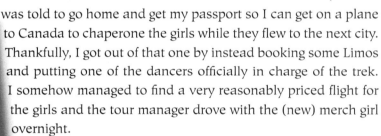

was told to go home and get my passport so I can get on a plane to Canada to chaperone the girls while they flew to the next city. Thankfully, I got out of that one by instead booking some Limos and putting one of the dancers officially in charge of the trek. I somehow managed to find a very reasonably priced flight for the girls and the tour manager drove with the (new) merch girl overnight.

Ah that brings me to another fiasco, the tour manager. We found a female tour manager who had previously been in the Israeli army, so we figured she'd for sure be able to handle some difficult dancers. We were wrong. While she seemed to be very on top of things the few days before tour when she was working from the office, once they got on the road, things slowly fell apart. Perhaps it was the fact that she was getting high before getting behind the wheel of the tour van, it could have had something to do with the fact that, as one of the dancers said, "she must have been on something. I never once saw her put anything in her mouth besides Red Bull." The girls were beginning to hate her for trying to drag them to the venues five or six hours before doors, they were also becoming a bit creeped out by her awkward stares in the dressing room, her absentmindedly leaving things, such as her laptop, literally on the side of the road, and her odd high school attempts to pit the girls against each other.

Missy decided she should get on the road herself and find out if the girls' complaints were valid. And they so were. Missy's first sign that things weren't right came when the TM told her that there were, "No more hotel rooms in the entire city of Chicago." Missy had no problem booking a room for herself. She arrived into Chicago on Friday night. The girls were supposed to get in Saturday morning, however, the TM decided to make an appointment first to get the van's brakes looked at, explaining that the girls are very worried about the brakes. This meant that Missy had flown out of LA earlier than she needed to and was now hanging out in a hotel in Chicago for a day and a half... five months pregnant.

She had planned to take the girls out for a nice dinner Saturday night, but they arrived into Chicago half an hour before doors. When the TM first saw Missy, she totally lost it (or maybe never had it to begin with). She started literally yelling at her "You're not going to ruin my reputation, I'm a good tour manager, how dare you think otherwise" and so on. Missy flew out there to get the full stories, not to accuse anyone of anything but because of this blow-up, she knew that she was going to have to learn all she could that night about being a tour manager so she can handle things after she fired this girl and searched for another. Missy sent the dancers off to have that nice dinner and she stayed at the venue to shadow the TM to learn as much about setting up a show as possible. During that night she spent quite a lot of time in the bathroom. Not because she was five months pregnant, but rather because she was on the phone interviewing new tour managers, which she found quite interesting, not knowing in the slightest what would make a good tour manager.

After the show she pulled an all nighter planning the next few days' schedules. It was planned out to the hour, everything from when they met at the lobby of the hotel, when they started driving, even the time they'd take to stretch before having lunch. She felt prepared and ready to fire that crazy tour manager; she just wasn't so sure about running the show until the next one arrived. The firing happened a bit prematurely, when Missy received a phone call from the enraged TM. One of the dancers had decided it would be a good idea to tell the TM that she was going to be fired. Missy somehow managed to get another Tour Manger out to Chicago for that night's show but he wasn't going to arrive until doors opened which meant that five foot tall, five months pregnant Missy had to drive the girls in the tour van. The trailer turned out to be her biggest nemesis, especially after she jackknifed it onto the sidewalk and had to enlist the help of a few men to actually lift it off the curb and back onto the road.

When they arrived to the venue that night, they discovered that the crazy Tour Manager had stolen the $500 *iPod*. One of the girls had an ipod shuffle, so they tried using that. The new TM attempted getting the shuffle to play the songs, but the thing with an ipod shuffle is: there's no screen. Not only did the new TM have no idea what he was doing because he had just been thrown onto this tour, he was also both not very technically adept and not able to see what songs were on the damn shuffle... because it has no screen.

Missy sat down with the new TM that night to settle up and prayed deep within herself that he knew what he was doing, because she certainly didn't. Thankfully he did, they got paid

> "...five months pregnant Missy had to drive the girls in the tour van. The trailer turned out to be her biggest nemesis, especially after she jackknifed it onto the sidewalk..."

correctly and went on to Detroit. Missy had to accompany them, because the girls didn't feel comfortable being left with a man they had only just met, makes sense, but for Missy that meant a five-hour drive in a van, and another night in a hotel room. At least the night in Detroit she was able to get some sleep, unlike the Sunday night after the final Chicago show, when she was kept up most of the night by a crying dancer. The one who was in charge of the ipod and was therefore going to get to keep it after the tour ended. She also happened to be the same one who told the crazy TM that she was being fired, giving her enough time to steal said ipod. That was another fun sleepless night for Missy.

The Detroit show went well and Missy was able to leave and come home…well, after a stop over in Chicago of all places. She also had about 70 grand in cash and checks from the venues as well as three laptops: hers, Peggy's old one and the one the merch girl managed to break. It was a very unnerving flight home.

Just before my two-week "vacation" was when Peggy was pulled off the tour, and about a week before my departure I was instructed to redo the budget and expenses to figure out just how badly we were in the hole. Missy and I sat down and went through the American Express bill, tallying up all the charges that this tour had incurred. I was both shocked and appalled by the spending that had been going on for this tour, even before they hit the road. A group of dancers, whose show includes taking off clothing spent nearly $8,000 on costumes and props. There was a misunderstanding with the girl we had gotten to do the dancers' hair, so for seven heads of hair, we spent $3,500. One of the girls had the company car while rehearsing and we mistakenly allowed her to hang onto the company credit card, so she easily raked up gas as well as some miscellaneous charges of $2,400.

Nixon and Regan

Peggy managed to spend over $1,000 herself in miscellaneous expenses during her "I don't want to go on tour" tantrums. Proclaiming she didn't even have enough time to do laundry, she was told she can send her clothes to the fluff n fold and put it on the company card. Unless she owns a ridiculous amount of clothes, I'm sure she dry cleaned her clothing instead, as it cost nearly $400.

Once the girls hit the road the expenses continued. There were some unavoidable but unexpected expenses, like over $1,000 for a trip to the emergency room when one of the girls couldn't see out of her swollen eye, another couldn't walk on her swollen knee and a third had a fever and apparently felt the need to accompany the others to the hospital to get it "treated." There were also many meal and travel expenses that probably could have been avoided if one of the dancers didn't have that damn company card. The total "incidental" expenses, as we ended up calling them, came to over $8,000, and that was for just nine weeks of touring.

We finally had a complete list of all these expenses, but sadly it was a bit too late to do anything about it. We made them promise to only put meals on the Amex when they had a long drive, and they were no longer allowed an extra hotel room when the rooms were cheap but that didn't really help much. We were already in the hole for over $50,000.

Thankfully, merch sales were good, so that helped, if only we could find a merch girl who A. accounted for all sales and B. sent us the cash when instructed. Why is it so difficult to send a FedEx, especially when you have pre-filled out FedEx forms? Our second merch girl was already eliciting complaints from the dancers, she was also constantly holding up the van both from the hotel and at the end of the night to count out. Furthermore, she would leave both the merch booth (the one job she has on the tour) and the cash box unattended. One night some of the dancers saw that she left the cash box and grabbed it. They gave it to the Tour Manager, and the merch girl never mentioned that the box was missing.

Several times she was instructed to FedEx the money to the office, and several times she failed. The last of these times, I wanted to make absolutely sure we received the money, so I called her the day she was supposed to get the FedEx out, three times – once in the morning, again early in the afternoon then again later in the afternoon. Each time, she assured me that the FedEx was going out. The last time, she even said that it was in the tour manager's hands and he was on the way to drop it off. When I didn't receive a tracking number though, I worried. When I spoke to her the next morning, she told me that the FedEx did not go out. She claimed that she gave it to the TM and he never dropped it off. I spoke to the TM (who I tended to believe a bit more) and he said she was still counting the money as she was speaking to me. I waited for her to count the money and hand it to the TM, then called her up and fired her. We were all so enraged in the office that none of us found any difficulty not buying her a plane ticket home. I later thought maybe that wasn't the best thing to do, but she wasn't doing her job and had already pretty much had a free ride on us. She also broke a $1,500 laptop which we had loaned to her to use (that fancy Excel document she also didn't bother to utilize) so my guilt quickly disappeared.

I thought that was the last of our problems with that girl, until I heard two days later from one of the other girls that the merch girl was still riding in the van with them, staying at their hotels and eating their food. This was bad in so many ways, not the least of which was the fact that the TM had neglected to tell us about it. Up until now, this new guy seemed to be doing pretty well. But he didn't even think there was anything wrong with someone who had just been fired off the tour to be still on the tour. I must admit that I was quite angry about this particular incident, and though I didn't want to search for another TM, I was ready to fire him. I nearly did due to the fact that he offered a couple of times to pack his bags and go if that's what we wanted... I think he was hoping I'd say no, but instead I believe I said something along the lines of "well I don't know how I can trust you anymore, so maybe that's best." He finally apologized, promised it'll never happen again, and assured me that the second merch girl would be out of our hands within five minutes.

I wouldn't say that left me happy, considering I then had to find another merch girl, but I had luckily been looking for a merch coordinator for the office, so I called up one of those candidates, and sent her on tour two days later.

> "I was both shocked and appalled by the spending that had been going on for this tour, even before they hit the road. A group of dancers, whose show includes taking OFF clothing spent nearly $8,000 on costumes and props."

As the SuicideGirls Live tour was coming to an end, and I continued my daily budget/expense checks to see how much deficit the tour had incurred for us, I received a call from our Booking Agent. It was the Wednesday of the second to last week of tour. He said that yesterday, he put us down just to see if anything would come of it, as possible support for Guns n' Roses and today he's heard that they may want us to go. The girls were already tired and wanting to come home. We knew there was no way we'd be able to get them to tour for another month and a half in a van. So I found a bus company and got a quote. I did a quick budget analysis and found that just for this leg of tour, we'd end up losing $16,000. We figured the publicity would be worth that amount, so we decided to go for it.

Or at least we decided to tell the GnR people that we were available. We then proceeded to bug them for an answer which we didn't receive until Thursday afternoon. I now had less than 1-1/2 business days to cancel a week of our current tour and prepare for another 5-1/2 week tour. And of course I had no idea what really needed to be done. Thankfully I had gotten involved in the previous tour, but I didn't know what had to be prepared, and I certainly had no idea how leasing a bus worked.

The girls headlined one last time in Las Vegas on Saturday, so I booked flights and limos to get them to Baltimore Sunday morning. The first gig with GnR was Monday night. That gave them 1-1/2 days to rework the routines for larger venues. We sent the choreographer out and hoped they could make it happen.

Thankfully, most of the props and costumes we were able to reuse, but I had a funny feeling that the bench and large folding ladder somehow wouldn't make it on the plane with the Tour manager and merch girl, who drove to LA on Sunday, handed me everything they wouldn't be needing, and got back on a plane that evening heading to Baltimore. I ordered a ladder to be delivered to the hotel in Batimore, which was probably one of the strangest conversations I've had: explaining to the hotel front desk that a large ladder would be delivered to one of their guests. We were able to check some hula hoops onto the plane, with only a few odd looks from the airline attendant and somehow managed to pack a few suitcases so full of costumes and props that I worried the over weight fees were going to be the least of our worries, as I had visions of stewardess costumes and stiletto heals sprawled across the tarmac.

The bus was probably the most difficult thing to wrap my head around. I had to learn what a "dead-head" day was, what it meant to owe the driver for an "overdrive" and I was praying that gas prices didn't increase any more than they already had. There were a lot of "hidden costs" with the bus that I didn't budget for, even though I had listened to the sleazy guy with the bus company yammer on about all sorts of things about busses he felt the need to enlighten me about, including one thing I heard more times than I had hoped to in my lifetime: the toilet is for pee only, otherwise there will be "plumbing issues." Apparently, the girls quickly learned that the sink also has similar restriction, it's for water only, not vomit, which they found out the hard way clogs up the plumbing as well.

Even once I understood what an overdrive cost is (when the bus driver has to drive more than 450 miles or 10 hours at a time) it was nearly impossible to avoid those charges. And at 185 a pop, they certainly increased our already swollen deficit.

We had an incident one drive where the bus actually broke down, due to the water lines freezing up. Of course, this meant having to pay the driver an overdrive cost, since he was behind the wheel for more than 10 hours. I didn't think it was very fair to have to pay because the bus broke down, but the damn bus companies sure set that up smartly, it's not the driver's fault either, so he deserves to be paid. When I asked the bus company if they'd give us some sort of credit for this incident, he had a think on it, spoke with his bosses, then spoke to the bus driver and told me that they had agreed that the driver would give us two overdrive's credit. I stupidly assumed that maybe the bus company was going to be crediting him this amount somehow...I was sadly mistaken. When it came time to settle up with the driver, he explained that he did indeed tell the bus company he'd credit us some overdrives, but in fact, those credits had already been made along the way, so I had to pay out another $370 I wasn't planning on.

The real fun part came when the driver handed me the receipt for this mechanical error as part of what he spent the float money on. We quickly got the bus company on the phone and the sleazeball denied having any knowledge of the fact that the driver used the float to pay the mechanic even though I later learned that the he had tried to get the driver to pay for half of it.

Lesson learned here: Bus companies are sleaze balls, budget an extra couple of thousand dollars to overdrives, cabs for the driver to and from the venue and extra fuel costs.

There was only one big "incident" that sticks out in my mind during this leg of the tour, and that began with the third merch girl not wanting to come home. It wasn't even that she wasn't doing her job, as I'd have guessed with our luck with these merch girls, but rather we just weren't selling enough merch to cover her weekly rate. She didn't want to come home, she was apparently having too much fun. I explained she was no longer needed on tour, I thanked her for everything, but reassured her that I needed her to go home. The day before she was supposed to leave, she just so happened to lose her purse, which contained her ID, and of course they were in Canada at the time, so she couldn't fly home. I didn't want to, but because I wasn't comfortable having someone who's no longer on tour in the bus, I ended up having to leave her without a wallet in a foreign country. I hear she had somewhere to stay and was there for over a week before she could get a replacement ID sent to her. We're not horrible people, just seem to have bad luck with merch girls.

The same flight that the merch girl missed, the choreographer was also supposed to be on to come home. She was on the first week of the tour reworking the numbers. I booked her flight, a hotel to stay in the night before she left (since the bus normally leaves at four in the morning), I booked her taxis and confirmed with her several times the week before, then Monday when I spoke to the TM, he said she didn't leave. He didn't seem very happy about it at all, said I should talk to her about why. So I did, and she told me that she couldn't get on her flight because Axl wanted all the girls to fly on his private jet with him to the next venue. To which I replied, "but you didn't need to go to the next venue" I think she came back with some bull shit about the bus not able to bring her to the airport, the plane was her only option or something. She pretended she didn't know she had a hotel room and basically didn't understand why she was "getting in trouble." In the end, she finally conceded and just agreed that she'd fly out the next morning.

I then spoke to the TM again and asked that he help make sure she gets on that plane (even though she's a grown adult who should have been able to take care of herself) and said that if she asks for cab fair, tell her no, it's her fault we had to rebook things. He responded with I think what's my favorite line of this whole tour, "Oh I'll give her money out of my own pocket if I have to, she's getting on that plane tomorrow. I want her out of here." Apparently, she wasn't as much an adult as we anticipated, she was as he called her "the leader of the three musketeers." I later heard that it wasn't actually all of the girls who went on Axl's plane, it was only three of the dancers plus the choreographer, the girls who apparently had something to provide to Axl, if you get my drift… but that's just what I hear.

All said and done, I think the biggest things I've learned on this tour are: it's hard enough to just break even, merch sales are much better when you're headlining and playing to your own fans, and merch girls are trouble.

"Sex is interesting, but it's not totally important. I mean it's not even as important (physically) as excretion. A man can go 70 years without a piece of ass, but he can die in a week without a bowel movement."

C·H·A·P·T·E·R ···· 29

ITINERARIES AND DAY SHEETS

"A well put together itinerary will make for a more successful tour. It's not going to eliminate all of the problems; it's just going to give you more time to deal with unexpected things that will crop up."

THE ITINERARY AS A TOOL

The itinerary should include basic information for anyone on the road: venue contacts, hotel information, departure times (if you know them), addresses, etc. In addition to the basic information, also include curfew, all ages, sound check, showers, dressing rooms, restaurants, limitations of venue (i.e. small stage). Do your work diligently and carefully. While you have the promoter's attention, and get the phone number for the production manager, the soundman man, the lighting guy, the number and the name of the person at the local hotel who will give you a good rate, etc. It's also a good place for helpful notes. If you remember that there's a great Thai restaurant around the corner or a fantastic laundromat with tvs and video games, put that in the itinerary. It might seem obvious if it's only one or two blocks away, but sometimes the artist and crew will never see the outside of the venue. Then, begin to use the itinerary as a bulletin board. If you've got two horrifying load-ins in a row, go back to a point before those two days where a warning (and some management sense!) would be useful. "Hey crew guys, we have a short drive and a hotel room so take advantage of the rest because

Looking at this itinerary from the 1980 PiL Tour, I see Larry White's hand all through this—late-night laundry, the phone card so we could have a clue how to call home, etc. The beginning of my education in all this was simply watching, he could turn an airline problem into an upgrade and a hotel problem into a later check-out. He showed me very early on that a problem is also an opportunity to do more than burst a blood vessel.

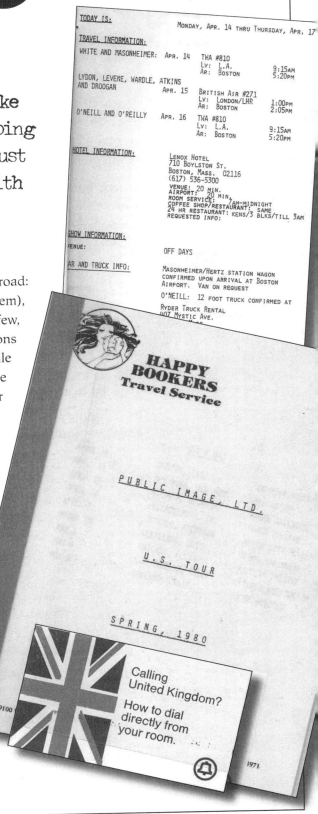

we've got two horrifying load-ins coming up," or "Hey it's a long drive tonight guys, don't go crazy. Tomorrow is an important show, we have journalists coming." The inclusion of all of this information in the itinerary will make it easier for everyone to do their job. Advance the tour dates, and it will make for a more successful tour.

Be careful. Anything you put in an itinerary may be used by anyone wanting friends or family to meet up. If you include show times, try to make sure they're accurate or at least put "subject to confirmation." Of course you won't know every piece of info before you leave, but try.

I've seen so many tours where the itinerary is the last thing to happen. The itinerary (at least the basic skeleton of it) should spring from and be fueled by the basic act of putting the tour together, talking to promoters, etc. Thus, it is just the printed form of a couple of month's worth of information and, as time goes on, the accumulation of year's worth of experience.

A good manager or tour manager knows that extra time spent on adding more to the itinerary could save hours of grief once on the road. This is not a holiday but, in some ways, you are a kind of spiritual travel agent. The temptation of four-foot deep Japanese baths and sushi on room service was the deciding factor for a Killing Joke tour of the U.S.

Putting itineraries together is a great way to see any holes in planning or information, and good practice for you to start to think through the tour on a day-by-day basis.

On a larger tour, the driver will refer to your itinerary and look at the directions. Put together three or four itineraries that have all the directions. If you are tour managing a package tour, do give the opening bands copies of the itineraries, and have one or two extras ready for when they are lost. Estimate travel time based on your information. Check with the venues, they will know better than anyone about the immediate conditions around the club (a street might be pulled up for construction or two bands might have been late because of a bottle-neck on a highway that week). Map-quest will not give you this information.

I like to put in bits and pieces that have to do with the enormity of the undertaking, like excerpts of Shakespeare's Saint Crispin's Day speech, which addresses the war-like nature of a large campaign, or photographs of band members who couldn't be with us (as a kind of tribute).

Include a section of useful phone numbers. Any information you have on interviews. Create a working itinerary to give to the crew at the beginning. And wait until a few days before the tour to give the band their copies with the most up-to-date information.

Timing can become a huge issue if you are in a union hall—one or two minutes over time and you might end up with 25 house crew hitting overtime. You could end up getting pulled off stage before you play an encore—or the hit—creating animosity in the audience who don't understand the time constraints. They just think you are dissing them or sitting in the dressing room drinking champagne with Elton John...

Be Smart. If everybody's traveling on a bus, a large itinerary is fine; people can leave it on their bunk. If everybody's flying, create something smaller, put useful phone numbers in it: emergency numbers, tour manager's cell phone, and all the band members' cell phones in case the tour manager is in a production office with bad reception.

We also started to put important numbers on laminates in case of emergency. Luggage tags can be used as inexpensive tour laminates.

ST. CRISPIN'S DAY SPEECH
WILLIAM SHAKESPEARE, 1599

KING.... he which hath no stomach to this fight,
Let him depart; his passport shall be made,
And crowns for convoy put into his purse;
We would not die in that man's company
That fears his fellowship to die with us.
This day is call'd the feast of Crispian.
He that outlives this day, and comes safe home,
Will stand a tip-toe when this day is nam'd,
And rouse him at the name of Crispian.
He that shall live this day, and see old age,
Will yearly on the vigil feast his neighbours,
And say 'To-morrow is Saint Crispian.'
Then will he strip his sleeve and show his scars,
And say 'These wounds I had on Crispian's day.'
Old men forget; yet all shall be forgot,
But he'll remember, with advantages,
What feats he did that day. Then shall our names,
Familiar in his mouth as household words-
Harry the King, Bedford and Exeter,
Warwick and Talbot, Salisbury and Gloucester-
Be in their flowing cups freshly remem'd.
This story shall the good man teach his son;
And Crispin Crispian shall ne'er go by,
From this day to the ending of the world,
But we in it shall be remembered-
We few, we happy few, we band of brothers;
For he to-day that sheds his blood with me
Shall be my brother; be he ne'er so vile,
This day shall gentle his condition;
And gentlemen in England now-a-bed
Shall think themselves accurs'd they were not here,
And hold their manhoods cheap whiles any speaks
That fought with us upon Saint Crispin's day.

MISTAKE TO AVOID

A creative itinerary from the same materials used to construct the *Damage Manual* CD (See on left). Very, very cool! Not when we still didn't have them the evening before the tour, though. Then, we discovered that some of the dates were wrong—talk about feeling like an idiot! Make sure your priorities are right! It does look cool though!

DAY SHEETS

You can supplement the itinerary with the use of a "daily fact sheet" or "day sheet." It seems like extra work for the tour manager, but the timely distribution of good information decreases the workload in the long run. It's a great way of preventing problems. Place notices around the venue and on each bus repeating some of this information—set times, meal times, etc.

I hadn't heard of a day sheet until my first tour with Jolly Roger, Ministry '91. In addition to the itinerary, he would put a day sheet on everybody's bunk at some point in the late evening. Usually assembled and fine tuned after the show, it would include comments (like "Great work from the crew!"), point out weak spots in the show, and call attention to new problems or high points to look out for. "Stop blowing pot smoke in the driver's face; he's getting upset," "Someone keeps leaving massive telephone bills on the day room," etc.

If you don't want to make a sheet everyday, think about doing one every week. It's a good chance to thank anyone that's been particularly helpful and loosely point out any seeds of problems before they become full grown oak trees. That reminds me of another quote I saw in an itinerary: "Don't be like an Oak tree, be like the Willow and bend!"

Time sheets should be posted around the backstage of the venue. If you're good and your advance work is on the ball, you can print a schedule at the beginning of the day (keep a template on your laptop), post it all over the backstage of the venue, on the buses, and in any other vehicle, and know that it's correct. If you haven't been doing your work, you're going to end up running

> **"Accurate information and early posting of these sheets will reduce the tour manager's workload substantially and the stress on all concerned."**

12/18/98 ATE DAZE FACTS

TODAY IS: FRIDAY, 12/18/98

WHERE WE ARE : IN THE LAND OF NEVER, NEVER !!! BETWEEN HITHER AND YON !!!

WHAT WE'RE DOING : SAYING GOODBYE TO THE GOOD PEOPLE OF THE TRIBE FENIX !!

SPECIAL EVENTS: EVERYTHING WAS SUPER SPECIAL THANKS TO RICK AND ALL THE STAFF !

HOTEL: THRIFT LODGE
949 E. BURNSIDE
PORTLAND, OR 97214
503-234-8411
FX CALL FIRST

GIG: ROSELAND BALLROOM
10 NW 6TH ST
PORTLAND, OR 97209
503-224-2038
503-221-0288

PROBLEMS WITH MOST OF THE PEOPLE BEING ABLE TO SEE US, WILL THEY STILL LIKE US IN PORTLAND ??

FLIGHT: NOT YET
HOTEL: IN PORTLAND IS IN A BAD PART OF TOWN SO USE YOUR COMMON SENSE
LOBBY: AT 9AM FOR TRIP TO PORTLAND
LOAD-IN: 2:00PM
BUS: WILL GO TO HOTEL FIRST TO DROP OFF YOUSE' POP STARS !!!!
S/CHECK: 6:00PM
DINNER: SOUTHWESTERN CUISINE
DOORS: 8:00PM
PROJ DRK: 9:00-9:20
SOW: 9:30-10:05
THEE: 10:15-10:50
PIGFACE: 11:00-1:00
CURFEW: 2:00AM

DIRECTIONS : SEE ITINERARY PLEEZ!!

WEIRD THINGS (NOTES): I'M STARTIN' TO SEE PIGFACE !!! YOU KNOW THE COUPLA THINGS THAT ARE STANDING IN MY LINE "O" SIGHT !!! FIX THEM PLEASE !!! AHHH!!! YES THAT'S BETTER ???? SERIOUSLY GREAT JOB & KEEP IT UP !!!! BACK TO BAD VIBES !!! SOME PEOPLE HAVE BEEN LEAVING INCINDENTALS SUCH AS PHONE BILLS & RESTAURANT BILLS !!! THIS HAS TO STOP !!! THIS IS NOT A VIABLE SOLUTION !!! OK WELL GOOD JOB !!! AND THIS IS ME OFF LIKE DIRTY UNDERWEAR !!!

DISTANCE: 3 HOURS AND A LAST CHANCE TO SEE MOUNT ST HELENS

QUOTE OF THE DAY: ON THE THIRD DAY OF PIGFACE MARTIN ATKINS GAVE TO ME THREE DRUMMERS DRUMMING MORE LYRICS DUDES

MORE TO FOLLOW JOLLY ROGER

PS: THANKS PINKY, BRAD, CHRIS, BILL, ROB, ROBIN, & "O" COURSE THE HONCHO OF THEM ALL !!! RICK !!!

Thursday 17th Jan

Leave Gunter Grove 9.45 am latest.

Depart Heathrow on flight AF 811 at 11.30 am, arrive Paris
Charles de Gaulle 1.30 local time.

Pierre Benain will collect us from the airport.

Hotel   :   Hotel Brebant,
                  59, Boulevard Poissoniere,
                  Paris 18.
                  (010 331) 770 25 55

Venue :   Le Palace,
                  8, rue du Faubourg Montmartre,
                  (Stage entrance at
                  3 bis Cite Bergere)
                  Paris 18.
                  tel: (010 331) 246 10 87

Soundcheck :   From 2.00 pm - 7.00 pm

Doors open :   7.30 pm

Support
  band   :   8.30 pm

PIL   :   9.45 pm

Polydor France will be taking us out to dinner   either Thursday
or Friday evening, as you prefer.

Friday 18th

Hotel, venue & times as above.

We have the following interviews to be done if possible over the
two days:

Rock & Folk   (monthly magazine)
Best   "   "
Actuel   "   "
Liberation   (daily paper)
RTL   (radio station who are recording the concert, would
                  need a short, 5 - 10 min. interview to go with the
                  concert)

**The day sheets
from our 1980 trip
to Paris with PiL.**

-2-

Actuel (copy attached) would like an interview of at least an hour,
as they intend to do a six page article and maybe front cover.

Saturday 19th

Lisa and Dave depart Paris Charles de Gaulle airport 10.30 am
flight AF 810, arriving London 10.30 am.

All others have open tickets (except Jo who returns on Wednesday
flight BA 329 departing 21.30)

Air France reservations (Paris):   533 61 61

around taking down the schedules you've put up, posting new ones, and then spending the rest of the day dealing with problems created by that, such as "The guitarist from the first band left to have Japanese food with his girlfriend because he thought (looking at the first schedule posted) that he had plenty of time. Now, his girlfriend is mad because he was called on his cell phone three bites into a $90 dinner and he hasn't eaten and who's going to pay for this mess?"

Pigface Tour
Monday, 14th, April

"As you all know, David Apocalypse got hurt bad falling into the crowd last night – here's an e-mail from girlfriend, Jenny."

Hello Martin,

I just left David in the hospital. He's busted the transverse process of one of his vertebrae, which, if you didn't know, is one of those little wing-like dealies sticking off the sides of a vertebra. He's in lots of pain and is now the bartender of his own personal keg of Dilotid. Poor sucker. His sense of humor is archaic and sickening as always, and it's sad to see such bent wretchedness wasted on student nurses who've had their funny bones removed.

I don't think I'll know anything more until he gets a CT scan on Monday. I'll keep you posted. For now I'm gonna moon around the house acting stricken, so it's up to you to rock hard for the both of us.

Thanks for your concern.

-Jenny

So let's rock this next few days for him. I REALLY wanted his spirit to be in LA with us. I forgot how cool and talented his vibe makes me feel inside. So now my bruises (you should see my ASS!) and strains seem like nothing. Let's rise above all of it and surf on the top of the vast pools of shit in the name of entertainment… and David Apocalypse!!

And, get your LA guest list shit together early – and the $$$ to pay for it – its going to be $15 per!

Bestest

MA

As a tour manager, you are gong to be dealing with opening bands that want to go on later, main bands who want to go on earlier, and the last thing you need to add to this soup is confusion or, especially with road-savvy people, the ability to pretend to be confused by your misinformation to suit their purpose.

The only other sheets you want to post around the venue are 'Band Dressing Room 1,' 'Band Dressing Room 2,' 'No Access,' and maybe, to avoid the "Spinal Tap Cleveland Situation," some arrows pointing the way to the stage if it is complicated or poorly lit. Throw down some light tape on the floor to point the way right before the stage.

You can put inspiring letters and e-mails onto the Day Sheet. Here's one from a Pigface Tour that turned into a t-shirt!

:SMART TIPS

- Make Day Sheets!

- The timely distribution of accurate information and early posting of these sheets will substantially reduce the tour manager's workload and the stress on all concerned.

- Be really careful with the info on the itinerary; it can prevent problems or cause them.

- Watch *Spinal Tap*.

- Use luggage tags as laminates.

C·H·A·P·T·E·R · 30

SETTLEMENT: GETTING PAID IS A BLOOD SPORT

Touring is like an expanded Kama Sutra Version 2.0, more ways to get shagged! It is never one big thing, because everyone is on the alert for that. It is death by 1,000 paper cuts.

Settlement is an opportunity for a decompression/ debrief between yourself and a promoter. It is also another chance not to be a prick. I have been a prick; a massive, glow-in-the-dark, Technicolor-disco prick! You do not always need to be. Promoters are people that you should hope to be seeing more of in the future. You are going to have to be making someone an awful lot of money for them to continue to deal with you.

Martin Atkins... the jaw is broken as well.

A bad show is an opportunity to man up. If you don't get defensive, you might get some great advice from an industry professional who has probably seen an awful lot. Be open: he or she might have some unexpected advice about something you might not be ready to hear. In all this talk about business, let's not forget that most of us are in this because we love it. Many people can look at a band for a few minutes and make some valuable suggestions.

> "Ditch that sound guy, he wasn't that good and one of my security guards said he was hitting on a couple of girls pretty aggressively."

> "Hey, your field rep is an asshole. He was demanding free drinks."

> "You should play with (band name here) next time!"

Walk around the venue and chat with everyone all day. Pay attention. How many loaders are there? Are they the same guys who are now doing security or lights? If you get chatting with a few of them see if you can find out what they get paid per day. This is very useful information to pull out of your ass at settlement... "$200 for the soundman, he told me he was making $110!"

Let's look at a settlement. Some will be much simpler, a record of tickets sold, expenses, and your percentage. Others will be much more complicated...

EXAMPLE

I chose this settlement because of the many elements it illustrates. We picked apart the settlement during class and stumbled upon one more way that the promoter shagged us out of another $200.

PROMOTIONAL BUDGET

The first thing I noticed about the settlement was that the venue did not spend all of the agreed upon advertising budget of $1,500.

Media Buys

Media / Vendor		Gross Cash
METRO TIMES	2/5/2003	$154.44
METRO TIMES	2/12/2003	$115.83
METRO TIMES	2/19/2003	$115.83
METRO TIMES	2/26/2003	$125.48
METRO TIMES	3/5/2003	$115.83
METRO TIMES	3/12/2003	$173.75
REAL DETROIT WEEKLY	2/19/2003	$5.00
REAL DETROIT WEEKLY	2/26/2003	$5.00
REAL DETROIT WEEKLY	3/5/2003	$20.00
REAL DETROIT WEEKLY	3/12/2003	$5.00
Total		**$836.16**

Expenses

Vendor Name	Expense Type	Gross Cost	Date Incurred
COPYMAX	Printing	$20.67	2/6/2003
COPYMAX	Printing	$11.40	3/5/2003
Kinkos	Printing	$7.81	2/28/2003
Kinkos	Printing	$12.81	3/3/2003
Kinkos	Printing	$6.96	3/11/2003
New Media	Advertising	$75.00	2/24/2003
GRAPHIC DESIGN	Flyers/Posters	$50.00	
DISTRIBUTION	Street Team	$50.00	
PRESS/FAX	Press Release	$50.00	
Total		**$284.65**	

Budget

Gross Budget	$1,500.00	
Actual Gross	**$1,120.81**	
Variance	$379.19	

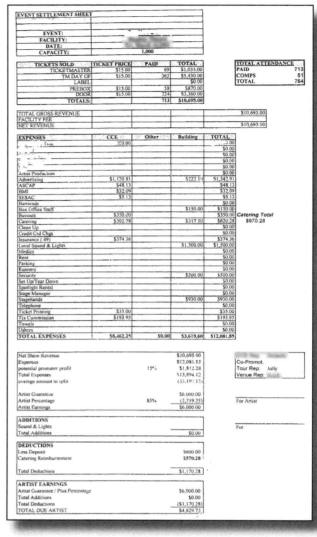

Even with a bunch of hogwash thrown in—like paying a company in Los Angeles $75 for including information on an e-mail list...

...paying their street team $50. Paying somebody for a press release,

...paying somebody $50 to typeset an ad that was already graphically completed!

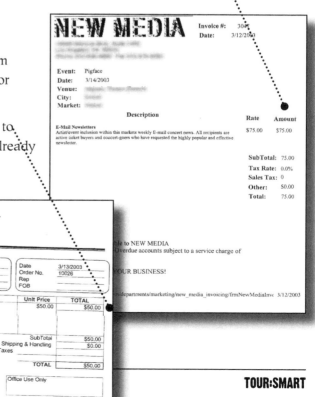

Right about now, I'm definitely having one of those "What the Fuck?" feelings. Waiting for a "beep, beep!" to wake me up from this bullshit-roadrunner-cartoon nightmare. Acme Digital Design, Inc., are you fucking shitting me? Then I saw a list of charges, which appeared to be around $20 for just placing an ad. This was not the fee that the paper charges, but the fee the venue charges for placing the ad.

The more you know, the more you do not want to know.

Promotion Expenses

	Pigface	
Show		
Date		
Venue		
Promoter		
Metro Times	3/12	$ 22.92
	3/5	$ 22.92
	2/26	$ 22.92
	2/19	$ 22.92
	2/12	$ 22.92
Real Detroit	3/12	$ 21.50
	3/5	$ 21.50
	2/26	$ 21.50
	2/19	$ 21.50
	2/12	$ 21.50
Total		$ 222.10

AD RATES

OK, so your bill is $695 for a quarter-page because that's the quarter-page rate. Here you see one of the ways a club makes money at settlement. They're buying a full-page ad and billing you for a quarter-page ad. By billing out 4 quarter-page ads for their full-page ad, they are charging $2,780. But, the full-page rate is actually $2,370, so they just made a profit of $410.

Worse still, they are probably taking out a full-page ad every week with a multiple-insertion discount. The rate drops to $1,805. So the club is really making $975 every week!

This is standard practice throughout the industry. Don't think for a second that you can use this information to get more money. But, you might be able to use it as leverage to avoid paying for the extra eight guests, the extra case of beer, or the broken microphone. This starts to cross over from "Interesting Bits of Touring Information" into a world where I know I'm going to get taken aside and punched in the nuts by somebody. So, please bring a bag of ice and be gentle when you see me.

CHICAGO READER	Average Circulation –	Over 120,000
Standard Sizes:	Non-prepaid Rates	
Size	Open	50x
Full Page	$2,370	$1,805
1/2 Page	$1,220	$930
1/4 Page	$695	$530
1/8 Page	$380	$290

CREATIVE LOAFING ATLANTA		
	Average Circulation –	129,592
Standard Sizes:	Non-prepaid Rates	
Size	Open	52x
Full Page	$4,725	$3,000
1/2 Page	$2,457	$1,560
1/4 Page	$1,139	$761
1/8 Page	$589	$383

3/4 Page*
7.4325 x 11.25

1/6V¹
2.3125 x 7.417

1/3H**
10 x 3.583

Junior*
7.4325 x 8.375

I used this information to secure one extra week of a half-page ad for a Pigface show. I wasn't interested in the money. I just wanted to make sure the show was promoted. We sent over the ad-mat to the venue (an ad-mat, either electronically or in print form, is a basic ad layout where the venue can insert their own information). How strange, then, and how short-lived the triumph when my name was spelled wrong in the ad. Understand, this wasn't somebody on the telephone that made a mistake. Somebody had to go into our design and change the spelling of my name. I've done some crazy fucked-up things in my time, but spelling my own name wrong is unlikely to be one of them.

Back to the original point about the advertising budget: if you are trying to break a band, gain some traction, or move forward in a market, the advertising budget is an important part of the overall deal. You have agreed to a $6,000 guarantee with a $1,500 advertising budget. We sold close to 800 tickets on a Friday night, at a venue with a capacity of 1,000 people. I wonder, if they had spent the additional money and used their abilities to promote the show instead of presenting strange invoices, if the show would have sold out? You can see that they only advertised for five weeks. Starting the campaign two weeks earlier would have made a huge difference.

CATERING

Another reason this show stands out in my mind is because the promoter was very upset that we went over-budget on the catering. The evening meal portion of the rider (See the Catering section in the Riders Chapter) was bought out at $10 to $12 dollars a head. This did not leave much room in a budget of $500 for 28 people. You see on the bottom of page 1 of the settlement there is a reduction of $570.28, that we paid the venue, because we ate and drank too much.

My first reaction was to apologize for my crazy drunken band mates until I looked at the catering invoice, which included $30 for a case of Heineken and a $10 case of water. Heineken is usually about $20/case in stores and water averages $5/case. Let's have a look:

So the overcharge is $5 for the 12-pack of Heineken, $17.50 for the three cases of domestic

DEDUCTIONS	
Less Deposit	$600.00
Catering Reimbursement	$570.28
Total Deductions	$1,170.28

beer, $40 for the 8 cases of water, and $20 for two more cases of Heineken for a total of $82.00. I can only assume that they overcharged us for the Skyy, the Absolut, and the wine as well. So, it was about $100.00. This became about the principle. We were, and you will be, handed pages of receipts, cross-referenced and allocated, to provide more and more crap to go through. I even started to think that the poorly-maintained drum tire marks on a couple of the invoices were actually some kind of Photoshop plug-in to make it look like invoices were generated from different offices and copied on different machines.

The rider provided for us upon arrival was horrifying and badly presented. Within minutes, packets of ham had spilled open, cheese was floating all over an inadequate cooler, and vegetarians delved into lukewarm ham filled water to retrieve what was, hopefully, wrapped cheese.

Someone in class once asked, "What do you mean by asking for clean ice?" Well, this would be it. Ice that isn't floating around with pieces of ham! Unfortunately, there was a fantastic restaurant in the same building as the venue and, for less money, we could have been well taken care of all day in terms of food quality and the removal of timing restrictions that an adjacent restaurant provides. More athletic members of the touring party need to eat sooner, some people party late and eat late; and the crew just has to grab a bite to eat when they can.

The other side to this has to do with our agent. Agreeing to a $500 catering budget, and a $6000 guarantee, his commission of 15% was $900. The tour had to reimburse the venue $570.28 for catering. Our agent should have insisted that the venue provide a realistic catering budget for such a large touring party and renegotiate with the venue to accept a $5,700 guarantee. However, that would have cost him $45 of his commission. In a way, he was getting money that should have been applied to the catering budget. How delightful it is to discover your agent is also taking a percentage of your soggy ham sandwich?

DEPOSIT

The idea of a deposit was originally to cement a deal and put everyone's mind at rest. If there is a problem with a show, the deposit is non-refundable. It used to be that the deposit was 30% to 50% of the total guarantee. Shifting the weight of responsibility onto the promoter to promote the show, to make sure that it happens, and to make sure he gets his money back. Now larger, more powerful promoters are only agreeing to a 10% deposit. However, it gets During settlement, if the promoter says he sent a deposit you have to see verifiable evidence of that: a Xerox of the bank transfer, Western Union receipt, something. And in the face of inconclusive evidence, weigh your response with your experience from throughout the day, and your knowledge of the venue. Understand that if you leave the venue without evidence of a deposit being made or the deposit itself, there is a chance you will never, ever see it. In this instance, these clever people did not mail out the deposit check until about ten days before the show.

> "How delightful it is to discover your agent is also taking a percentage of your soggy ham sandwich?"

This completely undermines the idea of a deposit. But what do they care? They are sure to have a copy of the check to prove it has been sent. It will probably arrive at the agency one to two days before or after the show. Of course, the check would have arrived earlier if it had been Fed Exed. So how do we know that it wasn't? Because if it was, you would have paid for it and there would be a Xeroxed receipt from Acme Shipping Company on fake invoice #1 or fake invoice #2 with poorly-maintained Xerox drum markings to prove it. Get the picture? Increased stress and a reverse effect on the cash flow of the tour occur as an out-of-state check is going to take ten business days to clear.

The end result of all of this was that what should have been a great show was marred by an argument at the end over $500 worth of catering that the agent should have made sure was provided within the budget anyway. At the end of a long day like this and an exhausting performance, that was the last thing that we needed. I was very, very tired and even though we put a lid on the argument before it escalated, it still left a very bad taste in our mouths. So, be careful, your battle is with the world and the machinery you need to get your music out there. Don't be so focused on the minutia that you end up losing a great relationship. It's all flexible, rubbery... a bit oily, and smells pretty bad, but you have to deal with it.

> *One of our publicists—Angelique from PromoHo—was out on the road with Cyanotic. She realized that a venue wasn't going to be able to pay them. The venue had a built-in restaurant so, during renegotiations, she asked the venue to at least feed the band. A good call—it didn't cost the venue very much to give the band $150 worth of items from the menu and the band got fed.*

TOUR:SMART TIP

Don Byczynski

After sound check or line check, have someone sit by the front door with a clicker and count everyone who walks through the door. I have had to settle with clubs who would claim that only 210 people paid at the door, but my counter shows 350. Most bands starting off in a new market will get a cut of the door, so this is getting you to the next show.

Another rule is: a good sound engineer will know who the owner is and what he looks like. I have been mixing during a show and seen the club owner leaving the club for the night. This will cause a big problem when it comes time to settle. I know audio gear very well and the value of it. If I was left alone to mix, I would have a screwdriver handy and loosen up the most expensive piece of gear in the rack. If the club owner was nowhere to be found after the show, I'd walk up to that piece, grab it, and sell it the next day at a pawn shop or call the club owner back. We got paid that way really fast.

TOUR:SMART TIP
for more information go to:
www.tstouring.com

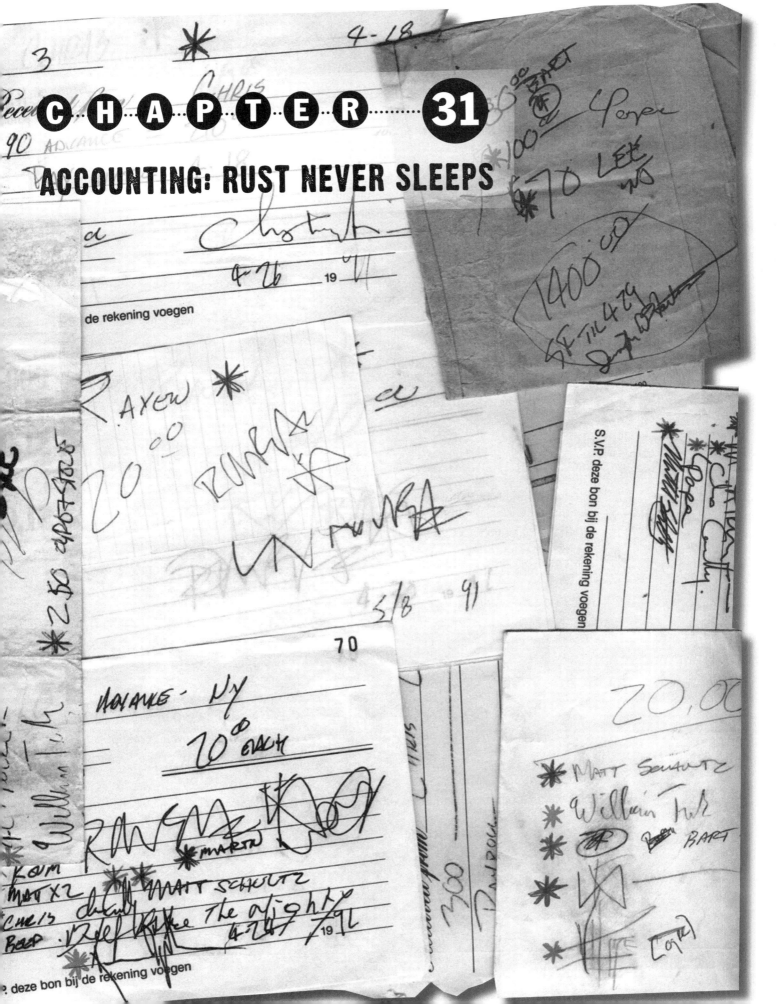

CHAPTER ···· 31

ACCOUNTING: RUST NEVER SLEEPS

> "It's like when you see the footage on the news of people weightless in space grabbing for different-colored floating M&Ms. Touring is just like that. Except that the M&Ms are replaced with exploding bags of shit."

Accounting is one of those rust-like things. It slowly creeps up on you and, before you know it, the bottom is rusted out of your vehicle. You've just got to grab it by the balls from the first day and not let go.

Write everything down. Everything. If you are advancing people money, get them to sign for it. You are not getting people to sign for it because they are dishonest or trying to screw you. Once you are on the road, everything starts to morph into a swirling kaleidoscope. It's like when you see the footage on the news of people weightless in space grabbing for different-colored floating M&Ms. Touring is just like that. Except that the M&Ms are replaced with exploding bags of shit.

After four or five days, you won't remember to whom you've given what and neither will they. So have a receipt book and get people to sign it. Write things on a piece of paper, on a napkin, on a paper bag, just write them down! There will be times when you give a runner the job of getting equipment or technical stuff and they will forget to get a receipt, just write it down! There! A receipt! If you've got a lot of stuff to keep track of, Quicken is a program that allows you to call up everything by category from any part of your budget, gas, hotels, food, etc.

In planning for the start of a tour, always bear in mind that everyone is going to come on the road broke. So, plan on advancing people money for wages, etc. Be prepared for more than just one entry at the end of each week for somebody's wages, you might have six or seven entries for small advances here or there. When the accounts are done diligently, they're the most accurate tour diaries I've seen. They include everything: the trip to the emergency room, the taxi for the trip to the emergency room, the two t-shirts you bought at Walgreen's to try and stop the blood flow, or the $200 you paid the hotel guy because you smashed the sink (marked N/R because he didn't give you a receipt!)

It's not a contest, the receipts and the final accounts don't exist to prove your budget right or wrong. They exist to teach you for the next time. You can look at all the taxi receipts backwards and forwards to the hotel that was the best price in town, but oh shit! While you saved $20 on a hotel that was ten minutes away, you spent $75 in cab fare. That's when you realize that the hotel that was two blocks away and $25 more would have been a better deal.

"I wish there had been a music business 101 course I could have taken." - Kurt Cobain

2 + 2 = 5
DARREN GUCCIONE

My name is Darren Guccione and I run a boutique financial services firm in Chicago that does accounting and tax work for corporate and individual clients. We specialize in working with musicians, actors, and professional management companies *(www.dsgfirm. com)*. Most often, our firm tends to stay out of the press and publication world to preserve the confidentiality of our client list and work product. We do not advertise and only accept new clients on a referral basis.

I am an avid musician. When I was 13, I sang in cover bands with names like Shag Nasty, Play Doctor, Yuppie Hippie, and The Shrine. When I graduated from college in Industrial and Mechanical Engineering, I went off to Hollywood to make it in the music world. It was at that point that I became enamored with the business and functional side of rock and roll and, generally speaking, the music industry.

The bottom line is that rock stars and musicians rule. Rock stars are eccentric. They tend to focus more on their art form as opposed to their financial form. I wanted to be of assistance to them. When I was in my early twenties, I met so many musicians that had made a great deal of money but for various reasons, they just could not find a financial balance in life. Most of them went. Frankly, they didn't know who to turn to, or they didn't know who cared. Musicians have always been our most revered yet difficult clients. In our business, a musician can make more on one tour than an accountant can make in an entire lifetime. A challenge in our profession is trying to get successful musicians to respect our knowledge, trust, and listen.

When I attended graduate school, no one could believe that I was studying to become a Certified Public Accountant. I just did not fit the mold. My hair was long; I drove a Harley

"We have seen people make and lose fortunes."

Davidson; and I wore ripped jeans. I had a different view of accounting, believing that it did not have to be so rigid or boring. Yes, there were rules but, this did not mean that one could not use the methodologies and beauty of accounting to design a financial framework or system for a musician or rock star. I wanted numbers to be laid out in such a way that they could tell a story. Receiving a Masters Degree in Accounting was not the hard part of accounting. The pure challenge was in communicating this with the client and really getting them to understand the importance of it and seriously sit down and listen.

We have seen people make and lose fortunes. Everyone has heard about it in the news. One day, a famous rocker or hip-hop artist was worth $30 million and then after a string of bad business deals, poor management, or theft, they are left with no money and no friends. The main reason for this was a result of simply not understanding what it takes to preserve wealth and listen to the proper professionals. There are several factors that we have seen which have essentially destroyed people's financial lives. These have included:

1. **Entering into business relationships with dishonest people:** unethical managers, poor accountants, and awful business advisory services putting rock stars in bad business transactions.

2. **Not receiving proper advice:** not listening to good advice when it is there because there is either a lack of comfort or lack of trust in an advisor. It is important that any client be totally comfortable with his or her financial advisor or CPA. Any great relationship, especially those that involve the management and tracking of one's money, starts with trust and comfort. Without that, forget about it. You'll be better off strapping yourself to the ass end of a donkey.

3. **Not properly guarding the checkbook:** there is a rule that I have established in this business: Never let your accountant have check signing authority on your accounts. Always sign your own checks. I cannot tell you how often I have seen this destroy a rock star or professional. When we handle a client's books for them when they are on tour, we receive the bills, process the bills, and write the checks. We then send a copy of the invoice, a stamped envelope, and the completed check to the client for signature. We do not sign checks, the client does. The bills are then deposited into the hotel's mail drop and sent to the vendors, etc. without delay. Any accountant or manager that demands check-signing authority on a personal rock star's account should be suspect immediately. This is like giving your advisor or accountant a license to steal.

4. **Not understanding your financial reports and tax returns.** We sit down with clients and explain their tax returns to them, even in the most general sense. Tax laws and the associated paperwork today are far more complex with each year. I cannot tell you how many new clients have never had anything in their financial lives explained to them other than a business advisor telling them, "I am sorry, you are broke. You're going bankrupt." Too often, the rock star is then hung up saying, "How could this be? I just sold 5 million records last year? Are you kidding me? I can't even buy a hot dog!"

5. **Not engaging in proper planning.** A plan is nothing—the act of planning is everything. It is imperative to sit down with your financial advisor and develop a road map that covers all sources of income and their timing. For example, music royalties tend to get paid every six months. This causes a problem in many cases because expenses are incurred on a more frequent basis. Without a budget coupled with monthly spending, insolvent situations can occur. The proper budget,i.e. "Here is what you can spend per month and this is what you should expect to pay in tax, etc. this year... Here is what our projected investment surplus will be and this is how I think we should deploy it for investment." These are the discussions that every client should have with their advisors, every month at a minimum.

> "Any great relationship, especially those that involve the management and tracking of one's money, starts with trust and comfort. Without that, forget about it. You'll be better off strapping yourself to the ass end of a donkey."

6. **Not staying healthy.** Drugs and booze can be a royal bitch. Once an addiction of this nature kicks in, everything else goes out the window. There is nothing more to say on this point except healthy mind, healthy body and think strong and live strong. Our most difficult client is one that has a chemical dependency problem, the best financial advice in the world is no match against a drug addiction.

Sometimes, things in business don't last forever. Bands and high-powered musicians can easily get wrapped up in today's excitement and the euphoria of fame. Too often, one can forget about some of the simple things in life that deal with self-financial preservation, growth, and one's overall well-being to solidify a comfortable future.

What more could I say on this topic? I suppose I could continue writing on this subject for weeks. Everyone's situation is different but the methodologies and disciplines that one follows are very similar. No matter what stage of the industry you are in, there will always be financial challenges that should be viewed as a priority.

ACCOUNTING SOFTWARE
CHRIS RAMOS

While this is not the most exciting topic you can think of, it is essential to maximizing profits on your current tour and setting up your next one.

Programs such as Quickbooks and Quicken can assist you in keeping track of merch sales, payments from venues, and miscellaneous payments you make along the way (gas, tolls, groceries, bail money, etc.). This is a basic function that you can use a program like Excel to perform. However, as Pigface's merch guys found out the hard way, using Excel will eventually get to a point where you are using a formula to calculate a formula that calculates another formula. All the while, you are wasting more time on data entry than analysis.

Quickbooks and Quicken will allow you to check inventory levels, average sales per night, and run reports. This can keep you from running out of items, as well as supply a basis for ordering merchandise for your next tour. For example, you look at your inventory and you have 45 belt buckles and ten days of touring left. It takes five days to get more belt buckles. You would probably think you can get through the rest of the tour. However, after running a report, you realize you are selling 12 of them per night at $5/unit profit. If you do not re-order, you will miss out on about five days of sales. That is essentially a $300 loss. This also shows you, for the next tour, that buying some belt buckles may be a better idea than buying more of whatever is at the other end of the spectrum (the pink XXL shirt with the pentagram).

ACCOUNTING ON THE ROAD TIPS
DAVE CALLENS

GIVING AN ACCURATE TOUR BUDGET IS A LOST CAUSE.

It is human nature to want to please your superiors and make them feel that they hired you for good reasons. Everyone in the chain has their own agenda with the tour accountant. It is easy to get the numbers, costs, and appraisals from all your vendors. However, it is more difficult to understand "how and why" it will cost more than it should. At any time, the schedule will change and costs never go down. Even if they do, you never divulge the fact. Managers, artists, and crew are not always as good at their budgeting as you are. They're not always as good at their estimated plans, either.

The main thing for an accountant on the road is to float the tour under any circumstances. If you can't, it exposes other people's mistakes. They don't like that and, therefore, never forget it. I have had problems with Production/ Crew Managers that forgot to express their real needs adequately and, when I could not come up with the money they wanted, found creative ways to make my life, somewhere down the road, a little more difficult.

Always over-budget by 5%. It may not cover all of the unexpected problems, but it adds up during the tour. Always add a 10% contingency to the final budget. If your superior doesn't understand, try asking him how he would feel asking for more money during the tour from the tour support people.

WHEN DEALING WITH MEALS, CATERING AND PER DIEMS ON THE ROAD, ALWAYS MAKE PEOPLE HAPPY!

Food is friendship. Whatever the cost, give people their per diem and meals. People cannot see the difference between per diem and free money. If per diem is paid daily, they also expect free food. I don't know where this turned around, but it has.

Just deal with it.

> **"Costs never go down."**

ACCOUNTING

JOLLY ROGER

MA: Accounting: how do you deal with it?

JR: I actually took classes. A long time ago. You can look back at the earliest tours we did together, I used those brown accounting books. And then it moved on to Quicken. Now that's all I use.

MA: And one piece of advice to anybody dealing with that?

JR: Be honest. That's it. Be diligent and honest. When there were discrepancies, I made up the discrepancies 'cause I was honest to the best of my ability.

MA: Where would you put the money?

JR: Nowadays, I sleep with my pants on and I leave it in my pants pocket.

MA: So there's only six or seven people with access!

JR: In those days, I would sleep with it in my pillow, but my pouch fell out of my pillow, so... in your pillow, or wear deep pockets. Some people use money belts. I don't find them comfortable. But, you have to know that you can carry $30,000 in your left front pocket and have like $2,000 to work out of in your front right pocket and nobody's gonna know you got your big pile. The whole thing is, when somebody asks you for more than you have in your right pocket you gotta follow through—you gotta turn around, say "I'll be back in a minute." You gotta go somewhere and make believe you're getting it from somewhere else and pull it out of your left pocket and then come back and nobody knows you've got $28,000 in your left pocket.

MA: Until now!

JR: (Laughs) Yea! But you really have to follow through with that. You have to write everything down the whole tour. Especially with the stuff that we did with people that are really hand-to-mouth. You have to keep a sheet on every penny you give everybody and show it to 'em. You know? And I still have some of those cheat sheets that are ten years old. But I can look at it right now and know that this person got $40; that person got $60; you know that kind of stuff. You have to back yourself up.

> "You have to write everything down the whole tour."

C·H·A·P·T·E·R ···· 32

MANAGEMENT: WHAT DO I GET?

"Band management is so much more than someone
just advising and counseling. It is the person
you trust to take you to the next level in your
career. A manager has to be mother, a father,
a psychiatrist and a baby sitter. What they need
to be is someone who can take a product (a band),
and marry art and commerce to perfection.
It is a difficult balance."
— Susan Ferris, Bohemia Management

If you don't already have a manager, first ask yourself, why do you need one? Are you so busy that you cannot do it yourself? Or is this manager so fucking amazing in terms of career development that you have to be involved with him/her for advice and direction? Because if all you really want to do is say to somebody at the bar, "I don't know, I'd really have to ask my manager," you can do that without hiring one. Managers are just human beings like agents. If you're paying your manager commission and you're not really earning anything, then your manager isn't either. Maybe he or she is just someone that wants to hang out in a bar and say, "Oh, well, I can't do that. The band I manage has an important studio date," or some other crap: checkmate!

Understand what you need and what makes that particular manager right for you. Then, give them the ability to act on your behalf. If you don't want to do that, don't hire them. A manager is useless without your trust (or at least a piece of it). So if you're not prepared to let go, don't. Otherwise, you are completely negating the manager's role. A band that has been running their own business for a while will have a better understanding of what they need in a manager.

"If you're not prepared to let go, don't."

It's not voodoo or secret code stuff, so be careful if someone comes at you with that angle, it's inspired but diligent hard work and follow-through, that makes the difference.

Anyone can see what's in the road ahead, if it's straight you can use binoculars to see further... a good manager can see around corners and through walls...

Here's an example of management styles:

> When alternate-side-of-the-street parking was introduced outside the old label offices, I could never remember to run downstairs at four o'clock to move my car. Usually at that time, I was in the middle of a mix session or something. A manager diligently collected all the parking tickets, paid them, filed the copied payment in a folder marked "Parking Tickets," and I'm sure at some point would have billed me for scanning and archiving the parking ticket file, which was clearly going to take up one entire side of the office. In the city of Chicago, if you don't pay your ticket within 30 days, the fine doubles. After 30 more days, it doubles again. So, it could be argued that the actions of this manager were saving me hundreds of dollars a month, the possibility of a clamp on my car, and untold buckets of stress. but that's really a good office manager. A great manager would have seen the longer term problem and would just walk into the office one day and announce that for the next two years I didn't have to worry because he had rented a parking spot from the guy at the liquor store or somewhere, a solution to not just my immediate problem, but the problem that was inevitably coming down the line... that's management.

MANAGEMENT IS CHANGING
SUSAN FERRIS

Management is changing. The old school way of thinking is long gone. Long considered the old boys club, the new face of management is young, mobile, and willing to take chances. Band management is so much more than just giving advice and counseling. It is being the person people trust to take them to the next level in their career.

It has often been said that if you want someone great to run a record label, get a band manager. They have to understand every aspect of how a band's career should function. They need to deal with every avenue from every angle.

A manager has to be a mother, a father, a psychiatrist, and a babysitter. Most of all, they need to be someone who can take a product (a band) and marry art and commerce to perfection. It is a difficult balance.

A GOOD MANAGER

A good manager will have patience. They will understand the artist without allowing the artist to get in his or her own way. They will listen to the needs and wants of the artist. A good manager will make sure an artist understands reality without discouraging the dream. You need to have the ability to put out fires and not be afraid to start them. As cliché as it sounds, you need to think outside the box but understand protocol. It is easy to describe what a good manager should do. It is not always easy to find a manager who encompasses all these things.

A BAD MANAGER

It would be easy to say that doing everything the opposite of what a good manager does is what makes a bad manager. Unfortunately, it is not that easy. The bad managers are sometimes very hard to spot, and worse, it can take a while to figure out that a band has found a bad one.

The bad ones tend to be the ones who "talk" too much. Making big claims of what they can do. Regaling bands with big stories of great success they have had. And ultimately weaving the web that bands think they are looking for. It's a very vaudevillian approach. These managers tend to have their own agenda. These are the managers who also tend not to listen. Or rather, listen selectively. What an artist doesn't say is as important as what they do say.

> Another band I know had been searching for a deal for a long time, over four years. They finally found an indie label that seemed to be a perfect fit. The band was manager-less at this time, so they made the deal with a lawyer. After the band was signed and in the studio working on their debut release, they collectively decided it was time to get a manager. With the advice of some of their friends in the business, they took a handful of meetings. When it came down to the best two, they asked if the label would, in fact, take a meeting with both managers. After taking the meetings, the label gave their opinion and the band made their decision. They picked the less favored manager who had the vaudevillian approach.
>
> The manager promptly caused problems with the label, tried to execute a coup with no success, started their own label, and bought the band back. The indie label made six figures and the band has still not put an album out. The record was done almost two years ago and the band has been sitting in their hometown scratching their heads trying to figure out what happened.

WHAT SHOULD A BAND THINK ABOUT BEFORE THEY GET A MANAGER?

It is easy for a band to say they want to play arenas and sell millions of records. The chances of it happening are slim. It is more important that a band have many goals and that each one is attainable. Not as simple as it sounds.

Why do you think you need a manager? What do you think a manager is going to do for you? What are your expectations? Is the goal to just get signed? Do think you manager is going to get you shows?

It may seem like common sense but a lot of times bands go into meeting managers with expectations that just don't make sense. A band should meet with a few managers, but not go overboard. Sometimes meeting too many is just as confusing. Do your homework. Who else does the manager handle? Is it someone big? Are they going to have time to build your career or are they going to pass you off to the new kid who is just learning? Something to consider, and not necessarily a bad option, as you are getting the knowledge of the old with the energy of the new.

I had a client who had been a member of a big band and had been fired. He came to me to manage him. We worked together for two years putting his new band together, getting him a lucrative six figure deal with a great record label, and traveling around the world on some incredible projects that he was a part of. We were on our way to big things. I had just started my own company and it was exciting to have it kick off so big. As the ball began to roll and he was getting more attention, a very famous band manager called my client and wanted to know why he had this young girl managing him. He should have someone like this guy to take him to the next level! So my client immediately saw stars and more dollar signs and fired me. At that point, I told him to get his checkbook out and pay me now because I would sue him and this would save us a lot of time and money. He did and no, the group never really went anywhere. They fizzled out after a few years and the big time manager got bored and moved on to other things.

It is OK to disagree with a manager. But if you disagree over fifty percent of the time, then neither of you are seeing eye to eye on things and it is time to move on.

Is having a new manager a bad thing? If you are a band that is just starting out, then having a manager who is just starting out can work in your favor. A manager should be someone you can grow with. If you have a good manager, then they should be with you for a very long time. It is important to know when to stay and when it is time to move on. If your manager is not growing with you, then it is time to move on. A new manager has a lot of energy and is willing to do things that a manager who is set in their ways may not be willing to do.

"In the height of the '90s, the manager could learn his craft by default from the record company people. That doesn't work today. The manager today really has to be the president of the independent artist's business."
- Jeff McClusky

SILENT PARTNER MANAGEMENT
WES KIDD

One thing I always say to artists is: it is your career. You should be working as hard as your manager. It is a team effort. If you think that because you have a manager now, whether or not they are new or experienced, it does not mean that you sit back and see what happens. That is a solid guarantee that nothing will happen. Communicate with them daily. You have to give them the tools to do their job.

MA: What do you think a good manager does, especially with a tour?
WK:

1. Help an artist do what they are already doing, but better.
2. Coordinate all the tentacles (label, publicist, marketing, etc.) to surround the shows and tour to create the biggest impact.

MA: Tricks and tips for the road?
WK: If you get a rider, make sure you put all the leftover beer, soda, etc. into a cooler. We used to save a fortune! •••••••••••••••••

MA: Ever had anything stolen?
WK: I've had guitars, amps, and merch stolen. It sucks! I'm still looking for the fucking assholes who took that stuff.

MA: Anything else that springs to mind from the real world of touring?
WK: Be great every night. No matter if you are only playing to the bartender, you never know who is in the room or where they will end up one day. You have to see everything as an opportunity. You know exactly what will happen if you say "No" (nothing) but you never know what will happen if you say "Yes."

WES KIDD

MANAGER, PRODUCER, MUSICIAN, NERD

TOUR:SMART TIP
for more information go to:
www.tstouring.com

> **"You know exactly what will happen if you say 'No' (nothing) but you never know what will happen if you say 'Yes'."**

"Whether you think you can or you think you
can't – it's true."
-Henry Ford

CHAPTER 33

SOUNDSCAN, POLLSTAR AND OTHER DATA

"Wal-Mart knows that people faced with the prospect of a hurricane will buy water and strawberry Pop-Tarts. The music business has its own data services too."

You thought that radio charts were the industry's radar? Read on.

NIELSEN SOUNDSCAN

Soundscan is an information system that tracks sales data for singles, albums, and music video products in Canada and the United States for Billboard and other music industry companies. MTV, VH1, and many other North American cable music channels use Nielsen SoundScan data as well. Nielsen SoundScan began tracking sales data for Billboard March 1, 1993.

How Nielsen SoundScan tracks sales:
Sales data from cash registers is collected from 14,000 stores outlets in Canada and the U.S. Though this includes all major brick-and-mortar retailers, it is not a 100% sample of record sales; it excludes music clubs as well as some independent retailers and online outlets.

POLLSTAR

POLLSTAR is an accurate source of worldwide concert ticket sales. In addition to publishing the concert industry's leading trade publication, POLLSTAR also maintains the world's largest database of international concert tour information. Concert tour information on that web site is updated daily with information gathered from thousands of music industry sources. POLLSTAR is a weekly media magazine geared for the concert industry. They also provide Artist Tour Histories for a small charge.

When I am looking at a band that wants to join a tour or buy on, I will look at Soundscan to see how well their CDs are selling (who needs who?) and then look at Pollstar to see how they have done in the past with concert ticket sales. This only takes a few minutes. Anyone in the business (that is still in the business) is going to run these reports to verify that you have indeed sold 10,000 CDs... and that your last tour was a huge success... the days of blagging it are over! You can help yourself by diligently reporting your live sales to your label, who can then report them to *Soundscan*.

"...the days of blagging it are over!"

SOME SOUND SCAN FACTS

CHRISTOPHER RAMOS

CHRIS RAMOS

**DOPE GEAR INC.
TOUR MERCH
WEB SALES**

In case you don't know, Soundscan is pretty much the Nielsen ratings of the Music Business. In fact, it's all part of the same company.

- If you are signing to a label, make sure they use Soundscan.

- **Get a scanner.** Scan and e-mail your Soundscan sheets from the road to your label. Fax machines suck. They're hard to find and they'll usually cost you more over the course of a tour than buying a scanner.

- **Don't lie.** Inflating your numbers may get you attention from larger labels, but it will also give them unrealistic expectations for you. If you tell a girl you're packing 12 inches, she'll be disappointed when she sees what you really have.

- **Get your reports in on time.** Find out when your label needs to send its weekly report and get your reports to them at least 18 hours before then. As much as they love you, it pisses them off when you send in reports five minutes before they need to create the weekly file.

- **Don't forget to include all the required info.** Do not count on anyone to fill in the blanks for you.

- **Get your Soundscan sheet signed when you get to the club.** There's nothing harder than finding club personnel after the show.

- **Be prepared.** Have a folder with a sheet for every club you are going to play before you leave. This will save you from running around the club looking for the one person that knows the zip code of the place. Save a master copy on the PC you'll have with you on tour. Also, bring a paper copy for when your hard drive takes a shit and dies.

- **If you only sell one CD** in Des Moines, IA, report it. It's one more than every lazy-ass band that didn't bother going there.

- **Print legibly.** You will be pissed when 96 CDs are counted as 46 CDs because you write like you have no thumbs.

- **Labels, Distributors, and Stores look at Soundscan** to see what you are doing and where you are doing it. Don't fuck around and forget to report your scans.

> "If you only sell one CD in Des Moines, IA, report it. It's one more than every lazy-ass band that didn't bother going there."

CHAPTER 34

EXCEL BASICS

"Sit and mess around with an excel sheet sometime and watch your drug money go up in smoke... before you can smoke it."

I used to think that Excel was the antithesis of anything we were trying to do at the sharp end of independent music. But, the more courageous the project, the more you need to be certain of as much as possible so that artistic risk is the only one you are taking. Excel needs to be your friend. By setting up very simple formulas and training yourself to create worksheets, you will be able to see the effect of changing gas prices, exchange rate, number of drummers, and transportation methods that all affect the bottom line and enable or disable future creativity.

You can go to *www.microsoft.com* to get the basics of Excel. If you work through the *Budgets* chapter and the Project .44 case study and spend 20 minutes with it, you'll get the idea.

One of my favorite uses for Excel is to handle the guest list. No matter how few people you think are going to show up for a show, get into the habit of typing out the guest list in an Excel format. In the case of a larger event, with guest list restrictions per band, it will enable you to bill back guests to each band and see which bands and publicists are really doing their job, and prevent problems at the door. (See the Chapter on *Guest Lists*.)

> "The more courageous the project you are undertaking is, the more you need to be certain of as much as possible so that artistic risk is the only one you are taking."

USING EXCEL TO SCHEDULE SHOWTIMES

When we put together larger package tours, we began to have a problem with show times. Within an hour of arriving at the venue, the tour manager would place day sheets with meal times and set times in each bus and the dressing rooms. Then, when he found out he'd scheduled our show to finish an hour after the club closed, he would reprint everything and walk around replacing all of the sheets he'd posted earlier. By this time, some people had read the information on the sheet, foolishly thought it was accurate, and gone off on errands (physical or spiritual) accordingly. Aside from the amount of time and energy the alleged tour manager was spending, the ripples of confusion (and then anger) were huge.

Certain things start to become routine: the changeover from the third band to the main band, the third band set time, etc. Instead of spending an hour or two collecting and distributing information, every time was dictated from one central time. The most beneficial time for the headlining band to be on stage. This time could be determined by how long the venue was open, the day of the week, curfew for minors if it was an all ages show, availability of public

TOUR:SMART TIP
............................•
for more information go to:
www.tstouring.com

transportation, etc. When creating the *Excel* sheet, I linked every time on the sheet with a formula to the cell containing this time. This saved tour management 24 work hours over the course of a tour, but more importantly, it saved everyone from the confusion that happens when incorrect information is posted early in the day and corrected three hours later.

You can solve a lot of issues before they become problems. When you type in the optimum time for the main band to be on stage, you may realize that the first band needs to be on stage a half an hour before the doors are scheduled to open. Use your skills to work this situation out. Perhaps the main band goes on 15 minutes earlier, while the opening bands cut one or two songs. Some band members can help the crew get the equipment offstage and save five minutes in the change over to make it work for everybody. Problem averted.

This is another one of those tiny, incremental factors that can screw everything up. How horrible is it to drive all the way to Salt Lake City to be at the right club, on the right night, and be on stage 45 minutes later than originally planned – with your explosive finale of dancing girls, smoke machines, and strobe lights being cut off by the club owners, fire marshals, security, or just because everyone had to leave to catch the last bus home?

	A	Length	Start Time	End Time	F
1	**Start Time Calcuation based on Optimum main band end time**				
2		30		7:15 PM	7:45 PM
3	Doors	25	**7:45 PM**	**8:10 PM**	
4	**1st Band**	15		8:10 PM	8:25 PM
5	Set Change over	25	**8:25 PM**	**8:50 PM**	
6	**2nd Band**	15		8:50 PM	9:05 PM
7	Set Change over	40	**9:05 PM**	**9:45 PM**	
8	**Main support**	15		9:45 PM	10:00 PM
9	Set Change over	90	**10:00 PM**	**11:30 PM**	
10	**Main band**				
11				11:30 PM	
12	Optium main band set END			12:00 AM	
13	Venue Close			1:00 AM	
14	curfew			3:30 AM	
15	Bus Call				
16	transportation issues:				

GUEST LISTS

Instead of thinking of *Excel* as some kind of mad accounting tool, I want to start with treating it as a flexible charting program—this is the way I use it most. Try this:

Open up the program and click on "New Workbook." You'll see letters across the top and numbers down the left hand side. Just like on a map, each of these gives you the coordinates of a cell—the box that is at a certain location. (Cell A1 or B4, etc.)

You can create a simple chart for mailing lists by expanding the size of the B and C columns. Put your cursor on the letter A. As you move it to the sides of the cell, you will see the cursor change to a line with arrows.

This is the tool that allows you to change the size of the

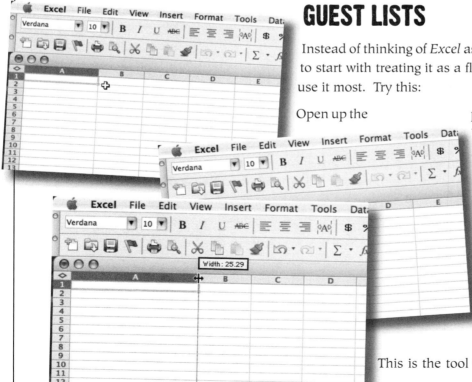

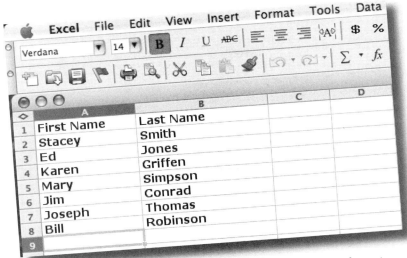

cells or columns. Click and hold down as you expand the width of the A column and then do the same with the B and C columns.

Title the columns: First Name, Last Name, and E-mail. (If you need to insert more columns later, there is an 'insert column' command under the 'insert' menu.) Maybe you'll need a space for Competition Winners or a space to mark people that have arrived (if it's a guest list), etc.

Let's take this another step. Select the entire sheet (Control-A), copy it (Control-C), and open another sheet. Then paste (Control-V) – See studio guys, copy and paste is the same world!

We are going to make this a guest list so delete the E-mail Column C. Add in a few guests – make sure to keep the first names and last names separated for easy sorting/ alphabetizing.

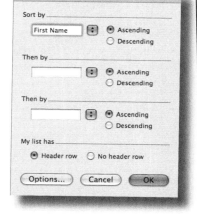

Now, you are out of tabs on the bottom of your screen. To insert a new sheet, go to the top menu and pull down the Insert Menu. Choose Insert Sheet. Now, copy and paste Sheet 3 into Sheet 4 using the same commands as before. (Now we are on Sheet 4.)

Let's sort the list alphabetically: Select the entire list use the sort command under the data menu.

Make sure the 'Header row' option is selected and sort by 'First Name' ascending... da-daaaaaaaaaa!!

You just sorted a guest list alphabetically!

You can impress the local venue so much that they might not charge you extra for all of those guests... But wait! You go to the door and it's kind of dimly lit and crowded. Let's reformat the sheet in a larger font. Choose Format > Cells > Font and bump it up to 14 or 16.

There you go!

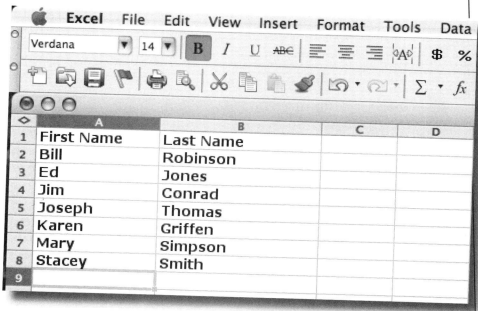

"People underestimate the massive cost of doing nothing it is huge in terms of cash and momentum."

-Martin Atkins

CHAPTER 35

SOFTWARE THAT'S AS HARD AS NAILS

There's just a staggering amount of software development that makes touring easier, more efficient, and more productive. There are new advances seemingly every day. Here's an overview of some things that are around right now: So we can look back on this in 18 months time and laugh our heads off.

EXCEL

It's useful for everything from guest lists to budgets and always easy to import to and export from.

MARKETWORKS

Marketworks is software that will automatically re-list an eBay auction as soon as it is purchased. This is pretty much essential if you're trying to sell a ticket package online. You can't afford to have the auction down from 2 a.m. Sunday morning until you remember to check it at 4 p.m. Monday afternoon.

MAP POINT

See Mike Johnson's piece on Map Point in this chapter.

PHOTOSHOP

The essential tool for visually expressing and marketing yourself

QUICKEN

No-brainer. Checkbook balancing and checkbook program.

AUTOMATIC POPSTAR

Builds an audience and songwriting skills while you sleep. If you just got excited, go back to the beginning of the book and start reading from page one. This software doesn't exist.

iMOVIE / FINAL CUT EXPRESS

iMovie comes with any new Mac. You can buy a mini-DV camera, it will plug straight into your laptop through a fire-wire port for a couple hundred dollars and boom!—you're creating your own documentaries.

MYNEWSLETTERBUILDER.COM

My Newsletter Builder and other contact managers

If you find yourself sitting behind the computer screen thinking, "This is taking forever," chances are that someone else thought the same thing and designed software to solve it.

One of your main jobs is to maintain communication not only with your fans, but with the rest of the outside world. If no one knows what your band is up to, no one can make a decision to support it. Most bands start their mailing list in Excel and it stays fairly manageable for a while. However, when you get 500+ names, addresses, zip codes, and e-mail addresses on that list, managing it becomes daunting. Pretty soon you have a batch of bad addresses to which you keep sending e-mails that continue to bounce back and clog your inbox. You have people who have asked to be unsubscribed from the list that you've forgotten to take out. Suddenly, sending an e-mail to your fans becomes such a task, that you don't want to do it.

This is where software like My Newsletter Builder (others include Constant Contact) comes in. It is designed to not only manage your mailing list by adding new subscribers, removing bad addresses, and handling bounces, but it has built-in, customizable templates you can use for your outbound messages. It has templates geared specially to bands, record labels, venues, promoters, and agents. It has an integrated "jukebox" that allows you to embed your new single, latest video, or cool photo collage directly into your e-mail. Additionally, it is designed so you don't have to be an html or any other kind of expert to use it.

Like most contact managers it works on a quote basis. In other words, you buy X number of e-mails that you can send per month. For example, if you have 2,500 people on your mailing list, you could buy 5,000 messages per month which would allow you to blast your list twice for $30/month (if you sign up for 12 months). Pricing schemes can vary from company to company but you get the general idea.

Take the time to investigate software solutions like this and insure that they meet your needs (most companies will have at free trial period). Consider the amount of resources you (or someone in your band) is spending on mailing list maintenance. Is your band at a point where the cost outweighs the benefit? Remember, your time is a scarce resource. Don't spend it on something that someone else has already put their time, their money, and their energy into developing. Understand the concepts of efficiency and effectiveness. Research your options and chose the ones that meet your needs.

MAP POINT
MIKE JOHNSON

Touring smart is not about going out and playing as many shows as possible all over the country and hoping that something is going to take off for you. It's about being selective: planning your shows and how they will benefit you in the context of an overall plan for promoting and growing your band in specific markets. Therefore, your best friend, as you move forward, is knowledge of your band and the ability to analyze and use that knowledge to help make your shows more successful. In that spirit, I give you one of the most useful computer program tools you will ever encounter: Map Point. This is a Microsoft program. (Unfortunately there is no Mac version, although I installed virtual PC on my Powerbook for the sole purpose of running Map Point, and it works just fine.)

At its most basic level, Map Point will remind you of Yahoo! Maps, in that you can enter addresses, zoom to street level detail, get driving directions and times, and allow you the added benefit of accessing real-time construction information from the internet to help you avoid travel delays. However, the value of this program is in its function to map data of any kind onto a national map, and to selectively export specific data back into a database format.

I am going to give three examples of applications for this program that either cannot be done any other way I know of, or which would take you hours of laborious work rather than four clicks of a mouse.

1. Identifying subscribers to your mailing list within a certain distance of upcoming shows. Hopefully, you are already doing your best to maintain an e-mail fan list for your band and you are sending out regular updates. If you are only collecting names and e-mails, you absolutely have to start collecting addresses, or at least zip codes, as well. When you are on a mailing list, the most annoying thing to receive are e-mail updates that have nothing to do with you (i.e. you live in NYC and get five e-mail updates about your favorite band's west coast tour). Sending out show-specific e-mails to only those fans who live near the event is the best way to get a positive response and a larger audience at the show. Before we discovered Map Point, we would typically search our mailing list for fans who lived in the city that the show was being held in.

Unfortunately, you miss out on a large number of fans that way because of suburbs, nearby markets, etc. For example, simply e-mailing all of our fans from Chicago for an upcoming show excludes people from Skokie, Evanston, Blue Island, Homewood, Cicero, Gurnee, all the western suburbs, etc., even though many of these people are only a 20 to 30 minute drive from the venue. So, how does Map Point help with this?

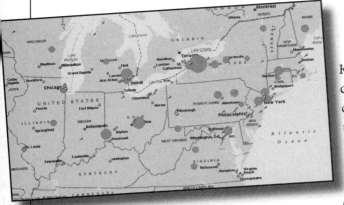

Keep your mailing list in a program like Excel (or any type of database file), with name, e-mail address, and zip code in separate columns. In Map Point, select the data mapping wizard tool and use it to import your contact database. All of your mailing list subscribers now appear on the map as push pins! Let's go back to the example of a Chicago show. Zoom in on the Chicago area and, on the drawing tool bar, select the "Driving Radius" tool. Click on Chicago and drag a radius to 30, 60, or however many miles you realistically believe that your fans will drive to see you play. (You can also use the "Pencil" tool to freehandedly draw an area around Chicago if there are specific suburbs and areas that you want to include that don't fit into a simple radius.) Once you have drawn your area on the map that you want to include in your e-mail blast, simply right-click on the shape you drew and select "Export Data" from the pop-up menu. What you get is a new Excel sheet with the names, e-mail addresses, etc., of everybody on your list who lives in the specified area. Now you can send out an e-mail to the people that live near the show without irritating people who don't. Including the show information in the subject of the e-mail personalizes it and makes it more likely to be read. Try to send these out a week or so prior to the show so people don't forget. (If you have a decent service for managing your mailing list, you should be able to set this up all at once, so even once you're out on the road, reminders will be automatically sent out to your fans in the cities you are playing.)

2. Mapping radio play and/or mail-order sales. When you have a college radio service working a release for you, you will get weekly reports detailing all of the stations that are playing your album. These reports are usually organized in long and cumbersome lists that don't lend themselves to doing anything productive with the data. First, enter all of your radio play data into an Excel spreadsheet. Include columns for station name, city, state, and number of plays, as well as chart position, if applicable. Now you have data you can use. As before, use the data mapping wizard in Map Point and import your radio play data onto a map to look for patterns, clusters of airplay, etc., that may be useful in helping you plan your tour route. You can even have the data represented by circles that are larger with more radio play, so that a station that has spun the record five times appears larger on the map than one which has only played it once. If you keep track of your website-based mail-orders in a spreadsheet, you can also import those individuals onto a map. (If you're using your existing fan distribution to decide where you are going to tour, consider that someone who has actually mail-ordered one of your CDs is probably as valuable as ten individuals who have simply signed onto your mailing list.)

>>> Map Point is Amazing Tip: You can simultaneously map multiple sets of data onto a single map and color code them! On one map, you can have your entire mailing list populated as red push pins, radio stations that have played your album represented by yellow dots that vary in size based on how many spins your album has received, and your mail-order customers represented by little green squares. Look at all of your data together and discover things about your band that you never knew before!

3. Maintain a visual database of venues for booking purposes. The first two applications for Map Point were for finding out information about your band: Where are your fans? Where is your radio play? And being able to look at this data graphically and pull out useful sets of information. Let's say now you're at a point where you have decided on the tour route you want, based on previous touring activity, fan distribution, radio play, strong distribution markets, etc. Now you need to start contacting venues. By the same logic as finding fans that surround the market you are playing, you will limit yourself severely if you decide "I'm playing Dallas on March 13th" and simply pull all of your Dallas venues from a list to start e-mailing them. Keep your venue database in an Excel spreadsheet (of course), and import it all into Map Point. You can then use the drawing tools to put little flags on all of the cities you intend to play. Then, looking at your map of venues, use the "Export Data Tool" we talked about earlier to find all the venues that fit within your overall tour plan. Maybe that means playing Denton instead of Dallas. That's OK! Chances are that if you e-mail only clubs in Dallas proper to start with, and you don't get a show offer, you are going to go back and contact Denton clubs later anyway, but without as much lead time and you will be less likely to get a show in the end. E-mail everybody right away. Having your venues mapped out in Map Point makes this quick and easy. You don't have to stop and think about which sub-markets are within a half hour of Dallas. Also, you can easily see which markets have 12 clubs you can e-mail and which markets only have one or two.

C·H·A·P·T·E·R 36

SEX: BETTER, SAFER SEX ON THE ROAD

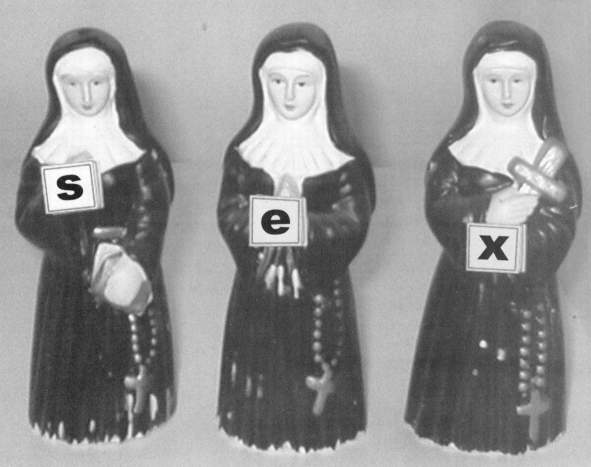

-Martin Atkins

TIPS FOR SAFER (AND BETTER) SEX ON THE ROAD

DR. DEBBY HERBENICK, PH.D., M.P.H

DR. DEBBY HERBENICK

INTERNATIONALLY KNOWN
SEX RESEARCHER, EDUCATOR
AND COLUMNIST
www.debbyherbenick.com

• **Check IDs.** Nothing spells drama like being charged for statutory rape by a 16 year old's parents (even if the 16 year old lied and said she was 18). The age of sexual consent varies by state and it is impossible to know the law everywhere you travel. To be on the safe side, set 18 as a minimum and ask for ID for any and all kinds of sex (including oral sex, the law sees it as a sex act, so you should too).

• **Stockpile condoms.** Even if you don't expect to need condoms on the road (either because your exclusive partner is with you, or you're staying faithful to a partner back home), someone at some point is going to need condoms. Keep them on hand. If your penis is the stuff rock star legends are made of (or if it falls a bit short), and standard condoms don't fit you well, keep sized-to-fit condoms *(www. theyfit.com)* on hand. They may break or slip off less often than typical condoms. Because infections can be passed from oral sex, stock up on flavored condoms *(www.condomania.com)*. Need extra sensation in order to come? Check out the Inspiral or Pleasure Plus brand. Use a condom correctly and every single time you have sex to reduce your risk of getting infected with chlamydia, gonorrhea, or HIV.

• **Get tested.** If you're having sex with random people, get tested regularly. Some infections (like chlamydia) rarely show symptoms in men, even though they may cause fertility problems later on. Plus, condoms cannot protect against all infections such as herpes and the human papillomavirus (HPV), which can cause genital warts. Call the Centers for Disease Control (1-800-CDC-Info; *www.cdc.gov*) to find testing sites in cities you travel to. If you're worried about being recognized, ask the CDC folks for several clinic numbers (many of the clinics provide a range of services other than infection testing, so no one would know why you were there). You can also call Planned Parenthood (1-800-230-PLAN; *www.plannedparenthood. org)*, which sees men as well as women, to find a health clinic where you or a partner can go for testing, treatment or other medical concerns. Or ask your tour manager if there's a doc who makes house calls.

• **Lube it up.** Not only does lube make for more pleasurable masturbation, but it also makes for more comfortable (and thus more memorable) sex for your partner. Some common brands contain ingredients that are irritating to women, so stock up on brands like Sweet Seduction (*www.pureromance.com)*, Pleasure Glide *(www.goodvibes.com)* or Sliquid *(www.babeland.com)* so that when they report back to their friends, the rumors are good.

• **Get creative.** Eager women are not always birth-controlled women. If you don't know your partner, why would you trust that she's on birth control? Or that she's using it correctly? Avoid paternity tests, law suits, stress (Is she? Isn't she?) and internet rumors by not getting someone pregnant in the first place. Once again, use condoms correctly and every time. Double up on your protection by getting creative about where you come (a secret used by many men who don't want to be dads). Come on her back, stomach, or in her hand, but not inside of her. Masturbation and oral sex have never looked so good.

• **Get a Boy Toy.** You've promised to be faithful, but everyone around you is getting laid. You're sick of your hand. Why not try a pocket pussy? They're available at most adult bookstores you'll find on the road, or stock up on a few before you leave (check out the Super Strech at www.pureromance.com, along with some creamy Whipped lube). The best models have an orgasmically tight fit and are ribbed inside. Not only are they good for masturbation, but they're fun to use with partners too. Just make sure to clean with soap and warm water after each use.

• **Go easy on drugs and booze.** Hello drugs, goodbye erection. Okay, that's not true for all drugs. But the term "whiskey dick" isn't for nothing. It's not like you can't drink or otherwise indulge. What happens, happens. But if you're wanting to spring into action later that day, go light on alcohol and avoid drugs known to kill erections (like adderall, various other amphetamines, and coke).

> "Hello drugs, goodbye erection."

• **Careful with Viagra.** Viagra and other erectile drugs do not mix with certain health conditions and party drugs. Some guys have trouble keeping their erections with partners they don't know well, or if they're having sex in front of their friends or band mates (privacy can be scarce on the road, it happens). Careful about leaning on these drugs as a crutch. If you think you need them, please get a prescription from a qualified physician—and not off the Internet, where you may get an inappropriate dose or a completely different (and possibly dangerous) drug.

• **Stay Off-Record.** Keep a journal, fine tune your memory, but please don't store your sex digitally. Regardless of your own reputation, remember that sex partners you meet on the road are real people with real lives (and occasionally, real spouses, parents or children). Even if you just want to record sex for personal use, sex tapes find their way onto the internet a strange amount of the time. For your own—and their own—mental health and well-being, safer sex is unrecorded sex.

• **Learn about sex.** Just because you're a rock star (or working with or wanting to be a rock star) doesn't mean you were born knowing how to have rock star sex. You or your partners are bound to have problems with orgasms, erections, ejaculation, lasting long enough, or otherwise feeling like it went the way you planned. You will have plenty of time on your hands while traveling, and books like *The Good Vibrations Guide to Sex* (Cleis Press, $25.95), *The New Male Sexuality* (Bantam, $16.00) and *The G Spot: And Other Discoveries About Human Sexuality* (Owl Books, $15.00) are sure to prime your appetite and your skills.

• **Don't leave home without it – birth control, that is.** Many clinics will only prescribe contraception to women who are already existing patients and it can take forever to get an appointment. Your best bet is to plan ahead. If you're on the birth control shot (Depo Provera), remember that timing is everything: you have to get that shot every 3 months, so plan accordingly based on where in the world you will be or use a different method. If you're on the pill, bring more than enough pill packs on the road. Planned Parenthood *(www.plannedparenthood.org)* can send you pills by mail, but you may not always know where you'll be. If you're traveling in other countries, you can't necessarily depend on the quality of the pills (medication consistency can vary dramatically in different countries). Bring condoms as a back-up, just in case.

• **On Your Guard.** You may feel on top of the world, but being a stranger in a strange town likely means that you don't know the safest parts of town and you are likely to meet all kinds of new faces. It is unlikely that you will be sexually assaulted, but it can and does happen to both women and men. General precautions include hanging out with friends and people you trust; staying away from deserted or otherwise scary looking parts of town; asking locals what's safe versus what's sketchy; accepting drinks only from those you know and trust, and bartenders too; and staying sober enough that you can make good choices. If you are assaulted, find support, information and other resources through the Rape, Abuse & Incest National Network *(www.rainn.org; 1.800.656.HOPE)* which was started by none other than Tori Amos.

• **Exercise and eat well.** Seriously. Not just for good health, but for your sex life too. It's hard to feel awesome about your body if you don't like the way that it looks or moves. You may have access to virtually no gym equipment while you're away but you can usually find a road to run on, a coffee shop to walk to, fresh fruit and low fat milk or yogurt at gas stations, and the occasional healthy but still tasty choice at fast food stops. Staying fit is good not only for body image but for your physical sexual performance too—erections, lubrication, and orgasm are influenced by having a healthy cardiovascular system to work with, so get moving and eat well.

** **Dr. Debby Herbenick, Ph.D., M.P.H** is a Research Associate and Lecturer in the Department of Applied Health Science at Indiana University. In addition, she coordinates The Kinsey Institute Sexuality Information Service for Students (KISISS; www.indiana.edu/~kisiss), a unique sexuality education service for college students provided by The Kinsey Institute for Research in Sex, Gender and Reproduction. She also serves as the Associate Director of the Sexual Health Research Working Group (SHRWG; www.indiana.edu/~shrwg), a collaborative of faculty and students conducting research on contemporary issues related to sexuality and writes regular columns about sexuality for various media including Men's Health magazine, Time Out Chicago, and Velocity Weekly. Dr. Herbenick has been awarded the William L. Yarber fellowship in sexual health at Indiana University where she has taught classes in human sexuality, sexuality education and research methodology. Her primary research interests relate to genital health and disease, the adult retail industry and its intersections with sexual health promotion, and condom efficacy.*

BE NICE TO GROUPIES: A WORD OF ADVICE TO ALL YOU ROCK STARS OF THE PRESENT AND FUTURE

CYNTHIA PLASTER CASTER

Be nice to your fans.

Treat us as you would treat yourselves.

Remember the way it felt after Keith Richards signed your guitar, and asked what kind of music you played? You couldn't believe he gave you the time of day.

Whether you wanted an autograph or sex from Keith, one thing's for sure—at one time, you were the adoring, starstruck fan.

And now the tables are turned.

So, what's the big deal about being nice to people who buy your music and go to your concerts, as long as they don't maul you?

When it comes to groupies, even if you don't care to partake in the gifts we offer, take our interest in you as a major compliment. Forgive us if we get a little excited meeting you, our hero, in the flesh. It only means that we think you rule.

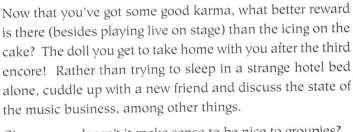

All right, maybe you've been feeling cranky and burned-out on touring your ass off. But don't vent your frustrations out on us, doll. Deal with it in a more healthy, productive way, like working out, playing soccer, writing even more fabulous music. Getting over yourself is good for the soul.

> **"Don't bite the hand that feeds you, pal. You may get your dick bitten off."**

Now that you've got some good karma, what better reward is there (besides playing live on stage) than the icing on the cake? The doll you get to take home with you after the third encore! Rather than trying to sleep in a strange hotel bed alone, cuddle up with a new friend and discuss the state of the music business, among other things.

C'mon now, doesn't it make sense to be nice to groupies?

Your record label might think so. Groupie interest in you is what interests the media. It's a publicist's dream come true. Hello, Random Notes.

Still have trouble being nice? Well...

Don't bite the hand that feeds you, pal. You may get your dick bitten off.

BE NICE TO GROUPIES AND OTHER FANS, OK?

Oh, and don't forget to be nice to your other long-suffering support system—your tour manager.

GROUPIES

> "Some people like to be backstage, some people like to be where they can't go. Some people just want free beer..."

There are famous groupies, drunken groupies, and people who are just trying to get the hell out of Dodge and make a connection. Be careful, not just because you might be breaking someone's heart, you might also be breaking the law.

Was it Groucho Marx that said, "I wouldn't want to be a member of any club that would want me for a member," or was it, "I wouldn't want to be in the back of the bus with anyone who has been with every member's member?" Remember?

And for every action there is an equal and opposite reaction. Your level of involvement is up to you, your God, and the STD clinic. Don't let this preoccupation upset the show, sidetrack a performance or a band itself. Remember, you are performing for the *entire* audience not just the person you want to be performing on later.

TOUR:SMART TIP
for more information go to:
www.tstouring.com

Spending an hour with one person means you don't have the time to spend five minutes each with 12 others.

Warning: if you think it's up to you whether your experience makes it onto the internet, think again. If you've already had a look at *smokinggun.com*, you'll have seen all of the details of a band's backstage requirements. Now imagine if what you were reading about was sexual technique and dick size. Metalsludge is one of many groupie sites and man, if you're off your game on stage, don't have much in your pants, and smell, are you in trouble! There's nothing quite like the combination of live show review, point-by-point sexual technique critique, and anatomic details. Seems like the most powerful ego-shredding lawn mower ever. Some of this stuff is just horrifying! Check out these excerpts from *metalsludge.com*:

This could be you:

What a fat lazy piece of shit. He has no charisma in the sack or on stage! After screwing thousands of chicks, he just doesn't put any effort into it anymore. If you hook up with XXXX, you deserve a painful yeast infection. Not to mention he has the build of Cartman from South Park.

...has nothing to be bragging about! Our source said he was a very lame lay, had an average cock, and lasted all of 2 seconds.

He has a very nice cock, above average in length and it's pretty thick. He can go ALL NIGHT! He's kinda aggressive, so beware. He will actually take time to get to know you, and is into anything you are into. He does like oral but will give it in return so that is a plus!

Reports are that he doesn't shower much. He does have an above average cock and can be a lot of fun, but his ego is totally out of line and out of control.

Maybe three inches if you pull on it. Could be the drugs though.

He will treat you as a prize the next morning and show you to the roadies like the catch of the day. Can be kind of crude that way!

C·H·A·P·T·E·R 37

DRUGS: HIGHS AND LOWS

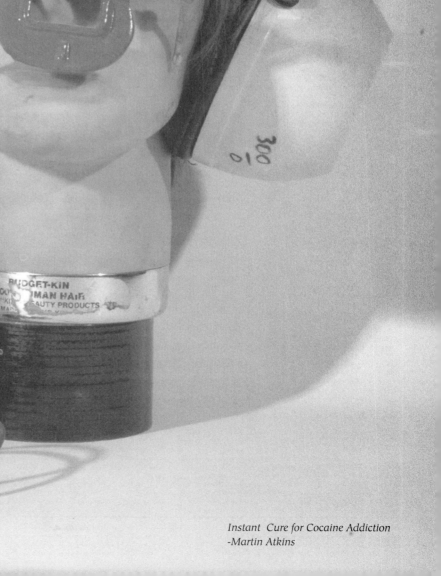

Instant Cure for Cocaine Addiction
-Martin Atkins

"Don't do coke in the front of the bus in the car park at Disneyland, you are on film... And in jail!"

My viewpoint on drugs, at this point, has distilled down to this: you can shoot heroin in your eyeball for all I care (that's none of my business) but it becomes my business when you are drooling on stage, playing perfectly in time with the song that the rest of the band played 20 minutes ago, transporting anything on the bus across borders, or exposing anybody else to risk or stress because of your own personal situation and the druggie fucks you hang around with. So, actually yes, I guess it is my business.

When I did drugs, I carried prescription speed in my pocket through airports and popped uppers in front of policemen with machine guns. That's fucking professional punk rock.

"Hey Kids - Don't buy drugs - become a Pop Star and they give you them for free!"
— Billy Mack, Love Actually

You might think you can play great on drugs... but you probably can't. If you were at a performance by PiL in the early '80s at Roseland Ballroom NYC, I'd like to apologize. It was nice to meet Harvey Keitel, but I was a little bit too coked-up to play so I smoked some weed to take the edge off and then had a couple of beers to take the smoke out of my throat and for that hour and a half my drumming was superb. I was the introduction to Hawaii 5 0. I was Ginger Baker reaching across the planet and shaking hands with Buddy Rich up in the sky, all four of my arms pounding my looking glass drum kit... until I heard the tape of the performance. If I had been performing with my drum kit nailed to the roller coaster at Coney Island I guess my performance could have been excused on those grounds but on no other!

I think, other than doing a few shots of Jäger on stage (before I stopped drinking), that's probably about it. So when somebody like me says be professional, that doesn't mean don't

"When I did drugs, I carried prescription speed in my pocket through airports and popped uppers in front of policemen with machine guns. That's fucking professional punk rock."

do drugs and don't do the things that make you happy and enable you. It means at least look at what you're doing and the people and circumstances around you and be professionally considerate about it.

> "Ambien is the savior of tours."
> – Nixon Suicide

TIME TO DROP

On tour with Pigface in '92, people on the bus were taking as much acid as they could. Several members would take 1,2,3,4,5 hits a day, several days in a row. I was as helpful as I could be. I would get on the bus at 5 p.m., and remind everyone, "Time to drop." At least everyone was high at the same time. If it's going to happen, make it happen as successfully and as safely as you can.

> "Don't mix drugs and touring. If you do, then don't expect to be very good for very long. You can try and have my band open for you and we'll blow your fuckin' doors off every night."
> – Henry Rollins

MUSIC ON DRUGS

LEE FRASER

> "For all the highs, you're gonna feel all the lows."
> – Sheep on Drugs

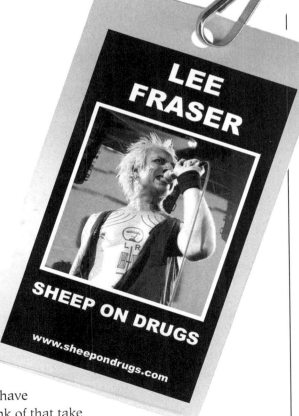

Music appreciation is based in the right side of the brain, along with emotions and dreams. Drugs can help you tap into the resources of the right hemisphere. Consequently, drugs and music complement each other and often go hand in hand.

Throughout history, musicians have used drugs to help them write music (in fact, I think music was invented by cavemen on magic mushrooms bashing bones together). Mozart used to sit down to compose with a bottle of brandy. Even The Beatles used drugs to influence their song writing. In fact, most musicians have used drugs at some point or other. How many musicians can you think of that take or have taken drugs (often to excess)? Quite a few, I bet.

The reasons for taking drugs and making music are therefore clear: Drugs help you think "out of the box" (i.e. "out of your head"). They can create new neural pathways, enabling you to literally think in new ways and, thus, have ideas you would never normally think of.

They can enable you to "distance" yourself from the song you're working on, giving you a new perspective on it. This is very important. Often, problems occur in song writing when you're "too close" to the song (i.e. "you can't see the wood for the trees"). Mentally taking a step back enables you to get an idea of what the song sounds like to the listener, not just the creator (i.e. you).

WHAT DRUGS DO (IN RELATION TO MUSIC CREATION):

All drugs affect people differently. This is a rough guide based on my own personal experiences. The effects of drugs also vary depending on how much you take and how quickly.

Cannabis, "Reefer," "Spliff"

Cannabis has a direct affect on one's hearing. It enhances it, making it easier to distinguish subtle tones within music and sounds. Much in the same way, it makes colors more vivid. Smoking cannabis also refreshes one's ears, almost as well as taking a break from listening to music. This is particularly useful when working on a mix in a studio, when there is no time to take a break (studio time is expensive, so you want to use all of it productively).

Some of the drawbacks of smoking cannabis include lethargy and impairment of motor skills, i.e. your playing can become sloppy. Some people also find it impairs their ability to concentrate. I personally have always found it an aid to concentration. That just goes to show how drugs affect people differently.

Amphetamines, "Speed," "Whizz"

Speed, as the name suggests, speeds up your mental thought processes, gives you extra energy, and enhances your ability to concentrate. This enables you to work for much longer periods than would normally be possible without a break.

Many times I have worked on a piece of music for over 24 hours straight with the aid of amphetamines. Drawbacks include getting "over-focused." Far too long can be spent on a minor detail of a song, something that ultimately only you will be able to notice once the song is completed.

> "Psychedelics, or "trips" as they are commonly known, have a profound effect on your hearing."

SHEEP ON DRUGS

Psychedelics – LSD, Magic Mushrooms, Mescalin, etc., "Trips"

Psychedelics, or "trips" as they are commonly known, have a profound effect on your hearing. Enhancing and distorting it makes things sound incredible. They also form new neural pathways in the brain, literally creating new ways of thinking —excellent for tapping into dreamlike states of heightened emotions. This is great for the enjoyment of music and getting new musical ideas.

There are drawbacks, however, in the fact that trips make it very hard to concentrate on something in a logical way. Things can become confusing to the degree where it becomes impossible to play / record music. I have been caught out with this. Once, while playing bass for a band, the bass guitar felt like it was made out of foam rubber. I also found it impossible to hear the beat of the song. I had to look at the drummer to try and get an idea of the beat. Not a good idea playing to visual prompts, especially as I couldn't see clearly. Trailing patterns were coming off of everything. Some of the other performers were also on acid. "Shambolic" is how I think you would describe that gig. I didn't do that again.

Duncan X and Lee Fraser of Sheep On Drugs.

Psychedelics can improve your ability to play for a few hours if you are playing / singing while you are "coming up" (as the drug takes affect). On the track "Slap Happy" on the "On Drugs" Album, both Duncan and I were tripping on six blotters each while recording the vocals. You can almost hear the acid on those vocal takes.

MDMA – "Ecstasy"

Although this drug enhances the enjoyment of music, it generally confuses you mentally too much to be able to play/write effectively. You can have creative ideas while on "E" but it is often difficult to remember what they were once the drug has worn off.

Cocaine – "Blow"

The Snorting Variety: Despite widespread use within the music business, I have never found it particularly useful in either mixing or performing music. If effects your hearing, making everything sound brighter than it is. Everything sounds a bit "toppy." Because mixing relies on you hearing sounds accurately, it hampers your ability to mix. Mixes generally come out sounding a bit weird. Dull, bass heavy mixes are common when mixing on cocaine. Playing / singing can also be affected. I personally find I make more mistakes. As far as performing live goes, it can lull you into a false sense of security. Consequently, you feel like you are doing a "blinding" gig, but the audience thinks you're a bit lame/untogether.

As far as crack goes, once you have smoked a pipe you're too out of it to do anything apart from enjoy the rush. Obviously, good musical ideas can be had on cocaine, but I would wait until the drug has worn off before mixing/recording. Although, each to their own.

> "The bass guitar felt like it was made out of foam rubber."

Opiates – Heroin, Opium, Codeine, "Smack"

These drugs, generally known as pain killers, work on the pain receptors of the brain. They give you a warm, comfortable feeling, removing anxiety and generally removing problems from conscious thought. How this drug (let's use heroin as the example, although all opiates have a similar effect) directly relates to making music is difficult to say. If you take enough, you enter a dreamlike state. "Couching" or "nodding" (as we shall refer to this state) appears to the outside world as if you're asleep, but inside, you're brain is active, having strange "dreams" normally of a dark, subversive nature. In this state it is obviously impossible to write, mix, or perform. The ideas you have when in this state can be carried through to a less "out of it" state and used in your music writing, recording, and performance. When you take less than enough to make you nod, heroin can be quite productive. You can think logically on "H" so you can think through complicated problems in the studio without the usual stress.

There are drawbacks, however, in that, unlike the other drugs mentioned (except alcohol), heroin is physically addictive. That means that after a few consecutive days of taking it, when you stop, you miss it. I mean really miss it, to the extent that you are unable to perform the simplest of tasks. You certainly don't feel like making music when you are withdrawing ("clucking"). You're physically in pain and your emotions are all over the shop—not a productive state.

Antidepressants

I've included this group of drugs purely because they have the ability to remove any creative urges you have. If you take antidepressants, chances are you won't create any music.

Having said all that, I am not a doctor. The effect drugs have on individuals varies enormously. "One man's meat is another man's poison." People have been known (people I have known) to completely "loose the plot," go crazy, and even die from taking drugs in even small amounts. I am consequently not advocating drug use. But if you want to take drugs and make music, remember those "out of the box" thoughts and good luck. Even if you don't write that smash hit, I'm sure you'll have a lot of fun. Also remember when you're broke and "clucking," don't blame me—I told you so.

That concludes the rantings of a drug addict.

"All illegal activities should be avoided while on the coach! (If you must smoke, do it in the rear lounge with the window open while the bus is rolling-not parked!)"

-Reggie Hall, Bus Driver

DISCLAIMER
MARTIN ATKINS

This is such a serious subject that I decided to ask a professional to give you the benefit of his opinion. I suppose I should take this opportunity to state that I'm not condoning or recommending any of the positions other people have taken in this book. I can't make you do anything. In fact, no one can effectively legislate and dictate behavior. It's your mind; it's your body to do with what you will.

If substances don't worry you then maybe the unfamiliarity with the source should. Being away from your hometown also means being away from relationships with trusted sources and they know you're not going to be in town tomorrow to complain about the quality of whatever it is they're selling you. Roll into all of that the more predatory nature of this business and life in general and it feels like you are diluting your ability to be more effective in all of the tasks outlined in this book. You're more likely to end up making a catastrophic decision with some people you've never met in a city you've never been to.

Lastly, I have a couple of things that may seem contradictory. If a member of your band gets in too deep with anything you have to stand by and help them through it, watch their back for as long as you can. Calling an intervention isn't the drug equivalent of snitching. You might be saving someone's life or at least giving yourself the knowledge that you rang the bell as loudly as you could. In terms of replacing a band member I'd advise going to great lengths to make sure that a new member is non-dependant.

You want everyone concerned about interviews, merchandise, songs, your street team, your fans, not just "Oh my God, does anyone know a dealer in the next two cities? We're heading for a problem." How sad to see an Excel spreadsheet proudly unfurled in front of me showing that we'd never be more than 100 miles away from a connection. I've heard the phrase used a lot, probably just in movies: "That thieving bastard is a genius. If he applied that brain to the business world, he'd be unstoppable instead of unusable." It's the same kind of deal with some of the most talented people on the planet. You just think if this person ever gets straight, fucking hell, the world had better look out.

JUST BECAUSE YOU'RE A ROCK STAR, YOU DON'T HAVE TO PARTY LIKE ONE
MATTHEW LEE SMITH, MPH, CHES, CPP

MATTHEW LEE SMITH

MPH, CHES, SPP
PRESIDENT/DIRECTOR
MLS HEALTH
SERVICES, INC.

ON THE ROAD...

Substance use has stereotypically been associated with the music scene since the beginning. Although sharing with us their vitalizing creativity, many talented artists have been tragically ripped from the scene, and this world, due to poor decisions, overindulgence, and lack of adequate knowledge. Drug consumption has led to the untimely demise of artists including Jimi Hendrix, Janice Joplin, John Bonham (Led Zeppelin), Hillel Slovak (Red Hot Chili Peppers), Bon Scott (AC/DC), Steve Clark (Def Leppard), Shannon Hoon (Blind Melon), Bradley Nowell (Sublime), Keith "Cowboy" Wiggins (Grand Master Flash & The Furious Five), Tommy Bolin (Deep Purple), Layne Staley (Alice In Chains), Bobby Sheehan (Blues Traveler)

The purpose of this article is to provide touring artists with the knowledge and awareness necessary to make informed decisions regarding substance use. We as humans have been privileged with "free will" and the ability to engage in behaviors that may be deemed undesirable by some. This freedom is accompanied by the need to assume responsibility for your actions. Thus, it is my task to arm you rockers with information about the physiological effects, consequences, and health risks associated with various substances you may encounter on the road.

MARIJUANA

420, Indica, Jive, Hydro, Kind Bud, Joint, Hemp, Home-Grown, Doobee, Mary Jane, Herb, Ganja, Grass, Dope, Shake, Maui-Wowie, Pot, Weed, Sinsemilla, Skunk, Reefer, Shwag, Chronic Cannabis Sativa

Marijuana is a plant used to get high. The buds, stems, and leaves of this flora may be smoked, ingested after mixing with food, or brewed into tea. Marijuana's primary active chemical, delta-9-tetrahydrocannibonol (THC), is responsible for producing "desired" effects.

Once THC enters the bloodstream, users experience increases in heart rate and blood pressure, blood-shot eyes, coordination loss, difficulty concentrating, short-term memory loss (damage to the hippocampus), and an increase in hunger. Despite a healthy appetite, marijuana contributes to more serious conditions including respiratory infections, chronic cough, increase phlegm production, panic attacks, depleted ability to learn, depression, anxiety, and decreased immune system functioning. Additionally, due to the overwhelming abundance of carcinogens present in marijuana smoke (approximately 50 to 70 more carcinogens than present in tobacco smoke), burning and inhaling this plant increases risk of cancers manifesting in the lungs, head, and neck.

Cocaine

Flake, Nose Candy, Devil's Dandruff, Horn, White, Yeyo, Pearl, Charlie, Coke, Blow, Toot, Snow, Yak.

Cocaine, a powerful central nervous system stimulant, is a white powder that is snorted, smoked, injected, or rubbed on the gums to produce physical effects. The effects of cocaine are short-lived, thus forcing users to frequently consume more and more of the drug to maintain the "desired" effects. This frequent and habitual use places users at risk for developing a dependency to the drug. Physical effects include increased heart rate and blood pressure, increased temperature, and blood vessel constriction. Users may feel irritable, paranoid, anxious, or restless.

Symptoms of smoking cocaine may take the form of shortness of breath, coughing, chest pains, or lung damage (accompanied by bleeding). Additional risks are associated with injecting cocaine. As with any behavior where a syringe is used to administer a substance into the body, risk of overdose and of transmitting blood-borne disease exponentially increase (especially if syringes and other injection utensils are shared).

CLUB DRUGS

Adam, Goop, Max, K, Go, Roofies, Burgers, Disco Biscuits, Eccies, Roaches, Soap, Echoes, Doves, Forget Me Drug, Jet, Super Acid, Fantasy, Hug Drug, XTC, Love Drug

Substances classified as "Club Drugs" include MDMA/Ecstasy (methylenedioxymeth-amphetamine), GHB (gamma hydroxybutyrate), Rohypnol (flunitrazepam), and Ketamine (ketamine hydrochloride). As you might expect (at least from looking at the scientific names), introducing this group of synthetic drugs into your body will manifest differing side-effects and greatly alter cognitive ability, decision making, and physiological functioning.

MDMA/Ecstasy is a psychoactive drug, typically consumed orally in pill form. Within 20-60 minutes after ingestion, users may experience an increased charge of energy, time distortion, altered perceptions, and increased enjoyment in physical contact. Short-term physical and psychological effects include increased heart rate and blood pressure, clenching of the jaw, blurred vision, hallucinations, confusion, profuse sweating, chills, nausea, muscle tension, anxiety, and dizziness. More serious, long-term effects include depression, insomnia, seizures, stroke, hyperthermia (core body temperature becomes too high resulting in kidney, liver, and circulatory system failure), addiction, loss of consciousness, and death.

GHB is a central nervous system depressant, which is consumed orally either as a white powder or as an odorless, colorless liquid. After consumption, users often experience drowsiness or unconsciousness, which makes GHB the culprit for sexual assault and date rape. Other side-effects include nausea, seizures, respiratory failure, and in extreme cases, coma.

> "The effects of hallucinogens may last for many hours, but in some cases, the associated chemicals will NEVER leave the body (they remain in your cells forever)."

Rohypnol, much like GHB, is a tasteless, odorless central nervous system depressant, whose sedative side-effects contribute to sexual assault and date rape. It is commonly taken orally in pill form or crushed to enable users to snort the powder. Side-effects include loss of muscle control, hypnotic effects, unconsciousness, and loss of memory. These effects may become more severe when combined with other substances, such as alcohol.

Ketamine is a powerful tranquilizer frequently used on animals. Available in solid and liquid forms, its users have used it to garnish drinks and smoking materials, powder their noses, and dissolve it so that it may be injected. Side-effects of Ketamine include "dream-like" states in which the user feels disoriented and uncoordinated, with distortions of sight and sound. Consumption of this sedative may result in abnormal heart rates, respiratory failure, and withdrawal symptoms.

Hallucinogens

Acid, Angel Dust, Boomers, Blotters Dots, Magic Mushrooms, Microdots, Hit, Peace Pill, Caps, Shrooms, Cactus, Buttons, Trips, Dose, Blotter, Windowpane

A classification of substances known to distort perceptions of reality and greatly alter moods, thoughts, and behaviors include LSD, PCP, psilocybin mushrooms, mescaline, AMT, DXM, Foxy, and DMT. Hallucinogens, as the name implies, are also known to make users see, hear, and feel stimuli that do not exist. The effects of hallucinogens may last for many hours, but in some cases, the associated chemicals will NEVER leave the body (they remain in your cells forever).

LSD is synthesized from ergot, a fungus found on grains, and capitalizes on lysergic acid. Typically consumed orally, LSD may be found in tablet or capsule form or less frequently in liquid form. This colorless, odorless drug produces a bitter taste, which may be added to small squares of decorative paper, each constituting one "hit" or "dose." Effects may be felt 30 to 90 minutes after ingestion and may last for up to 12 hours. Effects of LSD include increased heart rate and blood pressure, dilated pupil, increased body temperature, loss of appetite, sweating, dry mouth, tremors, and hallucinations.

PCP, also synthetic, produces unpredictable effects that are felt minutes after ingestion. Physical effects of PCP include increased heart rate and blood pressure, increased temperature, rapid and shallow breathing, dizziness, nausea, blurred vision, and in some cases, coma, convulsions, hyperthermia, and death.

Psilocybin mushrooms are consumed orally, with food to mask the foul taste, or brewed into tea. After consumption, users may feel the symptoms within 20 minutes. Physical effects include nausea, paranoia, panic, muscle weakness, and drowsiness.

PHARMACEUTICALS (AMPHETAMINES, BARBITURATES, BENZODIAZEPINES, & NARCOTICS)

Bennies, Reds, Oxy, Black Beauties, Downers, Bluebirds, Cottons, Blues, Copilots, Crank, Ludes, Crystal, Meth, Downers, Eye openers, Goofball, Ice, Yellow-Jackets, Wake-ups, Whizz, Uppers, Speed, Pep-Pills, Lid poppers, Barbs, Tooties, Scripts

> **"The dangers of drug use are very real and should never be down-played or overlooked."**

Amphetamines are stimulants that cause nervous system processes to function more rapidly than normal (hence its common reference…"speed"). This collection of chemicals is often presented as yellow or white pills/capsules that are orally ingested or crushed into powder, which is then either snorted or injected. Amphetamines make users extremely energetic, excitable, agitated, aggressive, and anxious. Symptoms include an increase in heart rate and blood pressure, rapid breathing, suppressed appetite, pale skin, insomnia, uncontrollable shaking, and enlarged pupils. In large doses, amphetamines cause irregular breathing and heart rhythm, dizziness, headache, hostile behavior, fever, heart attack, stroke, and even death.

Barbiturates and benzodiazepines, termed **hypnosedatives,** have sedative and hypnotic qualities and are often prescribed for their calming effects. They are presented as tablets, capsules, syrups, or suppositories and are either ingested or injected. Common hypnosedatives include chlordiazepoxide (Librium), diazepam (Valium), pentobarbital (Nembutal), secobarbital (Seconal). Other hypnosedatives that are neither barbiturates nor benzodiazepines include methaqualone (Quaalude) and mebrobamate (Miltown). Side-effects of hypnosedatives are similar to those of alcohol and include poor coordination, slurred speech, impaired judgment, and slow reactions to outside stimuli. Larger doses users clumsy and increase your risk of injuring yourself (falls, motor vehicle crashes), bronchitis, hypothermia, pneumonia, respiratory failure, unconsciousness, and death.

Narcotics are synthetic drugs intended to suppress pain. When taken in pill form orally, narcotics, such as oxymorphine (Numorphan), oxycodone (Percodan), and meperidine (Demerol), retard the natural function and reactions of the body. Effects may last up to six hours and include sweating, constricted pupils, slurred speech, suppressed appetite, nausea, vomiting, slowed reflexes, decreased heart rate and breathing, drowsiness, fatigue, depression, mood swings, apathy, and altered level of consciousness. Narcotic use becomes especially dangerous when combined with other depressant drugs and alcohol.

> **"Drug use won't define you or your worth, but your actions and decisions will!"**

In this article, you have been introduced to a wide range of substances with a variety of effects and health consequences. By now, you should feel a bit more knowledgeable about drugs you are likely to encounter while touring this vast and diverse nation. You should understand and accept why and how your decisions impact your health, the health of your bandmates, and the health of others you meet on the road.

The dangers of drug use are very real and should never be down-played or overlooked. What you may think is normal, low-risk, or acceptable drug use may carry enormous health consequences. The invincible mentality and thoughts that "it'll never happen to me" are foolish, irresponsible, unrealistic, and invitations for heartbreak, suffering, and compromised health. Although all effects and consequences of substance use may not be seen immediately, they may manifest themselves in the years that follow.

TO IMPART TO YOU SOME LASTING THOUGHTS TO PONDER:

• **Tolerance levels vary within individuals** (different tolerances for different drugs) and vary between individuals.

• **Combining different types of substances may have either "additive" or "multiplicative" properties.**

This means that the combination of two drugs will yield slightly larger effects (additive) or exponential effects (multiplicative), which increase health risks and the potential for fatal drug interactions. Never assume if the property of combining two drugs will be additive or multiplicative; rather, avoid taking or combining any drug in which the resulting effects are unknown or questionable.

• **The purity of a drug is not known, therefore you never know what unwanted chemicals are being ingested, injected, or smoked.** Drugs that have been "cut," or mixed, with other substances increase the already high risk with additional potentially adverse effects.

Life on the tour circuit has the ability to offer you a lifetime of experiences, memories, and friendships. After all the hard work you've devoted up to this point, it would be disastrous to drink, smoke, sniff, shoot, in other words, waste it all away.

Instead, allow your unique disposition and career choice to positively influence others, avoid peer pressures, and make healthy, informed, and responsible decisions. Remember you're an individual! Know yourself, love yourself, and don't let ANYONE tell you what to do or compromise your health! Drug use won't define you or your worth, but your actions and decisions will! Act right, be solid toward others, and live a life of health and prosperity in order to enjoy your success now and for years to come, but don't forget to tally up a few stories to entertain your grandchildren!

References:

Center for Disease Control and Prevention (CDC)- *http://www.cdc.gov*

Indiana Prevention Resource Center (IPRC)- *http://www.drugs.indiana.edu*

National Institute on Drug Abuse (NIDA)- *http://www.drugabuse.gov*

Office of National Drug Control Policy (ONDCP)- *http://www.whitehousedrugpolicy.gov*

"Remember not to get hammered neither because people who get hammered don't get to nail."
— The Streets

ILLEGAL DRUGS AND THE MUSIC INDUSTRY
CHRIS LEE, CHRISTOPHER LEE AND THE ODDITIES

I hate to feed a stereotype, but I can confidently say that illegal drugs are everywhere in the music industry. I am by no means encouraging this; I am merely going to pour out some of my thoughts on the subject.

Every tour needs someone who can keep the beast alive, namely a tour manager. People don't realize that this person is not always the most liked, and a lot of the times must act like a parent keeping the kids from doing something they are not supposed to. Once a tour commences, the tour manager needs to realize that for the next however many weeks, the bus or caravan that moves the tour has essentially become one big family unit, and one person's actions may affect everyone else.

If one member of the tour is using illegal drugs, this will affect everyone else. Of course there will be behavioral, social, and physiological side effects, but those are an inconvenience compared to the legal repercussions that could arise.

THINGS FOR A TOUR MANAGER TO KNOW ABOUT ILLEGAL DRUGS:

1. If a vehicle is "Hot Boxed," as in so many drugs have been smoked inside that vehicle that a police officer can detect the smell, that police officer has just gained the probable cause necessary to legally conduct a search of your vehicle and all of its contents. The occupants no longer have the right to say no to the search at this point, so get ready for every person on the bus to be contacted, identified, and questioned. If any of your performers have outstanding warrants or are on probation, don't count on them making the next show.

2. If a police officer conducts a traffic stop and has a police dog, you have no legal right to refuse that police dog the ability to sniff the air around your vehicle. If the police dog alerts for an illegal substance on the outside of your vehicle, just like the above situation, be prepared to have all of your belongings searched. This includes trunks and baggage storage on the undersides of a bus.

3. Depending on the state you are in, the officer you are dealing with, or the quantity and type of illegal substance found, your vehicle could be impounded, equipment and all. Not only does that mean someone is probably going to jail, it is going to take time and money to get your vehicle back, or to get new transportation. This situation could cost you the time needed to get to a venue, or multiple venues.

CHRIS LEE

FORMERLY OF CHRISTOPHER LEE AND THE ODDITIES HAS BEEN A LAW ENFORCEMENT OFFICER FOR THE PAST FIVE YEARS

> "Your vehicle could be impounded, equipment and all.."

4. The Supreme Court has ruled that if there are illegal drugs in a vehicle in such a place where more than one person knows of them and can exert control over them, no one has to claim ownership of the drugs for an arrest to be made. In this instance everyone with the knowledge of the illegal drugs existence could be arrested.

5. Lastly, and this one has nothing to do with the law: too many artists' lives have been cut short due to overindulgence of illegal drugs.

"...the best financial advice in the world is no match against a drug addiction."
    -Darren Guccione

"Sleep is my drug! You have your drugs! Let me have mine!!!"
    -Angelique Rickoff

CHAPTER 38

ALCOHOL: DRUGS PART II

-Martin Atkins

ALCOHOL
OK, SO ALCOHOL IS A DRUG. IT ABSOLUTELY IS A DRUG.

I stopped drinking about 12 years ago, it might be 14 years ago, I kept the very last bottle of Newcastle Brown Ale I drank and wrote the date on the label but I think it got thrown away in a tidy-up. Sometimes that makes me think "Ha, ha, ha the date and duration of my sobriety isn't important," but it is. I always thought I was dangerous when I was drunk and I certainly was. But I found I'm way more dangerous when I tap into that energy sober. It's like you find the keys to the secret room inside yourself where all the energy bombs are stored. If you're in that room drunk you could easily fumble one of the bombs and blow your own foot off. When you're sober, you can scientifically place the correct charge in the best place to create maximum creative devastation. Anyway, that's just me, you need to find your own path through all of this. The problem with alcohol is that it's not how much you can drink or how much damage that amount of alcohol will do to you... it's about the dangerous things that it will help you to try and rationalize are OK— dangerous sex, piles of drugs in untested combinations, etc. There's another good piece from Lee here and I wheeled in a guy with a bunch of letters after his name to give us some science about alcohol and he does the same thing with drugs, information, after all, is power.

Artwork by Mitch O'Connell

ALCOHOL
MATTHEW LEE SMITH

MATTHEW LEE SMITH

MPH, CHES, SPP
PRESIDENT/DIRECTOR
MLS HEALTH
SERVICES, INC.

"Brewskis, Hooch, Sipper, Freshie, Booze, Brew, Juice, Mixer, Coldie, Vino, Sauce, Spirits, Pops, Cocktail, Syrup, Snifter"

Alcohol is the drug of choice in the United States (and should not be consumed by anyone under the age of 21 years). Much of its appeal, other than being a legally possessed drug in America, is its social acceptance. Whether drinking beer, wine, or liquor, less social stigma surround this behavior when compared to using other drugs like marijuana, cocaine, or tobacco. Don't let this acceptability fool you! Alcohol consumption, although common, carries vast responsibility and potentially horrific ramifications.

It is important to know that one drink (serving) equates to 13.7 grams of pure alcohol. A serving is equivalent to: 12 oz. beer; 8 oz. malt liquor; 5 oz. wine, or 1.5 oz. hard liquor. The active ingredient in these aforementioned substances is ethyl alcohol (ethanol), which as ingested, increases a person's blood alcohol content (BAC), producing the intoxicating effect.

Everyone has their limit, although other factors influence the amount of alcohol one person can consume. Factors such as body size, gender, age, race or ethnicity, frequency of alcohol consumption, rate of consumption, food intake prior to drinking, and family history account for variances in a person's ability to process alcohol (and the side effects that accompany). Effects of drinking include slurred speech, drowsiness, blurred vision, slowed reaction time, increases in emotion, impaired judgment, decreased inhibitions, decreased equilibrium functioning, and memory lapses ("blackouts"). As alcohol consumption increases, users may experience nausea and vomiting, unconsciousness, and even respiratory distress. Intoxicated individuals should be monitored closely to ensure that they do not engage in other risky behaviors that may cause bodily harm to themselves or others.

Due to lowered inhibitions, those under the influence may partake in behaviors that they would otherwise avoid. Alcohol consumption has been linked to risky behaviors, which result in increases in unintentional injuries (e.g., falls, motor vehicle crashes, drowning), violent behaviors (e.g., homicide, suicide, assaults), unplanned pregnancies, and transmission of sexually transmitted infections. In addition to the short-term effects of alcohol, habitual use increases risk for heart disease, stroke, pancreatitis, cirrhosis (liver disease), various cancers, and social problems (e.g., fighting with friends or family, being arrested, depression).

"First of all, you have to be ready to wake up extremely early and immediately be ready to work. Your tour manager isn't going to care how many drinks you had the previous night or if you're suffering from a hangover. The amount of partying you do before you work again is completely your responsibility."
– Sarah Dope

ALCOHOL, "BOOZE" – LEE FRASER

Alcohol, the most commonly used drug, relaxes you mentally and removes inhibitions, which is good for creativity. It acts as a stimulant upon initial consumption for several hours, then as a depressant after that. It is best to use the creative energy of the stimulant part of the buzz. After you've had one too many and the depressant side kicks in, you can get sloppy, playing less well and prone to accidents (e.g. spilling beer into the mixing desk). Having said that, I have been in the studio completely drunk before. Listen to the song entitled "And More" a.k.a. "Sad Whiskey Song" on the double LP *Double Trouble* A lot of alcohol was consumed directly before we wrote and recorded that song. Although fortunately, we had a sober engineer to press record, otherwise it might never have been recorded.

Jack Sparrow: "Why is the rum always gone?"
– Pirates of the Caribbean: Dead Man's Chest

CHAPTER 39

HEALTH TIPS

It's easy to say, "Here are the top ten tips for staying healthy on the road: fruit, salads, water, no coffee, don't eat late at night (or early in the morning, right before you go to sleep), etc." But anyone who's been out on the road knows that, with the best will and intentions in the world, it can easily become fried chicken at 4 a.m., and more and more coffee, and anything to get you through however crazy the schedule might be—and you want it to be as crazy as possible. You want to have to miss dinner after sound check because you've got three interviews to do; you want to have two more to do almost as soon as you come offstage; you want to get a phone call at 5 a.m. from your publicist when you're still in your bunk because a magazine in Sweden really wants to talk to you. And the reality is you have to do what you have to do to get through it. So it just comes down to being as sensible as you can be, if you have a crazy three-day spell of constant demands, constant coffee, constant pizza, and constipation, deal with it on day four. As long as you are aware of how much of a toll all of this is taking, you can rebalance and start to find ways to exist healthfully in between the cracks.

> "At the end of a tour, you'll never want to eat pizza, tacos, or Denny's ever again for the rest of your life."
> --Lacey Conner, Nocturne

YOU MIGHT BE SURPRISED...

Two slices of Pizza Hut cheese pizza have about 480 calories, while a serving of Chinese chicken and broccoli can contain more than 1,100 calories...
www.living.aol.com/aolliving/main/slide

- **Don't buy your food where you buy your gas!**

- **Choose the salad if you have a choice between that and pizza.** For the next three days, you might not have the choice. Most fast food places will have something that at least seems like it is healthier.

- **Use your full-size refrigerator and microwave if you're traveling on a bus.** Instead of microwaving day-old pizza, you can find all kinds of healthy stuff from a Wal-Mart.

- **Microwave popcorn** is a favorite after-show snack.

- **Get a cooler,** if you are in a van. At least that will give you more of a chance to be healthy.

- **Grab a 30-minute power nap whenever you can.** Sometimes these naps might join together to form five uninterrupted hours of sleep per week.

- **Get earplugs or noise canceling headphones** to increase your chances of a productive nap.

When you sleep on a tour bus, your head is two feet away from somebody else's. That also means one person's super loud cell phone can wake up 12 people. Then, your

"It's more likely for someone to have a complete, total meltdown over the 100th tiny inconvenience, than it is that they'll lose it over one huge problem."

touring party will be just like the seven dwarves, except there's 12 of them and they're all named Grumpy. Create a phone recharging station in the front lounge of the bus, away from the coffee machine, and try to get people to keep their cell phones out of the sleeping area.

The same company that makes those cool Bluetooth walkie talkie headset things also makes Charge Pod. Most buses aren't equipped to deal with the outlet hungry needs of 8-12 touring entrepreneurs with laptops, cell phones, Blackberrys, iPods, and state of the art personal grooming devices. The charge pod can take care of six devices from a single outlet. A good investment for a tour manager to put one or two of these up front, close to the driver, away from the coffee machine so that when someone burns their hand on a joint and spills the coffee nothing gets damaged and when the guitarist's crazy, hysterical, jealous boyfriend calls for the fourth time in the early morning hours it's another gentle wake-up call for the snoozing driver.

chargepod™

PAY ATTENTION TO EACH OTHER.

Small stuff is huge. It's more likely for someone to have a complete, total meltdown over the 100th tiny inconvenience, than it is that they'll lose it over one huge problem. If you're tour managing and you have people who are sick or getting sick, call ahead, tweak the rider for the next day and the day after, and have nutritional and medicinal elements on hand to help when you arrive. If it is a combination of behavior, weather, scheduling, and nutrition, do what you can to address the behavior, too. Tell the bass player it's funny when he runs around the snow filled parking lot in his boxers, but you've got it on film already and it's on the web site, so he doesn't need to do it anymore.

"Small stuff is huge."

If it's a horrible load-in through snow and ice, I'm not suggesting that the lead guitarist help and smash his hand carrying a box so the tour gets cancelled. But he could walk around the corner to the hardware store and get some ice-melting crystals to throw down and, while he's out with the runner, blow $15 on clean, dry socks for the crew.

Greta Brinkman turned me onto Emergen-C. After a few tours, you'll discover everyone's secret formula for getting through it. Put together a small box of things you will surely need:

- Band-aids
- Antacids

- Imodium AD.

- First-aid Kit.

- Pain relievers (But remember not to take aspirin before you go on stage. Thanks Lee Popa for this tip. It slows the reaction time of your ears, just like alcohol, so when the monitor guy accidentally gives you the wrong feed and your monitor screeches at 180 dB you'll only be partially deafened for life).

- Basic Cold Remedies (Singers, take note: Chloraseptic might make your throat feel good for 20 minutes, but you'll end up doing more damage to your throat. See Chris Connelly's tips).

- Condoms.

- Morning-after Pills.

- Make sure anyone who needs a prescription has the prescription with them and/or the tour manager has a copy, so that when they run out or lose their medication they can deal with it.

And if you're a tour manager, make sure this box is clearly marked and that everybody knows where it is so you don't lose another 30 minutes of precious sleep telling someone where the aspirin is.

> Learn about your group's medical history and any allergies. I worked on an out-of-town show where I got a lot of grief about asking for this information. People seemed to think it was none of my business. I later learned that, within this cast of 12, there were three diabetics, two actors allergic to penicillin, one with asthma, and one more who was allergic to bee stings and had to have a shot of adrenalin within 45 minutes of a sting or his throat would close up and he'd die.
> *– Chris Tisone, Children's Theatre Tour Manager*

TOUR:SMART TIP
for more information go to:
www.tstouring.com

> "Tell the bass player it's funny when he runs around the snow filled parking lot in his boxers, but you've got it on film already and it's on the web site, so he doesn't need to do it anymore."

WATER

Make sure there's plenty of water everywhere: cases of the small bottles in the venue, gallon jugs, and small bottles on the bus. It used to be all about cases of beer; now it's about cases of water. The average person needs four or five handheld, average-size water bottles per day. On the road, you should drink way more. Depending on the energy level of your stage show and the proximity and number of lights in a venue, I know I've dropped pounds after two hours on stage with Pigface or Killing Joke where the drum riser has pushed me two feet closer to a spectacularly hot lighting rig. You cannot drink too much water. Worse case scenario, you pee a lot. (OK, actually, that's not true... someone just died from that!) When you're opening up a new case of water, hand out a few bottles to your heavy drinking band-mates. Someone might drink one.

One of the best ways to check to see if you are hydrated is to check the color of your urine (or your neighbor's). Clear to yellow is considered hydrated. Dark yellow indicates dehydration. Bright blue indicates a fountain pen has lodged in your penis. Just don't piss into a Gatorade bottle for later examination and leave it in the dressing room. And be careful with any drink in the dressing room, not just yellow fluids in a Gatorade bottle. If you have guests, any drink could be spiked. If you have ten cases of water, you could confuse your bottle with the unhealthy, wheezing guy's bottle of water. I always sharpie my name on the top any time I open a new bottle.

Invest in Mini-Sharpies on lanyards to go around your neck. Not only are you always prepared to sign autographs, but you can write your name or initials on the cap of your water bottle (or any beverage bottle for that matter).

TOUR MANAGERS

It's difficult to maintain the health of a band and crew. Handle it, not by being a, health-freak, but, as Jolly and I talked about in our interview, by gently steering. Hand people water. If you're in the middle of some unhealthy nightmare tour that you know is going to crash and burn because of health issues, start handing people 16 oz. bottles of water into which you've already put a pack of Emergen-C. Ask the driver not to stop at the horrifying truck stop. Does he know of somewhere within 50 miles that might be healthier and more comfortable? If your bus becomes "The Death-Bus Harbinger of Disease," bring in a crew to steam clean the fucker. Get the driver to wash all the sheets more often until the crisis has passed. You cannot have a passive role in any of this. Chastising band members for not being neat and tidy not only will not work, it will just be a huge laugh at your expense. Call a doctor out to sound-check at the venue to check-up on everyone before a particularly rough stretch. And after the half-hour consults about the singer's throat, the drummer's knees, and the guitarist's chesty cough, don't forget to treat the crew with the same respect and have the doctor look at them, too. With a bit of foresight, you can call ahead to even small venues and find one out of three or four that has a doctor who might be more willing to work with you on price and prescriptions if needed.

Amongst all of the craziness and constant need to push through barriers, ignore warnings, and go against the grain, don't let that artistic vision and your crusade as a band cloud your thoughts and influence your actions when it comes to a medical problem on the road. Call somebody as quickly as you can. If you're unplugged from a support network, call the promoter or the soundman or anybody whose number you have. Don't hesitate to call 911 or go to the emergency room. The worst thing that could happen is that you look back at the tour and laugh about the night that you didn't have to go to the ER and all of the wonderful people you met there.

> I had unbearable knee pain in '94 and the doctor who met us at the venue in Philadelphia gave me cortisone injections joined us on stage and played bass for the next three or four years.

"Do not get too worn-out before your important shows. Everything in moderation as you approach larger markets and industry shows along the tour."
  - Mark O'Shea, NIN Tour Manager

Cleanliness is...

Scrupulous cleanliness used to be an indicator of obsessive-compulsive behavior. These days, it's not a bad idea to make sure you carry hand sanitizers, anti-bacterial wipes, and if you're in close proximity to a member of a road crew, even some SOS pads.

You're not even safe in a hotel room. I just saw an episode of CSI (or something on the Discovery channel) where they went into what looked like a clean hotel room and turned on a special light to reveal any kind of fluid secreted by a human being (snot, cum, saliva, blood, urine, whatever). Any remnants glowed in the dark. This top quality hotel room looked like it had hosted the annual "Questionable Fluids Paintball Olympics."

So, you have a few choices:

1. Shortly after check-in, remove, shred, and burn every item in the room. Remove the carpets and completely redecorate.

2. Remove the bedspread (trust me, remove the bedspread), and use an antibacterial wipe to hit the hot spots: TV remote, computer keyboard, telephone, light switches, and, last of all, the Toblerone in the mini-bar. Everyone who has ever been in that room since the day the hotel opened has picked up that Toblerone and said, "Eight dollars? No fucking way!" And put it back. Do not touch the Toblerone. Step away from the Toblerone.

Another source of airborne and surface-borne germs would be any airplane. Take your own water. The flight attendants are touching everything you don't want them to touch. The guy three rows in front of you who has been coughing since takeoff just had his mucus-covered pop can tidied up by the flight attendant. The guy who just changed his baby's diaper and didn't wash his hands (because even his baby's poop is really cute) just handed the flight attendant a used cup. Now you're going to accept a germ-covered cup from them?

Another large health hazard when flying around the world is food poisoning. Everyone knows not to drink water from the faucet and not to eat salad or fruit that has been washed with tap water. That also applies to ice. What most people don't know is that airplane food originating in a country with different health standards than you're used to can also cause a bout of diarrhea. If all else fails, tuck your pant legs inside your boots.

Hotel rules apply to airplane bathrooms, too. Before you have sex in there, make sure to wipe off some of the surfaces with an anti-bacterial wipe. In fact, when you're finished put a condom over your head and don't breathe for the rest of the flight, you'll be fine. Cleanliness is no laughing matter... and I think I just proved that.

> " ...we'd stay up for two days speeding and get ridiculously drunk on the plane. That was either the best way to deal with jet lag, or I don't remember that it wasn't."

JET LAG

I just got back from Europe. There was a section in the in-flight magazine about jet lag. All the tips are the same tips I keep reading about and I keep getting jet lag! And it's horrible. There are pills you can take, diets, ways of trying to get your body thinking it's in another time zone by eating at the same time that somebody is eating breakfast in Spain. But then, when you think you're eating breakfast in Spain, you're actually late for a meeting in Los Angeles. I've seen an invention for pilots that shines light behind their knees—a place where UV Rays are absorbed more readily—and that seems to work. But, how long before we hear of a bizarre, florescent-tube-behind-the-knee accident? I know it's tough to sleep with jet lag, but is it easier to sleep with a florescent light behind your knee? So, now, I'm at this point: back full circle to my first couple of trips to the States, when we'd stay up for two days speeding and get ridiculously drunk on the plane. That was either the best way to deal with jet lag, or I don't remember that it wasn't. Anyway, here are a couple of ideas:

- Melatonin is supposed to reduce the effect. It is available at most drug or health food stores.

- Reset your watch to the time at your destination.

- Don't think about the time where you are. Think about the time where you are going to be... at the top of the Billboard Charts, baby!

- Drink Lots Of Water.

  - Dehydration will make everything worse. Jet lag is no exception.

- Sleep on the plane if you can, when flying at night. Use noise canceling headphones to help.

  - If you are arriving in the day, try and stay awake during the flight.

> "Think about the time where you are going to be... at the top of the Billboard Charts, baby!"

EFFECTS OF A SMOKE-FILLED ENVIRONMENT:

Another change, over the last 30 years, has occurred with smoking. I used to go from a tour bus where everyone except me smoked two packs a day into a venue full of smoke. Now, it's rare to find a musician over 25 smoking on a tour bus, either because they've chosen not to smoke anymore or they don't want the singer's boot hitting them upside the head. If you find yourself in Europe, try and stay out of the smokiest environments for as long as you can. Take the autograph meet 'n greet session outside (unless you're in China where it really doesn't make any difference).

"A clean coach is a healthy coach!"
-Reggie Hall, Bus Driver

NOISE AND YOUR HEARING:

Sounds louder than 85 decibels (dB) can damage your ears. A normal conversation is about 60 dB. Chainsaws, hammer drills, bulldozers, and EinstürzendeNeubauten ring in at over 100 dB. Loud noise does not have to be an everyday happening to cause damage. One-time exposure, such as the sound of a gun firing at close range, can harm your ears permanently (especially if the gun is aimed at your head).

From NIDCD: *National Institute on Deafness and Other Communication Disorders*

www.nidcd.nih.gov

VOICE TIPS
CHRIS CONNELLY

CHRIS CONNELLY

MINISTRY, REVOLTING COCKS, THE DAMAGE MANUAL, MURDER INC, PIGFACE

www.chrisconnelly.com

The best thing I ever found was that H2Ocean stuff that Curse Mackey's pal sold: salt water in an atomizer spray bottle. You cannot beat it. Tea feels nice, but ultimately that is all. Throat coat is good: make a flask of it, using boiling water and four teabags so it is very strong. This is excellent. I would spray the salt spray all the time and spraying it up the nose is excellent, too. Broadway night club singers will come home at night and snort warm salt water up their noses! Yuk! But it is the best thing to combat the smoky environments you find yourself in nightly.

These things have never done anyone any good:

- Cigarettes
- Marijuana
- Dry ice/booze (dehydrating)
- Coffee (dehydrating)
- Candy
- Dairy products
- And last, but definitely not least, talking! If you have to sing every night, talking for extended periods of time really fatigues the voice.

Of course, everything is fine in moderation, but before the last Pigface tour, I had to give up cigs or I simply would not be able to sing—end of story. It was really shit or get off the pot time for me.

Touring for a singer in winter is hard. A woolen scarf is essential to keep the throat warm.

A HORROR STORY

The most horrific of many stories was an outbreak of spinal meningitis on the Lowest of the Low Tour in '97. At the end of a show in Rochester, I was listening to Bagman, smiling to myself: "Another show completed!" When somebody grabbed my arm. "There's a problem with Dave Wright. He's freaking out at the hotel."

Dave had become delirious and violent in the hotel room to the point where the hotel had called the police. The police had Dave strapped to a gurney thinking he was on drugs, when his band mate assured the officer that he was the sweetest, gentlest guy in the world and something must be terribly wrong for him to have torn up a mattress and smeared shit all over the hotel walls. At the very last minute, the police took him to the hospital instead of jail, where he would have died. All of this is happening while the equipment still needs to be packed up and loaded. Total fucking freak-out is not the word. And if you have read this far in the book, you'll know that Murphy's Law was in full effect. This wasn't the night before two days off (because we never have days off on the road). It was the night before a long drive and a border crossing into Canada. The bus driver was legally required to notify the Canadian Board of Health and we were met by French-speaking medics who handed us information about spinal meningitis and some pills that made our piss fluorescent orange.

It's one thing to say "The show must go on." Give me a fucking break. Not only were we concerned for the condition of Dave Wright, but we had left his bandmate in Rochester at the hospital with him, along with Jim, my drum tech, who was exhibiting symptoms. The only conclusive test for spinal meningitis is a spinal tap, which is what Jim had that evening... and that was his birthday... Happy Birthday, Jim! I'm not sure if it was psychosomatic or what, but once the Canadian medics had sat down with each of us individually and asked us if we were feeling any one of a list of symptoms, most of us were. As the evening progressed, our numbers were thinning. Early in the evening, F.M. Einheit's drummer was rushed to the hospital and I took her seat, bumbling through the set, looking around anxiously to see who was left standing. F.M. Einheit returned the favor, acting as my drum tech for the Pigface show. I didn't really have peace of mind to appreciate the coolness of F.M. Einheit handing me towels and bottles of water.

We were anxiously awaiting news on Dave Wright's condition for several days. The only thing I could think to do in any way, shape, or form positive, was to insist that everybody in the venue chant "Wake up Dave, we love you!" before we would play any Pigface songs and try and send some positive vibrations his way. It was a week before we found out he was OK. He still has tinnitus in one of his ears which, for an electronic musician, is a pretty horrible thing.

MENINGITIS SYMPTOMS

- **Fever** – usually over 103.

- **Severe headache** – not a typical headache—extremely painful, caused by infected lining of the brain getting severely inflamed.

- **Vomiting –** the irritation in the brain triggers persistent vomiting.

- **Neck pain and stiffness –** severe pain in the back of the neck. Looking down at your stomach will cause severe pain. This occurs because the lining of the spinal cord is connected to the lining of the brain. When this infected and inflamed lining is stretched by looking down, it causes severe pain.

- **Photophobia –** extreme sensitivity to light. It hurts your eyes. Meningitis will cause someone to refuse to look into light, especially the bright sunlight. (someone needs to inject Brittany Spears and Paris Hilton with this....)

- **Confusion, or difficulty concentrating.**

- **Seizures.**

- **Sleepiness or difficulty waking up.**

- **Lack of interest in drinking and eating.**

- **Skin rash** in some cases, such as in viral or meningococcal meningitis

- **Sluggishness, muscle aches and weakness,** and strange feelings (such as tingling) or weakness throughout the body.

- **Dizzy spells.**

Check out *Stories from the Front Line* for more Horror Stories!

Illustrations by Adam Watkins.

- **Don't buy your meals where you buy your gas.**

- **Take time to power nap whenever you can.**

- **Get earplugs or noise canceling headphones.**

- **Watch Supersize Me.**

- **Don't drink coffee. (Yeah, right!)**

- **Try not to eat right before you go to sleep. (Yeah, right!)**

- **Drink lots of water.**

- **Watch each other's backs.** Be attentive to everyone's physical and mental state.

- **Do not get too worn out before your important shows.** Everything in moderation as you approach larger markets and industry shows along the tour!

- **Time your excesses wisely.**

- **Check to see if your hotel has health facilities and use them!**

- **Get over-the-counter meds from a nationwide chain like Wal-Mart or Walgreen's.** They keep your prescriptions logged into their computer network so it's easier to get refills on the road.

- **Try to get health insurance.**

"I've never had a problem with drugs. I've had problems with the police."
    -Keith Richards

CHAPTER··········40

BEING A GRRRL ON THE ROAD

PHOTOGRAPHY, GRAPHIC DESIGN, MODELING, AND MERCH
WWW.SARAHDOPE.COM

SARAH DOPE

Being a girl working in the industry is tough enough. Being that girl working on tour is even worse.

As a girl trying to be serious about work, you already have to deal with the stereotypes such as, "That girl's hanging out with one of the band guys. They must be hooking up," or "Oh, that girl's backstage. She must be a groupie."

At first, it makes your environment really hard to work in because you're dealing with these assumptions coming from just about everyone. The fans on the other side of the barricade (who don't know you and don't really understand everything about the industry), the security guards (who just automatically assume things and will give you a hard time no matter if you have a press pass or a tour laminate or even if you're carrying road cases), and yes, sometimes even the band and crew members (who only see you as a piece of ass, and will harass you to no end for sexual favors). Some will then even throw temper tantrums when you repeatedly turn them down. It gets frustrating. All you really want to do is get your work done and do some networking.

My advice to girls is: If you want to be taken seriously in the business, don't fuck around, and don't give up. Start by building yourself a good reputation; you will earn a lot more respect over time by respecting yourself and by the amount of determination and dedication you keep. You will make new friends, new acquaintances, and new business associates. When they hold great respect for you, they will be more willing to help you along your way to better your career.

As far as touring goes, I believe it takes a certain type of mentality for a girl to truly be able to handle the tour life, especially if you're on tour as a part of the road crew, not as a musician. It's not always clean and glamorous by any means.

- First of all, you have to be ready to wake up extremely early and immediately be ready to work. Your tour manager isn't going to care how many drinks you had the previous night or if you're suffering from a hangover. The amount of partying you do before you work again is completely your responsibility.

- I'm not saying don't have fun, but you better have your shit together if you have to work the next morning. Usually, I choose to only have maybe one or two drinks with my guys after a show if we have another show the next day, then go to bed an hour after bus call. Even the rare times I have decided to toss down a few more drinks and get drunk, I made sure I was up and ready by load-in time, and ready to carry cases and setup by myself.

- You have to be able to stay on track with time schedules (load-in time, load-out time, set time, bus call, etc). Nobody likes a late worker, and if you're late for bus call? Some bands will leave you behind, and it will be up to you to find a way to the next city on your own. You also risk getting fired.

> "If you want to be taken seriously in the business, don't fuck around, and don't give up."

- No matter what your job is on tour, you are responsible for what you work with: your "gear/equipment." You have to stay focused and aware of what technically belongs to you, because there will be no one else to do this for you. If you lose something that belongs to the band that is your responsibility to watch (like merch), chances are you will have to pay for it out of your tour salary. If you lose something that belongs to you, tough luck.

- If you are handling money for the tour, it is not a good idea to carry it with you everywhere. Invest in a lock for your luggage, suitcase, or money bag—whatever it is you decide to keep the money in. Keep this money in this locked container, and store it in a safe place on the bus.

- Keep track of your keys and always be sure to lock up. When you are handed copies of keys to the bus, the bays, and/or the trailer, keep track of them! If you lose them, you will have to pay for the lost copies. Also be sure to always lock up!

- If you are the last to leave the bus (or no one is in the front lounge when you leave), lock the door. There have been plenty of times random people have "broken into" a bus because of unlocked doors, and things get stolen. The same rule applies if you get on your bus, but won't be hanging out in the front to watch over things, and there's no one else there. Lock the door behind you. It takes two seconds.

- If you are getting equipment out of your bay or trailer, be sure to lock up when you leave the area, even if you still have more to grab for the show. When these are unlocked and unattended, things often turn up missing.

- No whining! You've got to be tough on the road and know how to take care of yourself. No one cares if you broke a nail or got a tiny little bruise, and honestly, no one has time to hear it. When carrying heavy gear, you are bound to receive road scars. I've gotten a bruise the size of a cantaloupe on my leg before from carrying a coffin-shaped table. It hurt like no other. Did I complain? No. It happens.

- Don't expect to get a shower that often. Unless you're working for a band of millionaires, you're most likely not getting a shower every night. Touring is like camping out for a few weeks. You might get a shower somewhere once a week, if even that. If this idea utterly disgusts you, you probably shouldn't go on tour then. Tip: those of us who can handle it usually bring antibacterial wet naps (a.k.a. "the poor man's bath"). And again, no whining about it!

- Girls, if you are going to go on tour, pack light. There is no need to bring your entire closet and two cases of makeup. You won't have the time to make yourself up and look like you're ready to go out to a nightclub with the girls.

> "... if you're late for bus call? Some bands will leave you behind,..."

> "Don't expect to get a shower that often."

MARGOT OLAVARRIA

THE GO-GOS
BRIAN BRAIN

GRRRRRL'S GUIDE TO THE ROAD:
MARGOT OLAVARRIA, BASS PLAYER

Back in the day when I was paying bass with Brian Brain, the road seemed endless. We would tour across the country and back again, coast-to-coast without passing GO or collecting any profits. It's easy to lose track of time and what is happening in the world. One seems sucked into a void of unending highways, motel rooms, and dark clubs wafting of stale beer. Most of this happened in a van named Doris, a 1960's Dodge camper painted blue with a white stripe with flapping fish decals on each side. On the inside, she had blue carpet that smelled of scorched antifreeze. In our years of touring, Doris survived an electrical fire, losing a wheel (not a tire), more than one transmission trauma, and constant overheating. But despite the many "disastours," we still managed to have fun and make lots of friends. And luckily, there is the almost-nightly reward of the 50 minutes on stage in front of an adulating audience. Having survived this and emerging a wiser person, I would like to share with you some of the things that spending the '80s on the road have taught me.

Time: Life on tour is like playing a waiting game—waiting to sound check, waiting to check into a motel, waiting to fill-up with gas, waiting for the van to be repaired, waiting to play, waiting to (hopefully) get paid, etc. Well, make sure you have plenty of good books. I discovered that thrift shopping is a great way to unwind and find treasures that time refuses to forget. It also satisfies the capitalist urge to consume without spending a lot of cash. After you check into a motel, look-up "thrift shops" in the Yellow Pages and maybe you'll strike a "fill a bag of clothes for five dollars" day. But please ask yourself "Will I really wear or use this item?" before jamming more junk into the packed van. Before we knew it, Doris was brimming with cha-cha shoes, martini glasses, and paint-by-number masterpieces.

Having time to yourself also becomes nearly impossible; sharing motel rooms, van space, stages, and the rest gets old super fast and you begin to feel that you are attached at the hips of four or five people. That's why it's important you love your band and crew. Spending even 24 hours of road time with someone you can't stand can make you physically sick, which brings me to the next important issue.

Health: Staying healthy on the road is a challenge. Late hours, bad food, booze, and other excesses damage mind and body and drain the energy needed to give your best stage performance. Sometimes even the most seemingly innocuous indulgence, like an eight ball, and a martini, can wreak havoc with your immune system and your liver and then come the sty on the eyes and the sores on the lips. I recommend daily doses of effervescent vitamin C of a thousand or more mg. to buttress the immune system and desiccated liver tablets to repair the liver. If you are a vegetarian, milk thistle and lecithin supplements for the liver will do the trick. (I am a doctor, you know, just not the medical kind.)

Good nutrition is very important. Stock up on snacks at health food stores and avoid fast food joints when possible. We learned the hard way after an existence that relied on microwave burritos and pizza. If you have a contract rider that states "the management will provide hot food for band and crew," for example, add the phrase "except pizza" in there. Clubs are only too ready to think that cheap pizza qualifies as a nutritious dinner, and you will find the pizza boxes stacked in the dressing room after sound check gig after gig. The club The Living Room in Providence, Rhode Island stands out in our memory because the owner's mother would layout a delicious spread of home-cooked chicken, green beans, salad, and other vegetables.

There were so many times when money was tight and we had to travel miles and miles to the next gig. I remember five of us surviving from South Dakota to Seattle on rice cakes, a jar of peanut butter, and a bag of oranges. As food is a great way to bond with people, friends and followers in different towns were gracious enough to offer their kitchens and Martin became famous for his culinary skills, especially for his Shepherd's Pie.

NIXON SUICIDE

Interviewed by Martin Atkins

Nixon has appeared in CSI and a new movie with Crispin Glover. Twelve hours after the current tour finishes, she's on a plane to head back to the store she works in to help out with the Christmas rush.

Nixon said it was hard going from six weeks of rehearsing eight to ten hours a day to just doing the show. I mentioned I had heard they had been thrown out of hotel. She said, "Well, you know, the hotel is your house. And naked girls running around the hallway don't go down very well!" They were thrown out of another hotel doing laundry early in the morning in party mode. Things got out of hand when the machines and the girls entered spin cycle. Nixon remembered someone screaming, "Dirty Lesbians!!" as they were thrown out of the hotel.

I asked about SuicideGirl groupies. She said she stopped off at Planned Parenthood before a tour to get bags full of (morning-after pills). And she spoke about the emotional cost of everyone being so far from their support system. By the time they get back from touring, she estimated that sixty percent of them would have lost their boyfriends. There's weirdness with exes, personality conflicts, and disapproval from mothers. I asked if they spent any time at the merch booth signing things. She said, "Oh, the 'meet-n-creep.' When the stalkers show up." But, it's almost always girls that do the creepy stuff: cop a feel or cut themselves open to prove their love.

MA: So how long have you been doing this?

Nixon: Now heading for four years. I got involved with SG way back. You know, I love the burlesque revival I love the whole concept of it. I think I'm naturally nomadic anyways so touring was a natural thing to do. The first time we went out, it was limited, you know, only a few weeks. But they got a great response! We've been building on it ever since!

MA: So, what was the first tour like?

Nixon: Well, the first one was a 15 passenger van, standard, pretty small venues, 300-500 capacity venues. And yeah! That was basically a hysterical disaster as I imagine first tours are for everyone.

MA: So, what went wrong?

Nixon: We had no basis from which to go on. It's not quite like touring with a band. And we found that the venues were totally ridiculous. We change outfits about every three minutes. Sight lines are built for bands, you know, so with bands you see from here up, and suddenly we were getting people walking out, loosing a third to half of the crowd sometimes because the sight lines were so poor. They couldn't see! So there were a lot of things we just hadn't thought about until we were actually out there in places that weren't made for the kind of show we were doing at all. We went through a lot of sound issues, trying originally to perform off a CD, that didn't go well. There was always skipping. So we ended up getting iPods. That was so much easier! I think that was one of the first major changes. We do a level check and that's all we need. Our load-in takes ten minutes. We have a box of costumes! Other things that we found were really weird. When you're doing choreography and every stage is a different size and shape, so that gets real exciting! We ended up doing a much tougher tour the year after that was literally almost everyday. And we were doing a promotion for a DVD we did during the first tour, so we were doing a show, a meet-n-greet, a signing, almost everyday. It was an absolutely insane schedule.

> **"We were doing a show, a meet-n-greet, a signing, almost everyday. It was an absolutely insane schedule"**

MA: How many weeks?

Nixon: That one was about six or eight weeks? Something like that. Tonight is our last show of this tour... very thankful for that! I've seen my house four days since August, so... (Laughs)

MA: So, on the third tour, the one when you were promoting the DVD, did you have an event in the afternoon?

Nixon: Yea, basically, sometimes we'd go straight to a signing or a meet-n-greet... try to hose off at a hotel... maybe hope for a shower, maybe not, maybe you're doing your makeup in the car. It happens! This last month is the first time we've had a bus.

Artwork by: Rion Vernon
Cards available on www.suicidegirls.com/shop

MA: And how was that?

Nixon: Um… well, getting the bus means we lost our hotel rooms. So, it's been a little strange. I like the bus cuz we have more time everywhere because we can travel at night, which is a big thing. But, that many girls trying to get ready as soon as we get somewhere where sometimes there were several showers, sometimes there was one.

MA: And sometimes there's none!

Nixon: Yeah! We've been doing arenas and they've been pretty good because most of them are sports. The first time we went out on tour, we did a lot of smaller clubs and we had chocolate sauce. They wouldn't have showers so we'd be in the sinks, dish washing sinks, trying to get the chocolate out of us. That and no laundry facilities, drawback from not having hotels. I think I've washed these pants once since New York!

MA: So are you Febreezing the hell out of things?

Nixon: Yeah! Just kind of dusting them off as we go! (Laughs) Like every other band, I think! The show we did with Guns 'n' Roses was much cleaner because we were on first and we couldn't make as much of a mess as we actually like to. We've had everything from chocolate, beer, whipped cream, every kind of liquor imaginable, fake blood, coffee at one point that we dumped on the audience… and the stage clothes would be soaking wet and all you could do was put them in the trunk and wear them again the next night! You want to stay away from the latex with cloth lining because it just holds stuff in! So gross!

MA: How was the bus driver?

Nixon: He was great! He was not around us that much because of course he was sleeping whenever we were awake and awake whenever we were sleeping, but he was a perfectly sensible bus driver. There were only a couple of nights when we woke up in the middle of the night going, "Um… did we just do something really bad?" But it felt much safer than the van. For sure. Our tour manager was driving and no one was getting any sleep at all. I actually ended up in the emergency room on the first part of this tour for getting an ulcer in my eye from staying up wearing my contacts all night trying to help everyone stay awake driving. We had an award winning day when three of us went to the emergency room in one day. I had the eye, Regan got a soft tissue tear in her knee, and one of the other girls had a cold that had settled so deep in her lungs that she couldn't even sleep at night. Neither could anyone else because she couldn't stop coughing.

MA: So, when you're doing the DVD promotion, that's in a van?

Nixon: Yeah.

MA: Fuck! So, were you getting out of the van into a store?

Nixon: Yeah! Quite literally.

MA: So you were getting ready in the van.

Nixon: Yeah!

MA: See that's where a bus would…

Nixon: …be helpful, yeah!

MA: And when you are doing that many events, how do people react to that? See I don't know what you guys are like. Is it just crazy and everybody's just drinking and it's just a blur? Or do people go the other way and try to be totally on it? Or is it a combination?

Nixon: I would say it's a combination of all of the above. The first couple of tours that went out, we took whoever was along for the ride. A bunch of punk girls basically. We'd be like, "OK, we need coffee and liquor if we're going to make it through this right now." But, this time out we've got trained dancers, so they're a little more about wanting healthy food and "Can we stop for a shot of wheat grass." While the rest of us are still going, "You get your wheat grass, get me a bottle of Ketel, and we'll be fine!" (Laughs)

MA: Do you have a rock tour manager?

Nixon: He came in actually halfway through this tour on 24 hours notice when we lost our old tour manager. She didn't work out. We discovered too many girls in one van with no balancing energy level just kind of makes everyone psychotic. It was nine girls in a fifteen passenger van. It didn't go real well. (Laughs) When we had the guy tour managing and we need things, the guy goes, "OK I'll walk through the rain to the bus and get you something." We had a girl tour managing, she goes, "Walk through the rain yourself! What the hell would I do that for?"

MA: Was she experienced?

Nixon: Somewhat. Not as much as the guy we have now, who's very calm under emergency situations, which is always nice because we've certainly produced some emergency situations. It's been pretty good.

MA: You've been to Australia, how were the Australian shows different from the American shows?

Nixon: They were actually pretty similar. They were real excited. Just really good crowds! Outrageous… I think they were just really happy that we came that far. We did eight or nine different cities in Australia, you know, we didn't just hit Sidney and Melbourne, we went to Brisbane and some of the other smaller cities.

MA: Did you do Newcastle?

Nixon: We did do Newcastle! We did Melbourne, Brisbane, Perth, Sidney. I can't even remember anymore! I'd have to go read the shirt to know. I don't even know what city I'm in most of the time!

MA: Well, at least you were there!

Nixon: Exactly! I didn't see any kangaroos, though. I was very sad.

MA: I put my sunglasses on a kangaroo that was sleeping under a tree and took some photographs. I saw the Gaudi Cathedral in, where the hell is that? Spain, Madrid, Barcelona… anyway, but I ran up one of the towers, ran back down, and was late to be on stage.

Nixon: Yeah, sometimes like, "You have four hours to play!" I was in Vancouver, two years ago, we had like half a day off. I ran out of the hotel first thing in the morning and got on one of those whale boats and went out and ended up in the water with 60 orcas in an inflatable boat. Yeah! That was really exciting when we got back to the shore. "Where have you been all day?" "Uh… uh… big things in the water…"

MA: What business are you running? Are you running the Nixon business and it's part of the SuicideGirls?

Nixon: Not really, I mean I'm a model for the site and I dance with the site. We're basically out to promote the site itself. The site functions in a lot of different ways, it's come to be a way for people who are looking for those types of girls to find them. Like in the last year, I did an episode of CSI: New York and I'm in Jerry Casten's new horror movie that's coming out next year. The more visible you are on the site, the more likely you are to get into extra projects. And I've met really cool people that show up at the shows and just tons of people that pop out of nowhere in the crowd! It's been really fun for that kind of thing, too, just meeting people. Plus, you know the money's good and it's a good excuse to be on the road. I like being on the road.

MA: What would you change about the touring experience? What would make it better?

Nixon: I would love to have both the bus and hotel rooms. I think one of the biggest problems we've had this last tour. We've been doing these arenas, we're literally all shut in a bus all day, then we're all shut in a dressing room for the evening, and then we're all back on the bus and there's no way to get away from each other so I think that's been… "God, we just want to escape from each other for awhile!" Beyond that, I don't know. I'd like more time to see things, I like when the routing gives us time to stop at roadside attractions and just have something to break the monotony and make you feel like you're having some fun out there; I'm sure for you, too, it just starts to feel like, "All I do is work!" And drink. (Laughs)

MA: So you kind of stumbled into this?

Nixon: Yeah, yeah, I really did. Right place at the right time.

MA: Is that just luck or were you busy getting ready to be lucky?

Nixon: You know, I was doing a lot of different things. I was really active with the Portland burlesque scene. I had been making up my own scenery and sewing all my own costumes and doing a full, new, completely different show once a month. So I had definitely put in my time and I'm lucky enough that my regular job is relaxed enough that I can do things like vanish for five months occasionally. Go, "Um… Hi, I'm… leaving… for five months." And they're ok with that, really supportive. I work for The Bone Room in Berkeley. We sell dead things. It's kind of like Necromance here. We do like, bones, custom skeleton preparation for museums and universities, fossil preparation, insect

mounting, things like that. But, I've been there since I was 18, so they pretty much let me get away with murder.

MA: So, this doesn't support you.

Nixon: No, no. It supports me when I'm doing it, but there's months in between tours where I definitely have to pick up a job.

MA: I come across people all the time who think it's easy and they're entitled.

Nixon: It's definitely something I can't imagine doing if you really didn't want to do it. It's leaving all your friends for months and months at a time, it's making personal relationships humanly impossible! I haven't seen my dog in months! I can't imagine people with, you know, families, husbands, wives, children, that kind of thing, even trying to survive this life.

MA: It's tough.

Nixon: But at the same time, if it's what you love to do, then it's certainly worth it. You tend to lose complete track of time, which I think is very hard for people back home to understand when they're like, "You haven't called in a month!" And you're like, "Really? Didn't notice! Sorry!"

MA: Has it been two days or a year?

Nixon: I have no idea!

MA: You get into that tunnel and time is different.

Nixon: Yeah, you know, I have no idea when normal waking and sleeping times happen at all. It's like, I sleep when I'm tired or there's nothing happening. I eat when catering shows up. That's been a plus to being on a real tour, the fact that someone feeds us!

2006
Martin Atkins Private Collection

C·H·A·P·T·E·R···· 41

PERSONALITY, EGO & CHARISMA

"A large ego is not charisma. Ego is not talent. Charisma is not talent – but it can override it."
    –Martin Atkins

PERSONALITIES AND EGO

To get in a van and tour across America, you have to believe somewhere that you could be massively successful. Just because you *believe* you can be, doesn't mean that you are. And even if you are, it doesn't mean you need to act like a prick to anyone. If you find yourself having to deal with some ridiculously-inflamed ego, in the case of a very small band, maybe it's just insecurity. In the case of Prince, well, he's Prince.

You're going to find all kinds of personalities on the road. Helpful, not helpful, bitter, nasty, unbelievably negative, unbelievably supportive, unbelievably kind, unbelievably trusting, and just plain unbelievable, cynical, bored, indifferent, stalker, thief, naked, and raw (and not always in a good way). You need to find a way to get the best out of each and every one of them without having their negatives contaminate your positive vision or dilute your purpose.

Mark O'Shea mentioned, "Kill everybody with kindness." I agree with fifty percent of that statement—the first half of it. That's how you might be feeling. You need to rise above this and put your music and your band first. Personalities within a band and within a tour can be interesting. On some levels, you strive for harmony, or if not harmony, space and distance. As it gets closer to show time, as John Lydon said, "Anger is an energy." If you're tour managing, understand that sometimes great performances need a spark. It might not mean that a band is breaking up; they might just be recharging their batteries.

CHARISMA

Search the web for "charisma" and you'll get everything from a wedding band in Boston to a stripper in New Orleans.

> "....you strive for harmony or if not harmony, space and distance."

John Lydon and Martin Atkins

Martin Atkins Private Collection.

It cannot be quantified and exercised like a muscle. I have seen instructions along side "Vocal Tips" for performers. Like charisma is a poodle you can put on a leash and take out for a walk. I think it's pretty simple—you either have it—or you don't. That's it.

There is a difference between stage presence and charisma. Stage presence trains you to make big gestures that can be seen at the back of the room, wave your arms around, and make a W and then an M shape with your head (thanks Dad for that) so that everyone in the room thinks you are addressing them individually. When someone has charisma, the audience wants to watch that person, there is a magical bond. Don't confuse the two. You can learn stage presence; you can't learn charisma— it is a rare jewel. As I got pulled further and further into a world of logistics, planning, business and the label, I found myself hoping for artists who were more organized, punctual, or more rational. I'm not saying pander to someone in a band, but pick your battles and have respect for something that can't be taught and just as importantly would be very difficult to replace. But, it's a left brain-right brain thing... and in the end, you can deal with a charismatic performers lack of organization or tardiness... there's not much you can do with a punctual organized singer that has negative charisma... I don't think it was ever said of Kurt Cobain that he was late or his shirt was wrinkled.

> **"You can learn stage presence; you can't learn charisma."**

That's the way it goes, sweetie... deal with it and be just happy anyone in the band has that light within and hope they shine it on you from time to time.

I saw John Lydon first hand for five or six years, at times PiL was just me and him. There was a fascination that people had with him. It wasn't just because he was Johnny Rotten of the Sex Pistols, it was a combination of elements. He could be what is called "charming and magnetic" in a hotel lobby or in front of 10,000 people... that's charisma. Sometimes that magnetism could turn around and polarize negatively...

> **"Caring about someone's emotional and mental state offstage can lead to greater accomplishments on stage."**

THE CODE OF THE ROAD

Take a band on the road for four days. And all of the dynamics and drama will be plain to see. If you're working with a band that you're not sure about, it's a good experiment before you go off on an 8-week long tour with them.

Some people can really snap, crackle, and POP under the harsh personality microscope of constant touring stress. This can manifest itself in many ways, from total stupidity; aggression directed at self, object, or others; to massive consumption of anything, and life-threatening behavior. I've seen it create diligent housekeepers out of amazing guitarists. Sometimes, it comes out in an embarrassing scene about nothing—absolutely nothing—it's just the last straw. It can be frightening and harmful to all concerned within hearing or splintered-glass range. I like to think of The Code of the Road applying to these moments, too, whether raging, tearful, or both. The idea that they occur under a blanket of camaraderie is comforting. It fuels the ability to open up on-stage and take a performance to another level. You need trust between everyone on the road to be able to do that.

TUFF LOVE

All of these things, all of these moments in people's lives can take on a physical energy and start to bounce tangibly around a vehicle or dressing room. Caring about someone's emotional and mental state offstage can lead to greater accomplishments on stage. The converse is also true. There are people out there who delight in needling and sometimes on tour the boundaries can get blurred. A collective concern is ideal. Watch each others backs… another reason to go on the road. If you want to unite your country said Shakespeare, "Take them to war!"

> "And, I'd suspect a few disgruntled band members are pissed off at their lead singer because, despite habits and lack of respect for their hard-won musical prowess, the fans still want the druggie fuck-up front man."
> – Martin Atkins

"Some people can really snap, crackle, and POP under the harsh personality microscope of constant touring stress. This can manifest itself in many ways, from total stupidity, aggression directed at self, object, or others, to massive consumption of anything and life-threatening behavior. "

TIPS FOR SELECTING NEW BAND MEMBERS

(Originally appeared in Martins' SuicideGirls.com column)

It is with great pride and my hand on my heart that I can honestly say, if you are auditioning singers for your band and you plan on going on the road and 'making it', here is my advice:

As the singer enters the room, listen for a while to the anecdotes of days gone by or days yet to come. Marvel as he or she weaves a tapestry of brilliant threads, joining words that were never before joined into songs that were never before sung. Look at the words as they appear to sparkle and dance in front of your eyes. Then punch the singer in the throat. I don't mean really hard, not as hard, say, as you might want to knee them in the nuts, but hard enough.

Why? (At least some of you are asking.)

Well, I've been looking at simple things you can do to better your chances of gaining popularity in this huge country without breaking, snapping, and then setting fire to the bank account and your partner's credit score. One of these things is to perform seven days a week instead of four or five. It's the easiest way to make more of the difficult real equations work. If you are a band gigging to 100 to 150 people on an OK night, then, this allows for some extra t-shirt sales and a few more CDs, etc. over the course of 40 weeks of gigging. This simple idea will put an extra $75,000 in your pocket—$75,000, OK?!! So, allowing for the fact that, in any larger city, there are hundreds of bands and hundreds of singers and, assuming that six out of the ten applicants are pretty good and not too insane, that's my advice. It's harsh, but fun as all hell. You have to make sure that they can deal with the throat stress that touring these days is going to rain down on them.

No sooner had I written this than I started to look at some e-mails from indie record stores across the country. Many of them have started to advertise early intimate/acoustic performances from bands performing at the larger venues. So, hell, that means another gig for your dulcet-toned singer. See what I mean? This started off to be a fun afternoon assaulting singers and now it has turned into some really good advice. You need someone fronting your band that can sing seven shows a week, hit a few acoustic afternoon shows, and do ten interviews a day without losing their voice – or at least losing it but getting it back by early morning...

Wasn't this part of the problem that really big band Creed had with their singer? By the time they were playing stadium shows, they realized the singer couldn't hack it. He was, err, hacking too much so they just gave him horse tranquilizer injections or something in his throat! All kinds of toxicity along with the idea that, when pain is diminished, then you are robbed of the bodies early warning system. Like when you have a broken leg, the body hints at you not to walk. Well, these drugs will make you want to snowboard on your twisted broken stumps—just like that for the throat: "Mama Mia! Mama Mia! Mama Mia let me go!" Anyway, here are some more ideas on the same theme:

Think before you start a band with nine members. It's going to sound amazing! Until you have to feed everyone. Any club owner is going to run screaming from giving you a shot at a first gig. You can try saying you only want pizza and beer—but, how many fucking pizzas is that? More than the DJ gets. Also, your chances of crashing at someone's apartment are severely limited.

> "It's the easiest way to make more of the difficult real equations work."

Anyone cool enough to let you stay is unlikely to have the room to accommodate nine of yas. (Unless it's on the king size water bed with the black latex sheets). Anyone with the room is unlikely to want to watch in horror as you trash one of their three bathrooms with your hair dye and the percussionist just threw up in the Jacuzzi and what was that again? Don't let the cat out and carefully close the microwave? Oops?

Multi-tasking is good. Think of yourself in the beginning of an episode of Mission Impossible. Think about the skills that might be needed on the road ahead: vehicle mechanic, computer nut, a bit of muscle here and there, a bit of sex appeal, a golden tongue for the interviews... Look at your choices as underlining the good points and balancing out your weak points (you probably do have a few). If you are totally shit at lyrics, then look for someone who has a rhyming dictionary. Get some balance so that you can be totally unbalanced in a deliberate way. Understand that chemistry is unfathomable and impossible to stage, direct, or plan for. There isn't a recipe for this stuff. So, let me sum all of this up into an easy to read checklist for greatness:

- **Choose the drummer** that shows up—if one does. Then, if you are struggling between two, choose the one with the smallest kit who doesn't want to change drum heads every day (ask them!) or the one that hears you when you ask if they can play a little quieter. Or choose the one with the ultra hot girlfriend.

- **Choose the bass player** with the van and the rehearsal space he built with the proceeds from the car accident settlement—unless he is totally shit and can't play bass. Then think about going all Human League and having him stand behind a keyboard with dark glasses and use a sequencer (and his van).

- **Choose the guitarist** that has several cup holders already built into his equipment with ashtrays and several cigarette lighters Velcro-ed to his amp along with a blender. This is the mark of a true professional. You are in the presence of greatness.

- **Choose wisely, surprisingly, and be understanding of the consequences** – one of them being that if you follow all of the rules of business and just choose two other people to be in your band based upon their assets instead of choosing the five nut jobs you really want to be in a band with, then you might be fucked before you start. But you'll have a hell of a time not getting there.

Man, is your head swimming now? Makes you want to hit a singer in the throat, doesn't it?

CREATIVELY MULTI-TASK

If you're a guitar tech in a sea of guitar techs, you can increase your chances of being hired by researching the kind of bands for which you want to work. A bunch of metal bands go to South America. So learn another language so you can be more useful to the crew. If you want to be Keith Richards' guitar tech, learn how to change an adult diaper. You could be a low calorie chef. You could do books as well as something else. Deal with the internet stuff and upload fans' pictures and information each night.

CHAPTER 42

KARMA: WHAT GOES UP...

Karma isn't some Eastern, hippie concept that only exists in a cloud of incense and lava lamps. It is as concrete as... a piece of concrete.

Karma can be less-exotically described as "What goes around comes around." Or, for every action, there's an equal and opposite reaction; except, the equal and opposite reaction is guaranteed by Murphy's Law to happen at a time that's ten times more damaging. Or, in its music business form, be careful who you tread on the way up, for they will surely delight in kicking you in the nuts and dancing on your head on the way down.

There are many times described throughout this book where the endless possibilities for karma are fully present.

A few instances in my career

Person:	Becomes:
Small Club Owner	Moves to a larger club, does well and becomes the lynchpin of the whole East Coast concert scene.
Fan who sent Demo	David Draiman, lead singer of *Disturbed*.
Crew Person you fired	General Manager of Grand Royal Records for the *Beastie Boys*.
Crappy Opening Band in New Jersey Club	R.E.M.
Assistant to the Promoter who you screamed at and punched the wall – drunk	Invents *Warped Tour*.
2 am Radio Guy at a College Station	The Number One Radio Personality at One of the Top Five Stations on the East Coast.
Worker at a Record Store	Owner of the Chain of Record Stores, a Record Label, or a Major Venue.
Street Team	Working for *Clear Channel*.
Guy Who Hands You a Demo at a Barbeque	Gains Critical Acclaim as *Nine Inch Nails*.

In my defense, I was pretty young (18) and pretty drunk (most of the time) and on prescription speed when most of this got crazy for me. I managed to piss upon and napalm some great relationships. Had I napalmed and then pissed upon, I would have been seen as a hero. I consider myself lucky to have a large degree of understanding and, hopefully, forgiveness from anyone on the receiving end. Thanks!

C·H·A·P·T·E·R····43

MURPHY'S LAW

- **If something can go wrong, it will, twice.**

- **If anything absolutely cannot go wrong, it will.**

- **Left to themselves, things will go from bad to worse.**

- **Equipment will be damaged, lost, or stolen in direct proportion to its value** and the size and importance of the show.

- **The chance of toast landing buttered-side down** is directly proportional to the cost of the carpet.

- **The first show to cancel will be the highest paying one.**

- **The only day off will be in a city during a massive convention** and rooms will be $350.

- **The bus will breakdown five hours away from the biggest show of your lives**, or the plane will run out of gas and crash. You survive but then you will be shot.

- **The best food you have ever had on the road will be served too late for you to eat.**

- **The worst food will be made available with plenty of time for you to eat and then throw up.**

- **There will be one horrible night when everything will go wrong:** snow, bad sound, wrong equipment, throat infection, tuning problems, weak batteries in effects, drummer with the runs, guitarist on bad drugs, intermittent microphones, malfunctioning smoke machine, strobe, projector, underwear, and you are on stage at the wrong time in front of the largest audience you have ever played to. This is the night that the record label, your family, the journalists, the radio promotions people and the person of your dreams will show up.

- **The night when everything goes amazingly well will be the night that no one is there.**

...AND HOW TO DEFEAT IT

WELL, FIRST UNDERSTAND THAT YOU CAN'T, THEN:

- **Have a spare everything.**

- **Instead of sleeping in the city before the long drive to the big show, leave that night.** You might need the extra hours. The information might be wrong. One of the other bands might not show up. I'm not contradicting the earlier advice to not show up four hours early. You can show up, but discreetly hang in the parking lot or something. Let the tour manager know you are there and take guidance.

- **Have a spare tire and always use a twin-axle trailer.** This means that when one of the tires does blow (not if!), you still have three wheels on your wagon – at least until you hit the tree/cat/central divide/toll booth/moose.

- **Krazy Glue for fingers!** It was invented as a surgical tool to replace staples and stitches, use it to repair wounds!

- **Double check everything.**

- **Leave plenty of time!**

- **Think!**

·PLAN AHEAD!

CHAPTER 44

TOURING AS A FAMILY MAN

"Diary Entry Beijing China Oct 2006: phew... I'm fucking exhausted! These days, I really hate being away from Trina and the boys. It kills me when little Sidney turns around when I walk in the door and says hi daddy."
— Martin Atkins

Touring as a family man is tough on everyone in the family. Jack Carson (one of Jäger's tour managers) told me about his pre-tour ritual of blasting "We Are the Road Crew" by Motorhead and how any time his dog hears that song he hangs his head understanding the solitude and loneliness that's coming. It might not be as obvious with your family, but the same emotions are in play. Throw into that soup the prospect of groupies, fun, financial hardship, stress, and risk, and it's a recipe that can decimate a relationship.

Financially, putting a tour together can be big stuff. You're balancing cost vs. time, art vs. business, and head vs. heart. While all of those equations can make sense within the tour office, it's really tough to balance that at the kitchen table where a two-for-one sale on gourmet soup is a talking point. It's tough to step between the two worlds.

During our last package tour, I signed over power of attorney to my wife so that, if necessary, she could sell our building halfway through the tour. The night before we left, I held our newborn on my chest wondering where I would be the next time I could do that. I certainly had the St. Crispin's Day Speech in my head. It felt like we were going off to battle. I used the energy to do the only thing I could under the circumstances which was to make every single show and every single moment count for something.

When you spend a lot of time on the road, family events (good and bad) will start to coincide with tour events, from breaking up with a girlfriend to a death in the family, from missing a birthday to missing a period. It's all just more important when other people's well being and security are tied directly to yours.

> "Financially putting a tour together can be big stuff. You're balancing cost vs. time, art vs. business, and head vs. heart."

KIDS ON THE ROAD

It was great to have my, then, two kids come out on the road.

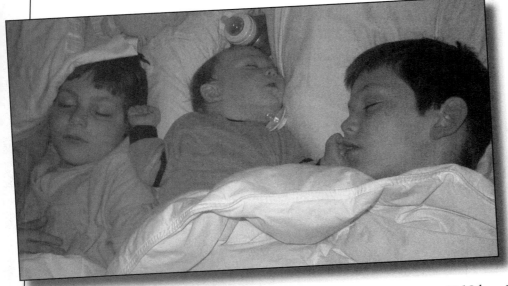

They believed that the tour bus was a pirate ship (because that's what I told them). But, you've gotta be careful. At a show in St. Louis, Harrison sat on my drum kit and pounded away. I didn't realize that my drum riser was at the back of the stage. So there was, in effect, a four foot drop behind the riser! He took a step back and grabbed for anything to keep his balance and pulled a brass snare drum onto his face as he hit the floor below giving him a fairly deep cut to the cheek. Later that same day, we went on stage behind the white screens and 16 or 18 band members, street teamers, and friends had flashlights to wave around behind Chris Connelly doing a 15 minute acoustic set. I bought Ian and Harrison their own special flashlights with plastic screens to project bugs and dinosaurs and footprints for them to enjoy themselves. It was delightful. I can still see the gleeful expressions on their faces. Then, Ian thought the smoke machine looked really interesting—it was a skull! With smoke spewing from it's mouth! I didn't know (and neither did he) that inside the skull's mouth, was a red-hot heating element which burnt his fingers quite badly and really freaked him out!

I forgot to mention that after sound check, Curse Mackey and some members of *Pigface* had helpfully rearranged Ian's hair to be a spiky, stand-on-end, look-like-you're-hanging-upside-down affair, which also left room for an upside down cross on his forehead. The burnt fingers were the last straw. He decided he'd had enough and found a bathroom backstage to wash off the cross and rearrange his hair. Except that he managed to get some of the industrial strength soap from the hand dispenser into his eyes and spent several dangerous minutes stumbling around backstage in darkness with his eyes closed.

So, it's fucking awesome to have your kids out on the road. But you have to be careful and realize that there are many dangers everywhere at a venue—push-to-open doors that don't let you back in, steps and stairs and drops not marked with tape, distractions, people wandering around not looking for things three feet high, not to mention lunatics.

> "...it's fucking awesome to have your kids out on the road. But you have to be careful and realize that there are many dangers everywhere at a venue..."

EXIT PLANET BUS

Be aware that you're body clock changes after a few days on the road. If you've been going on stage at around 11 or 12 each night, you'll get an adrenaline rush at that same time for a while after the end of the tour. If you're a family guy, it's not the last day of tour for you but the first day of your big return to your family. Plan for this in the same way that you would plan for the start of the tour. (Thanks to Doug Firley for this paragraph title).

I heard that when Bono returns from a tour—they check him into a hotel close to home for a few days—so he can acclimatize to family life—like a deep sea diver gradually rising to the surface…

TOURING AS A FAMILY MAN:
JASON NOVAK, ACUMEN NATION, DJ? ACUCRACK

JASON NOVAK

DJ?ACUCRACK
CRACKNATION RECORDS

www.cracknation.com

Touring as a family man sucks. And most guys on the road just don't get it, but if you are close to your kids like I am, every day is filled with heartache. There is a lot of guilt associated with it, wife at home handling everything, because whether or not you are working and making money on tour, there's still booze every night, people digging your shit, and weed! And most musos, if they are married with kids, will have cool wives who wish they could be partying too, so you have to be understanding. Also, we all know what a weird bond you create on the road, and what a really weird sense of humor you adopt, so coming off a tour and right back into daddy-mode is a bitch (anyone who has toured with Brits knows how damn hard it is to stop saying 'cunt' back in the real world, let alone with kids!).

Something that helps, something I have invested in, is cool Apple technology like a laptop and a couple of i-sights. Most venues have Wi-Fi, so during the afternoon, when I can, I set up the camera and let the kids see what's going on… it de-mystifies everything and really makes them a lot cooler with you being gone, and you get to see their faces, what they are wearing, and it is so much better on the soul for all of you, I highly recommend it.

In the end, if you are a good parent, it becomes harder to leave, and sooner or later you might have to wrestle with, for the first time in your life, something that has come along that is more important than playing music. It's also impossible to be a responsible parent and leave to tour if your band is making $100 a night and sleeping on people's couches, it can definitely limit your ability to tour with a small band. I have been fortunate enough to find situations where I can continue to make money on the road, be very careful how we operate financially, and have the support of a wonderful wife who knows, as hard as it is, how important it is for me to do this as long as I can, because the opposite would probably be a much fatter alcoholic with bitterness for breakfast every morning! However, a lot of band guys who actually can put food on the table in exchange for touring have families whose lives have become accustomed to it. It becomes part of their schedule, and actually becomes cool. Your kids appreciate what they have, the uprooting for a month or six weeks actually strengthens bonds and shows your family a different side to the day-to-day existence everyone else has (a.k.a.: the 'normies') and it builds character throughout your family.

"I never liked the end of a tour because it'll never happen again. You're either gonna have different songs, different venues, different drivers, different people in the band, it's never gonna be the same again. And when you have something that's really going good, I just wish it would never stop." **– Jolly Roger**

"Every single thing becomes more important to more people, except that if you are in a relationship or have a family, that's an area that can suffer. You need to balance the potential of this part of you with the need to show your children by example that you are prepared to work hard and to pursue a goal, with the possibility of emotional and financial hardship for them.

You've gotta learn 'em. You don't get given nothing."

-Martin Atkins

I think you forgot This.... we Miss you! ♡ Kat

CHAPTER 45

WHAT TO DO WHEN YOUR GEAR GETS STOLEN

When something gets lost or stolen it is one of the most horrible things that can happen on the road.

Sometimes it's just a CD player snatched from your bag at the airport but there's a good chance that anything you're carrying on the road is going to be very important to you, either personally or because of its role within your performance. It's not just a laptop, it's a laptop with the new tunes you're trying to edit, pictures of your girlfriend, the email addresses of all of the people who keep you sane while you're on the road—everything. The saved shortcuts that make life easy or bearable.

I don't know what the figures are for guitars or electronics but I read that there are over 1,500 laptops stolen every day which means if you're only touring for three days you're going to need 4,500 laptops. Every 25 seconds there is a motor vehicle theft.

It's not just an instrument, it might be an essential, integral part of the sound that defines you. The equipment in my studio is more closely related to a petting zoo than a rack of electronics. The combination of pieces relaxes me, joins together in certain different ways, that over the last 20 years has become part of my studio voice. So, loss or theft of any of this can be debilitating, especially in the middle of a tour. It's the worst kind of violation because of the above compounded by the ease of the target that any traveler presents.

Here are a couple of tips that might help:

1. If it's a laptop, make sure it's backed up in a different place.

2. If it's an essential part of a performance, have a back up or record and sample some of the audio flavorings of any instruments impossible to replace (financially or physically). Or hire more security. Or chain it to your wrist unless it's a piano and you're performing on a cruise ship.

3. Get insurance. This can be as an add on to your renter's, homeowner's policy or an add on to your vehicle policy or a specific equipment policy. In the case of more than a few thousand dollars, you might need to submit a list with serial numbers to the insurance company with specific values as an add on to one of those policies. It's never been easier to check out competing policies online. Make sure you're careful about the specific vehicle and who is insured for what. Your equipment might be insured, your lead guitarist's (who is traveling in the same vehicle) might not be.

4. Keep serial numbers, photographs, receipts, and any documentary evidence in a safe place away from the touring environment where it can be accessed by a phone call to a

management company, a friend, or relative. In the event of loss or theft the insurance company will approach you with the assumption that none of this equipment ever existed. You are a musician and therefore out of your mind on drugs or lying. They are not singling you out. That's how they treat everyone.

5. As soon as you find out that something has been stolen let everyone at the venue know. Chances are, they'll know some people to call or someone might have seen something. Jump onto Craig's list and post descriptions and serial numbers. Do the same on your website. File a police report which is essential to make any kind of insurance claim. If you don't file a police report, it never happened. Also try sites like *juststolen.net*. It's a data listing service that's more convenient for you than the police if they do find your laptop, camera, guitar, etc. Give and get as many phone numbers and email addresses as you can from anyone who wants to help. Get phone numbers for all the pawn shops and music stores in town and if it's not possible for you to stay until the stores open the next day start calling at 9 a.m. and be prepared to email or fax a list of the stolen items. One way to gain a few hours might be for one member of the touring party to stay behind. The band will probably need to be at the next venue between 4 p.m. and 6 p.m. to load in and sound check. The bass player or merchandiser might not need to be at the venue until half an hour before the band hits the stage so you might be able to arrange a ride with a fan or street teamer, or even a short, cheap flight. But it is those first few hours that could really make a difference.

6. Stupid, easy stuff. When you arrive at a venue and you get that feeling in your gut in the neighborhood surrounding the venue, you're getting it for a reason. Pay attention to yourself and pay more attention to everything once things get dark. Tell everyone in the band and make sure everything is locked. Talk to the promoter to see if your fears are justified, he might have a safe place where you could lock some things if you don't think they're going to be safe in your vehicle or in the dressing room. Worst case scenario—take it on stage with you. Make sure everyone has keys to everything. Get the good pad lock, not the one that saves you $4.99.

TOUR:SMART TIP
for more information go to:
www.tstouring.com

MARKETING IV – PACKAGE TOURS: A RELIGIOUS EXPERIENCE

10TH ANNIVERSARY TOUR
Pigface

w/ Meg Lee Chin, Chris Connelly & Many More!!!

with disciples:
GravityKills
gODHEAD

Come Join Us - Confess Your Sins

for more information: www.undergroundinc.com

a special limited edition print by Martin Atkins   777/1000   October 2001

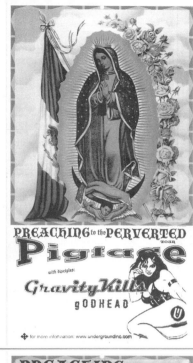

PREACHING to the PERVERTED tour
Pigface
with disciples:
GravityKills
gODHEAD

for more information: www.undergroundinc.com

PREACHING to the PERVERTED tour
10th ANNIVERSARY TOUR
Pigface
with disciples:
GravityKills
gODHEAD

Come Join Us - Confess Your Sins
for more information: www.undergroundinc.com

PREACHING to the PERVERTED TOUR
10th ANNIVERSARY TOUR
Pigface
w/ Meg Lee Chin, Chris Connelly & Many More!!!
with disciples:
GravityKills
gODHEAD

Come Join Us - Confess Your Sins
for more information: www.undergroundinc.com

ECONOMIES OF SCALE WORK

These ideas work for bands, comedians, golfers (you could have the same guy wash everyone's balls?) If you're running your band like a business, co-promoting your own shows, and creating your own events, this could be a step that you want to take. A package tour is a group of artists within a genre that join together to create an event with more momentum, greater possibility of success, and—of equal importance—less chance of failure than if each of the bands toured on their own. A creative theme or name for the tour can give the event more recognition.

There is strength in numbers. One band's weak market might be another's strong one. Additional elements added to the theme can both expand on the possibilities for success and mitigate risk. The success of these strategies is obvious with tours like Ozzfest, Warped Tour, and The Jäger Tour, where momentum built in previous years flows forward into the next and builds trust with a larger and larger fan base. On a much smaller scale, all of the ideas still work and, with clubs increasing the number of bands performing each night to try and ensure larger attendance, if you decide to avoid the prickly set-up problems of a package tour, you'll probably find yourself dealing with two to five different opening bands each night anyway.

> **"There is strength in numbers."**

So, grab the thistle!** It's going to happen one way or another; you might as well deal with it ahead of time in a way that can benefit you.

> ** *Next time you grab a thistle, do it boldly: All problems become smaller if you don't dodge them, but confront them. Touch a thistle timidly, and it pricks you; grasp it boldly, and its spines crumble.* **– Richard Denny http://www.denny.co.uk/:**

Build some alliances and understandings with other bands within your genre, you can create a strong package.

In terms of a touring situation, it is easier for a promoter to deal with a package (as long as it is organized) than it is for them to book a main band and then organize three locals around it. To an extent, you are selling an easier night for the soundmen, the crew, the catering, everyone. You are gathering momentum as the tour progresses and creating a slam dunk evening for them—and for yourself in the future.

STREAMLINING EQUIPMENT AND PRODUCTION ISSUES

You need to be a diplomat to deal with difficult issues. Everyone wants their own equipment, it's draining to wade through everyone's insecurities and shred some of their comfort blankets, but it's less work, less stress, and less damaging than dealing with a mediocre tour. You're better off dealing with problems, anxiety, and equipment logistics on the front-end than you are trying to deal with poor turn outs, reductions in fees, and eventually cancelled shows on the back-end.

> **"You're better off dealing with problems, anxiety, and equipment logistics on the front-end than you are trying to deal with poor turn outs, reductions in fees, and eventually cancelled shows on the back-end."**

> *On the United 2 tour, we had four bass players. There was no way we wanted to deal with carrying four bass rigs. So, we got everyone together and addressed the time and the craziness involved in loading them in. The bass players agreed to just take out two rigs. After a couple of shows, we started to leave one of the bass cabinets in the back of the equipment trailer. We knew it was there if we ever needed it, and we had two amps on stage. This was a great solution for everyone. We had the bands change over their stage positions so that the bass rig would stay on the same side of the stage all night. This was not always possible, but a great idea when we could swing it.*

TOUR:SMART TIP
for more information go to:
www.tstouring.com

Imagine the saved time, and stress relief. Every time something is moved on stage, something else is going to be unplugged, smashed, or plugged into the wrong channel. By working on these strategies before hand, you are reducing the number of emergencies you are going to have to deal with day by day . When you get to The Warehouse in Lacrosse, WI, you don't have to lug four bass cabinets up all of those stairs! Multiply this by all of the other changes you can make and it will add up to a safer, less stressful, more professional environment.

All of these principles apply to any multi artist situation. Time and motion is the potion! Preparation makes the difference. One day of work before a tour is the equivalent of five road days. Maybe more. Once the tour starts, you are in it neck deep. Start your planning earlier...

"Preparation is key. And like I tell my junkie friends... lose the H"
   - Martin Atkins

...and earlier. The bass player situation in the scenario above took several days to coordinate. People needed time to get used to the new and difficult ideas. You do not want to have very uncomfortable musicians... (slightly uncomfortable is OK). Keep people on their toes.

With a package tour, you can deal with all of these areas at the same time:

- **Working through difficult creative and business elements** with another band is an area that some agents and managers will be reluctant to get into. It's common for managers to simply ask for 200% of what they know their band to be worth to make sure that after harsh negotiations, they are still getting 125%. In practice, when faced with this approach, I don't have the energy to talk the manager off the ledge, and just move on. Try and talk directly band to band to create a scenario that can work logistically and artistically to everyone's benefit.

- **Maximize the poster power of a tour,** minimize the expenses, and build on each other's strengths. Split the cost of those posters and double the quantity.

- **Share a tour manager.** It's not twice as much work for a tour manager to deal with two bands.

- **Share transportation.**

> "One day of work before a tour is the equivalent of five road days — maybe more."

- **Share equipment.**

- **Share a soundman.** It's not twice as much work for one soundman to mix two bands. Sometimes, it can be less. Especially if there is a likelihood of two competing soundmen screwing with each other's settings and trying to outdo each other.

- **Share on stage crew.** This can be a much more sensitive area, but worth dealing with.

- **Share one merch person** or, if it's a higher profile tour, use each other's merch people to create a two to three person team that can more effectively deal with the ebbs and flows of the evening.

PACKAGE TOURS CHRON~OLOG~ICALLY FROM 1996:

666 TOUR

On our first package tour, we had a great logo, great t-shirts, and all the tools you'd want to promote a tour. We had awesome 8 x 10 images; we found a 666 cold remedy! There was a commercially released CD 66 minutes and 6 seconds long retailing for a price of $6.66. There were occasional appearances from myself doing my first set of spoken word gigs, a couple of shows from

Mark Spybey, Martin Atkins, Curse Mackey

Psychic TV, and even, fantastically, a fake liquor sponsorship from a champagne manufacturer 'Be-elze-bubbly'. However, all of this creativity wasn't enough to make up for the fact that none of the core bands on the tour had much drawing power. The day the posters arrived, Lab Report decided they didn't want to do the tour so we stayed up all night re-stickering posters.

ECSTASY UNDER DURESS

The following year, we paired Sheep on Drugs with industrial pioneers Test Department, who hadn't toured the U.S. in ten years. Great respect for both bands colored the arrangements we made for them. This, coupled with their reluctance to talk to journalists, didn't help. I guaranteed the bands wages and provided personnel, transportation, and hotels. With that kind of investment, I should have been on the tour to monitor progress. It generated quite a loss, partially offset by a double live album *Drug Test #1* recorded two sold-out Chicago shows. This acted as a safety net! Sometimes you have to dig deeper to break through to the other side... sometimes you are just digging deeper.

> **"Sometimes you have to dig deeper to break through to the other side... sometimes you are just digging deeper."**

LOWEST OF THE LOW

This was the tour that really started things off for us. A level above Route 666, we had video projections, our first real street team crew, and low-end reinforcement of at least 5,000 watts. Unfortunately after the posters had been printed, one of the acts from the U.K. decided they weren't coming. I spent the first 25 shows on the tour apologizing. It was tough. After all, we were all there, Mufti (F M Einheit) was there with torn ligaments, Curse was there with cracked ribs, I was there with kids at home, etc. In the end, when the artist eventually showed up for the last ten days of the tour, no one really cared. It was, I hope, a pretty good lesson for anyone around. With so many enemies to defeat you on the road, it's sad to see when the worst is yourself.

> "With so many enemies to defeat you on the road it's sad to see when the worst is yourself."

During rehearsals, we were about to hire a person whose only job would have been, running around, finding, and reminding everyone: "Fifteen minutes to show time!" With so many bands, I thought this would be essential for a smooth running event.

I realized that the video projections running in between each band were always the same length. So, we told everyone, "When you see the Ritalin album spinning towards you, or when F M Einheit blows up the hamburger restaurant, you have six minutes to your show time and pay attention because that's it baby!" And, fuck me, it worked! Halfway through the tour, one of the members of Not Breathing contracted spinal meningitis. You can read Mark Spybey's tour diary from that 1997 tour in *Stories from the Front Line* and my description of it in the *Health Tips* chapter.

Get an agreement from every band before you announce the package!!

MISTAKE TO AVOID

SOAP BOX BEAT BOX

Two prominent artists had important new releases but no band. We had to do something to promote their records. We threw them in a car and sent them out to hit two to four events a day: record stores at noon, cocktail parties at two in the morning, etc. The cost wasn't significantly less than if they'd toured with their bands, but the overall impact was.

PREACHING TO THE PERVERTED

This was a much higher level of visibility from the individual artists involved: Pigface, the gold-selling Gravity Kills (who had just signed a new deal with Sanctuary Records), and Godhead (who were signed to Marilyn Manson's label). It was not just a good lineup of bands, but a strong lineup of labels, too. I was excited to see what these other labels would bring to the promotional table. It turned out that it wasn't that much and we could have prepared a little better. Sanctuary decided to postpone the release of the Gravity Kills album and use the package tour as a setup for their release a few months later. It was a smart move—for them. Everyday they would put stickers and postcards all over the venue (flash back to Japan) and announce from the stage, "We'll be touring again soon!" The next surprise came from

> "Sometimes the solutions are staring you in the face; sometimes they're kicking you in the nuts."

Godhead's label. I was disappointed to find out that they didn't even have a street team in place for the tour. Lesson learned. You should check on all of these points before committing to a package tour, not just the bands, but the labels, too.

By this time, the workload of paying attention to all of the special areas of the tour was becoming overwhelming. 30 people, 3 buses, 5 bands and merchandisers. So, you look around and see who is really on it; then, delegate, and enable. For example, Kami from Pigface took care of the guest list and did a great job. Multi-tasking for a little extra money, the beginning of creating a tour managing team instead of one individual. Curse and I jointly TM'd the next one… its a great solution… if you're able to juggle the left brain, right brain switch. That's one of the reasons I'll head butt my cymbals. I'm switching my brain over. Sometimes the solutions are staring you in the face; sometimes they're kicking you in the nuts.

RED (NECK) WHITE (TRASH) BLUE (MOVIE)

I don't know how we did this, 18 of us hit all of the major markets in a two week period. Flying from Chicago to Seattle with over 20 oversized flight cases, each one of which was too large for the airline to take. Four bands: Project Dark from the U.K. (experimental turn table artists—instead of spinning vinyl they spin Scandinavian wheat crackers and sand paper— very interesting, thought provoking, but not really worth any ticket sales), Sow from France, Thee Majesty from New York City (which was supposed to be Psychic TV but it became a two-person art noise experiment and, although one tenth of the drawing power of P.T.V, of course they still wanted the same money), and Pigface.

> **MA:** To Jolly… I saw you give some skycap $500! I'm like, "What the fuck are you doing?!" And you're like, "Martin, this is, like, four or five thousand dollars in excess baggage and, most of it shouldn't even be allowed on the plane. Shut up!" And then I looked at these four skycaps wheel what looked like a semi's worth of flight cases past the astounded gate check people!
>
> **Jolly Roger:** You just gotta figure out how to do things and do 'em. That's all… there is no obstacle that's too big.

"…there is no obstacle that's too big."

Date	City	Venue
16-Dec-98	Eugene, OR	WOW Hall
17-Dec-98	Seattle, WA	The Fenix
18-Dec-98	Portland, OR	Roseland Ballroom
19-Dec-98	San Francisco, CA	Maritime Hall
20-Dec-98	Tusla, OK	Cain's Ballroom
21-Dec-98	Chicago, IL	House of Blues
22-Dec-98	Detroit, MI	St. Andrews Hall
23-Dec-98	New York, NY	Bowery Ballroom

Except you have to be careful how hard you push. We were OK in this instance because we were slightly overloading a commercial jetliner… but there have been recent incidences of small charter planes being overloaded without a great outcome.

In Chicago, December 21st, we had three bus breakdowns in 24 hours when the inexperienced driver turned off the bus and the fuel lines froze. To cut a long story short (and so I don't slash my wrists), the replacement bus broke down 50 yards further down Michigan Avenue (but at least we're making progress, right?). When the third bus was too far away to get the touring party to the Detroit show, we managed to get everybody on a plane, one person without a passport or any ID! You can read Dirk's account in "Stories from the Front Line," and Dave Baker's piece too.

The flight meant we couldn't carry scenery, so I built the screens (8' x 4' x 6-panels), hinged them together, and stretched and stapled fabric everyday, with tools that we asked for on the rider.

UNITED 1

My Life with the Thrill Kill Kult, Pigface, Zeromancer, and Bile made up the United 1 Tour. We had large bands, an accumulation of the promotional material elements we'd been building on, mass produced promotional CDs, advance promotional t-shirts from Jägermeister, three buses, and Pigface and TKK's large and connected but different fan bases. Zeromancer from Norway with a new U.S. label and release really elevated the quality of the package and Bile, showed just how powerful a package tour can be when all the elements are firing.

UNITED 2 TOUR – WHEN GENRES COLLIDE, LOOK OUT...

Dope had sold 70,000+ copies of their new album. They were crazy on stage, and had contributed a lot to the newest Pigface album. We all got along very, very well. We would end up congregating on stage during the Diablo Syndrome set (drum and bass low-end hypnosis) and we'd add seven drummers behind the screens. It became a musical and social sand pit—we loved it! But, when genres collide, look out... the Dope audience was used to very low ticket prices (and sometimes free) so 15 bucks in some markets was high (like the agent). Some idiot in New Jersey was charging $35 on a Tuesday night—not for long! Can you spell renegotiation? The Pigface fans were OK with a $15 ticket (after $50+ from NIN, Ministry, and Skinny Puppy that year) but they were used to staking out the first row, which, during the Dope set was mayhem—elbows and boots in the face territory. Throw in a war between the two agents and there's the shit flavored icing on the shit flavored cake.

> In 1983/1984, some lunatic decided to put together a metal/punk evening with the Circle Jerks and the Scorpions somewhere in Los Angeles. Well, spandex and Mohawks don't mix. Fucking chaos and, at times, hilarious. The manager of the metal band telling a bunch of punks to "keep off the stage" and that if any more of this insane behavior continued (I think someone trod on a wah-wah pedal}, then the band would leave. Yeah! I have no idea what happened when the Circle Jerks hit the stage—people left, lines were drawn, lines already drawn were kicked in...

It was incredibly naive of me to think that the agents would be able to get along. Anything was acceptable if it made one agent win a point over the other. The first week of shows were undermined by Dope having performed free shows a few weeks before in many of the same markets.

I can't count the number of days where I woke up (if I had slept) knowing that firing a hardworking crew member, restructuring, a leap of faith, and some good luck would be the least of it. With the addition of my wife experiencing a miscarriage halfway through the tour, I'd lock myself in the rear lounge and try to cry as quietly as possible so as not to create further problems and disruption. In hindsight, these problems seem like they could have been easily avoided. I'm a reasonably smart guy, but I got pulled into a situation that I was lucky to have only cost me $60,000. I share this story with you hoping to trade the embarrassment I feel now to help a more fragile person avoid such a catastrophic series of mistakes.

UNITED 2 – Mistakes To Avoid. Autopsy Blow by Blow

Fueled by the success of *United 1* and eager, maybe too eager, to create a new and powerful brand, we scheduled *United 2* within six to eight months of *United 1*. Here were the mistakes:

1. Too soon.

2. No new album from either of the main bands.

3. Different genre of main two bands.

4. Different age demographic.

5. War between the two agents.

6. One agent falls spectacularly off the wagon.

7. Three tour buses.

8. Feeling that the tour is strong enough, we take a buy-on from an unknown, un-staffed label to take their unknown band from the UK on tour with us.

9. Our new inexperienced tour manager begins flaking two weeks before the tour.

10. Our new TM is not around much one week before the tour.

11. See 1-10.

12. Realizing that it can't possibly get any worse, we fire tour manager the day before the tour begins. Curse and I split the duties.

13. Praising divine intervention, I immediately hire the band from the UK's tour manager after seeing him coordinate three buses and 30 people hours before the tour is scheduled to leave.

14. Newly hired tour manager falls spectacularly off the wagon

15. See 1 - 14.

"I think it was Curse that said 'it's like a digital Vietnam, except no one is dying'...but, I lost an arm and a leg!"
—Martin Atkins

"IT'S LIKE DIGITAL VIETNAM EXCEPT NO ONE'S DYING"

CLIFF SIELOFF PRESENTS

WITH UNDERGROUND INC./INVISIBLE RECORDS

A PIGFACE TOUR DOCUMENTARY

FREE FOR ALL

MARTIN ATKINS · CURSE MACKEY · HANIN ELIAS · EN ESCH
KRYZTOFF · CHARLES LEVI · LEE FRASER · SKOT DIABLO
CORIN JARENKA · CHAD WILDER · WAYLON BAYARD · JEFF WINFREY
JIM GOODMAN · LACEY CONNER · CHRIS TELKES · ROTNY · BEN GRAVES

V. MERCY
APOCALYPSE THEATRE

Survival for cutting edge bands, solo artists, and DJ's (plus others like filmmakers and performance groups), depends on paying the bills (gas, food, lodging, etc.) and this is improving. Every day on the road can cost a group of four to five in a van no less than $200 and usually more, depending on the distance between gigs. A collective can make between $200 to $800 a night and, if they work together, provide attractive merchandise and utilize every means possible to promote. If multiple bands and performers can share gear—even band or crew members—and avoid the usual pitfalls of ego and large contractual riders, the collective strategy will alleviate the risk. Then, the excitement in the venues, the feeling of being part of something by the staff, promoters, and locals could generate much more interest on return trips as the buzz spreads. The crowd feeds off of positive energy. Even when the content of the art form seems dark and angry, the nature of the beast is positive because it brings us together. You have to have faith that your hard work will pay off because, without that, you are staying at home, going to work, and paying bills. Fear has no place in this way of living. You can and might lose your life as you know it, once you step over that line. The edge is a dangerous place.

BENEFITS:

- Sharing crew.

- Reducing expenses to each band by reducing crew (sharing sound and TM).

- Maximizing everyone's advertising money—sharing posters so you can print more and utilize other avenues.

- Reducing the risk by creating an event with momentum for more than just one band.

- A larger event opens up the possibilities of sponsorships and other exposure.

- Time can smooth the operation into a self-running machine—instead of new bands and challenges every night (on top of the rest).

LIABILITIES:

- You have to supervise the other bands.

- You have to supervise the timetable. Get a non-competing clause signed, 60 miles/60 days. The bigger the event and the bigger the risk is to you, the longer and wider the extent of it should be.

- Make sure the labels and bands are doing what they agreed to and more.

- You are now supervising or policing 35 people.

"I can honestly say, all the bad things that ever happened to me were directly, directly attributed to drugs and alcohol. I mean, I would never urinate at the Alamo at nine o'clock in the morning dressed in a woman's evening dress sober."

— Ozzy Osbourne

C·H·A·P·T·E·R 47

SPONSORSHIPS AND ENDORSEMENTS

"When you are making music, standing on stage and, traveling around the country, you have something that larger companies want - grooviness, vibe, and an in with the hardest demographic to crack - other kids like you."

Look for things that are going on, things that you can plug yourself into, and start learning how to work with other companies. It isn't just about getting some kind of sponsorship. It's about getting it and giving back; delivering everything that the sponsor wants when they want it in a non-threatening way; and sowing the seeds for the next time, so that you can get to another level of sponsorship.

It might be just a small company that will pay you to place postcards at your merch booth or sign up people across the country, but what are you selling? Maybe it's just trustworthiness; the knowledge that if you say you are going to do this, then you will do it.

There are more and more companies getting involved in sponsoring music: from liquor to all beverages, most of the beer companies, car companies, clothing companies, and shoe companies...

You've just gotta open your eyes and find the opportunities.

Any help is more help than none and an opportunity for you to show that you can hold up your end of a relationship.

ENDORSEMENTS

Everyone looks to the big music instrument companies for endorsements. It's more of the inter-band, dick-length competition than anything else, remove the need for validation and concentrate on what's available. Every drummer wants a Pearl Drum endorsement. (Thanks Pearl, since 1983!) Every guitarist wants a Marshall Stack, a Line 6 something, a Hughes and Kretchnerr whatsit, etc.

It was the deal we struck with Aquarian drumheads that really helped the last few Pigface package tours, with three to seven drumkits on stage per night and 5 drumheads on each! It helped alot! Bass strings would have been great—especially when we had three bass players for fifteen or so shows: Andrew Weiss of Rollins, Paul Raven of Killing Joke, and Andy McGuire

> "You've just gotta open your eyes and find the opportunities."

from Dogzilla. All was well until Andrew carried on his usual practice of changing his strings every day! That was bad enough financially (bass strings were running $80 a set back then), but then Raven, who traditionally would change a string when it snapped (once a year or every 100,000 miles), started doing it, then Andy too! $250 a day... bang! Its the little things that add up, an endorsement with Trueline drumsticks has been really helpful too.

A full endorsement is an ambitious thing to try for, concentrate on establishing ANY relationship with equipment companies you are using on any level. Some of my deals are for equipment at cost, its great to get ANY support.

I have a relationship with Presonus Audio and Audix microphones because I use their gear in the studio and out on the road. One of the benefits is just knowing I'm plugged into a support network of cool people and, when you're however many thousands of miles away from home base recording bands in China, that's great to know!

So, aim low, get high!

HOW TO BE A BETTER SPONSORED BAND
ADAM GRAYER - JÄGERMEISTER

• **Love and use the product/company you have sponsorship from.** I have received many e-mail and phone call requests from people that do not like, drink, or have ever tried Jägermeister but want sponsorship. The best thing a company can hear is, "Your brand is the only one I live by. I eat, sleep, drink, and swim in your product."

• **Know a little about the company and know exactly how their sponsorships work before contacting them.** I have no problems explaining our program, but we keep all of our information widely available on our website, so do many other companies. It's so much easier to hear, "I know what you do and I love it."

• **Have a list of accomplishments when speaking to the representative,** but, do not be "currently recording your next record." Make sure to hit up a sponsorship when it makes best sense for the company and not just for the band. We look for bands that are out on the road touring. The band does not have to be signed to a major label at all, but playing lots of shows, yes. Too many bands want to be sponsored when there are no shows on the calendar—looks as if the band has nothing going on (not the best time to be looking for sponsorship). It is best to wait until there are so many things going on.

"Understand that as a sponsor of any company, when at a show or out in public, you are acting as a de facto employee of that company..."

• **Have your website completely up-to-date.** I've heard, "Our webmaster never gets things updated," many times. Send people to your website if there is something to see: mp3's, tour dates, photos, news, etc.

• **Sonicbids EPK:** Some companies like the physical press kit, and I rarely stand by another company, but SonicBids have a great EPK. It makes it cheaper for you to send hundreds of them out and easier for a company, as they do not have to wait for several weeks for it (it also can't get lost in the mail).

• **Follow up on any submissions,** but do so respectfully. Understand that any company that sponsors bands must receive hundreds of requests every week. After submitting, wait at least three weeks before following up. If you follow up within 24 hours of a submission, you risk harassing the sponsor and turning them off.

• **Accept rejection respectfully.** A company cannot sponsor every band that crosses their path (as much as we'd all like to). If you are rejected, thank them for their time and ask if there is anything that you can or should be doing that they would like to see to make a future submission more acceptable. Do not re-submit again for at least 6-12 months and make sure that you have something major to include if you re-submit

• **If accepted for sponsorship, do everything to include this company in all band promotions.** Include them on your web site, mention them in interviews (press and radio), on stage mentions, on flyers, posters, CD liner notes, etc.

• **Show the company you are promoting their product.** Regularly send every sponsor photos, audio and video of the band promoting their product, along with regular updates on the band. Constant communication between a band and sponsor is extremely important. The pictures and video show the company they are getting a lot out of the deal.

• **Understand that as a sponsor of any company, when at a show or out in public, you are acting as a de facto employee of that company.** While you do not work for the company and are not entitled to company benefits, anything the band does negatively reflects on that company. Always act with respect to anyone you deal with. If a band always causes trouble, it will get back to the corporate sponsors and embarrass them. If a band is always great to everyone, a company can be proud to have this band as a sponsored band.

CURSE MACKEY
OZZFEST AND SPONSORSHIP HELL

In 2006, I produced Six-String Masterpieces: The Dimebag Darrell Art Tribute. This is a collection of 60+ guitars that have been hand-painted by top rockers, artists, etc, original works of art painted on guitars. For six-months, I was the show's curator, eventually aligning an unprecedented artist list including Rob Zombie, Marilyn Manson, James Hetfield, Dave Grohl, Billy Corgan, Dave Navarro, Moby, Ozzy, Ace Frehley, Jerry Cantrell, tattoo artist Paul Booth, Bob Tyrrell, Guy Aitchison, Filip Leu, and more. We toured the thing all year long, finding ways to put together sponsorship deals to do NAMM, South by Southwest, MTV2, Fuse TV, The Family Values Tour and Ozzfest.

Ozzfest was a huge goal of mine for this exhibit. The ideal of taking an art gallery on tour and basically placing it in the moshpit was magnetic and it needed to happen. This exhibit has the potential to raise hundreds of thousands of dollars to support art and music education and also expose the next generation of rockers and metal heads to the world of fine art in a way that they otherwise may never know how fuckin' cool it is to look at paintings and go to galleries. It's enlightening and educational. Fortunately, I had a sponsorship relationship with a computer company and they were giving us $10,000 to do the Ozzfest tour. This amounted to about 50% of our budget. We also had a smaller sponsor and the rest of the funds would be raised by people making a contribution to the exhibit tour fund. A week before it was time to leave, I was informed that the sponsorship deal had fallen through, as the company had been bought by Dell, and all deals were cancelled that pertained to music-based marketing initiatives. My friend at the sponsor company said my check and agreement were sitting on the CEO's desk and the deal basically died there.

So basically that was it: we had zero dollars to leave with. It was over before it began. After a day of depression and feeling like I got kicked in the balls of my bank account, I began to devise a last minute plan. We set up a profile on MySpace with various levels of donation and offered incentives for the donations: posters, t-shirts, magazines, etc. and began reaching out to our closest fans, MySpace network fans of Dime, and all of the participating artists. We were able to raise enough money to get us to the first Ozzfest date in San Antonio to test the waters. We had a very successful day. The Ozzfest crew was totally supportive as were the Osbournes and, in the end, I had great meeting with Ozzy and Sharon and they were thankful for us bringing the exhibit. We had 3,000 to 4,000 people per Ozzfest event coming into our gallery zone. We ended with enough money to get us to the first family values date and we made it to the end of that without any sponsorship other than a small contribution from Dean Guitars. The rest was supported by the fans who believed in the exhibit and enjoyed the experience. Pretty amazing.

See Patrik Matas' interview in *Stories from the From the Front Line*.

> "Ozzfest was a huge goal of mine for this exhibit. The ideal of taking an art gallery on tour and basically placing it in the mosh pit was magnetic and it needed to happen."

CHAPTER 48

SEMINARS AND FESTIVALS

"Welcome to the Music Business... you're fucked."
- Martin Atkins

When faced with the reality of the hard work outlined in this book, most bands will thrash around trying to find the easy button. Many of them will think it's performing at a seminar, and if you don't know a lot about seminars, it seems like it might be a good idea. There'll be a lot of industry people there and... that's about as far as the thought process goes. But if you keep thinking for another four minutes, you might also realize that there will be over 1,499 other bands there too... one thousand four hundred and ninety nine!...

SOUTH BY SOUTHWEST 2007

If you don't like your chances of doing OK in a small bar in Albuquerque on a Wednesday night, what makes you think you'll do any better in Austin at South by Southwest when Pete Townsend is giving a keynote speech, several companies are giving away buckets full of alcohol, and there are bands from all over the world trying to split the same arrow you are. As far as all the business people are concerned, faced with the choice of standing underneath a demo waterfall and a barrage of 1,500 bands all wanting to explain why they are unique, many of them attend the seminars and conferences but have meetings offsite.

Martin Hooker who owns Dream Catcher Records in the UK told me that MIDEM in the south of France was so crazy he had someone from a band put headphones on his head while he was pissing in the bathroom!

If you already have a label and a great album, seminars can be a good idea to showcase the band and a new album six or eight weeks before you hit radio and go on tour. But, it's not a good way to be seen or get signed. There are over 100 American seminars; which one are you going to pick? On the way to SXSW or CMJ (two of the larger ones), it's very difficult, if not impossible, to get a show the night before in Philadelphia (in the case of CMJ in NYC) or in Houston, San Antonio, or Dallas (in the case of SXSW) and that effect ripples outwards.

This is a club in San Antonio letting us know that they are already bombarded with requests for shows around SXSW. This is November 8th – SXSW happens in March...

-----Original Message-----

Sent: Wed, 8 Nov 2006 15:34:24 -0800 (PST)

Subject: SXSW Holds

Hello, I hope this e-mail finds you well! We are getting tons of hold for South by Southwest here in San Antonio already , so if you need dates during this time period, please send your holds a.s.a.p. so we can fit you in as best as we can :)

Thank you so much

Veronyka Mezquiti

Ghost Cat Productions, San Antonio Texas 78228

South by Southwest is big business for the founders of the event and for the city of Austin, TX. Nearly 22,000 hotel rooms are booked per night. The three conferences that form *SXSW* *(Music, Film, and Interactive)* generate close to $40 million with participants from around the world spending just under an average of $300/day. Restaurants, bars, and music venues experience a close to 50% increase in revenues over their next highest month. If you think that events like this have a primary goal of helping you to get signed, then get a clue. If you're able to do so, it could be a good chance for you to do some research that is way more valuable than anything else you could take away from a seminar. You could get to see bands from all over the world and expose yourself to the people with whom you'll be competing. These events do provide opportunities; you just need to be clear on what those opportunities are.

CMJ

I performed at a Saturday night headline show for CMJ in New York a few years ago. It was a well-attended show with a prime time slot for my band, the Damage Manual, which was causing a bit of a stir at the time. "A bloody horse's head in between rocks' cozy blankets," *Kerrang Magazine* said. It was a great show. We were using the opportunity to promote an EP and an album. We invited representatives from radio stations from across the country.

At their worst, events will promise much and deliver little, although this isn't totally the responsibility of the festivals themselves... Another band performing the same night at the CMJ festival was away from the main stage in a basement room performing to six of their friends. The room was so heavy with shattered hope and desperation; I could only bear to stay for one song. I've had experiences of bands flying from England at their own expense to perform at a seminar in front of label owners, industry movers and shakers, etc., only to experience the reality of performing to 30 or 40 friends—the only label owner among them was me. Apply the "Think of your parents before you get shagged" rule on this one. Or start your own seminar.

> "These events do provide opportunities; you just need to be clear on what those opportunities are."

C·H·A·P·T·E·R ·· 49

TOURING INTERNATIONALLY

"The grass isn't greener it's just a different
shade of brown."
   -Martin Atkins

If the phrase "Don't run before you can walk" is true then "Don't fly before you can walk" is a fucking no-brainer. There is an undeniable benefit to international touring, but it has more to do with increasing the colors in an artist's palate than a cure-all for slow progress in an artist's home country.

Many bands look at foreign touring as if it isn't as massive a risk as touring at home. Compounded by the expense of flights and visas, the difficultly of language, voltage, and diet, etc., they somehow see it as the place where things will miraculously happen overnight. It's just not true. And it can be quite dangerous to neglect your home market and shred your financial resources to pursue something in a foreign land, unplugged from the support network of family and friends you've worked so hard to build.

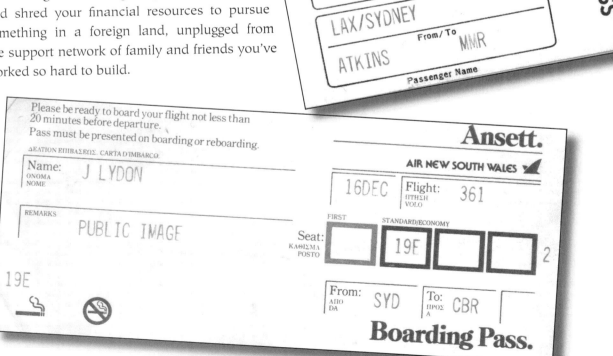

I began to work with the Evil Mothers very early in their careers. Over a three or four year period, they went from performing to seven people in Chicago to performing for a $1,000 guarantee to a substantial crowd. We spent a lot of time, energy, and money pushing the band forwards. When we finished the Spider Sex and Car Wrecks album. We started to get really good airplay on the album and a station in Phoenix, AZ, had the band at number one. It was shortly before the band was traveling to Europe, for an opening slot with Einstürzende Neubauten at The Astoria, an 1,800 capacity venue in London. I remember the call to the band's leader Curse Mackey very well. I said, "You have to go to Phoenix now. You're number one." Curse replied, "We'll get to it when we get back from Europe." I said something like, "I hope nothing crazy happens like the radio station goes out of business or changes format." The day the band arrived in London, a rift between the U.S. and the U.K. office of Alternative Tentacles became a gaping chasm when Jello Biafra filed a lawsuit. The dates in Germany didn't go very well. The Alternative Tentacles office in London didn't exist to help. Somewhere between arriving back in New York and driving back to Texas, the band disintegrated. All of its resources gone. Oh, and that radio station in Phoenix… went out of business before the band got back to the states.

So, while the allure of Austin Powers, kooky London Carnaby Street parties, decadent Berlin, any town, anywhere (just not here), exotic climates, and different languages, is real, it might be a whole lot fucking cheaper to send the singer of the band on a ten-day holiday, (or you could call it a fact-finding mission) before you send the band. The grass isn't greener. It's just a different shade of brown.

THE COFFEE LID TEST.

You can get a pretty good idea about how technologically advanced or service minded a country is by using the coffee lid test. I've spent hours hypnotized by all of the different designs of coffee cup lids with swivel mouths, buttons to press in if it's decaf, and different ways of opening and closing a disposable lid. But you only have to be in England for ten minutes, spend $7 for a cappuccino to then spill it all over your jet-lagged hand as you try and create some kind of an opening by tearing the plastic lid with your teeth, to realize it's the third world.

INTERNATIONAL DIFFERENCES

As the demographics of the U.S. and the world change, it's good to be aware of things outside of Toledo, it expands your mind, man. And you might have a situation like this:

I was having a conversation with the manager of a Scandinavian band called Zeromancer. We were negotiating the terms of their agreement to be on one of our package tours, when I mentioned that the band members would receive an evening meal or $10 per head (if the meal was "bought out") the manager flipped and said that "They couldn't even buy a Big Mac for that price!" Now, here is a potential problem. I am a Brit and so before I started in on the guy with some sarcasm, I realized (because I had been there) that Big Macs were, in fact, pretty close to $10 each in their home country and this guy wasn't being an asshole. I was able to point out to him that, at the moment, one could, if one wished, purchase probably three Big Macs, two fries, and a couple of gallons of pop for $10. Problem averted.

Did this mean we had a problem free day? No, of course not! It just meant that there was a little bit more time and brain space for the problems that needed it—each tiny one of which is the seed of the bean stalk climbing through the nebulous clouds of grooviness and good vibes...

THINGS TO PAY ATTENTION TO:

I know I've said throughout the book: "Never assume." But when you are touring internationally, you've got to check everything. For instance, what side of the road do you drive on? How much do you think a gallon of gas is in the U.K.? Look at the receipt. Convert liters to gallons and U.K. pounds to U.S. dollars. You know what? That's a lot of effort—it will probably be OK, right? In 2004, it was over $7 a gallon! And right now, it's well over $6. You can check the following website for useful information:

http://money.cnn.com/pf/features/lists/global_gasprices/price.html

Look at the other receipt for a sausage sandwich and a cappuccino for 5.94 U.K. pounds. That's $11.86 with the exchange rate of close to $2 to the pound! There is no such thing as a small detail.

AND CHECK EXCHANGE RATES!!

Foreign Currency Converter Site/Calculator

http://www.xe.com/ucc/convert.cgi

When traveling abroad, try and check out as many tourist deals as you can. There are usually large incentives for people from outside a country to travel inside a foreign destination. But you're going to need to book and investigate these before the tour starts as these options might not be open to everyone on the tour depending on which passport they hold.

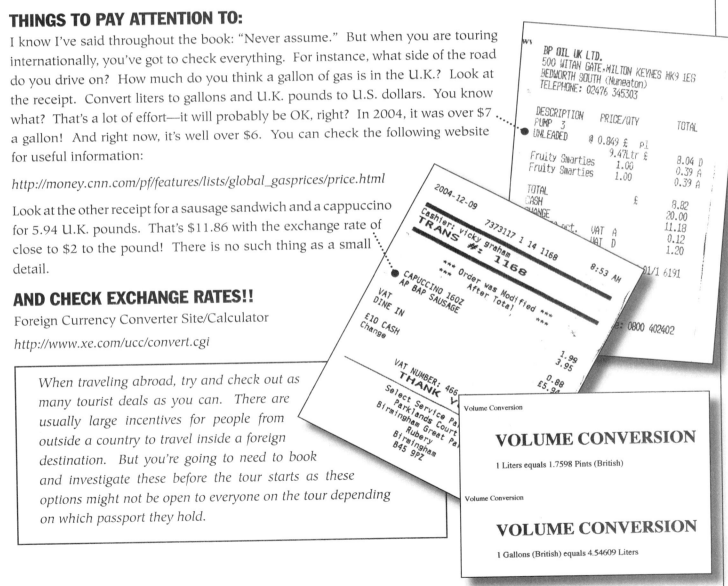

BP OIL UK LTD.
500 WITAN GATE, MILTON KEYNES MK9 1ES
BEDWORTH SOUTH (Nuneaton)
TELEPHONE: 02476 345303

DESCRIPTION   PRICE/QTY   TOTAL
PUMP 3
UNLEADED   @ 0.849 £ pl
              9.47Ltr £   8.04 D
Fruity Smarties 1.00   0.39 A
Fruity Smarties 1.00   0.39 A

TOTAL
CASH   £   8.82
CHANGE   20.00
              VAT A   11.18
              VAT D   0.12
                              1.20

2004-12-09
Cashier: vicky graham
7373117 1 14 1168
TRANS #: 1168
*** Order was Modified ***
*** After Total ***

CAPPUCCINO 16OZ
AP BAP SAUSAGE
VAT
DINE IN

£10 CASH
Change

VAT NUMBER: 466
THANK Y
Select Service Pa
Parklands Court
Birmingham Great Pa
Rubery
Birmingham
B45 9PZ

8:53 AM

1.99
3.95
0.88
£5.94

Volume Conversion

VOLUME CONVERSION

1 Liters equals 1.7598 Pints (British)

Volume Conversion

VOLUME CONVERSION

1 Gallons (British) equals 4.54609 Liters

TOUR:SMART Index

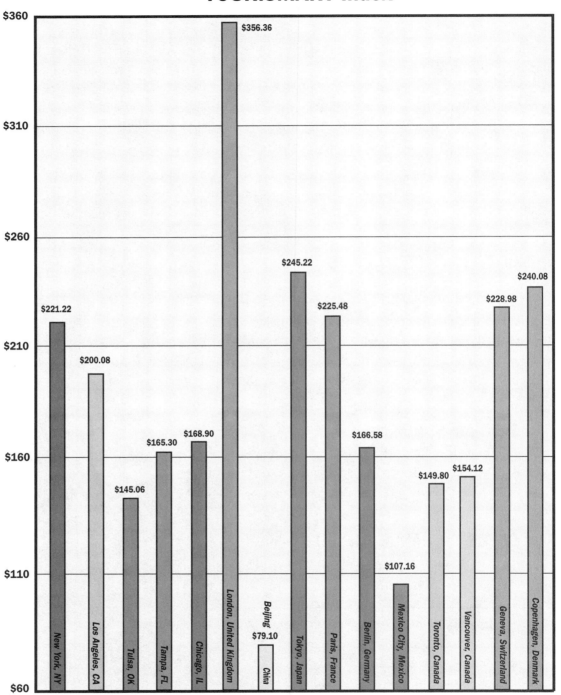

Location	Value
New York, NY	$221.22
Los Angeles, CA	$200.08
Tulsa, OK	$145.06
Tampa, FL	$165.30
Chicago, IL	$168.90
London, United Kingdom	$356.36
Beijing, China	$79.10
Tokyo, Japan	$245.22
Paris, France	$225.48
Berlin, Germany	$166.58
Mexico City, Mexico	$107.16
Toronto, Canada	$149.80
Vancouver, Canada	$154.12
Geneva, Switzerland	$228.98
Copenhagen, Denmark	$240.08

TOUR:SMART Index= *The total cost of 10 gallons of gas, 2 Big Macs, 6 bottles of beer and one hotel room.*

INTERNATIONAL TRAVEL TIPS
MARK WILLIAMS, PRESONUS AUDIO ELECTRONIC

TRAVELING ABROAD

Crossing borders can be an exciting adventure when handled correctly.

Nightmares can arrive from international travel when one is unprepared. Here are just a few tips to help get your thought process going in the right direction.

RESEARCH YOUR DESTINATION

Research the country where you are going before you go. It helps to know a little about the history, currency, and political atmosphere of a country before you go there. Also, you need to find to find out if you need a visa before you travel. Some countries, like Australia, will allow you to buy the visa at the airport. However, other countries require you to be invited by a citizen and to apply for a visa ahead of time.

Some helpful sites for when you are planning travel are:

https://www.cia.gov/cia/publications/factbook/index.html

http://www.timeanddate.com/worldclock/

http://www.x-rates.com/calculator.html

http://www.freetranslation.com/free/

http://www.worldwidemetric.com/metcal.htm

ITINERARY AND ADDRESSES

Keep all of your travel information on your person at all times. It is essential to have your hotel address and phone number on you at all times. If you don't speak the language, it's much easier if you can show someone the hotel address in writing. Some countries won't let you through customs if you do not have your hotel address. Also, always double check your flight and travel itineraries. Planes don't generally wait for passengers.

ELECTRICITY

Some electronic items will work at different voltages. You need to check them though to make sure the power range is not limited to 110/120. It is also important to know what voltage you are going to use.

FOOD

Be cautious about what you eat when traveling outside of the U.S. Ask your host or someone at the hotel for recommendations on where and what to eat. I generally try to eat three meals a day when traveling. This helps you get adjusted to your new schedule. Also, I try to locate a store close to the hotel as soon as possible and load up on bottled water and light snacks. This saves you money and can prevent you from getting sick from bad water.

FLIGHT

I always check the airline's web page and flight status frequently to make sure there are no delays and/or travel advisories. It is also important to check when you arrive in a country about any differences in rules or regulations for when you try to depart the country. In some instances, the carry-on rules are different for each country. For example, you are allowed to carry two items on board when departing Mexico, but only one when departing the U.K.

I have a backpack that I carry with me that is compartmentalized for accessibility. I generally carry my laptop, movies, a book (or two), and some sort of game or music player. This may sound like a lot of electronics, but being bored on a ten+ hour flight is like being imprisoned. I also carry extra batteries for the electronic . You never know when you will be stuck for an extra few hours at the airport or on the tarmac while the plane gets repaired. I also try to keep the following items in there as well:

- Umbrella
- Medicine, antacids, aspirin, etc.
- Power adaptors
- Small spare computer cables, firewire, USB, etc.
- Extra fold up bag

Always try to sleep some on the plane. This helps you adjust to the time zone you are flying into. Try to stay awake for the whole day when you reach your destination. If you sleep for the better part of the day when you arrive, you'll end up being up all night and this will make it even harder to adjust.

CUSTOMS CLEARANCE

Never make jokes with customs or airport security personnel. They don't respond well to this and it can sometimes create problems. Always have your passport and customs documents ready. Another good tip is to keep your phone off and definitely don't use your camera!

Declare only what you feel is necessary. Most of the times, customs officials are only concerned with agricultural items, prohibited items (contraband), etc. It's generally not necessary to declare the teddy bear you bought or the box of candy for the girlfriend.

EQUIPMENT

When traveling with commercial items, it is important to either bring an invoice to yourself for those items or a Carnet. Either of these will prevent you from having to pay customs/duties on the items you are traveling with.

These are only a few of the many, many items to keep in mind when traveling abroad.

Good Travels!

“...being bored on a ten+ hour flight is like being imprisoned. ...carry extra batteries for the electronics.”

ENGLAND

Lee Fraser told me that America really fucked him up because the common (-ish) language made him forget that he was 6,000 miles from home. At least when you're in Amsterdam, you hear a completely different language, there are hookers everywhere, and people are blowing pot smoke in your face. You know you're not in Salt Lake City. You're in a different country, and these subtle prompts remind you that other things might be different too. Not so between the States and the U.K. Two countries separated by a common language. So, bear that in mind. I just looked at the essay from Dee Generate and, in a page and a quarter, noted 17 things that I thought needed explaining to American readers. Throw into that some warm pints of stronger-than-you're-used-to-beer, the Brit's love of sarcasm, irony, and some cockney* rhyming slang** and you, my darling, my little bit of crumpet, are well and truly J-Arthured!***

*A cockney is traditionally someone born within the sound of Bow Bells church in London.

**Cockney rhyming slang was originally a device for the lower classes to talk more freely in front of the upper class. It's the removal of the rhyming word that creates the comic code. For example, a common phrase in England would be "Use your loaf" which means "Think."

Loaf of bread = head.

Another example: Geordie Walker said to me in a crowded bar, directly in front of a beautiful American girl with an amazing chest, "Fabulous thre'pennies, darling!" She was completely baffled by the combination of cockney rhyming slang and reference to a pre-decimalization UK currency.

*** J Arthur refers to the famous film producer J. Arthur Rank = wank.

DEE GENERATE, EATER

The Label had begun to show how bad they really were; Vinyl pressings that were as thick as dinner plates, crap distribution through a little outfit called Virgin, no money, dodgy [*shaky*] contracts and no attempt to get us better gigs and promote the single. So when they said that we would be going to Belgium to headline at Brussels first ever Punk Club I thought things were looking up.

We were told to meet the tour bus at Victoria, [*a train station*] all the equipment, including drums would be hired [*rented*] in Belgium, just bring guitars.

In a Situationist reference, 'The Sex Pistols' manager Malcolm Maclaren had 'Nowhere' and 'Boredom' printed on the destination board of The Anarchy Tour buses. Eater, and the sweetie shop svengali of the label, Caruzo, took a different approach, ours had National Express [*Bus Company. The UK's Greyhound*] emblazoned down the side and came with an entourage of the traveling public.

After queuing [*waiting in line*] for the tickets we were told the coach [*bus*] was an hour late so took refuge in a local pub where Dave was ordered to buy us beers which were drank surreptitiously while being watched by the worried landlord. [*because the band is underage*] When we piled onto the bus the other unsuspecting passengers began to fear that this would not be the opportunity for the bit of 'shut eye' that they were anticipating before the sea bound part of the journey. Dave's girlfriend had thoughtfully brought tangerines for the journey thinking us kids would tire and need a little snack along the way. There was a complaint from a bald pensioner [*retiree*] that had become the target in our tangerine peel recreation of The Golden Shot. [*A UK game show in which contestants shoot an apple with a crossbow.*] Without Bob Monkhouse's [*UK's Dick Clark (kind of)*] charm it was left to Dave and Curuso to negotiate our safe passage to the port.

On arrival the Hover Craft was delayed so a visit to the bar and more secret drinking ensued. We were ushered onto the craft and I was excited as I was shown to a seat next to the great Wolves [*Wolverhampton Wanderers soccer team*] centre forward the then retired Dereck Dougan. He was not so please to see me and shuffled uncomfortably as I recounted stories of collecting football [*soccer*] cards and how I had to swap Martin Chivers and Peter Osgood [*soccer stars*] for him to complete my set. During the journey the motion of the hover craft and the beer now swishing around in my stomach began to take its toll and the last thing I remember is seeing Mr. Dougan's lovely clean brown suede brogues swimming in a sea of Punk vomit.

We arrived in Brussels to be met by the local promoter who in either a misunderstanding of the etiquette of the Punk naming process or loss of meaning in translation introduced himself as Peter Penis. The hotel rooms were not ready for a couple of hours so Dave struck a deal with Peter who agreed to take us around Brussels to sight see while the adults got a rest from us in the hotel bar. We decided to take the guitars rather than leave them in the lobby. After some very token tourism a great photo opportunity at the 'Mannequin De Piss', well it had been a long journey and toilets [*bathroom*] stops were not too frequent, we went to a bar to eat and have a drink. Seeing the beer delivered in 2 litre [*2 liters=half gallon*] pitchers with smaller glasses was too much of a temptation so we ordered one each. After my mysteriously named meat dish 'Cheveux au Vin Rouge' [*horse with red wine*] and a few litres of Belgium beer we ambled back to the hotel. By the time we arrived at the lobby we were all dazed with a strange sense that something was wrong something was missing, maybe it was the combination of the beer, the tiredness from traveling or maybe.....where did we leave those guitars?

To be continued

I managed to avoid another "situation" when the Evil Mothers performed at The Foundry in Birmingham, U.K. It was a good show, not huge attendance, but good and definitely potential for a return visit. The owner of the club was very pleased and liked the band. When the band played the States, they would earn around $1,000 and get a few cases of beer, food, etc., and probably some Jim Beam. So, when I saw the smiling promoter taking a huge gift backstage after the show (four small warm cans of Long Life Lager), I knew I had to act swiftly. I could see the band throwing this guy out of the dressing room for being so insulting… they didn't realize that bands don't get shit over there… So I ran ahead of the promoter and said to Curse, "Oh look!" (Look, look, look, wink, wink, wink, are you getting the message here…) "The promoter is bringing you some beer—that's really unusual! Isn't that great guys?" (prod, prod, prod). Problem Averted.

JASON MILLER, GODHEAD

JASON MILLER

LEAD VOCALIST AND GUITARIST OF THE INDUSTRIAL ROCK BAND **GODHEAD**

The fans in the U.K., at least towards American bands, seem much more loyal and sincere. In America, it seems that fans are jaded and worried about what's cool right now, whereas fans in the U.K. are only concerned about what they actually like. It's a refreshing change from home, where as soon as you fall out of favor with the media, you are viewed as "uncool."

"Just nod a lot."

Accents are difficult to understand from region to region: A guy from London and a guy from Birmingham sound like they are from different planets! But with a little bit of concentration and a lot of "What?" you can make it through just about any conversation. Just nod a lot.

If you get hungry after about 10 p.m. though, all you are going to be able to find is a kabob shop. You'd better get used to it. Donner or Chicken?

BELGIUM
DEE GENERATE, EATER

DEE GENERATE

ORIGINAL AND CURRENT DRUMMER WITH EATER

www.myspace.com/deegenerate

The Label had begun to show how bad they really were: Vinyl pressings that were as thick as dinner plates, crap distribution through a little outfit called Virgin, no money, dodgy contracts, and no attempt to get us better gigs and promote the single. So when they said that we would be going to Belgium to headline at Brussels' first ever Punk Club, I thought things were looking up.

We were told to meet the tour bus at Victoria. All the equipment, including drums, would be hired in Belgium; "Just bring guitars."

In a Situationist reference, The Sex Pistols' manager, Malcolm Maclaren, had "Nowhere" and "Boredom" printed on the destination board of The Anarchy Tour buses. Eater and the sweetie shop Svengali of the label, Caruzo, took a different approach: ours had "National Express" emblazoned down the side and came with an entourage of the traveling public.

After queuing for the tickets, we were told the coach was an hour late so we took refuge in a local pub where Dave was ordered to buy us beers, which we drank surreptitiously while being watched by the worried landlord. When we piled onto the bus, the other unsuspecting passengers began to fear that this would not be the opportunity for the bit of "shut-eye" that they were anticipating before the sea-bound part of the journey. Dave's girlfriend had thoughtfully brought tangerines for the journey, thinking us kids would tire and need a little snack along the way. There was a complaint from a bald pensioner that had become the target in our tangerine peel recreation of The Golden Shot. Without Bob Monkhouse's charm, it was left to Dave and Caruzo to negotiate our safe passage to the port.

On arrival, the Hover Craft was delayed. So a visit to the bar and more secret drinking ensued. We were ushered onto the craft and I was excited as I was shown to a seat next to the great Wolves centre forward, the then-retired Dereck Dougan. He was not so pleased to see me and shuffled uncomfortably as I recounted stories of collecting football cards and how I had to swap Martin Chivers and Peter Osgood for him to complete my set. During the journey, the motion of the hover craft and the beer now swishing around in my stomach began to take its toll, and the last thing I remember is seeing Mr. Dougan's lovely clean brown suede brogues swimming in a sea of Punk vomit.

We arrived in Brussels to be met by the local promoter who, in either a misunderstanding of the etiquette of the Punk naming process or loss of meaning in translation, introduced himself as Peter Penis. The hotel rooms were not ready for a couple of hours so Dave struck a deal with

Peter who agreed to take us around Brussels to sightsee while the adults got a rest from us in the hotel bar. We decided to take the guitars rather than leave them in the lobby. After some very token tourism and a great photo opportunity at the "Mannequin De Piss" (well, it had been a long journey and toilet stops were not too frequent), we went to a bar to eat and have a drink. Seeing the beer delivered in two litre pitchers with smaller glasses was too much of a temptation, so we ordered one each. After my mysteriously named meat dish "Cheveux au Vin Rouge" and a few litres of Belgium beer, we ambled back to the hotel. By the time we arrived at the lobby, we were all dazed with a strange sense that something was wrong, something was missing… maybe it was the combination of the beer, the tiredness from traveling, or maybe… where did we leave those guitars?

To be continued

GERMANY

BERLIN

"If you live in Berlin," Universal Music Germany CEO Frank Briegmann says, "You are at the very heart of modern music."

"Yeah. But you're still in Germany?"
    - Martin Atkins

I remember a few things about Germany. It always seemed greyer and damper than England which was quite an achievement. Standing on stage at a club in Berlin with a hammer in each hand, smashing a metal coffee table, me and Paul Raven smiling. With Killing Joke, we had problems getting our vegetarian crew fed. The omelet was vegetarian… with just a little bit of bacon. This reminded me of another conversation where, of course, the ham wasn't vegetarian, but it was very thinly sliced!" This was a decade ago and Germany felt like a place that older bands would go to die. I don't know if the Michael Schenker Group is still performing live, but if they are, they're performing live in Germany.

BS-HU 481
MARTIN BOWES

HOOKERS.

That license plate is etched in my memory. It was the early hours of February 27th. 1997. We were half way through our fourth tour of Germany. Had just played at the Brain club, Braunschweig, Germany. Not a bad show. I was inside the club picking up the last gear and collecting the fee and the rest of the band were loading up the car outside…

Like a lot of rock clubs, this wasn't located in the best part of town. But you get used to that. You don't really care. Well, you hardly look like tourists. And as long as the gear is safe… There were a lot of red lights here. And women in short skirts over on the corner…

As I came out into the car park at the back of the club I heard screams and shouts. And they were English. Here we go again… One of the basic rules of touring is that if it can go wrong, it will.

But I didn't expect this.

The band were all round the car. The front passenger door was half hanging off, swinging from side to side. My singer, Julie, was crying. The rest of the band were shouting and pointing at a green Mercedes which was slowly lurching over the pavement and back onto the road. One of it's hubcaps was spinning in the road. Inside was a middle aged man and…well, one of those girls from the corner. It seemed like an age, but the Mercedes slowly gained speed and sped off into the distance…

Three of the band had read the license plate.

BS-HU 481. (BS meant it was a Braunschweig plate….)

Some of the green paint from the side of the Mercedes was scraped over our battered side door. We had the hubcap. It had been swerving wildly across the road as it approached our car and missed Julie by inches when it virtually took the door off. It could have easily have killed her.

MARTIN
BOWES

ATTRITION

www.attrition.co.uk

GESTAPO?

The police arrived. We gave them the details. We transferred our equipment to the road manager, Krisch's car and some to the opening German act, Morbus kitahara. The police towed our car to their station and we left for our hotel. It was one of those Formula 1 fully automated-self –service-plastic-box hotels you get a lot in Europe… I kind of like them.

Well some of us slept. Most people just drank a lot. Someone complained but we weren't really in the mood for that. I remember Will asking her if she was going to call Robocop…

Next morning I am on the phone to my insurance company. (Always. always. Have vehicle insurance if you tour. And get medical if it is the glorious USA as something will happen to you sooner or later.) We need a new car now. And we are taking it all over the country. They didn't know what we were doing. I hadn't had to tell them we were a touring band and it's not the best thing to do that if you don't have to. Well we got one, of course it was a smaller car. That always happens, too.

We got to the local police station. What was the news? Had they picked the drunk driver up? What was happening? They had checked the license plate number. It belonged to the ministry of the interior undercover affairs. It had definitely not been used for months. Three people had independently read the number wrong on a stationary car a few feet away.

OK. So it was a green Mercedes with a Braunschweig plate with a hubcap missing and massive scrapes down the side. Oh, impossible to trace. OK, we get it. The guy from the ministry shouldn't have been drunk in charge and picking up hookers on an undercover police license plate so he now just didn't exist.

We hadn't got time to argue. The insurance sorted the car to be taken to a garage until we return from the rest of the tour.

We could hardly do the tour. Julie was in no state to stay away for too long now. She was in shock.

We didn't have room in the new car and were relying on the other bands. We also had to get back soon to pick up our damaged car and take it back to England. Oh yes, I just lost £250 (U.K. pounds) as damage excess on that, too.

We agreed we could finish off the German dates, there were only a few left, but we had booked our first tour of Poland to follow, on our own. We faxed the Polish promoter to cancel. It just wasn't going to work out now. We arrived late for our sound check the next day in Rostock. The promoter decided we weren't going to get one now.

I fucking screamed. We got one. (That always seems to work. And I wish it didn't have to come to that. But we'd had a bad day.)

I AM A THIEF

We finished the tour. Pretty well, in the circumstances. There were a million other political issues on this tour but that was all to do with the German band and that can wait for the second book!)

Said our good byes to the other band and Krisch. Drove back to Braunschweig. Found our car out in the country somewhere in some weird old garage. The top box we had bought ourselves for the tour was missing. The German mechanic said it must have fallen off! It was held on top so hard it could never fall off. And there wasn't a scratch round the fittings. So it was an insurance job and he thought he'd just help himself to the extras. More calls. Another visit to the police station to report a theft.

The insurance company was going to look into it. The door was wired shut on our car so we took it and dropped off the replacement. We should have been home by now so we asked the insurance company if they will cover a nights hotel. In the circumstances they agreed. Drove back to England. Took the Dover ferry. At least customs didn't get their dogs out this time. Home.

AFTERMATH

I sent a threatening fax to the Braunschweig police. Told them what I thought of them. What did I care. I'm never going to live in Braunschweig. (Well not now…)

The insurance company paid for a replacement top box but refused to pay for that hotel and offered no compensation for the hassle their crooked mechanic caused us. I issued a press statement to all the German press, music and nationa, and even the U.K. and U.S. press that was interested. The German Green party asked questions about the incident in their parliament. I never heard an answer.

I contacted my member of the European Parliament. She looked into the whole secret police cover up. She asked what compensation I was after. What do you say? Well I said £10,000! I didn't get it.

Rock n roll.

Just enjoy every minute of it. We were back there the next year (but we missed out Braunschweig).

Martin Bowes. Coventry, England. 2006. *www.attrition.co.uk*

JAPAN

"I was born in Tachikawa, but seeing Tokyo for the first time as an adult was like visiting another planet. Sophia Coppola got it quite right with Lost In Translation."
- Jade Dellinger

The first time I went to Japan with PiL, I watched a group of people placing fliers on the seats while we were sound checking. When we finished, I went down to see what they were doing. It was a street team from the label putting fliers with information about the new PiL album, merchandise, other releases, and the next tour coming through. What an amazing idea—every seat of a 3,000 capacity venue! Every single one of these people was interested in what was going on (obviously, because they were going to be there!) The cheapest, most effective way to communicate with your fans is to get the information directly into their hands.

What else is special about these people (other then their fantastic taste in music)? Well, they put on their clothes, made sure they looked good and smelled nice, then drove and parked or took a bus or a train to get to see you. These are the people you need to take care of!

The second trip there, we recorded the first digital live album on a Mitsubishi 32 track tape machine. We mixed the live album there (*PiL Live in Tokyo*). We were accustomed to overnight sessions, which is what we'd done in the UK so we could use a great studio like The Townhouse to record *Metal Box* and *Flowers of Romance*. But in Japan, we were unplugged from our traditional bike messenger-ed supplies and it was tough. The last few sessions we were drinking cup-fulls of cough medicine with our sushi boxes sent over by the label and, desperate for any kind of dB level for monitoring. We ended up in a room two floors away from the control room slurring mix instructions via telephone.

By the time I got to Japan in 1983 with PiL, McDonalds, KFC, and Budweiser were already everywhere.

P.I.L

JAPAN TOUR

2

Van Production
TOKYO
☎ 03-470-0681

6月21日(火)　東　京・中野サンプラザホール

24日(金)　名古屋・名古屋市公会堂

閣ジェスパ　052(932)9500

大　阪・大阪厚生年金会館

・おやめ下さい!!・

ベッドでのお煙草

NO SMOKING IN BED PLEASE

It watered down the experience a little bit. It was also a little bit reassuring. Small things became fun. John's wife Nora was tall, very blonde, and stopped traffic. The custom of removing shoes before entering a bar enabled us to see who was in a bar before we went in. Our soundman's, huge cowboy boots were an invitation or a warning depending on how we felt. Part of me is still playing it back in my head now, almost 25 years later. Punk and June were representatives from Van Productions, translating and guiding, pointing out an interesting building on the left and a large office building on the right that was empty because it was haunted, we were matter-of-factly informed. Vending machines on the street sold beer. We had seven sold-out shows in one venue in Tokyo and we must have spent two full days of our time there sitting in traffic.

At the first show, we were feeling pretty good until the end of the first song. Nothing happened. I crashed the triumphant, "This is how it's done on our side of the planet" punk rock cymbal crash, to a chorus of nothingness. The silence was excruciating! I sat behind the kit, surrounded by the high-end wash of the cymbals, "Wow, what have I done? I'm shit. The band is shit. What are we doing here? We should never have come. Oh, please God, rewind my life so I can..." Then, as the last incremental part of a decibel of the cymbal crashes

Audience in Japan!

died away, massive applause (now that these discerning individuals had allowed the final nuances of the music to die down in reverent respect). "Oh yes, I am brilliant! I always knew this would be the case. More, more, more..." What a contrast when we performed in Australia (*PiL* '84/'85). If they liked you, it was mad! "I really like this, so I am going to jump up and down, pour this beer all over me, then throw the bottle at the band, because I love them!"

When Tub Ring went to Japan, we got off the plane at Narita Airport (Tokyo), loaded our equipment directly on a train, and were playing a show in downtown Tokyo within 45 minutes of first setting foot in Japan. That was wild.

I remember being surprised at how expensive shows were to get into, probably about triple our ticket prices. The other thing that really stood out was the bands that were our "local openers." In America, sometimes it seems like there are as many bands as there are people. Most of them are awful—bands that just go out and try to sound like what their favorite bands sound like, and don't do it very well. There are just as many independent bands and artists in Japan, but they weren't messing around. Every band I saw there was amazing. I don't know what it was, maybe they just all practiced more or were in general just more original. All the indie rock clubs there all have house amps and kits! Makes touring a ton easier. Jet lag didn't really affect us until we got back after being there for three weeks. We were out of commission for days!

ROB KLEINER

TUB RING

KEYBOARDIST
TUB RING

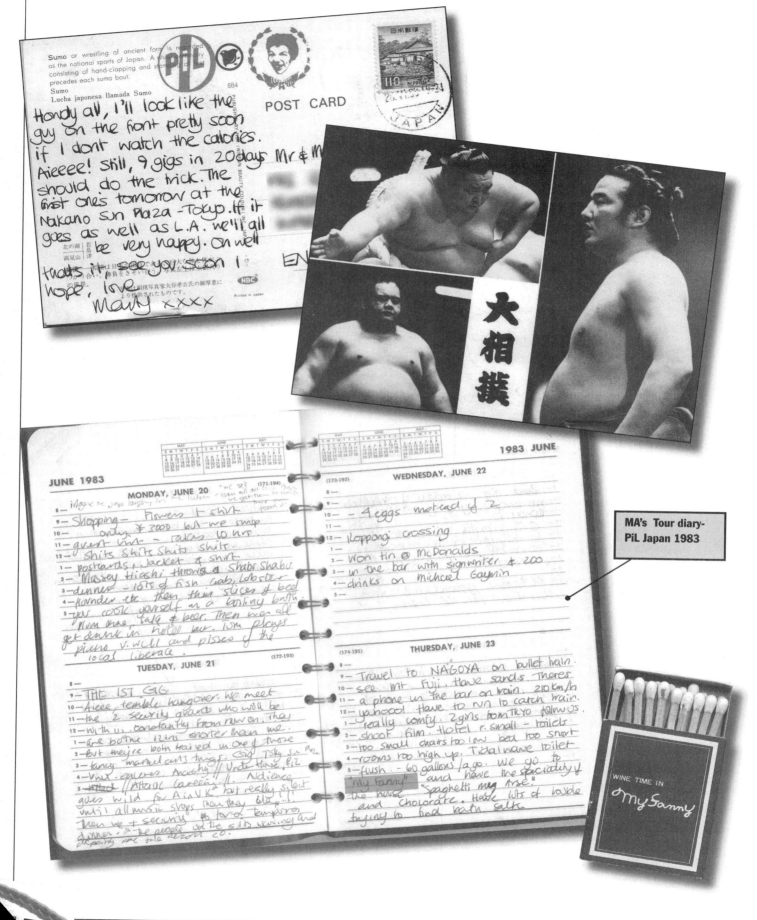

Sumo or wrestling of ancient form is regarded as the national sports of Japan. A ritual ceremony consisting of hand-clapping and stamping precedes each sumo bout.
Sumo
Lucha japonesa llamada Sumo

PiL
884

POST CARD

Howdy all, I'll look like the guy on the front pretty soon if I dont watch the calories. Aieeee! Still, 9 gigs in 20 days should do the trick. The first one's tomorrow at the Nakano Sun Plaza - Tokyo. If it goes as well as L.A. we'll all be very happy. Oh well thats it see you soon I hope, love Mary xxx

NBC
Printed in Japan

大相撲

1983 JUNE

JUNE 1983

MONDAY, JUNE 20 (171-194)
imagine the guys laughing in Rd Tutain 'we all then we'll all then we get hom to north
8—
9— Shopping — flowers + shirt
10— only ¥ 3000 but we swap
11— great bin — radios 10 hrs.
12— shits shits shits.
1— postcards + jacket + shirt
2— Massey Hiashi throw & Shabr Shabu
3— dinner — lots of fish crab, lobster
4— flounder etc then thin slices of beef
5— you cook yourself in a boiling broth. Num num, safe & beer. Then we all get drunk in hotel bar. Tim plays piano v. well and pisses off the local liberace.

TUESDAY, JUNE 21 (172-193)
8—
9— THE 1ST GIG.
10— Aieee, terrible hangover. We meet
11— the 2 security guards who will be
12— with us constantly from now on. They
1— are both 12 ins shorter than me.
2— but they're both trained in one of those
3— fancy marketl arts things. Gig Tsky se Plaza
4— Vinx. gauves machy // Unde time, PiL goes wild for A in VK but really silent until all music stops then they blip.!! Then we + security + taro tempura dinner. "the people at the record co.

WEDNESDAY, JUNE 22 (173-192)
8—
10— — 4 eggs instead of 2
11—
12— Roppongi crossing
1—
2— Won tin @ McDonalds
3— in the bar with signwriter & 200
4— drinks on michael Gaymin
5—

THURSDAY, JUNE 23 (174-191)
8—
9— Travel to NAGOYA on bullet train.
10— see Mt Fuji. Have sand-s. Theres
11— a phone in the bar on train. 210 km/h
12— yahooo! have to run to catch train.
1— really comfy. 2 gins from Tokyo follow us.
2— shoot film. Hotel r. small — toilets
3— too small, chairs too low, bed too short
4— rooms too high up. Tidal wave toilet
5— flush. — 60 gallons / ago. We go to "My tanny" and have the speciality of the house "spaghetti my arse." and chocorate. Have lots of trouble trying to find bath salts.

MA's Tour diary-
PiL Japan 1983

WINE TIME IN
my tanny

CHAPTER 50

CHINA

I am here to immerse myself in the music. The west is interested in China because they are excited to sell cigarettes, televisions and cars to Chinese people. (The car is our friend!) The record label executives are excited because they are interested in selling western music to a larger audience. the majority of the Chinese CD-buying public will be bombarded with George Michael, The White Stripes, and anything that the major labels want to SELL MORE OF or CAN'T SELL ANYWHERE ELSE. The question from the majors on a recent trip was, "Do you have someone who can translate these Madonna Lyrics?" The internal Chinese scene will be marginalized and suffer the same consequences that American musicians did in the late 60s; the arrival of the Beatles created THE BRITISH INVASION, no one, was interested in American bands for a decade!

THIS TIME IT WILL BE THE AMERICAN INVASION... and, that's the last thing anyone needs is more of that! I'm already seeing competitions from U.S. based companies for bands to submit (through Sonic Bids) to win the opportunity to perform at the Midi Festival (all expenses paid) so, one less slot for a Chinese band for now, until these bands go back to the States and tell all of their friends.

Anyway, what was it like? China was great—I had forgotten about the power of music in my life... put it this way, it made me smile inside and out. The experience is a real high for me—I mean HIGH! Everything that wankers say about music is actually true—you know when Stevie Wonder and Paul McCartney really get it on—it turns the idea of music into a bad hallmark card—but, the fact is—music is the most powerful thing—the chemistry and vibe that comes along with it is healing, joining, enlightening, compassionate and joyful—and transcends all boundaries... on a good day, music is the biggest best fighter on the block—choosing to help everyone with their struggles—not push them down the stairs... not a bunch of flowers in a vase—a seed in your heart...

"Russia is Russia - old hat. My new thing is China."

—Maureen Baker

GENERAL INFORMATION

BEIJING

Population: 14 million

Main Language: Mandarin Chinese

The flight to China is 18 hours and costs from $800 to $1,400 depending on the airline and the amount of time you leave yourself to book it. You can stop off in Tokyo, if you'd like, for a small fee.

Visas are easy to get, cost $60, and take a week or so to purchase. (Note: your passport must be valid for 6 months after you finish traveling.)

Beijing is 14 hours ahead of US central time (Chicago) and 8 hours ahead of London.

The exchange rate is $1 U.S. = 7.8 RMB Yuan Renminbi, called 'Kwai.'

A Starbucks coffee costs about the same as it does in the U.S. I guess they figured out that the only people buying it would be Westerners—good call. I had a moment where I was like FUUUUUCK the Americans have spoiled another part of the planet—then I looked around and jumped in for a double shot to the head! There are plenty of things to make the nervous comfortable—or jittery—7-11, Subway, and of course do you even have to ask? McDonalds, KFC etc.

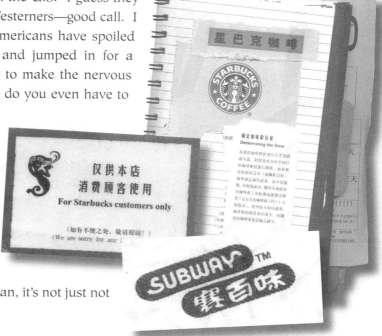

I saw 'boiled Coca-Cola with lemon and ginger' on a menu—I ordered it, because I couldn't work out what it might be. Well, it was boiled Coca-Cola with lemon and ginger! I felt kind of cheated... I wanted to be surprised or disappointed, not completely unable to complain! Seems like the perfect drink to put on the menu at a café in Paris so the waiters can ambush unsuspecting American tourists. "yes, excuse me waiter... garcon, my Coca-Cola is hot! I mean, it's not just not cold, it's HOT!"

HOTELS

The hotels are whatever you want them to be, from about $30 up. I was accidentally in a really nice hotel—one of the cheaper five-star hotels that had HBO and CNN... so, it's great to know that wherever you are in the world you can keep up-to the minute with the stupidity that is Washington DC.

PEOPLE

With the Westerners in Beijing there is the romantic idea of "re-inventing yourself"—as a few have done. There also seems to be some people who have completely fabricated a new person from nothing—so be careful if you are here doing any kind of business.

I met with labels, managers, magazine publishers, promoters, bands, educators, and others—much of what I saw and did has prompted more thought, investigation, and questions. I'm still wondering what defines Chinese entrepreneurial activity, what fuels it and what constrains it... not just physically or economically but psychologically and culturally too. The last few months back in the US we have done the things we said we would (and more) and the people who talked shit and promised other things haven't delivered anything (and worse). Maybe what was needed was time? It was difficult to see that when I was there—it is my nature to push—push—struggle. Sometimes, it's best to wait and let time do its job.

> **"The Americans have spoiled another part of the planet."**

> "There are just a lot of sketchy foreigners promising bands all sorts of things. I'm getting the feeling a lot of people have been burned before (by both foreign and local people) and are just generally nervous now. The bands don't get paid anything from the labels here, they just get 100 or so CDs to sell and that's it." - **Lindsay Tipping**

BUSINESS CARDS

Business cards are really important over there, a whole culture unto themselves. Know the little details (like how to ensure you don't make people lose face, how to hold your business card when you hand it to someone.

A QUICK CHINESE LESSON

Ni hao - Hello (pronounced "knee how")

Ni hao ma? - How are you?

Hen hao - Very good (Answer to ni hao ma?)

Zai jian - Goodbye (Hard z sound like -ds in beds, ai sounds like i in hi, jian like gee-N)

Xie Xie - Thank you (she-yeah, she-yeah)

POLLUTION

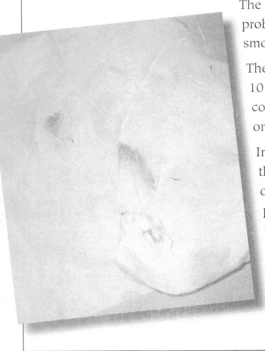

The pollution is overwhelming, especially if you have any kind of respiratory problem. It can trigger an asthma attack. Someone told me it's better to actually smoke—at least then you have a filter in your mouth for some part of the day!

There is a lot of smog in the air—I blew my nose and look what came out—and 10 weeks later there was still crap coming out of it. It was worse than a California coke binge (or at least what I imagine one of those might be like if I have ever had one, which I haven't and I haven't ever heard of a turbo-grinder either, OK?).

In the weeks leading up to the Olympics (which start on 08/08/2008 at 8 o'clock), the government will be closing down much of the industry within many miles of Beijing—but they are having difficulty controlling pollution from neighboring provinces who aren't going to see any of the benefits. The government controls the weather—not in the sci-fi way you might think—but they say that two-thirds of the days they have blue skies. That wasn't my experience—this is the one part of the world a proud parent can tell their children "look directly at the sun boys!" because you can't see it. It's like the showering bodies through the frosted glass at Crunch-much is left to the imagination.

As far as temperature is concerned—that's on the government too. If the temperature goes above or below a certain level then it's too cold or hot for people to work... so, errrrrrr, it doesn't. Get it?

They have electrically assisted bikes that re-charge each night, but the government has said that the batteries they use pollute the environment, so everyone should get a car (and a television and a refrigerator)! But meanwhile, keep on shoveling that dirty coal. There are 5% of all the world's cars there and 15% of the accidents, BICYCLES RULE!

I look at the video, its very interesting, Tristan does a great job of edit.t.t.t.ti/i/i/iNNNGGG some of the China footage—except that the coolest of computer visual effects is beaten hands down by the simple footage of a guy in China on a bike! Pretty cool. I love that guy. Where is he going? Where has he been?

WHY I WENT TO CHINA

It wasn't easy just to get on a plane from the US to China and be away from my family. In the past, I have packed up suitcases, moved to the U.S., and jumped on a plane back to the U.K. to join Killing Joke. So, I'm not new to risk but, SHIT, it was a LEAP. It's easy to look back on it and say, "Well, there's Starbucks and CNN," and the new documentary, but I didn't know that going in... I remember at one point I was just thinking that I'd get to see the Wall and maybe find a great hook up for cheap shirts!

See the *Tour Diaries* Chapter for more on Martin's trip to China.

XI
CHEN

SNAPLINE
BEIJING

XI FROM SNAPLINE, CHINA

1. Immigration issues: how hard is it to legally enter China to play for-profit shows as a touring band? What restrictions are placed on the songs you can play once you're there?

It's not very hard to bring a band to China for a tour. It's a very official thing to submit the lyrics and demos to the government before the gigs, especially the big shows (TV shows, or in a stadium of thousands of people). But I think you can skip this if you put the performances in small bars, such as D-22. Of course you better not freak the audience out.

2. Distribution: if you are going to go play shows in China, is there any realistic opportunity to get your CDs on sale there in order to capitalize on your Herculean touring efforts?

Of course it's a big effort to put the CDs on sale when touring. Sometimes we were asked whether we had CDs in the shop after gigs. But maybe the effort may not be that big: the touring indie bands can only perform in small venues and the audiences are not big. There will be less people who want to buy CDs after a gig. I think it depends on marketing methods (and also on whether the band is famous enough.)

3. Geography: how close together are cities in China? Is it feasible to go to China, get a van, and drive from show to show, or will they be 2,000 miles apart across rice fields and mountains and great walls? (Is it even possible for someone with a U.S. driver's license to rent a van in China?)

Big cities in China are not close. For instance, it takes 1-1/2 hours to fly from Beijing to Shanghai, 2-1/2 hours from Beijing to Guangzhou. By train, it's 12 hours from Beijing to Shanghai. We do have highways which connect the main cities, but if you want to tour to the west main land, there'll be lots of mountains... And, not all the big cities have good audiences. Actually we don't have a highway culture in China. It's possible to rent a van with an American driver's license in China, but you need a translated form from some certificated translation agency and to pass a stupid paper test from the traffic department.

4. Press and Publicity: is there college radio in China? Are there underground magazines, weekly music rags like The Reader and The Village Voice? Are there any alternative channels for advertising? Are there independent record stores in China?

We have radio broadcasts in college, but it seems nobody listens. There are some great programs in my university. For advertising, we have a most popular Chinese music channel, and another half English channel—CRI (China Radio International) (or CIR?? I don't remember). I always listened to this channel when I had a rented car. And I don't think there are any independent record stores here but there are many small stores which sell contraband CDs never published in China...

C·H·A·P·T·E·R ···· 50

IMMIGRATION: CROSSING THE LINE

"Do not screw around at border crossings. Have your paperwork in order. Never be under the influence at the border, never be disrespectful to either of the officer types (immigration and customs), never have drugs you're sneaking in or out, too many hassles can ensue, especially nowadays."

— Mark O'Shea — TM for NIN)

EQUIPMENT

If you're traveling to another country without bothering to get a work permit, any equipment you are carrying with you will be a sign post to problems, and you don't want to have a problem with an immigration or customs official. Use good judgment when thinking about work permits and talk with the promoter or agent from the country you're traveling to. They will have more experience with their country's laws and requirements.

If international travel is on your radar, then next time you have all your equipment out at rehearsals put together an Excel sheet (or just a list) with the:

Make
Model
Serial number
Country of Origin
Estimated replacement value

File the list away, you'll be glad you did. This is also a good thing to pass along to your insurance agent. Some countries will require a carnet or bond as evidence that you are not planning to import or export equipment. You pay the bond, fill out the paper work (make sure you get it stamped upon entering on the country, and just as importantly get it stamped as you leave the country as this is the proof you didn't sell any of it while you were there) and then you have the proof you need to file with your carnet agent for refund of your bond.

Be aware of size and weight restrictions with commercial airlines. It's not just a matter of the bigger the case, the more you pay. Over a certain limit a case has to go air cargo and could be delayed for several days. This can vary from airline to airline and country to country, so check.

MERCHANDISE AND OTHER GOODS

Some countries are more stringent about textiles then they are about anything else. Canada is a prickly place with this. Canadian dates are usually routed with one, two, or three border crossings. If you're beginning a tour with a large supply of merchandise you will be required to pay taxes on that merchandise as if you were importing all of it into Canada. Most bands leave merchandise in a hotel room on the US side of the border and pick it up upon re-entry. You can also deal with the problem by ground shipping merch into Canada, having your merchandise person meet you at the next show (rent a van). There's many ways to deal with this problem. However, the first part of it is knowing that there is going to be a problem.

Whatever you do, don't try smuggling merchandise into another country. Once pissed off, a customs or immigration official can decide to confiscate everything (including your equipment) and deny you entry to that country. The next time you try to travel to that country, the landing card will ask you, "have you ever been denied entry to this country before?" So, as I said somewhere else in the book—be careful. These decisions have consequences that can have a massive effect on your career.

So, you might think it's terrifically cool to shoplift, drive while you're drunk, spliff up or get into the kinds of trouble that Axl Rose or other pop stars get into, but the difference is that they can pay an immigration lawyer to make sure they get in and out of whichever country they choose. You can't. Don't underestimate the role of your criminal record. In terms of opening doors, it might be just as important as your debut album. I've recently come across artists who reside in the U.S. or Canada and are only achieving success in Europe. Imagine if you weren't able to travel to that *one* country in the world that loves you like France loves Jerry Lewis and Germany loves David Hasselhoff?... You'd be completely unplugged from all of that culture.

IF YOU ARE EVER LUCKY ENOUGH TO BE ASKED TO PLAY SOMEWHERE OUTSIDE OF THE COUNTRY:

MAUREEN BAKER, TRAFFIC CONTROL

I met Maureen over 20 years ago. She was working with Bob Tulipan, helping with the management of PiL, and shooting rolls and rolls of photographs. Our paths crossed again when we needed immigration help. Traffic Control became our go-to resource for any immigration issues and it's awesome that she's laying some advice on us all.

USA:

Immigration has been taken over by homeland security. There were a lot of changes made at the end of Clinton's era that were not enacted until Bush was in office. People think all the changes had to do with the 9/11 crisis.

There are two ways to file for Visas and we ask that people give as much time as possible for either process. A slow process takes anywhere from 3-6 months depending on which immigration office you use to file, but costs only $190 per petition.

Either way, if immigration has any questions about a petition, they will send a Request for Evidence. If they send a R.F.E. to you, their clock goes back an additional 15 days with premium processing or an additional 3-6 months for slow processing. If they send you an R.F.E. for a slow process case, you almost always have to pay the premium processing fee of an additional $1,000 to get the petitions processed in time even if you filed 6 months early. (You cannot file more than 6 months in advance of intended entry.)

Band and crew have to go on a separate petition because unions, having jurisdiction over the type of employment taking place, need to see what foreign workers are coming into the USA. The unions must provide a letter of advisory opinion as to whether or not they are taking work from union workers. This was one part of the new immigration law Clinton left us. However, a negative union letter will not mean a petition will be denied.

Immigration has categories for various people in the art and entertainment industry, but they do not have a category for a band or artist just starting out. It is quite different to obtain a visa for a "baby" band or artist because of this.

To apply for a band or artist, you must provide the artist's extraordinary merits and abilities or the band's outstanding merits and abilities. To do this, you must provide press and publicity attesting to said merits and abilities. If there is not enough press, you must provide letters from "experts" in the field stating that they're outstanding (in the case of a band) or extraordinary (in the case of a solo artist).

Press is an issue because the entertainment business tends to dwell on a band or artist's life outside of their musical abilities. Unfortunately, bands and artists do not always know when to shut up. The press can harp on drug use, alcohol abuse, or other issues that can be considered "issues of moral ineptitude" (a very broad matter)! Basically, if an immigration officer thinks an alien worker could cause problems for the American public, they can deny the visa petition. We prefer press that talks about musical abilities as opposed to the amount of drugs they can consume or the amount of alcohol they drown themselves in on a daily basis.

Other than the petition filing fee, you must pay the unions for their letters of opinion. Those fees range from $50 to $350 depending on the union and how quickly you want the letter.

> **"We prefer press that talks about musical abilities as opposed to the amount of drugs they can consume or the amount of alcohol they drown themselves in on a daily basis."**

MARGOT OLAVARRIA

THE GO-GOS
BRIAN BRAIN

GEOFF SMYTH

GUITARIST
BRIAN BRAIN

DETAINED FOR NO REASON

MARGOT OLAVARRIA ON IMMIGRATION

These are dangerous and intolerant times.

Stay Safe: In this post 9/11 time of increased violence and human rights abuses along the border, this is a special note to musicians of color. Unfortunately, racial profiling is inevitable and you may find yourself getting singled out by Border Patrol and detained for no reason. This, incredibly enough, is what happened to me while we were driving out of El Paso, Texas. Two very piggish border cops pulled us over and assumed that a British punk rock band was smuggling in a Mexican chula. They would not accept my California driver's license, the only I.D. I had, as proof that I was in the country legally. I argued that I was within the U.S. and that I was not required to carry my passport but they would not listen and detained me in a bungalow for hours, interrogating me on U.S. history and civics while the band and crew waited nervously outside fearing their bass player would be deported. May this not happen to you, my Black or Brown brothers and sisters. Carry your proof of legal residency or citizenship even if you do not plan to leave the country.

BRITISH PUNKS BORDER PATROL BROU HA HA

GEOFF SMYTH ON IMMIGRATION

Margot was wearing a very strange outfit concocted from thrift store purchases. Many layers, as I recall, to protect against an unexpected chill. Ironically she was the only American citizen aboard, but they were convinced she was a wetback and quizzed her on past presidents etc. The immigration man also quizzed me on my green card, saying the code numbers indicated that I received it because of my parents. I told them that was impossible because they were Scottish. I had received it because I married Margot, a US citizen. Then Martin piped up "Well, technically Geoff did receive it because of his parents. If it wasn't for them he wouldn't be here…" He was promptly ordered to leave the office, and thus avoided some tricky questions about his own rather dubious immigration status. Pretty clever.

> **"Carry your proof of legal residency or citizenship even if you do not plan to leave the country."**

IMMIGRATION
GARY TOPP

GARY TOPP

SNOW-SHOVELING, CONCERT PROMOTING, FILM DISTRIBUTING CANADIAN FROM TORONTO

www.myspace.com/garytopp

Immigration procedure coming into Canada is painless. I mean, all the promoter has to do is complete a pretty innocuous application to work in our country, supply contracts, and 1, 2, 3, the artist is granted approval. Upon crossing the border, work visas are granted and the show goes on. Clean, no hitches. Usually...

The other day I was talking to Arthur Brown. Remember him? The greatest psychedelic musician ever, the God of Hell Fire, The Crazy World Of, etc. the first guy to replace a drummer with a machine, a true artist, ahead of his time, one hit ('Fire'), he lived in Texas during the late '70s and early '80s. I'm bringing him over from the U.K. for three shows in Toronto and area. He sent me his details, I did the work, he got his approval. I have a friend in New York who was trying to string some gigs together while Arthur was over. Arthur was bemoaning the fact that immigration into Bush country was so ridiculously difficult. They wanted original press clippings in order to prove Arthur was legit. Arthur wasn't prepared to give them up, they were his only copies, he'd never get them back. Homeland security working overtime.

I've never had problems getting anyone into the country, Not Johnny Thunders who had a suitcase fill of no-no's, not Alex Chilton who was charged with alcoholic mischief when he was a teenager, not Hugh Cornwell of The Stranglers who also had been a bad boy. Not once. Well, once. When Eurythmics were crossing into Canada at Detroit, one of the roadies got popped doing some illegal drug snorting in a toilet stall at the US border. What a dumb fuck, we lost all our expenses on a sold-out show. But they returned, played a bigger venue and I watched Annie Lennox jack around a 10 year-old girl/fan who waited backstage with her dad for well over an hour after the show, way past her bedtime, for an autograph. Annie walked by her twice, told me to tell her dad to wait, joined some friends in the dressing room for a long drink, and finally signed the program. There's a lesson in manners there.

> **"They wanted original press clippings in order to prove Arthur was legit."**

THE MINISTRY TOUR:
JOLLY ROGER

JR: Sometimes you just have to say the tour is over. I said "I've got 160 grand of yours and we're all goin' home!" We're not gonna be out here... dealing with this stuff. We came through the border and I walked into the back of the bus and there were fresh syringes in the garbage can and we drove from there straight to New York City and I said we were goin' home. They quit that day and, you know, they'd go out front and they'd sing their song, and they'd go crawl in the back and puke in a garbage can until their next cue.

See Martin's excerpt from his Ministry tour diary.

> **"... I walked into the back of the bus and there were fresh syringes in the garbage can..."**

THE PAUL MCCARTNEY CLAUSE - MISTAKE TO AVOID

From: *stopthedrugwar.org*:

January 16, 1980: Paul McCartney is arrested by Japanese customs officials at Tokyo International Airport when they find two plastic bags in his suitcases containing 219 grams of marijuana (approximately 7.7 ounces). Concerned that McCartney would be refused a U.S. visa under immigration laws if convicted and be unable to perform in an upcoming Wings concert in the U.S., Sen. Edward Kennedy calls first secretary of the British Embassy D.W.F. Warren-Knott on January 19. McCartney is released and deported on January 25.

His arrest was a disaster for the former Beatle, It led to the breakup of his band Wings and cost him one million pounds in compensation to the group's Japanese tour organizer. "I was thrown into nine days of turmoil in that Japanese jail," McCartney recalled in a new documentary about Wings. "I don't know what possessed me to just stick this bloody great bag of grass in my suitcase. Thinking back on it, it almost makes me shudder."

:SMART TIPS

- **Never be disrespectful to an immigration officer.** They will use their power to mess you up.

- **Do not ever carry drugs of any kind across a border** unless you have a prescription and your name is on the bottle. You are putting your career and your band on the line. Not all of us are Sir Paul McCartney. They named a clause in all Japanese performance contracts after him!

- **Do not screw around at border crossings.** Have your paperwork in order.

- **Never be under the influence at the border.**

- **Do not ask Paul McCartney to play bass in your band.**

- **Be careful when assembling a press kit for immigration purposes.**

On the highway that runs from San Diego through Texas, even though you are well within the U.S. border...there is an immigration check point...BE CAREFUL, we stumbled across it drunk and more...

1982
Photo by Lisa Haun,
New York, NY

CHAPTER···· 52

MEMORABILIA

...ould be, I think.

What I've been doing with the new PIL album is ... I've done thre tracks, co-writen with John and Keith, but it's not drums. One trac I've got a Mickey Mouse watch I g from Disneyland, we put it on a floor tom-tom to get the resonance . liked it up, harmonised it in six different ways, mixed em all together ..I played drums to the clean recording of the watch, whic was in perfect time, then we lost th clean recording, mixed the drums in with the other watches, recorde some backwards trumpet .. I got a trumpet what when you blow into it, it plays a little disc; a recording of a trumpet. Backwards piano, fi extinguisher, aerosol sprays! I do

MEMORABILIA

It's great not to be dead. If you manage to avoid the burnout, freak-out, or bailout, ten, twenty, thirty years or more into your career, you can become the curator of your own museum of collectable crap. For some reason, despite a move to the States, a few years in Manhattan, Los Angeles, New Jersey, three different locations in Chicago, a move back to England, and then a move back to Chicago, I still have a ridiculous, somewhat frightening, amount of memorabilia: photographs, passes, ticket stubs, handwritten lyrics, buttons, t-shirts, scenery, the Mickey Mouse watch and the plastic trumpet I used on the *Flowers of Romance* album, a hat I wore in Prague while I was there with Killing Joke, diaries... How crazy is this: a receipt signed by John Lydon for an exercise bike in 1984!

> "...become the curator of your own museum of collectables."

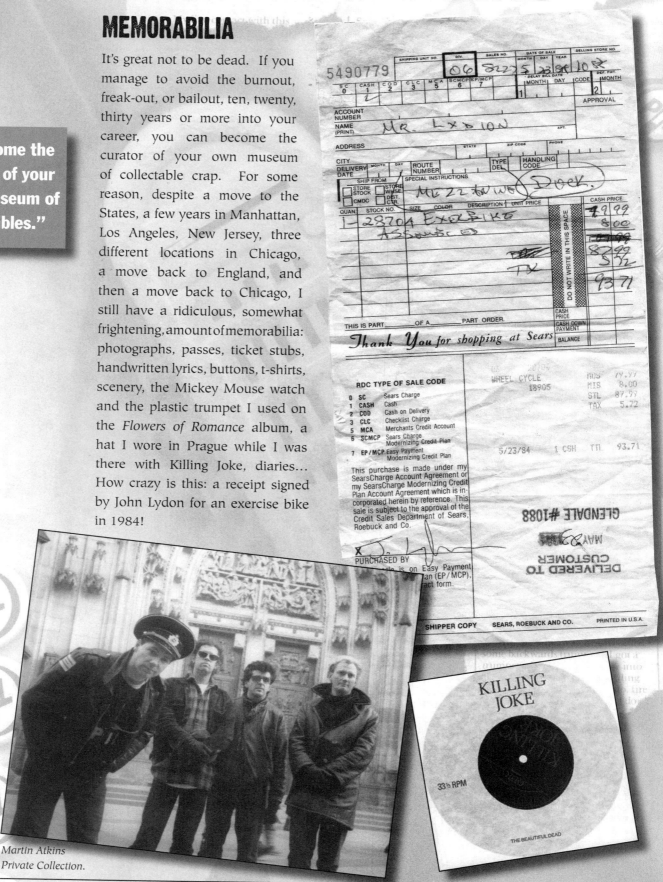

Martin Atkins
Private Collection.

It's hard to define the role of memorabilia. Some people collect it just to have it, a step beyond owning the obscure live bootleg or the re-mastered album on heavy weight German vinyl. For me, the combined little bits and pieces serve as memory flash cards to put me back in a place in time. In its coolest form, putting somebody else into that room, that head space, that creative atmosphere from which all of the ripples, echoes, and aftershocks come. It's some of the tiny stuff that becomes huge. A receipt from the Hard Rock Café Tokyo shows three people at the table—me, John, and Larry White, or little moments from my Japan diary, mentioning a restaurant, a mix, a show.

If an artist can't chronicle their own path, not just with materials, but with the insights and stories that embroider and illuminate, then who can?

While staying at a hotel in Seattle (I think it was the Edgewater Inn), I heard that The Beatles had stayed there. The promoter had bought all the carpets from the rooms, cut them up into one or two inch squares and sold them. When H-Gun Video left the 7th floor of a building we shared with them in Chicago (2024 S. Wabash), they left the cage from the 1991 Ministry tour. I put it in the hallway and kept it for several years. And then, tired of walking into it, catching my sweater on it, etc., I cut it up into 4" pieces, drilled a hole in one end and attached a laminated tag and gave a piece away to anyone who purchased a copy of the Ministry tribute album we released.

The *Extremities, Dirt, and Various Repressed Emotions* album I did with Killing Joke in 1986 is being reissued. I still have the scenery I made for the video shoot for the single "Money is Not our God," photographs, shirts, 7-inch flexi-discs, passes, buttons... It's not that any of these items are going to generate any money. But, they can generate interest and excitement. That's the currency we are all dealing with. These items will be part of a series of gallery shows I have coming up around the world. Don't just save stuff, write down your thoughts and save those, too. Keep a journal.

PiL Shower/Stamp/Detergent
Martin Atkins

PRESENTS

KILLING
JOKE
& LOUD

Tourleitung: Hammer Promotion GmbH, Frankfurt/M.
Örtliche Durchführung: Markthallen Betriebs-GmbH/Blindfish Prom

1034

21. Januar 1991
Einlaß: 20.00 Uhr • Beginn: 21.00 Uhr
HAMBURG • MARKTHALLE
Klosterwall 9-21

Vorverkauf: DM 21,- Abendkasse: DM 25,-
(zzgl. Vorverkaufsgebühr. (inkl. 7% MWSt.)
inkl. 7 % MWSt.)

The Religion of Marketing

NEWCASTLE BROWN ALE

1977-2007. 30 years of art, scenery, and memorabilia from Martin Atkins of PiL, Killing Joke, Pigface, and more.

C·H·A·P·T·E·R····53

TOUR DIARIES

MARTIN ATKINS' MINISTRY TOUR DIARY:

COMING ACROSS THE BORDER BACK INTO THE USA (JAN 8th or 9th, 1990)

"A very depressing experience: I am woken by all scurrying around; galvanized junkies methodically searching the bus for traces of each other's absentmindedness. I remember coming back to the PiL loft on 19th Street and 11th Ave. to see the holes in the blankets and sheets where Keith Levene had nodded. The noise of two vacuum cleaners wakes me up and trumpets their junkie fanfare. Al advises me to "Check my bunk for planted drugs" and something about a conspiracy. I am straight-edging and pretty pissed off at the suggestion that I should search my own bunk. Violation! Isn't it enough to have each city's uninvited junkie scum on our bus, in our home? Opening

> **"...the bleach mixed with the chemicals in the toilet to create a form of cyanide gas. Fantastic."**

the door to find a stranger playing a guitar—not getting nor wishing for an introduction. I couldn't even write down my feelings about it all until now—safely back across the border —in case the immigration officials read this! I feel trapped and upset. My friend Greg died last year. Keith was/is a junkie and this is all getting pushed back in my face. In Montréal, before we left, someone cleaned off all of the cooking spoons on the bus with bleach then flushed the toilet into the holding tank where the bleach mixed with the chemicals in the toilet to create a form of cyanide gas. Fantastic."

Wow, and we thought the golden rule was 'don't shit on the bus.'

DENVER

"Rick the driver freaks out, punches Jolly Roger proving he is certifiable, and then parks the bus across the entrance to the hotel and severs the fuel lines with a hunting knife. Then, he opens up all of the under-bus bays so that our belongings can be stolen. After the third punch, Jolly smacks him and he goes off to jail."

There is more...

> **Wow, and we thought the golden rule was 'don't shit on the bus.'**

MARK SPYBEY

Each day, a series of events. A succession of emotions. Rollercoaster? I spoke with Amy Gorman today, who is probably about as well known as anyone. Deservedly so. She reminded me about how emotional an experience it was. People actually wanted to work together. They actually did work together and pulled together. Laughed together. Became sick together. Recovered together. Musicians worry about such idiotic things. Idiotic. Trivial. Inane things. We're sitting in a diner in Arlington, VA, with my friends Nasty and Ralph. Elaine and I had arrived hours before the biggest thunderstorm I'd ever seen had tried to wash the Capital Ballroom fresh and clean. The show was unremarkable. Grilled cheese always tastes so much better in the USA.

DOCTORE

Please don't you laugh. Mother's son. Scott Walker repeated. Philadelphia. Doctor pays a visit. He examines swollen knees and head colds. Bruised and broken thumbs. Not exactly a clean bill of health. Most worrying is The Lady of Wright. He's looking green to the gills. We walk him back to a bus Stranded by zealot traffic cops. Flushed with bureaucratic pride.

We leave for a meal with Jarboe. A walk for coffee becomes a serialized adventure. Jarboe smiles and the air is punctuated with laughter. I say goodbye to James Plotkin. We exchange bear hugs.

IT IS MEAL TIME

Tacobox *(short haired Not Breathing)* and The Lady of Wright are curiously disgusted by my culinary expertise. Apparently peanut butter and salsa on rye is outlawed in Arizona. Illegal in Texas.

THEM CAMPBELL BOYS

Aaron and Kris Campbell with Driver Al come to see us In NYC. Aaron is the DVOA webmaster. I regret not being able to spend more time with them. Khan comes with Tetsou Innoue. Khan gives me a recent release of his, it's a 12 inch single, collecting bits of a riot recorded at a Black Sabbath show in Milwaukee, 1980.

B
E
A
U
T
Y

is a long ride across Utah.

DOUBLE----------TAKE
DOUBLE---------- TAKE

Golda Meyer dances with Charles Aznavour to the swing sounds of Jimmy Tenor. Charles enters into suicide pact with Golda, reluctantly.

NO

I am not Genesis.P.Orridge, nor have I ever been Genesis.P.Orridge. Despite the fact that you talked to me in Denver for like 20 minutes without realizing that I am not Genesis.P.Orridge. I am not he.

ORANJE TEST DEPARTMENT SCANDAL

I am curiously oranje. So is Martin Test and Gus Department. I gather we have some kind of loose affiliation with Dutch Protestants and Traffic Lights. I blame the very English affliction of reading the backs of cornflake packets at breakfast. Or wrapping chips in newspapers. Sportsnight with Coleman.

WRIGHT INVADES ROCHESTER HOSPITAL SHOCK

The good lady survived. He missed Tacobox, Elaine, and I walking the stone dead streets of Rochester, on a Saturday, searching for something to eat. All we could find were two exclusive restaurants, one with entrees starting at 27 bucks, the other with a "Imma sorree Senor, ah carn nurt pohsiblee gert urr a tabuhl untieel 9 ah clerk, "and a hotel with a dandy Ristorante. Kinda sucked Dave, where the hell were you? Sheesh. Ah jeah.

I spend the next few days pissing bright orange urine attached to a telephone with a lone voice saying, "Hi this is Scott at the Rochester Hotel South, how may I direct your call?" We were all worried, very worried.

The lady Wright awoke when we were in Detroit. I ran around the venue shouting at the crew, Mufti broke into a dance. I could smell the relief in Tacobox's voice.

WEAPONRY

Strange, but ironic how these venues supply you with salsa, beer, and children's toys from dollar stores. Three of life's essential requisites. Zaki and I spend a happy hour or two playing Power Rangers, shooting Qwak many times. Ambushing people. In Cleveland, Mufti pens the English into a stockade, resurrecting feelings inspired by that infamous English loss to Germany in Mexico City, 1970. Gerd Muller you bastard. Uwe Seeler, You little shite. Mufti patrols the pen with a sizeable flashlight and the look of man with a mission. He energetically eats cold chicken wings. In the middle of a Californian Walmart car park, we played soccer together. With obvious zeal, the Europeans outplayed their North American counterparts. Mufti is a midfield dynamo. Frazier, a pink haired tricky winger. Elaine toe hoofs. Tacobox besplendent in platform shoes scuff marked by Californian kick-abouts. He says that style comes first.

SLEEP SLEEP SLEEP GO TO SLEEP

Sleep, go to sleep, you are now in a deep sleep. This Heat should be mandatory listening. I grow weary of T shirts with the same slogans. Of knowing looks. Sinking boats in flame rivers. Youth should celebrate its infancy. Not seek to vent its churlish spleen on itself. I look at some of the people who I meet and think of the 17 year olds who were sent to Vietnam.

PRIDE

Besplendent. I'm not motivated by "that" much really. I'm very proud of my Galactus figure, given to me by the New York (and New Jersey) posse. The sword that Martin King gave to me in Pittsburgh. The orange clothes we proudly wear. Manchester United. The Cleveland Shouting Team. The callers in Salt Lake City. Montreal, Toronto, and Ottawa. Singing with Mufti.

Being with Jolly.

Meeting Freddie.

Harassing Josh.

Simple pleasures.

c. *spybey. 1998.*

DIRK FLANIGAN

Ok...way back when. 77 Luscious Babes was forming in the same building either upstairs or downstairs (can't remember) from Invisible on Wabash. It was the Gein Loft Inhabited by Matt Shultz and Eric Pounder, Oh shit, and Steve Silver. My mocking of Jello Biafra while Lard was rehearsing in the under construction Invisible space landed me a backing vocals on a song by Lard called "70's Rock Must Die." I met Martin Atkins and his cat Breakfast. I had met Raven at CRC down the street on Prairie rehearsing with 77. Martin told me a story about Raven and him dining at Raw Bar where I was the Cook. They were in the dining room and Raven was cutting his rare cooked tuna with spicy ponzu with a large steak knife, chewing, smacking with his mouth open, pointing in my direction with the same steak knife saying, "Martin, you know who we should take on tour?" and answering his own question, "That guy Dirk—he rocks. We should take Dirk on tour."

That was approximately two days before the second leg of the Fook tour, a 32-shows-in-30-days tour. The next day Martin called me and asked me to come down to Invisible. I arrived midday, 10 a.m. or so. Everyone was running around, packing gear, numbering cases, phones ringing. Martin and I, during our conversation, made a trip to the dryer where he was setting the ink on freshly screened t-shirts and I think some limited edition towels. He said, "Hey Dirk, do you want to come out on tour with Pigface?" I said, "To do what?" He: "Sing. Why, what else do you do?" The answer went something like this: "Uh whoa, yeah, yes, but there is one problem." Martin: "What's that?" Me: "I don't know any of the songs." Martin: "No problem!" We went into the old office and he handed me a proposed set list and three or four CDs and said "Learn what you can and be back here at noon." I stayed up all night and learned Auto Hag, Flowers, Murder Inc., Hips, Tits, 7 words, Satellite, Alles ist Mines (the Ground Zero Part), and parts of 10 ground. I learned the words to Weightless, but the timing still escapes me. I showed up at noon with lyrics written and enlarged them on the copier. I must have made 100 copies. I had them placed on every monitor, post, and speaker on stage. I was so nervous. I had never rehearsed with the band and we were on our way to the first of 32 shows. There were plants all over the stage; Martin was set up on stage left; the Fook twins hanging as the back drop; the ATG. Lab Report opened. Stick opened a show in Kansas City and after a fan took us to his Mediterranean restaurant across the street from the venue, we also recruited an additional cello player and had the tour bus pick her up in front of her house at like 3am on our way out of town. Roundhead, that was Barb's band, they opened in Cincinnati. 3 to the Head opened in Nashville after we had awesome sushi with Jolly Sushi in Nashville. That was the Exciting BJAM that started "Fuck it Up!" 3 to the Head came up with a groove. New Orleans, Alan Jeager, Harp Bitch and her boyfriend, a paper bag full of crawfish, two cases of Chimay... Martin obviously had some Hurricanes and some acid. Dean Ween had a bag of Mushrooms and Gooch was telling me the town and the stage time.

Washington, D.C., 9:30, Club in our Nation's Rat-infested Capital: We pulled up to the venue in broad daylight, rats all over the alley, all over the dumpster. Most of the Band is sick: Dean Ween, Andrew Weiss, Beef Cake from Gwar. Martin and I played the set. I was freaking. I knew about half the set! We pulled it off. I read something a few years ago and they were very vague like "a guy from Rollins band, a dude from Ween, Martin Atkins, and a guy with Long Red Hair and a ton of tattoos (me) fucking rocked, man, it fucking rocked!" En Esch may have been there.

Now time will get skewed if it hasn't already. Maybe the Notes Tour: Bagpipes start the show at Trocadero. About a third of the way through the set, Mary Byker and I set out on the Raft together. We were still in the air, about 200 feet from stage, the band fucking rocking, Bob Dog on a 15 foot riser, Martin has ice water flying off his drums, Trump is next to him, Levi being Levi, Tucker, the Kicker Bob Dogs' 55 gallon Drum is on Fire! Mary and I spoke after the show of what a rush it was to actually see Pigface in full effect, loud riffs, bangin' drums, tons of low, a lot of high! Fire, Water, Ice, Ink, Blood! Man, we were on! I almost passed out when we got back to the stage—it was such an adrenalin rush.

In Pittsburgh, at Electric Banana, a kid yelled out Cat Scratch Fever. Not a second later, En Ech kicks into the riff, Martin starts the beats, and Shultz shoves me out on stage. I sang. We played about three quarters of the song and it turned into something else. The crowd was laughing at the kid who made the suggestion. We were laughing. I think then Martin left the stage and En Ech got on the Drums and Suck ensued.

I lent Raven $75 on Miami Beach so he could buy Air Jordans. Surprisingly, he paid me back the very next day. Raven and I ate some cookies that were obviously laced with something. Then we ate Sushi! A lot of Sushi. My dad and sister came to the Miami show and tried to video it; I never saw the finished copy. My sister brought my mom to the Tampa show. Great moment: My Mom telling Marilyn Manson to be careful cutting himself and that he should use some ointment. Manson looks at me and whispers, "Dirk, please get your mom away from me. She's freaking me out."

Ogre and I had a three-hour conversation about the infectious hold music grabs us with and the inability of ever letting go of it. I swore I would never tell but I'm telling. I was dying my hair during the conversation. Ogre was helping—man, that guy is Evil. Pat Sprawl at the Fast Lane in Asbury Park, NJ, bowling with beer bottles. All I know is that Martin was not too happy about the situation. I was too busy spying on the crack house with binoculars from the bus, what a weird subculture. James Teitelbaum's in a bathroom with someone and his foot slips into the toilet. For the rest of the tour, Levi and I call him shitty foot. En Esch playing the first 30 seconds of the prodigy CD over and over and over. Martin suggesting that Tuesdays be quiet night on the bus... to no avail. That was a longer tour. Two months?

Hope and I collide on stage resulting in various injuries. A runner driving me to a Doctor for a cortisone shot... Results: vocals great, other results of all of the swelling in your body going away... a lot of unprotected injuries, results to this many phone calls for more muscle relaxers and pain killers to relieve the unbearable pain in my back and spine.

My Green Slicker (Rain!)
Tucker Peeking too early.
Theo Van Rock!
Fire Tribe. Ass light.
Sow.
Bellstarr
Air Freshener
Spray paint, hinges, screws, Martin's friends from England, "The Sex Pistols Fanatic"
Playing at Cains, the same stage as Elvis, Jerry Lee, Sex Pistols.
Phil.

HOB in the Dead of Winter: The Bus

#1 Hydraulics freeze: New bus

#2 called, never shows because we are underground, new bus

#3 shows with barely enough time to make it to the show, we repack everything onto the new bus and leave for Detroit. We got to about Wells or LaSalle, about six blocks away from HOB. Jared buys two bottles of Vodka, Genesis insists, "the Spirits don't want us to go to Detroit." A huge number of Phone calls between Martin, Me, Baker's voice mail! (Christmas shopping, his phone was off). Doors Open in Detroit I receive the phone call, grab all the gear, grab cabs, and Meet David Baker at Midway! Someone had no ID, but had a ticket Maybe Levi? We pulled a grift, yes ma'am that's all of the IDs, oh I'm sorry, here's mine, how silly of me. The Remainder of Pigface arrive at the Detroit Airport, a van arrives for the gear, and a fucking Limo—are you fucking kidding a Limo—with Food! Wine! Beer! Awesome! Nice one man.

I looked at my phone when we got off stage. We had been in Detroit for three and a half hours, two hours and forty-five minutes of that time was spent on stage!! I think the tour note from Jolly was something like, "Way to persevere guys, awesome show." I am sure there is more...

Oh, Jolly forgetting to wake me in London. I get a call in my hotel, the darkest room ever! Jolly on the other end, "We forgot to wake you… Send a car…traffic is fucked! You will never make it for the show. Go to the lobby get a cab, go to the train station!" A car and two trains later, I arrive at Clapham Junction just before doors and with a skeleton crew. We rocked the shit out of the set. I think we have a recording to prove it! Redneck, White Trash, Blue Movie. Our tour bus going off road on Easter Morning '02 or '03 Zeromancer, Bile, Pigface, very emotional because we could have died. Same event: Jolly Roger's in the air, flying at me, yelling off-road again, I could have died and cheated death twice in one morning on Easter!? Again, I think there is more…

MARTIN ATKINS' CHINA DIARY:

THE STUDIO

I'd had a bad day with my assistant Lindsay the day before. No directions to any of the appointments we had, really doing my head in. So, I really gave her the third degree about the studio—and she assured me everything was set.

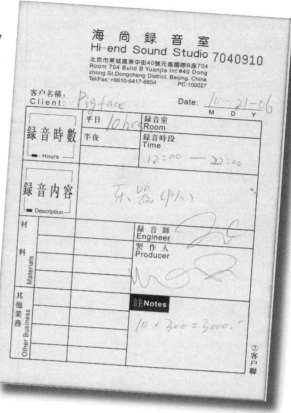

The studio was $300 per day (10 hours only) but we needed to rent drums and amps—a significant addition and of course a moving company to bring these items across town. They had nice Neve and API pre amps, pro tools set up, nice and roomy control room and reception area. The live room was described as being '12 orchestra members big.' Jovi, the engineer, and all the staff were very cool and everyone made a special effort. Shao Feng was on site most of the time with 303 at the ready to help. I get a little pissy when it turns out there aren't any cymbals! I ask Lindsay if she remembered to specify that we need oxygen.

It's difficult to stop my head from blowing off... stress sandwich??

Argument with Lindsay

On the way to the studio (and of course we are late and she doesn't have directions) Lindsay is filling the air with questions about me signing a band that she manages, and comments like "where are the hookers and the blow," like she has never been in a studio before in her life... because, well, she HASN'T! I inform Lindsay that if she mentions them ONE MORE TIME I will throw her out of the car. This is a great scene on the documentary.

The scene is set for a horrible day—so that when the ancient drummers show up - and turn out to be three young girls who play in the local orchestra—I have the length of a breath to understand what has happened (Lindsay fucked up! Mourn the loss of my drumming day in the studio where I magically re-connect with these drummers, myself at the age of 15) and SMILE—because all of this is GREAT! WELCOME!!!

This begins a new musical direction, the turntablists come in and spark.

There are so many surprises to overcome—so many unknowns. But all of this turns out to be not important anyway—the results are priceless.

Maybe that's a point to bring up to some of the audio/production classes I want to teach...yes, there's a great snare drum sound... now, lets do it upside down, jet lagged, stressed out on acid, on the moon and in a different language with the landlord knocking at the door and every time the phone rings it's not cool... it's someone wanting money—OK, NOW let's be creative. Oh yeah, here's a tissue and the number of the nearest International House Of Pancakes. Produce me an omelet motherfuuuuckerrrrrrrr, beat those eggs!

THE GREAT WALL

A gorgeous day for the wall... Writing a couple of postcards and thinking "I need to do more of that."

As TooKoo would say:

"Hold up your emotional faintness
Carry on and your desire
Plug me in and listen to my sad
Share my sorrow"

Exactly... Back to work.

It turned out there was a KFC there AND a fucking slalom ride down the hill for the youngsters, and those in need of entertainment... so all of the time I'm trying to meditate and write postcards and I'm thinking this and listening to some Italian tourists sing Ramones covers punctuated by the screams of the go kart thrill seekers hurling down the mountain.

THE BANDS AT D-22

"We opened D-22 on May 1, and we are doing this to really help improve/encourage and promote the music scene here in Beijing and China. We all have day jobs and are definitely not doing this for the money."
    - Charles Saliba from D-22

Drove straight to D-22, met Michael Pettis and Mark Addis, the soundman, very helpful, very nice, and accommodating. A strange good feeling to be home many thousand miles away from it, unless home is a feeling. This place and these people feel comfortable to me.

Michael told me about how he has told a bunch of bands to call the club their home, what a great idea—a community—their vision and vibe has fuelled a very interesting scene— (go to *www.myspace.com/chinamusicnetwork* to listen to some of the bands)

GENERAL BAND SOUNDS, ETC.

Saw and recorded: Hou Hai Sharks, Car Sick Cars, PK 14, Joyside, Hang On The Box, Honey Gun, Ruins, Caffe-In, Subs, Demerit, PK14, The Scoff, Tookoo, Snapline, Caffe-In... oh, you mean Caffeine? No, Caffe In

All great bands—different and great—from the Cilla Black-ness poppy-ness of Hou Hai Sharks to the frilly shirt drunken charismatic front-man of Joyside to the more measured early eighties vibe of PK14, the guitar twang of Car Sick Cars, and then the very ambitious collisions of Hang On The Box... I had expected a more all girl punk pop outfit—but the songs from the 3 piece were well crafted. With instrumentation ranging from pedal organ to ratchets and noise boxes: a nightmare for the soundman who handled it all with amazing humor and craft. Snapline—a three piece with a drum machine—I'd forgotten about drum machines... awesome— the girl that played drums with Car Sick Cars is playing guitar and I rub my eyes like I'm hallucinating or something. After one band pulls off the best western (no pun intended) band impression of the day - arguing for 20 minutes, not being happy with the monitors until, well, we'll never know because they spent so much time trying to get perfection that they ran out of time and indulgence from me, the club and anyone else that was still around— Demerit took the stage and 1-2-3-4'd straight into 12 songs in a row. I stood by the stage and filmed all of it then offered them a chance to join me in the recording studio and record a great album... which, made out of respect for their attitude more than a label affiliation with their punk sound - only reinforced an idea that I was there to sign EVERYTHING! What fucking long, long days —still horribly jet lagged. Did I even eat? Since arrival? I'd get back to the hotel and re-boot the computer and start to archive some of the live recordings and mix a couple of tracks. Oh yeah, jet lagged. Chinese jet lag is the worst of the species!

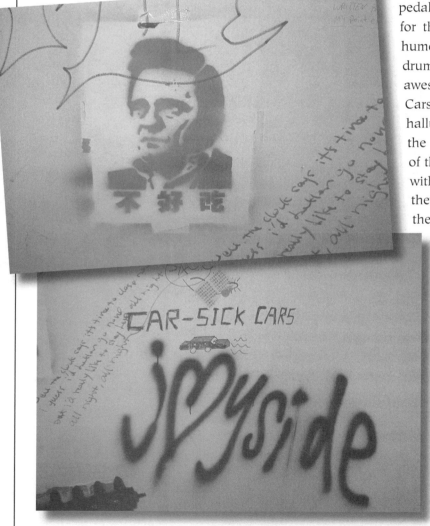

The following day The Subs are there early and I ask them to start immediately—with no audience in the venue—they are worried for a minute—but, I'm pushing and testing a little

bit—they rise above and slam out a great, emotional set; very, very impressive under the circumstances.

Kang Mao ROCKS! Johnny the drummer from PK14 is really helpful—he is from Sweden so speaks great English and becomes an interpreter for me—trying to help me explain my feelings and ideas... that's a pretty difficult gig... of course BO helps too.

Suddenly, the task of unraveling all of this on top of the language barrier, jet lag, and everything else, seems immense.

The laundry just called me up very worried—they had found a tear in my workshirt and were really freaked out!!!

Tibet CNN

Wow! Nothing gets your attention quite like the television being turned off. CNN had coverage of Chinese border guards allegedly shooting Tibetans at the border, the screen went blank for 20-30 seconds. It came back for a very short piece from a Chinese diplomat denying it all—then blank again. I sat up—I was eating breakfast in my room—and hit the top of the TV. When it came back on then I sat down just as it went off again—realizing that there was nothing wrong with the TV, sipping coffee wondering about the presence on the other side of the box. The government just cut the feed!

Later, I mentioned this to Michael from D-22. He informed me that no one except people staying at 5 star hotels gets to see CNN or any Western media anyway.

Hmm. Puts a twist on it for me in the studio... we have the Tibetan singers coming in later this week. This kind of sticks in my throat like, well, the duck foot that was stuck in my throat.

I get all kind of freaked out at the idea that another entity is controlling the media.

The next time I see CNN there is Patti Smith in NYC—crying because CBGB's is closing (and where will people get their drugs now??) It crystalmethylizes a thought for me: something is ending but something has very definitely begun—I jump in a cab and head down to D-22 where I end up jamming with Jeff from Car Sick Cars until the second drumstick breaks!

THEN, weeks later, we're sitting in the studio in Chicago and there is an item about Starbucks in The Forbidden City. People are wandering around there leaving their Starbucks junk everywhere (no, not the Starbucks Junk sponsored boat —Starbucks litter)! and some people are getting pissed off. So, I thought this would be a good item to flash in the background of my China Powerpoint presentation... except that after the first showing of this news item... it didn't appear on CNN for the rest of the day. Hmm... Strange for CNN, where ten dead dogs or one missing Boy Scout get hammered twice an hour on the half hour. I start to think, "Did Starbucks use some muscle to have the story pulled?" Later that day, a story hits that Starbucks is opening its own record label. I tracked down some of the people involved and the hysterical receptionist, clearly overwhelmed with a surge of unexpected phone calls, asks me to call back in five months. A bit of spin perhaps? Come back, heavy-handed Chinese government with the On-Off switch—all is forgiven. My definition of propaganda and media manipulation change.

Wow, so, maybe, Starbucks is as powerful as the Chinese government? Can it shut up CNN? If so, please, Starbucks, can you ask CNN if it could shut the fuck up about Suzanne Somers' burnt down career and Anna Nicole Smith and her Forbidden Titties?

Pigface Participants: Yi Yi Jun, Wang Li (DJ Wordy), Zai Wen Ting, Zhang Wei, Zhao Lan, Chen Xi, Kang Mao, Li Qing, Zhang Shou Wang, Li Qing, Li Weisi, Yang Haisong, CMCB (China MC Brothers), Snapline and TooKoo, Gangga Lamu, Tookoo, Yang Tan, Snapline, Subs, Cao Yang

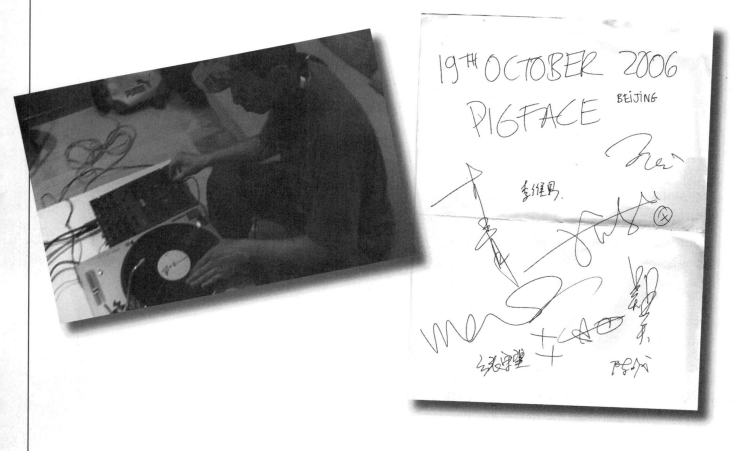

From: Martin Atkins
To: Katie Conlin
Subject: studio in Beijing

wow, after a week here seeing some AMAZING bands what a treat to be in a first class studio (Hi End Studios) with engineer Jovi and some great, open minded musicians from some of the bands.......just riffing on ideas - starting with a loop, layering traditional Chinese instruments over that (erhu and pipa and something else) then layering beats on top then a girl from a pop band wanders in and starts spluttering amazing chinese over the top - because I can't understand the words its just another instrument!, all the way through what is a VERY unusual situation for a top pop studio, Jovi records everything immaculately, or not as he dials in fabulous distortion on the drums - and, everybody gets it!!

SMILING, and groovyness all around and Pigface China Crew 2006 exists!!

Shao Feng and the other guys pull out Jovi's circuit bent 303, Jeff the guitarist from White starts twanging magnificent guitar, Chen Xi the singer from Snapline starts his monotone twang vocal about being in a car.......

ten minutes later - a track that doesn't have a name exists......pure _Pigface_.........
Kang Mao after singing all day with her band SUBS (fucking awesome) lays down another vocal........then we pull out some strange drums made of paper (I resist trying to set them on fire!) and Li Qing starts playing drums while the rest of us get hand cramps trying to deal with these weird new instruments...........the China M C Brothers amaze! 'who are these guys?' ask the studio cats...

GLORIOUS!

inspiring

tiring

fueling

love peace respect

humbled and happy.

End

66.7.11

I felt like I learned more about China in talking with Xi about a Pigface song called 66.7.11 than I would have if I'd had a conversation with him beginning, 'OK Xi - tell me some interesting stuff about China.' So, let me first explain the song so that everything that follows will make as much sense as it usually does.

It's a concept layered on a concept on a joke on an idea:

When you think about 666, then 667 you say the 'neighbour of the beast.' OK, we all get that—the concept of the devil living in a house—walking to the bottom of the driveway like Tony Soprano to pick up the newspapers, waving to the guy a few doors down washing his car. Talk about there goes the neighbourhood!

Now add the layering of a concept upon a concept—without the effort of a concept (as lcd sound system would say), with the attachment of a 24-hour convenience store next door... convenience store on one side, the devil on the other (the guy's property value is plummeting).

Assuming the convenience store is doing well - is the devil upset? Or is he just happy that his offspring can get Slurpees? And, is the owner of the store delighted on Friday the 13th when it's human sacrifice time and everyone wants baby wipes to get the blood off their outfits? And a bag of chips please...

OK, got the idea?

Let's take this concept to China... whadda we got? A big pile of nothing-ness and a cool learning experience. First off, 6 is lucky! 66 is luckier! 666 is so lucky you can't even fit into your pants and, even luckier is a 9... there are 9,9,9999 9 ninety nine and a HALF rooms in the forbidden city - one is a Starbucks. On the door of the Emperor's bedroom there are nine nines across and nine nines down. The luckiest room in the world... luckier than the champagne room (without the bubbles or the troubles). Maybe this idea was invented by the manufacturer of door numbers. "Mr. Chin, we have over-manufactured the 9's. Someone left the machine running all over the holidays." Well you can pretend that some of them are 6's but, maaan, you're drowning in 6's and 9's... like someone is at sixes and sevens over the 6's and 9's.

OK?

Then, let's add into this the idea that 4 is the unlucky number in China.

It is pronounced the same as the name for DEATH. (a Chinese retirement home situated on a golf course seems like unnecessary taunting, doesn't it?)

The movie 'Born on the 4th of July' becomes 'Born on the death death death die mother fuckerrrrrrrr'... even Tom Cruise's immense talent cannot save that one.

There are no 4th floors in China—so don't buy an apartment on that floor (especially one in Beijing with a great view of the Brooklyn Bridge). There's no 14th floor either, and, in deference to the west, no 13th floor. This is why it is possible to own a penthouse in Beijing and only be 17 feet off the ground... and don't worry about grandma up on the 15th floor with you down on the 12th... when there's a fire and all of the elevators are shut down... she's the luckiest burning grandma in Beijing... just inches above your head, one floor up.

In England, the emergency HELP number to dial is 999... unbelievably lucky! My house is burning down! And, we all know that nein nein nein in Germany means "please may I have another order of sausages."

Don't even start me in on 867-5309...

MARTIN ATKIN'S 1980 PUBLIC IMAGE LTD. U.S. TOUR DIARY

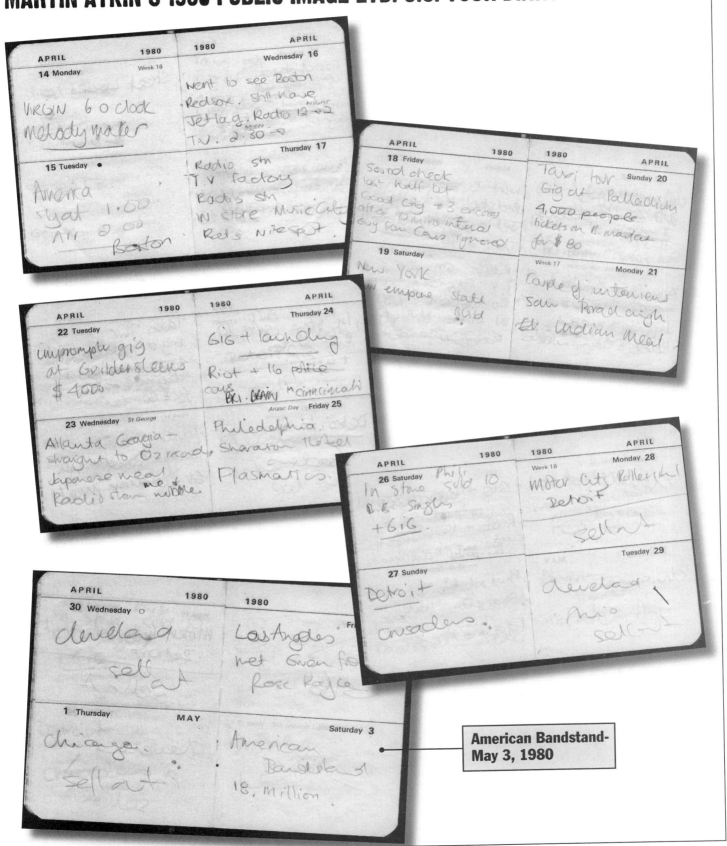

American Bandstand-
May 3, 1980

CHAPTER 54

HOW TO SCREEN PRINT

If you're taking control of your business and interested in expressing yourself artistically, learning how to screen print is great for both. You can screen print your band's logos on the oversized flight cases you should never have or on your favorite jacket. (But practice first because it's your favorite jacket). Once you know what you're doing, you can take an idea and turn it into a shirt overnight.

BLANK SHIRTS

There are plenty of places online where you can order blank shirts.

Blanktshirt.com – Choose the brand and color, from $3-$8.

Cheapesttees.com – Dozens of brand names, as low as $1.78.

Also look for hats, bags, work shirts, whatever!

One of the advantages of printing your own shirts is that you don't have to conform to the minimums that even smaller screen printing houses will make you order. You might have a great idea for a t-shirt, but you might not want to commit to buying 72 of them up front before the tour starts. Even if you do, maybe that means there isn't the money to take two or three other designs with you. And you need the spread.

You can also screen print scenery/backdrops and explore taking charge of the way your show is presented, heightening the overall production value without shredding the bottom line.

There are two kinds of inks you can use:

Water-based ink is fine for scenery, posters, and printing dark inks on light shirts. The only way to print white on a black shirt is to use a Plastisol ink. This is an ink that basically never dries; it's like tar. You have to dry it using a flash dryer, which cures the ink for about two minutes. Plastisol is the more professional medium and you will need a larger investment in basic equipment (around $1,500 total) or less if you look on eBay.

> "One of the advantages of printing your own shirts is that you don't have to conform to the minimums that even the smaller screen printing houses will need."

SCREEN FRAMES

These are the same whether you are using water-based inks or Plastisol inks. You can make them quite easily if you are handy. It's nice to have a power mitre saw and an electric stapler. If you don't want to deal with that, you can get pre-made, pre-stretched frames for around $22 for a 12" x 16" frame.

You will need one screen for each color. Depending on the size of your artwork you can probably fit two logos (or two elements) on one screen. To expose, I use the photo emulsion method, which consists of mixing two chemicals together—the emulsion and the photo sensitizer—in a 4:1 ratio. You don't need to be strictly scientifically accurate. I use plastic coffee spoons to measure. Work in a dimly-lit or light-safe room because once you combine the two chemicals, the mix is sensitive to light. I've never really had a problem with this. You will need an absolutely dark place once it has been coated to allow it to dry overnight.

NOW LET'S LOOK AT THE ARTWORK

You can do a special shirt for your crew without it being unreasonably expensive. You can do a nice shirt only for your street team. You can do anything you want. The good news is that you're learning a skill, which will be very useful when you want to print t-shirts for your second child's seventh birthday.

Most of our shirts that sell well do so because they say something clever, obnoxious, or they have the band's logo on them. Do yourself a favor and start out simple. Take the band's logo and make it a reasonable size on the chest or pocket of the shirt. Once you have a crisp black and white rendering of the logo, you can take it to Kinko's and ask them to simply copy the logo onto acetate, which is clear, overhead-projector film. They always seem to have 8.5" by 11" but check to see if they have 11" by 17." Print it as if it is color and you get a more dense black.

You can buy a printer that will handle 11" by 17" paper. There is a transparency paper that ink jet printers will print onto with enough black to be able to expose a screen. That's something to think about if you're going to be doing a lot of this and Kinko's is 20 miles away.

Pay attention to the distance you'll need to have the light bulb above the image. Follow instructions for exposing and washing out. Take your time! The black ink stops the emulsion from hardening behind it... it will then wash away.

The downside of self-printing shirts is that if you unexpectedly run out of shirts halfway through a tour, you don't have anyone to FedEx more shirts to you unless you plan ahead.

HOW ABOUT THIS

Bring the screen and a bottle of ink with you. What better, more productive way to trash a Super Eight motel room? Or during the day at the venue, you'll have plenty of space to screen print a few shirts. I've even seen people do them in the parking lot...

We printed a lot of merch ourselves, but sent three or four designs to a local printer just in case we did run out.

"Start simple. Most of our shirts that sell well do so because they say something clever, obnoxious, or they have the band's logo on them."

So here's a mini-snapshot of what a big deal the idea of spread and multiple use of screens is:

I got an e-mail from Nathan of Emulsion letting me know he was going to be on the road. There's one question I ask a lot, "Who's doing the merch? Do you have a spread (a range of different items)?"

Things had been so crazy that he actually didn't have any merch. I had him e-mail me the band logo in two different sizes and I shot two screens that evening. (There are often a few screens ready to go in the darkroom downstairs.) I did one screen on 110 mesh with the large Emulsion logo, 14" across on the top and a smaller logo on the bottom. Then I shot another screen on 65 mesh—which is a wider mesh—to allow the use of glitter inks, just because I was in the mood to do that. With the first screen, I made a simple black t-shirt with the band logo in white across the chest in two or three sizes. I made some DJ bags with a large band logo and ten work shirts: dark blue with a large band logo across the back and a small logo above the pocket on the front. With the broader mesh, I made some baby tees with a nice glitter logo across the chest. The quantity was good, but the spread was terrific. Although it was a short tour, it was the first time that Nathan had come back making a little bit of a profit. And there's the difference.

If you go on tour for ten days and lose $300 or $400, it'll take you a few weeks or a couple months to get back to zero to be ready to do this again. However, when you produce merch and bring in a profit, you can immediately start planning the next tour... not to mention, it feels good.

There's no reason that you can't do this. Along the way, you can experiment and maybe come up with some techniques that will make a really fantastic shirt or print down the sleeves or whatever! We're screening limited edition digipacks here, too.

If you want to get into more complicated designs and colors, a four-screen press isn't that expensive. But remember: for a four-color shirt, you'll need four screens and in between each pull of a color, you'll have to flash dry for one minute. Then when the whole shirt is done, you'll have to cure dry for two minutes. It could take an hour and a half to set up the four screens so they are all aligned, and then each shirt six or more minutes to print. That's only ten an hour... so, start simple.

CUSTOM PRINTED POSTERS

Early momentum is key. Information is needed in the marketplace 12 weeks ahead of time. It will be too early for you to have mass-produced posters in quantity and mass-produced promotional CDs. You can make sure that you have in advance: songs, electronic press kits, logos, artwork, and photos burned onto discs for the benefit of the clubs and the press. With the first Sheep on Drugs tour, we created a series of fluorescent original posters. It was at a time when I was messing around with screen printing and had found over 200 screens in the trash outside of a New Jersey screen printer. I started to create, with the theory that these

> "The downside of self-printing shirts is that if you unexpectedly run out of shirts halfway through a tour, you don't have anyone to fed-ex more shirts to you unless you plan ahead."

> "There's no reason that you can't do this."

TOUR:SMART TIP

screens represented a cross-section of American life. There were screens of trees for a landscaping company, steering wheels for the automotive industry, police SWAT teams, the word "fuck" for those outrageous people who wanted to do something to push the limits, and everything in between.

I shot a couple of Sheep on Drugs screens with the girl's face from their first U.S. LP over the text and background of Japanese lettering. This created a base of color without using tons of ink. Then I started to switch colors, basically went mad for a period of two days, and ended up creating four unique posters for each venue. They were awesome and invited, in fact, demanded that all four be put up as a Warhol-esque display!

FANTASTIQUE!

Once you master this very simple process, you can create your own environment on stage. How cool and trippy was it to make my Newcastle Brown Ale bottle cap sculptures, photograph them for album covers, and then end up on stage inside one of the album covers! There's a continuity, a grooviness, and a sense-out-of-nonsense that works in all of that.

C·H·A·P·T·E·R 55

WHEN YOU ARE THE OPENING BAND

"Sound checks are often non-existent. As a support band you have to learn to go with the flow."
— Mark Spybey

With more and more bands starting everyday, exposure becomes the most precious commodity of all. It becomes essential that if and when you do get a chance to play to a larger audience, you don't blow it. By paying attention to this chapter, you can absolutely decide where your band will be in a year's time.

DO'S AND DON'TS, GET MORE OUT OF IT:

- **Tell your drummer** not to put his new drum heads on in the middle of the auditorium and start pinging away to tune them up in the middle of anyone's sound check.

- **Be prepared to have no sound check.** If you don't get one, don't be upset. Get on with it. You've trained for this right? And don't mention the fact that you didn't get a sound check to the audience during your show. They probably had no idea… until then!

- **Help the other bands' merchandise person**, carry some boxes, etc. He or she might have something to do with who gets to play next time. Get him or her water or coffee, or if you are going out for Thai or pizza after sound check, offer to bring him and/or the soundman a slice!

- **Have a few different versions of your set** ready for an opening slot if you are using tapes or computers to supplement your live sound. If your set is going to be 30 minutes long, have a 20 minute version, even a 15 minute version ready. When the tour manager comes running into the dressing room and, because of any one of a hundred things outside of his control, gives you a choice of 15 minutes or nothing, you can be gracious under fire. You never know how he might show his appreciation—a six pack, a pizza, or a chance to be on the bill the following month when the band swings back, because you weren't an asshole!

- **Get an un-interruptible power supply** if you're using electronic reinforcement.

- **Turn on all the lights when sound checking!** That way you can see if the power of everything will cause a short circuit.

- **Pay for it if you damage a mic or a monitor.** (See U.K. 1995 – the Sheep on Drugs Story at the end of this chapter.)

- **Communicate with the label/management, etc.** Let them know if you are seeing good postering. Is the ad spelled correctly? Make sure the main band is on your flyer and it looks like you are opening. The band will get pissed if you do your own flyer that looks as if they are supporting you. Don't fuck with their logos and make it respectful. Set up a situation where, even if they don't love your music, they will say, "Hell, we need to make sure those guys are involved in the next date!" and ask, "Do you guys do well anywhere else?" Jackpot!

- **Be nice** and don't think that just because your album is good and you know the lead singer... It means shit!

- **Don't be negative... Never.**

- **Don't be too early.** Don't show up four hours early with 10 friends who want to see the main band sound check. Stay out of the way.

- **Don't call the tour manager or manager seven times.** Get all of your questions together and make one call, maybe with a follow up. Have one person do the communicating.

- **Don't disappear right before it's time to get on stage.** Get on and off stage at the correct time.

- **Don't ask for any more beer!** Is it worth saving $8-$10 to bother the tour manager or club owner and make the point to them that when you do bother them, it's going to be related to alcohol? Buy a fucking 6-pack!

- **Don't hang around in any of the other dressing rooms.** Get you and your band out of the way. If you stumble across a huge spread of hearty food and wonder if it's yours... it isn't!

- **Don't play the same city a week before or after a free radio show.** It will diminish your ticket drawing power and make you look like you just don't get it when the tour manager settles the show. "I thought that 'such and such' were a big draw, at least that's what they told me two months ago!" "Oh, yes they are," replies the club owner. "The show last week was amazing!" Ugh! End of story.

- **Don't complain** about anything to anyone.

- **Don't get drunk and start a fight**, as amazing as this might seem.

- **Don't bring the girlfriend or boyfriend you just broke up with** because she or he likes the main band. Social dynamics could get strange; you or they might get drunk and start a fight.

- **Don't slag off the main band** or a sponsor or anyone anywhere in the venue (especially over the PA system). This could be damaging to a potential relationship. You have no idea who anyone is. You might be talking to the band's publicist, or next to someone's brother... You don't know so shut up!

- **Don't be so insecure** that you have to put on a pop star front, you're not! You're opening!

- **Don't throw shit all over the stage** (literally or figuratively) unless you are the SuicideGirls and it's chocolate sauce. Don't go crazy and knock all of the mics over. The soundman will be pissed and he will remember you! The support network of people involved in these shows will be making decisions that directly affect your future and the success of your band.

See the Chapters on *Good Advice from Baad People* for more tips!

"If you stumble across a huge spread of hearty food and wonder if it's yours... it isn't!"

STRATEGY FOR SUCCESS:
PRACTICE FOR CATASTROPHE AND YOU WILL ALWAYS TRIUMPH

Over three days at the D-22 Club in Beijing, China, I recorded over 16 bands that went from basic four-piece drums/bass/guitar/vocals to bands almost insanely ambitious in their instrumental scope and variety: foot-pedaled organs, hand-cranked ratchets, and noise guitar. The club and the soundman were doing absolutely everything in their power to accommodate any direction anybody wanted to go in. So it was interesting and quite disappointing to encounter some of that uniquely Western-entrenched blaming, complaining bullshit from one of the bands. They spent 45 minutes complaining about the monitors, the mics, and pretty much everything before eventually launching into a song. The mix was nowhere near right. But, realizing this, and hearing an interesting tone between the two guitarists, I jumped to the front and positioned my head in between the two guitarists, closest to the one who was the quietest, creating my own mix in my head. I had just started to get into their sound when they stopped playing and started complaining again. I hung around for another four minutes wondering how these guys were so successful and confident in their future that they were OK with leaving the owner of a record label standing around by the front of the stage. Then I kind of just gave

up thinking about any of it and went outside to see what was going on in the streets of Beijing.

The manager came out onto the street 20 minutes later to see what I had thought of the band. I said that it really didn't matter. I honestly didn't care how good or bad they were. I had no idea what I could possibly do with a band with that attitude.

I took the time to do a drawing and explained: "Of course, you could be amazing under the best conditions, anybody can. That's not the game. You need to be amazing under the worst of conditions. There are many phrases that cover this: "When the going gets tough, the tough get going;" "Rise above;" or "Man up!" But I kind of like: "Don't be a fucking asshole, and get on stage, and do the best you can, you wanker!" I drew on a piece of paper the numbers one through ten, with one being the worst possible situation: bad or no monitors, bad PA, small audience, no food, diarrhea running down your legs. Number ten is an amazing show

> "Something is not beneath you if you are on the bottom!"
>
> Horace-Alexander Young

(10) BEST SITUATION!!!

(9) It will always be worse than 10.

(8) It's hardly ever going to be better than this.

(7) You'll be delighted when it's this good.

(6) Thrilling. Better than average!

(5) Remember when you complained when it was an 8?

(4) Hope for this level of mediocrity. Rejoice!

(3) Most times it will be better than 2.

(2) It will always be better than this.

(1) HORRIBLE SHIT!!!
but at least you have a gig!!

> **"Of course, you could be amazing under the best conditions, anybody can. That's not the game. You need to be amazing under the worst of conditions."**

at a venue like House of Blues Chicago, backstage showers, great food, great dressing rooms, wonderful monitors and PA, great crew. And I told them, "If you are planning for success, do you train to succeed at a ten out of ten venue, or a one out of ten venue?" Unbelievably, they and their manager chose the ten out of ten venue! And I said, "Look, if you train as a band and crew to pull off a fantastic show in a situation that's one out of ten, it will always be better. If you practice for a ten out of ten venue, it will always be worse. That's it."

"Be prepared, practice for catastrophe, and you will always triumph."
- Martin Atkins

HOW TO BE A BETTER OPENING BAND
JASON NOVAK, ACUMEN NATION, DJ? ACUCRACK

- **Advance your shows.** If you don't have a manager, do it yourself. Talk to the promoter a couple weeks before the show. Make sure they know you exist. If you are opening or supporting a bigger tour, fax or e-mail them your stage plot and input list needs. It's professional and means the house sound guy will at least know (even from a quick glance that afternoon) who you are and what you need.

- **Introduce yourself to all the house guys** if you are supporting or opening a tour. Be nice. Be humble. Make sure they know you exist and are on time, ready to work where and when they request. Most bigger tours have their own sound and light guys. These house guys are being paid to be there, so if they aren't running the headliner's shows, most often they will be happy to help you run yours. Some can be jaded dicks, but it never hurts to get on their good side right away.

- **Offer to help the headliner** if you are on tour with them for a while. Offer to carry some gear, grab a beer or water for the sound guy while he's working, whatever... Make friends and don't be shy. Headliners are always ready to take a shit on an opener, and even if your music sucks (in their opinion) they will be much more ready to help you get a sound check, hold doors if they took all day to check, or respect you, if you show them respect first.

- **Get road cases,** or at least have your shit together. You will be on time trial most nights. You will be setting up and tearing down your gear in record time, usually minutes before doors. If you are fumbling around with loose rack gear and cardboard boxes, it only adds to the confusion.

- **Have a merch person with you!** If you are making money with some decent merch, don't try and do it all yourself or trust the house guy or try to beg off the headliner's merch person. Paying a friend or someone close to the band (usually 10%) to sell your stuff will protect it, as well as get it pitched better, and allow you to concentrate on your set, your teardown, your music, and talking to kids who might eventually buy your shit!

- **Don't overdo your rider.** As opener or support, your needs will be met and respected if you show restraint. Don't be a dick and ask for stupid shit on your rider because you think it's cute and the hospitality chick will laugh—she won't. Keep it simple: basic beer and water,

> **"Make friends and don't be shy."**

TOUR:SMART TIP
for more information go to:
www.tstouring.com

access to a dressing room, and some simple meals or a $10 buyout. It's OK to specify the beer, or ask for vegetarian food if need be, but don't heap on the shit. If the headliner sucks up all the hospitality budget (and they usually do), your small respectable rider will be easy to handle, as opposed to easy to ignore because it's full of crap. Also, if you get fucked out of your requested beer or whatever, make sure to ask if you can get a band discount on drinks or a 12 pack of PBR behind the bar...

TOUR:SMART TIP
for more information go to:
www.tstouring.com

- **Don't get wasted before your set** unless you are fucking Van Halen, which you aren't because you are the opener! You have all night to get plowed after the show, and people can easily dismiss a band if they appear drunk. It's OK for the headliner to be wasted, but not for you.

- **Don't be an asshole.** Most nights you will be lucky to get a sound check, lucky to get your rider, lucky to get your full set. Shit happens all the time to hinder these things. They are not set in stone and the cooler you are, the more willing the people controlling the show will be to give you a hand, throw you a bone, hold the doors, order you some pizza, whatever.

- **Don't be late!** Just because you only ever have 15 minutes before doors, don't show up only a half hour before. The earlier you are, the more time you have to grease the local crew with your charm, suss out any problems, pre-set up all your shit on the floor, and show you care.

- **Don't overproduce your sound or your set.** Got eight keyboards and five samplers on your rig? Cut out most of that shit. Got two drummers? Send one home. Got anything that requires more than five minutes of troubleshooting once you are on stage? Forget it. This also goes back to the road case thing. Try and build touring racks with as much plugged in as possible. Use rack power conditioners, build pedal boards, and carry them in something that allows them to stay connected. Got a huge intro? Be careful, many nights you will get five minutes cut out of your set, so bring out your A-shit quick. You probably can't afford techs, so bring spare guitars and sticks, be prepared to work under shitty circumstances, be prepared to set up the drums on the floor in front of the riser (sucks ass, but is a fact of opening band life!) and make sure you can focus on your set, not fiddling with gear. Oh, are you using playback tracks? Bring a backup! And run it simultaneously (if you can) with your main source, so that if something goes down you can switch a cable or two and get on with it.

UK 1995

Pigface hadn't been in Europe for a few years and we decided to do a one-off show at a new rock venue called The Grand. I think it was in Clapham. The story is in two parts. Part one belongs in the *When You are the Opening Band* Chapter and part two belongs in the *Martin Atkins is an Idiot* Chapter.

PART 1

Ticket sales for the London show were a bit disappointing. We had had great shows in London before. So much so, that in '93, we were supposed to open for Siouxsie and the Banshees at Wembley Stadium until the show was canceled two days before because Siouxsie had a throat infection (See *Murphy's Law*). But, we immediately booked studio time and recorded the Fook album (see Triumph in the Face of Adversity). Except that the studio had a bar in the same building and our bar bill was larger than the studio bill (See *Martin Atkins is an Idiot)*.

Anyway, I digress. The point is, we had a show in London and, five weeks before show day, tickets weren't selling well. We decided to add a prominent London band to help with ticket sales and boost the show. Within a few hours, we had added Sheep on Drugs to the bill. At that time, they were flavor of the week with the U.K. press. We sat back, waiting for a bump in ticket sales. Two weeks later, ticket sales were still quite disappointing. I spoke to the agent in London about it. He explained that they hadn't been announced yet! It turns out that the last time they had performed for the same company, a microphone had been broken and the soundman had said that until the microphone was paid for, he wasn't going to allow Sheep on Drugs to set foot on his stage.

So, here I am with 12 international plane tickets, hotels booked, and a sound guy with a grudge over a $100 microphone is holding the entire event hostage. We immediately got the soundman on the phone and I tried to calmly explain how crazy this situation was and to personally guarantee payment for the microphone. The soundman then explained, in a way that only an English soundman can, that he had to receive the money personally from the singer of the band. Nothing else was acceptable. I'm not sure what happened after that. We eventually sorted it out, but not without losing a precious three weeks of ticket sales in the five weeks before the show.

Ticket sales were disappointing all the way up to the day of the show. I just couldn't figure it out. I wandered outside of the venue, took a 10 minute walk up the street while some rental equipment was being loaded in, and came across a small train station. Not an underground station, a regular above-ground station, and boom, that was it. The venue wasn't close to an underground stop and if this train stop was the closest link to central London, I knew that the regular trains stopped much earlier than the underground lines, much earlier. Brilliant.

It turned out that the show was just OK. Just enough people to make for a good evening; probably around fifty percent capacity. The agent told me it was a beautiful old theatre, and it was—just completely wrong for our purposes.

"The soundman then explained, in a way that only an English fuckhead can, that he had to receive the money personally from the singer of the band."

"The hardest thing in the world to do in this business is start a band nobody's heard of."
—Tom Whalley, Interscope Records

CHAPTER 56

MARKETING IV - 61 STRATEGIES FOR A MORE SUCCESSFUL SHOW

A lot of this might sound like economics, marketing, demographics, and whatever that you might not be interested in, but all of this enables a great show, sweaty bodies, and that magic that makes your head tingle. If you don't want to deal with this and other aggressive strategies, find someone in the band who does or put your Wal-Mart uniform in the washer—you're going to need it.

1. **Give your ticket-buying fans plenty of time to commit.** Time is a huge factor in determining the success of a show. And give yourself time to promote! There is an exponential growth curve to ticket sales. The sooner you begin the process, the more tickets you will sell. Unless of course, your band is shit.

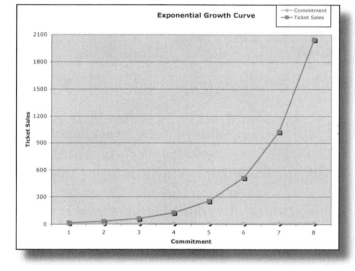

2. **Tour within a reasonable time of a new release.** You can gain some traction from a larger presence in stores and online and during a short window of attention and radio play. Take advantage of your record label (if you are signed). Enhance the chances of getting good reviews and having those reviews mention your live appearances. Tag a multi cut co-op ad with "Appearing at..." It is great for the venue owner to see that someone else is shouldering some of the financial burden and increases the chances of stores putting up your posters.

3. **Create Your Own Event!** (See that chapter).

4. **Play the right venue.** If you are a Country Western band, play a Country Western venue. It is very, very difficult to capitalize on a catastrophe . So don't have one. No one cares that you played the wrong club on the wrong night in a snowstorm during a curfew. All they care about is the fact that no one was there.

5. **Play the right venue on the right night!**

6. **Play where your fans are.** Use your web site or database to find out where your fan are—go play there! (Thanks Zim)

TOUR:SMART TIP
for more information go to:
www.tstouring.com

7. **Listen to Sun Tzu, "Don't take your country to war unless you are certain of the outcome."** If your band is based in the Midwest, why, why, why—other than hanging out with members of Ratt or buying speed from the waitress at some cocktail lounge on the Sunset Strip—would you go to LA? You should carefully expand your geographical range, you stand a chance of having your best street teamers and fans travel 50 to 100 miles to a city you have never played in before. Turn it into a crusade (because it is). Once you are more than 100 miles away from a place you have already played, it gets tough. Without any eyes and ears on the ground, you could be heading for a problem show. Do research on the web, and if you cannot guarantee success, at least avoid humiliating disaster.

8. **Advertise in Secondary Markets!** If you have covered all the bases in the city you are playing in, then before you spend ten more dollars in that city, spend that money in the closest secondary market. You will getter a better return.

9. **Be aware of larger tours** going though a big city or its secondary market within ten weeks of your show. One, you should avoid playing the same night as a much larger band in a similar genre—or in the event of a larger tour that milks all of the money from your scene, make sure you are at least one pay period away! Unless it's a late, late, after-show party with a $5-off-the-ticket stub. Two, use the event as a parking lot flyering opportunity. Use the huge following of the other tour as an easy opportunity for you or your reps to advertise your show. Put up posters in the toilets; buy a ticket for a rep to get into the show. Be careful if it's a competing promoter, they will not like you advertising in their venue. Talk to the promoter of your event—he might end up being the promoter of the larger event. Use a larger event like this as a genre boost and piggyback on its success.

TOUR:SMART TIP
for more information go to:
www.tstouring.com

10. **Involve a strong local band as an opener.** But be careful. Local bands often play their market too much. Confirm the information they give you: How many people are on their e-mail list? Do they have a local street team that will help? Have they played recently? Are there any other bands that would be good additions to the show? Sometimes a local band doesn't realize the full nature of their role in the success of a show. Explain to them that they have the opening slot not just because you like their music, but because they kick butt in the flyering department and are willing to travel to neighboring markets and you really need them to do that for this show, too. Be prepared to offer the band similar services and hospitality in your town (Oh my God, an alliance!). Suggest that you will open for them if they have a good local draw. The main thing is to play for people. Anything you can do to play to more people sooner will be beneficial.

11. **Plan, promote, push.** Use my five pointed star inward crush. This can be applied on a large scale with cities or on a smaller scale with suburbs and secondary markets. Each point of the star is a show within driving distance of a larger city or show, play each of the points of the star first then incentivize your new fans to come to the main show. Plan, promote, push! Use a venue or a night that has developed a loyal following (a built-in) to

your advantage. Look at the strategies in the booking chapter to increase the chances of success.

12. Provide a service to another, larger band that needs help. Offer your resources, whether they be equipment, transportation, or road crew help. Buy a larger vehicle and offer space to another band if there are four of you and you can afford a vehicle. This can also help you cut costs… if you do it right. Make sure to include all expenses involved (gas, repairs, etc.). See the *Transportation* Chapter for more.

13. Give your show a name. Five or six disconnected small events in New York City became a week long assault when Jaz, the singer from Killing Joke, titled the week "Days of Sweat and Madness."

14. Involve a sponsor! If you know ahead of time about any support you are getting, it might make it easier for you to get a decent show and a decent offer. There is no shortage of companies looking to involve themselves in the promotional power of music. Make sure there is some kind of a fit and give value and courtesy to the sponsor. Send them pictures, keeping them involved even after the time for their help is over. Take any help that is offered. If it isn't exactly what you need, it is still the beginning of a relationship—and more help than none.

> **Sunkist, Visa, Absolut, Smirnoff, Jägermeister, Monster, No Fear…**

15. Involve a local radio station! It doesn't have to be a commercial radio station to be of assistance to the success of your show. Commercial stations might have a show such as "Local 101" on Chicago's Q101, where they feature local bands (another reason to involve a local band in your show). If you are getting airplay at the college level, talk to the promotions department about giving away free tickets with CDs or shirts for the show. This way every time they give away a ticket they will be announcing the show. Do this as early as possible. The promotional materials have to be at the station before they begin to give anything away.

16. Save some resources to kick into higher gear in problem markets. Make sure you have something left in your war chest for problems.

17. Talk to the promoter. Sometimes a DJ from the venue might also be a DJ at the radio station, a bartender, a journalist, or work at the record store. It's the same amount of effort to send a package to the right person as it is to the wrong person.

18. Get a media list from the venue. The venue is going to be your best source of the top five or ten places you need hit. This helps you allocate your resources and send packages to the right people. If the venue cannot send you a media list or come up with one off the top of their head it is a red flag and you need to be on your toes.

19. Get information out to local press. Keep the information simple and direct. Bullet points. No one has time or desire to learn how you and the guitarist met. Provide links to easily downloadable graphics and help them fill their paper with things people want to see. Make sure the listing goes out and the information is correct.

20. Send the venue elements for their website. Well-mastered music that slams and sounds good on the web—not the song with the really long, quiet, acoustic intro. And all the bullet points of good promotion: photographs, a few sentences for some respected resources, links to reviews, etc.

21. **Get information to the local record store – and any other stores.** Call. Send a poster. Tell them when you are playing. Maybe someone there works at the venue or is in the band opening for you (ask the promoter). These types of contacts could give you feedback on the venue such as, "Oh God, you are playing there! On a Tuesday!" Good stores are happy to help, within reason. Do not, not, not suggest an in-store appearance unless you are, in fact, Michael Stipe of REM. There is no such thing as a "moderately well-received" in-store or a "good" in-store. They are either fantastic or catastrophic. If in doubt, watch *Spinal Tap*. There are some record stores in remote parts of the country who have stages and welcome touring bands. This is because there are no alternatives close by. Take this opportunity to dazzle, amaze, and befriend an audience (hopefully) and a record store owner at the same time.

22. **Track your packages**. If you wait two weeks to call to make sure a package has been received, that's when you find out the person who does the booking is only there on Thursday and you called on a Friday, so you call back the following Thursday and that's when you find out that the package hasn't been received, and you just blew three weeks. FedEx is expensive. You can FedEx Ground something for $7 or $8 or add delivery confirmation from USPS for $0.60 then you can allocate your resources. FedEx packages to the 10 or 20 most important venues and use a cheaper method for the additional packages. Follow up within a few days of the venue receiving the package. That way, if they say they didn't get the package, you can refer to your organized notes and let them know who signed for it. This might lead them to finding your package and opening it.

23. **Make sure that you "guest list" people from these outlets that want to take the time to come and support you.** It is not enough to put somebody on the guest list. Make sure the guest list gets to the door before the doors are open. Also, make SURE it is typed and alphabetized and your band leader, manager, or rep checks with the door man frequently in the first hour or two, less frequently after that. Use the guest list to help a show that needs an attendance boost.

24. **Type the guest list.** Even if you only have seven people on the guest list—still type it. You'll get into the habit and what was a seven person guest list at 3 p.m. might explode into a 58-person list by the time the three radio stations that you didn't know about bring you their give-away lists. Bonus: When you are typing up the seven person guest list, you realize that your ink cartridge is fucked. Even though you bought three (like I'm going to tell you somewhere else in this book), you realize that the keyboard player has stolen them again so he can print more "Bass Players Suck" stickers to plaster in the bus toilet, and it's the night before the big LA show. You don't want to be tooling around LA at 4 p.m. looking for an Office Depot, do you?

25. **BUY ON.** If you are independently wealthy or injured in a car accident, you can buy on to a larger show or event with a guaranteed attendance for an evening.

26. **Give away free tickets.** There is nothing as bad as a poorly attended show. And now you get to go up one of the ladders on the Chutes and Ladders board.

27. Sell tickets to an event through your own website. Once you realize that getting people to commit early is essential to a successful show, begin to guarantee success by pairing up tickets on a deal: "Two for One," "Buy a ticket, get a free shirt," "Buy a pair of tickets at full price, get a free shirt and a laminate." These are all strategies that don't cost very much, but are very effective. Not only do advance ticket sales help with your cash flow and the financial crunch of getting the tour out the door, they also open up lines of communication with fans from other cities. If you have never played in Atlanta before and 20 tickets sell quickly, give these eager fans information (now you have their e-mails) and they can help boost word of mouth and create success. Present this as a "Free ticket to the show when you buy a CD" or "Free ticket to the show when you buy a T-shirt" deal. Let the promoter know that you are aggressively promoting the show on the web by giving away t-shirts and CDs with the purchase of tickets and that you will be ready to make a ticket buy the day of the show if necessary. Track sales by city—you can use this information to allocate funds accordingly.

28. eBay a ticket or a concert! See the story about Local H in the *Using the Web* chapter. They auctioned a concert on eBay and were wildly successful.

29. Give away an iPod. Advertise a free iPod on the web. You can also offer prizes: get some giveaways from local sponsors like gift cards from a music store, clothing store, or tattoo shop. Put the logo of the shops who donate gifts on the flyer. When people buy tickets to your show from your site, enter their name into a drawing. This enables you to see how well the show could do (or not) and act accordingly.

30. Bundle – This is a new trend for concert tickets. Prince did it first—I think with no label. Every concert ticket came with the new CD. Good idea removing the choice, removing the Soundscan hassle, and jacking up sales.

Be careful — overaggressive bundling can cause a backlash. Make sure you are giving value to your fans, not ripping them off.

> *I just called to get tickets for the Chicago FIRE soccer team playing Chelsea FC– one of the best teams in the UK premiership division. "Great!" I thought. "$70 isn't bad for two tickets." The girl told me that was part of the "two-for" deal. Err. No, she called me back to tell me it was actually $90 – you get tickets to see The Fire play DC United in September... ugh! It's not a rip off as such; I can tell myself that at $20 a ticket, I'll take the family, etc. But it certainly is outside-of-the-(penalty) box thinking and aggressive as fuck! At the Chelsea game, there were license plates from New York and Minnesota... you can bet none of those people came back up to see DC United.*

31. Have a contest. I know it seems like maybe it's lame and one step away from bingo, but these strategies work - especially when they are smart and imaginative. You can read about Luke's strategy with Dope in the merchandising section and Local H's eBay strategy earlier in this section. Here's a great one from Pegasus Unicorn, a band in Erie, PA. They had a gumball machine on stage. The person with the prize winning gumball (like the Willy Wonka Chocolate bar) got a song written about them on their new album. See? It doesn't have to cost a fortune to be priceless.

> **"It doesn't have to cost a fortune to be priceless."**

32. **Don't ever be an**

cut this out and staple it to the singers forehead

...to your fans! Don't be an asshole to anybody who shows up. They showed up!

If only 50 people show up to see you in a 400 capacity venue, it's 50 people more than NONE. Don't sit in the dressing room for an extra hour waiting for another 300 people to show up from nowhere, because the promoter said, "It's a late crowd." (He or she is correct—the Tuesday night crowd is so late you won't see them 'til Friday.) Instead, rise above. This is your mistake, not theirs. Given a chance, and some help and encouragement, a small crowd will go to great lengths to prove that each one of them equals five in number—which is great, especially if they buy stuff. Don't tell them to come to the front... they won't. Don't be an asshole to the promoter, nobody needs it. You are going to have to make them a lot of money to make them consider dealing with you again. You may not get the chance to apologize. Promoters are people, too, running their own business in a very competitive field, overworked and stressed.

33. Recognize and reward. If you are in a city for the second time, stay on top of your database and make sure that people who have helped you in the past are recognized and rewarded on the guest list. If you cannot give them a shirt, do something that at least lets them know they are valued. Spend some time; they have earned it.

34. Get and give accurate information. It is difficult for one person to tell another person (you) that ticket sales are bad and no one really likes your band. If a promoter knows he or she is talking to the artist, your request for a ticket count will probably elicit the response that everything is fine or some nebulous feel-good response. What you have to get from them is an accurate and up-to-date count of the actual number of tickets sold. This will enable you to use your limited resources wisely, in the place where they are most needed to prevent problems.

35. Think about alternative places to promote. Local press, radio stations, and record stores are constantly bombarded by bands, managers, etc., daily and hourly. You could target nontraditional outlets such as tattoo and piercing, hair, clothing, and the skate/snowboard markets. Sending out hundreds of promotional CDs to record stores is like sending buckets of stupidity to President Bush. When we sent CDs to clothing stores, we got phone calls thanking us. Anytime you can ignite a reaction from anyone, it is a good beginning of something, which is more than nothing. And by constructively forming relationships with retailers, you might get plugged in to more opportunities that could be helpful later on.

36. Do a Promotional Postcard!

37. Print your poster in small quantities. If you're a new band, make your posters at Kinko's or somewhere that allows you to print a small quantity. As soon as you get good press, put this information on your poster so that you can adapt, react, and regurgitate. People want opinions of the band that aren't from the band.

38. Partially underwrite some of the expense of the tour by selling the other side of the promotional postcard to a band that's too lazy to leave home. Remember: you are not just offering half of the postcard; you are offering to place that postcard at the center of a group of fans. You will be saving them a ton of postage and spreading seeds on fruitful ground. You might find a clothing company, a printer, a graphic artist, anyone who might be interested in a real concrete promotional opportunity.

39. Make the booth the reason to go to the show. Cool shirts, free samplers, free stickers, etc. are all extra incentives to come to a show. Make sure people know you're going to have a cool booth to add one more reason why they should not miss your show. Make the booth the only place to get the new CD with three songs from the upcoming album.

40. Get as many email addresses as you can when you have people assembled to see you. Make sure you use this opportunity to say hello. You will need these emails when you begin the

> "Anytime you can ignite a reaction from anyone, it is a good beginning of something, which is more than nothing."

process all over again. Be prepared to give stuff away when you begin. No one is going to buy an album from a band they've never heard.

41. **Pay attention to age limits, curfews, and transportation availability** so you can advise your fans and compensate when possible.

42. **Pay attention to routing and your fans' income streams.** Sarah Williams, a student in my class, suggested that if your band is doing the flower petal routing on the weekends you should either: avoid the end of the month and hit the middle of the month when everyone has more money or...

43. **Play for free.** As a new band, you're not going to get paid much (if at all), so why not just bite the bullet and play for free? At the end of the month no one has any money. You can understand and avoid this fact by using the strategy above or understand and use it by playing at the end of the month for free. The bands that have the most to gain by this strategy also have the least to lose. If you're only making $150/show, that means that after gas and fog juice you're only putting $15 a piece in your pocket anyway. So be heroes—play for free. It'd be popular as all hell with fans, help you get some new fans, and make all of the other bands in town look like bourgeois money grabbing fuckheads..........and, the upside could be huge! If it goes off well and people drink a lot you might even end up getting paid.

44. **Always double double-check everything!** See the Cyanotic example in *Case Studies*.

45. **Use a hot issue to your advantage.** Global warming, politics, voting, human rights, animal rights, education, music—but mean it!

46. **Hire a celebrity to sit in with your band.** "Featuring a special sit in from Mr. xxxx xxxx on xylophone."

47. **Create a smaller event four weeks before the main event as a satellite publicity device.** Be your own advance man. This could be a small acoustic show, a reading, a DJ night, a BBQ in the park, a lecture, an art event—anything that gets people out. So now you're saying "What, I was happy blaming my agent, but now in addition to suggesting I create my own event, now you want me to create another event four weeks before my other event?" Yes!

48. **See the "Experience Is Good" list in the appendix...**

49. **Don't travel too far away from your home base.** When you create an accidental collision of events you have to be able to go back to that city to put that smoke in a jar. See the Project .44 Case Study as an example.

50. **Stay sober.** In his piece about accounting, Darren Guccione advised taking care of mind and body and pointed out that even the most amazing accountant is no match for drugs. For a band starting off it seems that all kinds of problems would be helped if they were dealt with by at least one or two members of the band being sober. It's easy to get pulled into the world of sex, drugs, and rock'n'roll and get swept up into the idea of what you think it is. The reality is that it's very hard work, the pinnacle of three-dimensional-multi-tasking, and next to impossible if you don't know exactly what you're doing all of the time. Instead of having a designated driver in the band, I'd suggest the opposite; a designated idiot. It's that person's job to get drunk that day; insult the soundman; accidentally unplug something on stage; trash a mic, a guitar, a monitor, something to the value of around $150: insult some fans; puke in someone's car; get lost; fall asleep; delay the band's departure by several crucial hours; piss themselves, and then puke in the van.

51. **Get GPS.** Here's a really easy way to have a better show: Don't get fucking lost on the way there, you stupid fuck! Someone in the band needs to get directions to the venue from Mapquest, a road map at the library, or your $300 GPS system. If you're late to the venue, you're not going to get a soundcheck, you're going to be stressed, and you're going to sound like shit.

52. **Don't think of the promoter as a promoter.** That's as misleading as calling a guarantee a guarantee. The safest philosophy for you is to think of them as door openers and remind yourself that that is the only thing you are relying on them to do. Anything else will be a pleasant surprise. As your experience of different promoters grows you'll find some who are fantastic and some who don't care. If in doubt, use this strategy.

53. **Don't give up your day job.** Once you give up your day job you have to invest completely in the idea that one day you're going to be huge and you become susceptible to pie in the sky philosophies. With the grounding of a day job, or two, or three, you're more likely to have the resources you need to make smarter choices about touring. You'll be able to play for free and start the building process.

54. **Create a guest list of the twenty-five coolest people you know** three to four weeks in advance of your event. Then these influential types will become part of your promotional team (See more from Curse Mackey in the Chapter on *Creating Your Own Event* chapter).

55. **Put a celebrity in your merch booth.**

56. **Be your advance/promotions team.** Create a reason to be in a tour city six to ten weeks ahead of your show: a DJ slot, spoken word appearance, anything. While you are there you can do a radio interview, stop by local stores to tell them about the show and leave postcards, meet with your street team and play them new tracks from your new album, give them the materials they need, and plant the seeds for greater success.

57. **Tour in the smallest, most efficient vehicle you can - not the coolest.** One of our bands had a 1970's bus and they spent more time painting the flames down the side than they did planning their tour or making sure the brakes worked (which they didn't).

58. **Tour in the coolest vehicle you can.** Never mind efficiencies and size - this will become your unique signature.

59. **Don't play a market too often, especially your own.** An exciting event is one that doesn't happen every three weeks.

60. **Buy on to a larger tour for regional dates. Then book shows in smaller venues in each of those markets four weeks later.** Use your buy-on as the reason to get the smaller club shows that have previously eluded you.

61. **Have a new shirt for every new home market show.** This does two things: it makes you have a new shirt for every show, and it might make you stop playing your home market to the point that all of the people that used to love you more than any other band on the planet now hate you because of the impositions you are making on their time. Go and ask your biggest fan right now, "Would you like it if we played every two weeks?" They'll say yes… then move to another country. You might say, "We could only have a new shirt designed, printed, and ready for a show every three months" … OK! Maybe your fans will get into the habit of collecting the shirts from each show. As long as it's four per year, it's special and cool. And you'll be the band that has special stuff at every show… someone will wear the shirt from the show two years ago and people will talk about it .

And for heaven's sake, try writing a Thank You Card!

Check out the one the artists from the 2003 Pigface *United Tour* sent to all the venues who welcomed them:

I'm not saying that a thank you card is an unusual thing… but we should have included an oxygen tank with each one!

CHAPTER 57

GOOD

Advice

...FROM BAAAD PEOPLE

MUSIC AS "ART" NOT "PRODUCT"

ZIM ZUM

ZIM ZUM

MULTI PLATINUM MUSICIAN / SONGWRITER

www.myspace.com/ThePopCultureSuicides

As a band, we follow a simple yet, at least to us, obvious approach: bringing what we do directly to the people that want to hear it, see it, and truly be a part of it. It stems from simply writing music and being a band without ever taking into account where the music will go or how it will be received.

MUSIC AS "ART" NOT "PRODUCT"

Interesting concept, no? Certainly not an "industry standard" by any means, but the thought and time that is put into being creatively unique with the music that I write has to carry over into bringing that music to the masses with an equally unique approach. Being an independent and completely self-supported band that can look at 90% of the tour packages out today and not see where we would fit in, we pay very close attention to what our fans say and do.

Beyond a cult-like gang, along the lines of a well-organized social movement, the fans are thousands of publicists and promoters, extremely viral on the Internet and in the cities they live in, and even more passionate than anyone you could ever hire because they are connected to it in a personal way. The perfect balance is to bring what we do to the places that they want us to do it in. They dictate exactly where we play regardless and in spite of the major market. You can easily get lost in the shuffle of a major market venue schedule because of the amount of bands that come through the doors or you can stand out and change the scene by taking a different approach. A lot of the focus in the industry is to specifically target major markets and demographics and that does work for a lot of bands. But there are actually bands that don't fit the "industry standard" and we are certainly one of those bands. We are working with the knowledge and experience of how the industry works but also going around the industry formats and trying things that are out of the box but work well for us.

The first 15 shows we did had no product, no CD—the live shows being the only place you could hear the music, and playing one hour and forty-five minute nonstop sets. They were all in places that 99% of bands don't look to as places that they would play as they are trying to play the places that the bands they emulate play and marketing to get a respectable amount of people into those venues.

We do the exact opposite. We bring an arena-sized show that translates just as effectively into a club that usually requires the stage to be built out, the PA and lighting to be brought in, as well as all of the promotion to be done by us and the fans. At any given moment, any part of the club could be, and usually is, the stage. Why? Because you simply can't buy or manufacture the vibe of a room where everything is unexpected, unknown, and extremely combustible. I will always prefer the entire venue to feel like they just spent the evening in

> "...you simply can't buy or manufacture the vibe of a room where everything is unexpected, unknown, and extremely combustible."

"Shatter the mold and build a new model." the front row rather than a handful of people who actually did. Bringing 500 people into the standard major market 800-1,200 capacity ten foot barricade, six foot stage room is one thing, but bringing full production into a 300+, face to face with the band, room that should hold 250 at best and has never seen anything other than cover bands and $1 beer nights, is the way to shatter the mold and build a new model in a way that most bands won't do. Maybe they don't want to; maybe they won't translate as well in that environment; maybe playing the standard venues symbolizes a certain status that means more than longevity. All you have to do is pay even a little attention to what major bands do when they want to "do something for their fans" ... they play the small, unexpected venue.

Building a militant following and carving out our own path means sticking to an alternate approach that is truly dictated by the people that make the regional, national, and international exposure of this band more than standard marketing formats ever could. In 15 shows, we have changed the general mindset of almost every single club we have played in that they see what they have become accustomed to and what can actually be done if approached with an open mind. Maybe we are alone in this way of thinking, but there is a new strategy—not one solely based on markets and demographics, but based on alternate approaches. Bridging the gap between what you want to present with where your fan base really wants to see it because that experience goes a long, long way in a day and age where the separation between bands and their fans is much larger than the barricade in between them.

LOVE WHAT YOU DO
STEVE TRAXLER, JAM USA

1. Love what you do, regardless of what you are paid. It will show and you will grow and go far.

2. Learn everyday and make friends on the road. Take time to learn what everyone else does both alongside you and in each city you visit. It's a great opportunity and no matter how far you go in the business, you will learn more each day.

3. Follow your gut instinct. It's probably the right one.

4. Always deal with honesty and integrity. Your credibility is your most important asset.

5. Make good people choices, whether you are being hired or doing the hiring. Surround yourself with great people.

6. When issues arise on the road, treat others as you would want to be treated, never lose your cool, and put yourself in the other person's shoes before acting. By understanding all perspectives, a solution usually becomes obvious.

7. Pay attention to the details. In this business, the devil is always in the details and there are many devils along the way.

8. Its OK to make mistakes in this business and still be extremely successful as long as you do the following: a) learn from your mistakes so you never repeat the same one twice—eventually you will start to run out of things to mess up and b) if you make a mistake, go to the person you report to (or those impacted) and explain the situation and how you are going to fix it. It's amazing how fast the problem will go away with quick and open communication.

9. Be on time. The touring business relies on everyone working together. Being on time and ready to work is important; from the person who unlocks the venue to the roadies to the headliner, being on time is critical and ensures financial responsibility to the tour.

10. There are few academic rules of touring. It really boils down to common sense and being able to think on your feet. Solve issues using logic and leave emotions at home.

TIPS FOR THE ROAD

MICHELLE CHO, PETA

- **Stay hydrated!** Drink plenty of water.

- **Eat!** Nutrition will make or break you on tour. I highly recommend a vegetarian diet. Better for your health, better for the environment, and better for animals. Visit *www.GoVeg.com* for your free vegetarian starter kit!

- **Don't talk shit!** This is difficult for a lot of people. The others you're on tour with are your family. You may just find that you need a favor one day, so be courteous to everyone, including crew.

- **Shower daily!** In the event that the venue doesn't have a shower and your drive is a long one, at least be sure to sink shower and use plenty of non-animal-tested baby wipes! There's nothing worse than a stinky bus mate.

- **Be nice to your bus driver!** Just do it…

- **Follow bus rules!** No exceptions! No poop in the potty.

- **Clean up after yourself!** Don't trash your bus, don't trash venues, and don't trash hotels.

- **Bus call means have your ass on the bus at the posted time;** otherwise you're getting left behind!

Nothing can truly prepare you for life on the road. But, who better to prep you than musical genius and industry mogul Martin Atkins?

www.goveg.com

www.PETA2.com

10 THINGS I LEARNED FROM TOURING

CHRIS TISONE

1) Everything is not a half hour away. I worked with a manager once who, no matter where we were going, told everyone it would take a half hour. After several half hour drives that were more like two to three hours, people started to get upset. People can deal with a lot if you are up front with them, but they get downright angry when you lie.

2) Never distribute per diems in lump sum. Actors will spend their first couple of nights drinking the entire amount away, and have nothing left for the rest of the tour. It may be more work for you, but distribute the cash in installments, or else by midweek you'll be buying everyone dinner.

3) People need to eat. For whatever reason, people tend to turn their brains off when on tour and forget to take care of their basic personal needs. This leads to extremely cranky behavior that can be detrimental to the group. When planning a tour, it's wise to designate or schedule meal times in advance and stick to them. If you are doing a lot of traveling, bring along a cooler with water and some snacks to eat in the car. Don't be afraid of healthy stuff either. You tend to eat a lot of fast food when touring, and it helps to have something healthy to munch on.

4) Have at least one zero balance credit card with you at all times. You just never know what is going to come up on tour and having a credit card that you know is available for emergency use can be essential in a crisis, as well as give you personal piece of mind.

5) Learn about your group's medical history and any allergies. I worked on an out-of-town show where I got a lot of grief about asking for this information. People seemed to think it was none of my business. I later learned that, within this cast of twelve, there were three diabetics, two actors allergic to penicillin, one with asthma, and one more who was allergic to bee stings and had to have a shot of adrenalin within 45 minutes of a sting or his throat would close up and he'd die.

6) Map quest can be a useful tool, but it can also suck. Sometimes it will lead you to a field in the middle of nowhere and it does not account for traffic congestion and construction. Always

> " Never distribute per diems in lump sum. Actors will spend their first couple of nights drinking the entire amount away, and have nothing left for the rest of the tour."

CHRIS TISONE

CHILDRENS GROUP TOUR MANAGER

check with the venue 24 hours before you are scheduled to arrive; double check your directions with them and ask if there are any construction projects or detours on the way.

7) **Be nice to the Union guys.** If you are a non-union company working in a union house, you have to work with these guys and they can be your best friends or your worst enemies. What determines how they treat you, is how you treat them.

> " What determines how they treat you, is how you treat them."

8) **On a longer tour, you must have back-up cash for incidentals.** You simply can't depend on payment from the venues as it is hard, if not impossible, to cash checks on the road.

9) **Confirm, confirm, confirm.** Hotels, cars, plane tickets, whatever. It's always best to confirm everything at least a week before the tour goes out and then again about 24 hours in advance. This is one area of touring that you can have some amount of control over. Take it!

10) **Coordinate your tour so that you are not constantly backtracking.** People just can't handle being in cars for too long and they get frustrated driving back and forth across a state when they have no control over it. Also, if it's a really hectic tour schedule, make some time for R&R. People can't go from venue to venue without some kind of break and relaxation.

DO'S AND DON'TS
FROM MOOSE

DO:

- **Make friends with every person at the club:** merch handler, loaders, ticket person, promoter, runner, owner, opening bands, everyone.
- **Play your best show no matter how many people are there.**
- **Make the effort to personally promote the show through any means available.**
- **Spend the time to develop a band logo, album art, and T-shirt art.**
- **Trust the members of your team.**
- **Second guess every decision made,** especially when someone else is telling you to do it.
- **Be willing to take risks that will assuredly cost money.**
- **Keep the groupies out of the van.**
- **Get paid upfront.**
- **Call the local radio stations as part of advancing a show** to let them know you're playing and invite staff to the show. Offer, but don't push, to do an in-studio interview and/or performance.

DON'T:

- **Trash talk the opening bands, headliner's venue, promoter, fans, or sound guy,** whether at the show or afterwards.
- **Expect anyone else to do it for you.**
- **Plan on being in a band to make money.**
- **Make yourself so sick that the band is affected by it.**
- **Open yourself to situations that will likely result in legal action.**
- **Fuck your bandmates' significant others.**
- **Let the 10th interview or hand you shake** be less important than the first.
- **Assume someone else is taking care of everything.**
- **Sneak in underage audience members.** Ask the doorman and then walk away from it.
- **Complain about anything for any reason** while you are a guest in someone else's town.

TIPS FOR TOURING:

JARED LOUCHE, CHEMLAB

These are just a few things that came to me in a flash. They're not must-have guiding lights or screaming common sense like "Don't shit on the bus!" They're not the quintessential do's and don'ts for the young guns as they trip ecstatically out onto the road. They're just a few things that I've found are important to keep in the back of your mind.

JARED LOUCHE

SINGER, LYRICIST, CONCEPTUALIST
FOR CHEMLAB, ALTERED STATEMEN,
H3LLB3NT
FIFTH COLUMN RECORDS
www.hydrogenbar.com
www.myspace.com/chemlab

1. **Don't get wasted before the show.** Celebrate afterwards, when there's something to celebrate. Johnny Thunders puking all over his amp during "Chinese Rocks" (how apropos) is really only barely on the edge of being cool. All the rest of us mortals look like wasted idiots. Never mind the fact that afterwards you have nothing to celebrate and you have to pay for the trashed keyboard you fell on top of. Good thing you didn't borrow it from the other band on the bill.

2. **Don't borrow gear from the other bands if it can be helped.**

3. **Bring a toothbrush to clean puke out from between the keys of the keyboards** you borrow from the other bands.

4. **If a promoter points a surprisingly large gun at you,** while one of his gorilla doormen looms, and screams at the top of his lungs: "I'm not paying you fucks a dime! Now get the fuck out of my office!" the proper response almost certainly isn't to tell him to his face that he's an asshole, his club blows, and that you're going to smash out his windshield with a baseball bat, especially when his office is at the top of a very long flight of stairs.

5. **Don't get off the bus at 5am, one hundred miles from anywhere, in Texas,** without making sure that at least two people know that you're leaving. Preferably they are awake, or sentient enough to recognize who you are. Don't get off the bus without your cell phone or credit card. And bring a jacket. And a pair of underpants. What the hell, bring that "keyboard" toothbrush with you, too.

6. **Don't let your label bosses fly "tastemakers and label reps" in from the home office in LA.** Especially for your show in Moscow. No matter what they tell you, that's a recoupable expense and will be coming out of your hide until it's paid back. So are the 5-star hotels they're staying in. Besides, "tastemakers" have invariably bad taste, even if they swear up and down that they "love your band, man." I mean, who wears a leopard-print jacket without a profound sense of humor about it?! If you're staying down the hall from each other in that 5-star hotel you're inadvertently paying for, always offer to let them borrow your toothbrush if they seem to have "mysteriously lost theirs."

7. **On hills with steep gradients, don't drive the van loaded with gear full-speed** onto one of those enticing-looking, and hilariously labeled, "Runaway Truck" ramps no matter how much fun your drummer thinks it would be to ram into the water drums at the far end of it. Remember, he's a drummer and, while talented in some areas, he's limited in common sense. A bit like your singer, but without the pretension and feather boas.

8. **Don't ignore that funny smell in the back of the van any longer.** It's almost certainly something unpleasant rotting in some secret corner. Left to its own devices, it'll become virulent and start taking over. Root it out and face the mucus. Don't ignore that funny sound coming from the engine and keep driving for another hundred miles, either. Though if I have to tell you that one, you really shouldn't be on the road at all, and if that noise continues unchecked you won't be for much longer.

9. **Don't pick up socks in the hallway of the bus. No, really. Think about it.** Touring can be a lonely business. Guys tour a lot. They get lonely. Think about socks and girls. Think about what uses socks have. Then think about why one wouldn't want them to remain in the bunk with you… afterwards. Then think about why you really don't want to pick one, or loads of them up, even if you're fresh out of socks. Really, don't put your foot in… never mind.

10. **Don't listen when other bands tell you what you should watch out for on the road.** You'll work it out soon enough. Good luck though. Maybe you should write a book about it.

CHAPTER 58

CASE STUDIES: AN OUT-OF-BAND EXPERIENCE

PROJECT 44

PEGASUS
UNICORN

CYANOTIC

PIG

CASE STUDIES

CYANOTIC CASE STUDY
CYANOTIC TOUR 2006

The band, Cyanotic, were having some problems right before the beginning of their tour. So, I started to take some notes at the same time as trying to help them. They were definitely conflicted between their entrenched plans to tour and what they thought would be the long-term consequences of cancelling. In our first real conversation about these issues, they admitted, "some of theses shows are like, fuck we're only going to play to, like, three people." So, I raised the point that they could very well be doing more damage by performing the shows than not. It was three days before they were due to leave and they still had no information from the agent!

Note the dates were listed without the days off "so it looked better." There were three days off on a twenty-one day tour and nine TBA's which means "To Be Arranged" or "Not Confirmed." These were the dates listed as of July 8th—two weeks before the band was supposed to leave.

They were aware that they still needed to send out promotional materials for Florida and South Carolina. I told them, "The show should have been on sale eight weeks ago!" They should have had posters eight weeks ago! It seemed like the singer was coming down with hives or some stress-related freak out. "This shouldn't be my job," he said. But it was. I suggested that their tour manager call three venues to find out how tickets were selling to get an idea of what they were heading into.

Twenty-four hours later, they hadn't.

I sent them an e-mail link to a club I had never heard of in a city I had never been to, where their show, five days away, was not listed. And I saw such horrifying information as: "the largest rock venue" in wherever the fuck it was. I bounced the information to the band. Twenty-Four hours later, it turned out that the club was no longer open.

So, maybe this is a good time to talk about a real mindset which is: "inability-to-cancel-a-tour-itis." And whilst any label-owner or manager wants a band to be stubborn, to laugh at the prospect of adversity, to swim through mud and shit, to

CYANOTIC TOUR AS OF JULY 8th	
07/21	Grounds Sphere Rhythm - Allegan, MI
07/22	High Five - Columbus, OH
07/23	Garfield Artworks - Pittsburgh, PA
07/24	The Penny Arcade - Rochester, NY
07/25	
07/26	**TBA** - Boston, MA
07/27	Bottom's Up - Flushing/Queens - New York, NY
07/28	The Sterling [Rock Room] - Allentown, PA
07/29	**TBA** - Baltimore, MD
07/30	**TBA** - Raleigh, NC
07/31	**TBA** - Charlotte, NC
08/01	
08/02	Ground Zero - Spartanburg, SC
08/03	**TBA** - Tampa, FL
08/04	Saints & Sinners - Spring Hill, FL
08/05	**TBA** - Atlanta, GA
08/06	**TBA** - Nashville, TN
08/07	
08/08	**TBA** - St. Louis, MO
08/09	Double Door - Chicago, IL
08/10	**TBA** - South Bend, IN

make their music and perform on stage, and basically suspend logical, realistic, not to mention pessimistic, thought, there also needs to be some kind of reality check. When along the way did "the show must go on" come to mean "kamikaze pilot?" That's not what it's supposed to mean! You have to understand that it takes more than a couple of well-placed comments and a reality check to convince a band or a tour manager or an agent that following a laid-out path might be fool-hardy. You have to remember that relatives, girlfriends, peers, bartenders, and all kinds of people have probably been telling this band, for years, to "wake up and smell the napalm." At least in this case, the band got to quickly arrange two internet-promoted shows and managed to deal with some of the fallout before it fell out.

> Four days before the tour starts:
> "We calculated the mileage today."
> Traveling by Van 110 miles = $800-900
> "Kinda sucks to find that out now." 7/17/06

> "When along the way did "the show must go on" come to mean "kamikaze pilot.""

MA: Hang in there—don't let everyone's hopes influence what really is the situation here... You might also want to watch out for a guarantee—that has already had 50% paid to the agent as deposit!

Please be very, very careful and remember I am here to help if you and the band want to do it right.

Cyanotic: Thanks very much—I'll be in touch, and let you know what I find out.

MA: And, just in case you didn't realize *1/3rd *of your dates are still open - in class and in the new book - we recommend at least 10 weeks lead in time.

MA: You know what I said about the night before or after being a huge industrial night....?

The Hottest Monthly Industrial Party in the Tri-State!!! Saturday, July 22nd!!

...the band is performing there on the 28th!!

RIGHT PLACE, WRONG NIGHT:
MERCH DISASTER: $1,300 OR NOT?

MA: did you need any shirts?

Cyanotic: we have shirts coming

MA: Some work shirts or chick shirts? To broaden your merch extravaganza?

Cyanotic: it would be cool

Cyanotic: but my budget...is...yea...ouch

MA: I can look at fronting them - what sizes worked for you b4?

MA: you gotta have the spread dude!!

Cyanotic: I am just worried about owing you more than I have

Cyanotic: how much would 20 work shirts be? those did sell well.

MA: dude!! do you know how many you sold? what sizes? does Ang have that

Cyanotic: no idea

MA: can you ask her? I'm sure she kept records of it—and you need to know what sizes sell......!

MA: 20 work shirts would be 150. BUT—if you sold 5 per night... you should be ordering 100... with 20 you make 250 profit. With 100 you make $1,300, selling them at $20. That's for 18 shows

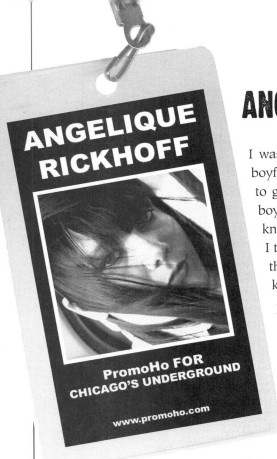

ANGELIQUE RICKHOFF

PromoHo FOR CHICAGO'S UNDERGROUND

www.promoho.com

ANGELIQUE RICKHOFF

I was asked to join the *Cyanotic Transhuman Tour* in the summer of 2005. My boyfriend at the time was their live drummer and I figured it would be a neat way to get away for a little while and see some different places. Besides all that, my boyfriend is straight edge and if you know anything about the Cyanotic crew, you know that they enjoy their drinking and drugs quite a bit. I'm a happy medium so I thought maybe I could bring some balance to the situation. A few weeks before the tour, I was asked by Cyanotic's manager to be the touring manager. Little did I know what that would mean.

In prep for the tour I mapped out all the dates, figured out gas costs with average gas prices, and made a list of things that should be brought on any trip (like a map!). We got lost in every single city! Getting lost means wasting gas. Getting lost means being late. Promoters don't like when you are late. Sound guys don't like when you're late for sound check. If you are too late for sound check, you just don't get one and you sound like shit.

While I'm on the subject of promoters I'll give you a little insight into what my job entailed. Though Cyanotic had a rider with a guarantee, few promoters/ clubs acknowledged it. I had to chase down more than a few promoters for water and money. In Ithaca, the promoter actually left without paying us. After talking to the club owner in person the next day, he admitted they hadn't made enough money to pay us. He offered to send us the money later, but seeing as though we were all starving and low on cash, we compromised and he fed our seven-person crew. In the end we actually got more money in food.

The party factor did become a problem at times. Since my boyfriend was the only sober band member at the end of shows he was often the stuck loading the gear back into the van by himself. He also became designated driver since the van was a little too large for me to drive. Some nights we got our own hotel room just so we could get some down time. I recall screaming at some point "Sleep is my drug! You have your drugs! Let me have mine!"

Other highlights on this tour were: playing a barn show at the hippy commune (chickens and all!), the guitarist taking off with the van before every show and returning it once with a huge dent in the side, following some coke crazed promoter in our van in the rain at about 90 miles an hour to find a hotel, same coke crazed promoter buying the band a hooker.

I was happy to get home, but I knew I going to miss parts of it. Let's just say it's not easy for one straightedge, one or two obsessive-compulsive people, and two - four addicts to spend 24 hours a day for a week and a half together. But we did! I got some tour managing experience under my belt, I met a lot of cool people, and I got to see some places that I might not have otherwise. I just wish I could've been more involved with pre tour planning but from what I hear it was kind of last minute as far as when dates were announced. There were a few disappointing shows. And there were some clubs that had their shit together. Sound along the tour tended to vary. I think I'd do it again if I had the chance, but with more planning before hand to save on those preventable problems.

> "I'd do it again if I had the chance, but with more planning before hand to save on those preventable problems."

"The other thing that really sucks about this tour is that we only have 60 'Tanshumans' (their CD) left." — Sean Payne, singer of Cyanotic

TOO MANY COOKS...

MA: who is the one person i can talk to about a deal??

Cyanotic: myself and my management are the best

MA: ok, whats your managers e mail and #

Cyanotic: management's e-mail is abcdefg@123.com and his number is 312.555.1212... his name is Jason... he's also on AIM... RevHydra

MA: is he managing you or the label or everything?

Cyanotic: at this point, everything with me... and he's co-managing the band with Jon from InYurFace mgmt

MA: now theres another person! this is silly

Cyanotic: yeah... but all he does is handle our booking

Cyanotic: co-handle our booking

MA: so why is he co-manager?

Cyanotic: well... I guess I meant co-managing in the way that he's managing to get us shows :)

MA: too many cooks mate

Cyanotic: well... for the live aspect, Jason makes sure we get what we need and looking at the contracts, while John is put in charge of actually getting us the shows, because he's got WAY more contacts than Jason, but he doesn't do the paperwork

MA: so, what do you need?

Cyanotic: as far as...?

MA: for a show

Cyanotic: I don't even remember right now, as we just revised our rider, but my management can tell you everything and anything you would need to know

MA: can you send me the rider?

Cyanotic: Jason most certainly can, but since my last laptop was stolen last month, I don't have a copy right now

MA: ok i'll talk to you laterrrrrr

CYANOTIC END OF TOUR WRAP UP E MAIL:

The booking agent's incompetence overshadowed everything. We found out he had been straight-up lying to us and venues/promoters – telling us that the venues had been promoting the shows and that he had gotten radio ads and promo, and then telling the venues that we'd promote it and we had gotten radio ads – so in some cities, there had been -literally- zero promotion.

With that said, the shows that we had booked ourselves went very well. We're looking at playing a small number of make-up dates in November in the cities we cut from this tour, and several venues that we played have asked us to come back in a few months, so that the show can be properly promoted.

Jairus

PIG CASE STUDY

PIG TOUR 2006

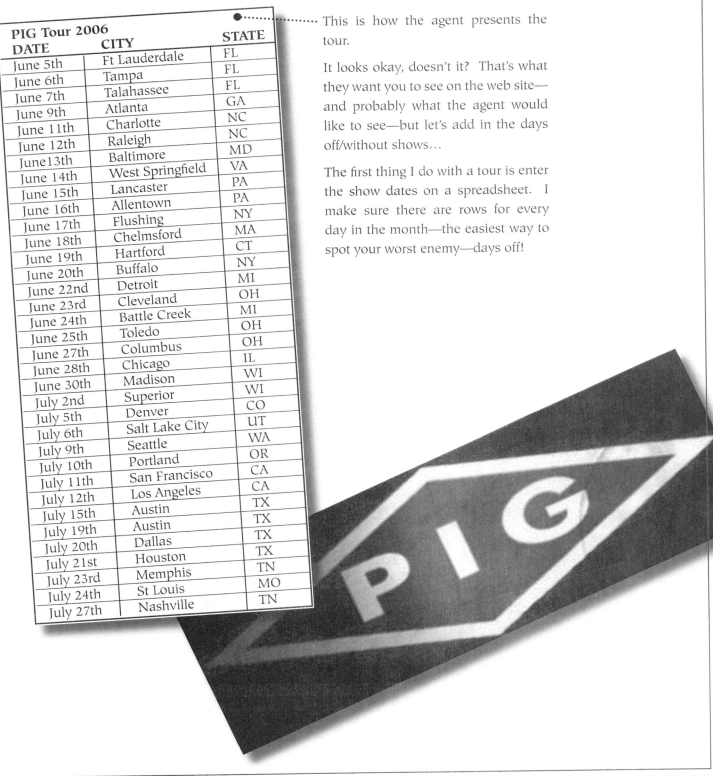

PIG Tour 2006		
DATE	**CITY**	**STATE**
June 5th	Ft Lauderdale	FL
June 6th	Tampa	FL
June 7th	Talahassee	FL
June 9th	Atlanta	GA
June 11th	Charlotte	NC
June 12th	Raleigh	NC
June 13th	Baltimore	MD
June 14th	West Springfield	VA
June 15th	Lancaster	PA
June 16th	Allentown	PA
June 17th	Flushing	NY
June 18th	Chelmsford	MA
June 19th	Hartford	CT
June 20th	Buffalo	NY
June 22nd	Detroit	MI
June 23rd	Cleveland	OH
June 24th	Battle Creek	MI
June 25th	Toledo	OH
June 27th	Columbus	OH
June 28th	Chicago	IL
June 30th	Madison	WI
July 2nd	Superior	WI
July 5th	Denver	CO
July 6th	Salt Lake City	UT
July 9th	Seattle	WA
July 10th	Portland	OR
July 11th	San Francisco	CA
July 12th	Los Angeles	CA
July 15th	Austin	TX
July 19th	Austin	TX
July 20th	Dallas	TX
July 21st	Houston	TX
July 23rd	Memphis	TN
July 24th	St Louis	MO
July 27th	Nashville	TN

This is how the agent presents the tour.

It looks okay, doesn't it? That's what they want you to see on the web site—and probably what the agent would like to see—but let's add in the days off/without shows…

The first thing I do with a tour is enter the show dates on a spreadsheet. I make sure there are rows for every day in the month—the easiest way to spot your worst enemy—days off!

...and you can now easily see what a fucking nightmare this was, 19 days off out of 52. The budgetary Hiroshima that they created was cited as the main reason that the tour was cancelled half way through! Who couldn't see where this was going? Remember, a day off isn't just a day without a "guarantee," it's a day without food being supplied, ditto beer, and much less likelihood of staying with someone, and much greater chance of boredom, more alcohol consumption, over indulgence, and jail! ...etc., etc., etc. So, adding in a line for every day is a top tip to avoid disaster.

TOUR:SMART TIP
for more information go to:
www.tstouring.com

Now, let's look at the days of the week, too—see if we learn anything from that...>>

"19 days off out of 52."

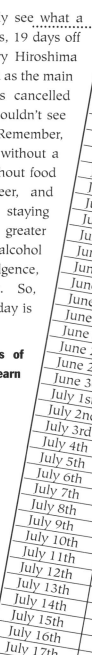

PIG Tour 2006 DATE	CITY	STATE
June 5th	Ft Lauderdale	FL
June 6th	Tampa	FL
June 7th	Talahassee	FL
June 8th		
June 9th	Atlanta	GA
June 10th		
June 11th	Charlotte	NC
June 12th	Raleigh	NC
June 13th	Baltimore	MD
June 14th	West Springfield	VA
June 15th	Lancaster	PA
June 16th	Allentown	PA
June 17th	Flushing	NY
June 18th	Chelmsford	MA
June 19th	Hartford	CT
June 20th	Buffalo	NY
June 21st		
June 22nd	Detroit	MI
June 23rd	Cleveland	OH
June 24th	Battle Creek	MI
June 25th	Toledo	OH
June 26th		
June 27th	Columbus	OH
June 28th	Chicago	IL
June 29th		
June 30th	Madison	WI
July 1st		
July 2nd	Superior	WI
July 3rd		
July 4th		
July 5th	Denver	CO
July 6th	Salt Lake City	UT
July 7th		
July 8th		
July 9th	Seattle	WA
July 10th	Portland	OR
July 11th	San Francisco	CA
July 12th	Los Angeles	CA
July 13th		
July 14th		
July 15th	Austin	TX
July 16th		
July 17th		
July 18th		
July 19th	Austin	TX
July 20th	Dallas	TX
July 21st	Houston	TX
July 22nd		
July 23rd	Memphis	TN
July 24th	St Louis	MO
July 25th		
July 26th		
July 27th	Nashville	TN

PIG Tour 2006 DAY	DATE	CITY	STATE
Mon	June 5th	Ft Lauderdale	FL
Tue	June 6th	Tampa	FL
Wed	June 7th	Talahassee	FL
Thu	June 8th		
Fri	June 9th	Atlanta	GA
Sat	June 10th		
Sun	June 11th	Charlotte	NC
Mon	June 12th	Raleigh	NC
Tue	June 13th	Baltimore	MD
Wed	June 14th	West Springfield	VA
Thu	June 15th	Lancaster	PA
Fri	June 16th	Allentown	PA
Sat	June 17th	Flushing	NY
Sun	June 18th	Chelmsford	MA
Mon	June 19th	Hartford	CT
Tue	June 20th	Buffalo	NY
Wed	June 21st		
Thu	June 22nd	Detroit	MI
Fri	June 23rd	Cleveland	OH
Sat	June 24th	Battle Creek	MI
Sun	June 25th	Toledo	OH
Mon	June 26th		
Tue	June 27th	Columbus	OH
Wed	June 28th	Chicago	IL
Thu	June 29th		
Fri	June 30th	Madison	WI
Sat	July 1st		
Sun	July 2nd	Superior	WI
Mon	July 3rd		
Tue	July 4th		
Wed	July 5th	Denver	CO
Thu	July 6th	Salt Lake City	UT
Fri	July 7th		
Sat	July 8th		
Sun	July 9th	Seattle	WA
Mon	July 10th	Portland	OR
Tue	July 11th	San Francisco	CA
Wed	July 12th	Los Angeles	CA
Thu	July 13th		
Fri	July 14th		
Sat	July 15th	Austin	TX
Sun	July 16th		
Mon	July 17th		
Tue	July 18th		
Wed	July 19th	Austin	TX
Thu	July 20th	Dallas	TX
Fri	July 21st	Houston	TX
Sat	July 22nd		
Sun	July 23rd	Memphis	TN
Mon	July 24th	St Louis	MO
Tue	July 25th		
Wed	July 26th		
Thu	July 27th	Nashville	TN

OK, well, we can see **four Saturdays and two Fridays off in the first 5 weeks?**

If you have to have one or two days off – then wait, take days off on the days that, whatever you try, you cannot find a place to play!

OK, let's go to the next level with this: Refer to the list of cities by population table (See *Appendix*). These markets are organized by the largest cities/markets first in descending order.

If I was in a band traveling from the U.K. for the first solo tour in however many years, I would certainly have some markets that, based on past touring or record sales, I would definitely want to hit. I'm not sure that Allentown, PA and Superior, WI would be on that list. I'd also want to see San Diego, Phoenix, or Tucson for better coverage overall.

One way to have increased attendances might have been to have had less than the three shows in Ohio, four shows in Texas, and three shows in Florida. Talk about an easy way to make the shows go better or worse.

TOUR:SMART TIP

for more information go to:
www.tstouring.com

TRYING TO KEEP UP WITH PIG ONLINE

RAYMOND WATTS

KMFDM, CHEMLAB,
FOUNDING MEMBER OF
INDUSTRIAL ROCK BAND
PIG

Jesus man,

One thing I learnt. Don't work with an insane booking agent. Talk about a bad routing! We were in the same city as NIN three times and one or two days before/behind ministry! All the way up the east coast, if she'd done the tiniest bit of research we would have started on the west coast and all would have been OK.

Can you believe that?

Anyway,

Hope all's good with you,

Raymond

" Don't work with an insane booking agent."

CASE STUDY PROJECT .44

I want to thank Chris Harris for allowing me to use this as an example. Next time you see Project .44 coming through town go out and support them as a thanks for sharing and caring. If you see them in LA, kick their asses.

This is a real case study, for a real band with real consequences. It's a small band but don't worry the mistakes are huge and surprisingly common. I called the band leader and his manager into the office for a meeting with myself and Chris Ramos to discuss strategy and make sure that we were all on the same page. In the preamble to the meeting we were talking about some possible scenarios and I jokingly said "you guys should do anything, just as long as you don't head out to the West Coast for Christmas." There was

p44_dist_o_m

Day of Week	Date	City	State	Venue	Support
		Chicago	IL		
	30-Dec	Salt Lake City	UT	Club Vegas	Digital Mindy
Friday	31-Dec	Las Vegas	NV	Divebar	Digital Mindy
Saturday	1-Jan				
Sunday	2-Jan	Hollywood	CA	The Whisky	
Monday	3-Jan	San Diego	CA	Brick by Brick	
Tuesday	4-Jan	Phoenix	AZ	Chasers	
Wednesday	5-Jan	El Paso	TX	Lucky Devil's	
Thursday	6-Jan				
Friday	7-Jan	Kansas City	MO	TBD	Digital Mindy
Saturday	8-Jan	St. Louis	MO	Creepy Crawl	
Sunday	9-Jan	Indianpois	IN	Melody Inn	
Monday	10-Jan	Chicago	IL	Double Door	Apocalypse Theatre
Tuesday					

a split second of silence where I realized that's exactly what they were planning, although planning is no-where near the correct word to use for this kind of sillyness.

I asked if they knew how much the fuel would cost. They didn't. They said the guarantees would cover the fuel and the venues were providing hotel rooms. This was alarming as first of all, guarantees don't exist. And if the guarantees were covering fuel then the band were getting paid substantially more than $200/night, throw in $150 for hotel rooms and the promoter is going to have to elevate the price of tickets to cover these losses. It is the last thing a band needs when trying to grow. Chris Ramos and I worked out the mileage and cost in minutes and then suggested if they wanted to tour beginning Dec. 30 they might not want to go through the mountain passes of Colorado and Utah—dangerous in December and in January. We also noticed there wasn't a show on one of the Fridays and that perhaps two days after New Year's Eve wasn't a good time to do anything anywhere. The manager assured us the club was opening especially for them. Even though it was normally closed on that date! We also noted that we never heard of the opening band and that P.44 might be better off with a strong local opener. By this point, the defenses were up and the manager proudly told us that another band had bought onto the tour. This was alarming. I didn't see Project .44 playing to many more than 30-50 people anywhere. Not an opportunity I'd be happy buying, nor one I'd be proud to sell. So now you have the problems of geography, weather, and most definite financial problems layered with a support band that is no help whatsoever to the drawing

TOUR:SMART TIP
for more information go to:
www.tstouring.com

power of the evening but who is going to be upset that the opportunity they've purchased might not be what they thought. Let's look at the mileages:

First, grab your *Rand McNally Dist-O-Map* and dial up the mileage:

It just took six minutes to add in the numbers. In a vehicle getting 15 miles to the gallon at $2.50 a gallon, that's $788.00 except, they told us they had a great deal on two small vehicles, so double the gas—$1,577.00.

Chris and I are problem solvers and suggested they head east instead of west and

Dist-O-Map® is a registered trademark of Rand McNally & Company.

p44_dist_o_map_P44.xls

	A	B	C	D	E	F	G
1	Day of Week	Date	Miles	City	State	Venue	Support
2			Start				
3				Chicago	IL		
4	Friday	30-Dec	1458	Salt Lake City	UT	Club Vegas	Digital Mindy
5	Saturday	31-Dec	439	Las Vegas	NV	Divebar	Digital Mindy
6	Sunday	1-Jan					
7	Monday	2-Jan	289	Hollywood	CA	The Whisky	
8	Tuesday	3-Jan	121	San Diego	CA	Brick by Brick	
9	Wednesday	4-Jan	398	Phoenix	AZ	Chasers	
10	Thursday	5-Jan	402	El Paso	TX	Lucky Devil's	
11	Friday	6-Jan					
12	Saturday	7-Jan	942	Kansas City	MO	TBD	Digital Mindy
13	Sunday	8-Jan	255	St. Louis	MO	Creepy Crawl	
14	Monday	9-Jan	239	Indianpois	IN	Melody Inn	
15	Tuesday	10-Jan	189	Chicago	IL	Double Door	Apocalypse Theatre
16	TOTAL MILES		**4732**				
17							

quickly dialed up an alternative. East of a line from Minneapolis to Houston every show you have will be closer. If there's a problem with a show there will be many alternate cities with an easy driving distance. Let's have a look at that sheet.

p44_dist_o_map_P44.xls

	A	B	C	D	E	F	G
1	Day of Week	Date	Miles	City	State	Venue	Support
2			Start				
3				Chicago	IL		
4	Friday	30-Dec	92	Milwaukee	WI		Digital Mindy
5	Saturday	31-Dec	79	Madison	WI		Digital Mindy
6	Sunday	1-Jan	269	Springfield	IL		
7	Monday	2-Jan	101	St. Louis	MO		
8	Tuesday	3-Jan	309	Nashville	TN		
9	Wednesday	4-Jan	179	Louisville	KY		
10	Thursday	5-Jan	110	Cincinnati	OH		
11	Friday	6-Jan	306	Pittsburgh	PA		
12	Saturday	7-Jan	131	Cleveland	OH		Digital Mindy
13	Sunday	8-Jan	175	Detriot	MI		
14	Monday	9-Jan	152	Grand rapids	MI		
15	Tuesday	10-Jan	173	Chicago	IL		Apocalypse Theatre
16	TOTAL MILES		**2076**				
17							

So, by heading east instead of west it saves the band $885.33 in gas alone, and even though its still winter the drives are much less risky and much shorter so there is less chance of the band arriving late, missing a show completely when one of the mountain passes in Colorado is closed. Or maybe the band makes it and nobody in the audience does, or, just in case you've forgotten this is the real world, there's less of a chance of someone dying in a horrible road accident. Although, risking life and limb to go and perform to an enthusiastic crowd has never seemed crazy to me. This west coast trip is just completely fucking insane. If they head east they could add two more shows. Let's be pessimistic, $250/night door money and $300/night merch—that's $1,100 difference. A total of slightly under $2,000 on a ten day tour. Also, there's much more chance, assuming you have some fans, that some of the Louisville kids will drive to Cincinnati and some of the Pittsburgh fans will drive to Cleveland and some of the Detroit fans will drive Cleveland and Grand Rapids, increasing your attendance by 10-15%. There is no fucking way anyone's driving from Salt Lake City to Las Vegas.

There's a much better chance you will arrive in a city early enough to sound check so you're going to sound better.

There's a much better chance you will have had time to shower so you're going to smell better and have a much better chance of finding a place to stay the next night.

There's a much better chance you'll have time to visit a local record store, a tattoo parlor, a Starbucks, and hand out hundreds of free tickets if you need to. Simply put, heading east is a much better idea.

Despite all of this, the band and their manager decided to head west. It seemed like they were unable to think things through with the new information. They just made a plan for whatever reason (palm trees, California girls, the amazing pizza in Los Angeles?) And by golly they were going to stick to it. One of the first repercussions was Chris Ramos disillusioned, left the label. After all, what's the fucking point? At least I had the germ of an idea this would make one hell of a case study.

I'm not saying that all travel like that is bad. For P.44, traveling to Los Angeles to do a show at Christmas was an event. But they failed to make it an event for anyone else. There should have been a Farewell P.44 "California or Bust" Party two weeks before hand where they could have sold some shirts, and got people invested in the idea. The ticket could have included admission to their final show where they would have slide shows of their crazy tour to the west coast. But they didn't do any of that. This business is all about creating events. They didn't.

> "...just in case you've forgotten this is the real world, there's less of a chance of someone dying in a horrible road accident."

TOUR DIARY—CHRIS HARRIS *PROJECT .44*
Wednesday, January 11, 2006
Propaganda Tour (phase 1) *tour diary*
Category: Travel and Places
Ahh the ups and downs of life on the road.

15 states, 5000 miles and 3 major flesh wounds.

Denver– OK denver where were you? late arriving crowd, felt bad for Digital Mindy—good warm up for things to come.

Salt Lake City– day before new years is typically a tough day to get anyone out but SLC showed up—great crowd (enthusiasm wise—non stop movement), great club & owner (sorry the backstage party went so long Dusty!)—thanks to paul for helping out. We will be back, I like the SLC.

Vegas– there is a diamond in the desert and its name is Dive Bar, if you go to Vegas find this place—a very cool vibe, not your typical Vegas B.S. small stage intense show, I wind up in the ER all night on NYE, oh well the first of the flesh wounds.

LA– The Whisky sucks—this isnt the place Van Halen, The Doors & Motley Crue played—this is place out for $$. They 'pay to play' the openers and F the bands, horrible experience—don't want to play there again. On the bright side thanks to Andrea for her hospitality.

San Diego– San Diego puts LA to shame, small but loyal scene—great bunch of people will P.44 play ComiCon? Negotiations have started. Thanks to Bryan for his hospitality.

Phoenix– Phuck Phoenix.

El Paso— I enjoyed being a 'minority for a day' as this is pretty much a mexican town. GREAT bunch of people fantastic show pone of the best on the tour. met some great people— 'L' have fun in Dallas ;-)

KC– for a last minute show this was fun, some loyalist came out again, and Brandon is a class guy, this was a small show but a great time. it ended like an episode of cops and we all hope Angel is OK (major flesh wound 2) cant wait to get back to KC.

St Louis– Back at the creep crawl! we learned that this was one of the last shows at the legendary creepy crawl—we will sad to see it go. Jeff runs a nice club there. We will back to the 'new' creepy this spring looking forward to it.

Indianapolis– ahhh Indy was great. Gretchen and Dave worked their asses off and had the place packed on a Monday–great crowd and great people . Cant wait to get back and support DJ Copper Top!!!

Sidebar annotations:

This is brilliant. Not only was there nobody there, now everybody knows it.

NOW you have an awareness of the marketplace?

Great crowd 'enthusiasm wise' = entertainment code for nobody there.

Wow, this is the venue that agreed to open especially for you. Was there another way to find out it's not the same place is was 15 years ago other than driving there?

OK. So I'm guessing this was bad?

Wow! There is a chapter about the random collision of events. Congratulations, you made one happen. ONE THOUSAND FOUR HUNDRED AND THIRTY NINE MILES away from home.

Easiest way to create a catastrophe.

Three good shows but how are we defining good at this point? More than 50 people? A good show isn't just a show that isn't just a catastrophe. It is a show that puts the band in front of more people than the time they played the city or venue before with a broader array of merchandise and a more successful overall result. If it's an early crowd with an early curfew, you get there early, etc. The one surprising high point—El Paso so far away from home that the band are unable to capitalize on a favorable collision of events that they stumbled into like a drunk being hit in the side of a face with a revolving door.

Summary

Salt Lake City, UT	Small Show
Las Vegas, NV	OK
Hollywood, CA	Terrible
San Diego, CA	OK
Phoenix, AZ	Terrible
El Paso, TX	Good
Kansas City, MO	Small Show
St. Louis MO	OK
Indianapolis, IN	Good
Chicago, IL	Good

CHRIS HARRIS:
A FEW QUESTIONS TO CLARIFY THE CASE STUDY

MA: How did Digital Mindy, the opening band, react to everything?

CH: DigMin expected much more promotion. They didn't know the label was not fully supporting the tour and when we got to cities, it was hit or miss on whether there were even posters up that we had sent. Some cities, we would roll in and hear radio ads… those were good shows. When you don't even see the poster up at the club? Bad show.

MA: Were there any unforeseen expenses?

CH: Not really, I had budgeted for the gas and rentals fairly well, we had accommodations set for the most part. Aside from having to get one $30 hotel, we were good.

MA: How did merch do?

CH: Some cities great, some so-so, some sucky. All ages in El Paso—great, an OK-attended show in San Diego—great, no crowd in AZ—no real sales!

MA: Do you have the actual attendance figures?

CH: No.

MA: How much money was made or lost?

CH: After all expenses, we made about $135.

> "A good show isn't just a show that isn't just a catastrophe."

STORIES FROM THE FRONT LINE #3

MURDER INC.
we're
here
to
fuck
you
over
ALL ACCESS
summer premier 1992

TEST DEPT
AFTER SHOW
invisible
x-tacy under duress 1996

KILLING JOKE
BACKSTAGE
EXCESS
ALL AREAS

SEE The DAMAGE MANUAL
@WETLANDS N.Y.C. 10/21 11pm
Call The Syndicate
1-888-666-2061

DAMAGE ADDICT
THE DAMAGE MANUAL
GUEST

CONCERT PASS
MARTIN ATKINS
Van Production

DAMAGE ADDICT
THE DAMAGE MANUAL
ALL ACCESS

PIGFACE
SCORN
FM EINHEIT
BAGMAN
NOT BREATHING
PHVLR
DEAD VOICES
ON AIR

THE DAMAGE MANUAL
Chris Connelly Ministry
Geordie Walker Killing Joke
Jah Wobble Public Image Limited
Martin Atkins Pigface
AAA

MCP MI CONCER
STAFF PASS
ACCESS ALL AREAS
Date Venue
Date Authorised by

CHRIS CONNELLY TOUR 1992

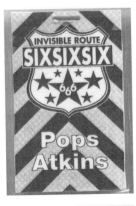

INVISIBLE ROUTE
SIXSIXSIX
666
Pops Atkins

SHEEP on DRUGS
AFTER SHOW
invisible
x-tacy under duress 1996

pigface
Sounds the Staff
AFTER show

ALL ACCESS

Pigface Team '94
Notes from thee underground
BAND

working together to tear things apart
inc. underground
UNITED II TOUR 2003
U
DIFFICULT FUCKHEAD

Pigface Team '94
INDEPENDENCE AND STRENGTH
invisible
THROUGH DIVERSIFICATION
ALL ACCESS

PIGFACE
HOUSE OF BLUES
CHICAGO
IN BLUES WE TRUST

pigface
dope
PROFESSIONAL MURDER MUSIC
RACHEL STAMP
DIABLO SYNDROME
TEAM 03
THE UNITED TOUR
PRESS

tour 1990
MINISTRY
all access all areas

AUSTRALIA
TOURING BANDS THE UNDER-GROUND WAY IN AUSTRALIA!
JEFFREY HALLS - BLAKHOLE

I started the old traditional punk 'DIY' way in 1987 from just helping load bands' equipment that I was a fan of to booking shows for them as a way to see more music I loved and help the scene prosper. First by asking the bands if they would be interested and then going to the bar person at various venues, I would find out how they ran their gigs. This was definitely a simpler time. You have the room, organize the bands, promote it, and collect all the door takings. The admission would always be low as it wasn't about the money but just making a good show happen. Often, if there was a loss at the end of the night, people would pass a hat a r o u n d to cover the PA and flyer printing so the bands went home with something! I didn't care if I got paid. I usually got some free beers, saw some great bands, and felt a sense of self achievement in making the show happen.

Things started to change in the late '80s with the more "Commercial" promoters sensing that something was brewing. Throughout the '80s, they would tour the more major "Alternative" acts. Venues started offering guaranteed "fees" for certain bands as this was before the time of electronic gambling in bars, cable TV, the internet, and other distractions! Live music, in any form, was a contender for dance clubs and provided great opportunities for "social" scenes with people you could relate to.

Then came Nirvana! Or, as Sonic Youth put it as the title of their video release "1990 – The Year That Punk Broke" and boy did it break – things would never be the same!

At the beginning of '90s, I took the next step up and started managing and "touring" bands. Using what I had learned from booking local shows and from networking with interstate bands I had worked with or just became friends with, I was able to start working on a national level. The punk/hardcore/noise scene of the 80's was great for this. No one had egos and everyone was willing to help each other out to make things happen. This would change through the 90's as people who were interested in making money, taking drugs, and getting groupies saw the form of "mainstream" music change into something we lived our lives by.

JEFF HALLS

...IS PROUD TO PRESENT REAL ALTERNATIVE ENTERTAINMENT

I was offered some of the more "popular" alternative acts to tour but now it had become a situation where I was dealing with major booking agencies, instead of dealing directly with the band or manager, and would often find myself in bidding wars against commercial touring companies. The type who might do a band like Green Day one week, then do something like Bruce Springsteen the next! Other individual promoters would also appear who would have a "mysterious" financial backer who would throw around a lot more money then promoters like myself could.

I had to remember that the main reason I started doing this in the first place was that I was a fan of music! I continued to search for music that would stimulate me and this is the music I decided to tour. Everything from Japanese noise to garage rock, from black metal to experimental. Originally taking the ethic that if you did these shows at a reasonable price, people would be interested in coming to see something different. Unfortunately, a lot of people were being confused by the mass advertising of major labels that were now signing "alternative" acts that people couldn't distinguish from the real deal. When these acts toured, they were asking for ticket prices which were over the top. Often on the back of one single!

Luckily, there were faithful audiences who were interested in the acts I was touring. Some tours made money and some lost. That's business. My partner, Julie (in life and business), made a concerted effort in 1999 to pick up the tempo of touring bands. We did eight tours that year with more losing than making money. We had to close the business down. On top of this, it cost me a relationship. Luckily, I kept a best friend. Bring on the new millennium!

The most ironic thing is seeing similar types of bands that I toured in the past now doing major shows that I would never even have considered. After learning some hard lessons and seeing how the music industry had changed over the last decade, I had to adapt the way I approached any future tours. I took a year's break because I wanted to enjoy working on tours again. It had to be a joint risk between the act and the promoter. Looking once again to quality acts, not only bands, that were inexpensive to tour and weren't driven by the almighty dollar! I have been able to do this at the scale which I enjoy, but it doesn't necessarily provide a living. But what is most important in life? Hey, I'm celebrating my 20th anniversary this year!!

ESSAYS & DEEP THOUGHTS
FAKIE WILDE

TRIUMPH IN THE FACE OF ADVERSITY

AUSTRALIA... COOL STUFF!!!

It's funny; I was lying in bed watching the morning squeeze itself to life on my ceiling, thinking about my "worst/best" gig experiences. It occurred to me that I always seem to have been able to turn bad things into good in retrospect. I guess I'm lucky that I haven't been stung that badly! For example, one show in a Brisbane pub, I think it might have been New Year's Eve; I got word back that nobody would be getting paid for the show. The band agreed to go ahead and play anyhow, a) because we were already there and "Fuck it, we like to play, let's play!" and b) because we had a stack of our friends coming. As a consequence, I snuck out the back of the club and let in heaps of people (including some of our friends) through the back door for free (it must've been an $8 or $12 entry fee). The club got really pissed at me, but we still played and I no longer felt quite as cheated.

One time I did a gig at some beach side club and the bouncers wouldn't let me in unless I paid. Damn! Bouncers can be so fucked up! My "I'm with the band" totally failed to impress them, so I said "OK, here's what I'll do. See that park bench over there in the park across the road? I'm gonna go over there and have a sleep (big party the night before). You come get me when you decide I'm in the band." Twenty minutes later, a humble bouncer wandered over, apologized, and asked could I please hurry in because the band won't play without its singer and everybody in the crowd was getting pissed off... I wandered in, the band saw me and gave me an intro, big cheers, big applause, had a great gig. Got paid!

There was a show on an outdoor stage in the middle of a city park in Brisbane one Saturday afternoon; I think the city council must've been running it or something. It was free for people to just wander down and dig the music, so we wouldn't have been getting paid anyhow. We were just having a good old time belting out the songs, until I realized that the sound guy (city council employee?) had instinctively worked out every time I was going to swear and kept pulling my vocal out of the mix every time just before I said "...fucking my clown..." in this good old song. I got hip to this very quickly and started throwing in extra "cunts and arses" all over the place in first that song and then the following song. All eyes on the soundman, he put his hands in the air, surrendering. At the end of the set, we played the "censored" song again including all the "clownfucks."

Played a midnight gig in an outdoor city mall fiesta once. That was such a great show. The mall was packed big-time. Thousands and thousands of people all bouncing around. Before we played, I saw a couple of cops backstage talking to the other band members. They shook their head and pointed at me at the tent door. The cops told me that when I sang that night, I had to try and calm everything down so that nothing got out of hand. They didn't expect this many people to come and see the bands. I told them there was nothing I could do; I was there to hype them up. They said if it got too bad out there, they'd stop the fiesta. So, the band set up and we were all ready to go in front of the biggest sea of people I'd ever played to. Then, the keyboard player, Peter, came up beside me and said, "Hey man, all my gear just crashed. The band is just gonna jam some riffs—you'll have to make something up!" Fuck! Biggest gig I'd ever played at that point, all rehearsals out the window, here we go! The band played, I did a big Iggy Pop impersonation and jumped up and down and ran around and screamed, shouted, hyped up the crowd, the police backed away, and everybody had a good time. Then, at the end of the jam, the crashed gear got fixed and we got to play our songs. Good gig, got paid! *(I think...)*

Maybe I'm just lucky but, also I think, in a sense, it's about not losing your head. In each of these three instances (and I'm sure if I think about it, we've had hundreds of occasions like these!), we could have been all hot-headed and just gone, "Nah! Fuck this! We aren't going to play!" But that just makes it worse! We like to play. We just go with it and try to make the gig work itself out. It's always a free rehearsal and there's usually a few free drinks about. (Oh! It's usually pretty bad if there are no free drinks. What sort of place hasn't got drinks on for the band? Ha, but then the band just buys their own drinks and gets happy again, anyhow!) Sitting in a dressing room or in the corner of the club being angry does not help.

> "Sitting in a dressing room or in the corner of the club being angry does not help."

POLITICAL CAMPAIGNING
JIM HOLAHAN

Campaign events and rock concerts have similar goals: to promote a person or group by bringing attention to their views, art, and issues and hopefully gain them an office, fame, or fortune.

A friends' description of past and current campaigns he worked on sparked my interest. He described the excitement of planning and executing political events. Tired of my apartment renovation work in the East Village, I was ripe for a change and signed on for my first foray into the world of political campaign planning. My job was to help set up events in NYC. The candidate was unknown and had a small staff, which allowed more opportunities for my participation.

The goal at this point was exposure and recognition of the candidate seeking public office. We walked in parades, visited landmark sites, and even hired a group of models to accompany us to Albany to carry signs. It became evident that a component of a successful campaign was good scheduling and proper planning. There wasn't a designated scheduler, so I stepped into the position and learned scheduling as I went along. This experience prepared me for my next venue, the Mark Green for U.S. Senate campaign. As an advanceman, I would make sure events were set up for the candidates' arrival and escort him through them. I always tried to drive to the location the day before at the same time of day to check the route and traffic patterns and to look for potential problems like construction or detours. This aided preparing the schedule with realistic times and exact locations.

While working for Mark Green, I met someone who worked in Senator Gary Hart's office in Washington. I wanted to join a presidential campaign and I thought Hart was going to win. I decided to volunteer for a month at his campaign headquarters in Denver and it paid off: I was hired to be an assistant scheduler and help with advance. After three months in Denver, I found myself heading back East to Washington. Hart was out of the race and I secured a job working for Al Gore as the Deputy National Scheduler for his presidential campaign. "Wow," I thought, "How did I get here?"

The scheduling department was set up with one head-scheduler and two assistants. The head-scheduler worked on the big picture—geographic regions, major events, and political issues. My role was to deal with the barrage of requests for the candidate's appearance. Our most important function was to write the candidate's daily schedule and to make sure everything was in place so it ran smoothly. Overseeing events from a remote office can be challenging, so you coordinate an advance staff to arrive days before to help execute the event. They work with local volunteers, build crowds, and determine driving routes, entrance and exits, holding areas, and where the nearest bathrooms are.

Typically, the candidate was on the road six days a week. The two assistant schedulers would alternate developing and overseeing a three-day trip. A three-ring binder was assembled for each trip with all the information needed for the candidate's events. Each book, called a "Trip Book," included a minute-by-minute schedule, speeches, issue papers, political notes, and notes about people and officials he was to meet. It was truly amazing what the candidate had to go through on a daily basis. He would be "on stage" sixteen hours a day. We would schedule a jogging partner and radio interviews all before his first breakfast meeting. Every waking minute was filled.

As the campaign grew, so did the need for more transportation. Volunteers' cars and commercial flights were not enough. As more staff and press began to travel, we began to rent vans and private aircrafts. When a certain point in the campaign is reached, Secret Service protection is available. This added a whole new dimension to my job as scheduler. The Secret Service would provide transportation and security for the candidate. Schedules needed to be created earlier in order to secure hotels and to pre-check event areas. They really didn't like changes. One of the toughest jobs of the scheduler is dealing with unpredictable complications and to keep things running smoothly. Gores' trips to NYC were always full of changes. While I was in NYC setting up events, he came to town a day and a half earlier than planned. This meant that previous efforts were useless. We only had a few hours to reschedule the events. We succeeded in accomplishing most of the tasks and had to whisk him out during rush hour. This was a challenge with a police escorted secret service motorcade: two police cars, five secret service cars, two press vans, and two staff vans winding through grid locked, snarled traffic on the way to the Lincoln Tunnel. There, Port Authority police took the lead and guided us through a tunnel cleared of traffic. On the other side, we were met by New Jersey State Troopers who escorted us to the airport—the only way to travel.

Political events have to take into consideration current events or what is happening in the area, which can determine the direction of the speech. For example, if a plant closes in the area the speech might be changed to talk about labor and unemployment instead of education. The issue staff has to keep the speeches current. It is the nature of a political campaign that the staff must be aware of all local, physical, political, and emotional tenor at the location of the event.

Eventually, the campaign progresses to the point where you have either won or lost. If you lost, you go back to your life before you started, if you can remember it, or you find another campaign to work on. There are many people who go from campaign to campaign or get a job working in a congressional office until it is campaign time again. If you win, in the words of Paul Newman in the movie The Candidate, "What Now?"

After two years of travel, planning, and sleepless nights, I decided not to join another campaign. I needed a long break. I found the skills I learned useful for a variety of other jobs: working

"He would be 'on stage' 16 hours a day."

"We were met by New Jersey State Troopers who escorted us to the airport— the only way to travel."

as a Trade Show Coordinator for a national clothing company and for my current campaign, *www.mudroomstudios.com*. I am now scheduling tours and traveling to shows to exhibit the home and garden sculptures and accessories we make. I'll never forget the adrenalin rush, excitement, and feeling of being at the right place at the right time. I still consider getting involved again, but for now, West Wing reruns take the edge off. If I were to go back, I would make sure that I was up to date on communication systems and the Internet. It is clear that organizations like *Moveon.org* add an entirely new level of outreach to the public.

A background in promotion or stage production can be an edge in obtaining campaign work. They easily link to the scheduling, advance, press, and fundraising departments on a campaign. If you are not sure what part of a business you are interested in, whether it is rock touring or politics or whatever, getting exposure in the field will open doors. The best tools are creativity, a willingness to learn, and tenacity.

ENDORSEMENT WHORING
PATRIK MATA , KOMMUNITY FK

One would think that, after surviving 30 years in what was once called the "record industry," that somebody such as myself would have tons of procured endorsements to boast about. I never ever have... Until now. It is now the year 2007.

I was blessed firstly with an endorsement from the awesomely and appropriately monikered COFFIN CASE company. I had just started a West Coast tour in Hollywood and was in L.A. a few days ahead of schedule so I e-mailed a very kool kat who was the head salesman there. He happened to be a huge fan of mine from the Old School days of the Kalifornia Deathrock/Gothik scene. I made a deal with Coffin Case that I would be one of their promo whores by not only using their killer guitar cases, mic cases, pedals, etc, but, I would also have images of me wearing their cool line of t-shirts.

On *MySpace.com,* I received an e-mail from a foot pedal designer who is the owner of PRO TONE PEDALS. I asked if he would allow me to have an endorsement and in return I would completely promote everything that he would let me use. Due to the fact that the original pedal that I used to play through doesn't exist anymore, he and I have designed a new and improved one together. Not only that, but he says that there will not be another one like it in the Universe!

I realized that I would need some new clothing so I asked a company called LIP SERVICE. I wore those skull dagger stretch cotton pants when they first ever came out back in 1984 and I loved them. All they ask of me is to promote, take publicity shots in their lovely and deadly attire, post the pix at all of my official website, be seen on tour wearing them, and share their company name.

Basically, you need to sell yourself as a media product to any company. Place on your show flyers that you use their products so this can be included in any promo pack you may need to use to get in their door. Let any company know that you can boost their products sales by you being their endorseé. All in all, anybody can procure any type of endorsement or sponsorships if they just put their pure efforts into it.

But, you must have something to offer.

More from Patrik at *www.tstouring.com,* including his story about Phil Spector.

EUROPE, 1991

MARTIN ATKINS

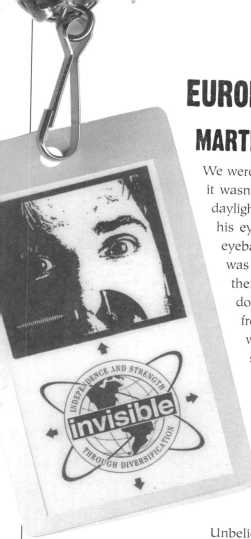

We were touring Europe in 1991 with Pigface. We were all on an evening schedule and it wasn't until seven or eight shows into the tour that I saw a band member's face in daylight. His eyes were yellow. I don't mean his eyes had a tinge of yellow to them, his eyes were yellow. His fucking eyeballs were yellow. Like "don't eat the yellow eyeballs" yellow. We rushed him to the emergency room in Malmo, Sweden, where he was diagnosed with advanced Hepatitis. The only thing we could do was leave him there. The promoter assured us he'd look after him and there was nothing for us to do except continue. Meanwhile, the office in Chicago was scrambling to find flights from Malmo to someplace else to someplace else to someplace else to Canada. You want to book a flight like that with 48 hours notice? You better have yours and someone else's credit card ready.

It didn't end there. We found out that we all had to have precautionary shots as soon as we arrived back into the U.K. Our merch girl absolutely freaked out. She'd been bitten by a rabid dog when she was a child and the cure involved twelve injections to the stomach three times a day. Two days later, we found out that the Wembley show (which was a large reason for the tour) had been canceled because Siouxsie had a throat infection. Later, I found out that a compassionate girl who had stayed by his bedside listening to him babble was actually a reporter conducting an interview on cassette tape. Unbelievable! And just another day on the road.

HORROR STORIES

Horror stories don't have to be medically related. Let me catalog a few of mine—not to try to be the guy with the most road stories—but I think with more and more and more examples, you might get to understand that this isn't as random as it might appear.

- Main member of second band on bill decides not to get on the plane and misses the first 2/3 of a tour. Eventually joins the tour by which point it is meaningless. Most people have heard through the internet that he is not on the tour and his presence is just a meaningless reminder of what a complete asshole he is.

- Band member has an epileptic seizure at the U.S. Embassy in Canada.

- Freak out in the bus three nights before border crossing. It turns out there is a fully fledged doctor on board who will lose his license if discovered on a bus with drugs, not to mention that they were aboard a bus full of drugs.

- Band member burns hand on crack pipe and fractures elbow before important Chicago show.

- Incompetent soundman blows up PA system at another important Chicago show.

- Three buses in a row breakdown in a 24-hour period and, Murphy's Law in full effect, right before a spectacularly well-promoted Detroit show.

- Trying to be responsible and conduct some preventative maintenance on a vehicle I bought for one of our bands, I get a phone call from the mechanic's shop that the vehicle has been listed as stolen. Turns out the band didn't actually give all of the money to the guy they were buying the van from. Situation made slightly worse by explaining to some woman on the phone that the mechanic involved was obviously a fucking crack-head speed freak. He was, of course, her husband.

- A few PA's on fire, Killing Joke in Pittsburgh, twenty grand, and an enthusiastic crowd turning on the fire hose at The Olympic Auditorium with PiL in '81. The waterfall looked really pretty before it started cascading directly onto the mixing console.

- Two lost PiL shows, delirious, don't remember much except drums changing size and density before my eyes; ditto Killing Joke, somewhere in France.

- Fractured knee on tour with Chris Connelly, this time Murphy's Law not in full effect (aside from fracturing my knee...) it was the last night of the tour, last song of the set.

- Scratched cornea, Killing Joke—the worst pain I have ever experienced. I scratched my cornea during the filming of the "Money Is Not Our God" video..

- 666 Tour: Lab Report pull out one week before the dates, of course just after the posters arrive.

Throw in a few tour managers falling off the wagon, sometimes worse on the wagon, break-ups the night before a tour, smashed doors, smashed mirrors, smashed equipment, smashed hotel rooms put back together with blue tack long enough to get out of the country, exploding transmissions, hanging out with the bus driver in Portugal just long enough to see him pouring whiskey in his can of non-alcoholic beer. Or, in St. Louis the night before a Chicago show, the last night of a 50 night tour, making the mistake of relaxing and thinking 'we did it'! Humorously enough, I think that is the same mistake the bus driver made. An hour outside of Chicago, I woke up—reflex—bracing my arms across the top and bottom of the bunk to prevent my wife from being launched out of the bunk as the bus began to tilt from side to side. The keyboard player from Zeromancer was not so fortunate. He was catapulted into a door. As soon as I knew Katrina was OK, I opened the door to the front of the bus in time to see a Spielberg-esque shot of things floating in the air and Jim, yes the same Jim from the spinal meningitis story, staring at me, his head surrounded by the entire contents of the front of the bus: sugar, coffee, shoes, cell phones, cameras. I think that the bus came within an inch or two of toppling. When we arrived in Chicago, there were clumps of dirt and mud four feet high on the front of the bus. At least this one has a funny ending apart from the keyboard player from Zeromancer collapsing twice that day. The bus driver handed me his card, hilarious that he would think we would ever want to see him again, more hilarious when I read his name...

Michael L. Hunt
Coach Driver

A CHAINSAW, A BLACKOUT, A FREAK, AND WHY!

A little advice from your blue pal, The Enigma

I don't know a lot about chainsaws, but this little morsel might come in handy for those that need know. Here is the lesson I learned during the summer of 2003. Do not operate a chainsaw in the middle of the night during a blackout on a pier while running from the sideshow tent to the haunted house next to it. Do not, I repeat do not, do this even if you are blue skinned, and even if customers are complaining about having paid to see a show you can't deliver due to lack of electricity.

THE ENIGMA

MORTAL DJINNI (A DEVIL APPEARS UNDER THE BLUEBACKING OF A JIGSAW)

MUSICIAN / DAREDEVIL / ICON / ARTIST / HORNED TATTOOED SIDESHOW MUSICIAN

www.theenigmalive.com

I learned this lesson after I had been surrounded by security and police aiming guns and flashlights on me at the entrance to the haunted attraction. The only sound breaking the blackout silence was the yelling of "Drop your weapon!" by the policy enforcement agents. This would have been too extreme even for the TV show COPS. Lucky for me, after being handcuffed they found the "weapon" to not have a blade on it. They decided to walk me to the end of the pier in cuffs and released me on the pretense that I hide out until every one left the pier. I guess bringing me in would have made us all look stupid.

Another piece of advice I might give to those gracing the stage is to never throw anything to the audience that you don't want coming back to you.

> *I found this out with Brian Brain in London 1979 …we threw bananas into the audience stenciled with 'Buy My Single'… we were surprised when all the bananas came back…*
> *-MA*

People think its fun to throw back and forth an item, especially when they are intoxicated. Sometimes they will throw a t-shirt or some other promo product to you and if you throw it back they will continue the game of it. This can pose a risk when performing a stunt that needs your full attention. If, for instance, you are blindfolded with an apple in your mouth and carving that apple with a running chainsaw, do not end up throwing the apple to the audience. That same apple may be tossed back to the stage while you are slicing a cucumber on the back of an audience member's neck resting on a pitchfork.

Oh, and one more thing, never, never, never jump into a mosh pit wearing a straight jacket. You just might break your back. I saw this stunt performed first hand while playing on tour with PigFace.

These are the risks of employment that few have the opportunity to experience. That having been said I must remind you all of whom I am and what I do.

I am "The Enigma," not just "a" or "an" enigma, and I am an entertainer. More precisely to the point I am a musician and a sword swallower by trade. I am tattooed from my horn implants to my toes with a blue jigsaw puzzle pattern, with over 200 tattoo artists around the world having had a piece of the action.

In this way I am a walking psychological experiment. The reactions of my tattooing are everything from total avoidance to absolute shock. These days however, since I have been seen so much on the television, many people even know my name. Currently, cell phone cameras are a bane and a bounty to my social interactions.

Every one wants to take a photo of me at the most inopportune times; however, they use them as their Myspace photo, which helps me acquire more notoriety.

I am a product of a double rebellion. My mother wanted to be a music teacher and her father wouldn't let her. She had her two sons take music lessons and dance lessons at the age of six. My older brother is currently a sound track composer in Los Angeles. I took to the arts in a slightly different fashion.

While in a magic club as a kid, I stumbled upon sideshow stunts at the age of fifteen. Here for me was "real" magic. I went to school exchanging dreams of boundless grandeur for realities of very little worth. I grew up going back and forth to private lessons and living off of comic books and casseroles. I was never in any scholastic peer group. My peers were the X-men and other such marvel comic characters. I believed in my world, and the power to believe is just as strong as the power to disbelieve. Upon reading of sideshow stunts, I held it to myself as worth risking my life for the chance to do something that everyone around me told me was impossible. When the truth is revealed and everyone believes otherwise then it appears as magic. At only 15 years of age, I learned to swallow swords, eat and blow fire, and drive spikes into my skull with a hammer. My mother was not pleased. It's not like I was in my room studying to be a football star. I joined a few bands hoping to incorporate the stunts and music together. Later I joined up with the Torture King, Mr. Lifto, and Matt the Tube Crowley. We became "that Lollapalooza Sideshow" in 1992. I had finished the jigsaw puzzle outline tattooed all over my body by Feb 93. Since then I have toured the world many times over, inspiring and surfing on a revival of live primitive art and performance.

In a magic show you wonder, "How is it done?" In a sideshow you merely wonder, "Why is it done?" Now I am alone on my quest of giving the audience not just the flourish of my skin, or the gimmick of sideshow stunts, but the "why?" of it all, through music to round out the performance. Between that and trying to get into films and music scores I keep a full plate. Come and smell the fun at *www.TheEnigmaLive.com*.

MARTIN ATKINS ASKS:
CHUCK SUBER

MA: We were talking about the future and how much has changed. Do you have any interesting stories or a valid lesson from twenty years ago?

CS: In 1972, the Chicago Board of Education cancelled all funding for the arts from the budget. Because of certain circumstances, I was appointed executive director of S.O.M.E.—Save Our Music Education—by the American Music Conference Public Relations Wing to get the money back!

I was good friends with the superintendent of music. We called an emergency meeting of the shakers. They came up with a budget. More importantly, they gave us the services of their public relations firm, which was the largest in Chicago at that time. And they came up with S.O.M.E. The first thing that we did was to reserve time at the open meetings of the council. I think in a two day period, there were some 60 openings and we were able to grab 58 of them to have various people testify about protecting the arts. We had a meeting of music educators in Chicago—the high school music teachers—and had them contribute. The art teachers had a tea. I had Benny Goodman come in! We had a spot for him on the board.

I had written out a speech for him. He used it, but with good embellishments of his own—particularly the first opening remark, "So, I understand that you're going to take music away from the students of the city of Chicago?" A lot of press! The astronauts were in town that week. Benny Goodman got front page of the *Sun Times* and the Tribune – astronauts on page three! We got the lead stories on the six o'clock news and the nine o'clock news.

We arranged for a parade, organized by the music educators who knew what parades were like. It came down State Street. Leading the parade were all the students. In front was color guard with flags dipped, the drums playing a dirge. They had bass cases acting like coffins with instruments and sheet music inside. Little kindergarten kids held up signs saying, "Don't take music away from me!"

They all came into Daley Plaza, organized. We had each group choose one student to say something into a mic—no faculty, just students. An 11 year old kid picked up the microphone and said, "I don't wanna join a gang, I wanna join a band!"

CHUCK SUBER

ARTIST-IN-RESIDENCE
1978-
AEMMDEPT, COLUMBIA
COLLEGE OF CHICAGO

MA: Wow!!

CS: They got out of Daley Plaza at about quarter to eleven. At high noon, everything was quiet and we blew echo taps out of all the windows and so forth. We boarded buses for Springfield. A team consisted of a music educator, parents, and students. They were prepped by our representatives in Springfield how to get reps and senators out of their meeting rooms to chat to pass this message. The governor, Ogilvie, was out of town at this time. The superintendent and I arranged to meet with his deputies. The deputies said, "This is the way it's going to work. Governor Ogilvie will announce next week that he is taking the problem of the arts in the city of Chicago and he will do the utmost to get it done and will allow Mayor Daley to make the announcement. We'll get it done in a few weeks."

So, we won. But we only won the battle. We didn't win the war. The war was something that the governor said he would look into but probably couldn't accomplish. And that was to have music and the other arts written into the mandate for each school in the state, in the minimum curriculum requirements. That's the war that we never won. We were able to get a sixteen page insert that the music educators came up with. The superintendent and I had a lot of speaking engagements with music educators, "How did you do it? We had the same problem…" And so forth.

It was a missed opportunity, but absolutely understandable. High school music teachers are not good political advocates, regardless of what their political philosophies may be. They are certainly not used to doing this kind of thing. The band parents associations are not used to doing it either. There was a great deal of press on this. There were very few examples of any kind of similar action to bring music back into the schools.

By 1972, the white flight was in its full flower. And it came, not just to the suburbs, but to so-called academies, which were really private high schools. Those high schools certainly did not have music. The only reason you could have music was if you paid extra. We've had many experiments throughout the years—good scientific experiments about music in particular that helps reading. Principally, the main use of the arts is motivation. They have lots of statistics. For any students involved in the arts, performing arts, whatever else, the rate of graduation is higher; the attendance is higher; everything is higher. One of the specific things is increasing reading. It was in Chicago—we did a control experiment. One class got guitars and a plan and the other one did not. A special instructor read poetry to the students. "Just go ahead and put some music to this." They gave them a reading test before the six weeks—whatever grade level they were reading at—and then we'd give them one afterwards. Then we gave them one six months after that! The reading level was a minimum of a one year upgrade. This was all throughout the country.

MA: I heard it helped with math.

CS: Yes! Yes, certainly with math! Music, 2, 5, 7 progression; it helps stuttering.

MA: How so?

CS: Robert Merrill, the great tenor stuttered until he started to sing! I myself stuttered the first year of high school. I got over it by reading poetry aloud. You get yourself in a rhythmic pattern. The rhythm takes over—it eliminates the block.

This whole business of No Child Left Behind and that whole federal funding has been a disaster for the arts, as it has in many other sectors, but particularly for the arts. Maybe, with the Democrats coming in and some other changes, there may be some changes in the No Child Left Behind Act that, as long as there's a threat of war, the general public is not going to want to sacrifice math for... they're not going to realize that you can have both! That you really need both. As well as you need recess which is being cut out in lots of the schools. I'm pretty optimistic about it, but that's my story for you.

MA: **I think that this is what's happening around the world and an education system is hurting. The two major exports now are what, intellectual property and...?**
KC: Weapons.

CS: Weapons is number one, intellectual property is two.

MA: **But, intellectual property, where's the intellect? You've got to build that! I got a phone call from a charity that was holding auctions to bring music to kids.**
KC: Rock for Kids.

MA: **Rock for Kids! And all they were trying to do was to bring music into kids' lives and it's become a private charity.**
CS: Isn't that something? It's great that they are contributing!

WOODSTOCK TATTOO & BODY ARTS FESTIVAL
CURSE MACKEY

This event was a collaboration with tattoo artist Bruce Bart, owner of the Woodstock Tattoo Co. and the Woodstock Chamber of Commerce and Art. I designed a town-wide festival that featured various art exhibits, bands and performers, and world-class tattooing. Activity was scheduled in 15 local clubs, theaters, and art galleries. It was basically like a South by Southwest for the tattoo industry.

Six months into the creative and promotional development of our event, my daily flow was harshly interrupted by a visit from the Woodstock Code and Safety Supervisor, the Fire Inspector, and the Police Chief. It turns out in this eclectic haven of art and commerce, there was a faction of people that were sick and tired of the "radical art lifestyle" that was invading the Catskill Mountains. It was recommended by these old-timers that I take my event somewhere else, as visions of 100,000 mud-covered, drug-fueled metal heads and hippies set the quaint township on fire while having orgies in their front yards.

It was requested that a town meeting take place in two weeks that would include the mayors and all chief safety personal from Woodstock and four connecting towns to discuss the future of the Woodstock Tattoo Festival. I was given a list of demands for safety maps, parking plans, traffic flow plans, insurance, venue diagrams for 15 venues, and more.

Dick Goldman, my attorney, was also the attorney for Michael, the producer of the original Woodstock Music Festivals, and had some solid rapport with the safety officials. Also, the local county legislator who had built all of the roads and temporary buildings for Woodstock '94 and '99 had become a close advisor. Together with my partner, the four of us entered a meeting with 32 top area officials. As I said, this room was filled with mayors, town supervisors, emergency medical technicians, fire chiefs, code enforcement officials, the New York State Police, the Ulster County Sheriff Department, and the Woodstock Police Chief.

For 90 minutes, I answered darting questions like "How do I plan to help 88 year old Mrs. Smith get to the hospital if she has a heart attack?" and "What if we can't get an ambulance to her because your tattoo fest has all of the town's roads clogged up?"

"How do you plan to park cars for 10,000 people?" "What about all the bikers?" "Do you have a million dollar liability insurance policy?" Etc., etc. Bullets, knives, and arrows aimed to make us look like we were neophytes that were planning an art-themed Armageddon that would surely end in disaster or bad taste.

> "How do you plan to park cars for 10,000 people...? What about all the bikers? Do you have a million dollar liability insurance policy? Etc., Etc."

CURSE MACKEY

TOUR MANAGER
WOODSTOCK TATTOO &
BODY ARTS FESTIVAL
EVIL MOTHERS / PIGFACE
www.actionartsagency.com

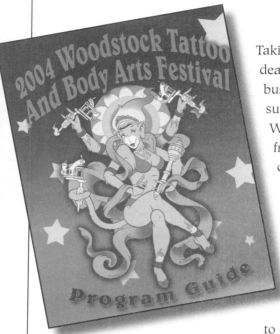

Taking a cue from Gene Simmons, who always deals with the powers that be in proper business attire, I dressed in a kick-ass black suit. I was fully prepared for most questions. We had hired a Manhattan traffic architect friend to come on board, and together we counted every parking space available and did traffic flow studies and maps. We blew them away with information. I had a town map designed with all the venue layouts, event schedules, shuttle schedules, security detail, and insurance certificates.

Any time things got a bit whack, my attorney or the legislator were able to step up and speak of witnessing our research and belief in the safety of the community. The meeting ended with a series of follow-ups scheduled right in the middle of peak promotion and deadline times. It was hell; they made us jump through flaming hoops. At times, I wanted to scream at them for their lack of artistic vision and for being redneck assholes but over time, I understood that these people's sole job was to protect the public and town property and citizens. Once they got to know me, they realized that we had gone through the process and delivered answers and solutions to all of their concerns to the point that we got all of our approvals. The weekend of the festival, these guys treated me as a good friend that they could trust and slapped high five saying, "I knew we could do it," under baited breath. I smiled. Goddamn right!

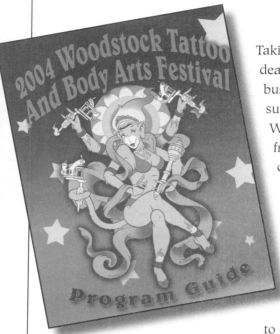

For a while, my new art became public speaking on architecture and politics and public safety in order to be able to put on an event that featured 100 tattoo artists from around the world, 40 bands on six stages, and five separate art exhibits, including one of the largest exhibits of H.R. Giger to have taken place in America, as well as the *Rides Of Passage* exhibit, which I also published a book on. In order to get to that point, I had to adapt or die to new influence and rules. I had to pull all resources and favors to get through and it was extremely difficult. Had we not been able to gain the trust and support of the powers that be, we would have lost our ass as we had been working on it for six months. It would have potentially sent me into oblivion mentally and financially. Instead, I have traveled the globe fueled by these lessons and have since applied them to all future events and projects with much success and momentum.

GOING AND GOING AND GOING...
JOEL GAUSTEN

I first met the stripe-shirted Energizer Bunny known as Martin Atkins in 1993 after a Pigface performance at the New Orleans Music Hall. What a fucking show! In true fan boy fashion, I bum rushed Martin after the show in search of an autograph, which he graciously gave me. (To find out what else happened to me that night, read my quote in the liner notes to *The Best Of Pigface—Preaching To The Perverted*.)

By 1995, I had started a little gig for myself as a concert promoter, booking 300-4000 seat venues throughout North Jersey. One night, I decided to leave a phone message at Martin's label, Invisible Records, asking if any Invisible acts were available to play for me. Since it was late, I didn't expect anyone to pick up, let alone hear a Birmingham accent excitedly proclaim, 'We've got Sheep on Drugs coming over! It's gonna be huge!"

He remembered our talks nearly five years later, when I interviewed him about The Damage Manual for *The Aquarian Weekly*. I loved the first Damage Manual EP but I can now freely admit that I had ulterior motives.

Thanks to Martin's performance on *Extremities, Dirt & Various Repressed Emotions*, my already-strong love of Killing Joke became an obsession when I first heard that album in 1990. At that precise moment, I had seriously considered abandoning my drums lessons completely. After all, how would I ever be that fucking good? I ultimately decided to keep playing because, well, I wanted to play with the guy!

"Thanks for the interview, Martin. By the way...out of curiosity...you know, I'm a drummer, and I've always been into what you do...Is there room for one more in Pigface?"

"Sure! Keep in touch."

Well, shit, that was easy!

About a year later, I got an invite from Martin to play in Pigface at a show at the Limelight in NYC. Of course, in true Pigface fashion, I had no fucking clue what to expect...or what I would even be doing once I walked onstage. A few hours before show time, I ran into Atkins on the street and asked him the Million Dollar Question:

"So...what do you need me to do?"

Guess it was the wrong thing to ask, since all the guy did was stare at me like I was from Mars.

"Um, should I just wing it, then?"

"Just wing it, man!"

Oh, okay.

And that's exactly what I did. Before I knew it, I was onstage playing toms to "Stateless" alongside Martin and Dickless, the tour's other drummer. Then came the flood of "Murder Inc," "Weightless," "Nutopia," and the rest of the glorious noise. Every so often, I'd catch a peak at Atkins behind his kit – blonde hair and black stripes flying with every blast. Surreal.

Oh, yeah, I think a didgeridoo player hopped onstage for the encore, but I was way too deaf at that point to know for sure…

The best part? When I'm an old man someday, I can tell the little ones about the time a half-naked woman spat fire above my head while I improvised drums to a cover of Black Sabbath's "Supernaut."

So why I am bringing all this up? Well, each one of the above stories in some way sums up why Mr. Atkins has survived in this insane biz for so long. In 1993, he was an independent bandleader responsible for the day-to-day lives of God knows how many people on the Pigface tour. Even with that on his mind, here he was after playing a show taking the time to talk with an excitable 15-year old uber-fan like me in the street. In 1995, there he was answering a late-night booking call at the offices of his independent record label. In 2001, there he was inviting a player he'd never heard before to join his band onstage at a major NYC gig. And if you've ever seen a Pigface gig, you already know that it's a pretty chaotic experience… so just imagine being in charge of that logistical fiasco!

Obviously, there's a pattern here: After nearly three decades, Atkins is still keeping his ear to the ground, constantly maintaining personal contact with his friends and fans while also welcoming new ideas into his world… and somehow keeping the wheels of his independent music enterprise spinning with unbridled enthusiasm. Above all else, he's actually enjoying this shit! I'm not talking about somebody who'd cancel a gig over a headache here—I'm talking about the real deal.

So read this guy's words and take them to heart. He knows of what he speaks (or writes, as the case may be). He's got the battle scars, bruises, and endless road tales to prove it. And more than a few sweaty black-striped shirts in his laundry hamper…

Joel Gausten is the former managing editor of Liner Notes Magazine. A longtime musician, he has appeared on over 40 releases and has worked with a vast array of artists including Pigface, The Undead, and Electric Frankenstein. He got his start in the music business as a promoter for The Misfits. He can be contacted at www.myspace.com/gaustenbooks.

C·H·A·P·T·E·R····60

THE FUTURE OF TOURING

The future of touring belongs to innovative companies and individuals that create new opportunities for themselves. More and more, this innovation is coming from a new breed of creative thinkers and entrepreneurs outside of traditional channels. It might be because it's difficult for the people in it to evolve as things change and blur the traditional music business. Innovation used to prompt a period of satisfied reflection and some resting on the laurels, now the speed of change is dizzying and innovation creates innovation.

> "Innovation sparks more thought. One man's ceiling becomes the next man's floor. One mans wall another mans door."

I remember hearing that quote at a conference of educators in Nashville. On the same panel, renowned engineer George Massenburg stated that, over his career, he's had to relearn his skill set every three years. It seems like that cycle has accelerated. I can best describe the task of learning about the music business as learning to skateboard on the Orange Line in Chicago while balancing a cup of steaming-hot coffee. By the time you master this and jump off the train, your instructor informs you that while you have been practicing, the industry has moved along and hands you an extra cup and a blindfold...

THE CW AND SUNKIST

The CW (which used to be the WB and will probably be something else by the time you read this) and Sunkist have created a new model for product promotion. Sunkist sponsored a band on *One Tree Hill* with all of the usual paraphernalia, shows, banners, and backstage product placement. Then, they created a real concert tour using the actors to enhance the events. It's like the new answer to the question, "What came first – the chicken or the egg?"... McNuggets.

Adam Grayer from Jägermeister told me about all of the wild cross-promotional inter-connected levels of the Sunkist/CW alliance. His enthusiasm and ability to appreciate a good idea from another company perhaps marks one of the true differences between the music business and other businesses. You have to acknowledge the other guy's ceiling exists if you're going to use it as a floor.

> **"It's like the new answer to the question, "What came first – the chicken or the egg?"... McNuggets."**

> **"You have to acknowledge the other guy's ceiling exists if you're going to use it as a floor."**

JÄGERMEISTER

Jägermeister is on the front line of the future of touring. Much of what they do comes from a love of music and a desire to help young bands keep moving forward. There are currently over 200 Jägermeister-sponsored bands at different levels. They started off in competition with other liquor distributors, sponsoring and paying bands, being looked upon as a revenue stream. They developed the Jäger tour, a twice-yearly event that guarantees sellout crowds. Bands and labels are looking to make concessions in order to have their bands play. This is what happens when smart, passionate people engage brain in a field plagued with dogma and entrenchment. That's a pretty awesome achievement... and one hell of a growth curve. But it doesn't stop there.

Currently, I believe Jäger has five or six RVs out on the road. They are currently customizing a new vehicle which, instead of a notoriously unreliable RV or an expensive bus, has the front end of a freight liner truck. It is automatic. You don't need a CDL license to drive it. The projected life of the engine is over 2,000,000 miles and they can be serviced at any truck stop. At about $200,000, that's pretty cool and innovative.

But it is their answer to the question: "How do we get people to come to this venue?" that rocks my world. You just take the venue to where the people are.

The project is the baby of Jack Carson, Rick Zeiler and Adam Grayer. They showed me blueprints and animations of the trailer they have built: a $450,000 custom trailer housing a 30 foot wide stage, side and front extensions, and PA, which will open up at the push of a button. With an automatic roof, PA and monitors are all hard-wired so there's no set-up time   The trailer has its own custom generators in a sound-proof enclosure and once the stage is set, the Toter-Home can pull around to the side to become the dressing rooms. A safety railing assembled on the reinforced roof creates a VIP viewing deck. Jägermeister expects about six months of 2007 from its first vehicle combo and it intends to have up to five on the road for 350 days a year by 2009. The basic idea isn't new. Companies have customized trailers before, but the vision and insight from Jägermeister is unique. They already have agreements in place with ABC parking lots, the San Diego Chargers, NASCAR, Sturgis, and the second stage at OzzFest. In just seven years, they've created a very powerful brand in rock music. By aggressively creating a valuable opportunity that they can leverage instead of being leveraged themselves. For those of

you looking to work in a venue, it seems like Jägermeister could have some of the busiest. Job descriptions are going to change, you might want to look at some of the skills you are planning on adding to your tool belt.

THE FIRST ROCK CONCERT ON THE MOON

In an effort to open some minds and create a realistic learning opportunity in a field that is moving faster than the traditional educational system can keep up with, I'm developing two ideas. One involves a regular Rock 'n' Roll Tour. Everything is as usual – the guitarist is a prick, the drummer's a drunk, and the tour manager is MIA. The only difference being we are not touring in a van, a bus, or a plane. We are touring on board the Santa Maria, the Nina, and the Pinta, Punk Rock Pirates'. (Thanks Ian).

Then, I came up with the "First Rock Show on the Moon!" Same idea, faster transportation, better toilets. Although the uniforms aren't as cool, you're less likely to have problems with your new electronic equipment, but perhaps more likely to have crazy stalker female astronauts in NASA diapers. Stay tuned as this idea develops on the web. I already like two of the comments that surfaced. One was from Mark Williams at PreSonus who said, "Count me in. I already have enough frequent flyer miles." And one from me, which was, "If there are two venues on the moon, we know for a fact that our agent will book us into the wrong one."

"Take the venue to where the people already are."

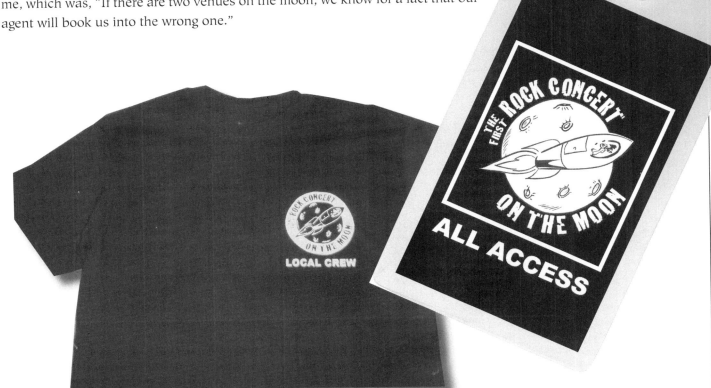

APPENDIX
LIST BY CHAPTER:

CHAPTER 2
BUILDING BLOCKS: BASIC CONCEPTS AND IDEAS

EXPERIENCE IS GOOD

Sometimes it might not seem like there is a direct path from where you are to where you want to go. Try not to get discouraged. Take a job or internship in a seemingly unrelated field. You might be surprised how useful this could be. Send me more examples!

Learn a second language. In a number of fields the language requirement seems to be first. So, if you're fluent in Chinese but just a mediocre drum tech - that combination of skills could make you more useful than an amazing drum tech who can't communicate.

Fashion design/seamstress. When the crotch of the lead singer's pants gets ripped again you'll be indispensable, thrilled, and a little bit frightened.

Veterinarian. Barbara Streisand is taking her 15 dogs on the road and your skills, along with your piano tuning ability and fluent Polish mean that you will be sending postcards from Warsaw telling people about the funny incident with Barbara Streisand's dogs' poop.

Nanny/Teacher. As artists get older, they have kids. If the kids are on the road, so are you.

Pizza/Restaurant. During a panel discussion at Belmont University in Nashville, one of the producers was asked how someone could better prepare for working in a studio. One of the panelists unhesitatingly replied, "Work in a pizza restaurant on a Saturday night." So, in addition to gaining experience at dealing with a stressful environment, you'll have no problem making a mix sound cheesy.

Office/Legal/Filing/Organizing/Administrative. No brainer. This area is always in short supply.

Film/Video Editing. You could be the person who films the road clips, edits them together for the website and creates special materials that are great for any sponsors to receive during a tour. "Here's some footage of the still smoldering wreckage of the bus. But look! – the amps are still in perfect working condition."

Computers. Any kind of knowledge in this area, hard drive maintenance, laptops, replacing keyboards, cabling, voodoo, is priceless and can allow you to be helpful to anyone on the tour with IT issues.

Cab Driver. This increases your tolerance of being in close proximity to large amounts of vomit amongst other useful attributes.

Bartender. Duuuuuh!

Retail Experience at Clothing Store. Useful to help with some aspects of the merchandising, either with the display content, etc. Access to another group of highly influential, groovy people. You'll also gain people management skills.

Database Management. You can assist with the massively growing e-mail list, mail merge, and essential fan communication.

Tattoo. Everybody gets tattooed on the road and this skill also plugs you into another great, musically aware community.

Carpentry. Not only does this increase your value to the crew in some obvious ways like repairing a drum riser or making a reliable ramp to make load-in quicker and easier but it also decreases the chances of some enthusiastic idiot cutting off their thumb with a circular saw. Any kind of construction skill imparts a kind of, "can we do it? Yes we can!" mentality that is useful on the road.

Security. Not just for the implementation of amazing choke holds and pressure points but great people management skills.

Paramedic. From injuries caused by over-exertion, over-extension, over-indulgence to just stupidity. It's great to know that the guy standing next to you has a paddle in each hand already charged.

Crisis Management. It's all crisis.

Publicist. Great to see what happens on the other side of a tour. You can sharpen your people skills and database.

Screen Printer. A simple skill that, with a day's worth of effort and a couple of hundred dollars, you could not just unplug your band from a limited range of t-shirt designs but you could also create backdrops and scenery that elevate the experience.

Moving Company. Great for developing muscles, attitude, and organizational skills.

Travel Agency. Experience in this field can create huge savings, not just in hard cash but in stress. People's downtime can be maximized and you can pre-plan built-in flexibility so that when things do go wrong, changes are simple and inexpensive.

Electrical/Electronics. With a band coming up the difference between a good and a bad a show is as simple as finding reliable electricity or just making sure that turning the lights up doesn't trip the power.

Telemarketing. Phone skills/Sales Skills, fingerwalking.

Accounting/Financial Services. You could be the tour manager's best friend. You can spend 45 minutes per day helping him with the books.

Booking Agency. Develops a wide variety of skills – planning, organization, people skills, sales, marketing, boat payments – real world stuff.

Fitness Instructor. Some people get fit on the road, some fall apart. An increasingly important area – either from the ultra competitive pop-end with a performer striving for a higher leap and a more defined ab, or at the other end of the age spectrum just struggling to get through a show.

Writer (newspaper/magazines). You can help a band express themselves more effectively or more carefully. You can help create content with a road diary and plug into a community of writers around the world.

Mechanic – no brainer – and you are showing a perspective employer that you are not afraid to get your hands dirty!

Hair Stylist – cut cut cutting – always useful – and, all you need is a pair of scissors and a razor and some spray and those weird scissors with the teeth and a hair dryer and some hair gel and glue and …….

Chef/catering – everyone likes to be catered to.

MOVE TO BOISE: EXPANDED

		Music Events (3-5 Acts)	Movie Theaters	Theatrical Shows	Art Events	Comedy
3/8/07	Boise, ID	2	12	15	40	2
	Los Angeles, CA	110	108	60	250	35
	New York, NY	48	196	122	419	42
3/9/07	Boise, ID	4	12	20	42	2
	Los Angeles, CA	125	108	80	250	35
	New York, NY	49	196	139	415	42
3/10/07	Boise, ID	5	12	20	45	2
	Los Angeles, CA	116	108	80	326	35
	New York, NY	50	196	148	399	42
3/11/07	Boise, ID	1	12	20	42	2
	Los Angeles, CA	70	108	35	328	35
	New York, NY	34	196	71	142	42
3/12/07	Boise, ID	0	12	7	40	2
	Los Angeles, CA	48	108	45	280	35
	New York, NY	30	196	21	80	42
3/13/07	Boise, ID	1	12	4	40	2
	Los Angeles, CA	59	108	8	253	35
	New York, NY	27	196	60	305	42
3/14/07	Boise, ID	0	12	4	40	2
	Los Angeles, CA	60	108	11	250	35
	New York, NY	9	196	78	358	42

Sources: Boiseweekly.com, LA Weekly, Villagevoice.com

CHAPTER 3
PLANNING AND ROUTING

LIST OF U.S. CITIES BY POPULATION

Rank	Metropolitan Statistical Area	July 1 2006 Population	July 1 2005 Population	Change In Population (Number)	Change In Population (Percentage)
1	New York-Northern New Jersey-Long Island, NY-NJ-PA	18,818,536	18,813,723	4,813	0.0
2	Los Angeles-Long Beach-Santa Ana, CA	12,950,129	12,933,839	16,290	0.1
3	Chicago-Naperville-Joliet, IL-IN-WI	9,505,748	9,446,565	59,183	0.6
4	Dallas-Fort Worth-Arlington, TX	6,003,967	5,823,043	180,924	3.1
5	Philadelphia-Camden-Wilmington, PA-NJ-DE-MD	5,826,742	5,806,092	20,650	0.4
6	Houston-Sugar Land-Baytown, TX	5,539,949	5,352,569	187,380	3.5
7	Miami-Fort Lauderdale-Miami Beach, FL	5,463,857	5,424,697	39,160	0.7
8	Washington-Arlington-Alexandria, DC-VA-MD-WV	5,290,400	5,251,629	38,771	0.7
9	Atlanta-Sandy Springs-Marietta, GA	5,138,223	4,972,219	166,004	3.3
10	Detroit-Warren-Livonia, MI	4,468,966	4,479,254	-10,288	-0.2
11	Boston-Cambridge-Quincy, MA-NH	4,455,217	4,448,884	6,333	0.1
12	San Francisco-Oakland-Fremont, CA	4,180,027	4,158,012	22,015	0.5
13	Phoenix-Mesa-Scottsdale, AZ	4,039,182	3,878,525	160,657	4.1
14	Riverside-San Bernardino-Ontario, CA	4,026,135	3,909,903	116,232	3.0
15	Seattle-Tacoma-Bellevue, WA	3,263,497	3,207,892	55,605	1.7
16	Minneapolis-St. Paul-Bloomington, MN-WI	3,175,041	3,141,050	33,991	1.1
17	San Diego-Carlsbad-San Marcos, CA	2,941,454	2,936,609	4,845	0.2
18	St. Louis, MO-IL	2,796,368	2,782,411	13,957	0.5
19	Tampa-St. Petersburg-Clearwater, FL	2,697,731	2,646,540	51,191	1.9
20	Baltimore-Towson, MD	2,658,405	2,651,069	7,336	0.3
21	Denver-Aurora, CO	2,408,750	2,361,778	46,972	2.0
22	Pittsburgh, PA	2,370,776	2,381,671	-10,895	-0.5
23	Portland-Vancouver-Beaverton, OR-WA	2,137,565	2,096,571	40,994	2.0
24	Cleveland-Elyria-Mentor, OH	2,114,155	2,125,138	-10,983	-0.5
25	Cincinnati-Middletown, OH-KY-IN	2,104,218	2,090,968	13,250	0.6
26	Sacramento--Arden-Arcade--Roseville, CA	2,067,117	2,041,701	25,416	1.2
27	Orlando-Kissimmee, FL	1,984,855	1,931,479	53,376	2.8
28	Kansas City, MO-KS	1,967,405	1,944,690	22,715	1.2
29	San Antonio, TX	1,942,217	1,888,047	54,170	2.9
30	San Jose-Sunnyvale-Santa Clara, CA	1,787,123	1,761,164	25,959	1.5
31	Las Vegas-Paradise, NV	1,777,539	1,709,364	68,175	4.0
32	Columbus, OH	1,725,570	1,706,913	18,657	1.1
33	Indianapolis-Carmel, IN	1,666,032	1,640,029	26,003	1.6
34	Virginia Beach-Norfolk-Newport News, VA-NC	1,649,457	1,641,543	7,914	0.5
35	Providence-New Bedford-Fall River, RI-MA	1,612,989	1,619,440	-6,451	-0.4
36	Charlotte-Gastonia-Concord, NC-SC	1,583,016	1,521,474	61,542	4.0
37	Austin-Round Rock, TX	1,513,565	1,454,706	58,859	4.0
38	Milwaukee-Waukesha-West Allis, WI	1,509,981	1,509,388	593	0.0
39	Nashville-Davidson--Murfreesboro, TN	1,455,097	1,421,124	33,973	2.4
40	Jacksonville, FL	1,277,997	1,247,828	30,169	2.4
41	Memphis, TN-MS-AR	1,274,704	1,256,631	18,073	1.4
42	Louisville-Jefferson County, KY-IN	1,222,216	1,210,182	12,034	1.0
43	Richmond, VA	1,194,008	1,173,410	20,598	1.8
44	Hartford-West Hartford-East Hartford, CT	1,188,841	1,185,700	3,141	0.3
45	Oklahoma City, OK	1,172,339	1,154,991	17,348	1.5
46	Buffalo-Niagara Falls, NY	1,137,520	1,144,796	-7,276	-0.6
47	Birmingham-Hoover, AL	1,100,019	1,088,218	11,801	1.1
48	Salt Lake City, UT	1,067,722	1,046,685	21,037	2.0
49	Rochester, NY	1,035,435	1,036,890	-1,455	-0.1
50	New Orleans-Metairie-Kenner, LA	1,024,678	1,313,787	-289,109	-22.0
51	Raleigh-Cary, NC	994,551	951,809	42,742	4.5
52	Tucson, AZ	946,362	925,000	21,362	2.3
53	Honolulu, HI	909,863	904,645	5,218	0.6
54	Bridgeport-Stamford-Norwalk, CT	900,440	901,086	-646	-0.1
55	Tulsa, OK	897,752	885,778	11,974	1.4
56	Fresno, CA	891,756	878,089	13,667	1.6
57	Albany-Schenectady-Troy, NY	850,957	847,421	3,536	0.4
58	New Haven-Milford, CT	845,244	844,510	734	0.1
59	Dayton, OH	838,940	841,240	-2,300	-0.3
60	Omaha-Council Bluffs, NE-IA	822,549	812,830	9,719	1.2
61	Albuquerque, NM	816,811	797,517	19,294	2.4

Rank	Metropolitan Statistical Area	July 1 2006 Population	July 1 2005 Population	Change In Population (Number)	Change In Population (Percentage)
62	Allentown-Bethlehem-Easton, PA-NJ	800,336	789,695	10,641	1.3
63	Oxnard-Thousand Oaks-Ventura, CA	799,720	796,348	3,372	0.4
64	Worcester, MA	784,992	781,704	3,288	0.4
65	Bakersfield, CA	780,117	756,981	23,136	3.1
66	Grand Rapids-Wyoming, MI	774,084	770,171	3,913	0.5
67	Baton Rouge, LA	766,514	731,322	35,192	4.8
68	El Paso, TX	736,310	721,183	15,127	2.1
69	Columbia, SC	703,771	690,959	12,812	1.9
70	Akron, OH	700,943	701,435	-492	-0.1
71	McAllen-Edinburg-Mission, TX	700,634	678,652	21,982	3.2
72	Springfield, MA	686,174	686,491	-317	0.0
73	Greensboro-High Point, NC	685,378	674,219	11,159	1.7
74	Sarasota-Bradenton-Venice, FL	682,833	671,371	11,462	1.7
75	Stockton, CA	673,170	664,796	8,374	1.3
76	Poughkeepsie-Newburgh-Middletown, NY	671,538	667,259	4,279	0.6
77	Knoxville, TN	667,384	655,905	11,479	1.8
78	Toledo, OH	653,695	655,617	-1,922	-0.3
79	Little Rock-North Little Rock, AR	652,834	642,630	10,204	1.6
80	Syracuse, NY	650,051	650,434	-383	-0.1
81	Charleston-North Charleston, SC	603,178	591,792	11,386	1.9
82	Greenville, SC	601,986	590,622	11,364	1.9
83	Colorado Springs, CO	599,127	586,719	12,408	2.1
84	Wichita, KS	592,126	586,933	5,193	0.9
85	Youngstown-Warren-Boardman, OH-PA	586,939	590,968	-4,029	-0.7
86	Cape Coral-Fort Myers, FL	571,344	544,196	27,148	5.0
87	Boise City-Nampa, ID	567,640	545,141	22,499	4.1
88	Lakeland, FL	561,606	541,910	19,696	3.6
89	Scranton--Wilkes-Barre, PA	550,841	550,539	302	0.1
90	Madison, WI	543,022	536,990	6,032	1.1
91	Palm Bay-Melbourne-Titusville, FL	534,359	528,640	5,719	1.1
92	Des Moines-West Des Moines, IA	534,230	523,366	10,864	2.1
93	Jackson, MS	529,456	520,680	8,776	1.7
94	Harrisburg-Carlisle, PA	525,380	520,690	4,690	0.9
95	Augusta-Richmond County, GA-SC	523,249	517,855	5,394	1.0
96	Portland-South Portland-Biddeford, ME	513,667	512,992	675	0.1
97	Modesto, CA	512,138	505,492	6,646	1.3
98	Ogden-Clearfield, UT	497,640	486,428	11,212	2.3
99	Chattanooga, TN-GA	496,704	491,758	4,946	1.0
100	Deltona-Daytona Beach-Ormond Beach, FL	496,575	487,875	8,700	1.8
101	Lancaster, PA	494,486	489,936	4,550	0.9
102	Provo-Orem, UT	474,180	461,020	13,160	2.9
103	Santa Rosa-Petaluma, CA	466,891	466,970	-79	0.0
104	Durham, NC	464,389	456,180	8,209	1.8
105	Winston-Salem, NC	456,614	448,220	8,394	1.9
106	Lansing-East Lansing, MI	454,044	454,668	-624	-0.1
107	Spokane, WA	446,706	440,434	6,272	1.4
108	Flint, MI	441,966	442,732	-766	-0.2
109	Pensacola-Ferry Pass-Brent, FL	439,987	438,066	1,921	0.4
110	Lexington-Fayette, KY	436,684	429,679	7,005	1.6
111	Fayetteville-Springdale-Rogers, AR-MO	420,876	406,521	14,355	3.5
112	Visalia-Porterville, CA	419,909	411,131	8,778	2.1
113	York-Hanover, PA	416,322	408,182	8,140	2.0
114	Corpus Christi, TX	415,810	413,107	2,703	0.7
115	Vallejo-Fairfield, CA	411,680	410,786	894	0.2
116	Salinas, CA	410,206	412,340	-2,134	-0.5
117	Canton-Massillon, OH	409,764	409,527	237	0.1
118	Fort Wayne, IN	408,071	404,182	3,889	1.0
119	Springfield, MO	407,092	397,869	9,223	2.3
120	Mobile, AL	404,157	399,851	4,306	1.1
121	Manchester-Nashua, NH	402,789	400,516	2,273	0.6
122	Reading, PA	401,149	396,236	4,913	1.2
123	Reno-Sparks, NV	400,560	393,820	6,740	1.7
124	Santa Barbara-Santa Maria, CA	400,335	400,908	-573	-0.1
125	Asheville, NC	398,009	391,850	6,159	1.6
126	Port St. Lucie-Fort Pierce, FL	392,117	379,252	12,865	3.4
127	Brownsville-Harlingen, TX	387,717	378,905	8,812	2.3
128	Shreveport-Bossier City, LA	386,778	382,048	4,730	1.2
129	Salem, OR	384,600	376,268	8,332	2.2
130	Beaumont-Port Arthur, TX	379,640	383,140	-3,500	-0.9
131	Davenport-Moline-Rock Island, IA-IL	377,291	375,972	1,319	0.4
132	Huntsville, AL	376,753	368,641	8,112	2.2
133	Peoria, IL	370,194	368,364	1,830	0.5

Rank	Metropolitan Statistical Area	July 1 2006 Population	July 1 2005 Population	Change In Population (Number)	Change In Population (Percentage)
134	Trenton-Ewing, NJ	367,605	366,070	1,535	0.4
135	Montgomery, AL	361,748	355,932	5,816	1.6
136	Hickory-Lenoir-Morganton, NC	359,856	355,966	3,890	1.1
137	Anchorage, AK	359,180	351,586	7,594	2.2
138	Killeen-Temple-Fort Hood, TX	351,322	349,664	1,658	0.5
139	Evansville, IN-KY	350,356	349,087	1,269	0.4
140	Rockford, IL	348,252	342,058	6,194	1.8
141	Ann Arbor, MI	344,047	342,124	1,923	0.6
142	Fayetteville, NC	341,363	339,702	1,661	0.5
143	Eugene-Springfield, OR	337,870	334,486	3,384	1.0
144	Tallahassee, FL	336,502	333,112	3,390	1.0
145	Wilmington, NC	326,166	314,608	11,558	3.7
146	Savannah, GA	320,013	313,456	6,557	2.1
147	Kalamazoo-Portage, MI	319,738	318,836	902	0.3
148	South Bend-Mishawaka, IN-MI	318,007	317,572	435	0.1
149	Ocala, FL	316,183	303,448	12,735	4.2
150	Naples-Marco Island, FL	314,649	307,864	6,785	2.2
151	Charleston, WV	305,526	306,179	-653	-0.2
152	Kingsport-Bristol-Bristol, TN-VA	302,451	300,946	1,505	0.5
153	Green Bay, WI	299,003	297,083	1,920	0.6
154	Utica-Rome, NY	297,286	297,566	-280	-0.1
155	Roanoke, VA	295,050	292,490	2,560	0.9
156	Columbus, GA-AL	288,847	282,495	6,352	2.2
157	Fort Smith, AR-OK	288,818	284,404	4,414	1.6
158	Huntington-Ashland, WV-KY-OH	285,475	285,458	17	0.0
159	Lincoln, NE	283,970	281,440	2,530	0.9
160	Boulder, CO1	282,304	279,508	2,796	1.0
161	Erie, PA	279,811	280,184	-373	-0.1
162	Fort Collins-Loveland, CO	276,253	271,842	4,411	1.6
163	Duluth, MN-WI	274,244	274,991	-747	-0.3
164	Atlantic City, NJ	271,620	270,318	1,302	0.5
165	Spartanburg, SC	271,087	266,764	4,323	1.6
166	Norwich-New London, CT	263,293	264,265	-972	-0.4
167	Lubbock, TX	261,411	258,974	2,437	0.9
168	Holland-Grand Haven, MI	257,671	255,187	2,484	1.0
169	Hagerstown-Martinsburg, MD-WV	257,619	250,836	6,783	2.7
170	San Luis Obispo-Paso Robles, CA	257,005	255,538	1,467	0.6
171	Lafayette, LA	254,432	246,855	7,577	3.1
172	Santa Cruz-Watsonville, CA	249,705	249,420	285	0.1
173	Cedar Rapids, IA	249,320	246,992	2,328	0.9
174	Binghamton, NY	247,554	247,896	-342	-0.1
175	Merced, CA	245,658	242,249	3,409	1.4
176	Gainesville, FL	243,985	240,189	3,796	1.6
177	Amarillo, TX	241,515	238,807	2,708	1.1
178	Bremerton-Silverdale, WA	240,604	241,525	-921	-0.4
179	Clarksville, TN-KY	240,500	242,884	-2,384	-1.0
180	Lynchburg, VA	239,510	236,015	3,495	1.5
181	Myrtle Beach-Conway-North Myrtle Beach, SC	238,493	227,520	10,973	4.8
182	Greeley, CO1	236,857	228,158	8,699	3.8
183	Olympia, WA	234,670	228,881	5,789	2.5
184	Yakima, WA	233,105	230,937	2,168	0.9
185	Laredo, TX	231,470	224,874	6,596	2.9
186	Macon, GA	229,326	227,969	1,357	0.6
187	Topeka, KS	228,894	228,253	641	0.3
188	Gulfport-Biloxi, MS	227,904	254,616	-26,712	-10.5
189	Waco, TX	226,189	224,365	1,824	0.8
190	Kennewick-Richland-Pasco, WA	226,033	220,892	5,141	2.3
191	Barnstable Town, MA	224,816	226,161	-1,345	-0.6
192	Appleton, WI	217,313	215,150	2,163	1.0
193	Champaign-Urbana, IL	216,581	215,469	1,112	0.5
194	Chico, CA	215,881	214,153	1,728	0.8
195	Sioux Falls, SD	212,911	207,882	5,029	2.4
196	Prescott, AZ	208,014	198,841	9,173	4.6
197	Saginaw-Saginaw Township North, MI	206,300	207,846	-1,546	-0.7
198	Springfield, IL	206,112	205,276	836	0.4
199	Burlington-South Burlington, VT	206,007	205,222	785	0.4
200	Longview, TX	203,367	201,112	2,255	1.1
201	Houma-Bayou Cane-Thibodaux, LA	202,902	199,004	3,898	2.0
202	Florence, SC	198,848	197,628	1,220	0.6
203	Tuscaloosa, AL	198,769	196,259	2,510	1.3
204	Elkhart-Goshen, IN	198,105	195,276	2,829	1.4
205	Medford, OR	197,071	195,151	1,920	1.0

Rank	Metropolitan Statistical Area	July 1 2006 Population	July 1 2005 Population	Change In Population (Number)	Change In Population (Percentage)
206	Racine, WI	196,096	195,219	877	0.4
207	Tyler, TX	194,635	190,501	4,134	2.2
208	Las Cruces, NM	193,888	189,306	4,582	2.4
209	Lake Charles, LA	192,316	194,319	-2,003	-1.0
210	College Station-Bryan, TX	192,152	189,960	2,192	1.2
211	Johnson City, TN	191,136	188,905	2,231	1.2
212	Charlottesville, VA	190,278	188,016	2,262	1.2
213	Yuma, AZ	187,555	181,598	5,957	3.3
214	Fargo, ND-MN	187,001	184,171	2,830	1.5
215	Bellingham, WA	185,953	183,363	2,590	1.4
216	Lafayette, IN	185,745	183,493	2,252	1.2
217	Athens-Clarke County, GA	185,479	182,464	3,015	1.7
218	St. Cloud, MN	182,784	180,973	1,811	1.0
219	Kingston, NY	182,742	182,433	309	0.2
220	Fort Walton Beach-Crestview-Destin, FL	180,291	181,221	-930	-0.5
221	Redding, CA	179,951	178,970	981	0.5
222	Rochester, MN	179,573	176,994	2,579	1.5
223	Bloomington, IN	178,714	177,734	980	0.6
224	Anderson, SC	177,963	175,258	2,705	1.5
225	Muskegon-Norton Shores, MI	175,231	174,971	260	0.1
226	Gainesville, GA	173,256	166,302	6,954	4.2
227	Monroe, LA	172,223	170,587	1,636	1.0
228	Joplin, MO	168,552	165,968	2,584	1.6
229	Terre Haute, IN	168,217	168,104	113	0.1
230	Greenville, NC	165,776	162,359	3,417	2.1
231	Albany, GA	163,961	162,805	1,156	0.7
232	Jackson, MI	163,851	163,432	419	0.3
233	Panama City-Lynn Haven, FL	163,505	161,322	2,183	1.4
234	Waterloo-Cedar Falls, IA	162,263	161,857	406	0.3
235	Yuba City, CA	161,806	156,149	5,657	3.6
236	Parkersburg-Marietta-Vienna, WV-OH	161,724	162,247	-523	-0.3
237	Niles-Benton Harbor, MI	161,705	162,090	-385	-0.2
238	Bloomington-Normal, IL	161,202	158,977	2,225	1.4
239	Oshkosh-Neenah, WI	160,593	159,535	1,058	0.7
240	El Centro, CA	160,301	155,862	4,439	2.8
241	Janesville, WI	159,153	157,324	1,829	1.2
242	Abilene, TX	158,063	158,155	-92	-0.1
243	Columbia, MO	155,997	153,273	2,724	1.8
244	Eau Claire, WI	155,041	153,779	1,262	0.8
245	Monroe, MI	155,035	153,772	1,263	0.8
246	Vineland-Millville-Bridgeton, NJ	154,823	152,905	1,918	1.3
247	Punta Gorda, FL	154,438	154,340	98	0.1
248	Pueblo, CO	152,912	150,974	1,938	1.3
249	Pascagoula, MS	152,405	156,742	-4,337	-2.8
250	Blacksburg-Christiansburg-Radford, VA	151,524	150,927	597	0.4
251	Jacksonville, NC	150,673	150,508	165	0.1
252	Alexandria, LA	150,080	147,325	2,755	1.9
253	Decatur, AL	149,549	148,264	1,285	0.9
254	Bend, OR	149,140	141,288	7,852	5.6
255	Billings, MT	148,116	146,481	1,635	1.1
256	Dover, DE	147,601	143,462	4,139	2.9
257	Wheeling, WV-OH	147,329	148,297	-968	-0.7
258	Bangor, ME	147,180	146,817	363	0.2
259	Johnstown, PA	146,967	147,804	-837	-0.6
260	Madera, CA	146,345	142,530	3,815	2.7
261	Rocky Mount, NC	146,276	145,194	1,082	0.7
262	Hanford-Corcoran, CA	146,153	143,467	2,686	1.9
263	Wichita Falls, TX	145,528	146,116	-588	-0.4
264	Jefferson City, MO	144,958	143,737	1,221	0.8
265	Sioux City, IA-NE-SD	143,474	142,457	1,017	0.7
266	Burlington, NC	142,661	140,227	2,434	1.7
267	Florence-Muscle Shoals, AL	142,657	142,041	616	0.4
268	Santa Fe, NM	142,407	140,801	1,606	1.1
269	Springfield, OH	141,872	141,908	-36	0.0
270	State College, PA	140,953	140,313	640	0.5
271	Iowa City, IA	139,567	138,566	1,001	0.7
272	Dothan, AL	138,234	136,167	2,067	1.5
273	Battle Creek, MI	137,991	138,543	-552	-0.4
274	Hattiesburg, MS	134,744	131,402	3,342	2.5
275	Texarkana, TX-Texarkana, AR	134,510	133,164	1,346	1.0
276	Dalton, GA	134,397	131,913	2,484	1.9
277	Grand Junction, CO	134,189	129,746	4,443	3.4

Rank	Metropolitan Statistical Area	July 1 2006 Population	July 1 2005 Population	Change In Population (Number)	Change In Population (Percentage)
278	Napa, CA	133,522	132,516	1,006	0.8
279	Morristown, TN	132,851	130,640	2,211	1.7
280	Coeur d'Alene, ID	131,507	127,722	3,785	3.0
281	Pittsfield, MA	131,117	131,783	-666	-0.5
282	Anderson, IN	130,575	130,389	186	0.1
283	Wausau, WI	130,223	128,850	1,373	1.1
284	Sebastian-Vero Beach, FL	130,100	127,357	2,743	2.2
285	Glens Falls, NY	129,455	128,576	879	0.7
286	La Crosse, WI-MN	129,236	128,748	488	0.4
287	Warner Robins, GA	127,530	125,576	1,954	1.6
288	Odessa, TX	127,462	125,267	2,195	1.8
289	Mansfield, OH	127,010	127,585	-575	-0.5
290	Lebanon, PA	126,883	125,429	1,454	1.2
291	Altoona, PA	126,494	126,572	-78	-0.1
292	Farmington, NM	126,473	125,820	653	0.5
293	St. George, UT	126,312	119,188	7,124	6.0
294	Valdosta, GA	126,305	124,753	1,552	1.2
295	Auburn-Opelika, AL	125,781	123,122	2,659	2.2
296	Weirton-Steubenville, WV-OH	125,168	126,296	-1,128	-0.9
297	Flagstaff, AZ	124,953	123,826	1,127	0.9
298	Midland, TX	124,380	121,480	2,900	2.4
299	St. Joseph, MO-KS	122,306	121,811	495	0.4
300	Winchester, VA-WV	118,932	116,081	2,851	2.5
301	Rapid City, SD	118,763	117,908	855	0.7
302	Sherman-Denison, TX	118,478	116,763	1,715	1.5
303	Salisbury, MD	117,761	115,918	1,843	1.6
304	Williamsport, PA	117,668	118,102	-434	-0.4
305	Idaho Falls, ID	116,980	113,315	3,665	3.2
306	Mount Vernon-Anacortes, WA	115,700	113,181	2,519	2.2
307	Morgantown, WV	115,136	114,644	492	0.4
308	Muncie, IN	114,879	116,203	-1,324	-1.1
309	Sheboygan, WI	114,756	114,406	350	0.3
310	Victoria, TX	114,088	113,395	693	0.6
311	Goldsboro, NC	113,847	113,827	20	0.0
312	Harrisonburg, VA	113,449	112,058	1,391	1.2
313	Jonesboro, AR	113,330	111,919	1,411	1.3
314	Bowling Green, KY	113,320	110,944	2,376	2.1
315	Anniston-Oxford, AL	112,903	112,242	661	0.6
316	Lawrence, KS	112,123	111,519	604	0.5
317	Owensboro, KY	112,093	111,396	697	0.6
318	Jackson, TN	111,937	110,548	1,389	1.3
319	Logan, UT-ID	111,156	110,768	388	0.4
320	Elizabethtown, KY	110,878	110,488	390	0.4
321	Michigan City-La Porte, IN	110,479	110,281	198	0.2
322	Cleveland, TN	109,477	108,159	1,318	1.2
323	Decatur, IL	109,309	109,835	-526	-0.5
324	Lawton, OK	109,181	110,629	-1,448	-1.3
325	Kankakee-Bradley, IL	109,090	107,824	1,266	1.2
326	Bay City, MI	108,390	108,896	-506	-0.5
327	Lewiston-Auburn, ME	107,552	107,061	491	0.5
328	Danville, VA	107,087	107,452	-365	-0.3
329	Wenatchee, WA	106,806	104,854	1,952	1.9
330	Lima, OH	105,788	106,051	-263	-0.2
331	San Angelo, TX	105,752	105,157	595	0.6
332	Sumter, SC	104,430	104,909	-479	-0.5
333	Pine Bluff, AR	103,638	104,201	-563	-0.5
334	Gadsden, AL	103,362	102,920	442	0.4
335	Missoula, MT	101,417	100,033	1,384	1.4
336	Bismarck, ND	101,138	99,398	1,740	1.8
337	Kokomo, IN	100,877	101,268	-391	-0.4
338	Brunswick, GA	100,613	98,113	2,500	2.5
339	Ithaca, NY	100,407	100,104	303	0.3
340	Longview, WA	99,905	97,178	2,727	2.8
341	Cumberland, MD-WV	99,759	100,185	-426	-0.4
342	Fond du Lac, WI	99,243	98,911	332	0.3
343	Ocean City, NJ	97,724	98,805	-1,081	-1.1
344	Grand Forks, ND-MN	96,523	96,293	230	0.2
345	Rome, GA	95,322	94,362	960	1.0
346	Hot Springs, AR	95,164	93,436	1,728	1.8
347	Dubuque, IA	92,384	91,603	781	0.9
348	Elmira, NY	88,641	89,005	-364	-0.4

CHAPTER 4
TRANSPORTATION

SENATORS COACHES, INC. – LEASING INFORMATION

Reservations – Senators Coaches requires a one-week deposit to hold the equipment. This will be applied to the last week's payment. Your reservation is not guaranteed until deposit is received. All leases are to be paid one week in advance and kept current until final payment is made.

Insurance – Senators Coaches provides a $5,000,000 liability coverage at a cost of approximately $36 per day.

Travel or "Deadhead" – All tours have a travel charge for the travel time from Florence, Alabama to the appointed pick-up location, as well as the travel time from the appointed drop-off location back to Florence, Alabama. The daily rate is figured with 450 miles being one day. Fuel expense is additional.

***Driver receives single hotel room per night.

Bus Lease – Approximately $475 - $500 a day.

Driver's Wages – Drivers receive approximately $185 per day paid directly to the driver; $10 more if there are 15 bunks (and 15 people to deal with) and $25 extra a day to pull a trailer (not for trailer rental, but to pull it.)

- Drivers of Star Coaches get $210/day. Lessee will be charged for filters and/or parts on bus or generator.

- Driver receives an additional day's pay for drives that exceed 450 miles. For drives that exceed 600 miles, the driver will receive another day's pay.

- Driver may not drive over 10 hours in accordance to DOT or over 625 miles without an 8-hour hotel break.

Weekly Charges – Drivers will charge $45 for one bus wash per week, $45 for generator service every 100 hours of use, and $45 per week for interior cleaning to include linen change. The cost of laundry is in addition to this fee. The driver must receive a cash advance float from the Lessee at the beginning of the tour to cover all incidentals (fuel, permits, hotels, and tolls, etc). This amount should be settled with the driver, and they will turn in receipts on a timely basis. The driver is also to be given an end-of-tour float for the return to Florence and cleanup costs.

Carpet Steam Cleaning – The price and frequency of carpet cleaning will vary depending upon the amount of use, weather, and the local economy. (Under normal conditions, the carpet should not need to be cleaned more than once every three weeks. Under heavier or more extreme use, the carpet may need more attention. The average cost is approximately $60.)

End Of Tour Cleaning – This involves steam cleaning, laundry, and a bus wash (Anything needed to return the bus to the condition it was in at the start of the tour). The driver will estimate end-of-tour cleaning costs and fuel back to our shop before the tour ends.

Tracking Satellite Service – Activation is $10 per day per satellite.

www.senatorscoach.com

GAS MILEAGE CHART

VEHICLE	CITY (mpg)	HWY (mpg)
Toyota Prius	60	51
Honda Civic	30	40
Honda Civic Hybrid	49	51
Honda CRV	21 - 23	26 - 29
Ford Escape Hybrid	40	31
Ford Escape	18 - 22	22 - 25
Dodge Caravan	20	26

CHAPTER 26
SCENERY AND STAGE DECORATION

FIRE RETARDANTS

So we talked a lot about covering the stage in your branded logos and cool art – but all of this, in the post Great White World, needs to be treated with fire retardant chemicals and certified as such. I found a company that will do this for you: NTG products. You can find them on the web at Fire-Retardant.biz. I spoke with Lisa there to get some broad strokes for you.

You can order the basic materials from them to coat your scenery. I was talking with her about the kind of scenery we make: backdrops and banners. They have an odorless non-toxic fluid that you coat onto the fabric with a garden sprayer kind of device. One quart is under $100, a gallon will cost you around $200 and will cover 500 to 600 sq ft. It will work on any material that will absorb it. Then, you can print the certification that is online.

If you are performing on larger, more sensitive venues, I would suggest completing the backdrop and then shipping it to the company for treatment there. The cost is $200 for the first 100 sq ft then 80 cents per foot thereafter. You should allow at least 2 -3 weeks plus shipping

CHAPTER 29
ITINERARIES AND DAY SHEETS

THE HOTEL ROOMING LIST

Should you be fortunate enough to have a hotel anywhere, have the tour manager send rooming lists ahead. If and when you do arrive at a hotel, you are probably going to be exhausted. As soon as someone gets a room, they will disappear; probably without telling you which room they are in. When you check with the front desk, all of the rooms will probably be registered under the band name or touring company, so you'll end up waking everyone to try to find the one person you need. So, send a rooming list ahead – ask the front desk to fill it out beforehand and give copies to everyone along with the keys. This way each person knows where everyone else is. You can also let them know that you are the tour manager and you would like to be as far away from the band as possible - different floor, different side of he building

CONTRIBUTOR LIST

AME was the merch girl for Aqualung and HeeBeeGeeBeez Independent Record Store in Salt Lake City.
www.myspace.com/aimles0923

JOHN AIKIN is the Vice President of Leasing at Senator's Coaches, the company that provides the largest fleet of Prevost motor coaches in the entertainment industry.
www.senatorscoach.com

PATRICK ALBERTSON is the Associate Art Director at Revolver Magazine, the world's loudest rock magazine.
www.revolvermag.com

STEVE ALBINI is a singer, songwriter, guitarist, audio engineer and music journalist. He was a member of Big Black and Rapeman and is still a member of Shellac. He is founder and owner of the company Electrical Audio, which operates two recording studios in Chicago.
www.albinimusic.com

KATRINA ATKINS has been married to Martin for 11 years and together they have three lovely boys. She is CEO of the Atkins' household and has coordinated, pre-production arrangements, hotels, and air travel for package tours for the five years.

DAVE BAKER was Label Manager for Invisible Records from 1994 – 2000.

MAUREEN BAKER is an immigration consultant and logistics coordinator for Traffic Control Group. TCG is one of the entertainment industry's leading visa coordination agencies. With over 20 years of experience, the company serves U.S. and international clients in all of their visa/passport issues worldwide.
www.tcgworld.com

WILLIAM BASTONE is the editor of smokinggun.com, a website that features exclusive, confidential, accurate, and quirky documents and information that cannot be found anywhere else on the web.
www.smokinggun.com

STEVE BEATTY is the director of England's Plastic Head Distribution which exclusively handles sales and distribution in the UK for 170 record and DVD labels (over 30,000 titles), a range of over 3,000 titles of merchandise and 4,000 titles of specialist vinyl from limited edition 7 inch box sets, picture discs to electronic 12's. Plastic Head is a music distributor, not a carrier of "product." Extreme metal to hip hop, techno to reggae, ambient chill out to hardcore punk, it matters not, but quality is top priority. He plays bass with his band October File.

www.plastichead.com

TAMAR BERK is a singer, songwriter and multi-instrumentalist and has been a fixture in the Chicago music scene since 1996. She and her husband, Steve Denekas, formed The Countdown in 2001 (Invisible Records).

www.thecountdown.net

BRADLEY BILLS is a drummer, performance artist, and creator of CHANT, the solo drum project that is a new invention of the Industrial machine, a refined view of performance art, and a tribal/electronic showcase of sonic energy that intrigues audiences by its sheer power. He has contributed to the Pigface studio album '6.' Check out his contribution online at tstouring.com.

www.chantproject.com

STEVE BLUSH is the author of *American Hardcore: A Tribal History* and *.45 Dangerous Minds*. Throughout the early 1980s, he promoted hardcore punk shows in Washington, DC, and later went on to found and publish for *Seconds Magazine* from 1986-2000. Blush has written for *Interview*, *Village Voice*, *Spin* and *The Times of London*, and he currently serves as contributing music editor at *Paper Magazine*.

www.newyorkwaste.com/nyw_main/underground/americahc.html

MARTIN BOWES is the co-founder of the British electronic music band Attrition, formed in 1980 and still touring the world. He is an educator at Tile Hill College in Coventry, England.

www.attrition.co.uk

KATHLEEN "BURT" BRAMLETT is the Production Manager for Penn and Teller.

www.pennandteller.com

GRETA BRINKMAN is a bass player who has performed with Moby, L7, Debbie Harry, Pigface, and more. She has recently recorded some vocals and keyboard parts on Jayne County's new EP.

www.bassgoddessgreta.com

DON BYCZYNSKI is a once death metal/hardcore guitarist, for Fleshold, turned swing producer. He has engineered and/or produced bands such as The Atomic Fireballs and Blue October, and mixed live sound for The Damage Manual and more.
web.mac.com/producedb

DAVE CALLENS is a professional tour manager, accountant, and has been employed in every known touring position. For 34 years he has worked with a variety of artists, corporations, and agencies on many different levels including: Barry White, Coolio, Motley Crue, Everlast, Kenny Wayne Shepherd, Pointer Sisters, Paul Anka, George Benson, A.J. Croce, Arrested Development, Christopher Cross, Nell Carter, Sarah Vaughan, Tavares, Bobby Sherman, Roger Williams, The Monkees, The Carpenters, Paul Revere & the Raiders, and Tangerine.

JACK CARSON is a tour manager for Jägermeister Music Tours and one of the creators of Jager's Mobile Stage.
www.jagermeistermusictour.com

XI CHEN is the singer from the band Snapline from China.
www.myspace.com/snapline

JOHN CHMIEL is the owner of Water Street Music Hall in Rochester, NY. He also makes great soup!
www.waterstreetmusic.com

MICHELLE CHO is an activist for People for the Ethical Treatment of Animals (PETA). She attended Columbia College Chicago for music business.
www.peta.org

CHRIS CONNELLY is a Scottish singer/songwriter known for his industrial music work with Ministry and The Revolting Cocks and his critically acclaimed solo albums. He is also an author.
www.chrisconnelly.com

LACEY CONNOR is a singer and songwriter who founded the band Nocturne and toured with Pigface on the *Free for All Tour*.
www.nocturne.cc/

JIM DARDEN is the Production Manager at House of Blues Chicago. House of Blues Chicago is one of the busiest venues in the country with over 600 events per year between its downstairs restaurant and upstairs venue.
www.hob.com

JADE DELLINGER is an art curator and the co-author of *We are Devo!* He has collaborated with the German musical group Kraftwerk on archiving their collection.
www.devobook.com

SARAH DOPE is a photographer, graphic designer, model, and merchandise specialist. She has photographed many bands including Incubus, Jane's Addiction, and Megadeth.
www.sarahdope.com

RAMONA DOWNEY is in charge of booking at the Bottom of the Hill Club in San Francisco, CA. Their website with detailed instruction for bands is so well put together that it has become an industry standard.
www.bottomofthehill.com

JEAN ENCOULE runs the British webzine trakMARX.com: "Where writing about music is like dancing to architecture: for punk rockers & poseurs past, present, and future – the diseased artery at the heart of the underground! 6 years! 29 issues! 1 agenda!"
www.trakmarx.com

ENIGMA is a horned, tattooed sideshow musician, not to mention a daredevil, icon, artist, original member of the Jim Rose Circus and sideshow, and featured on *The X-Files* and NBC's *Identity*.
www.TheEnigmaLive.com

MARIA FERRERO is the owner of her company Adrenaline PR which represents artists like Metallica, Anthrax, Ministry, Lamb of God, and many more. "Turning artists into household names since 1983."
www.adrenalinepr.com

SUSAN FERRIS, former manager of the band Slayer, is now Partner at Bohemia Entertainment Group, "Mob Boss" of Long Live Crime Records, and has since birthed another record label as well as a publishing company.
www.longlivecrimerecords.com

DOUG FIRLEY is the producer and keyboardist for Gravity Kills. He is also the co-owner and producer for Shock City Records. He gave us the title "Exit Planet Bus." Awesome.
www.shockcityrecords.com

DIRK FLANIGAN has been the singer in 77 Luscious Babes, High Plains Drifter, Pigface, and more, not to mention being "one of the best chefs in Chicago!!!" He is now Executive Chef at The Gage Restaurant and Tavern, across from Chicago's Millennium Park.

LEE FRASER is the guitarist, keyboardist, and co-founder of the British industrial group Sheep on Drugs and his own project Bagman.
www.sheepondrugs.com

MICHAEL GALLINA is a street teamer for Invisible Records, creator of indeterminism.org, and general technology anarchist.
www.indeterminism.org

JOEL GAUSTEN has been the drummer for The Undead and Electric Frankenstein. He is also a promoter and author of such books as *Tales of Horror: The History of THE MISFITS & THE UNDEAD* and *Pandemonium: Inside Killing Joke.*
www.myspace.com/gaustenbooks

DEE GENERATE taught by Rat Scabies, Dee is the original and current drummer with the British punk band Eater, one of the youngest punk bands on the scene in 1977.
www.myspace.com/deegenerate

ANDREW GOLDBERG is the managing editor of smokinggun.com, a website that features exclusive, confidential, accurate, and quirky documents and information that cannot be found anywhere else on the web.
www.smokinggun.com

ADAM GRAYER is in charge of sponsorships for Jager Music Tours that sponsors more than 150 bands across the country.
www.jagermusic.com

DARREN GUCCIONE is an Illinois licensed certified public accountant, business broker, real estate broker, mortgage broker and loan originator who heads up the DSG Accounting Firm in Chicago.
www.dsgfirm.com

JEFFREY HALLS is the proud owner of Australia's Blakhole Record Label, presenting real alternative entertainment.

CHRIS HARRIS is the lead singer of Project .44, a Chicago band who joins metal guitar with captivating dance beats to create an aggressive alternative sound.
www.project44music.com

DR. DEBBY HERBENICK, PH.D., M.P.H., is an internationally known sex researcher, educator, and columnist. She is a research associate and lecturer in the Department of Applied Health Science at Indiana University. She coordinates The Kinsey Institute Sexuality Information Service for Students (KISISS; www.indiana.edu/~kisiss.) She also serves as the Associate Director of the Sexual Health Research Working Group (SHRWG; www.indiana.edu/~shrwg), a collaborative of faculty and students conducting research on contemporary issues related to sexuality and writes regular columns about sexuality for various media including *Men's Health* magazine, *Time Out Chicago*, and *Velocity Weekly*.
www.debbyherbenick.com

JIM HOLAHAN was the Deputy National Scheduler for Al Gore's Presidential campaign, and is now a co-owner and Design-maker for Mud Room Studios.
www.mudroomstudios.com

MIKE JOHNSON, formerly of Reckless Records, is now label manager of Invisible Records, Chicago.

JAIRUS KHAN is Ad·ver·sary, an independent Canadian industrial project. With output ranging from ambient to rhythmic noise and industrial rock, Ad·ver·sary has joined several acts on tours of the United States and Canada. He has also done tour management.

WES KIDD is a manager, producer, and musician. He manages bands such as Local H and Cheap Trick for Silent Partner Management.
www.silentpartnermanagement.com

NATHAN KOCH is the electronic pop music band Emulsion and promoter of RAMP Chicago at Sonotheque. He is currently expanding his digital horizons.
www.emulsionmusic.com

KAMELA LISE KOEHLER is the vocalist for the industrial gutter gothic band Apocalypse Theatre, the gypsy punk troupe The Hellblinki Sextet, and the Honky Tonk Angels' "The Shed Keys."
www.apocalypsetheatre.com

CHRIS LEE, formerly of Christopher Lee and the Oddities, has been a law enforcement officer for the past five years.

KEN LOPEZ is an entrepreneur, explorer, inventor, and musician. He is a professor and Associate Director of the Music Industry Program at the University of Southern California's Thornton School of Music. For 15 years, Mr. Lopez served as vice president of JBL, a world-renowned manufacturer of professional audio equipment. He has an extensive background in professional audio and musical equipment product development, distribution, and marketing.
www.usc.edu/music

JARED LOUCHE is the singer and songwriter of Chemlab. He is also a writer, conductor, father, mythomaniac, painter, storyteller, and conceptualist.
www.hydrogen.com

KEVIN LYMAN is the founder and promoter of Van's Warped Tour, which has featured as many as 100 bands every year since 1993. Van's Warped Tour continues to sell over 500,000 tickets a year.
www.warpedtour.com

CURSE MACKEY is a vocalist, composer, art curator, DJ and producer, currently based in Tampa, Fl. He is also the Creative Director of the Action Arts Agency and curator of Six-String Masterpieces: The Dimebag Darrell Art Tribute. Curse also founded the Woodstock Tattoo & Body Arts Festival where "artists who also tattoo," illustrators, graffiti artists, and other visionary artists come together to display and share their art.
www.actionartsagency.com

PATRIK MATA is an American anti-art, anti-pop singer/guitarist who formed the post punk rock band Kommunity FK that helped establish what came to be known as the death rock scene in Los Angeles.
www.kommunityfk.com

MAT MATLACK is the drummer and co-founder of The Follow and the founder of Space 380, a music promotion website that offers promotion services for radio airplay, press reviews, tour and retail, TV coverage, and more.
www.space380.com/MatBio.html

SIMON MATTOCK, a.k.a. Suburban Kid, has played in a number of bands; managed bands including Fudge 45, dragSTER (with Jah Wobble), and the legendary '76 punk outfit Eater; and toured with bands including Pigface. He has promoted shows in the UK for over 25 years and made/edited promo videos for bands including The Damage Manual. He just finished co-writing the first full account of Public Image Ltd.: *John Lydon's Metal Box* through Helter Skelter publishing (release date June 2007). He occasionally DJs as DJ Virus in the UK and the US and is currently involved in the following projects: trakmarx.com, UK singer/songwriter Pete Molinari, Eater, Black Noise Records, and Deadly Long Legs.
www.myspace.com/suburban_kid77

STEVE MCCLELLAN was the General Manager and Talent Buyer at First Avenue Nightclub in Minneapolis, MN for most of its life. He is an advisor to the Diverse Emerging Music Organization, a non-profit focused on connecting independent venues and new artists. He also teaches classes at McNally Smith College of Music in Saint Paul, Minnesota in the business department and introduced Martin to White Castle.
www.first-avenue.com

JEFF MCCLUSKY is the owner of Jeff McClusky & Associates, the only comprehensive entertainment promotion and artist exposure company with music, broadcast, and new media expertise, with clients including major and independent record labels, publishing companies, Internet music companies, artist management firms, and film companies among others.
www.jmapromo.com

V. MERCY is the co-founder of Apocalypse Theatre, a traveling caravan of musicians, and promoter of the U-35 corridor, an alliance of artists dedicated to the ultimate American touring experience.
www.apocalypsetheatre.com

ADRIAN H. MERRILL is Metal Chef. He provides on-site catering to bands on the road such as As I Lay Dying and Exodus. The "Cuisine To Mangle Your Mind" menu ranges from proscuitto-wrapped baby greens to Frangelico-infused chocolate Ganache with crushed pecans.
www.metalchef.com

JASON MILLER is the lead vocalist and guitarist of the industrial rock band Godhead. He has also been selected as music producer for a film written and directed by Andy Dick. He is also a voice-over artist who owns his own studio in Los Angeles.
www.godhead.com

MOOSE is the Editor-in-Chief of the *College Music Journal*, the authority on new music, college radio, and music industry charting. CMJ also holds the CMJ Music Marathon where over 1,000 bands play all over Manhattan and Brooklyn.
www.cmj.com

DAVID NICHOLAS is a street teamer for Invisible Records, Washington DC anti-scene agitator, and dub addict.

JASON NOVAK is a producer, father, and co-founder of the industrial rock band Acumen Nation, the drum and bass-driven DJ? Acucrack, and Cracknation Records.
www.cracknation.com

MITCH O'CONNELL is a Chicago artist whose illustrations have appeared everywhere from "traditional" comics by Charlton and DC to Heavy Metal to "cutting edge" publications like *Deadline* and *Juxtapoz*. He published his first "graphic novel," *The World of Ginger Fox* in 1986 and followed that with two collections, *Good Taste Gone Bad* in 1993 and *Pwease Wuv Me!* in 1998. He has recently been concentrating on tattoo designs which can be seen in his new book, *Mitch O'Connell Tattoos* available from Last Gasp Publishing. To see more about the Man, the Myth, the Legend, please visit www.mitchoconnell.com today!

MARGOT OLAVARRIA, PH.D., was the bass player for The Go-Go's and Brian Brain. She currently resides in NYC and is a writer, Doctor of Philosophy, entrepreneur, activist, and party girl.

MARK O'SHEA is the former tour manager for Nine Inch Nails, Pigface, and The Damage Manual among many others. He is also an adjunct instructor at Cuyahoga Community College in Cleveland, OH, where he teaches a course on Concert Tour Management.

CHRIS PAYNE is the DJ for Local 101, a radio program that showcases local bands on Chicago's Q101, one of the leading radio stations for new music in Chicago and one of the top stations in the country.
www.q101.com

SEAN PAYNE does vocals and programming for Cyanotic, an electronic metal band. He also owns of the label Glitch Mode Recordings based in Chicago.
www.cyanotic-online.com

ERIC PERINA has been involved in all aspects of touring, from working for a local PA company carrying gear to tour management and drum tech for Cheap Trick, Survivor, Run-DMC, Local H, Kanye West, and many others. He mixes for major label executives throughout the country and has done runs as a drummer for bands such as Killjoy, Voodoo Rain, and Dirtbag. He owns/operates "Chicago Music Service," a full service production company.
www.q101.com

JASON PETTIGREW is Editor-in-Chief of the Cleveland, Ohio-based *Alternative Press*. Since its debut as a photocopied fanzine handed out at a punk show in 1985, AP has been the publication where the honest word, the correct word, the authoritative word has been spoken on new music and youth culture.
www.altpress.com

CYNTHIA PLASTERCASTER is an artist, fan, collector, author, and rock/cockumentarian – immortalizing rock star's "very special appendages" for the last 30 years, from Jimi Hendrix to Martin Atkins.
www.cynthiaplastercaster.com

JONO PODMORE, also known as Kumo, is a composer, producer, programmer, engineer, orchestral arranger, and professor of music at Germany's Cologne Musikhochschule, (the Cologne University of Music), the largest academy of music in all of Europe.
www.spoonrecords.com

LEE POPA has been in charge of Front of House Sound on tour for Ministry, KMFDM, Killing Joke, Zilch, Living Colour, Lollapalooza, Pigface and more.
www.myspace.com/popasound

JONATHAN PUST is the owner of the Independent Record Store HeeBeeGeeBeez in Salt Lake City and the vendor coordinator for the Curiosa Festival, a tour headlined by The Cure.
members.aol.com/hebgbz23/homepage.html

CHRIS RAMOS is former label manager of Invisible Records and tour merchandiser for Pigface, Dope, and other bands. He is currently working with Dope Gear, Inc.
www.dopegearinc.com

ANGELIQUE RICKHOFF is the owner of PromoHo, an ever-growing network of businesses and artists providing a one-stop for affordable service and promotion for musicians in Chicago's Underground. She is also a graphic designer, web designer, merch girl, and photographer.
www.PromoHo.com

URSULA RODRIGUEZ is in charge of booking at the Bottom of the Hill Club in San Francisco, CA which was chosen as "the best place to hear live music in San Francisco" by *Rolling Stone* Magazine.
www.bottomofthehill.com

JOLLY ROGER is an imposing legend in touring circles. He has been the tour manager for Cheap Trick, Kansas, Styx, Foreigner, Hart, Ozzy, Ministry, Pigface, and more.

HENRY ROLLINS has been touring steadily since 1981. His various roles include: vocalist of Rollins Band, Black Flag, radio DJ, author, actor, spoken word artist, and several television and movie credits. He also heads up 2.13.61 Publishing Company.
http://21361.com/

CARLTON P. SANDERCOCK is a UK promoter.

VICTORIA SANTINO is the production manager for the SuicideGirls, an online community that features profiles of goth, punk, emo, and indie-styled young women, who themselves are known as the "SuicideGirls." The website also features interviews with major figures in popular and alternative culture.
www.suicidegirls.com

CHRIS SCHLEYER was the guitarist with the bands Prick and Zeromancer, rehearsal guitarist with A Perfect Circle, and guitar tech for Nine Inch Nails. He is currently promoting his new band Affected and working with NIN on their current tour.
www.affectedband.com

RANDALL SCOTT is the front man of Portland-based rock band, Railer.
www.myspace.com/railer

JOE SHANAHAN is the owner of the Metro in Chicago, a concert hall that features live alternative/rock acts on the verge of breaking into the big time. Joe started what soon became the Metro in 1982 and it has been going strong ever since.
www.metrochicago.com

CLIFF SIELOFF is a filmmaker with such credits as *GothicFest, Terrorvision*, and the *Free for All Documentary*.
www.cliffsielofffilms.com

MATTHEW LEE SMITH is the former President and Director of MLS Health Services, Incorporated. Currently, he is a doctoral student in the Department of Health & Kinesiology at Texas A&M University, College Station. He has achieved distinction as a Certified Health Education Specialist (CHES) and Certified Prevention Specialist (CPP) with research experience in fields surrounding alcohol, tobacco, and other drug (ATOD) use and abuse, human sexuality, minority health, health disparities, youth problem gambling, and injury and violence prevention
www.tamu.edu

GEOFF SMYTH was the guitarist with Brian Brain, assisted with tours and accounting and whatever the band were throwing at the audience.

JIM SOCHACKI is a drum and guitar tech. He has worked with Gravity Kills, Evil Mothers, Dry Cell, Godhead, Test Department, Sheep on Drugs, and Pigface, among others.

MARK SPYBEY is the creator of Dead Voices On Air, an experimental and industrial project formed after his departure from Zoviet France, an ambient industrial music group from England. He has also toured with The Legendary Pink Dots and Can. He is an industrial psychologist.
www.spybey.net

BRAIN ST. CLAIR was the drummer for Triple Fast Action and Local H. He was the drum tech for Bun E. Carlos of Cheap Trick and has been the tour manager for Liz Phair, Triple Fast Action, and Local H. He works with Tour Time Productions, a professional tour management company for bands on a budget.
www.tourtimeproductions.com

DAN STEINBERG is a concert promoter at Square Peg Concerts (Seattle, WA), producing live events all over the country.
www.squarepegconcerts.com

MICHE STIRLING is a promoter, DJ, and owner of the company Mother's Cupboard Productions – an "international DJ rescue service." Check out her contribution online at tstouring.com.
www.myspace.com/mama_miche

LUKE STOKES is a tour manager, merchandiser, Chicago-based DJ, and owner of Deezal Records. He has also been co-hosting a radio show called Abstract Science since 1999 on WLUW 88.7.
www.abstractscience.net

CHUCK SUBER has been an Artist-in-Residence in the Arts, Entertainment, and Media Management Department at Columbia College Chicago since 1978. He is the Director of Publications at AEBMedia.
www.aebmedia.com

NIXON SUICIDE is one of the first SuicideGirls. She has been featured in *CSI: New York* and *Jeremy Kasten's Wizard of Gore* with Crispin Glover. She also works at The Bone Room in Berkeley, CA.
www.suicidegirls.com

JEFFREY A. SWANSON is the creator and promoter of GothicFest, North America's largest gothic festival and expo.
www.gothicfest.com

LINDSAY TIPPING is a band manager and has worked in music promotion and tour management in Beijing, Shanghai, and Vancouver.
www.myspace.com/lindsaytipping

CHRIS TISONE is the tour manager of a Children's Theater Troupe. He is currently working to establish a new theater group in Chicago.

GARY TOPP is a concert promoter and film distributor from Toronto.
www.myspace.com/garytopp

MIGUEL TORRES is an engineer at Chicago's Mattress Factory Studio.

STEVE TRAXLER is the president and co-founder of Jam Theatricals, a Chicago-based entertainment company that produces Broadway engagements throughout the country. Jam has presented programs such as *CATS*, *STOMP*, and *Hairspray*.
www.jamtheatricals.com

PAT VAN HULLE is Director of Online Marketing at Underground, Inc. in Chicago and does booking for Grow Fins.
www.growfins.com

RION VERNON is the creator of PinUp Toons, which brought the punk rock-driven style of SuicideGirls to the digital canvas. Creating pinup portraits for 54 of the SuicideGirls, this unique, glamour-caricature technique focuses on the diverse personalities of these fascinating girls.
www.pinuptoons.com

ADAM WATKINS is a St. Louis-based multimedia artist and is an art instructor at East Central College (Union, Missouri). He graduated with an MFA in 2000 from the Kent Institute of Art and Design in Canterbury, UK (BFA Webster University 1997). His work deals with the notions of the post-pop culture that we live in and the constant re-contextualization of it.
www.tonerodent.com

RAYMOND WATTS is founding and sole member of the industrial music project PIG. He has also collaborated with KMFDM and Chemlab.
www.theswining.com

REV. JOHN WHEELER is the lead singer and keyboardist for the metal band Screaming Mechanical Brain.
www.smbband.com

EMILY WHITE was the tour manager for The Dresden Dolls and Imogen Heap's last tour. She currently works with Madison House Management Co. in New York.
www.dresdendolls.com
www.madisonhouseinc.com

FAKIE WILDE was a member of Spank Sinatra (the Australian one), Hayward 5000, Visitors & More. He is also an author and poet.

MARK WILLIAMS is the Director of International Sales for PreSonus Audio Electronic. He is an entrepreneur, engineer, and musician.
www.presonus.com

GAIL WORLEY is a writer and Rock Critic at Large. She has interviewed artists such as Marilyn Manson, Dweezil Zappa, and Ryan Roxie from Alice Cooper. She also runs her rock journalism website The Worley Gig.
www.worleygig.com

MICHAEL YERKE is the #1 Talent Buyer in the country at House of Blues Chicago.
www.hob.com

MICHELLE YOON is a touring merchandise manager and has traveled the world for a variety of organizations including Warped Tour and Shirts for a Cure doing merchandise and management. She is currently pursuing her Master's of Arts Management.

HORACE ALEXANDER YOUNG teaches woodwinds and jazz studies at Washington State University and tours the world as a member of Abdullah Ibrahim's jazz sextet, EKAYA. He plays woodwinds, keyboards, and percussion. He also sings and composes, and has done arrangements for and performed with a variety of musical artists including the Madd Hatta, Nancy Wilson, and B.B. King.
horacealexanderyoung.com

ZIM ZUM is a multi-platinum musician and songwriter, Marilyn Manson's former guitarist, and member of The Pop Culture Suicides, an American experimental rock band from Chicago, Illinois.
www.myspace.com/thepopculturesuicides

Please e-mail info@tstouring.com for unlisted or updated web links for any of the contributors above.

STOP PRESS!

Things are moving so quickly that by the time we formatted the book more amazing new developments would demand that we did it again. This is why we created the *Stop Press* section. Check out the website for updates so new that they didn't even make it into the *Stop Press* section.

SCENTS AND MEMORY

The following marketing phrase became a central part of the presentation of my three-piece post-punk band Brian Brain:

BUY MY SINGLE
BUY MY ALBUM
BE MY FRIEND
AND MAKE ME RICH

It was different than any other catchphrase or marketing pitch that was out there. The traditional punk ethos was, "We don't fucking care if you buy the records or not. Fuck off." For the very first show in 1979, I bought 30 pounds of bananas and stayed up all night hand-stenciling the phrase "Buy My Single" into the skin of the banana in ballpoint pen. I went to bed exhausted at four o'clock in the morning and woke up to a Christmas-like surprise. What had previously been ink on yellow bananas had turned into bruised bananas with the lettering taking on an almost branded appearance, as if the message was coming from inside the banana, like some inherent banana DNA. That's a happy accident.

The idea to have a real drum kit professionally recorded but playing back on a quarter-inch reel to reel tape machine was revolutionary in 1978 when drum machines had just appeared. It freed me up to dance around and drink.

At the end of the set, instead of leaving the stage and sitting in the dressing room hoping, opening our ears to try and catch every single piece of applause to justify an encore, we'd already inserted over three minutes of rapturous applause onto the tape. We were always guaranteed to get an amazing ovation. This wasn't some cut and paste from a sound effects CD (in fact CDs didn't exist back then). We went into a 16-track recording studio and created an audience of over 100 by multi-tracking and layering. The applause slowly grew along with some whistles and occasional shouts of "Yeah, Brian." Then, it built to a soccer-style chant to an incessant, "Bri-an Bri-an, Bri-an." Then fell apart and died down only to build back up twice as loud.

So, we haven't even done the show yet and we're smiling. But, as is my nature, my question was, "What else can we do?" Now, we weren't waiting for the audience to tell us whether we could play one more song or not. We unplugged them from the power they had over us. What would be more natural then to come back out on stage and pelt them with bananas?

We didn't really think it through. We were just happy with our dali-esque art performance piece. But, as Enigma pointed out in his piece, anything you throw into an audience is likely to come back. Within minutes, the pissed-off crowd is pelting us with bananas. The three of us, Bobby on guitar, Pete on bass, and I were very energetic and pretty much drunk. Throw into that mix, literally, 30 pounds of bananas and you have all the ingredients of an Animal House food fight.

After two minutes of banana exchange, the banana started to disintegrate. Bobby, Pete, and I were slipping and sliding all over the stage. People were scooping handfuls of banana mush off the floor and throwing it at us like snowballs. It was everywhere. Somewhere I have a receipt from a hi-fi equipment repair shop in London. I'm sure it was the only time that a Revox tape machine repair specialist has ever written, "Removing banana pulp from the play back heads - £75."

At settlement, the 30 lbs of bananas became the 300 lb gorilla in the room. The ceiling fans above the stage had done their job well, splattering the velvet curtains that surrounded the stage. Of course, they had just been cleaned the week before (once a year maybe) for £200. I think we were paid £50 for that show, less the £75 for the revox repair, taxis, beer, and £200 for cleaning.

If that was all of the story, it would be pretty good. But it gets better:

A year or so later, Martin Hooker, the owner of Secret Records (Brian Brain 7" was catalog # SHH001) called me, laughing his head off. He had gone to see a band in London and had a strange feeling of déjà vu in the venue. It was familiar but he didn't know why. It was bugging him until the first band came on. As the stage lights came on, the room slowly filled with the scent of bananas – still gently cooking on the lights over 12 months later.

I guess we invented Smellyvision.

I used sense-prompting during some of the early Pigface shows. While scratching government pregnancy advisory cassettes, we emptied four or five full cans of lemon air freshener to wake the crowd up. Before the final part of the show with sitars and belly dancers, we lit hundreds of sticks of incense to promote the feelings floating through the room.

I'm creating a scratch and sniff 7" single for The Countdown.

All of this seems like crazy punk rock performance art but then I read about the role that smell is having with new marketing campaigns: Starbucks has gone to great lengths to find the best smell to have on a sticker on complimentary newspapers – blueberry it seems is the best smell to make you want to go get a muffin. Supermarkets use smells that are known to stimulate shopping (or spending) and now Omni hotels is branding a specially created smell for their lobbies.

To prevent accidental exposure for anyone who might be allergic to the scent (or to at least say that they tried to) companies are now using a protective sticker over the odorant – "Pull off the sticker and release the smell."

Now I'm going to go and develop a new pair of pants for myself with a scratch and sniff crotch... oh hang on, I already have one.

NINE INCH NAILS - YEAR ZERO
PAT VAN HULLE

The marketing campaign behind Nine Inch Nails' 2007 release, Year Zero, was noteworthy for many reasons. It was able to develop an online fantasy universe to coincide with the concept of the dystopian future covered in the album. The campaign netted great press for the release from MTV, Rolling Stone, CNN, and the blog community, to name a few.

The campaign began on NIN's European tour where a t-shirt sold at the merch booth had highlighted letters that spelled out iamtryingtobelieve. This led people to iamtryingtobelieve.com which opened the door to other websites that laid the groundwork for the dystopian future that Trent Reznor, the man behind NIN, prophesizes in Year Zero. It is an Orwellian future where the government has put mind-controlling substances into the water supply, morality reigns supreme, and a strong "underground resistance" to the corrupt government is growing.

Through hidden secrets in each of the websites, more websites were uncovered. One website, Anotherversionofthetruth.com, included what appears to be a propaganda poster that when clicked and drug upon, tears away the image and reveals a website-behind-a-website with audio files and links to other sites. One of the sites had a phone number that people could call and hear a distorted version of the album's first single "Survivalism." Even the band's DVD, Beside You In Time, released during this period, contained hidden text that led to another website.

The sites encourage exploration and set up the viewer to become part of the "resistance." This, in turn, created a rabid following throughout and outside of the NIN fan community. The message boards were abuzz with theories and tips on how to dig deeper into the universe. A NIN wiki (http://www.ninwiki.com/Main_Page) was created to keep up on the progress of this campaign.

With high-speed internet being so prevalent, every album is leaked at some point prior to release. To use this to their advantage, NIN started leaking songs through hidden flash drives found at their concerts. The fans who found some of these drives discovered that they contained songs off of the new album. The fans then disseminated the track throughout the fan community. Even though NIN had leaked the tracks themselves, the RIAA, ended up sending cease-and-desist letters to many of the websites that were hosting the "leaked" tracks. The fact that NIN had leaked these on their own, presumably with their label's, Interscope Records, permission, garnered more press for the release.

One of the discovered websites, OpenSourceResistance.com, allowed viewers to submit their emails. In March, 2007, people received an email that told them to meet in LA at a certain corner and wear something that will identify them as part of the resistance. When people showed up, a van pulled up and handed out ammunition boxes full of stencils, fliers, stickers, buttons, and for a lucky few, a cell phone. The phone received a call the next day and the person was told to meet up at a location in LA for a resistance meeting. Once at the location, the fans were treated to a resistance meeting and then carted off to a warehouse. When they walked into the small dark room, about 50 fans were treated to a short-NIN show. The show was then broken up by sirens and a SWAT team that pushed the fans out of the warehouse. For a full account check (http://www.ninwiki.com/2007/04/18_LA). A video of the show was posted onto opensourceresistance.com.

The record's release did not end the campaign. The CD case itself has a phone number to call that contains a voice that states that the government is now watching you because you bought this immoral material. The CD booklet contains a few hidden characters that lead to other sites and the CD itself has a thermochrome covering that, when warmed up, reveals some binary numbers that hides the clues to another site.

NIN also used some more traditional means to promote the record. A strong Myspace.com push, a Year Zero website linked off of the nin.com site, outdoor posters, radio play, a music video, and listening parties were all used for promotion.

It is safe to say that this campaign has been very successful at getting the NIN community to actively participate in the album's release. It was also creative enough that the music press and blogs wrote many articles about the release. This was able to incorporate more than just the large NIN fanbase, but involve people who had not been a fan before. As for sales, the album debuted at number 2 and the Billboard charts with 187,000 units sold, behind a new release from Avril Lavigne. The band's 2005 album, With Teeth, had debuted at number 1 with 272,000 records sold. That album came after a 6-year hiatus from NIN and had a much more straightforward sound to it. The album's official single, "Survivalism" has been at the top of the Modern Rock charts since its release.

WHAT THE HELL DO I KNOW: EXPANDED

TOURS:

PUBLIC IMAGE LTD. (1979 – 1985)
Europe
United States
Canada
Australia
Japan

BRIAN BRAIN (1979 – 1989)
United States
Canada
Europe

KILLING JOKE (1988 – 1991)
United States
Europe
Canada

LUNAR BEAR ENSEMBLE (1986 – 1988)
One-off shows in New York and New Jersey with Henry Rollins and Lydia Lunch

PIGFACE (1991 – PRESENT)
United States
Canada
Europe
Mexico

MURDER INC (1992)
United States
Europe

THE DAMAGE MANUAL (2000 – PRESENT)
Europe
United States

MINISTRY (1991 CAGE TOUR)
United States
Canada

MARTIN ATKINS (DJ, PRODUCER, SPOKEN WORD) (1995 – PRESENT)

United States

Canada

Europe

China

...And working on art work, sculptures, scenery, and t-shirt designs, and performance art since 1980

TOUR MANAGEMENT

Killing Joke: booking, management, set design, t-shirt design

Pigface: booking, management, set design, t-shirt design

PACKAGE TOURS (1995 - PRESENT)

Conception, production, logistics, graphics, marketing, routing, and some booking, etc.

- Free for All (2004)
- United I (2003)
- United II (2003)
- Preaching to the Perverted (2001)
- Soap Box, Beat Box (1999)
- Red Neck, White Trash, Blue Movie (1998)
- Lowest of the Low (1997)
- Ecstasy Under Duress (Sheep on Drugs, Test Department) (1996)
- Route 666 (1995)

GUEST LECTURES

2005
- Underground Inc. Seminar, Chicago, IL: Welcome to the Music Business - You're Fucked
- University of Southern California Los Angeles, CA: 15 Strategies for a More Successful Show and an overview of the music industry

2006
- Midi School Beijing, China: State of Industry in the United States and Opportunity
- Underground Inc. Seminar Chicago, IL: Welcome to the Music Business - You're Fucked II

2007
- NAMM Anaheim, CA: Two Weeks in China presented by PreSonus Audio
- Underground Inc. Seminar, Chicago, IL: Welcome to the Music Business - You're Fucked III

- Belmont University, Nashville, TN: Indie Record Label Operations and Two Weeks in China
- Underground Inc. Internship Seminar, Chicago IL: Current State of the Music Industry
- University of Southern California, Los Angeles, CA: Songwriting
- University of Colorado, Denver, CO: Current State of the Music Industry
- University of Colorado, Denver, CO: MEISA seminar - The Nature of Opportunity in the Music Business
- Conservatory of Recording Arts and Sciences, Gilbert, AZ: Two Weeks in China & Opportunity in the Business, China and Current State of Industry
- Rock for Kids, Chicago, IL: Battle of the Bands Celebrity Judge
- Chicago Cultural Center's Musician's at Work Forum, Chicago, IL: The ABC's of Touring
- Creative Chicago Expo, Chicago, IL: Art vs. Business
- DePaul University, Chicago, IL: Entrepreneurship
- Columbia College Chicago, Chicago IL: Record Label Strategies and the Digital Domain
- Martin's first gallery show presented by the Chicago Arts District featuring his work from the last 30+ years including: photographs, scenery, and sculptures with workshops and special events throughout the month.

INDEX

Buttons, 116, 426

Buy-Ons, 103-106, 119, 465

    Pay to Play, 106, 219, 492

Cars, 33

Case Studies, 477-494

Catering, 82-88, 99, 286-287

    Cutting Down the Catering Rider, 86-87

    Evening Meal, 85, 286, 397

CDs, 114, 118, 186-187, 193-194, 418

Celebrities, 130, 464

Cell Phones, 160, 225, 254, 341-342

    Chargepod, 342

Chain Stores (See Record Stores)

Chargepod (See Cell Phones)

Charisma, 361-366

Charles Bukowski, 238

Charles Saliba, 437

Checkbooks, 292

Chemlab, 130, 475-476

Chicago, 39, 61, 63, 182, 198-200, 271-272, 311-312, 508-510

Chicago Music Service, 260-261

Children's Touring Group, 264-266, 343

China, 413-418, 436-442, 451

    Beijing, 414-418, 436-441, 451

Chris Connelly, 248, 347

Chris Harris, 489-494

Chris Lee, 53-54, 335-336

Chris Payne, 4, 186-187

Chris Ramos, 132-134, 181, 294, 304

Chris Schleyer, 240

Chris Tisone, 253, 264-266, 343, 472-473

Christmas Lights, 250

Chuck Suber, 508-510

CIMS (See Record Stores)

Cincinnati, 100

Circle Jerks, 383

Cleanliness, 345

Clearing the House, 75, 125

Cliff Sieloff, 210

Climate Control, 74

CMJ (See Seminars and Festivals)

CNN, 439-440

Cocaine (See Drugs),

Cockney Rhyming Slang, 401

Code of the Road, 256, 257, 363

Coffee, 86-87, 341, 347, 396, 415

    Coffee Lids, 396

College Radio, 185, 188, 418, 459

Columbia College of Chicago, XXV

Commmercial Radio, 185-192, 459

Condoms (See Sex)

Confirming Shows, 73, 109, 254, 473

Consignment, 194

Contests, 461

Contracts, 73-94, 256

Co-Op Advertising (See Advertising)

Creating Your Own Event, 207-212

Credit and Blame, 70, 108

Credit Cards, 120, 124, 133-135, 221, 254, 472

Crew, 90, 150-151, 218-219, 235-246, 421

Curfews, 15, 464

Curiosa Festival, 140

Currency Exchange Rates, 150, 397, 415

Curse Mackey, 151, 208, 221-222, 236, 238, 254-255, 392, 511-512

Customs Officials, 55, 257, 400, 419-420

Cutting Down the Catering Rider (See Catering)

CW, 515

Cyanotic, 288, 479-484

Cynthia Plastercaster, 319-321

D-22, 418, 437-439, 451

Daily Expenses, 142-143